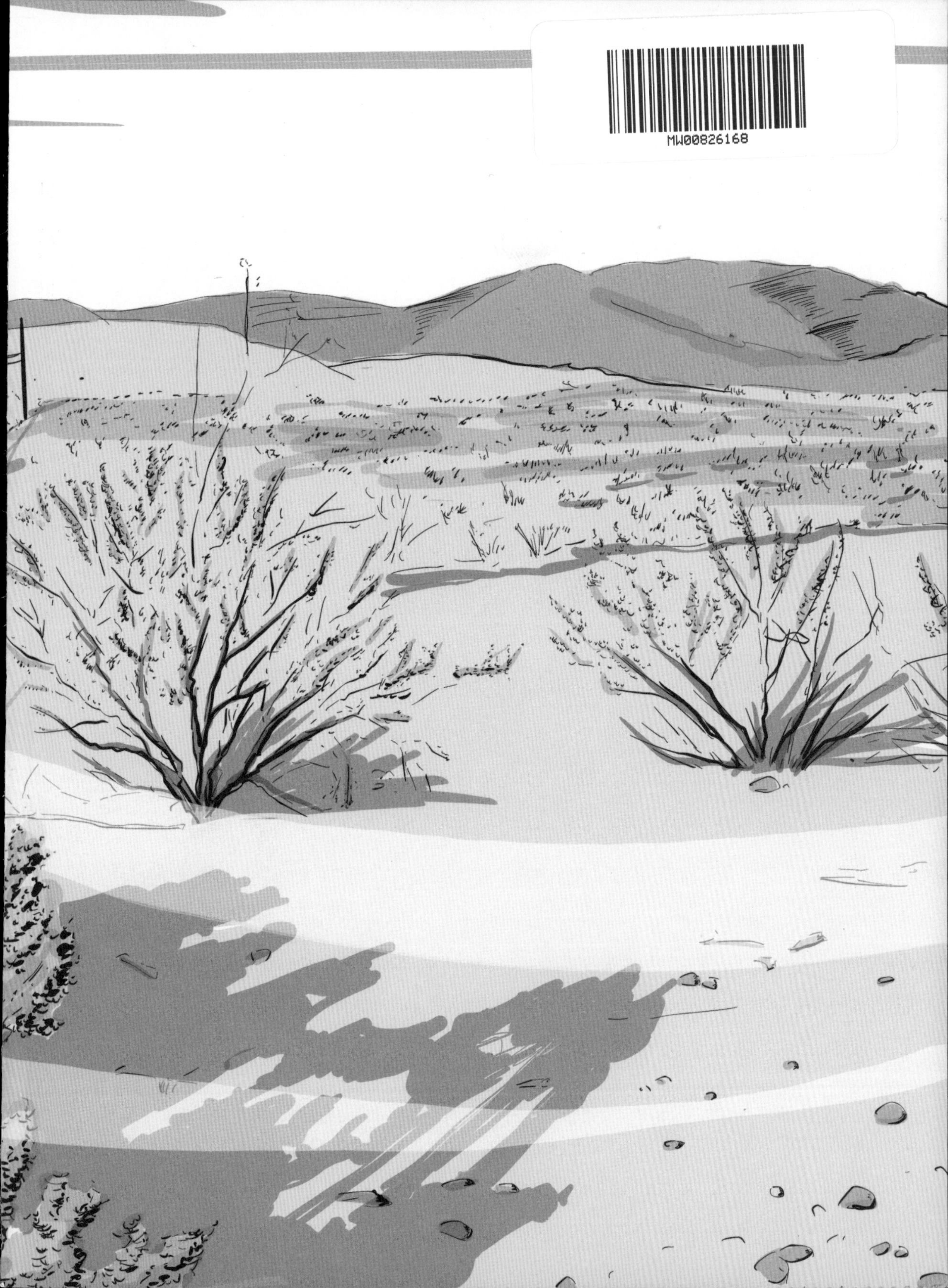

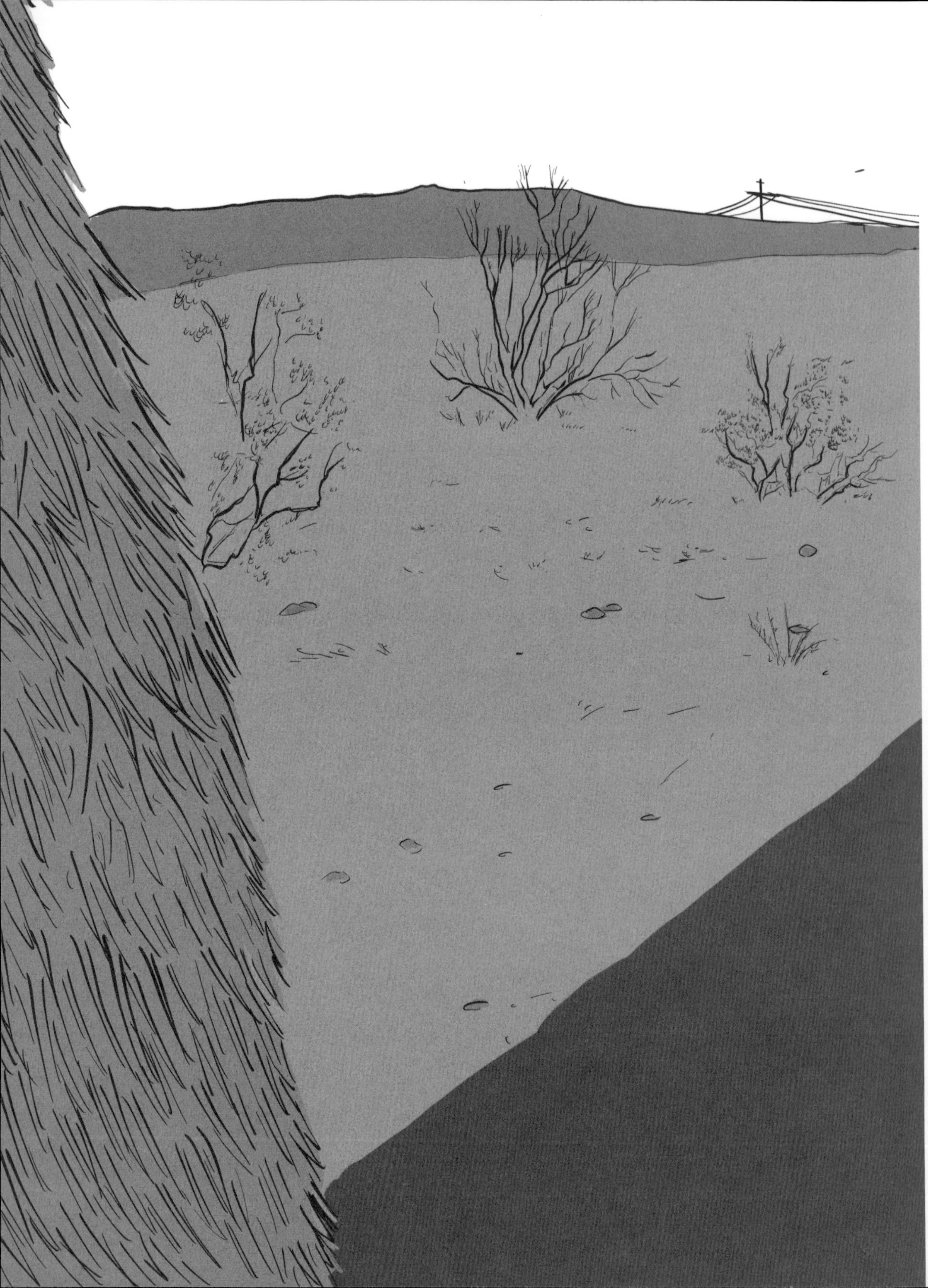

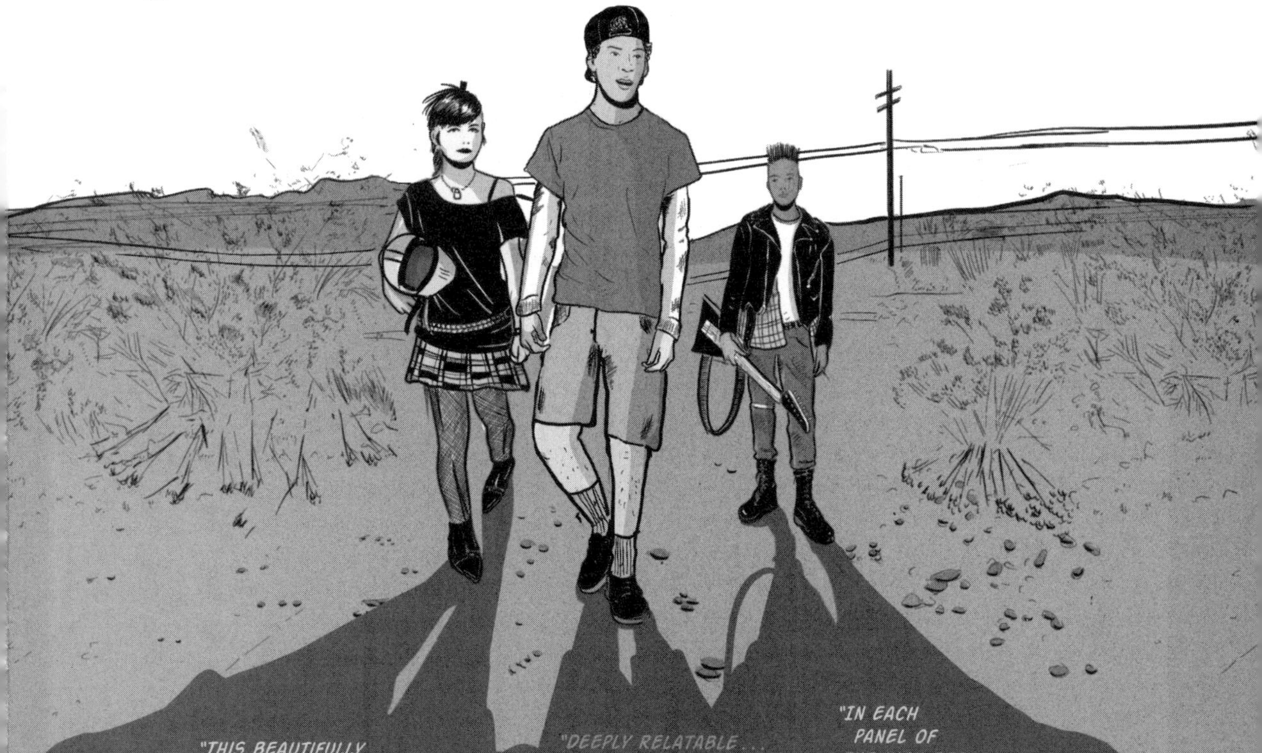

"THIS BEAUTIFULLY PACED GRAPHIC MEMOIR ILLUSTRATES THE STRUGGLE AND JOY OF FINDING SELF-ACCEPTANCE AND COMMUNITY ON THE FRINGES. IT PERFECTLY CAPTURES THE INNOCENCE, CAMARADERIE, AND TRAUMA OF BEING A PUNK OF COLOR IN THE LATE EIGHTIES AND EARLY NINETIES. I COULDN'T LOOK AWAY."

—MariNaomi, author and illustrator of *Losing the Girl*

"JAMES SPOONER CAPTURES AN OFTEN OVERLOOKED WEST COAST SLICE OF MODERN AMERICAN CULTURE AND SUBCULTURE. MISFITS, NERDS, SOCIAL OUTCASTS, AND REBELS: MR. SPOONER HAS DELIVERED A WELL-NEEDED ROAD MAP FOR FUTURE GENERATIONS OF KIDS WHO DON'T QUITE FIT IN, ESPECIALLY KIDS OF COLOR."

—John Norwood Fisher, Fishbone

"A MASTERFUL DEBUT THAT'S JUST AS CAPTIVATING AS IT IS INSPIRING. SPOONER PAINTS A WORLD THAT'S IRRESISTIBLE AND HARROWING, AND FILLS IT WITH THE KIND OF HONESTY THAT DEFINES EVERY GREAT GRAPHIC MEMOIR."

—Ezra Claytan Daniels, author of *BTTM FDRS*

"DEEPLY RELATABLE . . . IT IS GENUINELY THERAPEUTIC TO READ ABOUT JAMES SPOONER'S EXPERIENCES: BEING IN PROXIMITY TO WHITE SUPREMACY, THE EXCEPTIONS THAT ARE MADE IN SMALL TOWN, USA, AND HOW QUICKLY VIOLENCE CAN ESCALATE. MAN OH MAN. *THE HIGH DESERT* HITS SO DEEP."

—Kimya Dawson, Moldy Peaches

"A COMING-OF-AGE TALE OF THE VERY PRECARIOUS FAULT LINES OF GROWING UP AN OUTSIDER AMONGST OUTSIDERS: *THE HIGH DESERT* IS AN AMERICAN TALE OF RACE, POLITICS, COUNTER-CULTURE, AND THE TENDER AND PERSONAL STORY OF BLACK ADOLESCENCE RARELY TOLD."

—Brontez Purnell, author of *100 Boyfriends*

"PUNK IS JAMES SPOONER'S SALVATION AS HE COMES OF AGE IN A RACIST WORLD, BUT PUNK CULTURE IS ALSO A MICROCOSM OF THAT WORLD. THE PATH TO RECONCILIATION—WITH HIMSELF, HIS PARENTS, HIS PEERS—IS NAVIGATED WITH EXQUISITE NUANCE AND COMPASSION. A BEAUTIFULLY DRAWN STORY."

—Alison Bechdel, author of *Fun Home*

"IN EACH PANEL OF *THE HIGH DESERT*, JAMES SPOONER DELIVERS MAGIC BETWEEN HIS ART AND HIS WORDS, MIXING THE INTENSE PASSIONS OF YOUTH WITH THE HINDSIGHT OF THE WISE. GORGEOUSLY DRAWN, BRUTALLY HONEST, AND AS EMOTIONALLY RAW AS YOUR FAVORITE PUNK SONG."

—Dawnie Walton, author of *The Final Revival of Opal & Nev*

"JAMES SPOONER'S DOCUMENTARY *AFRO-PUNK* INSPIRED A MOVEMENT THAT CENTERED BLACK AND BROWN PUNKS EVERYWHERE. IN HIS NEW MEMOIR, WE LEARN ABOUT THE MAJOR PITFALLS AND MINOR TRIUMPHS THAT PUT SPOONER ON THE PATH TO REALIZING HIS DREAM OF AN ALL-BLACK MOSH PIT."

—Kathleen Hanna, Bikini Kill and Le Tigre

"THERE'S SOMETHING SO RECOGNIZABLE IN *THE HIGH DESERT* . . . I SUSPECT IN A WAY WE WERE ALL THERE AT ONE TIME IN OUR LIVES, NAVIGATING AND NEGOTIATING AS WE FIGURED OUT JUST WHO THE FUCK WE WERE AND WHO WAS WITH US. I LOVED THIS BOOK."

—Ian MacKaye, Minor Threat and Fugazi

AUTHOR'S NOTE: THIS MEMOIR IS BASED ON A TRUE STORY. SOME EVENTS AND CHARACTERS ARE COMPOSITES. ALL NAMES, EXCEPT FOR THE AUTHOR, HAVE BEEN CHANGED. THE SEQUENCE OF EVENTS MAY BE OUT OF ORDER FOR DRAMATIC EFFECT.

HARPERCOLLINS BOOKS MAY BE PURCHASED FOR EDUCATIONAL, BUSINESS, OR SALES PROMOTIONAL USE. FOR INFORMATION, PLEASE EMAIL THE SPECIAL MARKETS DEPARTMENT AT SPSALES@HARPERCOLLINS.COM.

FIRST EDITION

DESIGNED BY KERRY RUBINSTEIN

LIBRARY OF CONGRESS CATALOGING-IN-PUBLICATION DATA HAS BEEN APPLIED FOR.

ISBN 978-0-35-865911-2

22 23 24 25 26 LSC 10 9 8 7 6 5 4 3 2 1

FOR HOLLIS AND ISSA

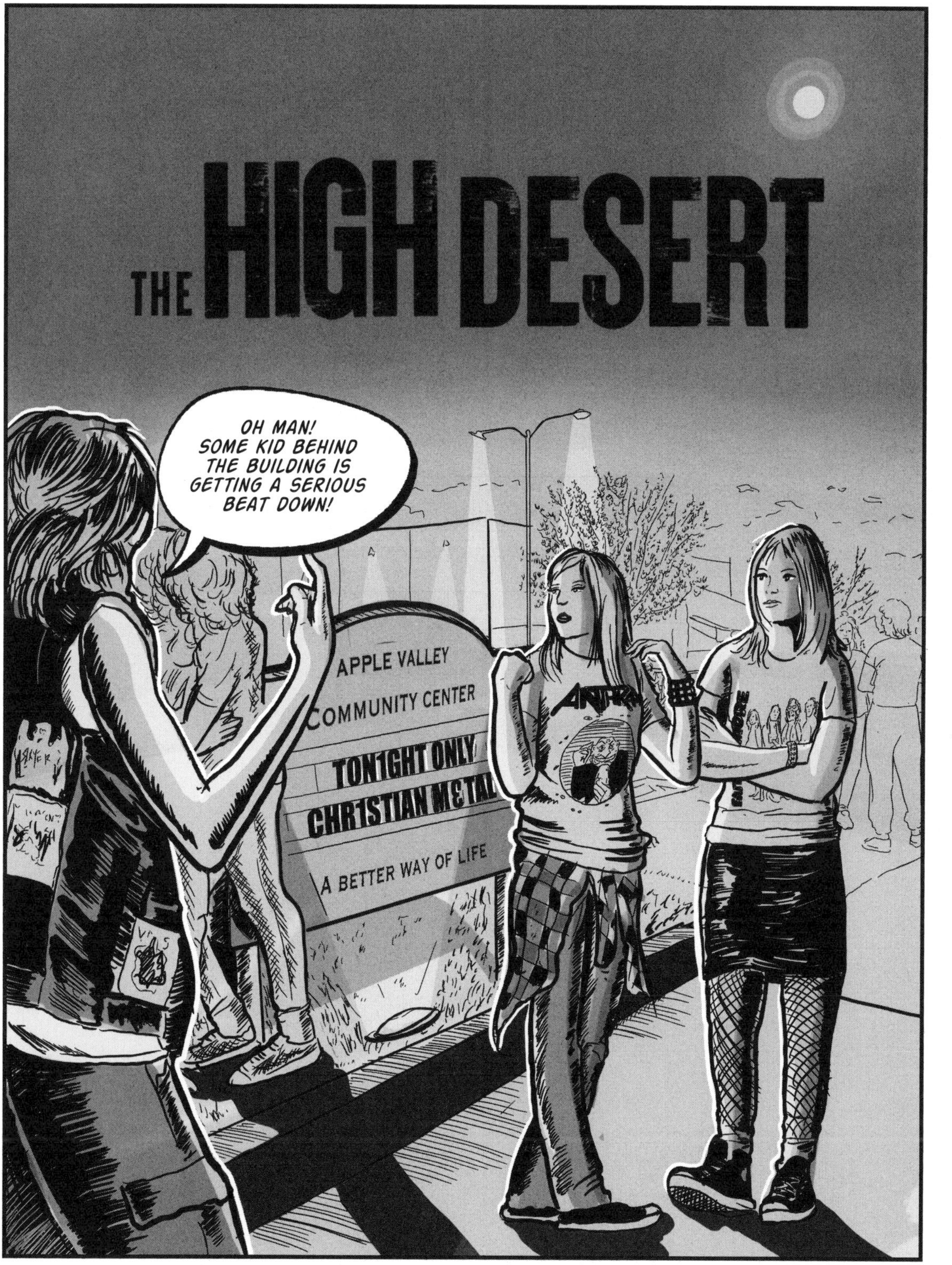
THE HIGH DESERT
OH MAN! SOME KID BEHIND THE BUILDING IS GETTING A SERIOUS BEAT DOWN!
APPLE VALLEY COMMUNITY CENTER
TON1GHT ONLY
CHR1STIAN METAL
A BETTER WAY OF LIFE

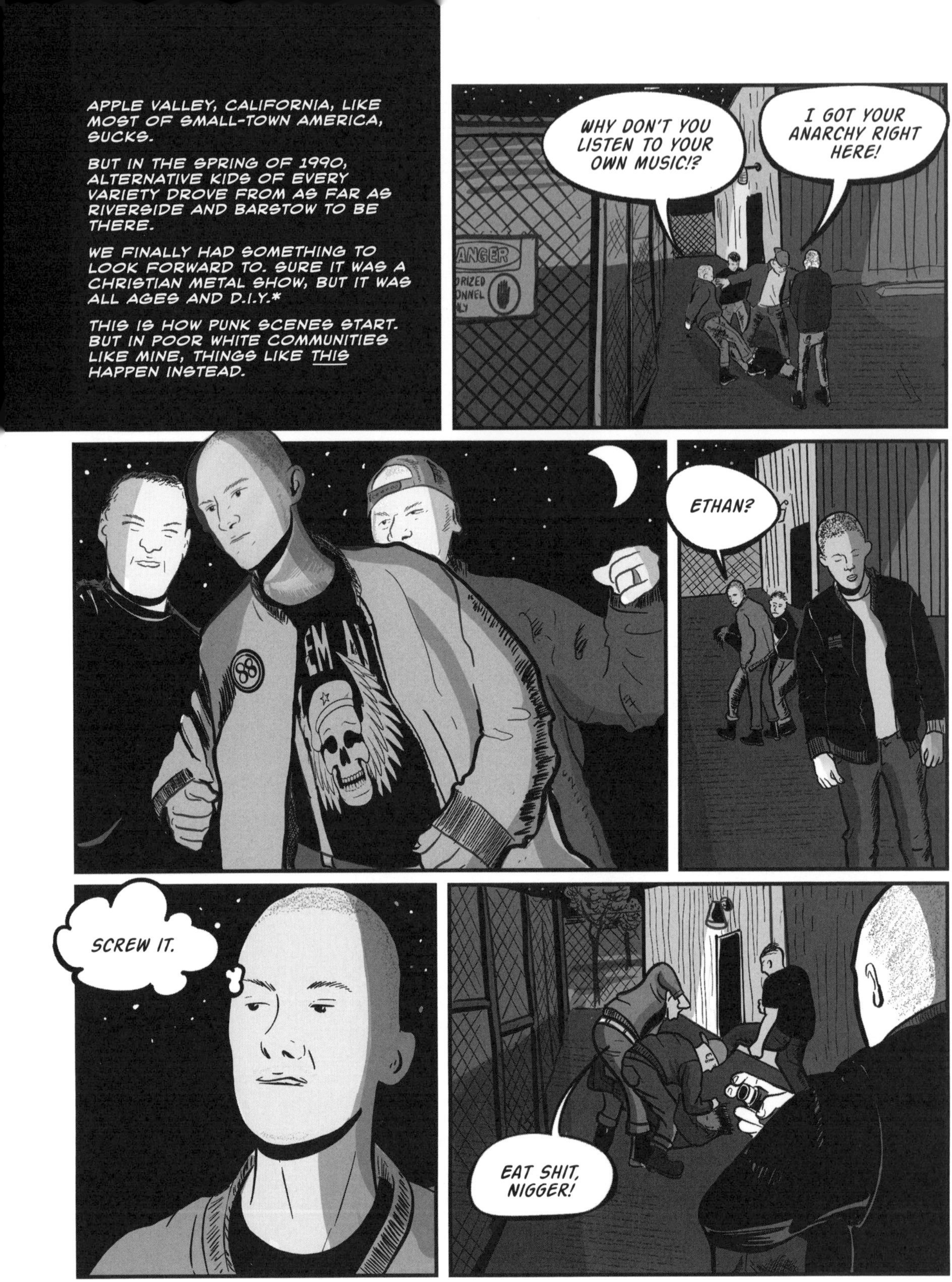
APPLE VALLEY, CALIFORNIA, LIKE MOST OF SMALL-TOWN AMERICA, SUCKS.
BUT IN THE SPRING OF 1990, ALTERNATIVE KIDS OF EVERY VARIETY DROVE FROM AS FAR AS RIVERSIDE AND BARSTOW TO BE THERE.
WE FINALLY HAD SOMETHING TO LOOK FORWARD TO. SURE IT WAS A CHRISTIAN METAL SHOW, BUT IT WAS ALL AGES AND D.I.Y.*
THIS IS HOW PUNK SCENES START. BUT IN POOR WHITE COMMUNITIES LIKE MINE, THINGS LIKE THIS HAPPEN INSTEAD.
WHY DON'T YOU LISTEN TO YOUR OWN MUSIC!?
I GOT YOUR ANARCHY RIGHT HERE!
ETHAN?
SCREW IT.
EAT SHIT, NIGGER!

*REFERRING TO THE "DO-IT-YOURSELF" MOVEMENT

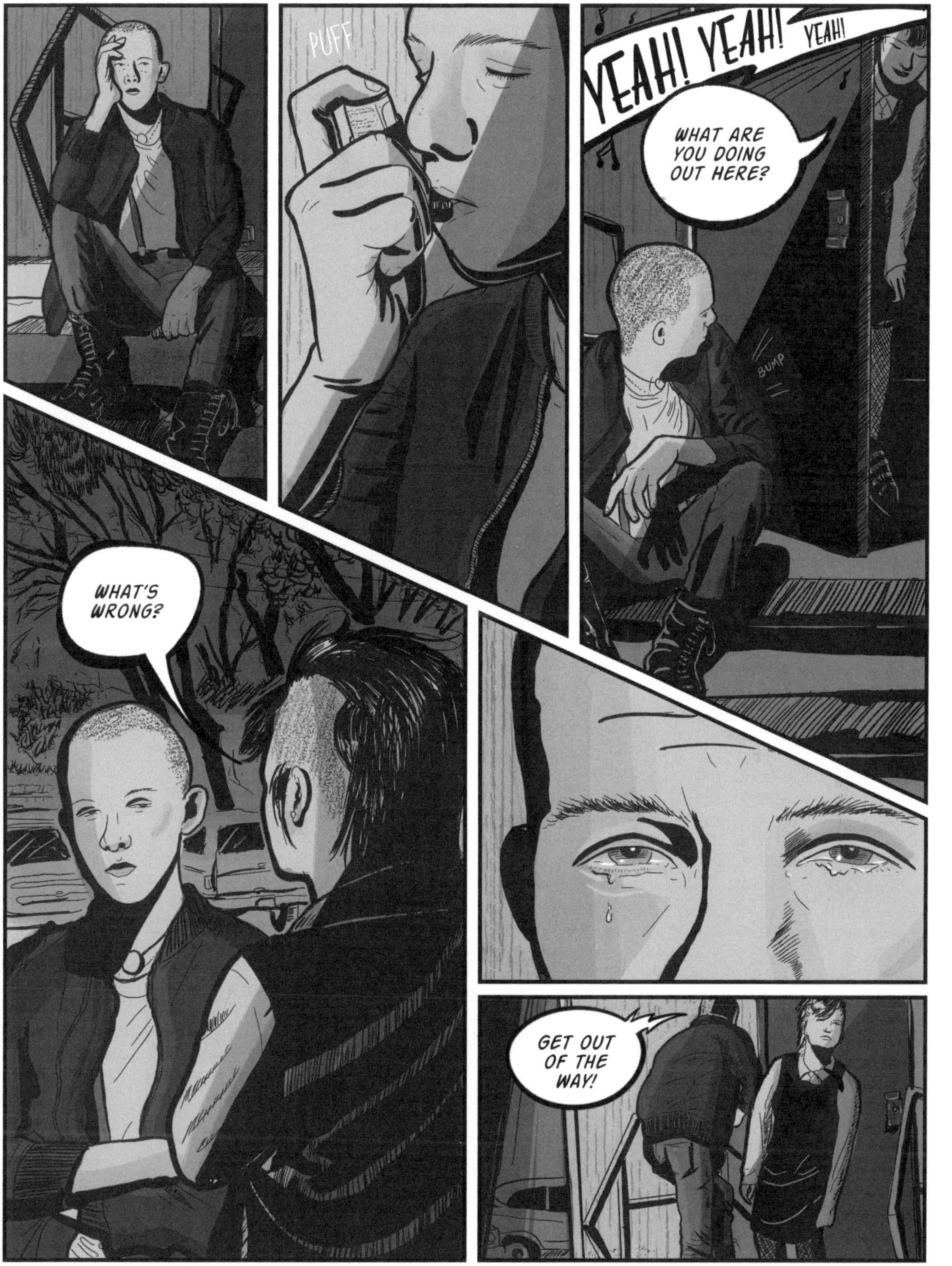
PUFF
YEAH! YEAH! YEAH!
WHAT ARE YOU DOING OUT HERE?
BUMP
WHAT'S WRONG?
GET OUT OF THE WAY!

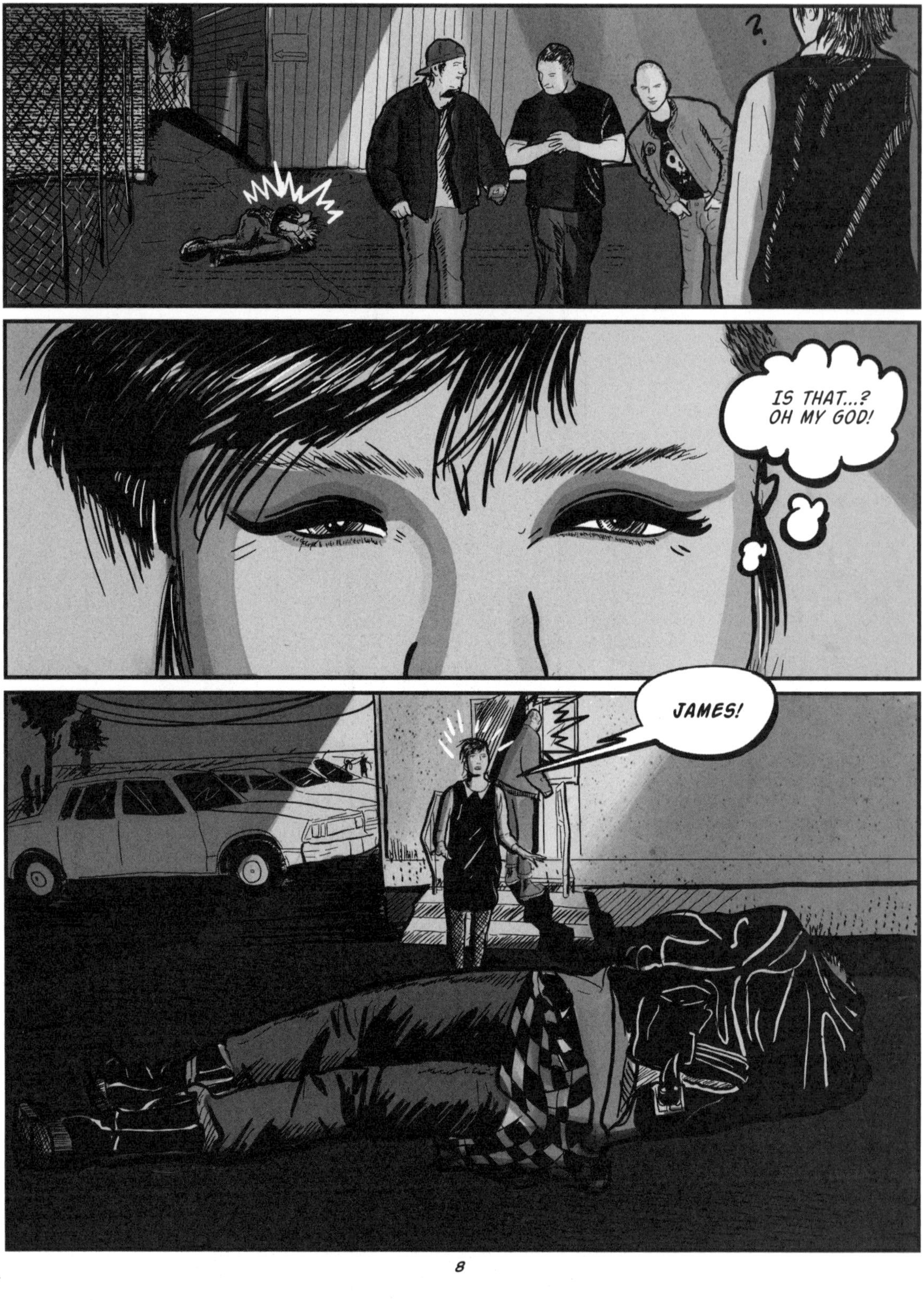
?
IS THAT...? OH MY GOD!
JAMES!

THE HIGH DESERT

HARPER

An Imprint of HarperCollins*Publishers*

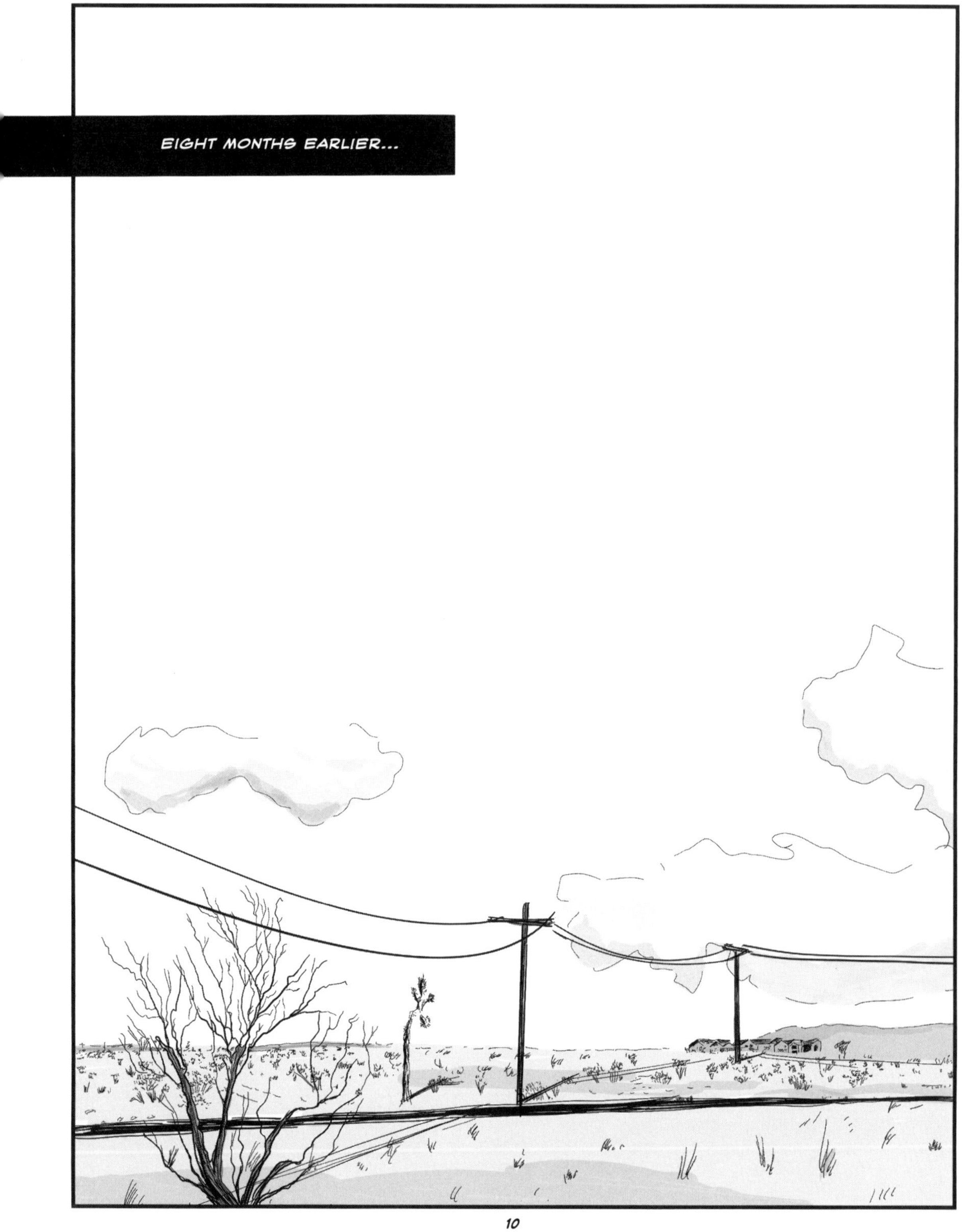
EIGHT MONTHS EARLIER...

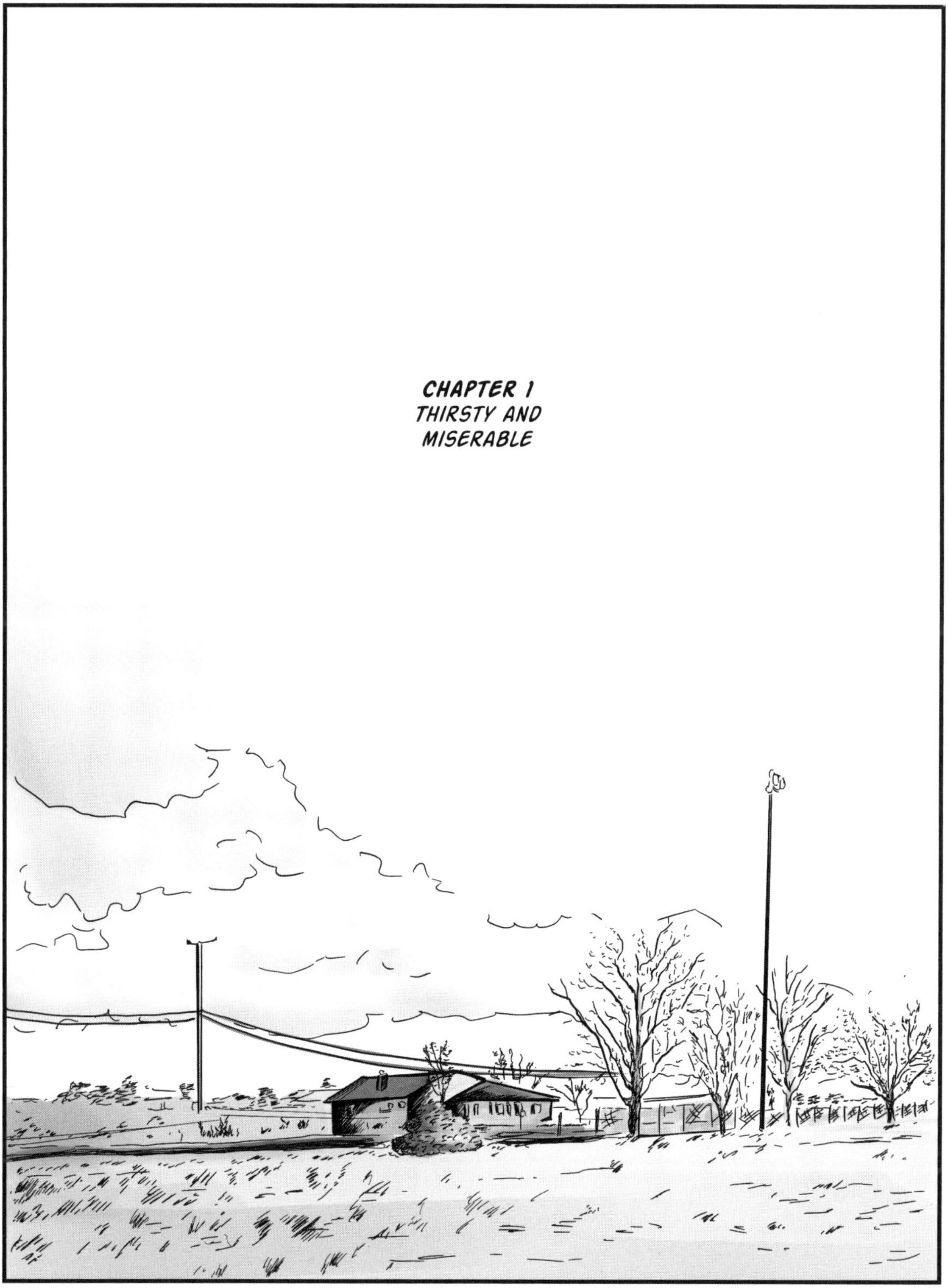
CHAPTER 1
THIRSTY AND
MISERABLE

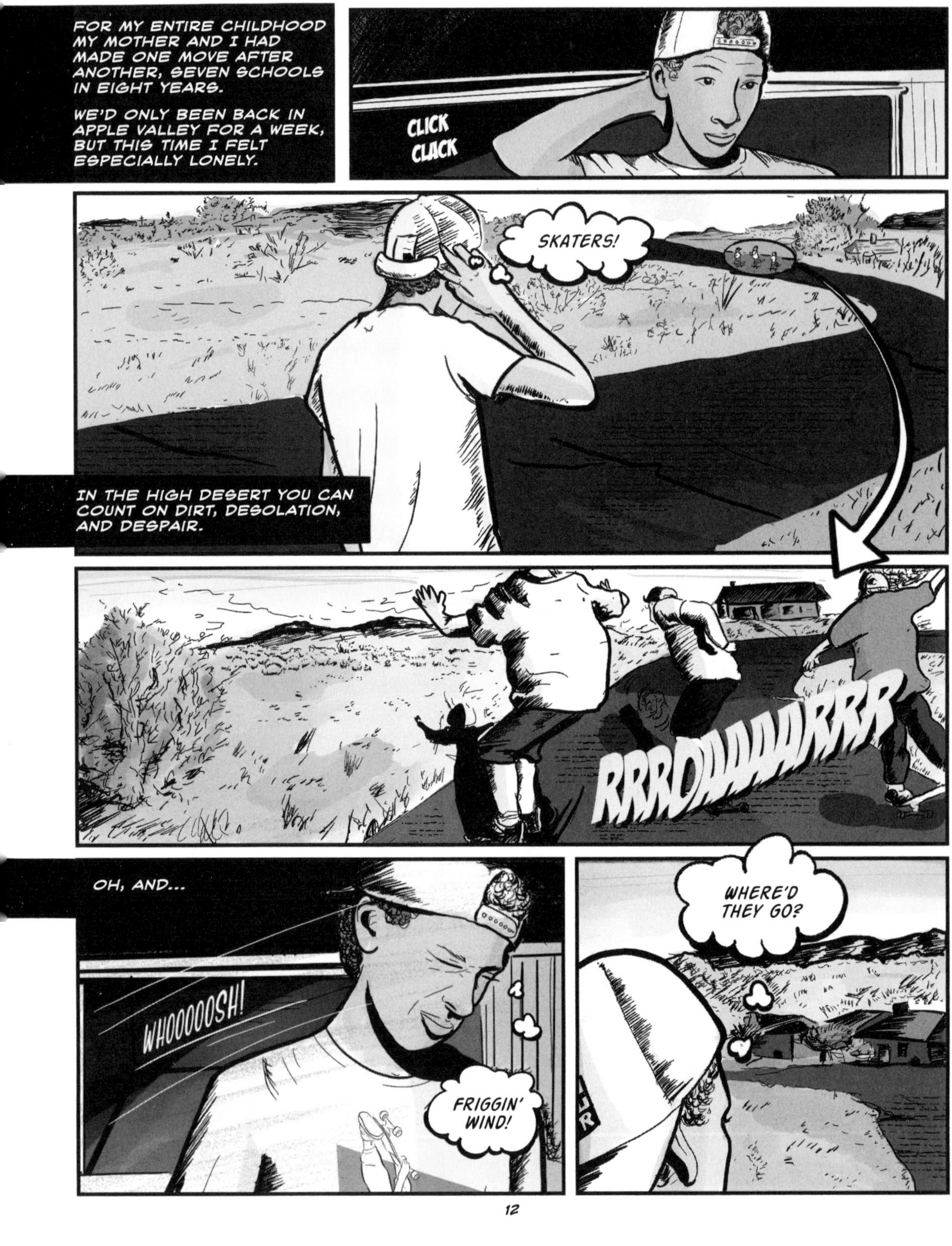
FOR MY ENTIRE CHILDHOOD MY MOTHER AND I HAD MADE ONE MOVE AFTER ANOTHER, SEVEN SCHOOLS IN EIGHT YEARS.
WE'D ONLY BEEN BACK IN APPLE VALLEY FOR A WEEK, BUT THIS TIME I FELT ESPECIALLY LONELY.
CLICK CLACK
SKATERS!
IN THE HIGH DESERT YOU CAN COUNT ON DIRT, DESOLATION, AND DESPAIR.
RRROAAAARRR
OH, AND...
WHOOOOOSH!
FRIGGIN' WIND!
WHERE'D THEY GO?

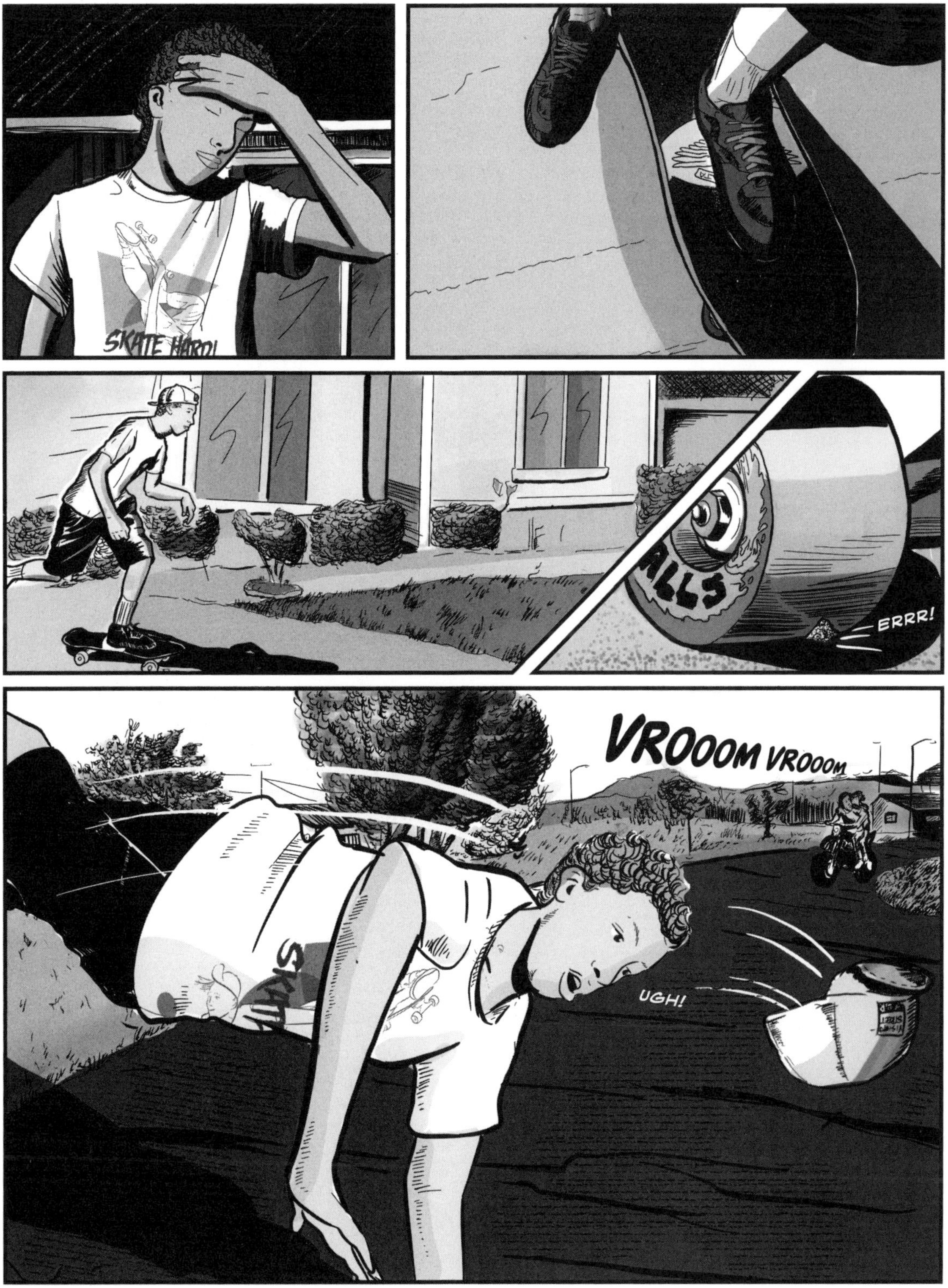
SKATE HARD!
ERRR!
VROOOM VROOOM
UGH!

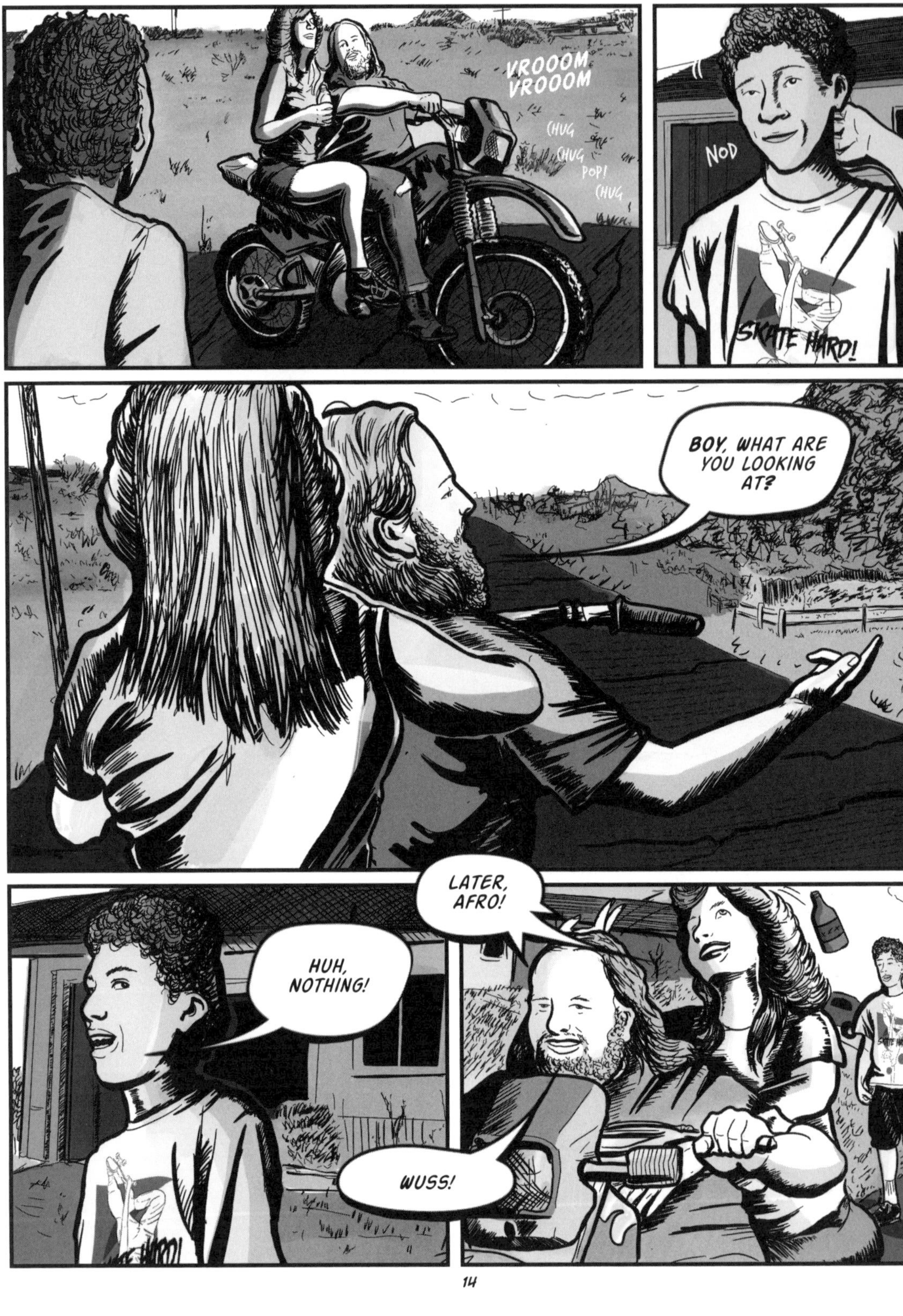
VROOOM
VROOOM
CHUG
CHUG
POP!
CHUG
NOD
SKATE HARD!
BOY, WHAT ARE YOU LOOKING AT?
HUH, NOTHING!
LATER, AFRO!
WUSS!
SKATE HARD!

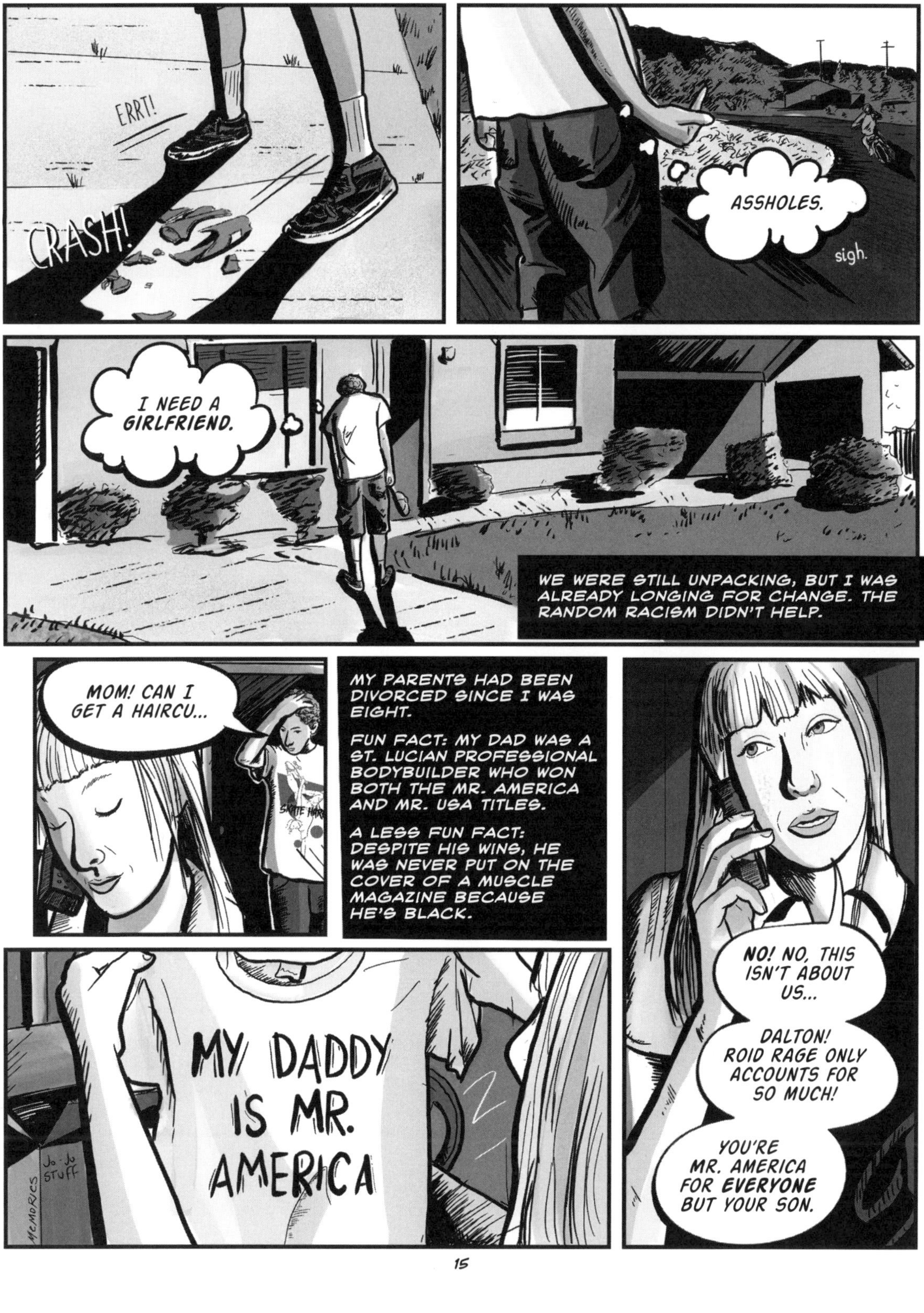

ERRT!
CRASH!
ASSHOLES.
sigh.
I NEED A GIRLFRIEND.
WE WERE STILL UNPACKING, BUT I WAS ALREADY LONGING FOR CHANGE. THE RANDOM RACISM DIDN'T HELP.
MOM! CAN I GET A HAIRCU...
MY PARENTS HAD BEEN DIVORCED SINCE I WAS EIGHT.
FUN FACT: MY DAD WAS A ST. LUCIAN PROFESSIONAL BODYBUILDER WHO WON BOTH THE MR. AMERICA AND MR. USA TITLES.
A LESS FUN FACT: DESPITE HIS WINS, HE WAS NEVER PUT ON THE COVER OF A MUSCLE MAGAZINE BECAUSE HE'S BLACK.
NO! NO, THIS ISN'T ABOUT US...
DALTON! ROID RAGE ONLY ACCOUNTS FOR SO MUCH!
YOU'RE MR. AMERICA FOR EVERYONE BUT YOUR SON.
MY DADDY IS MR. AMERICA
JO-JO STUFF
MEMORIES

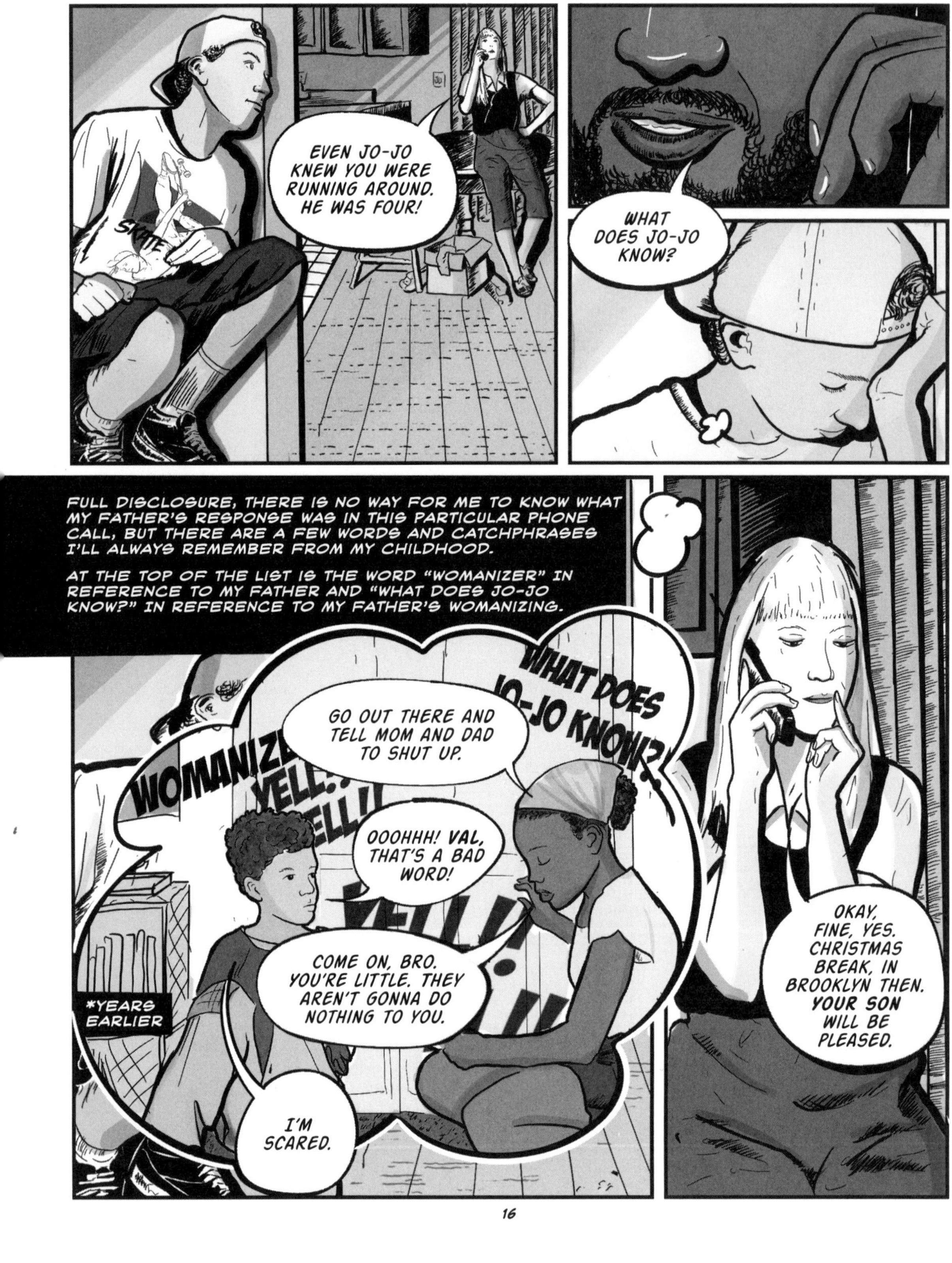
EVEN JO-JO KNEW YOU WERE RUNNING AROUND. HE WAS FOUR!
WHAT DOES JO-JO KNOW?
FULL DISCLOSURE, THERE IS NO WAY FOR ME TO KNOW WHAT MY FATHER'S RESPONSE WAS IN THIS PARTICULAR PHONE CALL, BUT THERE ARE A FEW WORDS AND CATCHPHRASES I'LL ALWAYS REMEMBER FROM MY CHILDHOOD.
AT THE TOP OF THE LIST IS THE WORD "WOMANIZER" IN REFERENCE TO MY FATHER AND "WHAT DOES JO-JO KNOW?" IN REFERENCE TO MY FATHER'S WOMANIZING.
*YEARS EARLIER
WHAT DOES JO-JO KNOW?
GO OUT THERE AND TELL MOM AND DAD TO SHUT UP.
OOOHHH! VAL, THAT'S A BAD WORD!
COME ON, BRO. YOU'RE LITTLE. THEY AREN'T GONNA DO NOTHING TO YOU.
I'M SCARED.
OKAY, FINE, YES. CHRISTMAS BREAK, IN BROOKLYN THEN. YOUR SON WILL BE PLEASED.

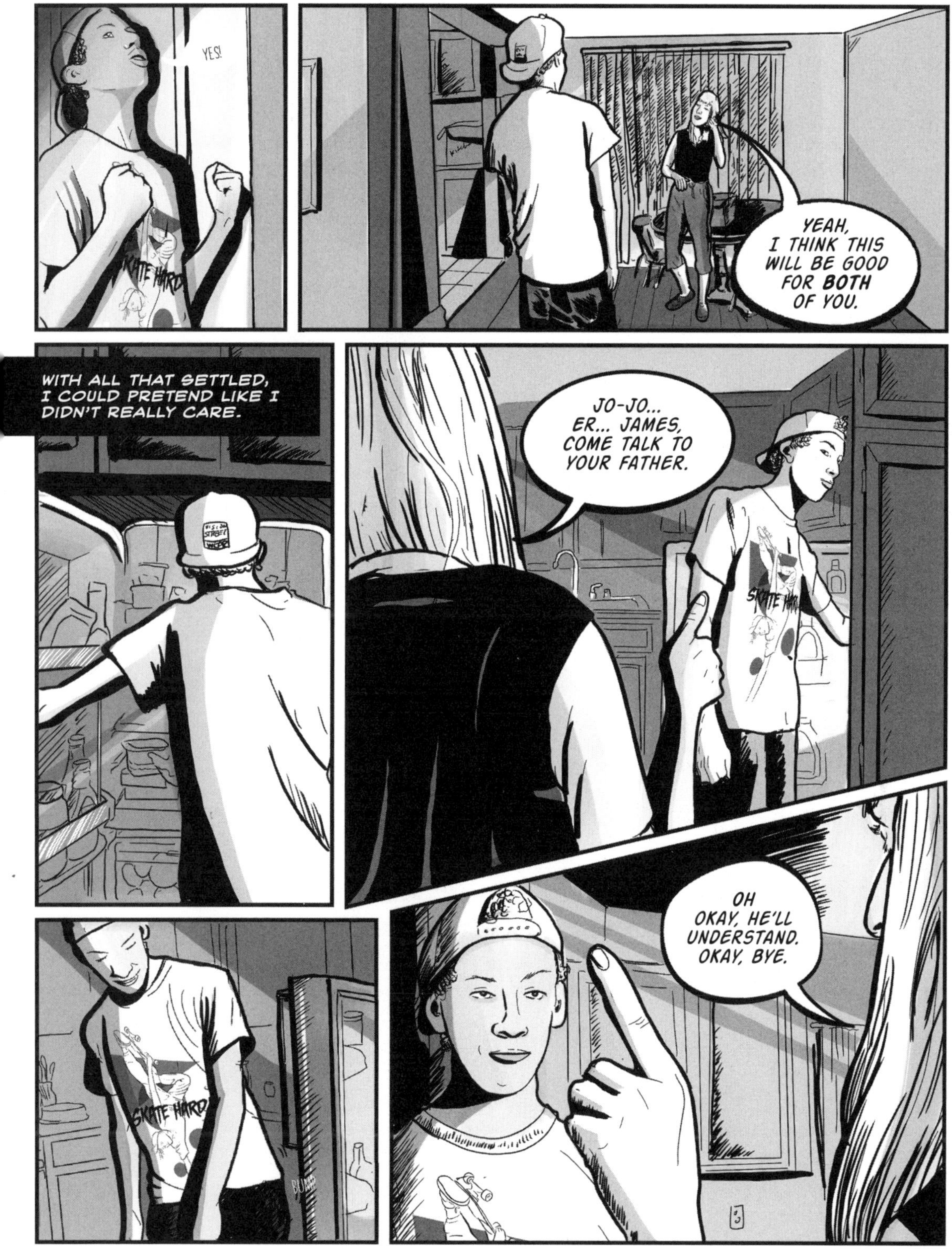
YES!
YEAH, I THINK THIS WILL BE GOOD FOR **BOTH** OF YOU.
WITH ALL THAT SETTLED, I COULD PRETEND LIKE I DIDN'T REALLY CARE.
JO-JO... ER... JAMES, COME TALK TO YOUR FATHER.
SKATE HARD
OH OKAY, HE'LL UNDERSTAND. OKAY, BYE.

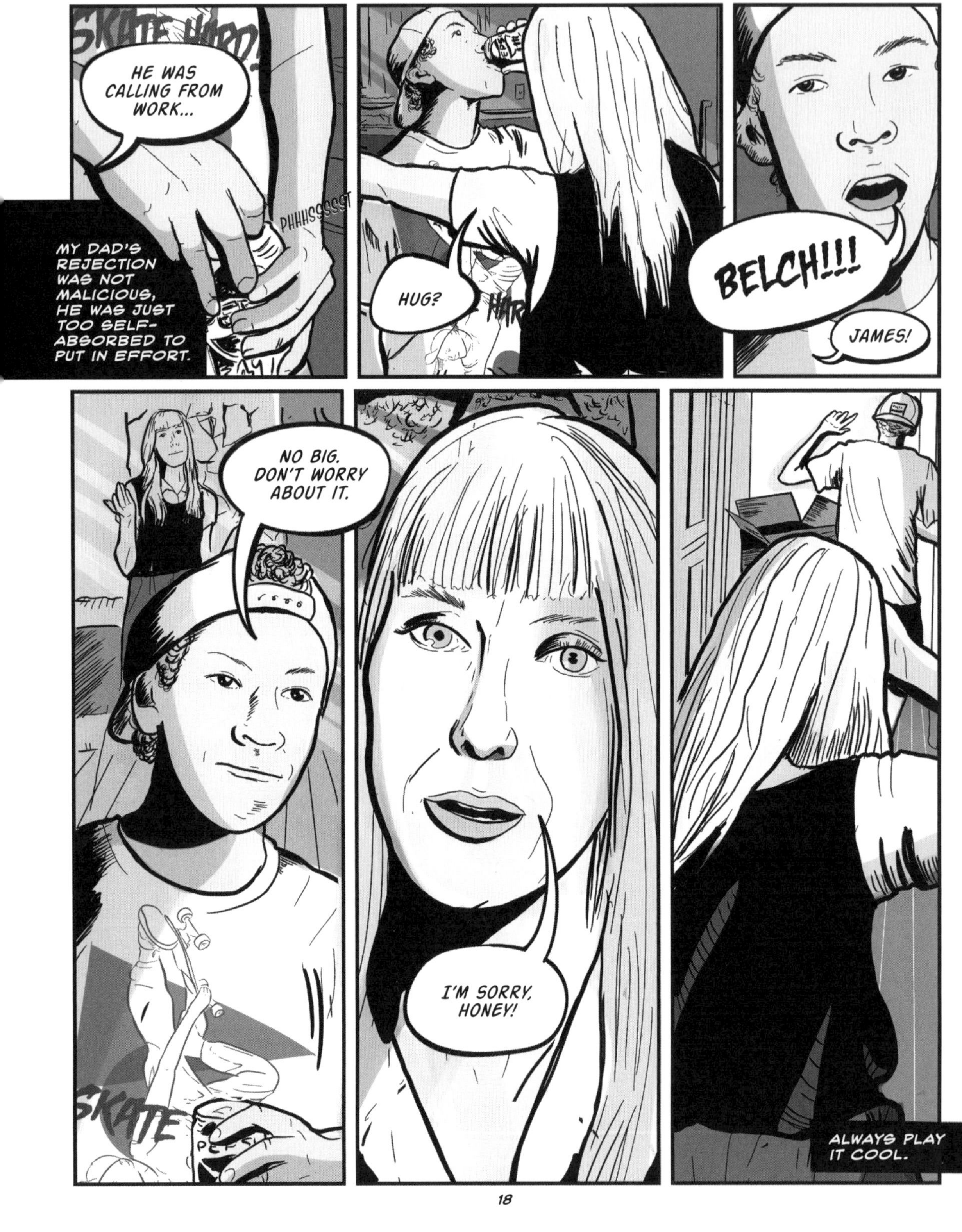

SKATE HARD!
HE WAS CALLING FROM WORK...
MY DAD'S REJECTION WAS NOT MALICIOUS, HE WAS JUST TOO SELF-ABSORBED TO PUT IN EFFORT.
PHHHSSSSST
HUG?
BELCH!!!
JAMES!
NO BIG. DON'T WORRY ABOUT IT.
I'M SORRY, HONEY!
SKATE
ALWAYS PLAY IT COOL.

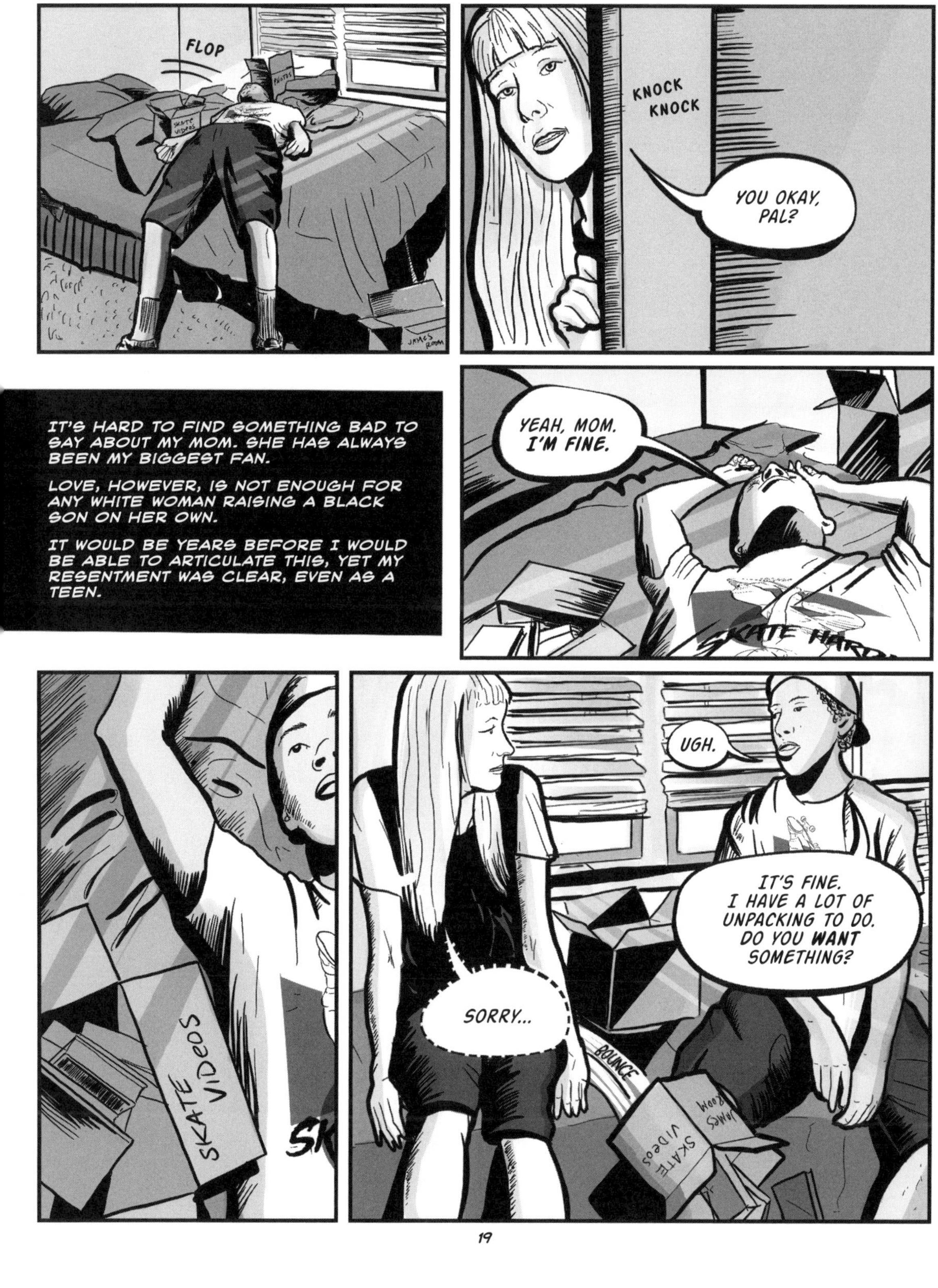
FLOP
PHOTOS
SKATE VIDEOS
KNOCK KNOCK
YOU OKAY, PAL?
IT'S HARD TO FIND SOMETHING BAD TO SAY ABOUT MY MOM. SHE HAS ALWAYS BEEN MY BIGGEST FAN.
LOVE, HOWEVER, IS NOT ENOUGH FOR ANY WHITE WOMAN RAISING A BLACK SON ON HER OWN.
IT WOULD BE YEARS BEFORE I WOULD BE ABLE TO ARTICULATE THIS, YET MY RESENTMENT WAS CLEAR, EVEN AS A TEEN.
YEAH, MOM. **I'M FINE.**
SKATE VIDEOS
UGH.
IT'S FINE. I HAVE A LOT OF UNPACKING TO DO. DO YOU **WANT** SOMETHING?
SORRY...
BOUNCE
SKATE VIDEOS

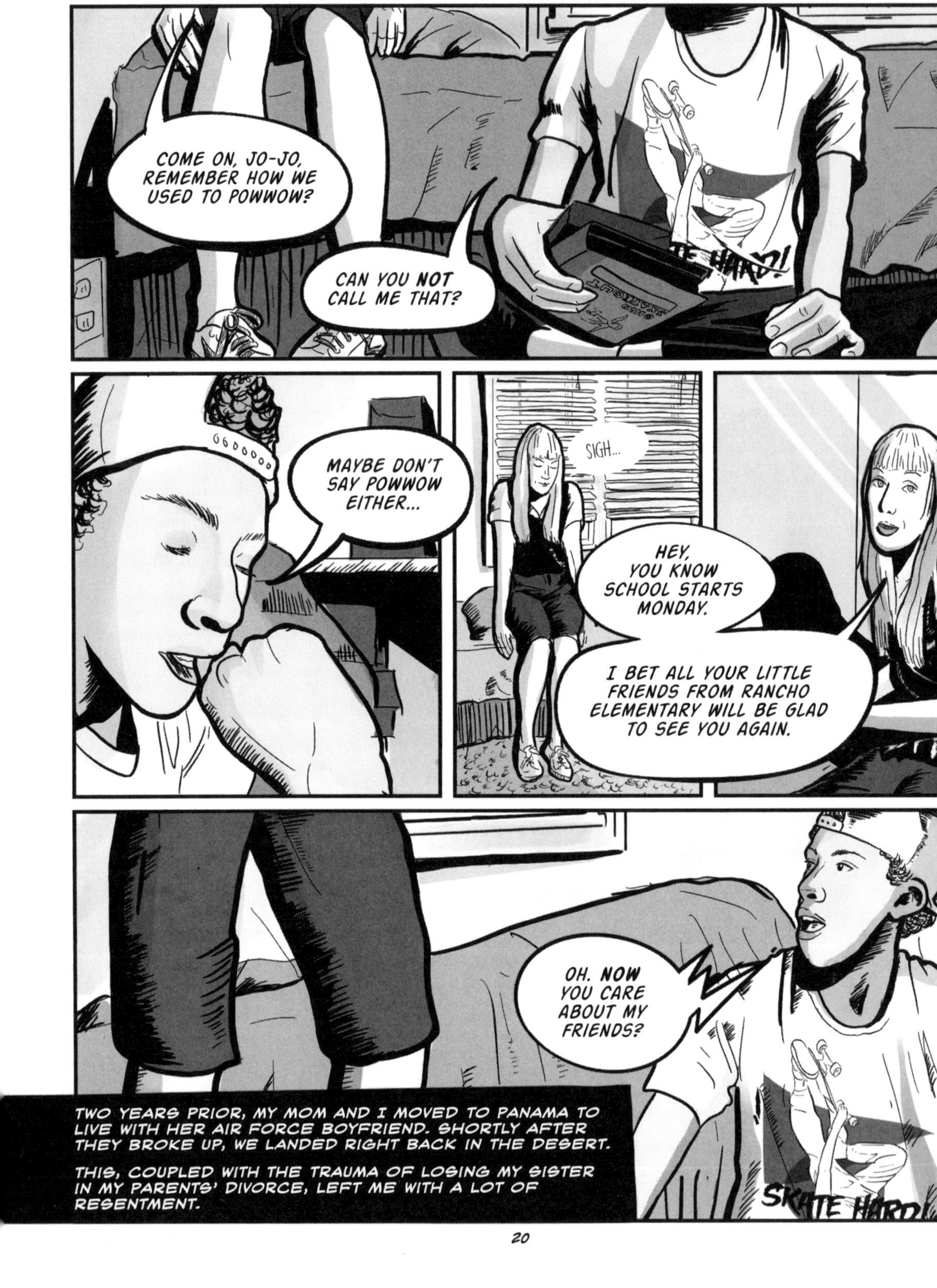
COME ON, JO-JO, REMEMBER HOW WE USED TO POWWOW?
CAN YOU **NOT** CALL ME THAT?
MAYBE DON'T SAY POWWOW EITHER...
SIGH...
HEY, YOU KNOW SCHOOL STARTS MONDAY.
I BET ALL YOUR LITTLE FRIENDS FROM RANCHO ELEMENTARY WILL BE GLAD TO SEE YOU AGAIN.
OH. **NOW** YOU CARE ABOUT MY FRIENDS?
TWO YEARS PRIOR, MY MOM AND I MOVED TO PANAMA TO LIVE WITH HER AIR FORCE BOYFRIEND. SHORTLY AFTER THEY BROKE UP, WE LANDED RIGHT BACK IN THE DESERT.
THIS, COUPLED WITH THE TRAUMA OF LOSING MY SISTER IN MY PARENTS' DIVORCE, LEFT ME WITH A LOT OF RESENTMENT.
SKATE HARD!

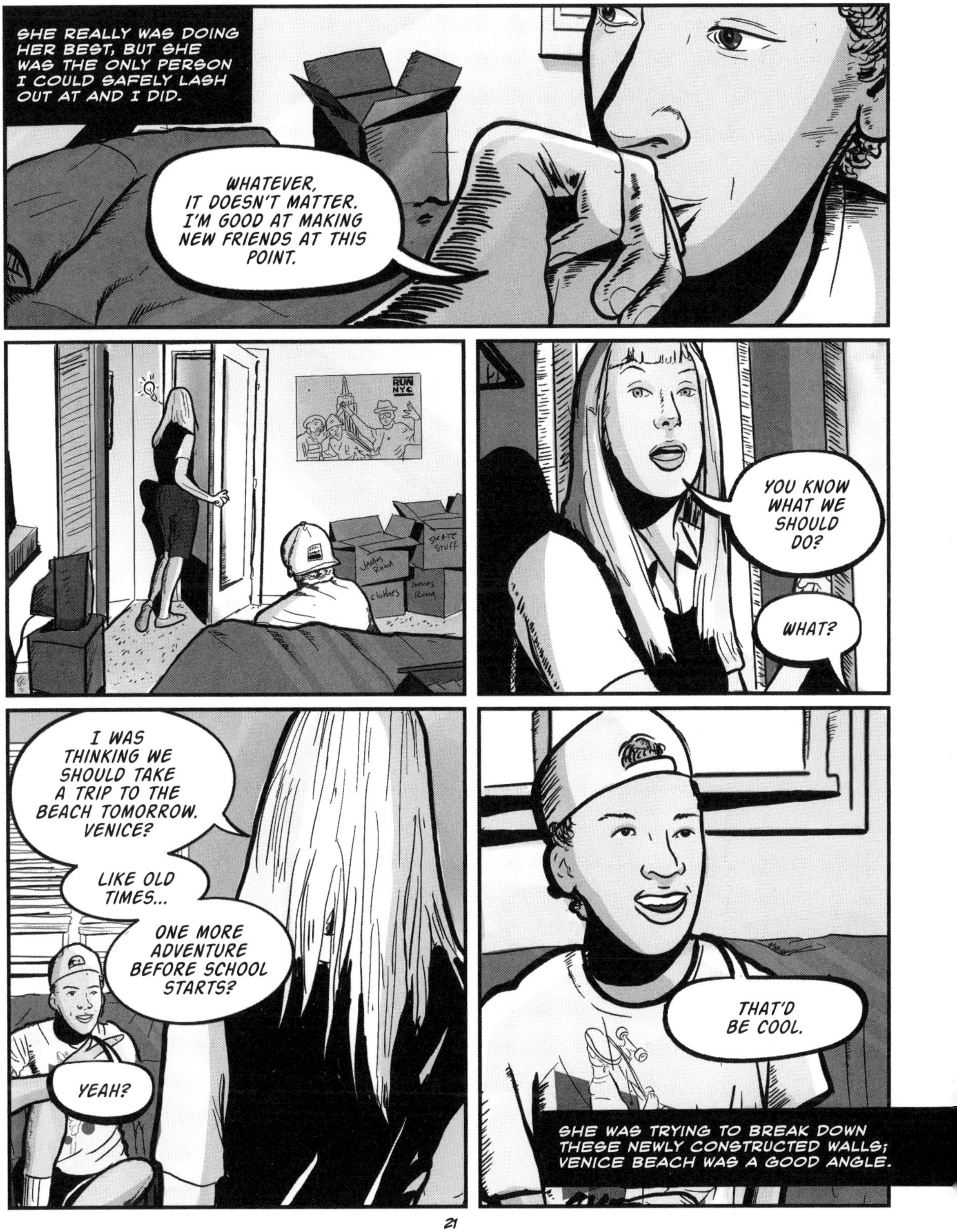
SHE REALLY WAS DOING HER BEST, BUT SHE WAS THE ONLY PERSON I COULD SAFELY LASH OUT AT AND I DID.
WHATEVER, IT DOESN'T MATTER. I'M GOOD AT MAKING NEW FRIENDS AT THIS POINT.
RUN NYC
SKATE STUFF
JAMES ROOM
CLOTHES
JAMES' ROOM
YOU KNOW WHAT WE SHOULD DO?
WHAT?
I WAS THINKING WE SHOULD TAKE A TRIP TO THE BEACH TOMORROW. VENICE?
LIKE OLD TIMES...
ONE MORE ADVENTURE BEFORE SCHOOL STARTS?
YEAH?
THAT'D BE COOL.
SHE WAS TRYING TO BREAK DOWN THESE NEWLY CONSTRUCTED WALLS; VENICE BEACH WAS A GOOD ANGLE.

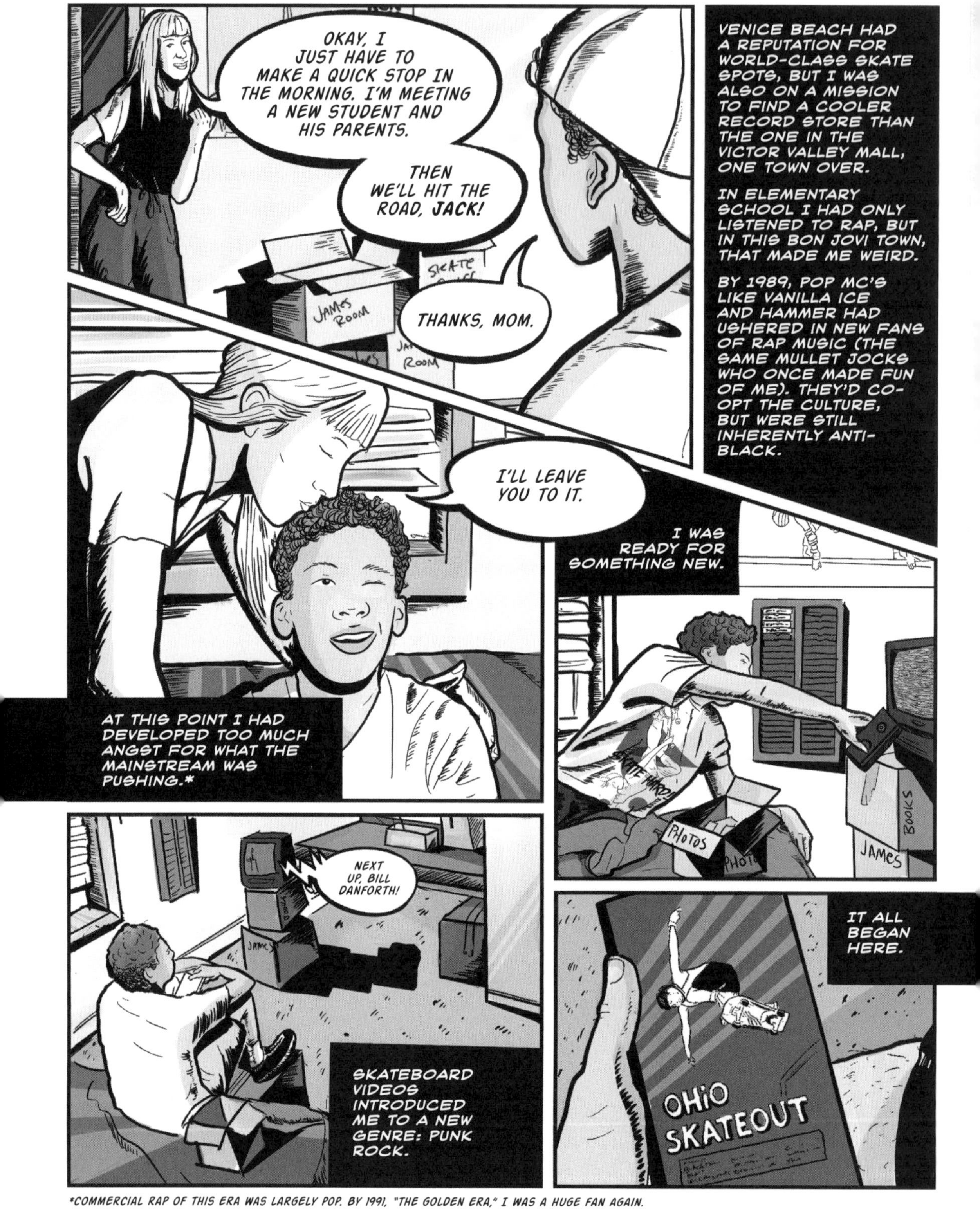
OKAY, I JUST HAVE TO MAKE A QUICK STOP IN THE MORNING. I'M MEETING A NEW STUDENT AND HIS PARENTS.
THEN WE'LL HIT THE ROAD, JACK!
THANKS, MOM.
VENICE BEACH HAD A REPUTATION FOR WORLD-CLASS SKATE SPOTS, BUT I WAS ALSO ON A MISSION TO FIND A COOLER RECORD STORE THAN THE ONE IN THE VICTOR VALLEY MALL, ONE TOWN OVER.
IN ELEMENTARY SCHOOL I HAD ONLY LISTENED TO RAP, BUT IN THIS BON JOVI TOWN, THAT MADE ME WEIRD.
BY 1989, POP MC'S LIKE VANILLA ICE AND HAMMER HAD USHERED IN NEW FANS OF RAP MUSIC (THE SAME MULLET JOCKS WHO ONCE MADE FUN OF ME). THEY'D CO-OPT THE CULTURE, BUT WERE STILL INHERENTLY ANTI-BLACK.
I'LL LEAVE YOU TO IT.
AT THIS POINT I HAD DEVELOPED TOO MUCH ANGST FOR WHAT THE MAINSTREAM WAS PUSHING.*
I WAS READY FOR SOMETHING NEW.
NEXT UP, BILL DANFORTH!
SKATEBOARD VIDEOS INTRODUCED ME TO A NEW GENRE: PUNK ROCK.
IT ALL BEGAN HERE.
OHIO SKATEOUT

*COMMERCIAL RAP OF THIS ERA WAS LARGELY POP. BY 1991, "THE GOLDEN ERA," I WAS A HUGE FAN AGAIN.

I DID HAVE A COUPLE GLIMPSES INTO PUNK PRIOR...

FIRST WAS SPUD, MY FOURTH GRADE SUMMER CAMP COUNSELOR.

HIS IDEA OF A WAKE-UP CALL WAS TRACKS OFF SUICIDAL TENDENCIES' FIRST LP.

ALL I WANTED WAS A PEPSI, AND SHE WOULDN'T GIVE IT TO ME!*

WAKE UP!

NOT THIS PEPSI SONG AGAIN!

I WASN'T READY.

A FEW YEARS LATER I NOTICED THE OLDER COOL KIDS WEARING LOGOS I DIDN'T RECOGNIZE.

I WONDER WHAT THAT SKULL IS FROM?

BUT NOTHING WOULD KICK DOWN THE DOOR LIKE "OHIO SKATEOUT."

THIS VIDEO HAD MY FAVORITE PROS DOING ACID DROPS, BONELESSES, AND CHRIST AIRS TO MUSIC I NEVER HEARD BEFORE.

THE SNOTTY TONE OF BLACK FLAG'S KEITH MORRIS SCREAMING "I DON'T CARE" OVER AND OVER WAS EXHILARATING!

OHIO SKAT

MUSIC BY BLACK FLAG BL'AST DESCENDENTS

The Hottes Ever

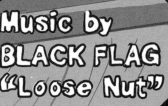

Music by BLACK FLAG "Loose Nut"

GOOD CHOICE, MAN!

WITHIN A WEEK OF MOVING BACK TO THE STATES, I FOUND MYSELF IN THE MALL BUYING MY FIRST PUNK TAPE... BLACK FLAG'S "EVERYTHING WENT BLACK"...

23

*SUICIDAL TENDENCIES "INSTITUTIONALIZED"

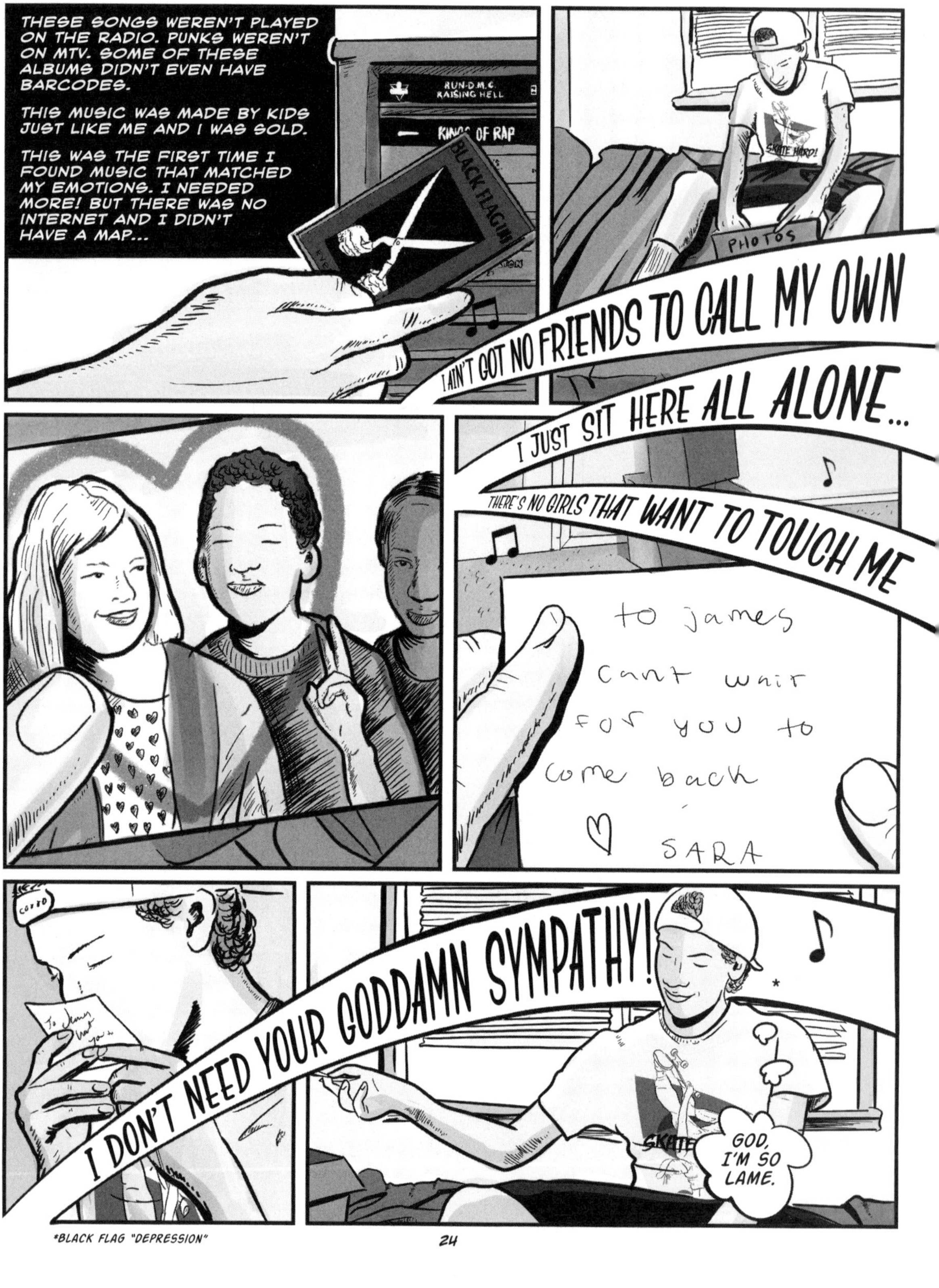
THESE SONGS WEREN'T PLAYED ON THE RADIO. PUNKS WEREN'T ON MTV. SOME OF THESE ALBUMS DIDN'T EVEN HAVE BARCODES.
THIS MUSIC WAS MADE BY KIDS JUST LIKE ME AND I WAS SOLD.
THIS WAS THE FIRST TIME I FOUND MUSIC THAT MATCHED MY EMOTIONS. I NEEDED MORE! BUT THERE WAS NO INTERNET AND I DIDN'T HAVE A MAP...
RUN-D.M.C. RAISING HELL
BLACK FLAG
SKATE HARD!
PHOTOS
I AIN'T GOT NO FRIENDS TO CALL MY OWN
I JUST SIT HERE ALL ALONE...
THERE'S NO GIRLS THAT WANT TO TOUCH ME
to james
cant wait
for you to
come back
SARA
I DON'T NEED YOUR GODDAMN SYMPATHY!*
SKATE
GOD, I'M SO LAME.

*BLACK FLAG "DEPRESSION"

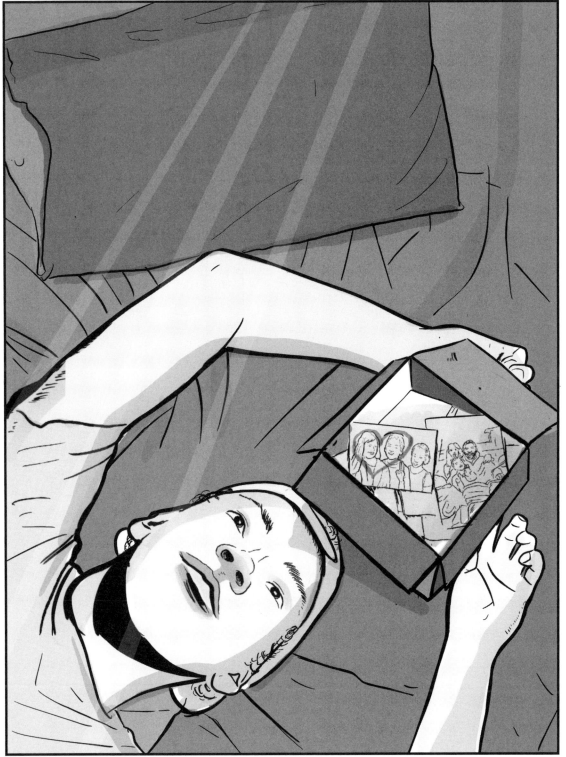

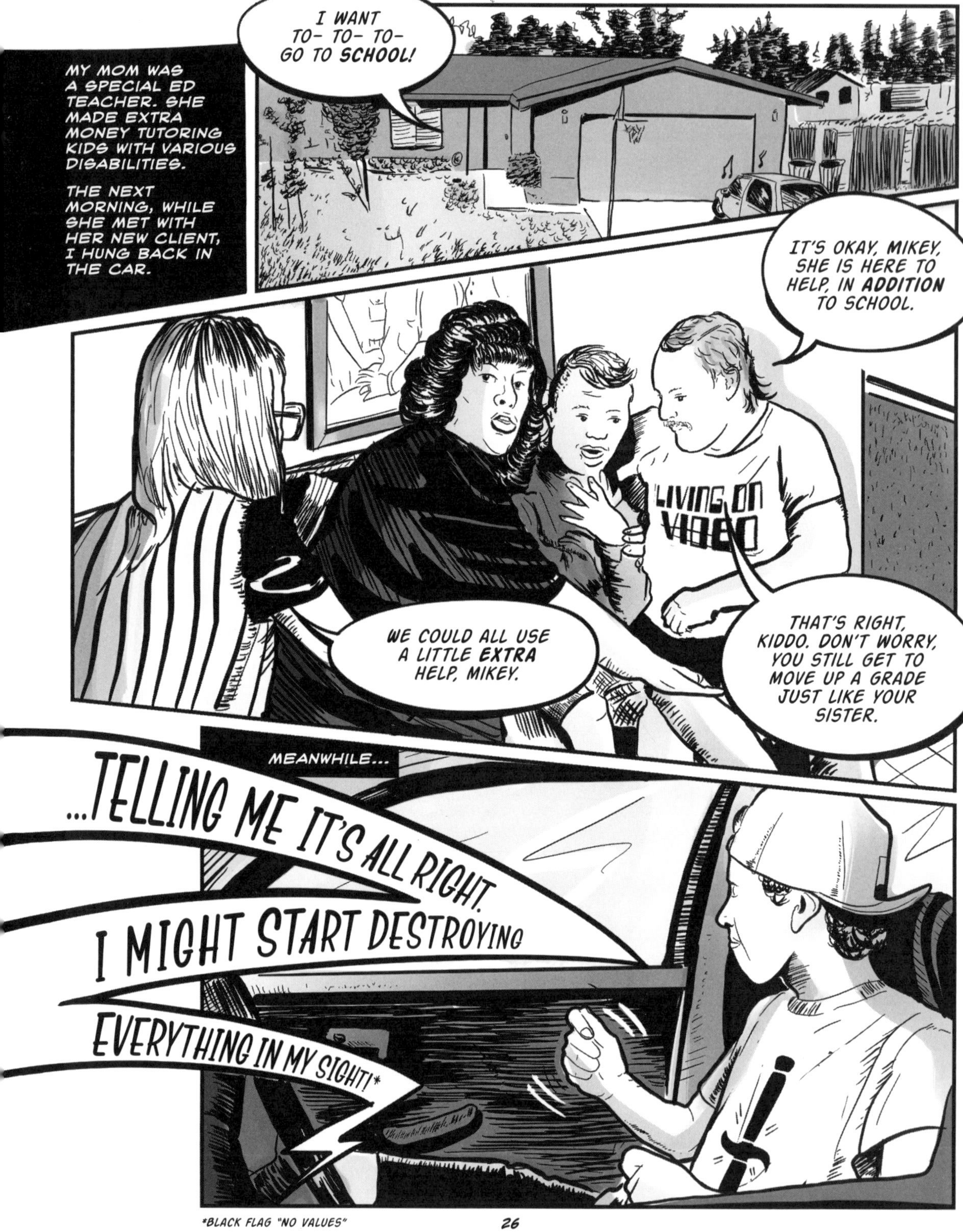
MY MOM WAS A SPECIAL ED TEACHER. SHE MADE EXTRA MONEY TUTORING KIDS WITH VARIOUS DISABILITIES.
THE NEXT MORNING, WHILE SHE MET WITH HER NEW CLIENT, I HUNG BACK IN THE CAR.
I WANT TO- TO- TO- GO TO SCHOOL!
IT'S OKAY, MIKEY, SHE IS HERE TO HELP, IN ADDITION TO SCHOOL.
LIVING ON VIDEO
WE COULD ALL USE A LITTLE EXTRA HELP, MIKEY.
THAT'S RIGHT, KIDDO. DON'T WORRY, YOU STILL GET TO MOVE UP A GRADE JUST LIKE YOUR SISTER.
MEANWHILE...
...TELLING ME IT'S ALL RIGHT.
I MIGHT START DESTROYING
EVERYTHING IN MY SIGHT!*

*BLACK FLAG "NO VALUES"

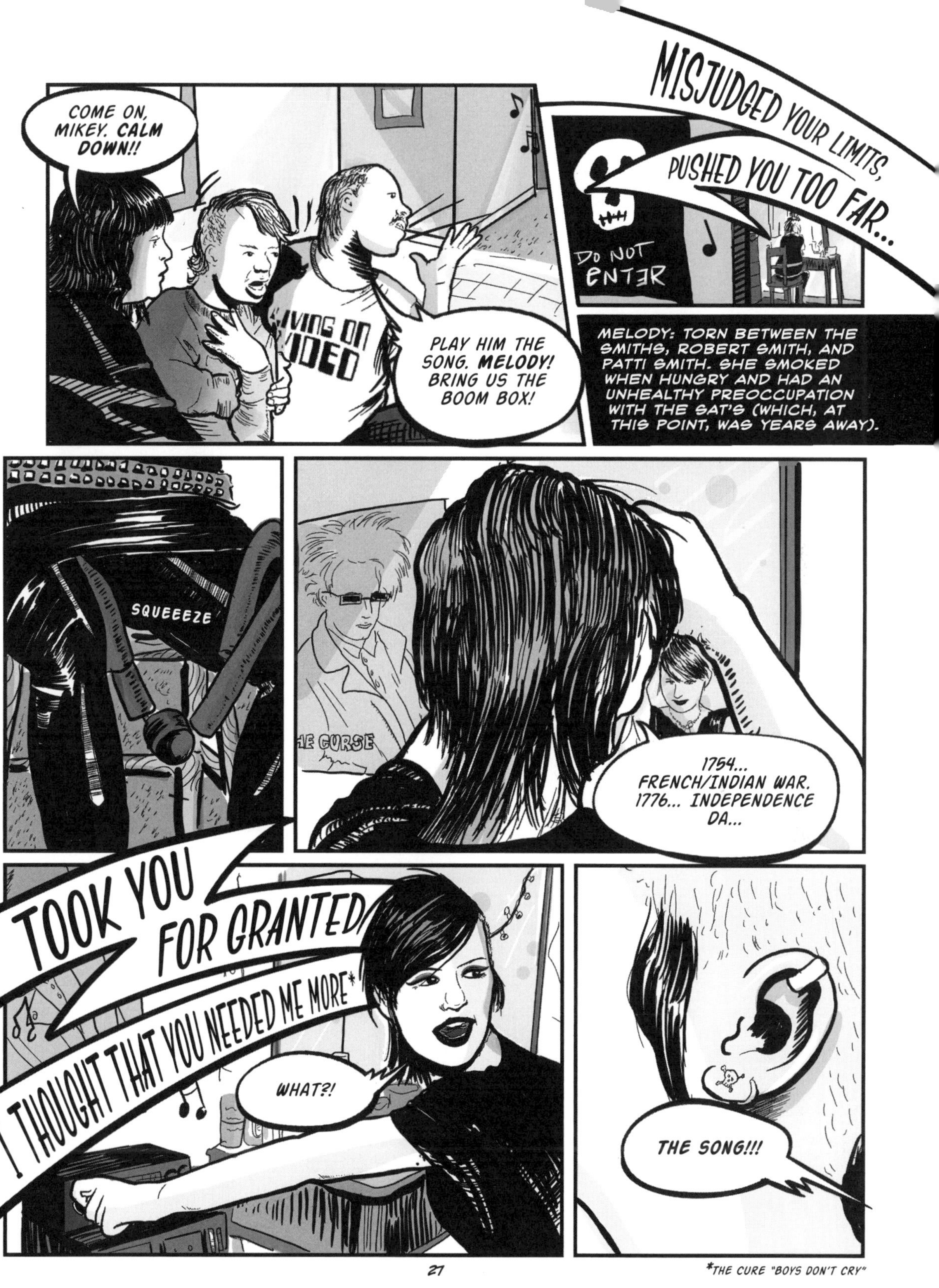
COME ON, MIKEY. CALM DOWN!!
LIVING ON VIDEO
PLAY HIM THE SONG. MELODY! BRING US THE BOOM BOX!
MISJUDGED YOUR LIMITS, PUSHED YOU TOO FAR...
DO NOT ENTER
MELODY: TORN BETWEEN THE SMITHS, ROBERT SMITH, AND PATTI SMITH. SHE SMOKED WHEN HUNGRY AND HAD AN UNHEALTHY PREOCCUPATION WITH THE SAT'S (WHICH, AT THIS POINT, WAS YEARS AWAY).
SQUEEEZE
HE CURSE
1754... FRENCH/INDIAN WAR. 1776... INDEPENDENCE DA...
TOOK YOU FOR GRANTED
I THOUGHT THAT YOU NEEDED ME MORE*
WHAT?!
THE SONG!!!

*THE CURE "BOYS DON'T CRY"

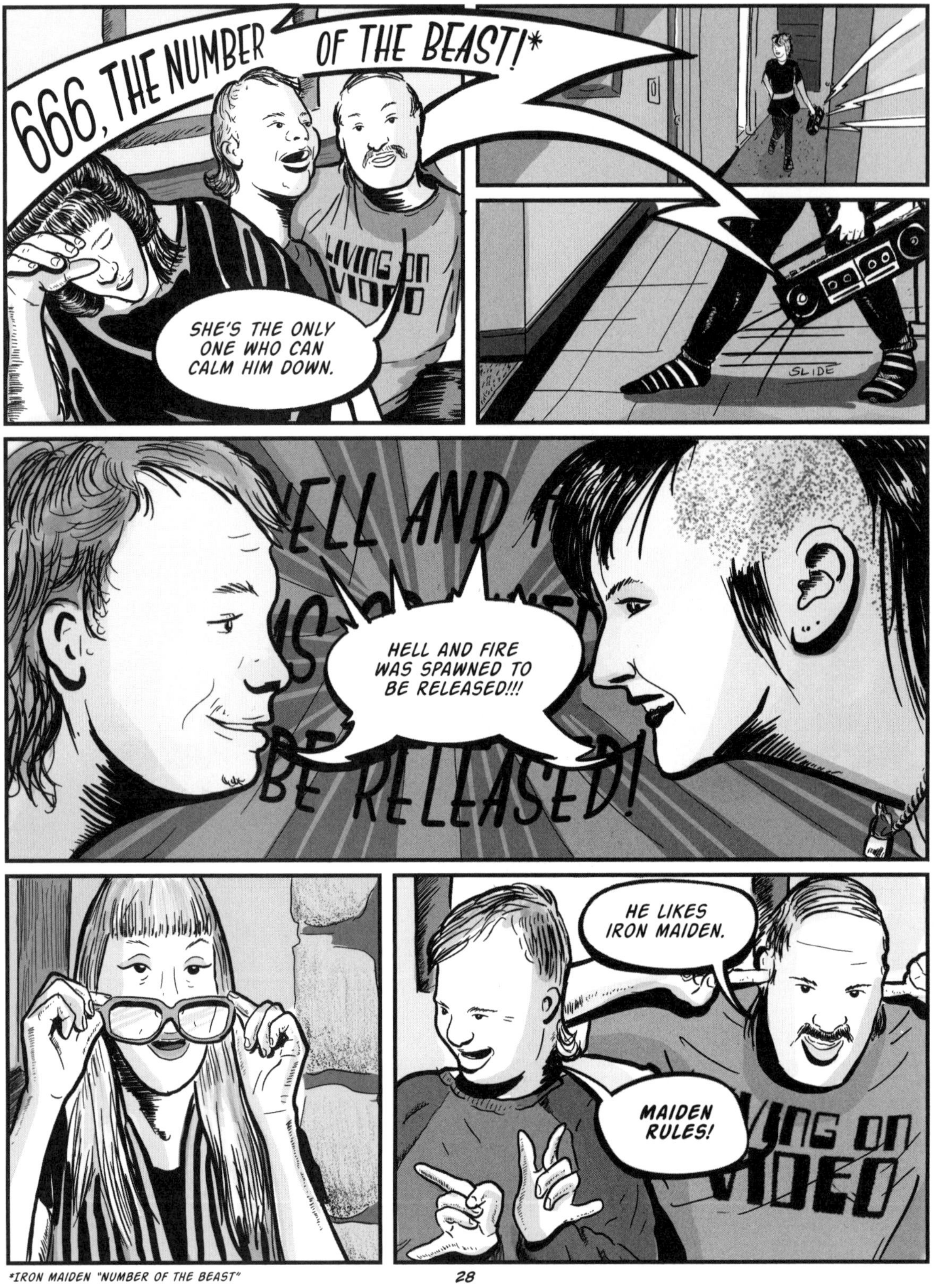
666, THE NUMBER OF THE BEAST!*
SHE'S THE ONLY ONE WHO CAN CALM HIM DOWN.
SLIDE
HELL AND FIRE WAS SPAWNED TO BE RELEASED!!!
BE RELEASED!
HE LIKES IRON MAIDEN.
MAIDEN RULES!

*IRON MAIDEN "NUMBER OF THE BEAST"

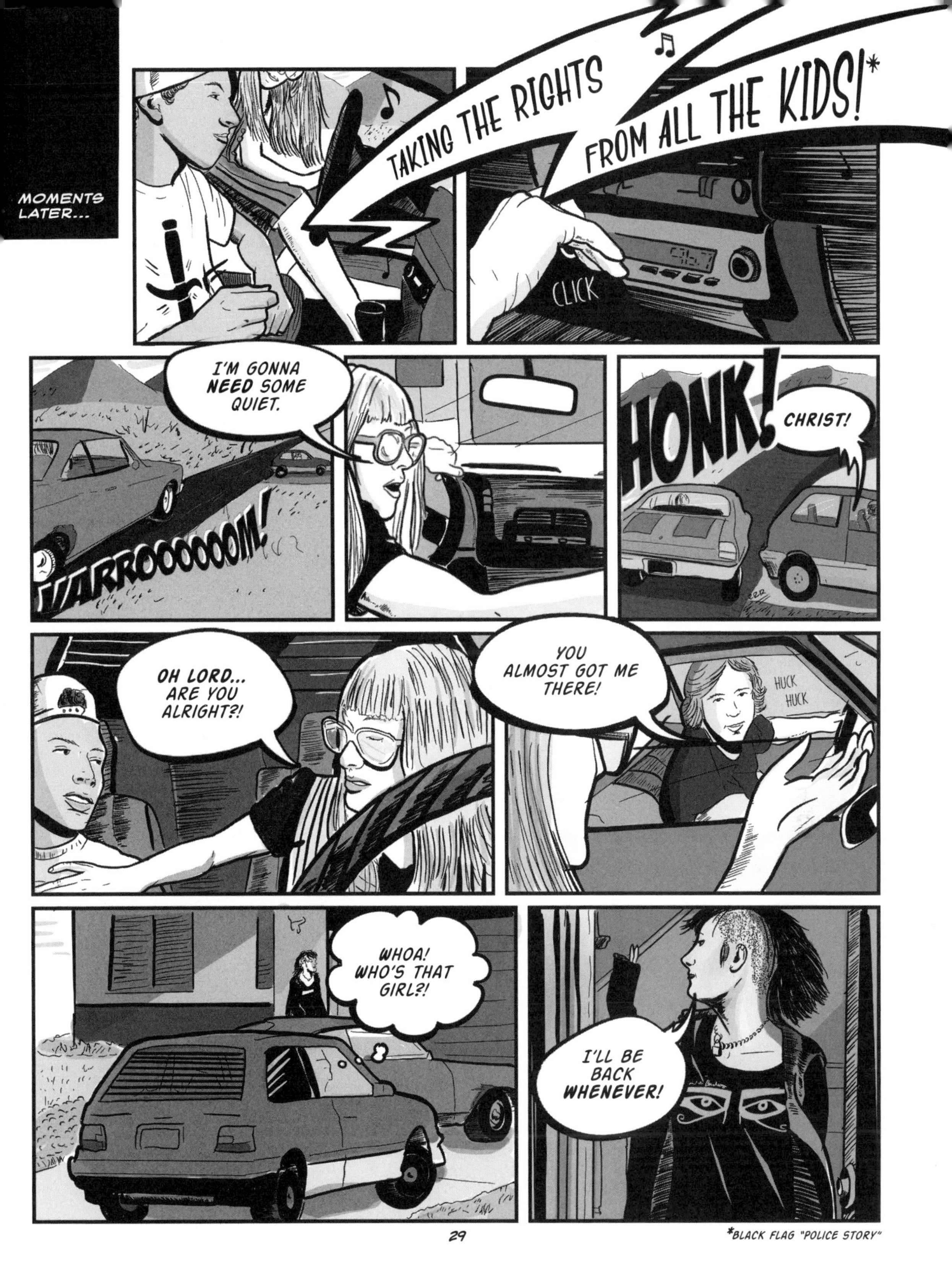
MOMENTS LATER...
TAKING THE RIGHTS
FROM ALL THE KIDS!*
CLICK
I'M GONNA NEED SOME QUIET.
VARROOOOOOM!
HONK!
CHRIST!
OH LORD... ARE YOU ALRIGHT?!
YOU ALMOST GOT ME THERE!
HUCK HUCK
WHOA! WHO'S THAT GIRL?!
I'LL BE BACK WHENEVER!

*BLACK FLAG "POLICE STORY"

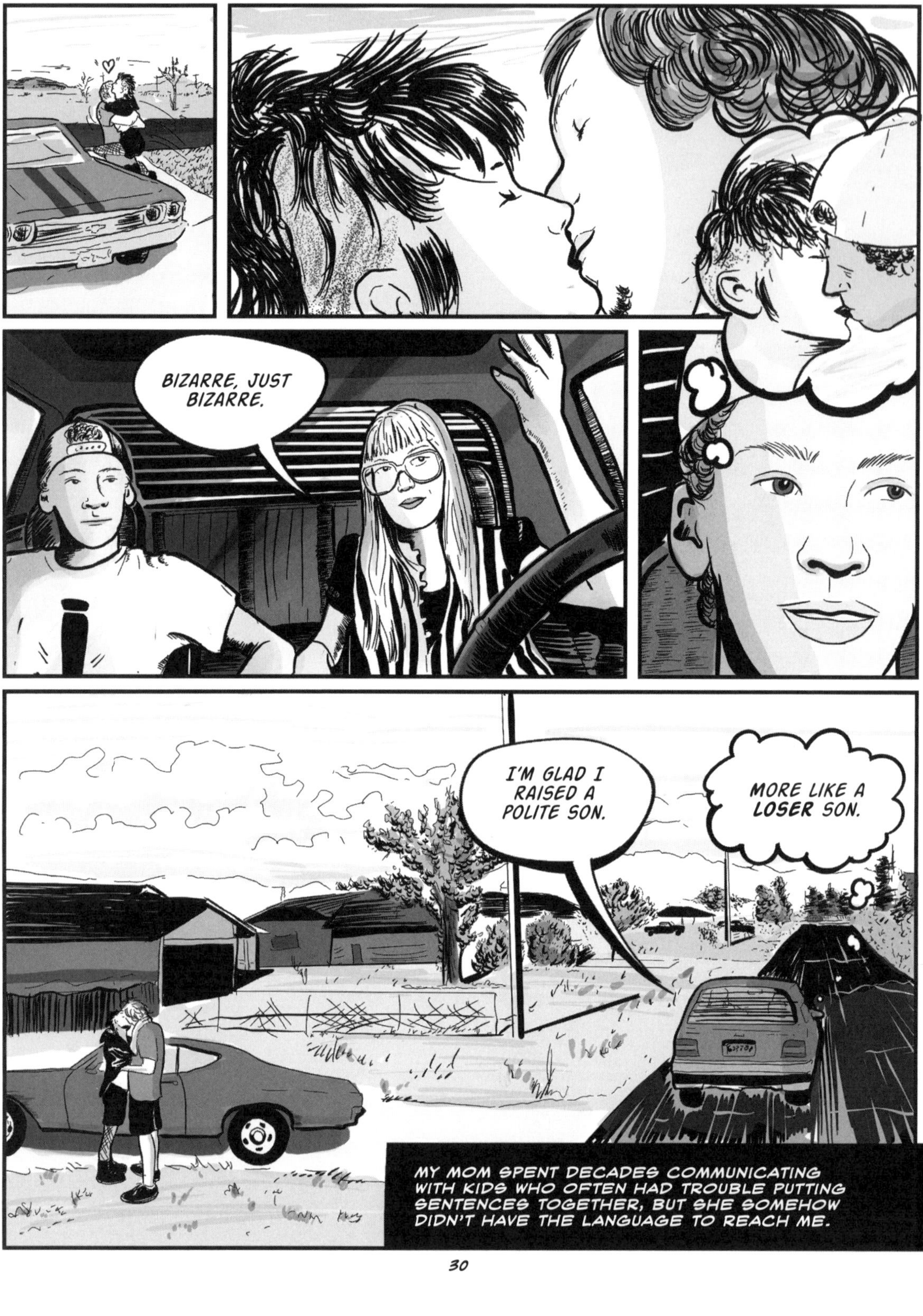
BIZARRE, JUST BIZARRE.
I'M GLAD I RAISED A POLITE SON.
MORE LIKE A **LOSER** SON.
MY MOM SPENT DECADES COMMUNICATING WITH KIDS WHO OFTEN HAD TROUBLE PUTTING SENTENCES TOGETHER, BUT SHE SOMEHOW DIDN'T HAVE THE LANGUAGE TO REACH ME.

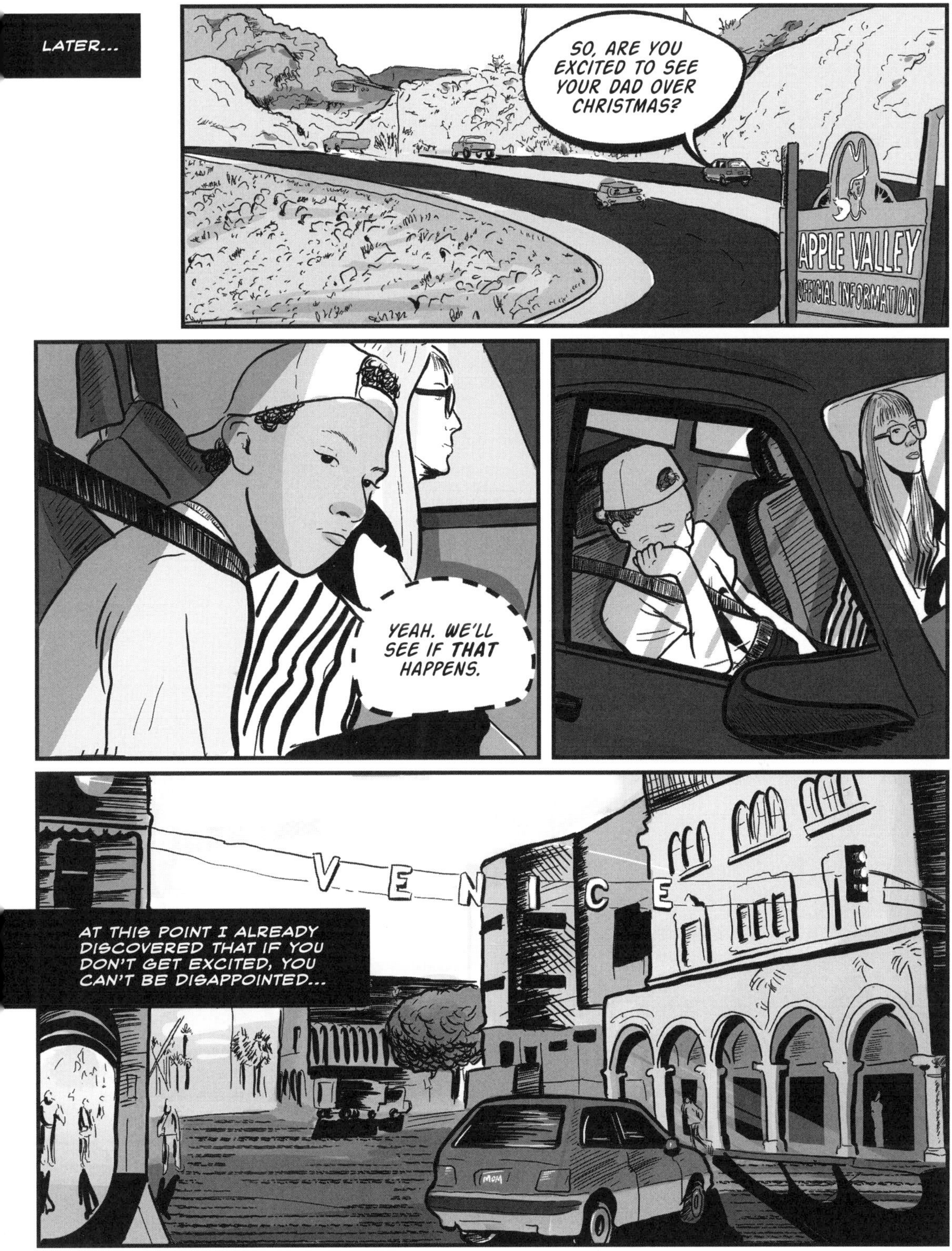
LATER...
SO, ARE YOU EXCITED TO SEE YOUR DAD OVER CHRISTMAS?
APPLE VALLEY
OFFICIAL INFORMATION
YEAH. WE'LL SEE IF THAT HAPPENS.
VENICE
AT THIS POINT I ALREADY DISCOVERED THAT IF YOU DON'T GET EXCITED, YOU CAN'T BE DISAPPOINTED...
MOM

... I'VE FOUND THAT KIND OF CYNICISM TO BE A COMMON DENOMINATOR IN A LOT OF PUNK AND HARDCORE KIDS.

FOR MOST OF US, OUR DISTRUST FOR THE GOVERNMENT SOCIETY, AND AUTHORITY, BEGAN AT HOME.

ARE YOU SURE YOU WANT TO WANDER AROUND ALONE?

WHAT, ARE YOU GOING TO **SKATE** WITH ME?

OKAY, FINE. I'LL MEET YOU BACK HERE IN TWO HOURS.

K.

JAMES?

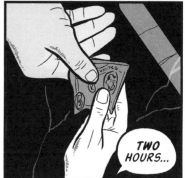

TWO HOURS...

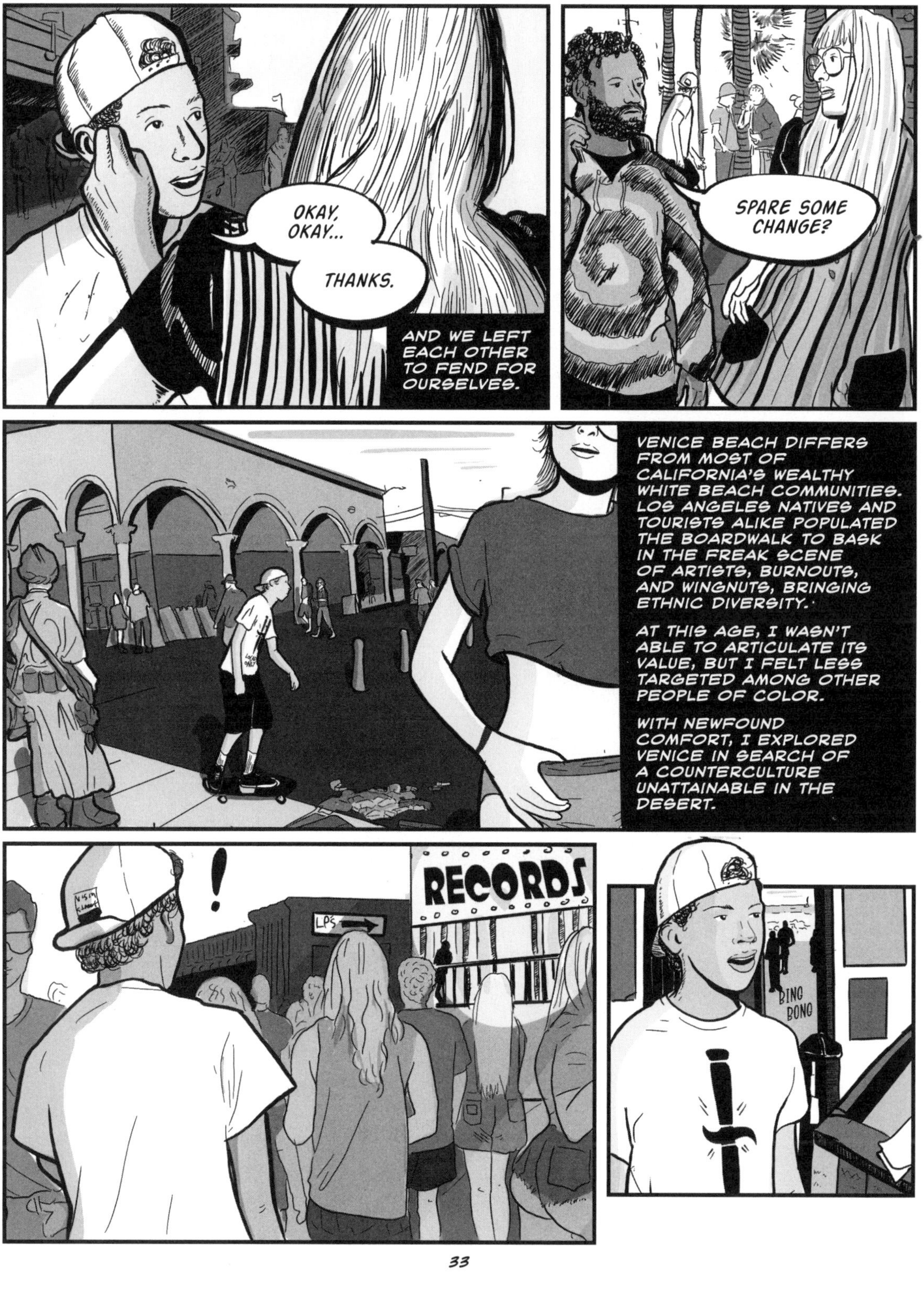
OKAY, OKAY...
THANKS.
AND WE LEFT EACH OTHER TO FEND FOR OURSELVES.
SPARE SOME CHANGE?
VENICE BEACH DIFFERS FROM MOST OF CALIFORNIA'S WEALTHY WHITE BEACH COMMUNITIES. LOS ANGELES NATIVES AND TOURISTS ALIKE POPULATED THE BOARDWALK TO BASK IN THE FREAK SCENE OF ARTISTS, BURNOUTS, AND WINGNUTS, BRINGING ETHNIC DIVERSITY.
AT THIS AGE, I WASN'T ABLE TO ARTICULATE ITS VALUE, BUT I FELT LESS TARGETED AMONG OTHER PEOPLE OF COLOR.
WITH NEWFOUND COMFORT, I EXPLORED VENICE IN SEARCH OF A COUNTERCULTURE UNATTAINABLE IN THE DESERT.
!
RECORDS
LP'S
BING BONG

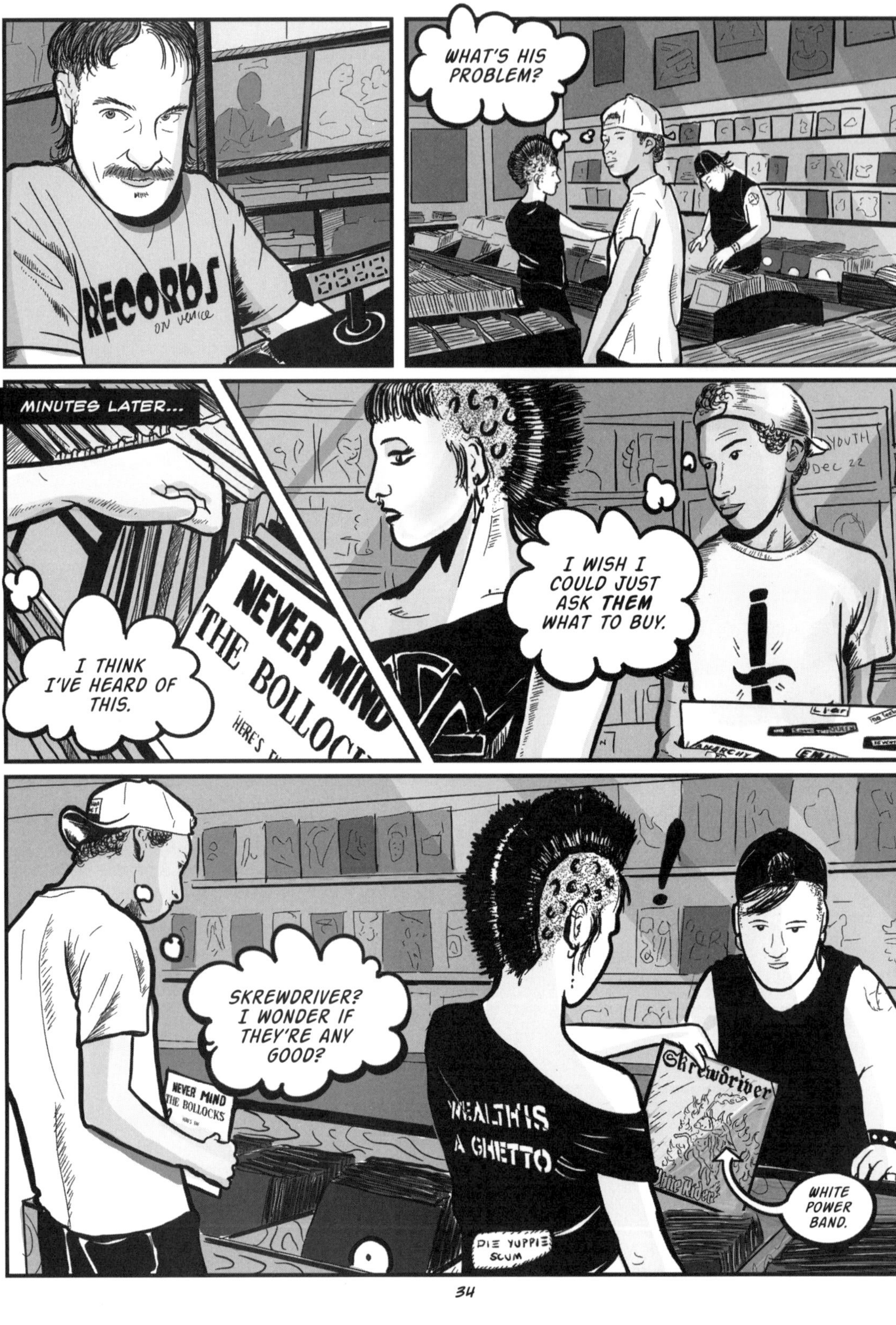
RECORDS
ON VENICE
WHAT'S HIS PROBLEM?
MINUTES LATER...
YOUTH
DEC 22
I WISH I COULD JUST ASK THEM WHAT TO BUY.
NEVER MIND THE BOLLOCKS
I THINK I'VE HEARD OF THIS.
ANARCHY
SKREWDRIVER? I WONDER IF THEY'RE ANY GOOD?
NEVER MIND THE BOLLOCKS
WEALTH IS A GHETTO
Skrewdriver
DIE YUPPIE SCUM
WHITE POWER BAND.

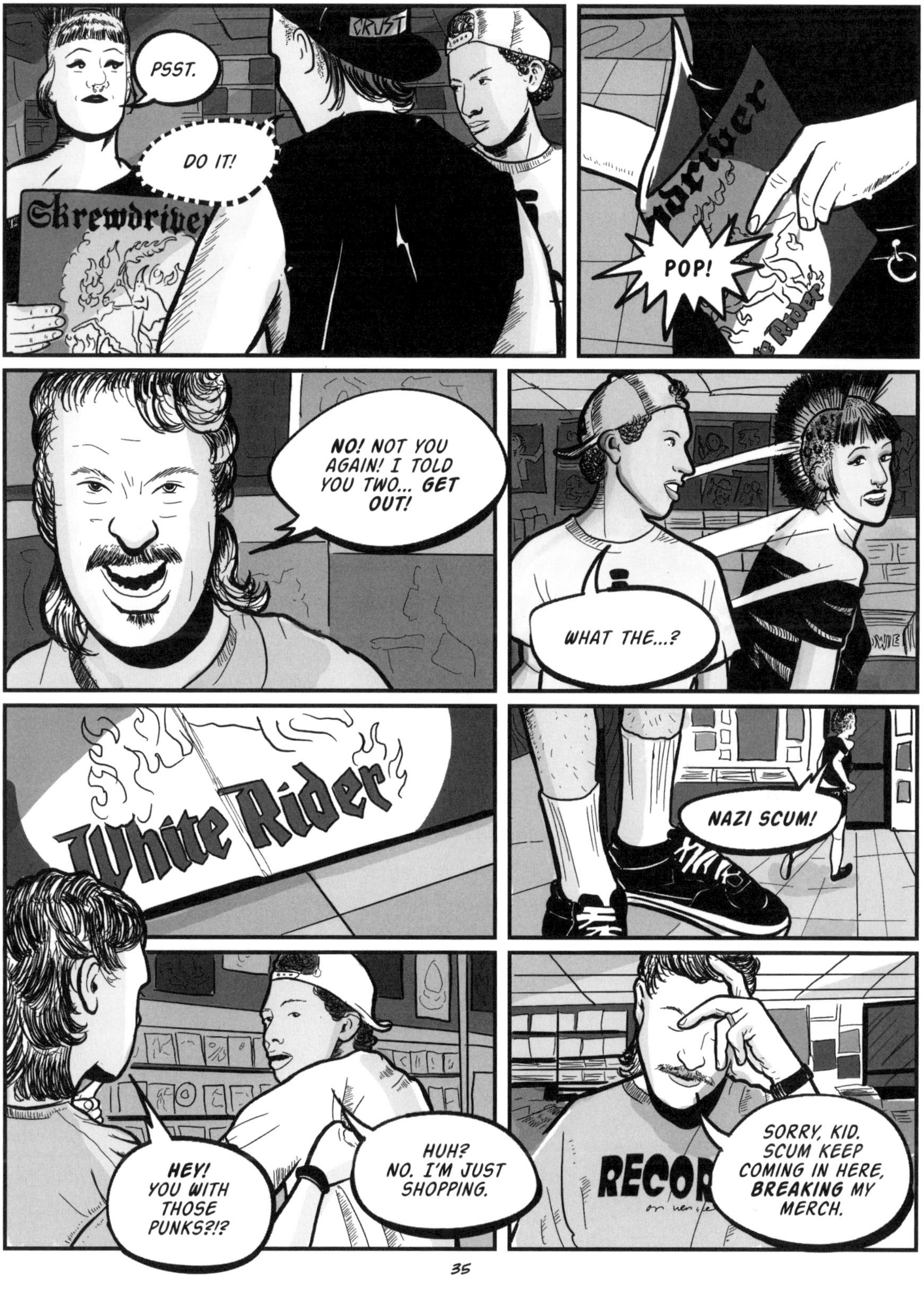
PSST.
DO IT!
CRUST
Skrewdriver
POP!
White Rider
NO! NOT YOU AGAIN! I TOLD YOU TWO... GET OUT!
WHAT THE...?
White Rider
NAZI SCUM!
HEY! YOU WITH THOSE PUNKS?!?
HUH? NO. I'M JUST SHOPPING.
RECOR
SORRY, KID. SCUM KEEP COMING IN HERE, BREAKING MY MERCH.

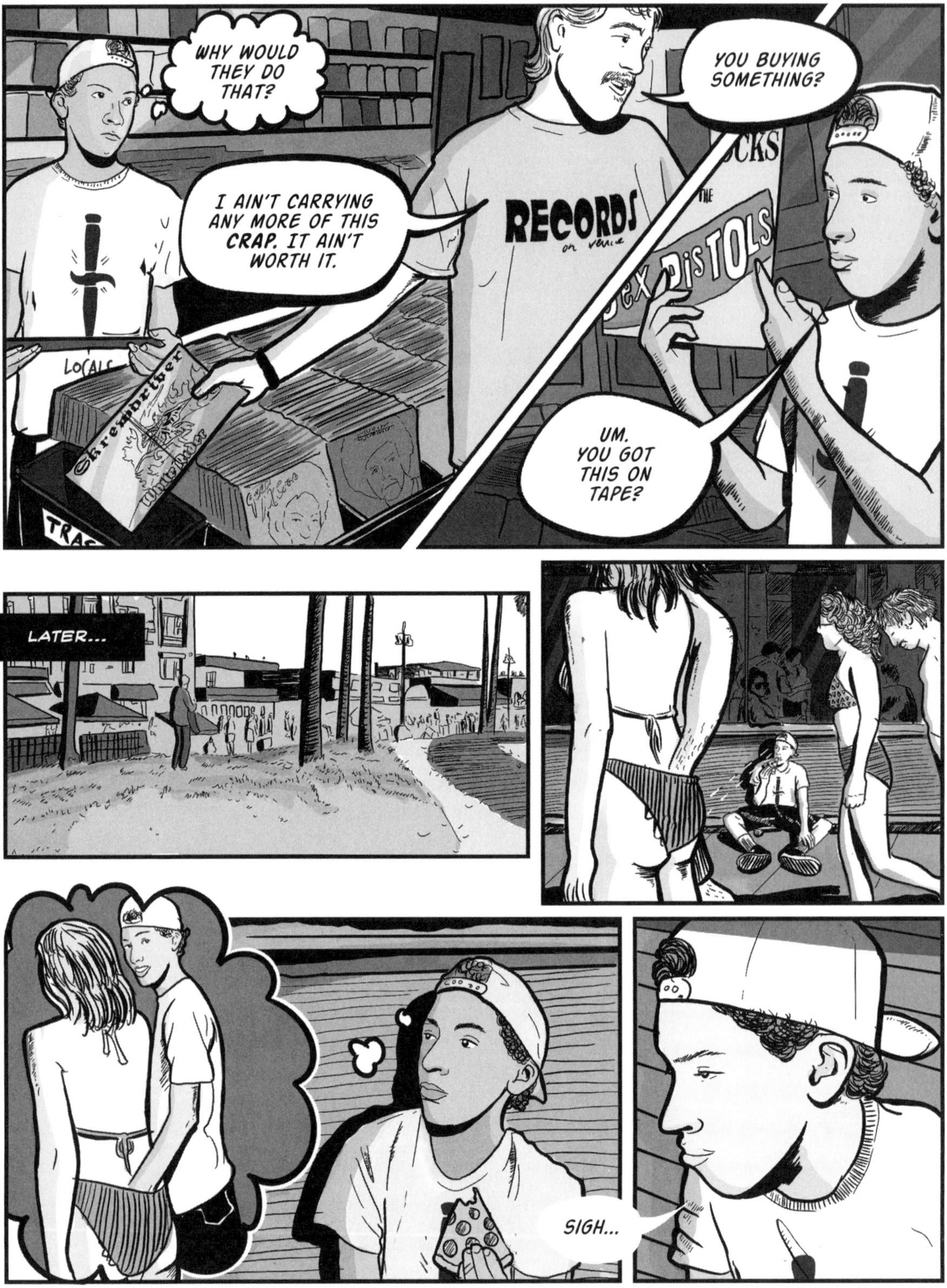
WHY WOULD THEY DO THAT?
I AIN'T CARRYING ANY MORE OF THIS CRAP. IT AIN'T WORTH IT.
YOU BUYING SOMETHING?
UM. YOU GOT THIS ON TAPE?
LATER...
SIGH...

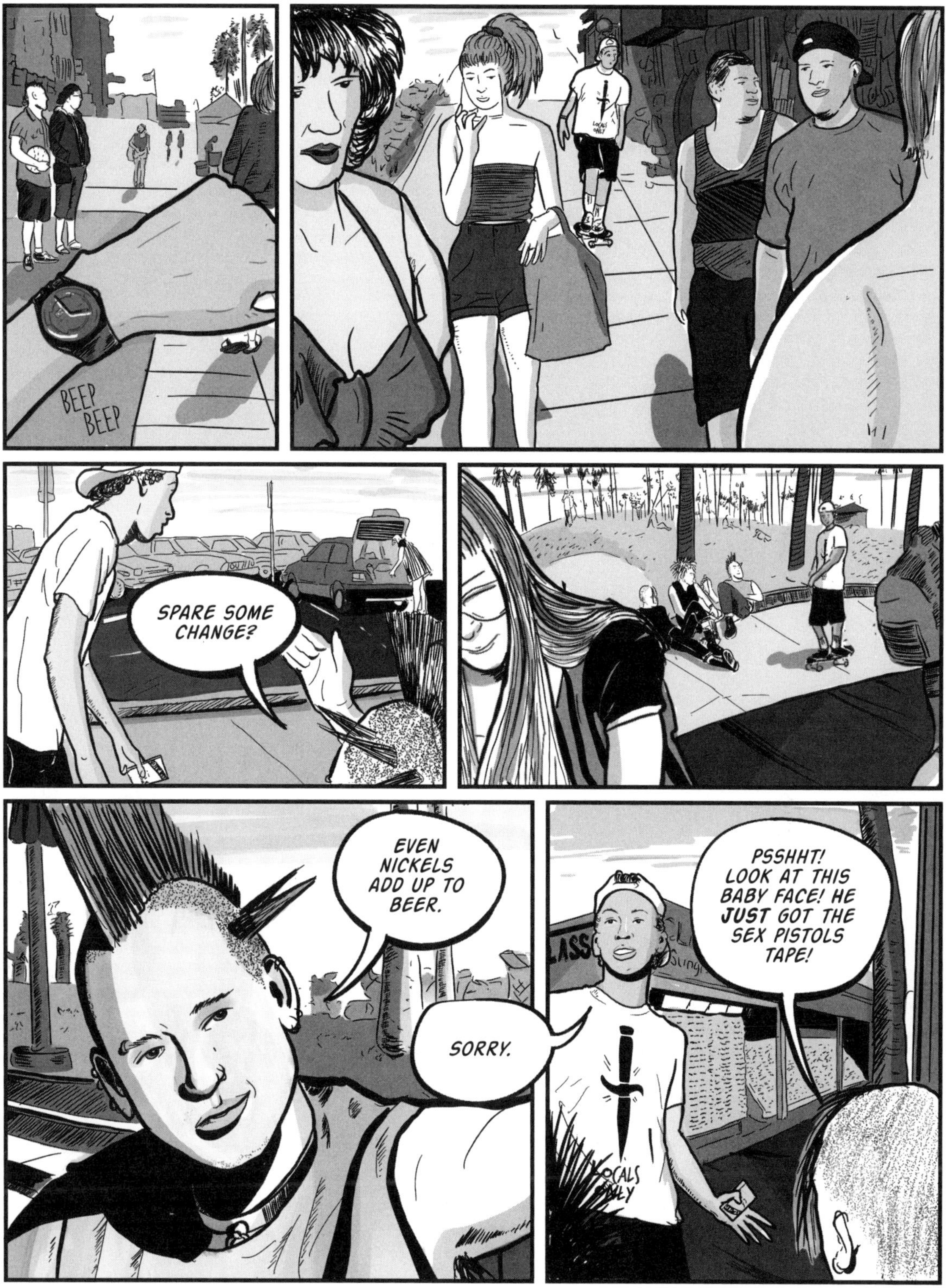
BEEP BEEP
LOCALS ONLY
SPARE SOME CHANGE?
EVEN NICKELS ADD UP TO BEER.
SORRY.
PSSHHT! LOOK AT THIS BABY FACE! HE JUST GOT THE SEX PISTOLS TAPE!
LOCALS ONLY

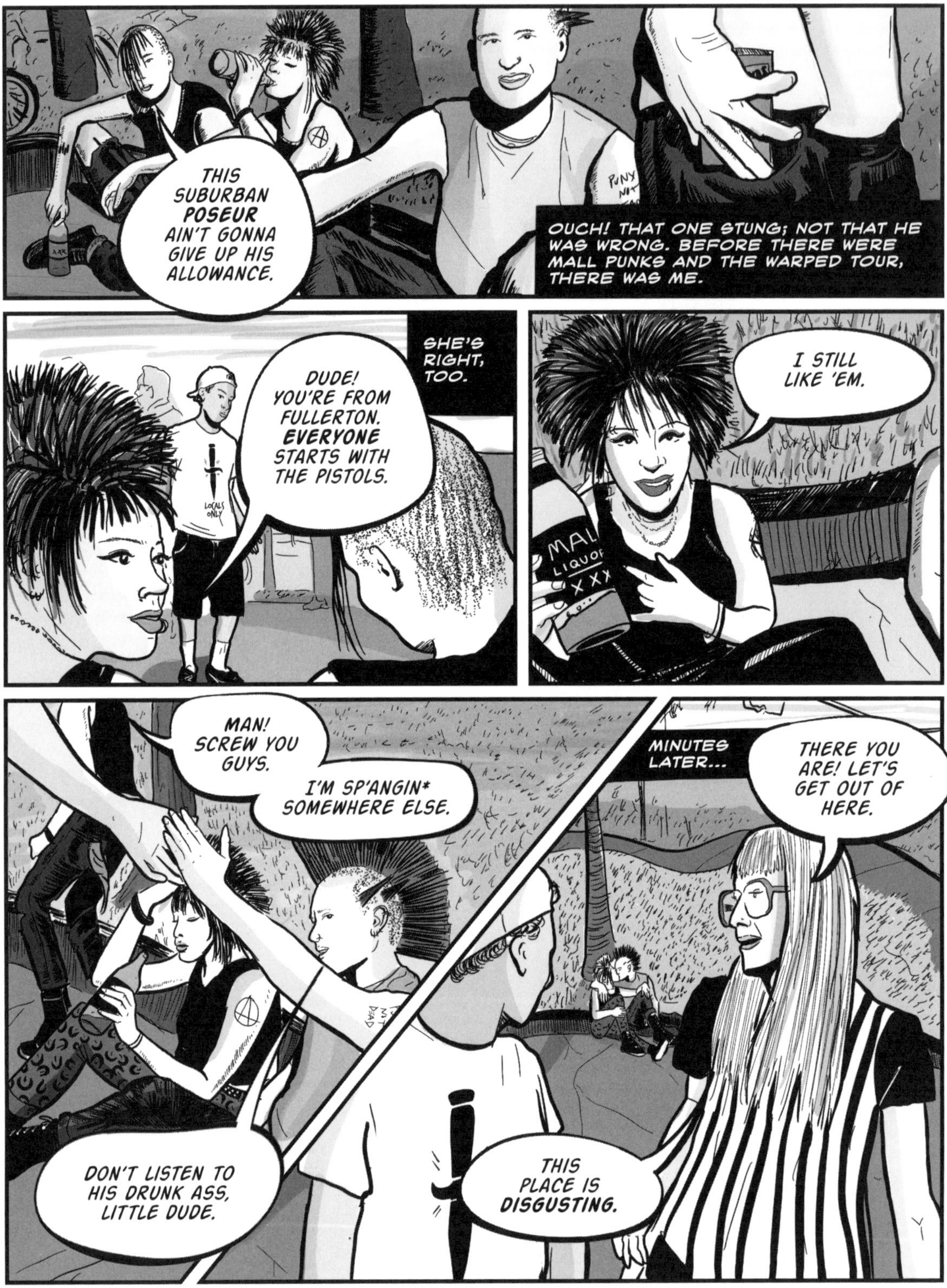
THIS SUBURBAN POSEUR AIN'T GONNA GIVE UP HIS ALLOWANCE.
OUCH! THAT ONE STUNG; NOT THAT HE WAS WRONG. BEFORE THERE WERE MALL PUNKS AND THE WARPED TOUR, THERE WAS ME.
SHE'S RIGHT, TOO.
DUDE! YOU'RE FROM FULLERTON. EVERYONE STARTS WITH THE PISTOLS.
LOCALS ONLY
I STILL LIKE 'EM.
MAN! SCREW YOU GUYS.
I'M SP'ANGIN* SOMEWHERE ELSE.
DON'T LISTEN TO HIS DRUNK ASS, LITTLE DUDE.
MINUTES LATER...
THERE YOU ARE! LET'S GET OUT OF HERE.
THIS PLACE IS DISGUSTING.

*SPARE CHANGING

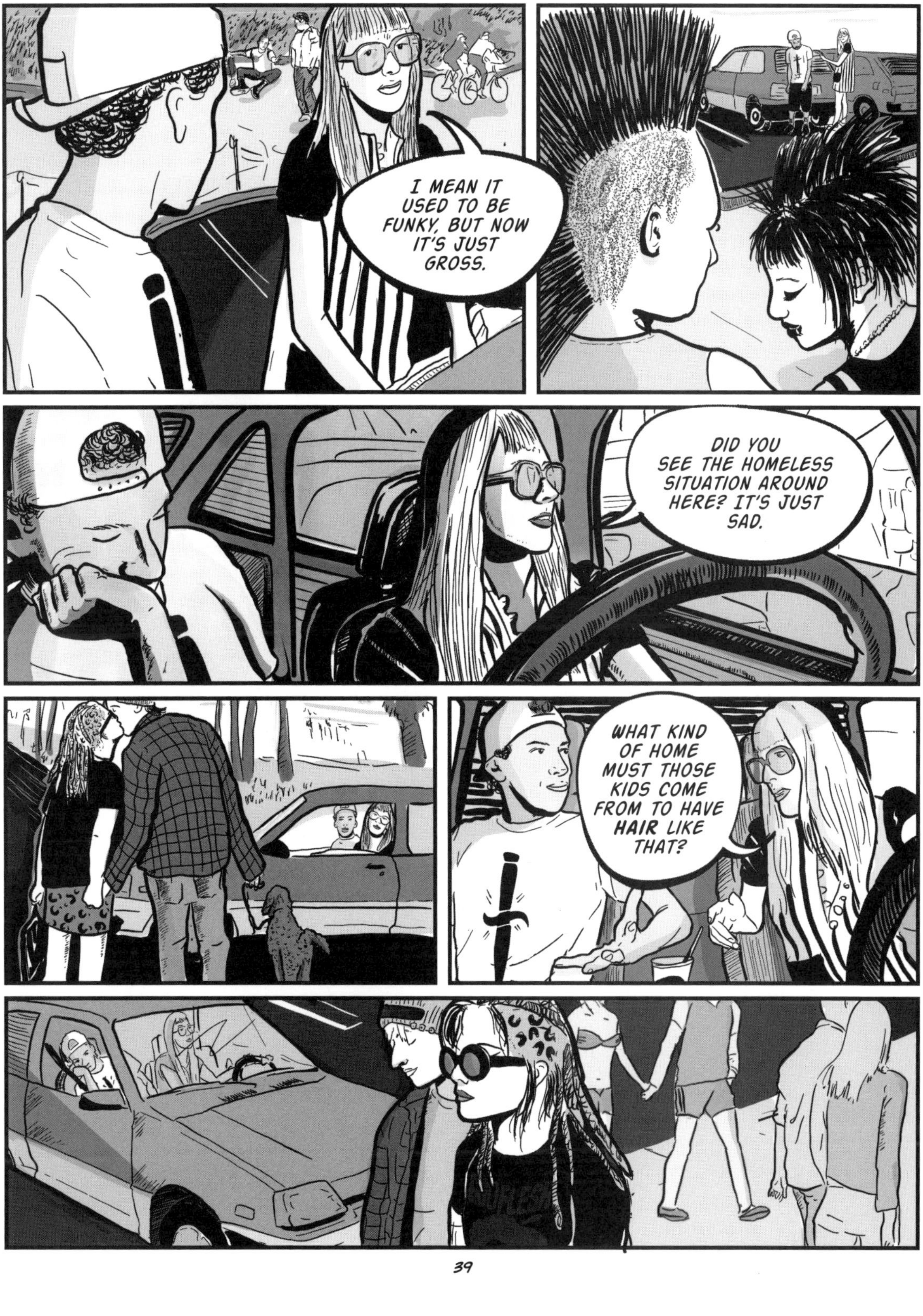
I MEAN IT USED TO BE FUNKY, BUT NOW IT'S JUST GROSS.
DID YOU SEE THE HOMELESS SITUATION AROUND HERE? IT'S JUST SAD.
WHAT KIND OF HOME MUST THOSE KIDS COME FROM TO HAVE HAIR LIKE THAT?

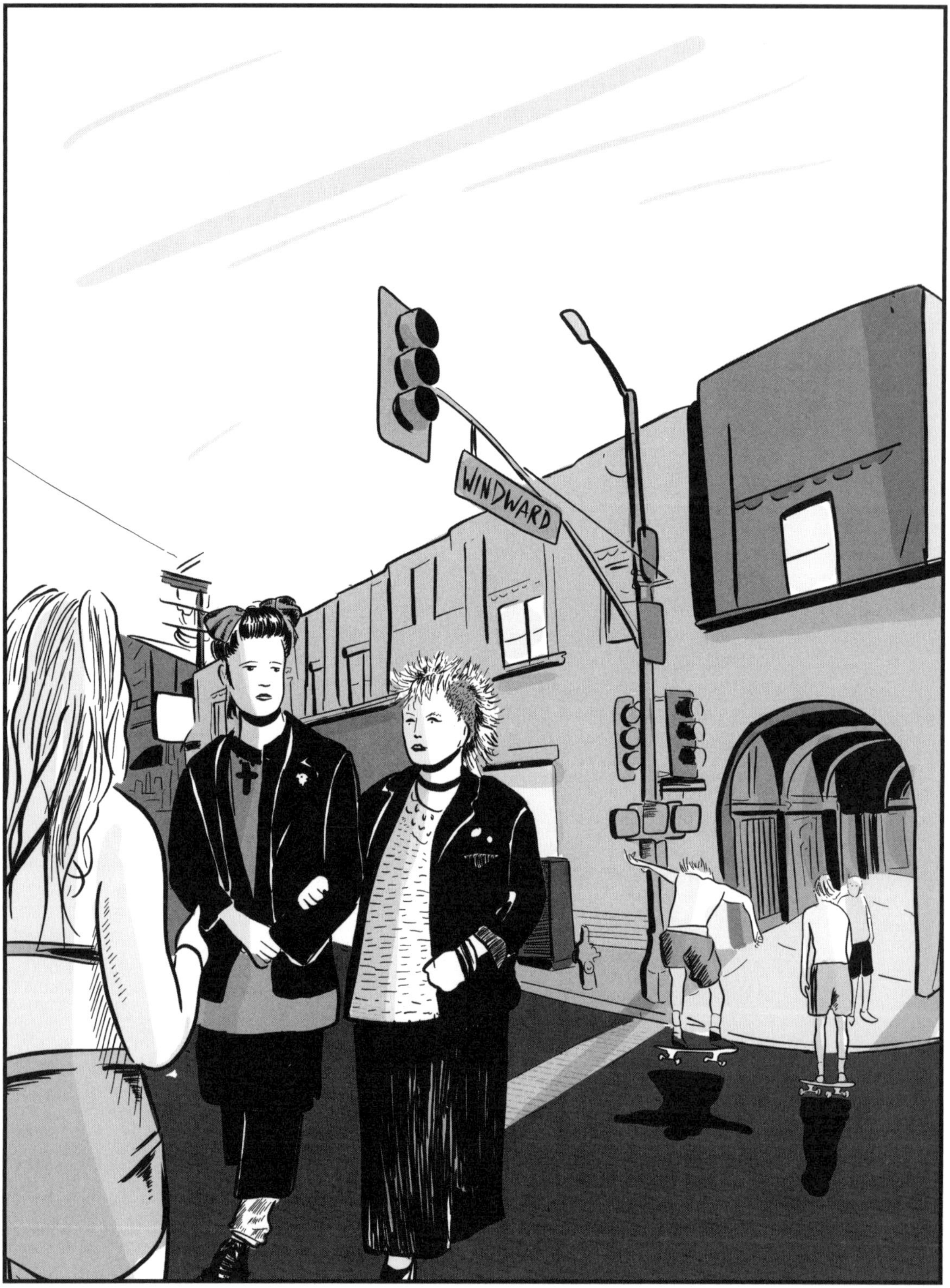
WINDWARD

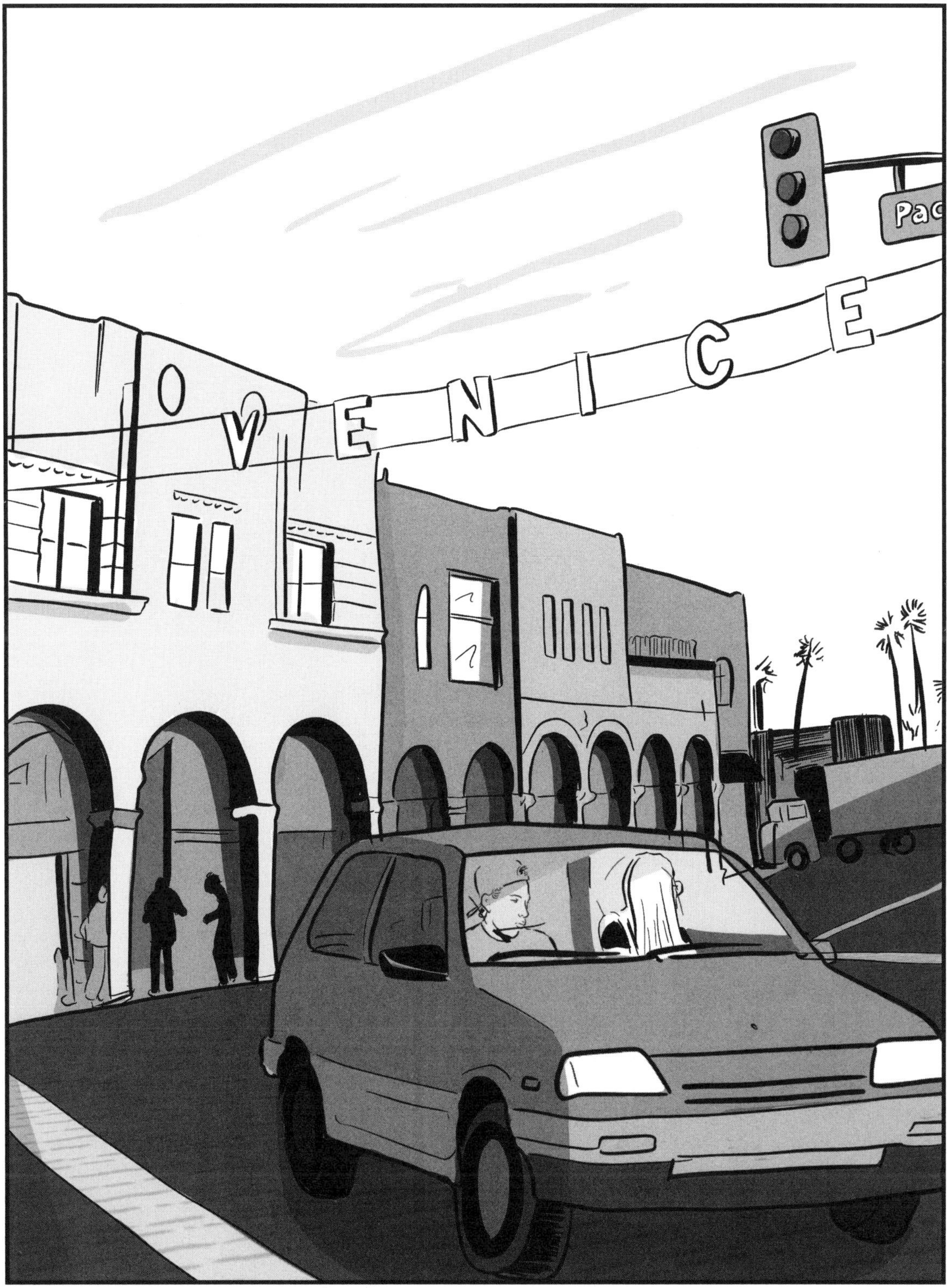
VENICE

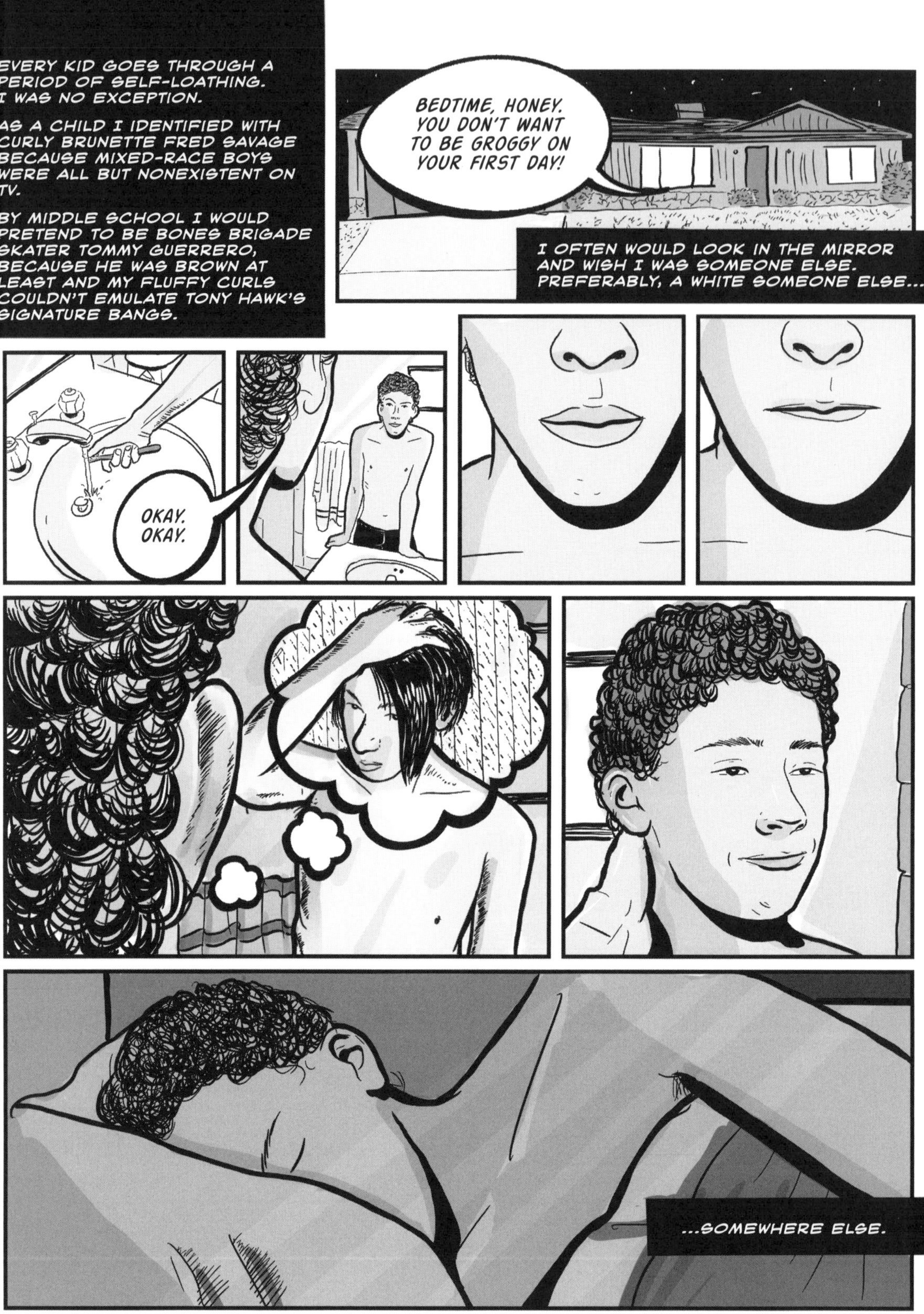
EVERY KID GOES THROUGH A PERIOD OF SELF-LOATHING. I WAS NO EXCEPTION.
AS A CHILD I IDENTIFIED WITH CURLY BRUNETTE FRED SAVAGE BECAUSE MIXED-RACE BOYS WERE ALL BUT NONEXISTENT ON TV.
BY MIDDLE SCHOOL I WOULD PRETEND TO BE BONES BRIGADE SKATER TOMMY GUERRERO, BECAUSE HE WAS BROWN AT LEAST AND MY FLUFFY CURLS COULDN'T EMULATE TONY HAWK'S SIGNATURE BANGS.
BEDTIME, HONEY. YOU DON'T WANT TO BE GROGGY ON YOUR FIRST DAY!
I OFTEN WOULD LOOK IN THE MIRROR AND WISH I WAS SOMEONE ELSE. PREFERABLY, A WHITE SOMEONE ELSE...
OKAY. OKAY.
...SOMEWHERE ELSE.

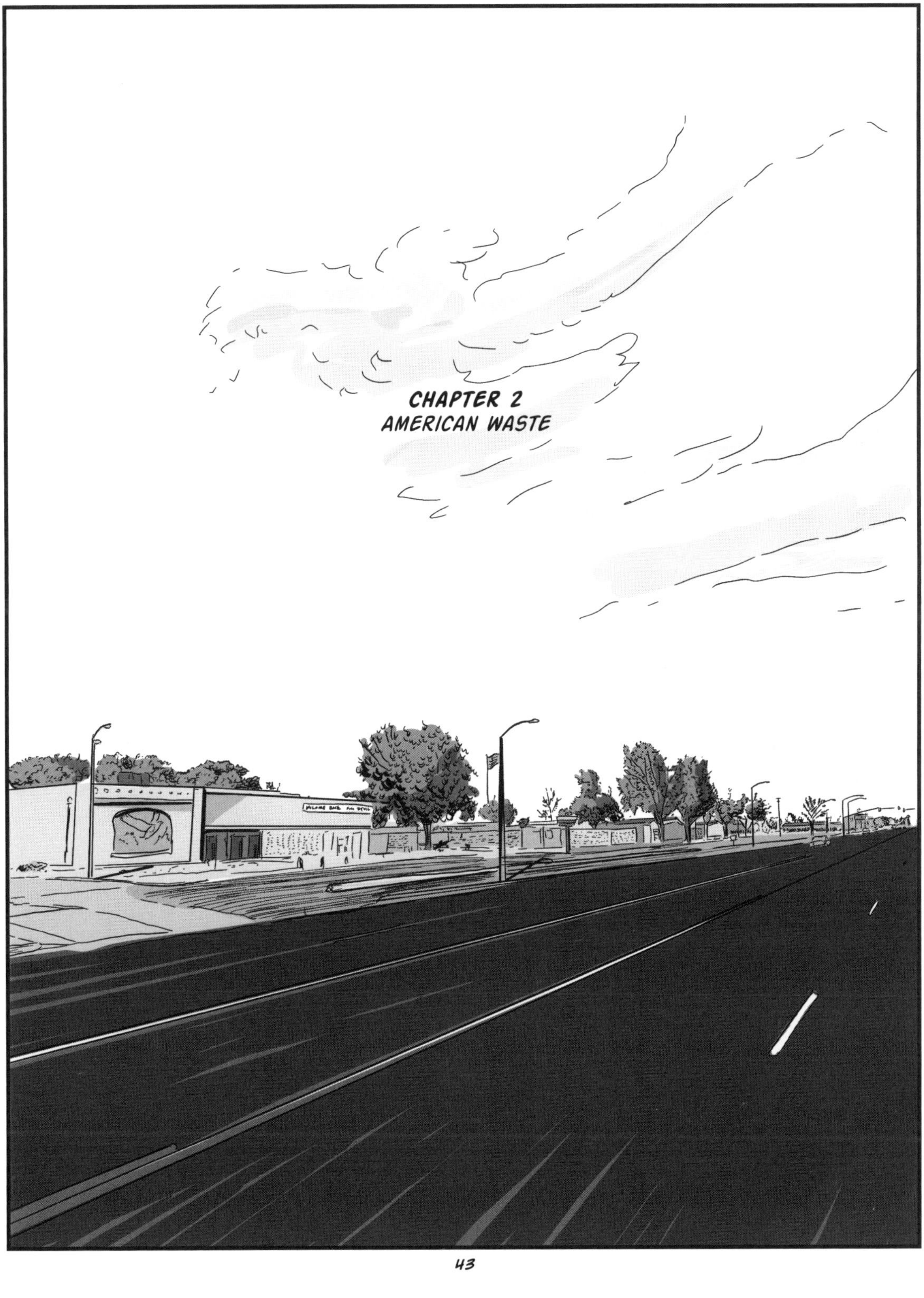
CHAPTER 2
AMERICAN WASTE

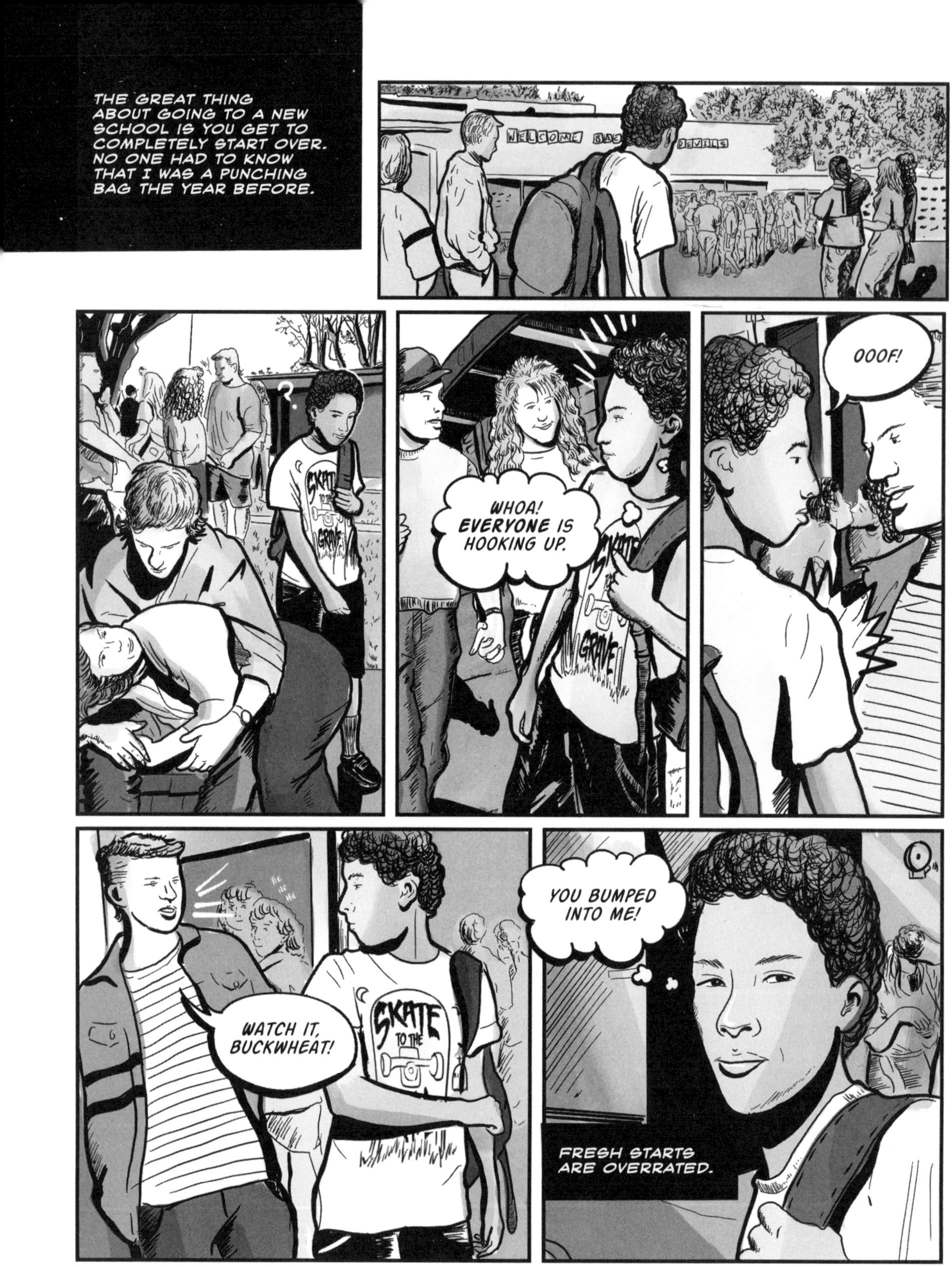
THE GREAT THING ABOUT GOING TO A NEW SCHOOL IS YOU GET TO COMPLETELY START OVER. NO ONE HAD TO KNOW THAT I WAS A PUNCHING BAG THE YEAR BEFORE.
WHOA! EVERYONE IS HOOKING UP.
OOOF!
WATCH IT, BUCKWHEAT!
YOU BUMPED INTO ME!
FRESH STARTS ARE OVERRATED.

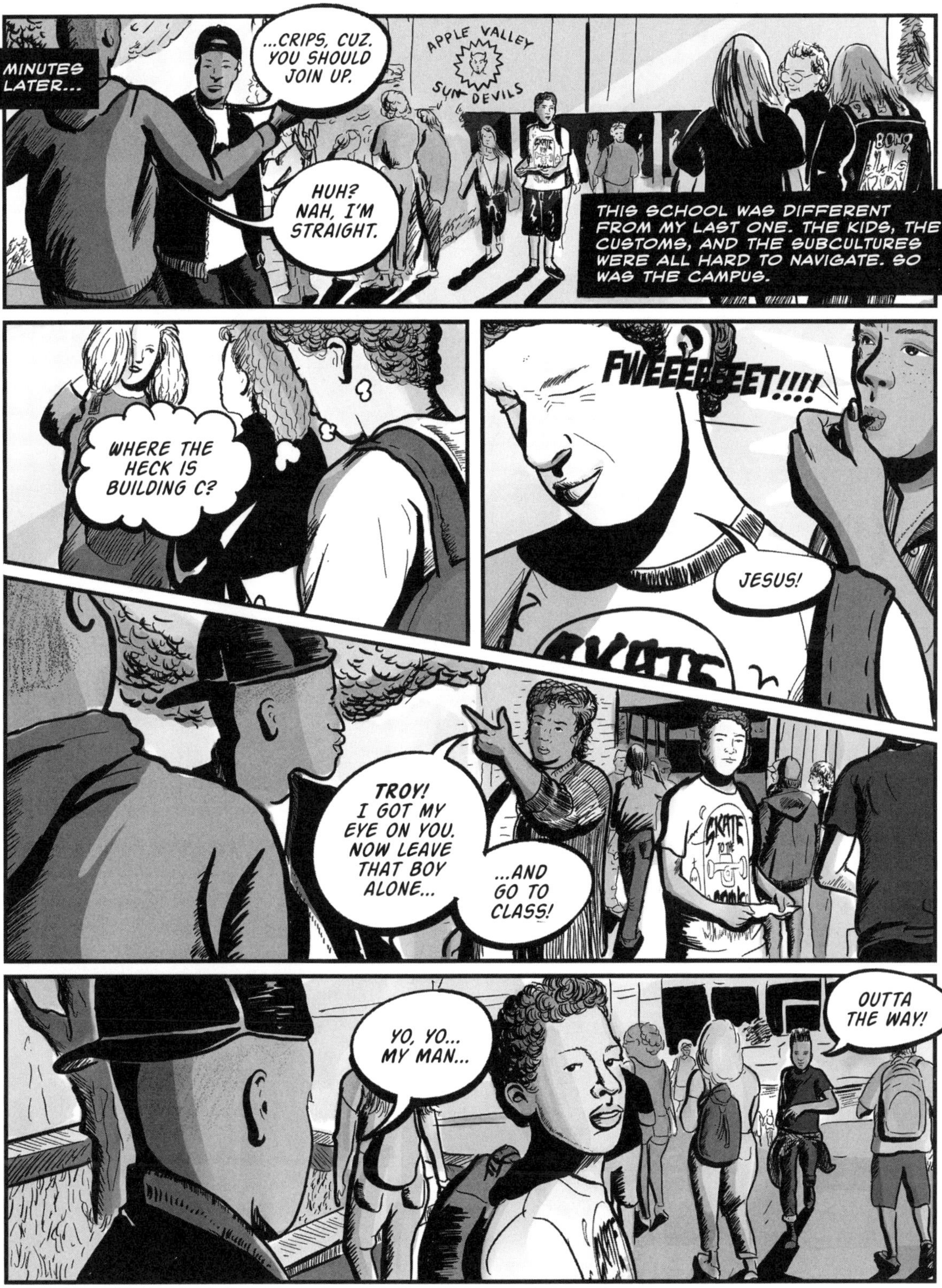
MINUTES LATER...
...CRIPS, CUZ. YOU SHOULD JOIN UP.
APPLE VALLEY SUN DEVILS
HUH? NAH, I'M STRAIGHT.
THIS SCHOOL WAS DIFFERENT FROM MY LAST ONE. THE KIDS, THE CUSTOMS, AND THE SUBCULTURES WERE ALL HARD TO NAVIGATE. SO WAS THE CAMPUS.
WHERE THE HECK IS BUILDING C?
FWEEEEEET!!!!
JESUS!
TROY! I GOT MY EYE ON YOU. NOW LEAVE THAT BOY ALONE...
...AND GO TO CLASS!
YO, YO... MY MAN...
OUTTA THE WAY!

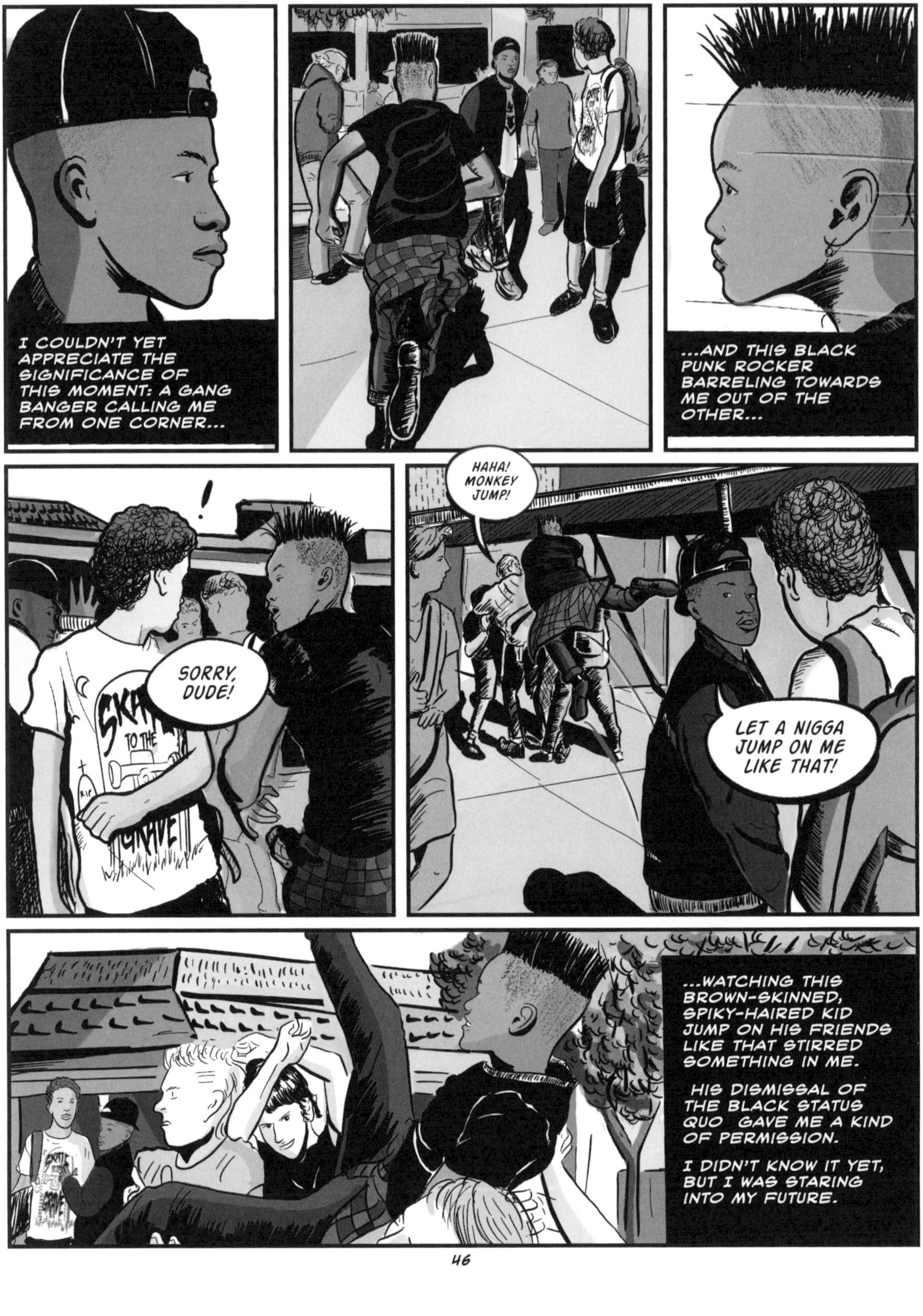
I COULDN'T YET APPRECIATE THE SIGNIFICANCE OF THIS MOMENT: A GANG BANGER CALLING ME FROM ONE CORNER...
...AND THIS BLACK PUNK ROCKER BARRELING TOWARDS ME OUT OF THE OTHER...
!
SORRY, DUDE!
HAHA! MONKEY JUMP!
LET A NIGGA JUMP ON ME LIKE THAT!
...WATCHING THIS BROWN-SKINNED, SPIKY-HAIRED KID JUMP ON HIS FRIENDS LIKE THAT STIRRED SOMETHING IN ME.
HIS DISMISSAL OF THE BLACK STATUS QUO GAVE ME A KIND OF PERMISSION.
I DIDN'T KNOW IT YET, BUT I WAS STARING INTO MY FUTURE.

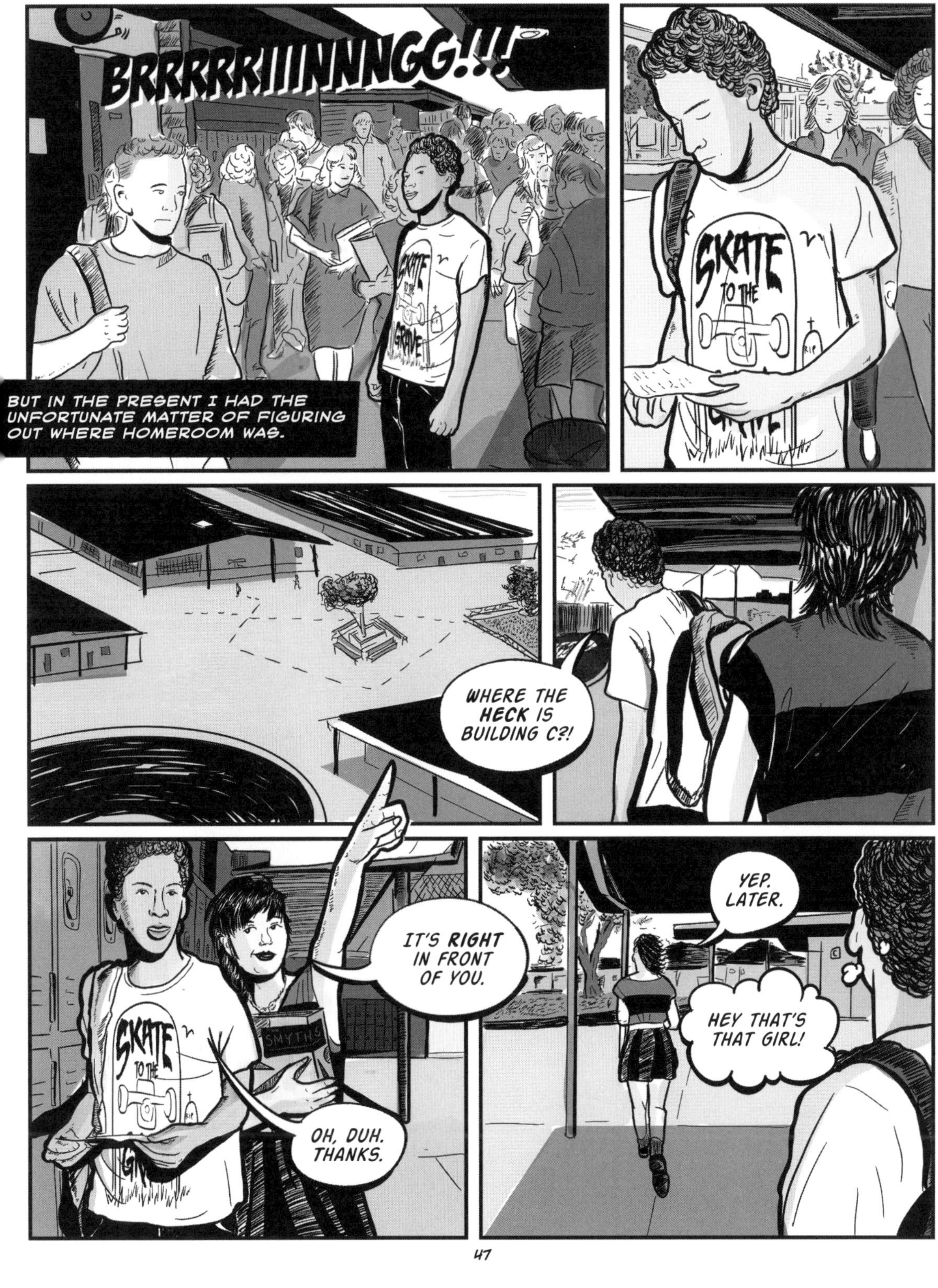
BRRRRRIIINNNGG!!!
BUT IN THE PRESENT I HAD THE UNFORTUNATE MATTER OF FIGURING OUT WHERE HOMEROOM WAS.
SKATE TO THE GRAVE
WHERE THE HECK IS BUILDING C?!
IT'S RIGHT IN FRONT OF YOU.
SMYTHS
OH, DUH. THANKS.
YEP. LATER.
HEY THAT'S THAT GIRL!

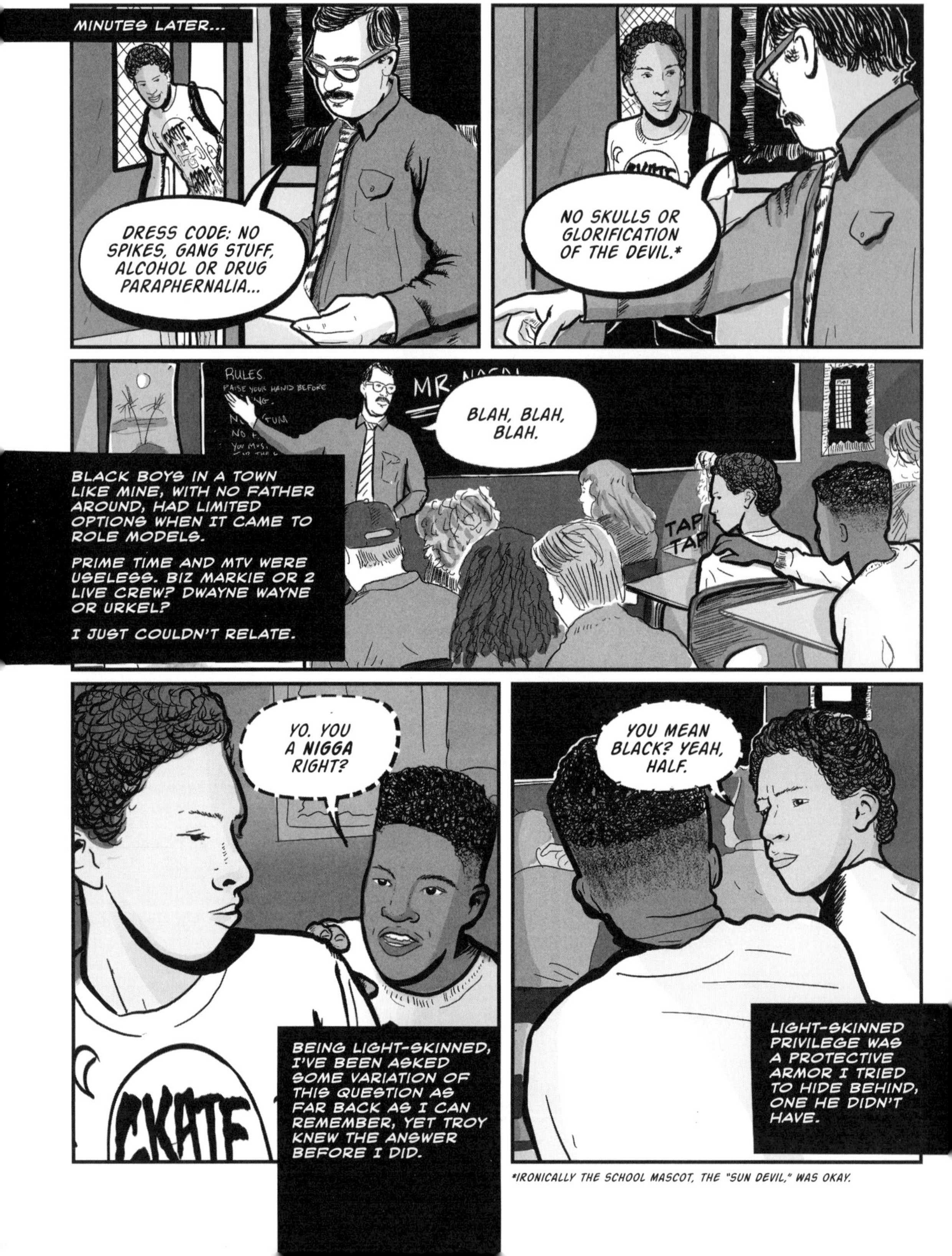
MINUTES LATER...
DRESS CODE: NO SPIKES, GANG STUFF, ALCOHOL OR DRUG PARAPHERNALIA...
NO SKULLS OR GLORIFICATION OF THE DEVIL.*
RULES.
RAISE YOUR HAND BEFORE
BLAH, BLAH, BLAH.
BLACK BOYS IN A TOWN LIKE MINE, WITH NO FATHER AROUND, HAD LIMITED OPTIONS WHEN IT CAME TO ROLE MODELS.
PRIME TIME AND MTV WERE USELESS. BIZ MARKIE OR 2 LIVE CREW? DWAYNE WAYNE OR URKEL?
I JUST COULDN'T RELATE.
TAP TAP
YO. YOU A NIGGA RIGHT?
BEING LIGHT-SKINNED, I'VE BEEN ASKED SOME VARIATION OF THIS QUESTION AS FAR BACK AS I CAN REMEMBER, YET TROY KNEW THE ANSWER BEFORE I DID.
YOU MEAN BLACK? YEAH, HALF.
LIGHT-SKINNED PRIVILEGE WAS A PROTECTIVE ARMOR I TRIED TO HIDE BEHIND, ONE HE DIDN'T HAVE.

*IRONICALLY THE SCHOOL MASCOT, THE "SUN DEVIL," WAS OKAY.

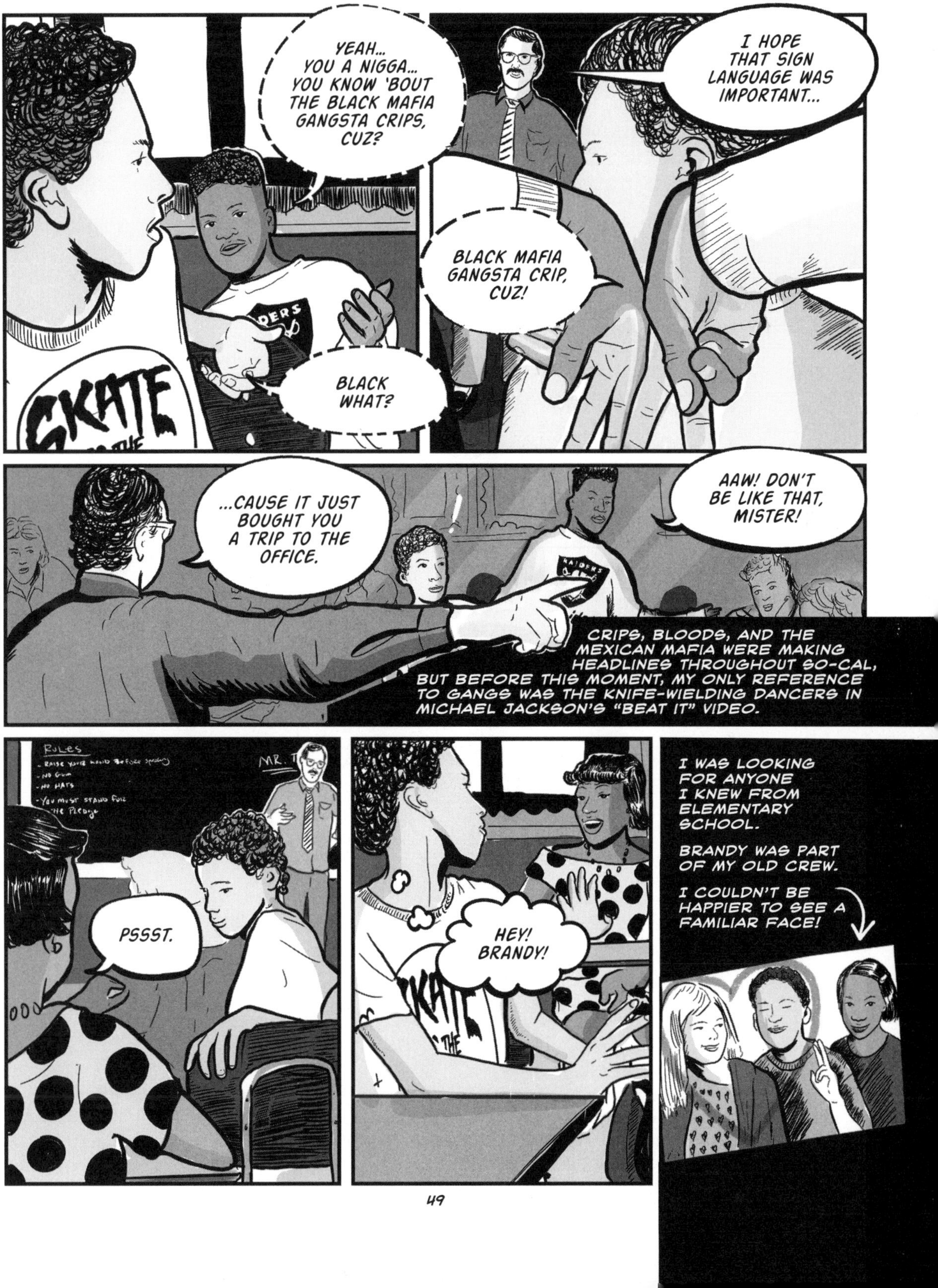
YEAH... YOU A NIGGA... YOU KNOW 'BOUT THE BLACK MAFIA GANGSTA CRIPS, CUZ?
BLACK WHAT?
BLACK MAFIA GANGSTA CRIP, CUZ!
I HOPE THAT SIGN LANGUAGE WAS IMPORTANT...
...CAUSE IT JUST BOUGHT YOU A TRIP TO THE OFFICE.
AAW! DON'T BE LIKE THAT, MISTER!
RAIDERS
CRIPS, BLOODS, AND THE MEXICAN MAFIA WERE MAKING HEADLINES THROUGHOUT SO-CAL, BUT BEFORE THIS MOMENT, MY ONLY REFERENCE TO GANGS WAS THE KNIFE-WIELDING DANCERS IN MICHAEL JACKSON'S "BEAT IT" VIDEO.
RULES
- Raise your hand before speaking
- No Gum
- No Hats
- You must stand for the Pledge
MR. T
PSSST.
HEY! BRANDY!
I WAS LOOKING FOR ANYONE I KNEW FROM ELEMENTARY SCHOOL.
BRANDY WAS PART OF MY OLD CREW.
I COULDN'T BE HAPPIER TO SEE A FAMILIAR FACE!

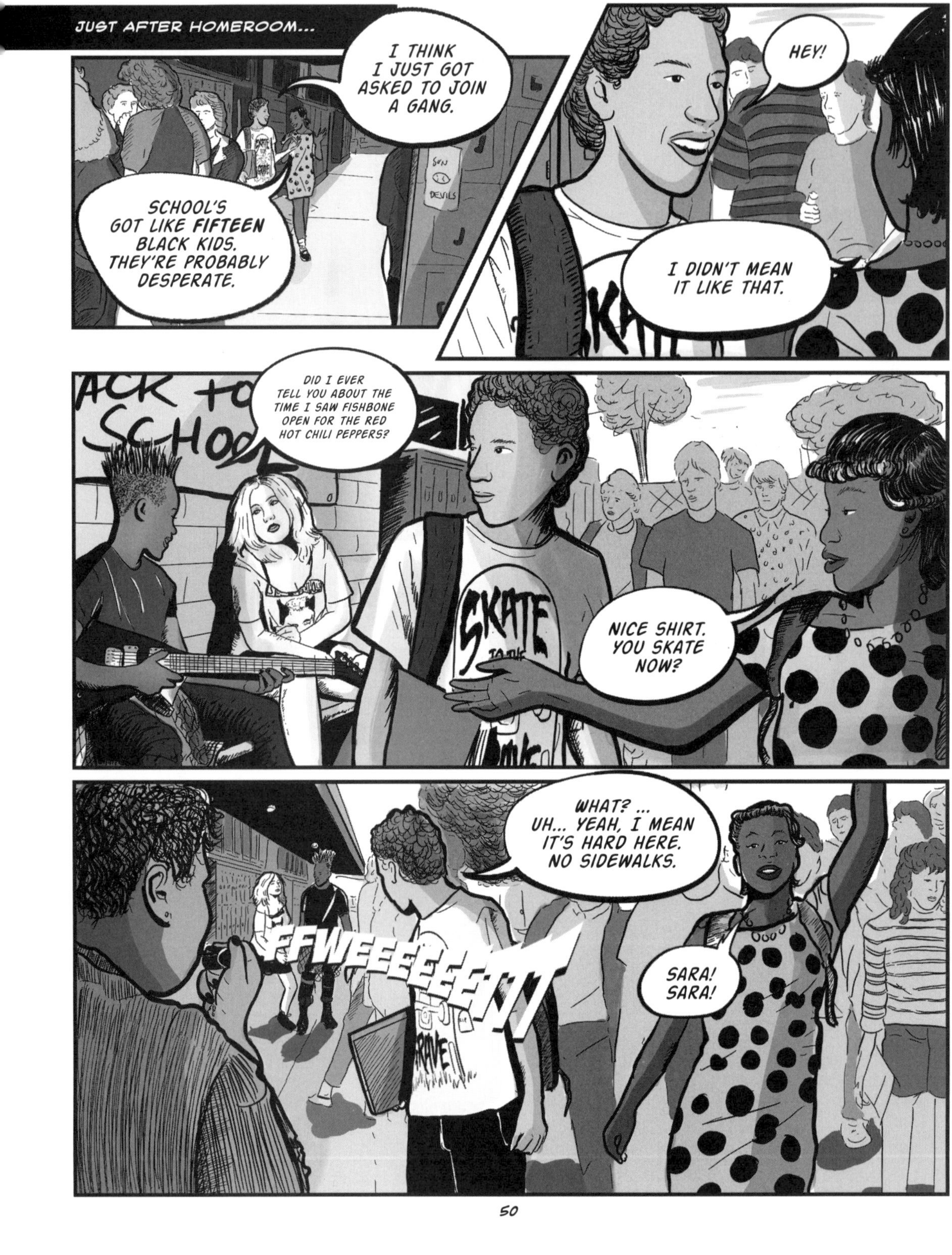
JUST AFTER HOMEROOM...
I THINK I JUST GOT ASKED TO JOIN A GANG.
SCHOOL'S GOT LIKE **FIFTEEN** BLACK KIDS. THEY'RE PROBABLY DESPERATE.
HEY!
I DIDN'T MEAN IT LIKE THAT.
DID I EVER TELL YOU ABOUT THE TIME I SAW FISHBONE OPEN FOR THE RED HOT CHILI PEPPERS?
NICE SHIRT. YOU SKATE NOW?
WHAT? ... UH... YEAH, I MEAN IT'S HARD HERE. NO SIDEWALKS.
FFWEEEEEEET!!
SARA! SARA!

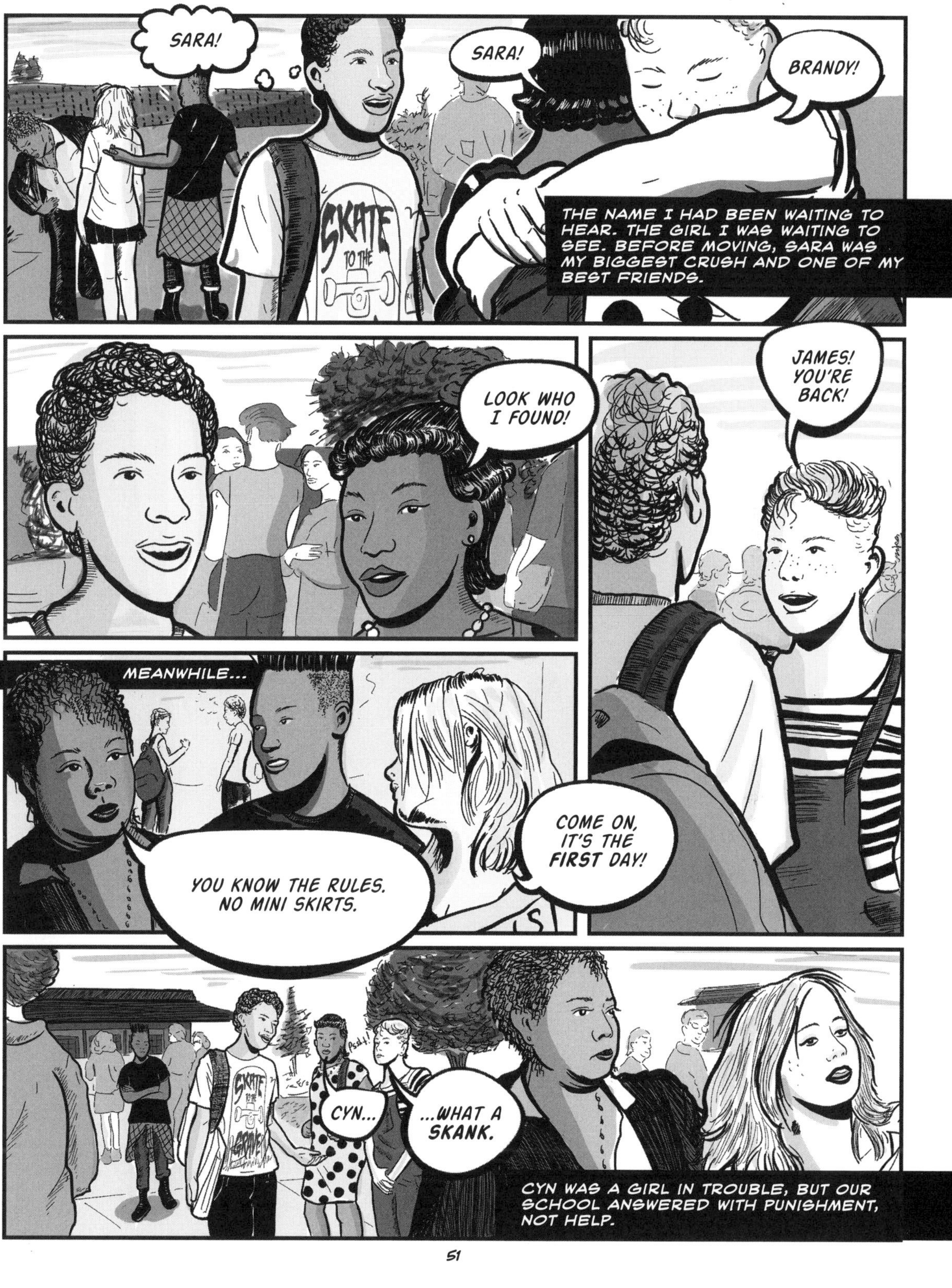
SARA!
SARA!
BRANDY!
THE NAME I HAD BEEN WAITING TO HEAR. THE GIRL I WAS WAITING TO SEE. BEFORE MOVING, SARA WAS MY BIGGEST CRUSH AND ONE OF MY BEST FRIENDS.
LOOK WHO I FOUND!
JAMES! YOU'RE BACK!
MEANWHILE...
YOU KNOW THE RULES. NO MINI SKIRTS.
COME ON, IT'S THE FIRST DAY!
CYN...
...WHAT A SKANK.
CYN WAS A GIRL IN TROUBLE, BUT OUR SCHOOL ANSWERED WITH PUNISHMENT, NOT HELP.

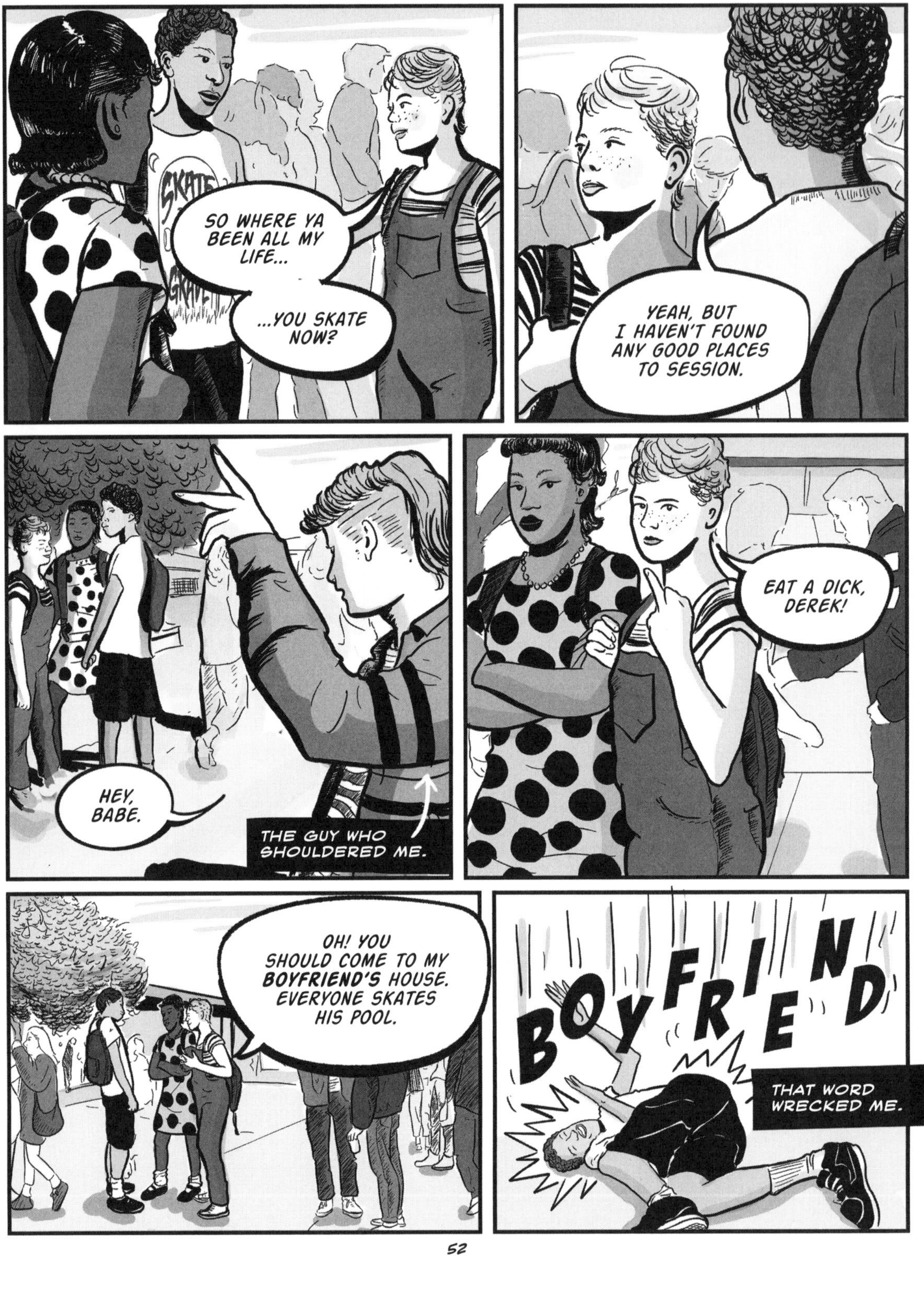
SO WHERE YA BEEN ALL MY LIFE...
...YOU SKATE NOW?
YEAH, BUT I HAVEN'T FOUND ANY GOOD PLACES TO SESSION.
HEY, BABE.
THE GUY WHO SHOULDERED ME.
EAT A DICK, DEREK!
OH! YOU SHOULD COME TO MY **BOYFRIEND'S** HOUSE. EVERYONE SKATES HIS POOL.
BOYFRIEND
THAT WORD WRECKED ME.

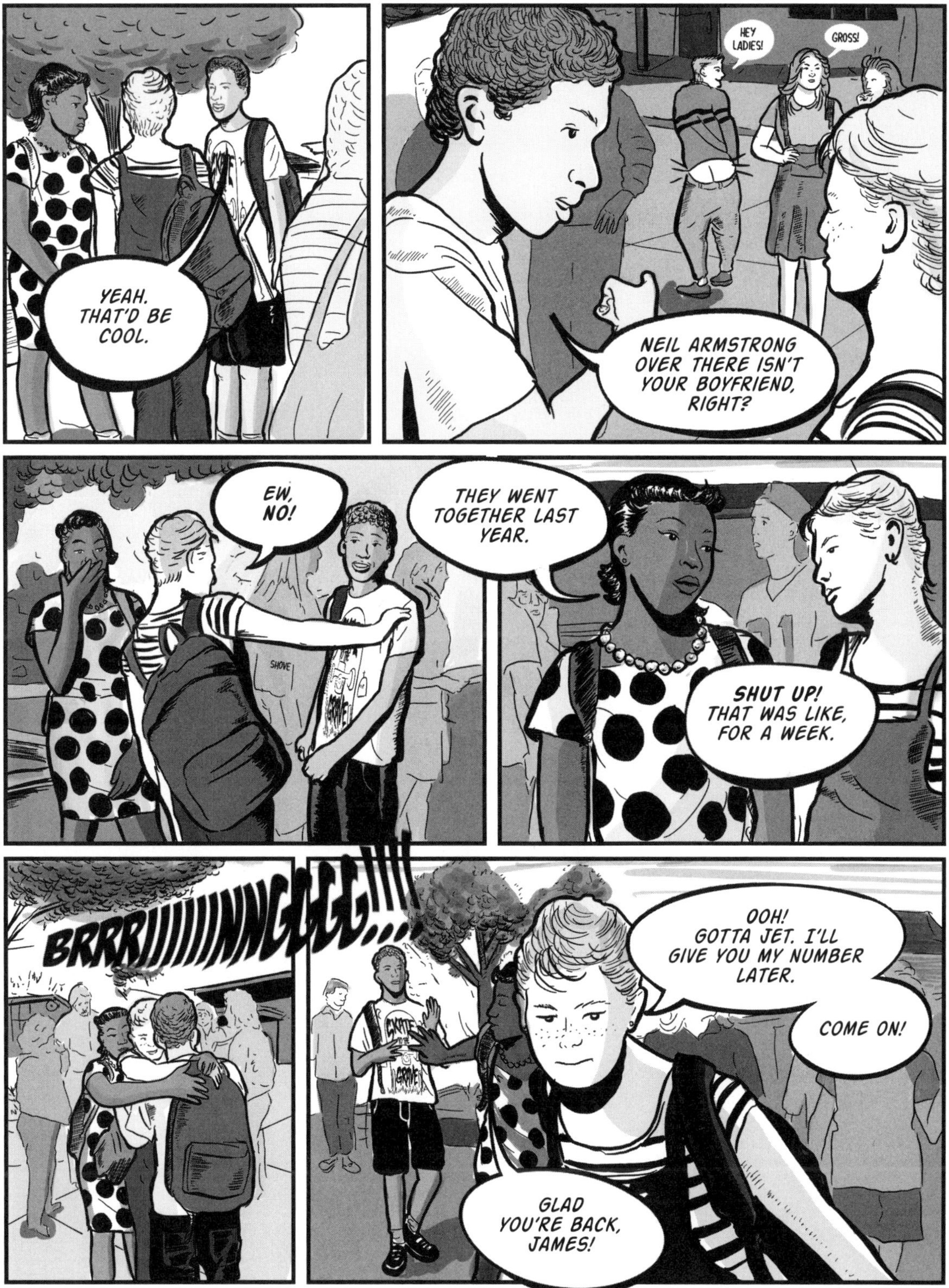
YEAH. THAT'D BE COOL.
HEY LADIES!
GROSS!
NEIL ARMSTRONG OVER THERE ISN'T YOUR BOYFRIEND, RIGHT?
EW, NO!
SHOVE
THEY WENT TOGETHER LAST YEAR.
SHUT UP! THAT WAS LIKE, FOR A WEEK.
BRRRIIIIIINNGGGG...!!!
OOH! GOTTA JET. I'LL GIVE YOU MY NUMBER LATER.
COME ON!
GLAD YOU'RE BACK, JAMES!

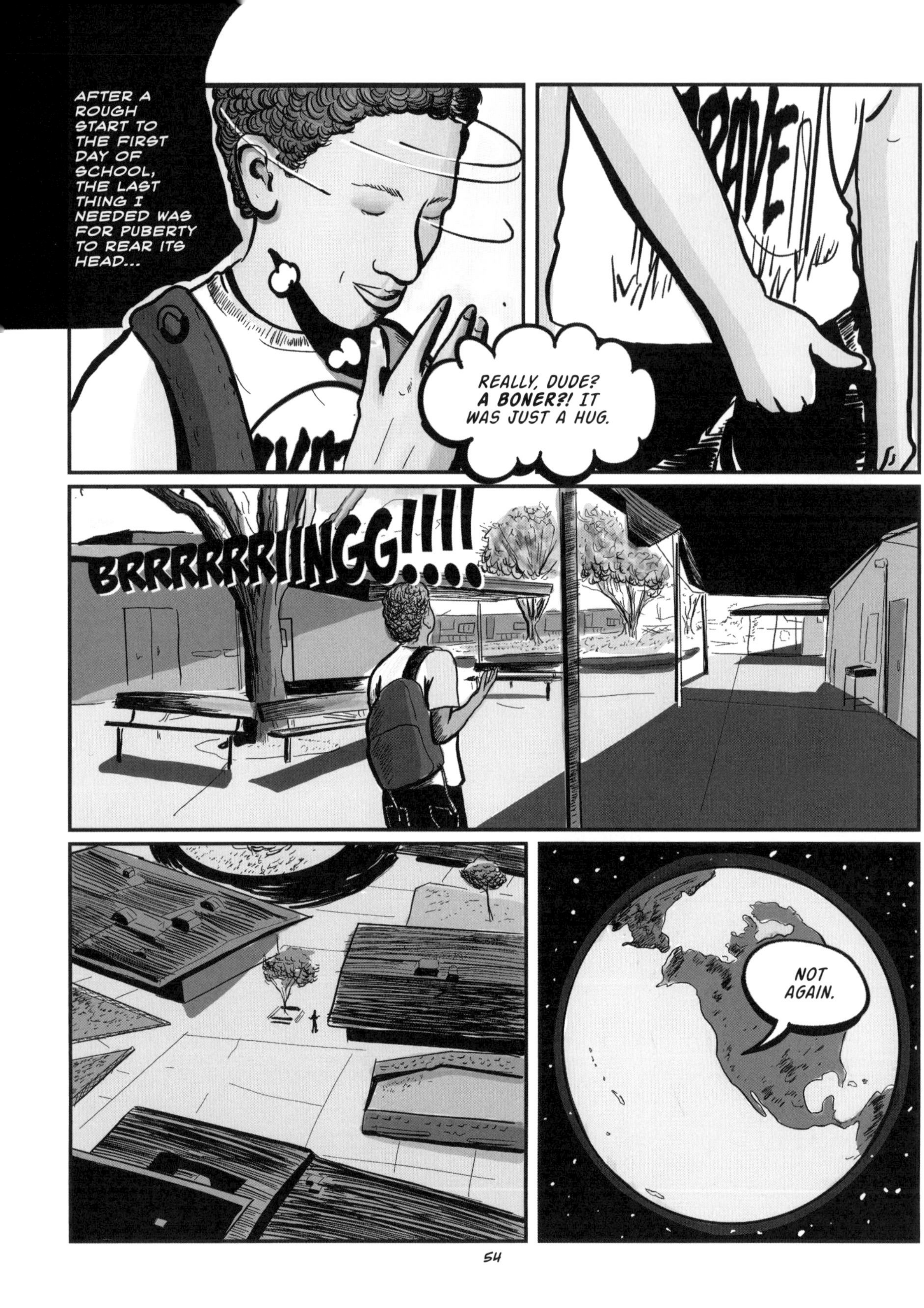
AFTER A ROUGH START TO THE FIRST DAY OF SCHOOL, THE LAST THING I NEEDED WAS FOR PUBERTY TO REAR ITS HEAD...
REALLY, DUDE? A BONER?! IT WAS JUST A HUG.
BRRRRRRIINGG!!!!
NOT AGAIN.

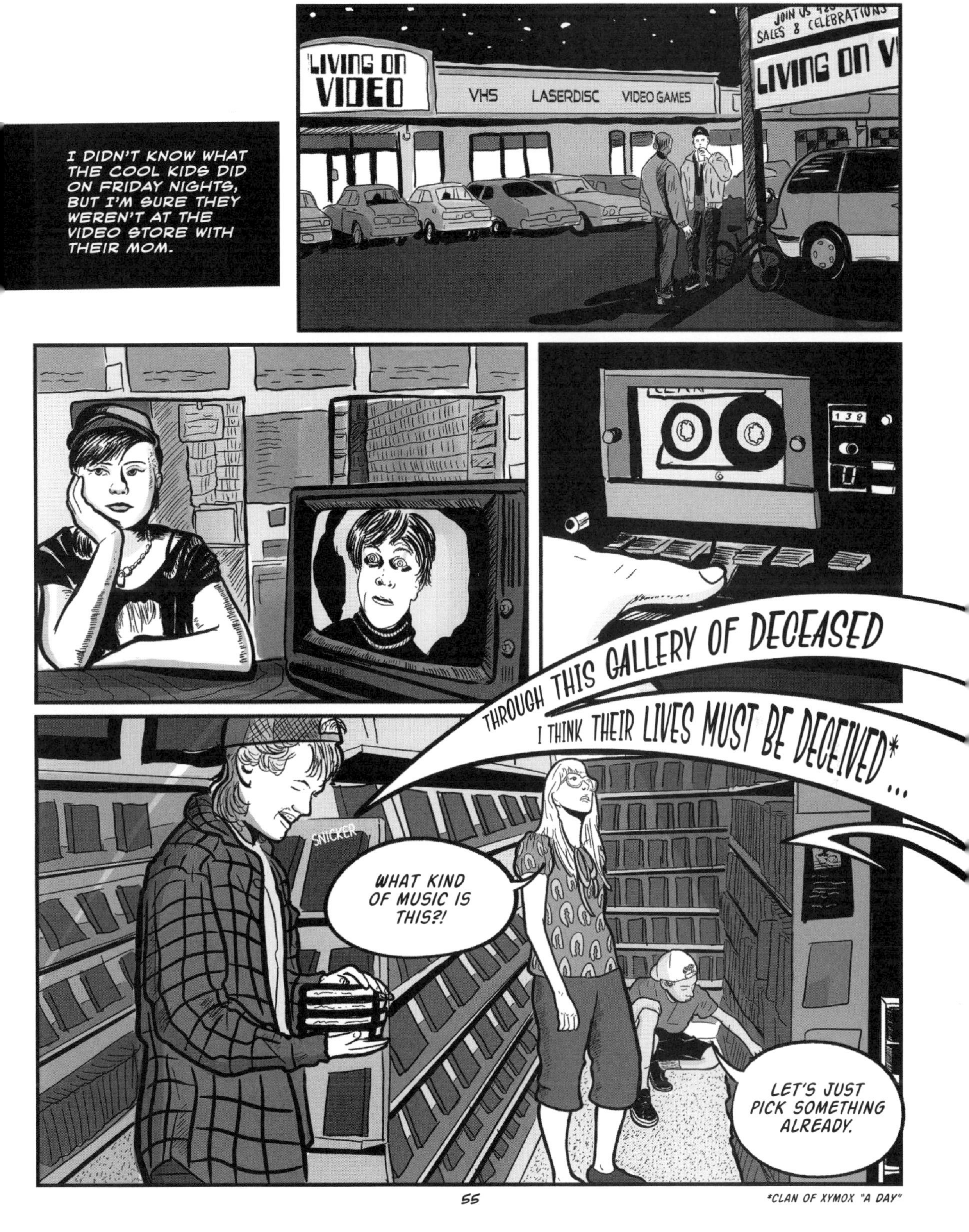
I DIDN'T KNOW WHAT THE COOL KIDS DID ON FRIDAY NIGHTS, BUT I'M SURE THEY WEREN'T AT THE VIDEO STORE WITH THEIR MOM.
LIVING ON VIDEO
VHS
LASERDISC
VIDEO GAMES
SALES & CELEBRATIONS
LIVING ON V
138
THROUGH THIS GALLERY OF DECEASED
I THINK THEIR LIVES MUST BE DECEIVED*...
SNICKER
WHAT KIND OF MUSIC IS THIS?!
LET'S JUST PICK SOMETHING ALREADY.

*CLAN OF XYMOX "A DAY"

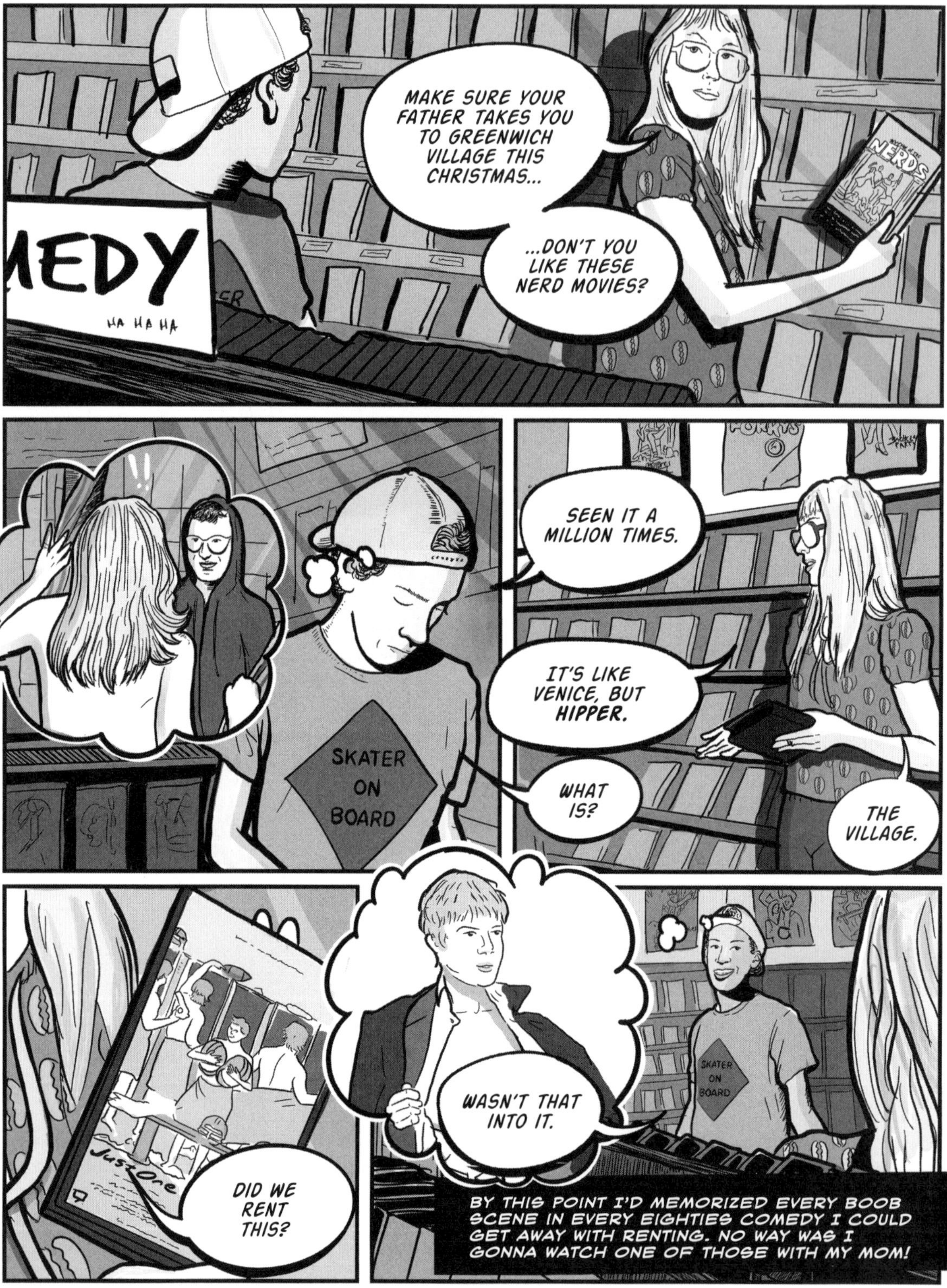
MEDY
HA HA HA
MAKE SURE YOUR FATHER TAKES YOU TO GREENWICH VILLAGE THIS CHRISTMAS...
...DON'T YOU LIKE THESE NERD MOVIES?
NERDS
SEEN IT A MILLION TIMES.
IT'S LIKE VENICE, BUT HIPPER.
SKATER ON BOARD
WHAT IS?
THE VILLAGE.
WASN'T THAT INTO IT.
Just One
DID WE RENT THIS?
SKATER ON BOARD
BY THIS POINT I'D MEMORIZED EVERY BOOB SCENE IN EVERY EIGHTIES COMEDY I COULD GET AWAY WITH RENTING. NO WAY WAS I GONNA WATCH ONE OF THOSE WITH MY MOM!

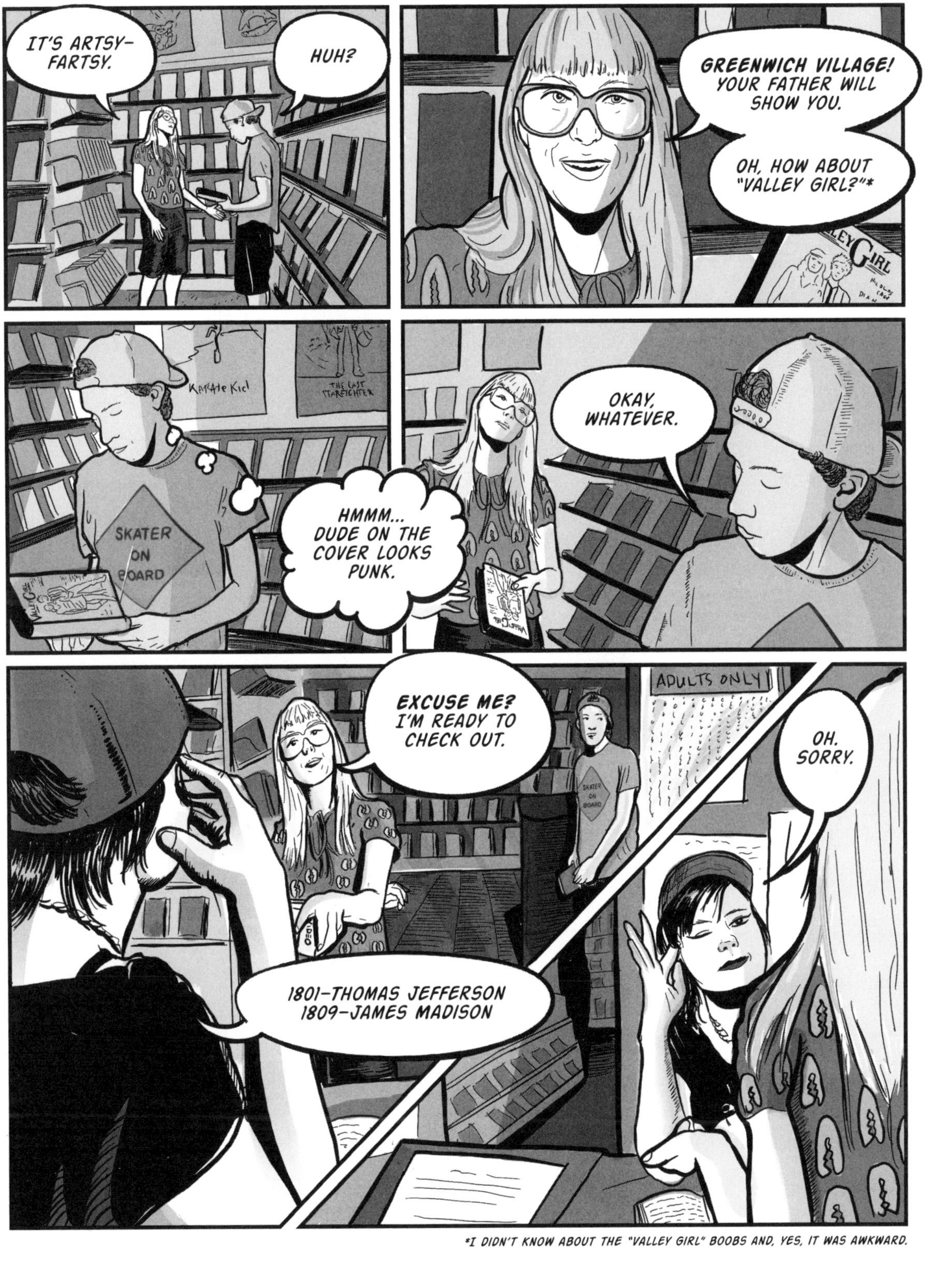
IT'S ARTSY-FARTSY.
HUH?
GREENWICH VILLAGE! YOUR FATHER WILL SHOW YOU.
OH, HOW ABOUT "VALLEY GIRL?"*
Karate Kid
THE LAST STARFIGHTER
SKATER ON BOARD
HMMM... DUDE ON THE COVER LOOKS PUNK.
OKAY, WHATEVER.
ADULTS ONLY
EXCUSE ME? I'M READY TO CHECK OUT.
OH. SORRY.
1801–THOMAS JEFFERSON
1809–JAMES MADISON

*I DIDN'T KNOW ABOUT THE "VALLEY GIRL" BOOBS AND, YES, IT WAS AWKWARD.

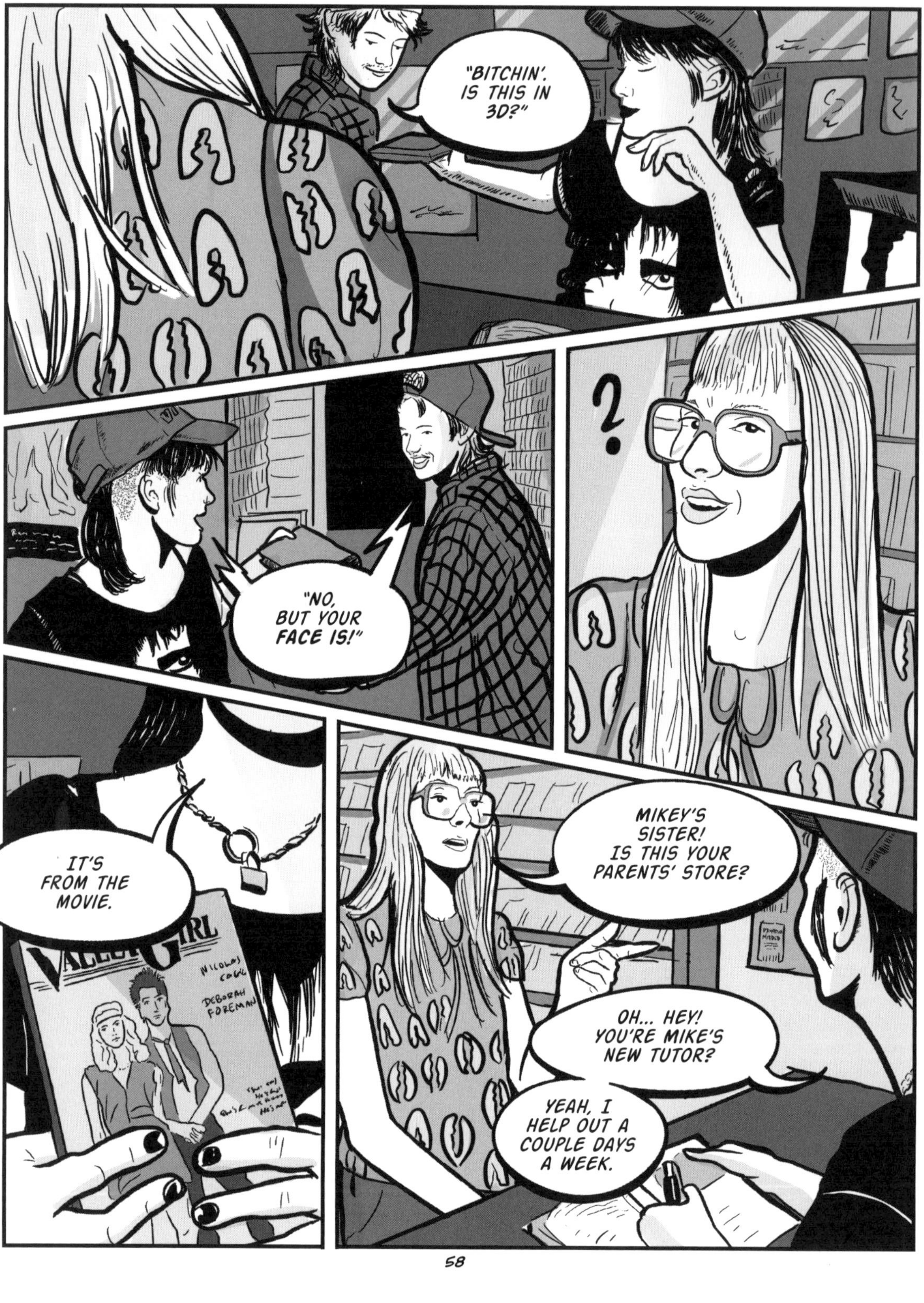
"BITCHIN'. IS THIS IN 3D?"
"NO, BUT YOUR FACE IS!"
?
IT'S FROM THE MOVIE.
MIKEY'S SISTER! IS THIS YOUR PARENTS' STORE?
OH... HEY! YOU'RE MIKE'S NEW TUTOR?
YEAH, I HELP OUT A COUPLE DAYS A WEEK.

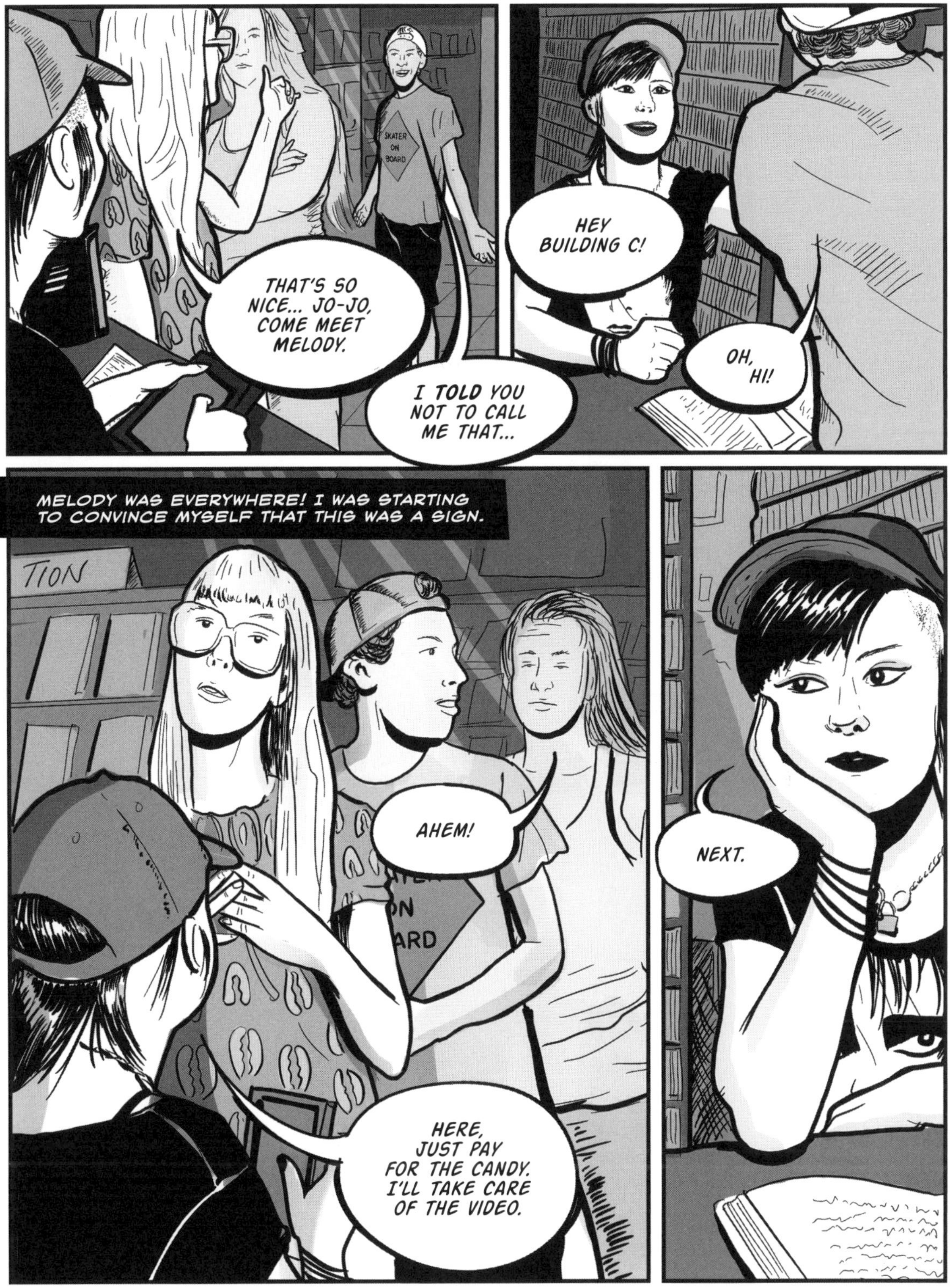
SKATER ON BOARD
THAT'S SO NICE... JO-JO, COME MEET MELODY.
I TOLD YOU NOT TO CALL ME THAT...
HEY BUILDING C!
OH, HI!
MELODY WAS EVERYWHERE! I WAS STARTING TO CONVINCE MYSELF THAT THIS WAS A SIGN.
TION
AHEM!
HERE, JUST PAY FOR THE CANDY. I'LL TAKE CARE OF THE VIDEO.
NEXT.

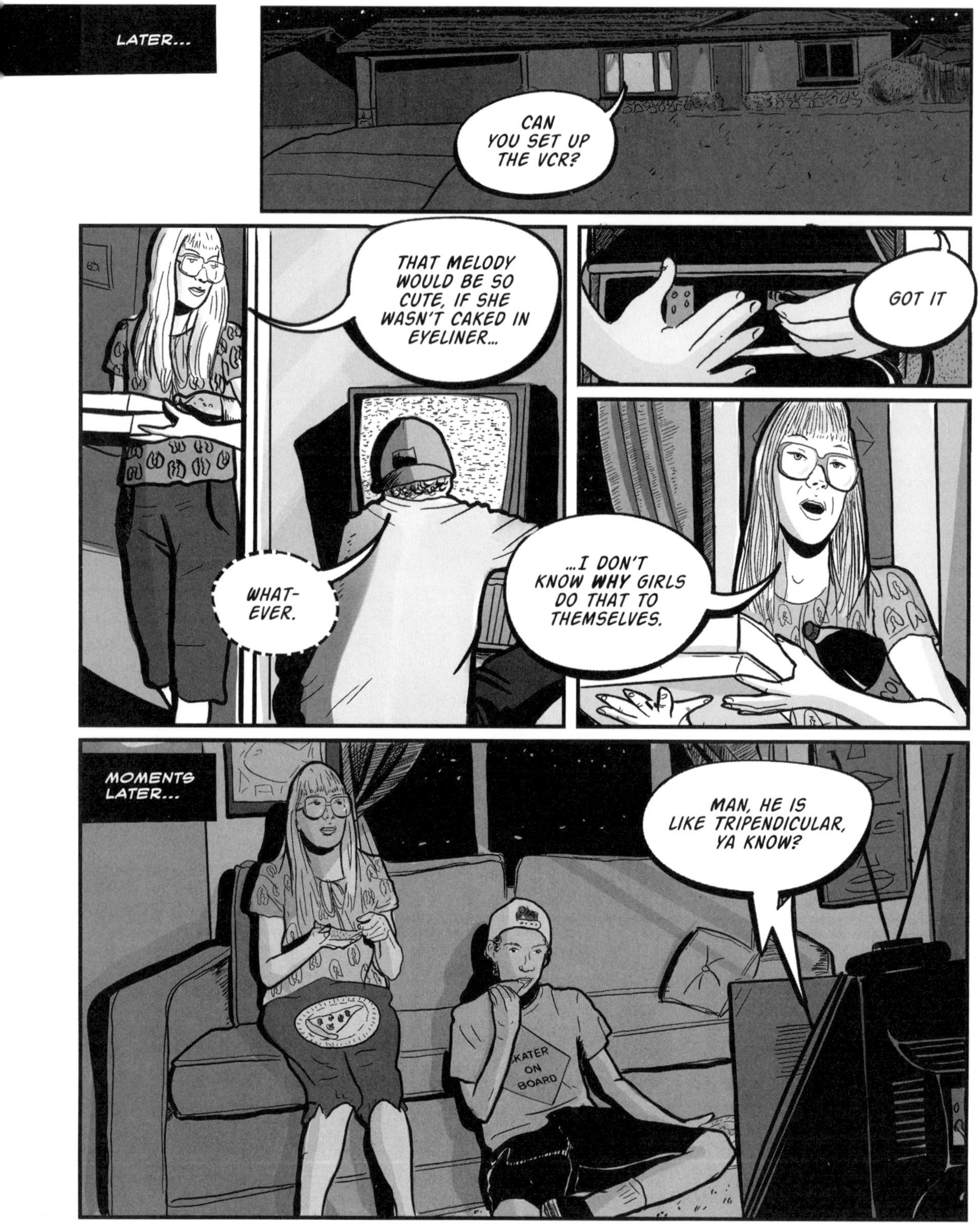
LATER...
CAN YOU SET UP THE VCR?
THAT MELODY WOULD BE SO CUTE, IF SHE WASN'T CAKED IN EYELINER...
GOT IT
WHAT-EVER.
...I DON'T KNOW **WHY** GIRLS DO THAT TO THEMSELVES.
MOMENTS LATER...
MAN, HE IS LIKE TRIPENDICULAR, YA KNOW?
SKATER ON BOARD

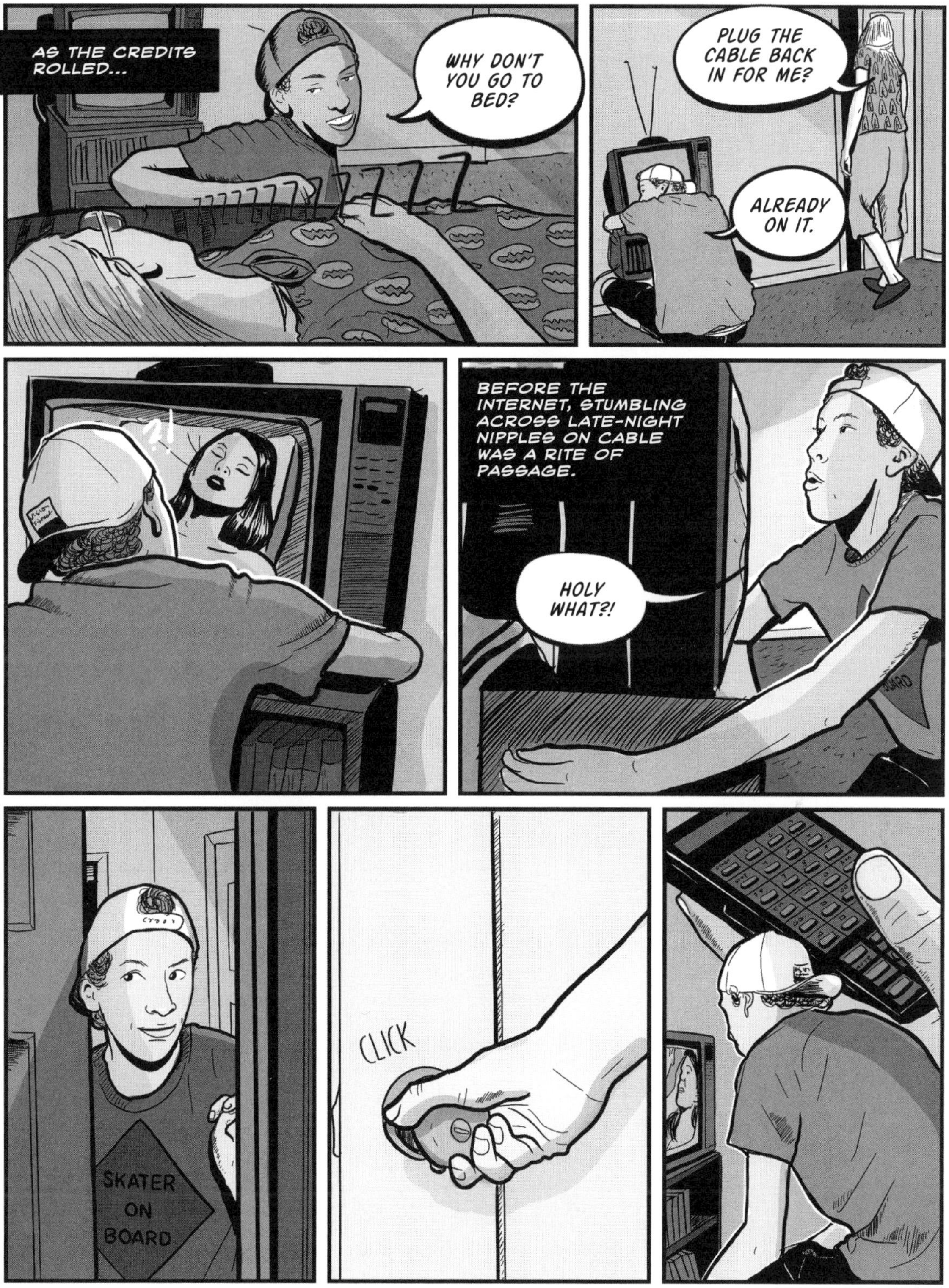

AS THE CREDITS ROLLED...
WHY DON'T YOU GO TO BED?
ZZZZZZZZZZ
PLUG THE CABLE BACK IN FOR ME?
ALREADY ON IT.
BEFORE THE INTERNET, STUMBLING ACROSS LATE-NIGHT NIPPLES ON CABLE WAS A RITE OF PASSAGE.
HOLY WHAT?!
SKATER ON BOARD
CLICK

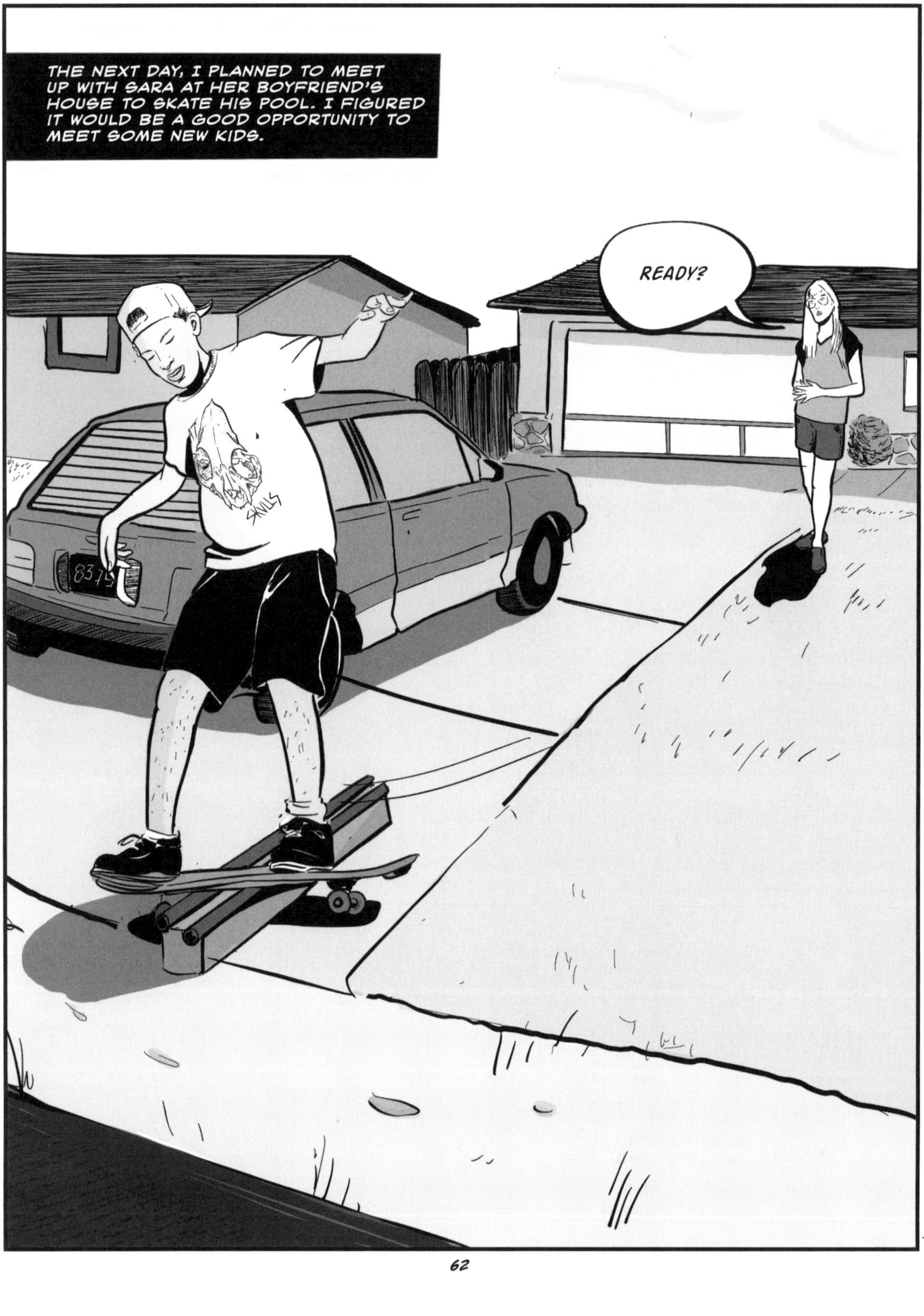
THE NEXT DAY, I PLANNED TO MEET UP WITH SARA AT HER BOYFRIEND'S HOUSE TO SKATE HIS POOL. I FIGURED IT WOULD BE A GOOD OPPORTUNITY TO MEET SOME NEW KIDS.
READY?
SKULLS

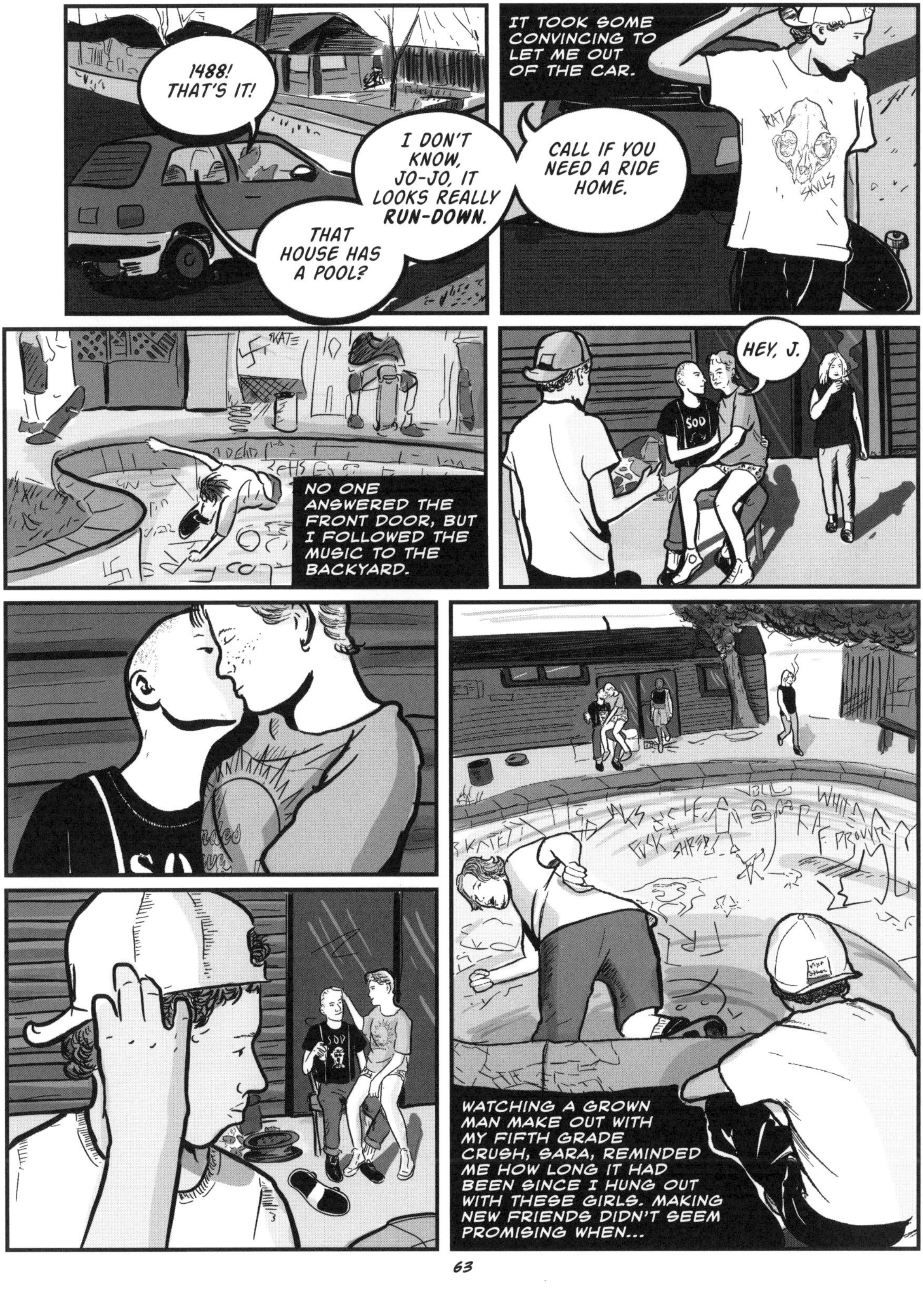
1488! THAT'S IT!
I DON'T KNOW, JO-JO, IT LOOKS REALLY RUN-DOWN.
THAT HOUSE HAS A POOL?
IT TOOK SOME CONVINCING TO LET ME OUT OF THE CAR.
CALL IF YOU NEED A RIDE HOME.
NO ONE ANSWERED THE FRONT DOOR, BUT I FOLLOWED THE MUSIC TO THE BACKYARD.
HEY, J.
WATCHING A GROWN MAN MAKE OUT WITH MY FIFTH GRADE CRUSH, SARA, REMINDED ME HOW LONG IT HAD BEEN SINCE I HUNG OUT WITH THESE GIRLS. MAKING NEW FRIENDS DIDN'T SEEM PROMISING WHEN...

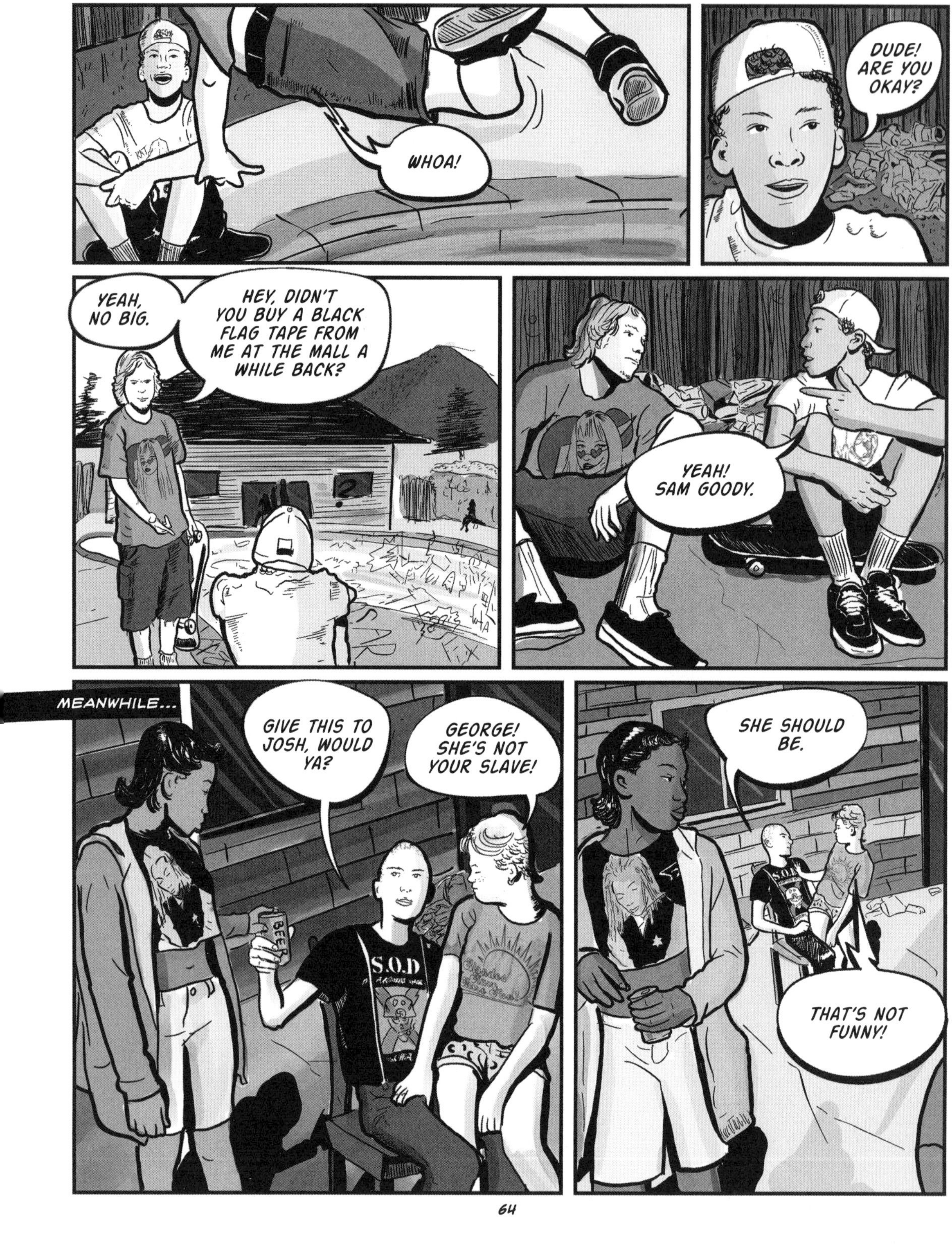
WHOA!
DUDE! ARE YOU OKAY?
YEAH, NO BIG.
HEY, DIDN'T YOU BUY A BLACK FLAG TAPE FROM ME AT THE MALL A WHILE BACK?
YEAH! SAM GOODY.
MEANWHILE...
GIVE THIS TO JOSH, WOULD YA?
GEORGE! SHE'S NOT YOUR SLAVE!
SHE SHOULD BE.
THAT'S NOT FUNNY!

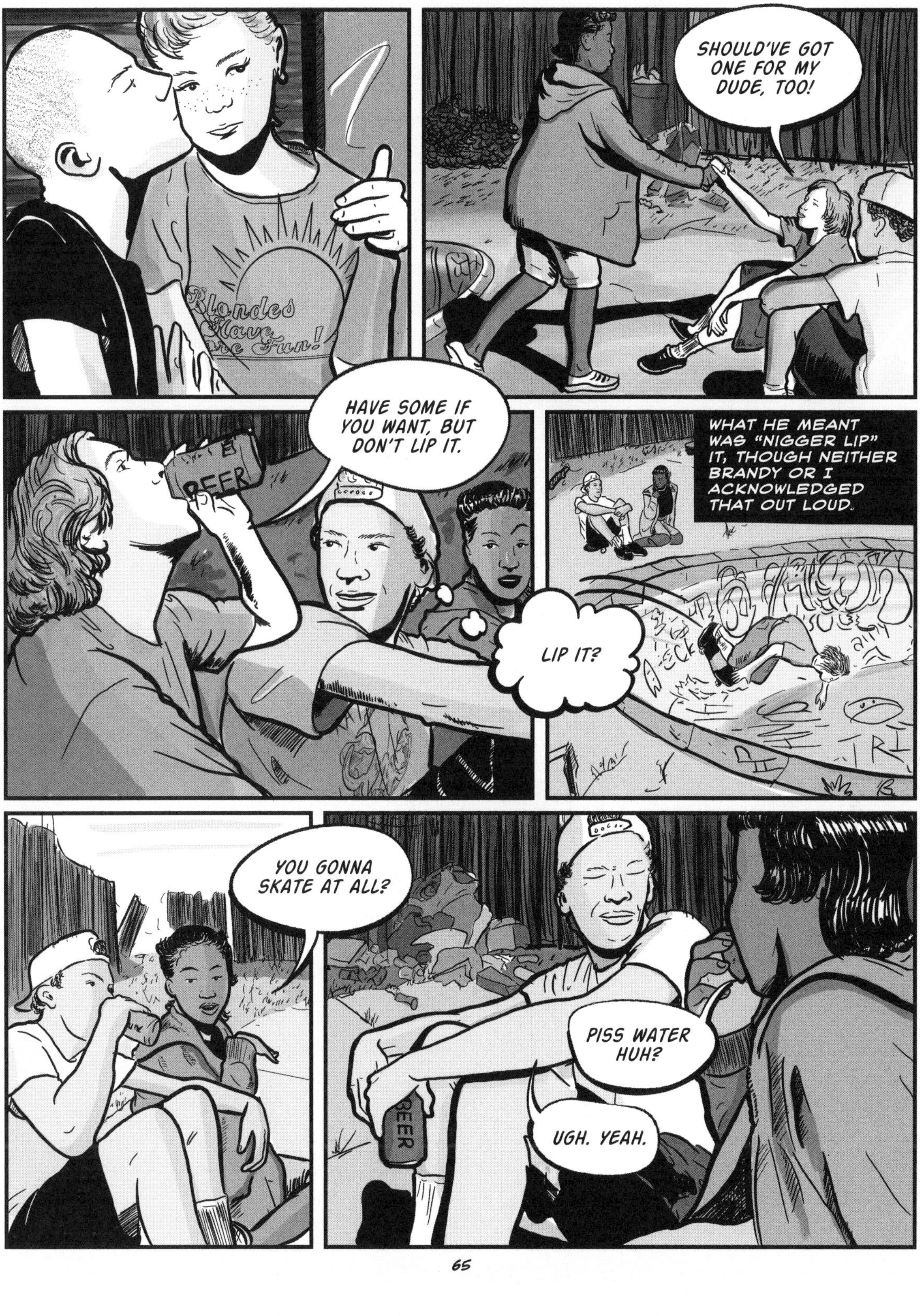
SHOULD'VE GOT ONE FOR MY DUDE, TOO!
HAVE SOME IF YOU WANT, BUT DON'T LIP IT.
BEER
LIP IT?
WHAT HE MEANT WAS "NIGGER LIP" IT, THOUGH NEITHER BRANDY OR I ACKNOWLEDGED THAT OUT LOUD.
YOU GONNA SKATE AT ALL?
PISS WATER HUH?
UGH. YEAH.
BEER

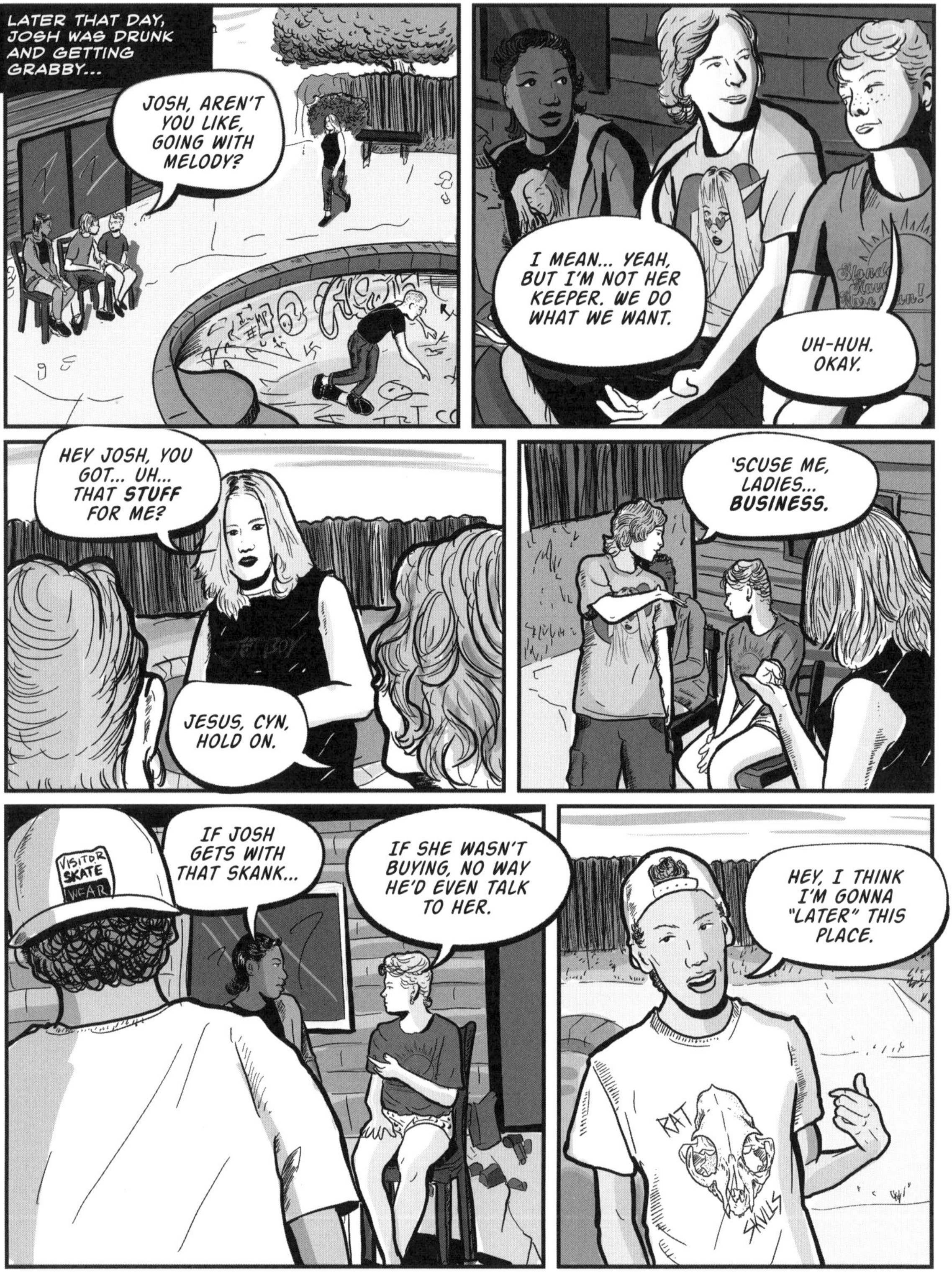
LATER THAT DAY, JOSH WAS DRUNK AND GETTING GRABBY...
JOSH, AREN'T YOU LIKE, GOING WITH MELODY?
I MEAN... YEAH, BUT I'M NOT HER KEEPER. WE DO WHAT WE WANT.
UH-HUH. OKAY.
HEY JOSH, YOU GOT... UH... THAT STUFF FOR ME?
JESUS, CYN, HOLD ON.
'SCUSE ME, LADIES... BUSINESS.
VISITOR SKATE WEAR
IF JOSH GETS WITH THAT SKANK...
IF SHE WASN'T BUYING, NO WAY HE'D EVEN TALK TO HER.
HEY, I THINK I'M GONNA "LATER" THIS PLACE.
RAT SKULLS

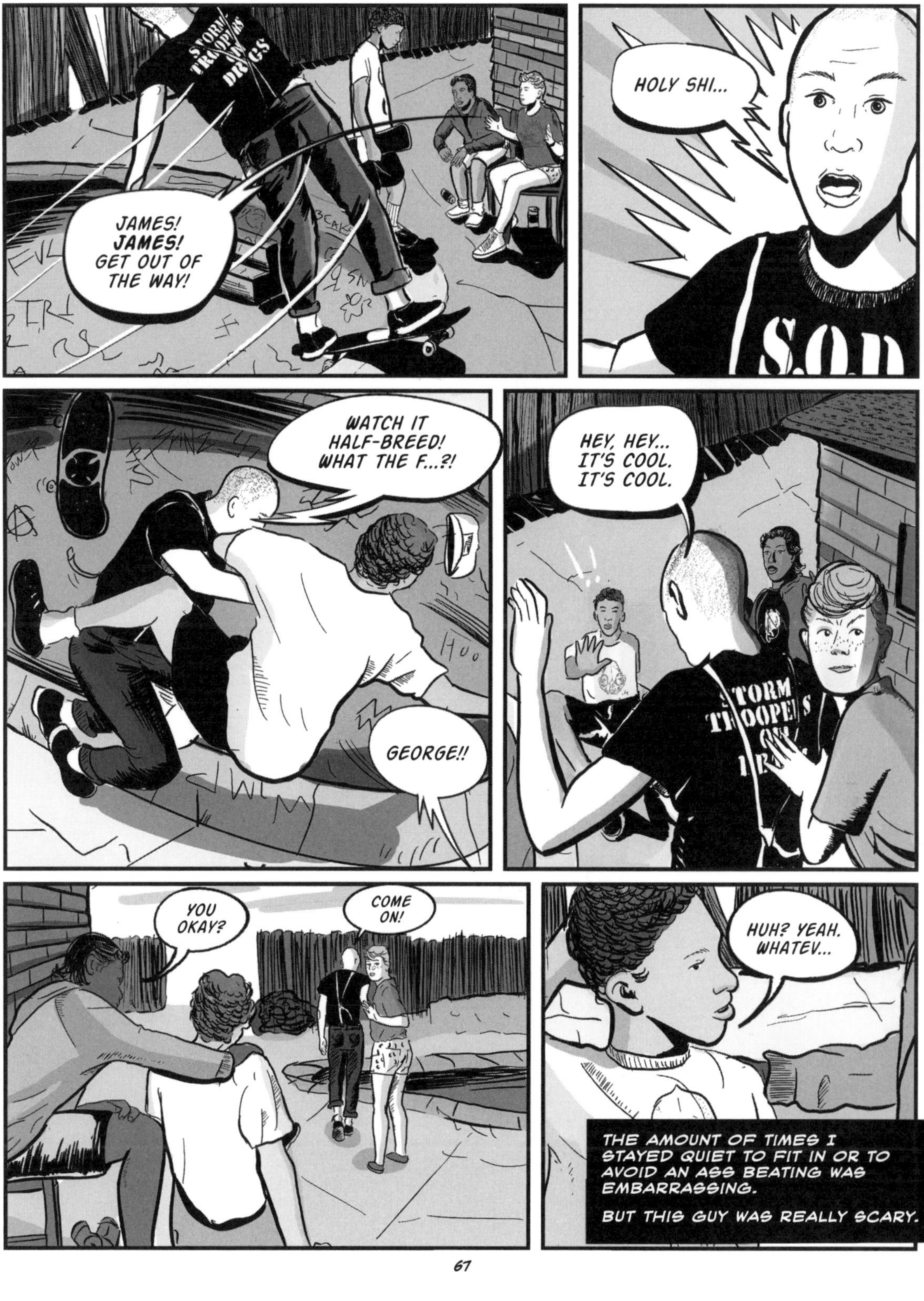
JAMES! JAMES! GET OUT OF THE WAY!
HOLY SHI...
WATCH IT HALF-BREED! WHAT THE F...?!
GEORGE!!
HEY, HEY... IT'S COOL. IT'S COOL.
YOU OKAY?
COME ON!
HUH? YEAH. WHATEV...
THE AMOUNT OF TIMES I STAYED QUIET TO FIT IN OR TO AVOID AN ASS BEATING WAS EMBARRASSING.
BUT THIS GUY WAS REALLY SCARY.

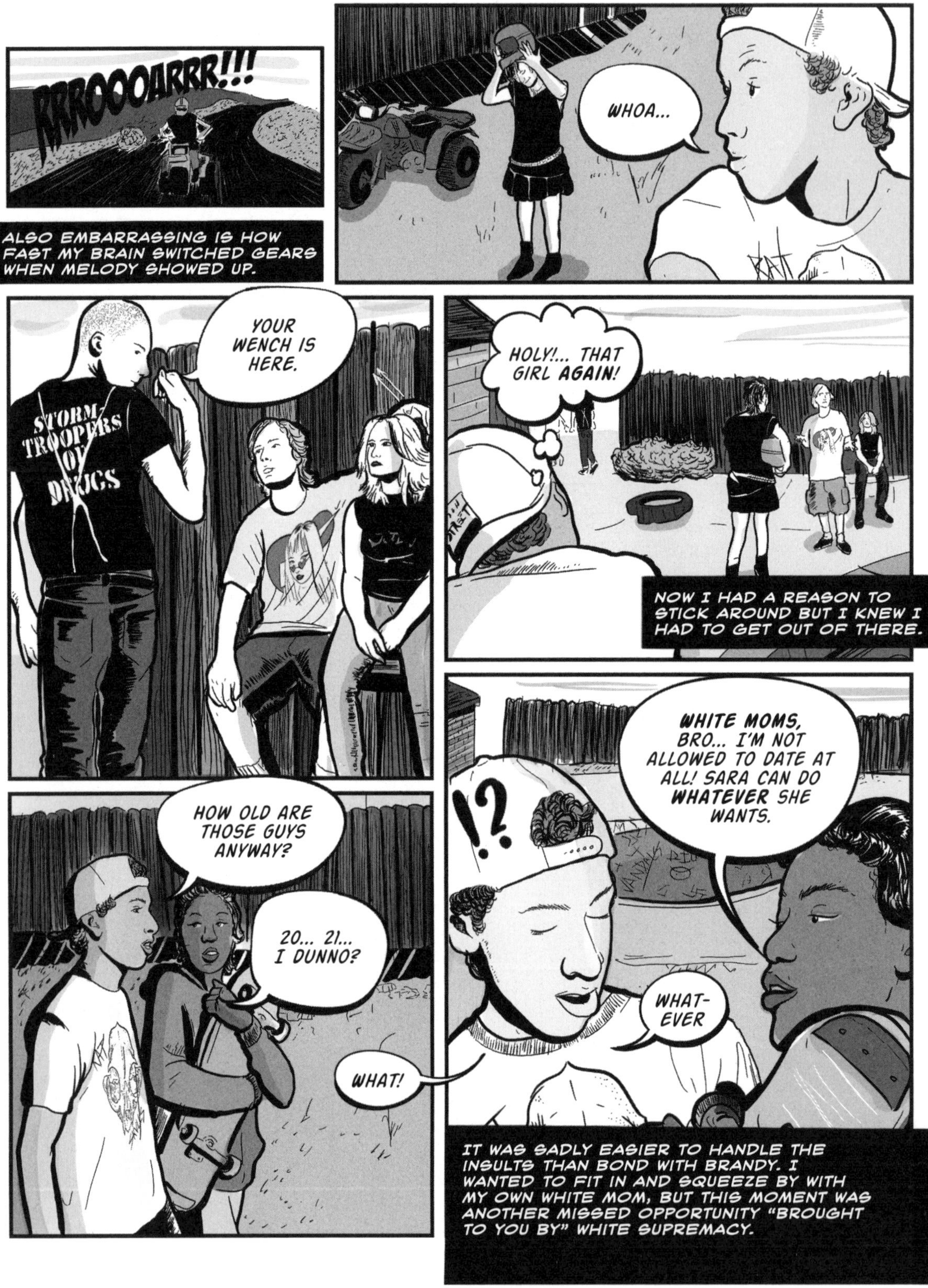
RRROOOARRR!!!
ALSO EMBARRASSING IS HOW FAST MY BRAIN SWITCHED GEARS WHEN MELODY SHOWED UP.
WHOA...
YOUR WENCH IS HERE.
STORM-TROOPERS OF DRUGS
HOLY!... THAT GIRL AGAIN!
NOW I HAD A REASON TO STICK AROUND BUT I KNEW I HAD TO GET OUT OF THERE.
HOW OLD ARE THOSE GUYS ANYWAY?
20... 21... I DUNNO?
WHAT!
!?
WHITE MOMS, BRO... I'M NOT ALLOWED TO DATE AT ALL! SARA CAN DO WHATEVER SHE WANTS.
WHAT-EVER
IT WAS SADLY EASIER TO HANDLE THE INSULTS THAN BOND WITH BRANDY. I WANTED TO FIT IN AND SQUEEZE BY WITH MY OWN WHITE MOM, BUT THIS MOMENT WAS ANOTHER MISSED OPPORTUNITY "BROUGHT TO YOU BY" WHITE SUPREMACY.

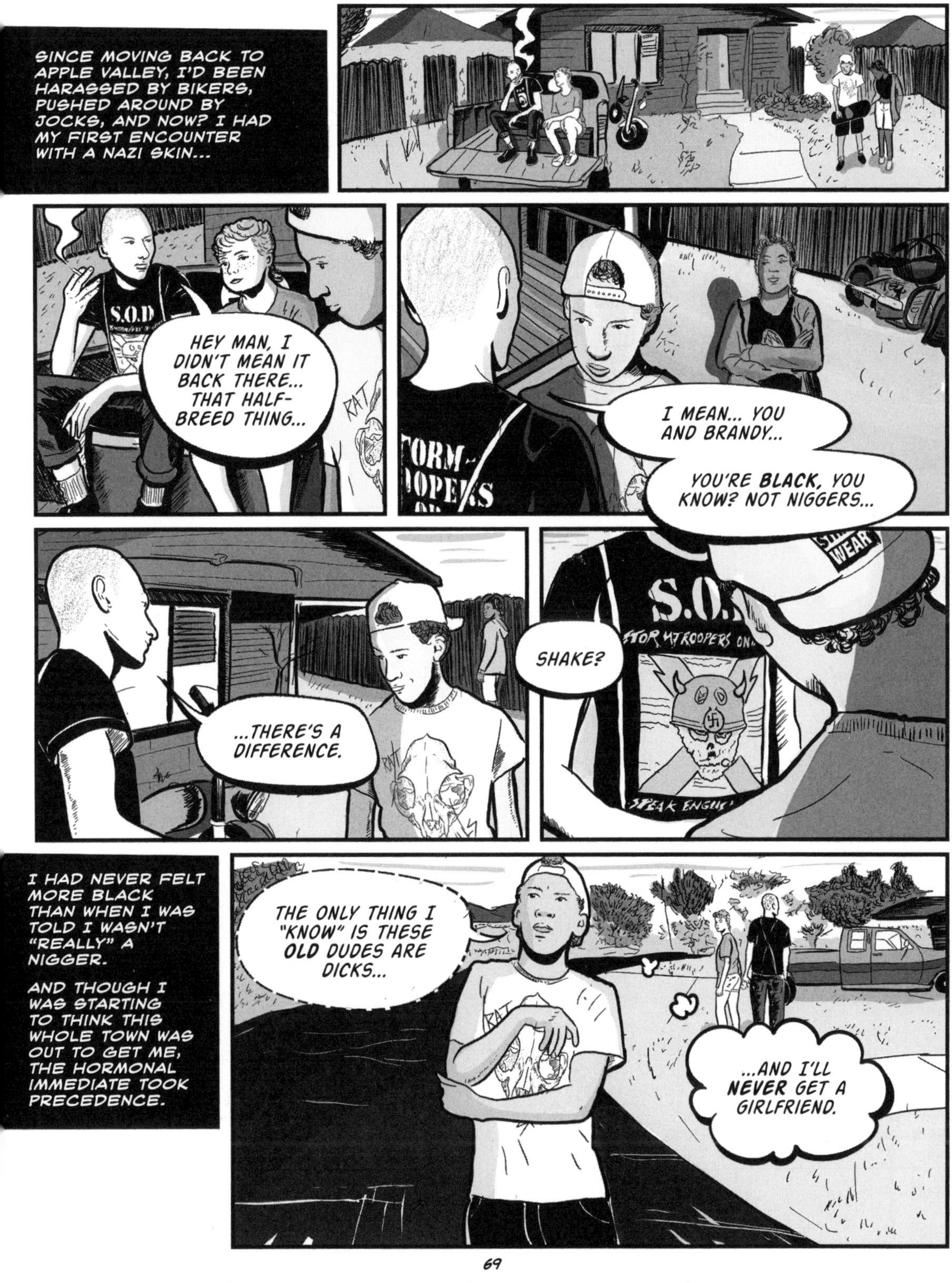

SINCE MOVING BACK TO APPLE VALLEY, I'D BEEN HARASSED BY BIKERS, PUSHED AROUND BY JOCKS, AND NOW? I HAD MY FIRST ENCOUNTER WITH A NAZI SKIN...
HEY MAN, I DIDN'T MEAN IT BACK THERE... THAT HALF-BREED THING...
I MEAN... YOU AND BRANDY...
YOU'RE BLACK, YOU KNOW? NOT NIGGERS...
...THERE'S A DIFFERENCE.
SHAKE?
I HAD NEVER FELT MORE BLACK THAN WHEN I WAS TOLD I WASN'T "REALLY" A NIGGER.
AND THOUGH I WAS STARTING TO THINK THIS WHOLE TOWN WAS OUT TO GET ME, THE HORMONAL IMMEDIATE TOOK PRECEDENCE.
THE ONLY THING I "KNOW" IS THESE OLD DUDES ARE DICKS...
...AND I'LL NEVER GET A GIRLFRIEND.

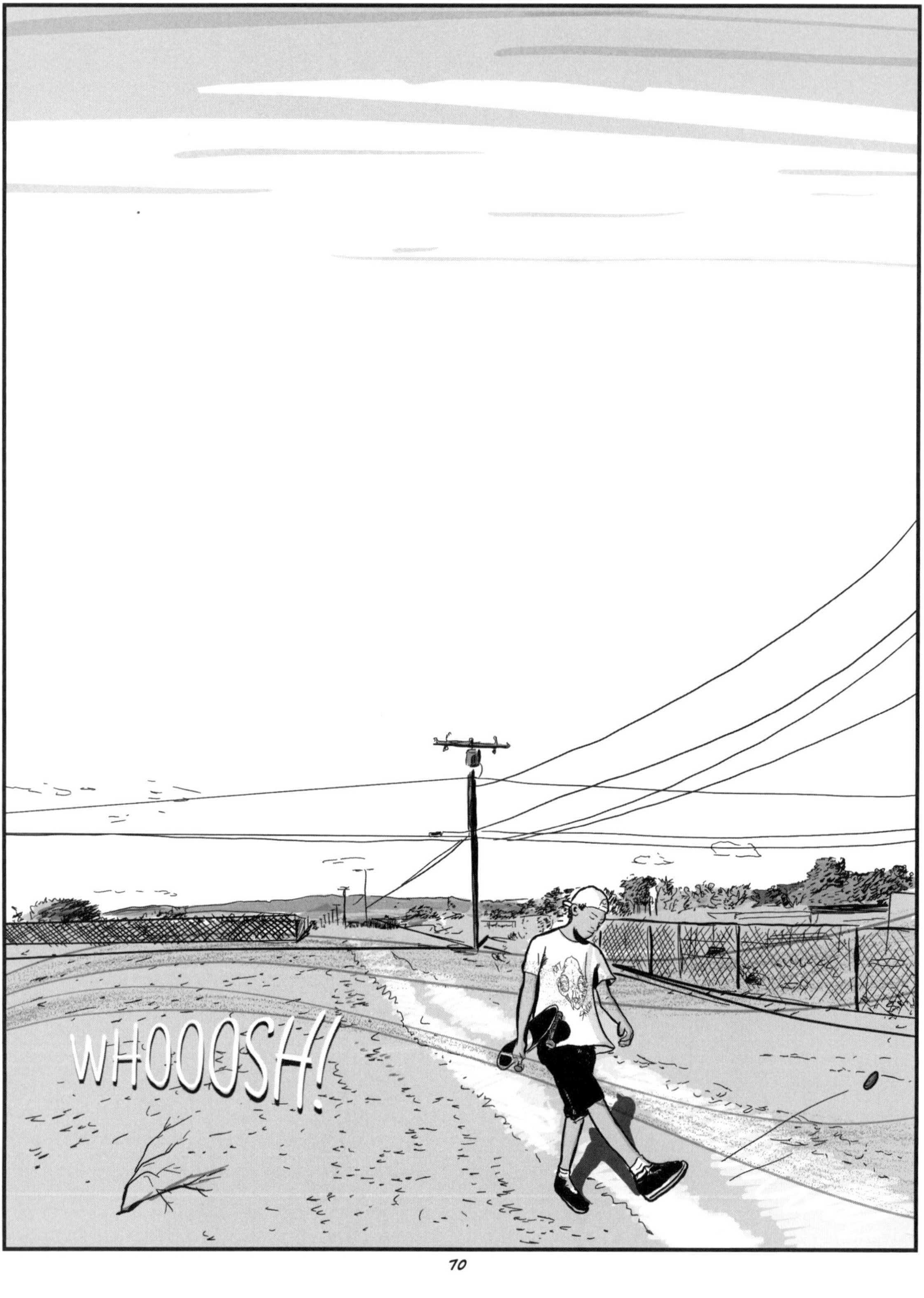
WHOOOSH!

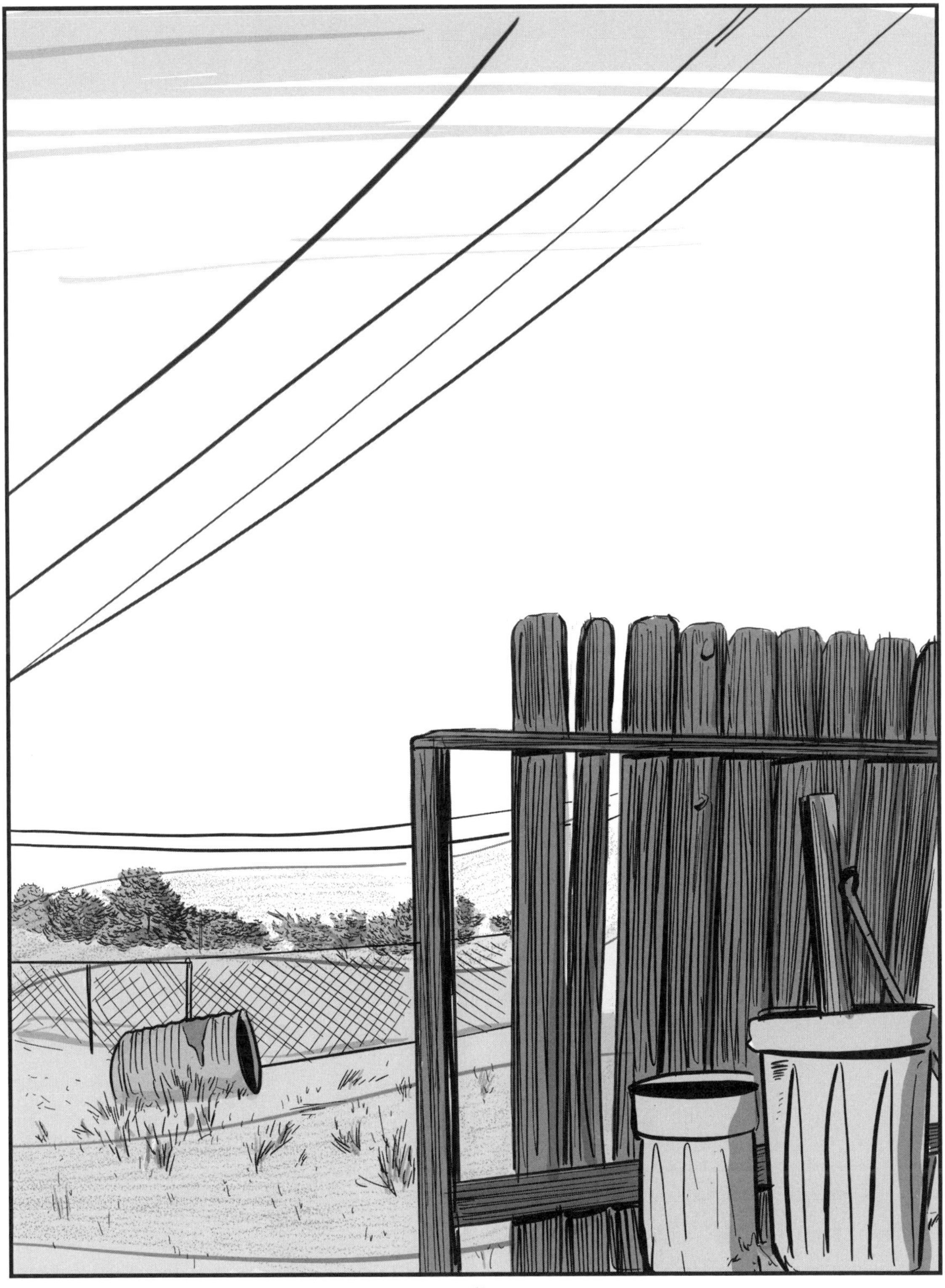

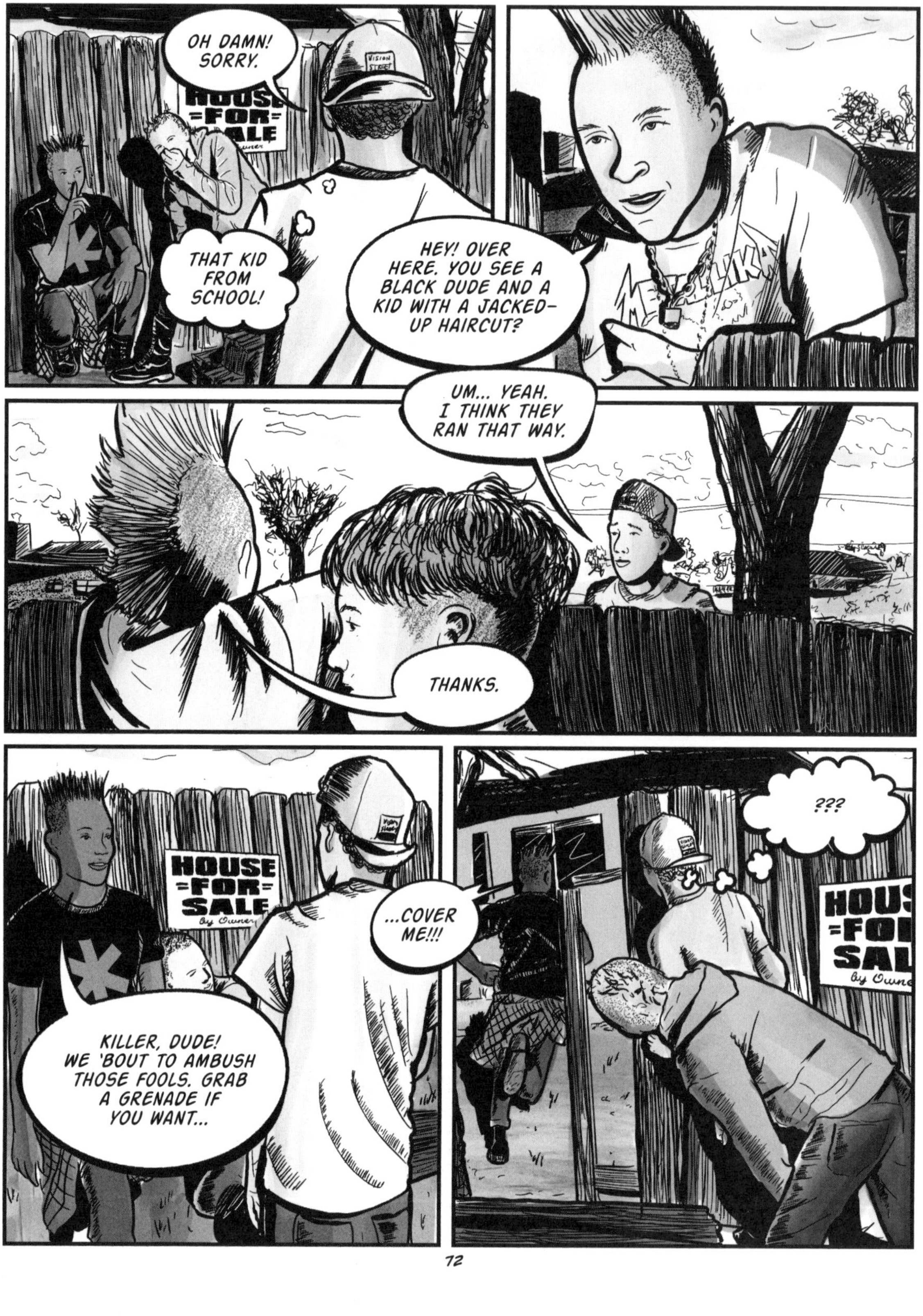
OH DAMN! SORRY.
THAT KID FROM SCHOOL!
HOUSE FOR SALE
HEY! OVER HERE. YOU SEE A BLACK DUDE AND A KID WITH A JACKED-UP HAIRCUT?
UM... YEAH. I THINK THEY RAN THAT WAY.
THANKS.
HOUSE FOR SALE By Owner
KILLER, DUDE! WE 'BOUT TO AMBUSH THOSE FOOLS. GRAB A GRENADE IF YOU WANT...
...COVER ME!!!
???
HOUS FOR SAL by Owne

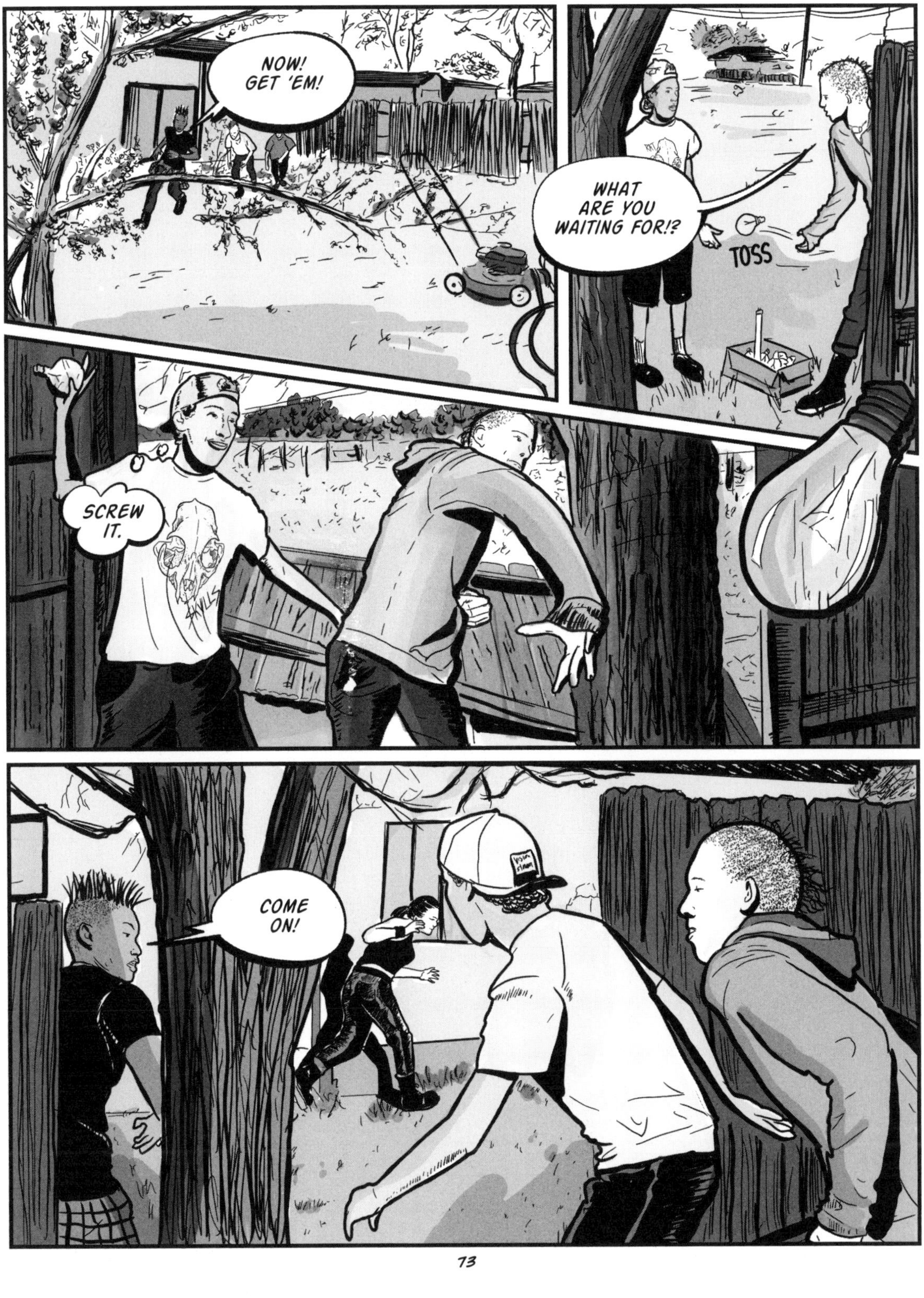
NOW! GET 'EM!
WHAT ARE YOU WAITING FOR!?
TOSS
SCREW IT.
COME ON!

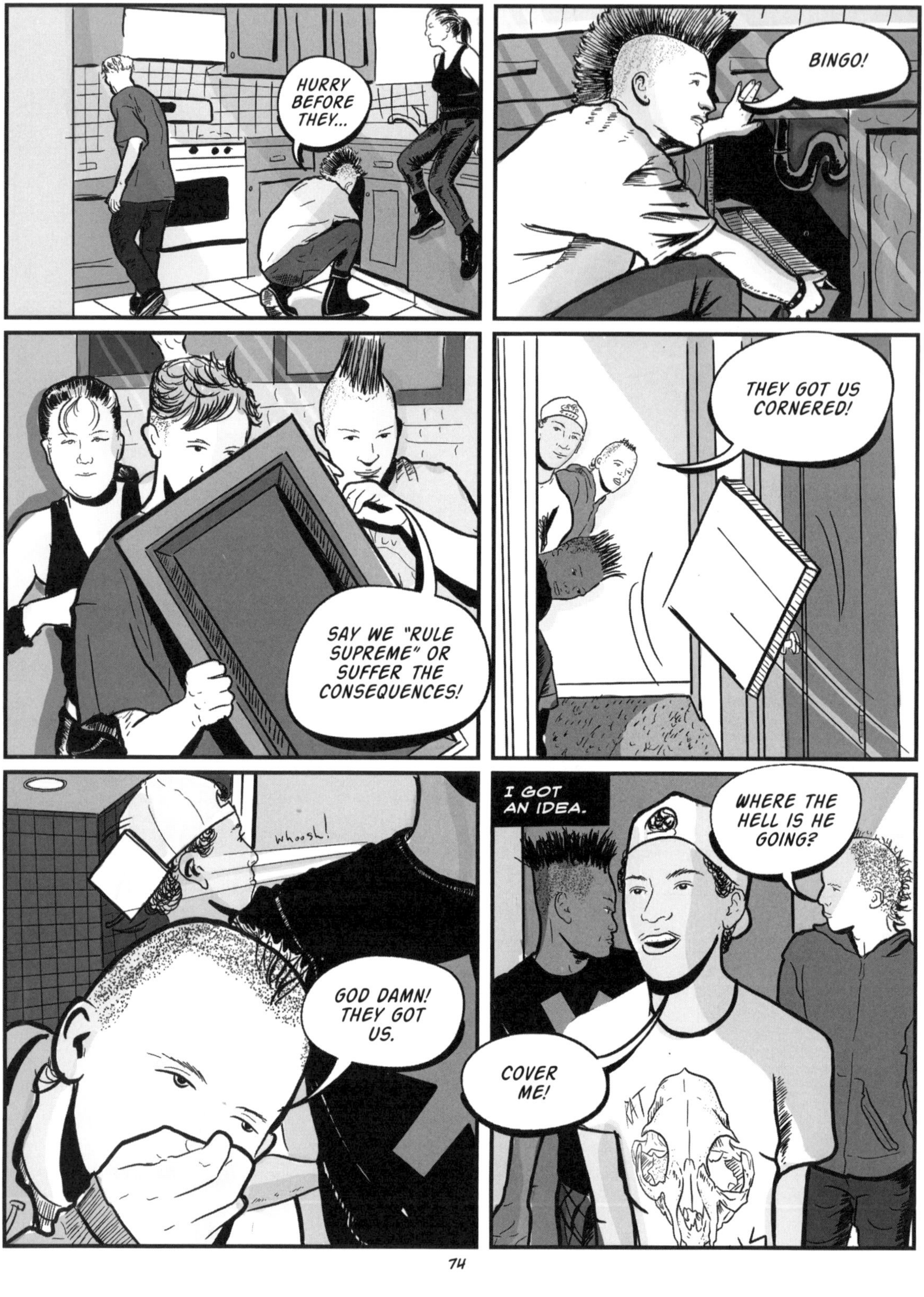
HURRY BEFORE THEY...
BINGO!
SAY WE "RULE SUPREME" OR SUFFER THE CONSEQUENCES!
THEY GOT US CORNERED!
whoosh!
GOD DAMN! THEY GOT US.
I GOT AN IDEA.
WHERE THE HELL IS HE GOING?
COVER ME!
RAT

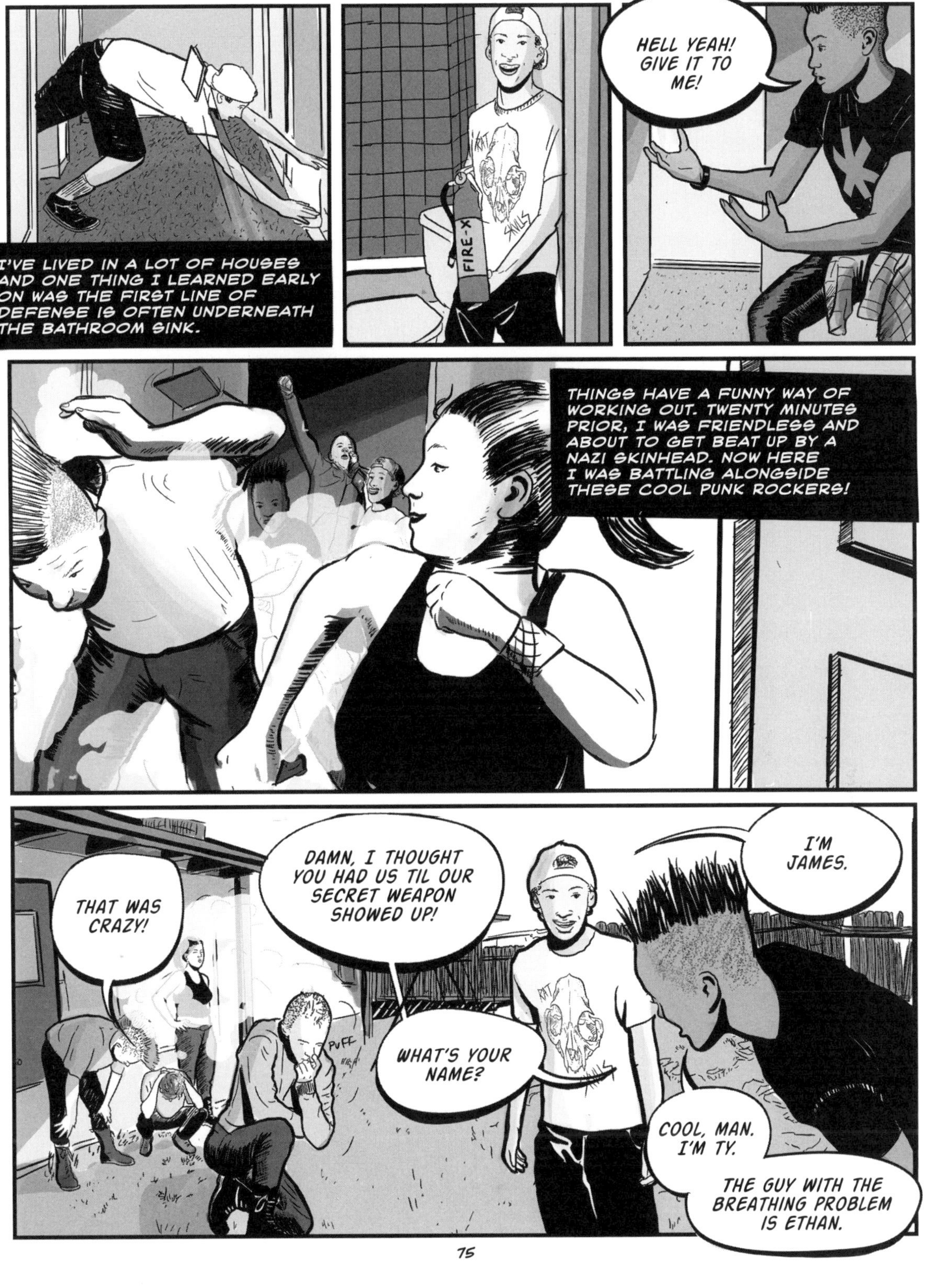
I'VE LIVED IN A LOT OF HOUSES AND ONE THING I LEARNED EARLY ON WAS THE FIRST LINE OF DEFENSE IS OFTEN UNDERNEATH THE BATHROOM SINK.
FIRE-X
HELL YEAH! GIVE IT TO ME!
THINGS HAVE A FUNNY WAY OF WORKING OUT. TWENTY MINUTES PRIOR, I WAS FRIENDLESS AND ABOUT TO GET BEAT UP BY A NAZI SKINHEAD. NOW HERE I WAS BATTLING ALONGSIDE THESE COOL PUNK ROCKERS!
THAT WAS CRAZY!
DAMN, I THOUGHT YOU HAD US TIL OUR SECRET WEAPON SHOWED UP!
PUFF
WHAT'S YOUR NAME?
I'M JAMES.
COOL, MAN. I'M TY.
THE GUY WITH THE BREATHING PROBLEM IS ETHAN.

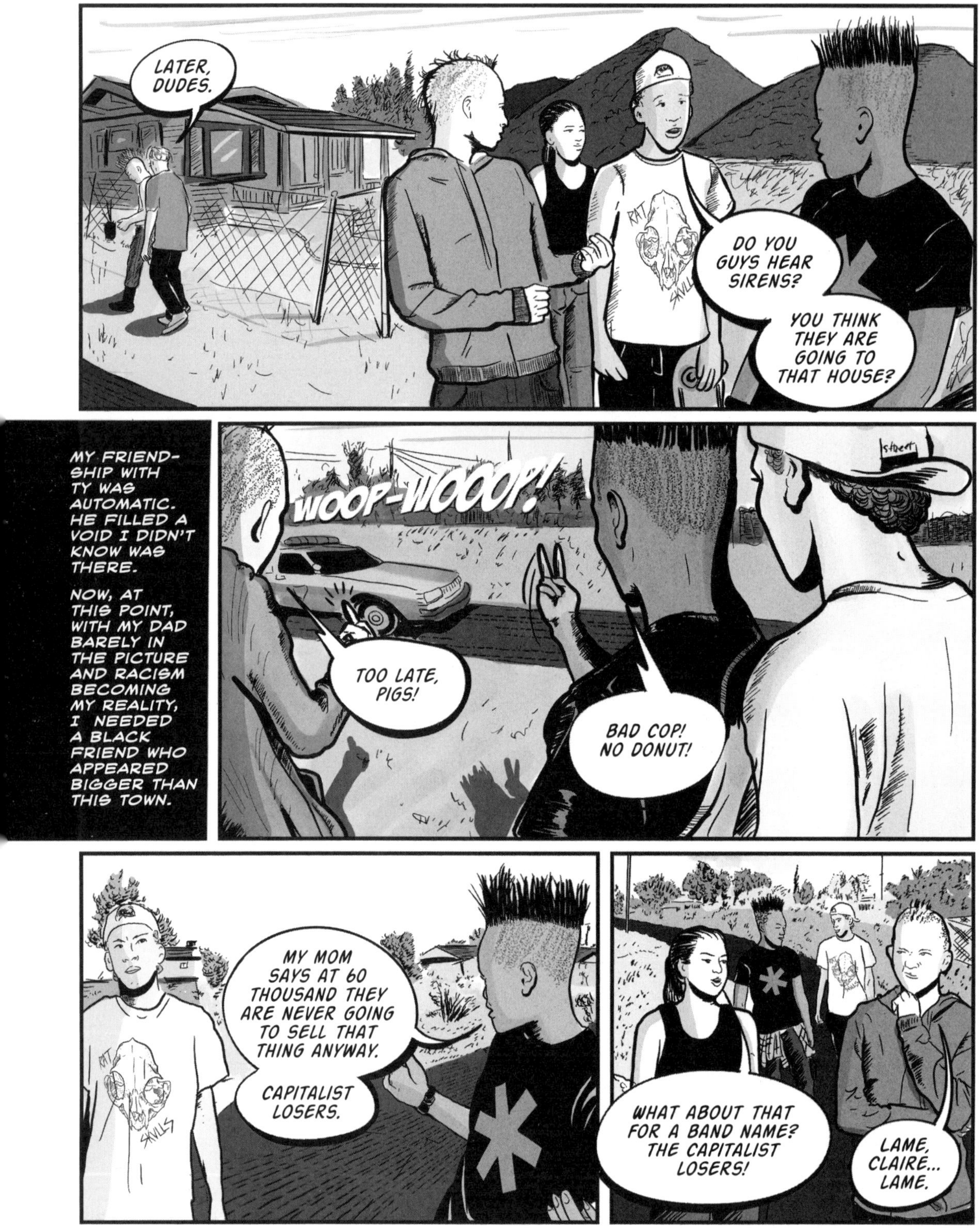
LATER, DUDES.
DO YOU GUYS HEAR SIRENS?
YOU THINK THEY ARE GOING TO THAT HOUSE?
MY FRIENDSHIP WITH TY WAS AUTOMATIC. HE FILLED A VOID I DIDN'T KNOW WAS THERE.
NOW, AT THIS POINT, WITH MY DAD BARELY IN THE PICTURE AND RACISM BECOMING MY REALITY, I NEEDED A BLACK FRIEND WHO APPEARED BIGGER THAN THIS TOWN.
WOOP-WOOOP!
TOO LATE, PIGS!
BAD COP! NO DONUT!
MY MOM SAYS AT 60 THOUSAND THEY ARE NEVER GOING TO SELL THAT THING ANYWAY.
CAPITALIST LOSERS.
WHAT ABOUT THAT FOR A BAND NAME? THE CAPITALIST LOSERS!
LAME, CLAIRE... LAME.

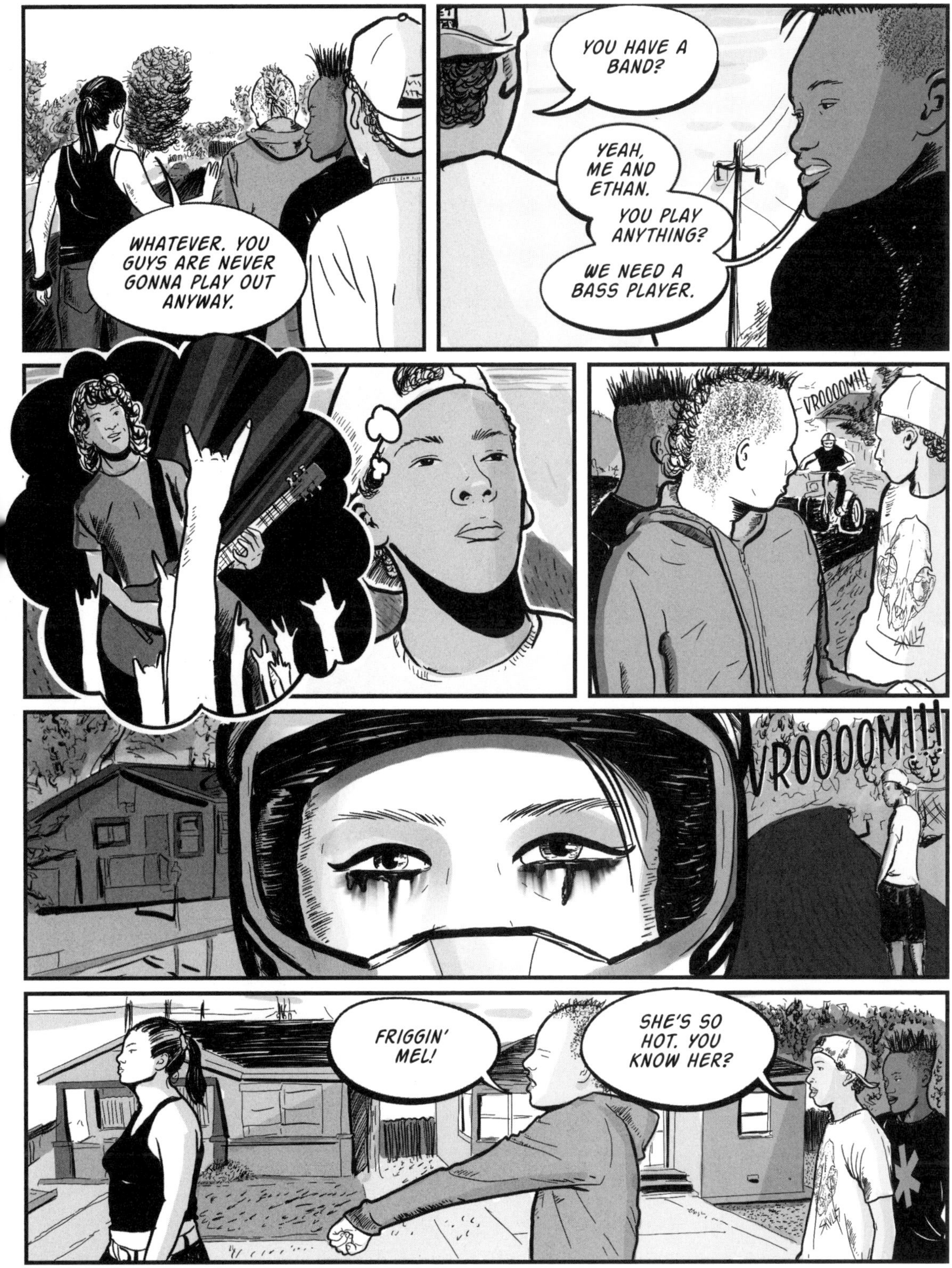
WHATEVER. YOU GUYS ARE NEVER GONNA PLAY OUT ANYWAY.
YOU HAVE A BAND?
YEAH, ME AND ETHAN.
YOU PLAY ANYTHING?
WE NEED A BASS PLAYER.
VROOOOM!!!
VROOOOM!!!
FRIGGIN' MEL!
SHE'S SO HOT. YOU KNOW HER?

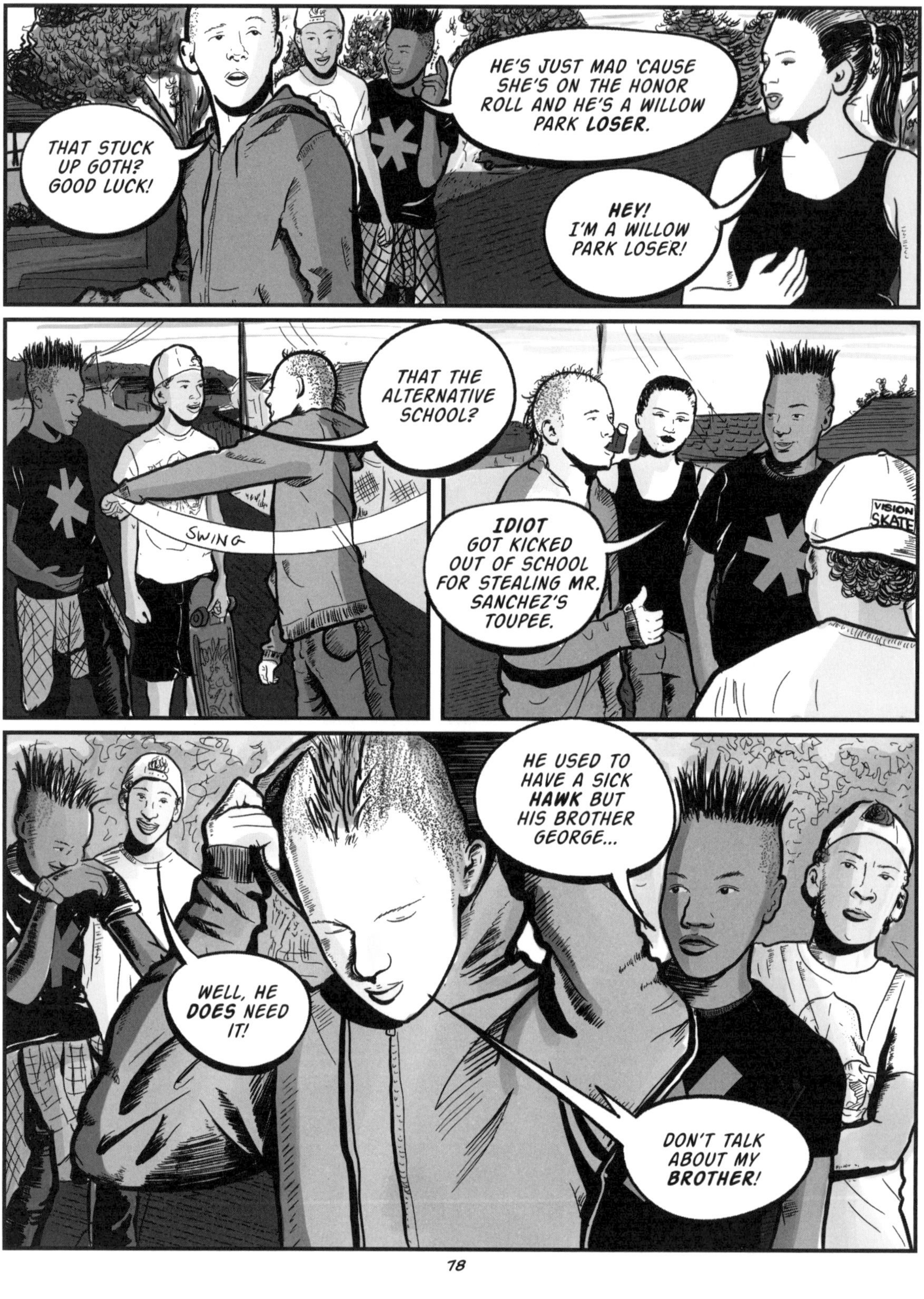
THAT STUCK UP GOTH? GOOD LUCK!
HE'S JUST MAD 'CAUSE SHE'S ON THE HONOR ROLL AND HE'S A WILLOW PARK LOSER.
HEY! I'M A WILLOW PARK LOSER!
THAT THE ALTERNATIVE SCHOOL?
SWING
IDIOT GOT KICKED OUT OF SCHOOL FOR STEALING MR. SANCHEZ'S TOUPEE.
VISION SKATE
HE USED TO HAVE A SICK HAWK BUT HIS BROTHER GEORGE...
WELL, HE DOES NEED IT!
DON'T TALK ABOUT MY BROTHER!

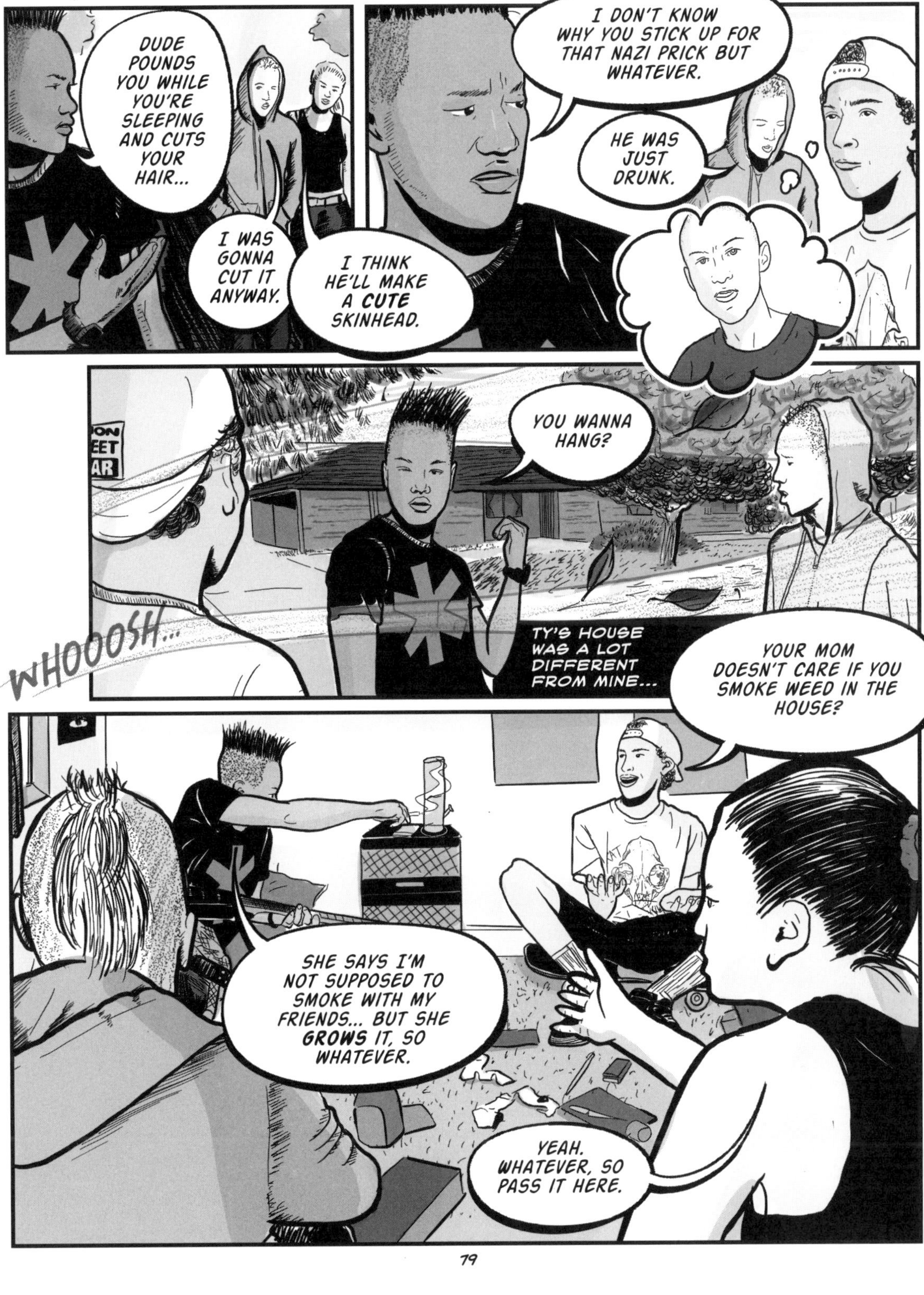

DUDE POUNDS YOU WHILE YOU'RE SLEEPING AND CUTS YOUR HAIR...
I WAS GONNA CUT IT ANYWAY.
I THINK HE'LL MAKE A **CUTE** SKINHEAD.
I DON'T KNOW WHY YOU STICK UP FOR THAT NAZI PRICK BUT WHATEVER.
HE WAS JUST DRUNK.
YOU WANNA HANG?
WHOOOSH...
TY'S HOUSE WAS A LOT DIFFERENT FROM MINE...
YOUR MOM DOESN'T CARE IF YOU SMOKE WEED IN THE HOUSE?
SHE SAYS I'M NOT SUPPOSED TO SMOKE WITH MY FRIENDS... BUT SHE **GROWS** IT, SO WHATEVER.
YEAH. WHATEVER, SO PASS IT HERE.

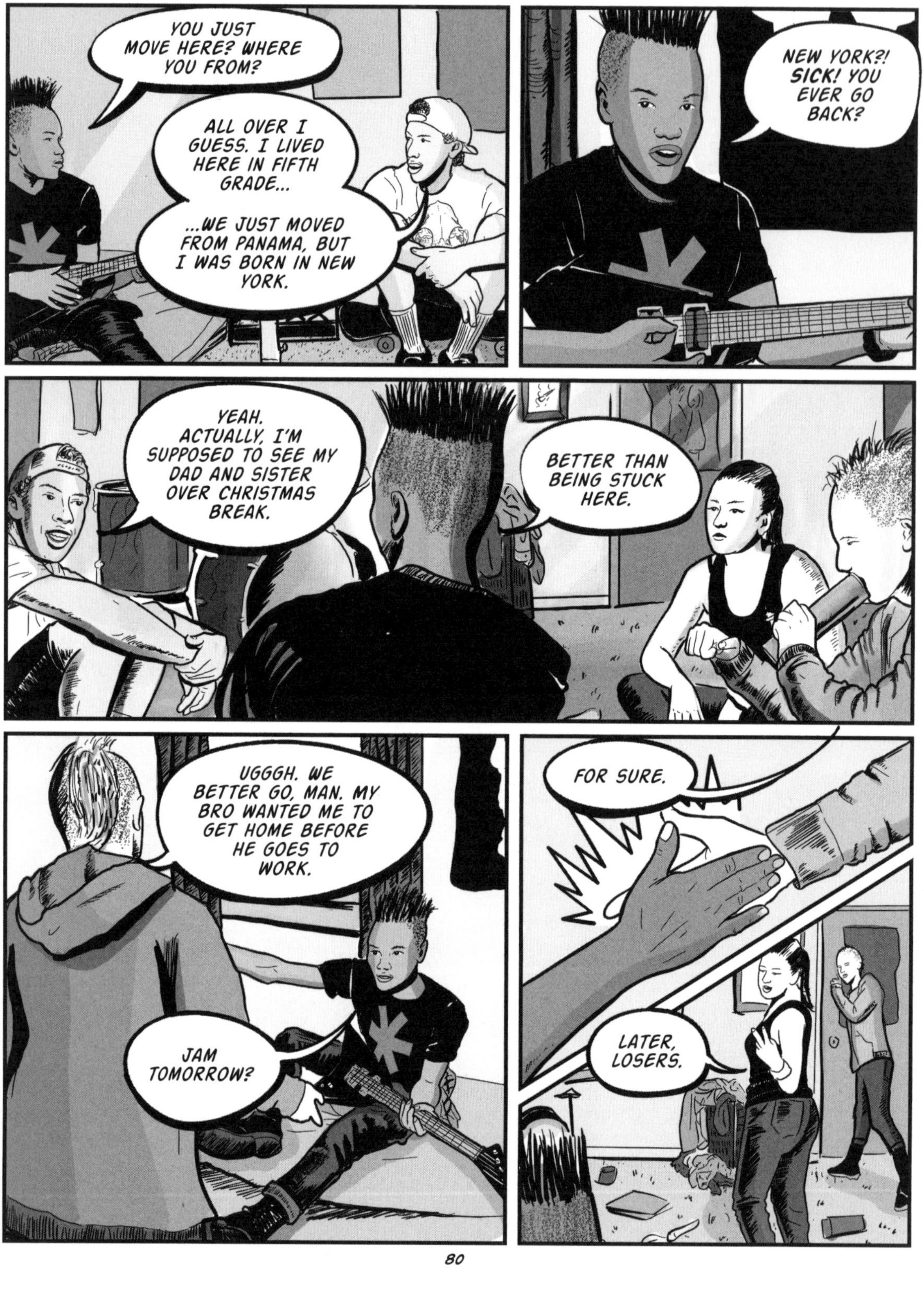
YOU JUST MOVE HERE? WHERE YOU FROM?
ALL OVER I GUESS. I LIVED HERE IN FIFTH GRADE...
...WE JUST MOVED FROM PANAMA, BUT I WAS BORN IN NEW YORK.
NEW YORK?! SICK! YOU EVER GO BACK?
YEAH. ACTUALLY, I'M SUPPOSED TO SEE MY DAD AND SISTER OVER CHRISTMAS BREAK.
BETTER THAN BEING STUCK HERE.
UGGGH. WE BETTER GO, MAN. MY BRO WANTED ME TO GET HOME BEFORE HE GOES TO WORK.
JAM TOMORROW?
FOR SURE.
LATER, LOSERS.

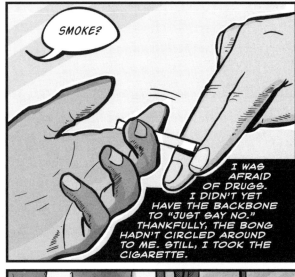

SMOKE?

I WAS AFRAID OF DRUGS. I DIDN'T YET HAVE THE BACKBONE TO "JUST SAY NO." THANKFULLY, THE BONG HADN'T CIRCLED AROUND TO ME. STILL, I TOOK THE CIGARETTE.

HACK!

IF YOU DON'T SMOKE, DON'T WASTE MY CIGS.

I'M JUST NOT USED TO THIS BRAND.

TY COULD SEE RIGHT THROUGH ME.

OKAY...

...I DON'T THINK YOU TOLD ME, YOU PLAY ANYTHING?

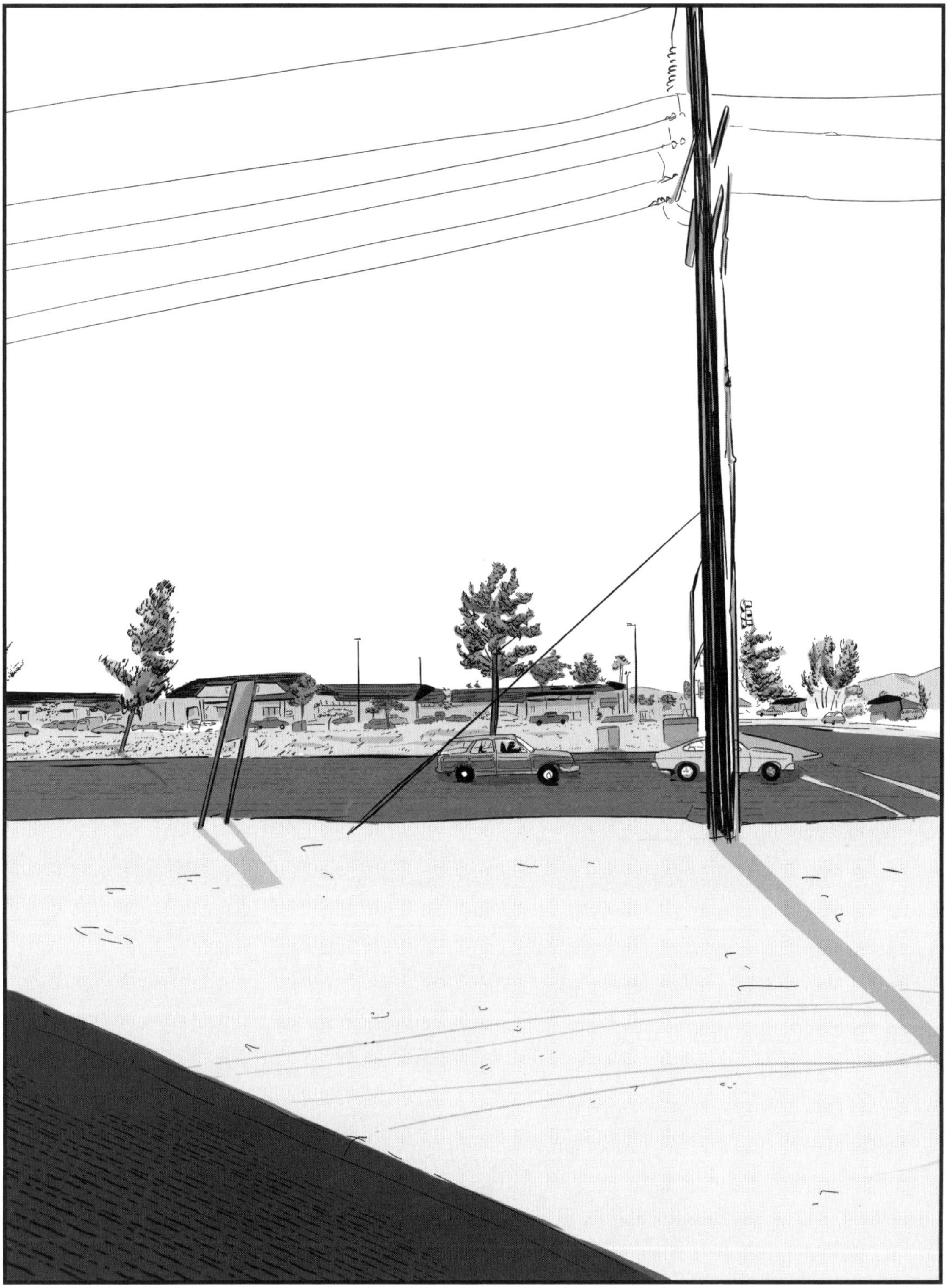

CHAPTER 3
TV PARTY

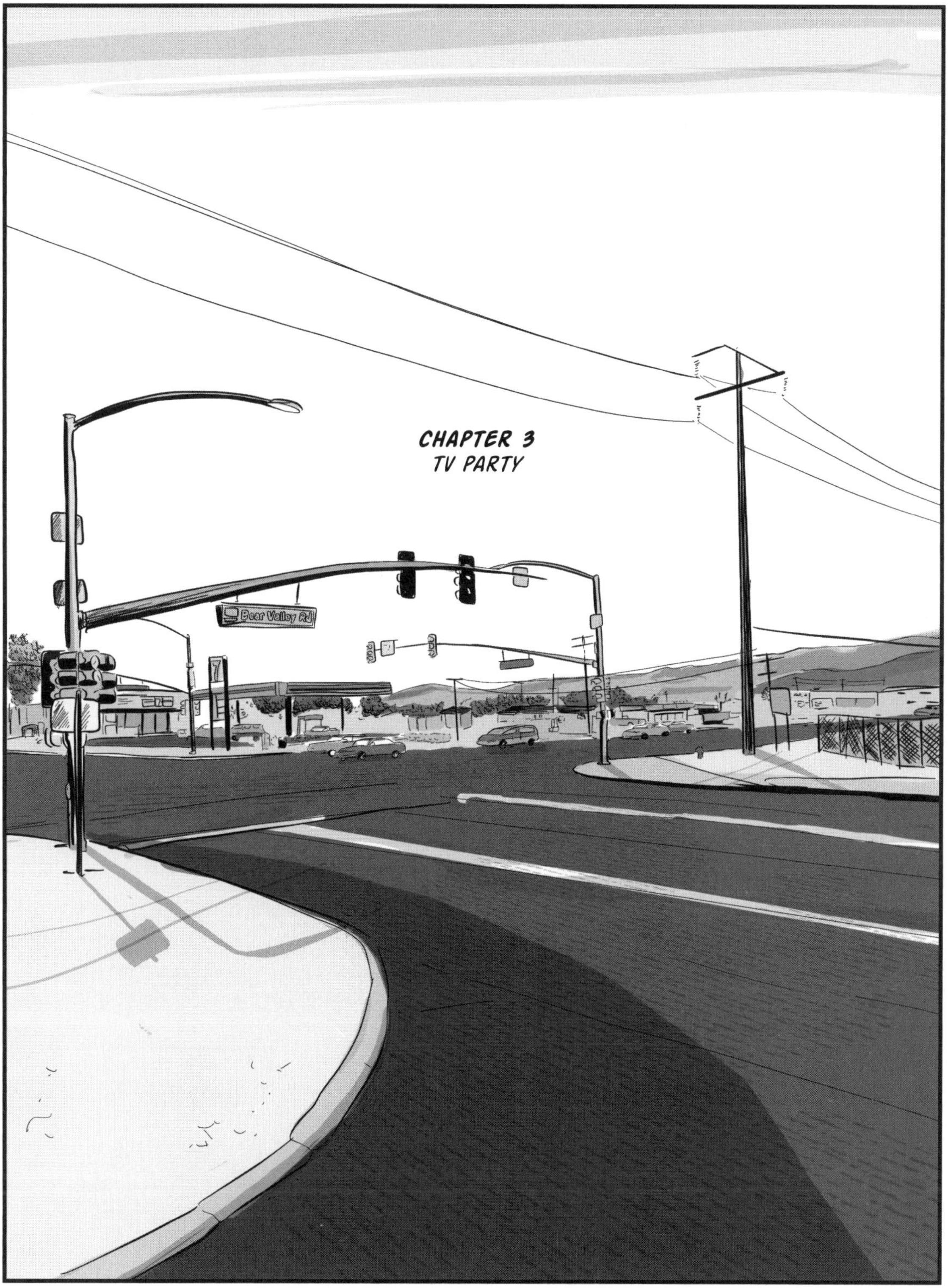
Bear Valley Rd

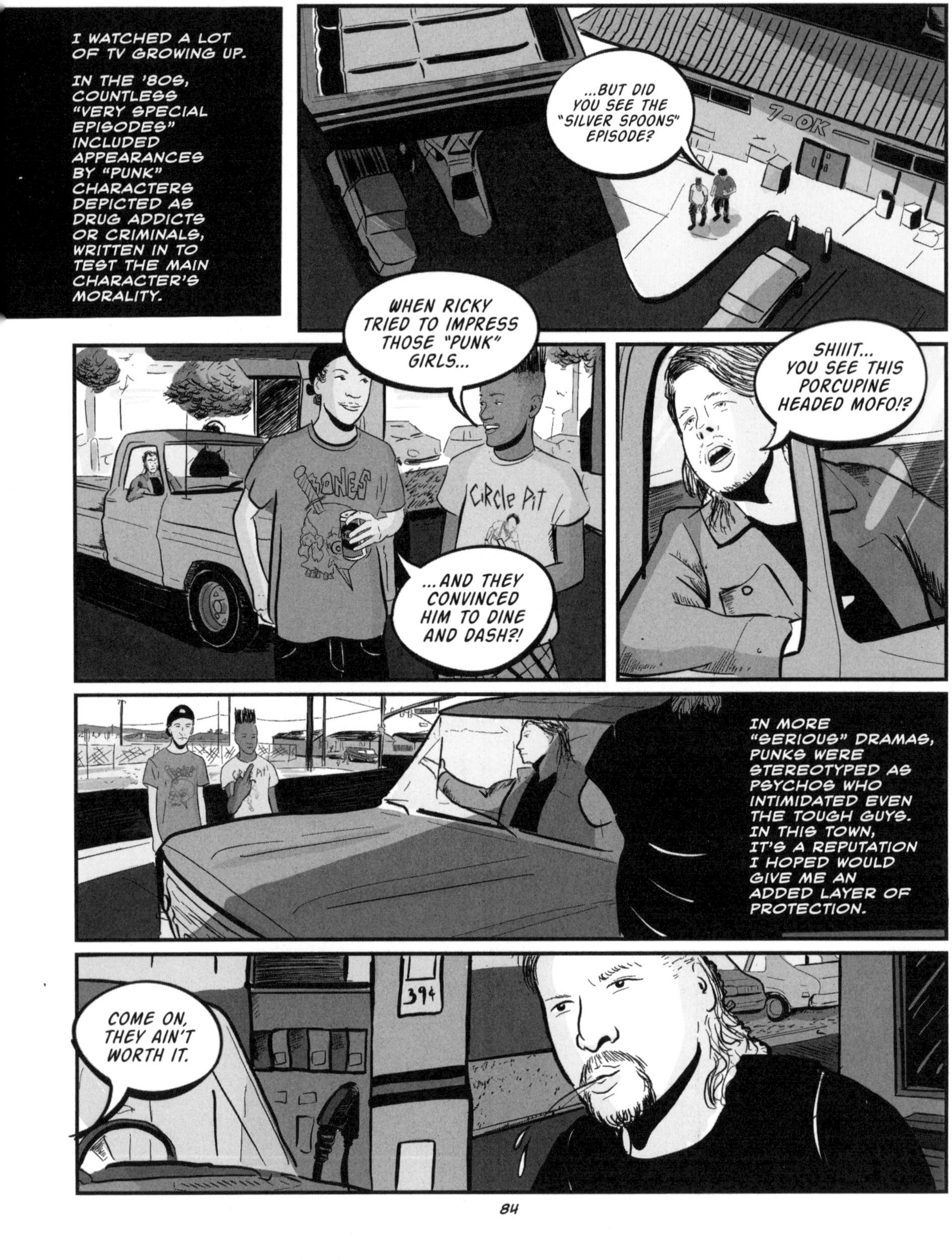
I WATCHED A LOT OF TV GROWING UP.
IN THE '80S, COUNTLESS "VERY SPECIAL EPISODES" INCLUDED APPEARANCES BY "PUNK" CHARACTERS DEPICTED AS DRUG ADDICTS OR CRIMINALS, WRITTEN IN TO TEST THE MAIN CHARACTER'S MORALITY.
...BUT DID YOU SEE THE "SILVER SPOONS" EPISODE?
7-OK
WHEN RICKY TRIED TO IMPRESS THOSE "PUNK" GIRLS...
...AND THEY CONVINCED HIM TO DINE AND DASH?!
CIRCLE PIT
SHIIIT... YOU SEE THIS PORCUPINE HEADED MOFO!?
IN MORE "SERIOUS" DRAMAS, PUNKS WERE STEREOTYPED AS PSYCHOS WHO INTIMIDATED EVEN THE TOUGH GUYS. IN THIS TOWN, IT'S A REPUTATION I HOPED WOULD GIVE ME AN ADDED LAYER OF PROTECTION.
39¢
COME ON, THEY AIN'T WORTH IT.

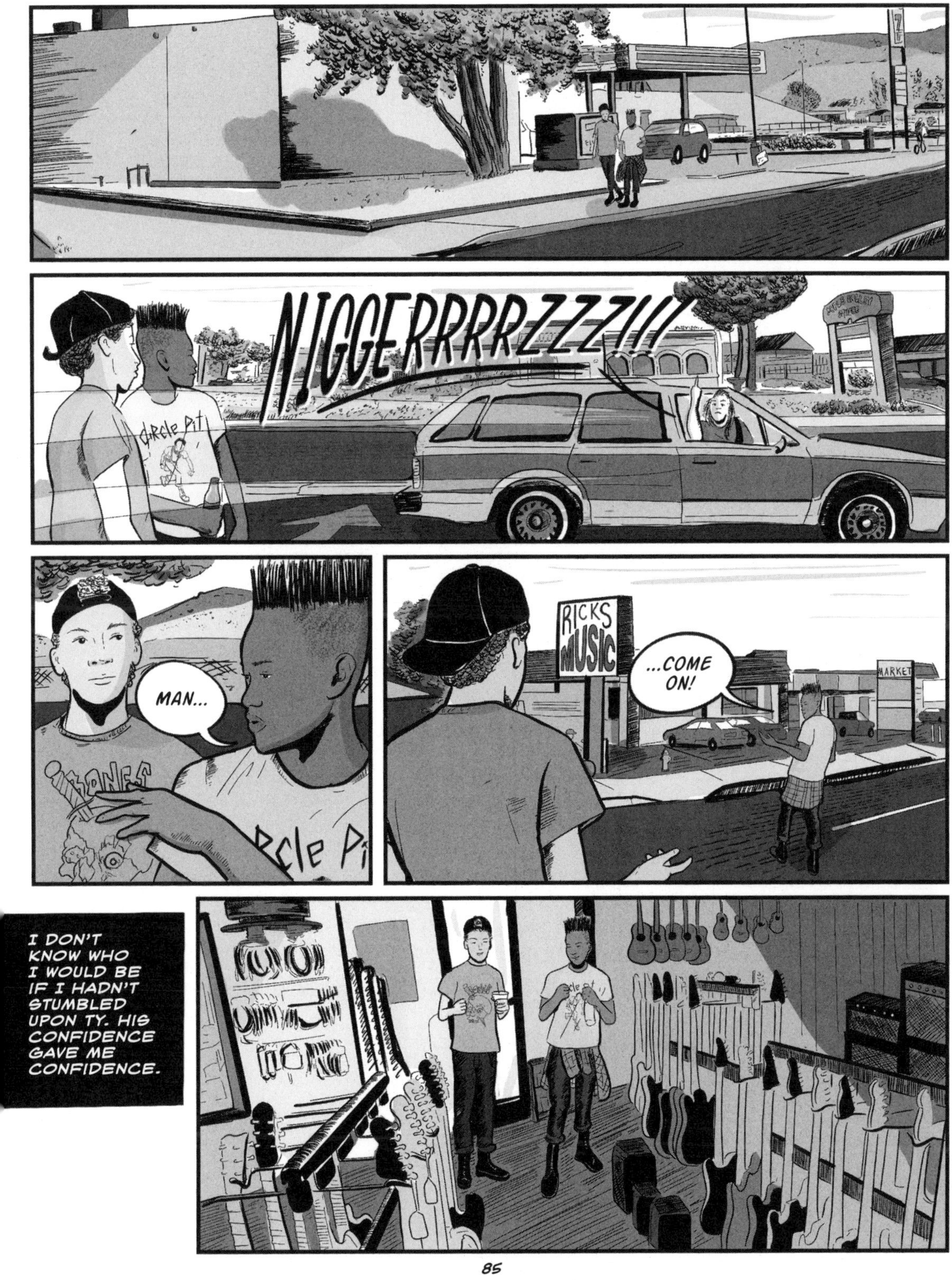

NIGGERRRRZZZZ!!!
Circle Pit
MAN...
RICKS MUSIC
...COME ON!
MARKET
I DON'T KNOW WHO I WOULD BE IF I HADN'T STUMBLED UPON TY. HIS CONFIDENCE GAVE ME CONFIDENCE.

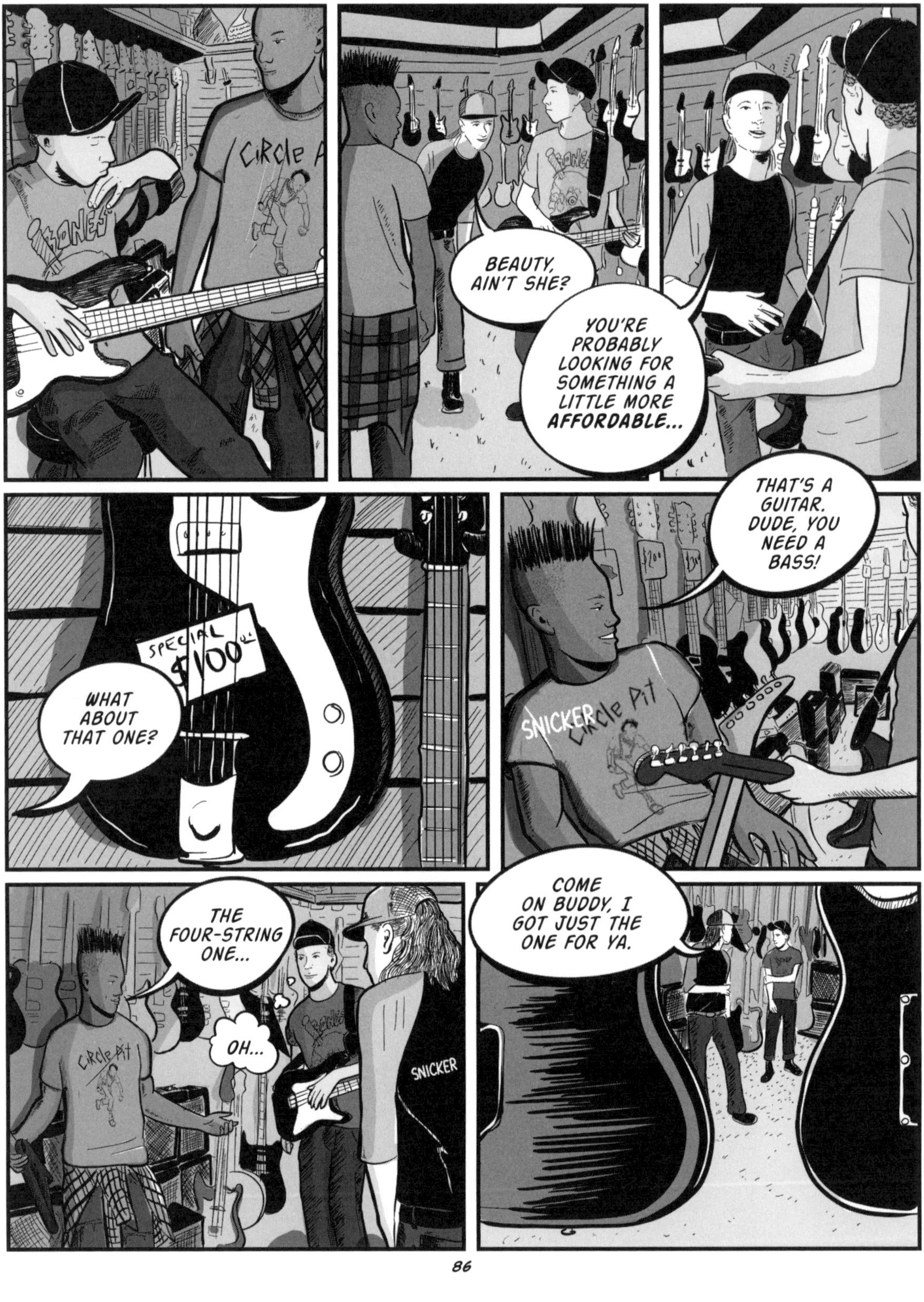
CIRCLE A
BONES
BEAUTY, AIN'T SHE?
YOU'RE PROBABLY LOOKING FOR SOMETHING A LITTLE MORE **AFFORDABLE...**
SPECIAL $100
WHAT ABOUT THAT ONE?
THAT'S A GUITAR. DUDE, YOU NEED A BASS!
SNICKER
CIRCLE PIT
THE FOUR-STRING ONE...
OH...
SNICKER
COME ON BUDDY, I GOT JUST THE ONE FOR YA.

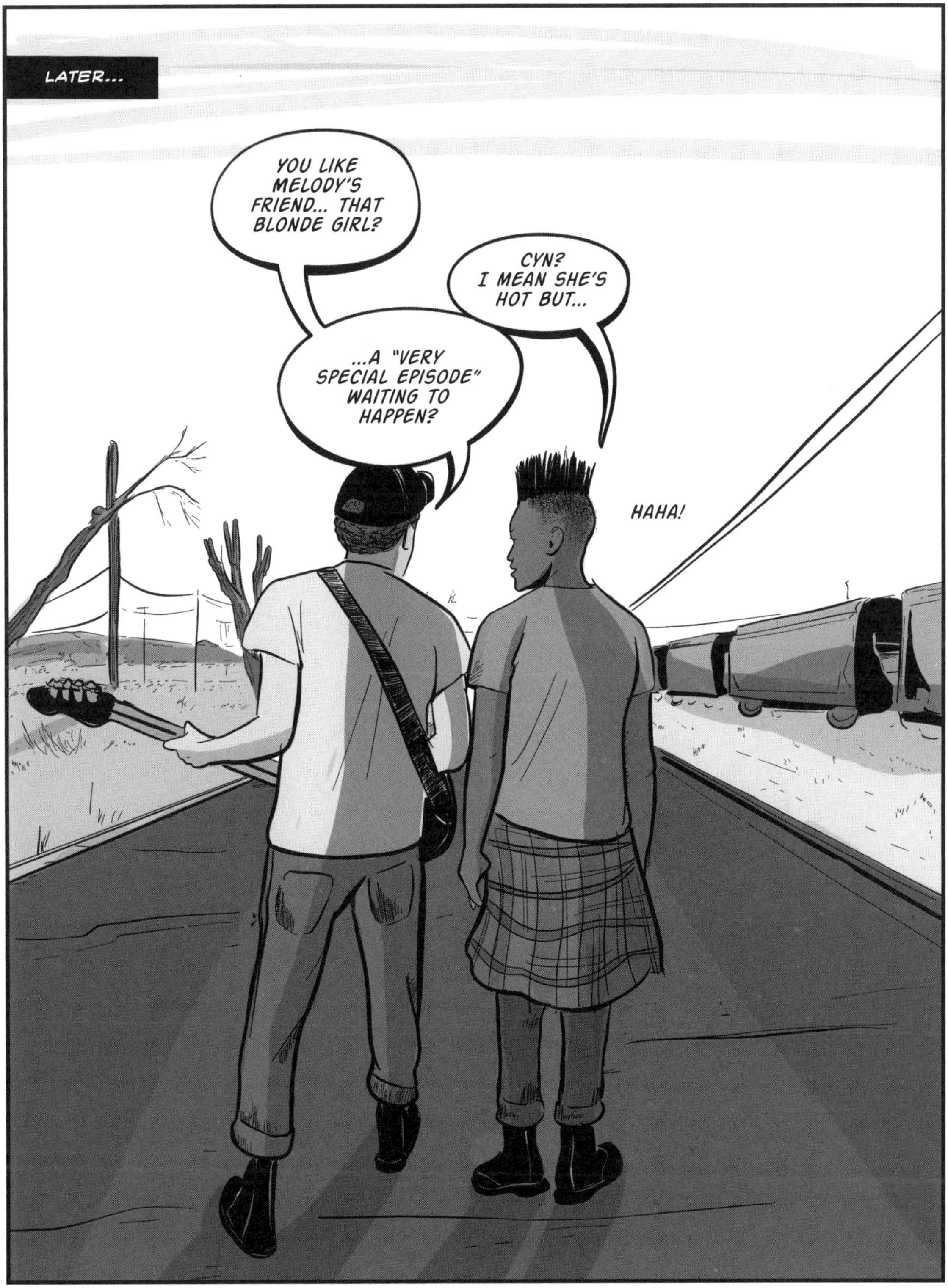
LATER...
YOU LIKE MELODY'S FRIEND... THAT BLONDE GIRL?
CYN? I MEAN SHE'S HOT BUT...
...A "VERY SPECIAL EPISODE" WAITING TO HAPPEN?
HAHA!

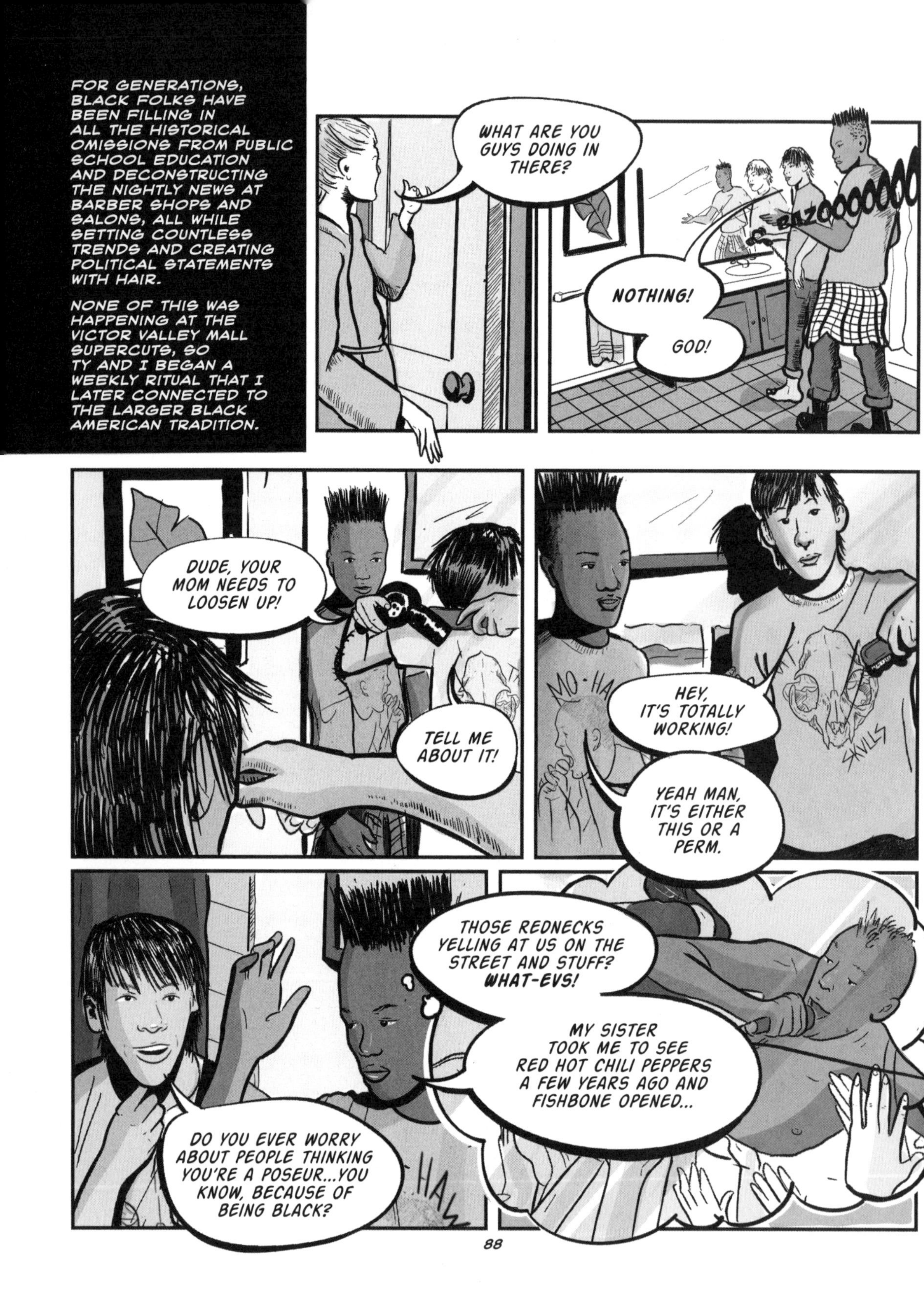
FOR GENERATIONS, BLACK FOLKS HAVE BEEN FILLING IN ALL THE HISTORICAL OMISSIONS FROM PUBLIC SCHOOL EDUCATION AND DECONSTRUCTING THE NIGHTLY NEWS AT BARBER SHOPS AND SALONS, ALL WHILE SETTING COUNTLESS TRENDS AND CREATING POLITICAL STATEMENTS WITH HAIR.
NONE OF THIS WAS HAPPENING AT THE VICTOR VALLEY MALL SUPERCUTS, SO TY AND I BEGAN A WEEKLY RITUAL THAT I LATER CONNECTED TO THE LARGER BLACK AMERICAN TRADITION.
WHAT ARE YOU GUYS DOING IN THERE?
NOTHING!
GOD!
DUDE, YOUR MOM NEEDS TO LOOSEN UP!
TELL ME ABOUT IT!
HEY, IT'S TOTALLY WORKING!
YEAH MAN, IT'S EITHER THIS OR A PERM.
DO YOU EVER WORRY ABOUT PEOPLE THINKING YOU'RE A POSEUR...YOU KNOW, BECAUSE OF BEING BLACK?
THOSE REDNECKS YELLING AT US ON THE STREET AND STUFF? **WHAT-EVS!**
MY SISTER TOOK ME TO SEE RED HOT CHILI PEPPERS A FEW YEARS AGO AND FISHBONE OPENED...

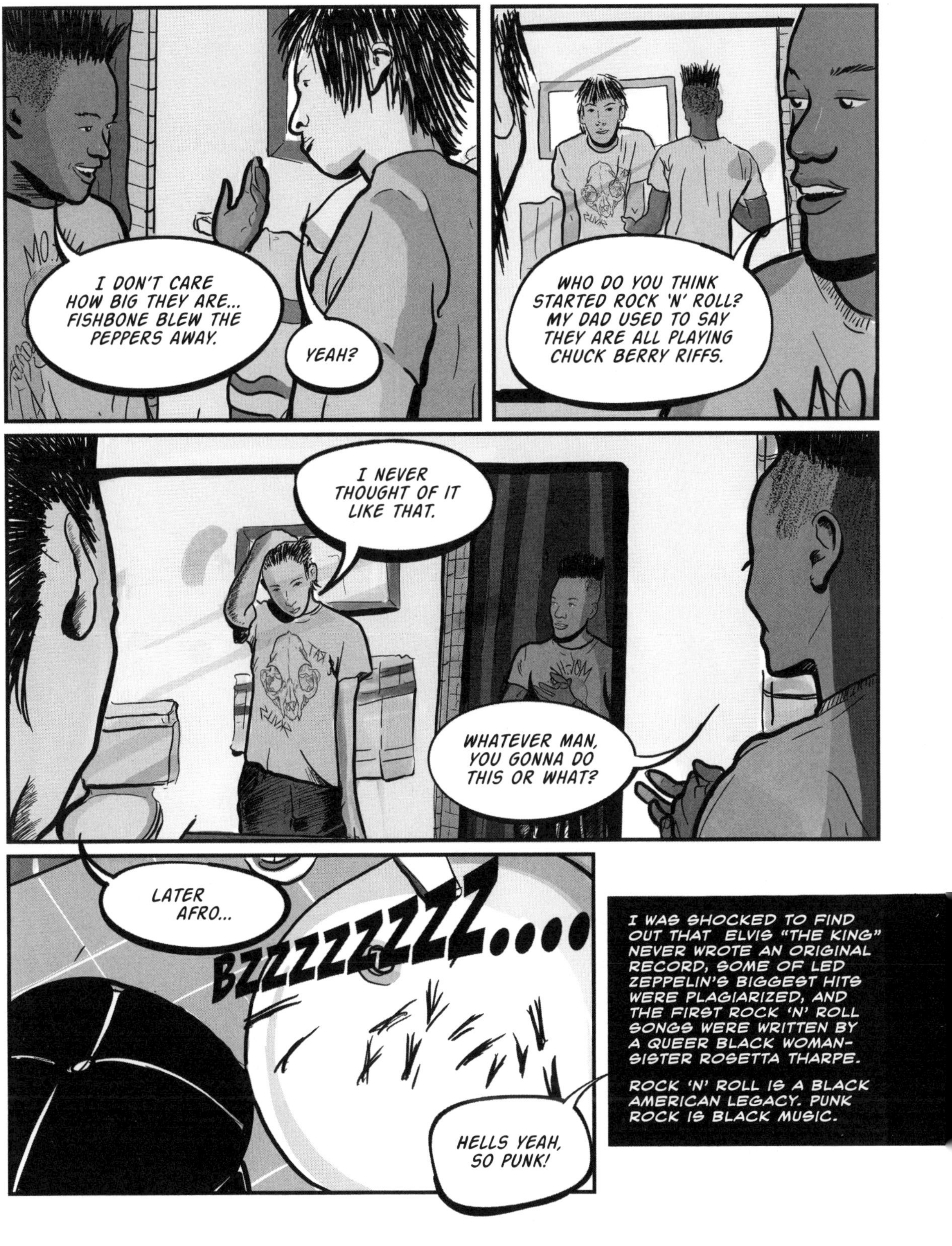
I DON'T CARE HOW BIG THEY ARE... FISHBONE BLEW THE PEPPERS AWAY.
YEAH?
WHO DO YOU THINK STARTED ROCK 'N' ROLL? MY DAD USED TO SAY THEY ARE ALL PLAYING CHUCK BERRY RIFFS.
I NEVER THOUGHT OF IT LIKE THAT.
WHATEVER MAN, YOU GONNA DO THIS OR WHAT?
LATER AFRO...
BZZZZZZZZ....
HELLS YEAH, SO PUNK!
I WAS SHOCKED TO FIND OUT THAT ELVIS "THE KING" NEVER WROTE AN ORIGINAL RECORD, SOME OF LED ZEPPELIN'S BIGGEST HITS WERE PLAGIARIZED, AND THE FIRST ROCK 'N' ROLL SONGS WERE WRITTEN BY A QUEER BLACK WOMAN- SISTER ROSETTA THARPE.
ROCK 'N' ROLL IS A BLACK AMERICAN LEGACY. PUNK ROCK IS BLACK MUSIC.

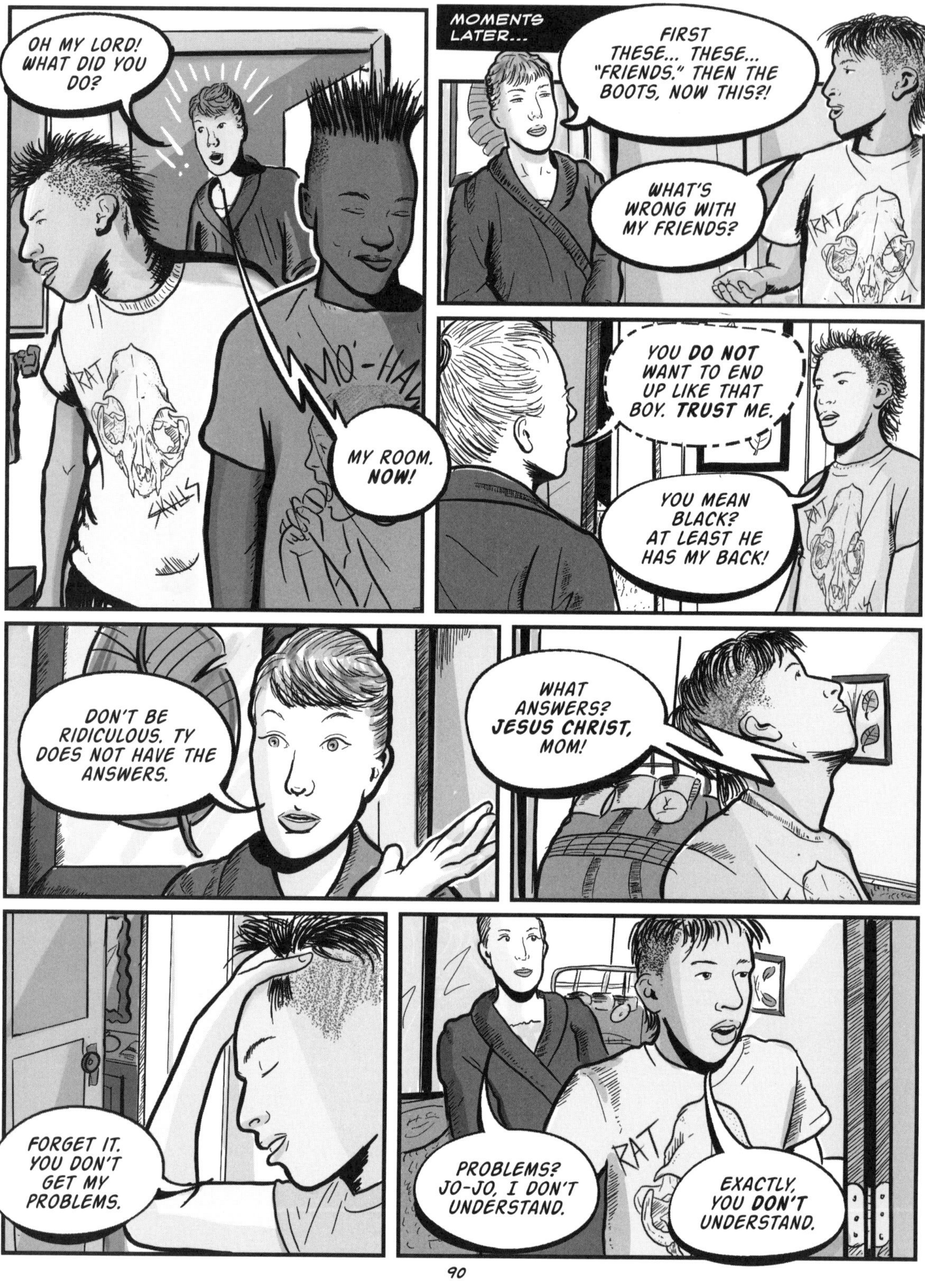
OH MY LORD! WHAT DID YOU DO?
MY ROOM. NOW!
MO'-HAW
RAT
SKULLS
MOMENTS LATER...
FIRST THESE... THESE... "FRIENDS." THEN THE BOOTS, NOW THIS?!
WHAT'S WRONG WITH MY FRIENDS?
RAT
YOU DO NOT WANT TO END UP LIKE THAT BOY. TRUST ME.
YOU MEAN BLACK? AT LEAST HE HAS MY BACK!
DON'T BE RIDICULOUS. TY DOES NOT HAVE THE ANSWERS.
WHAT ANSWERS? JESUS CHRIST, MOM!
FORGET IT. YOU DON'T GET MY PROBLEMS.
PROBLEMS? JO-JO, I DON'T UNDERSTAND.
EXACTLY, YOU DON'T UNDERSTAND.
RAT

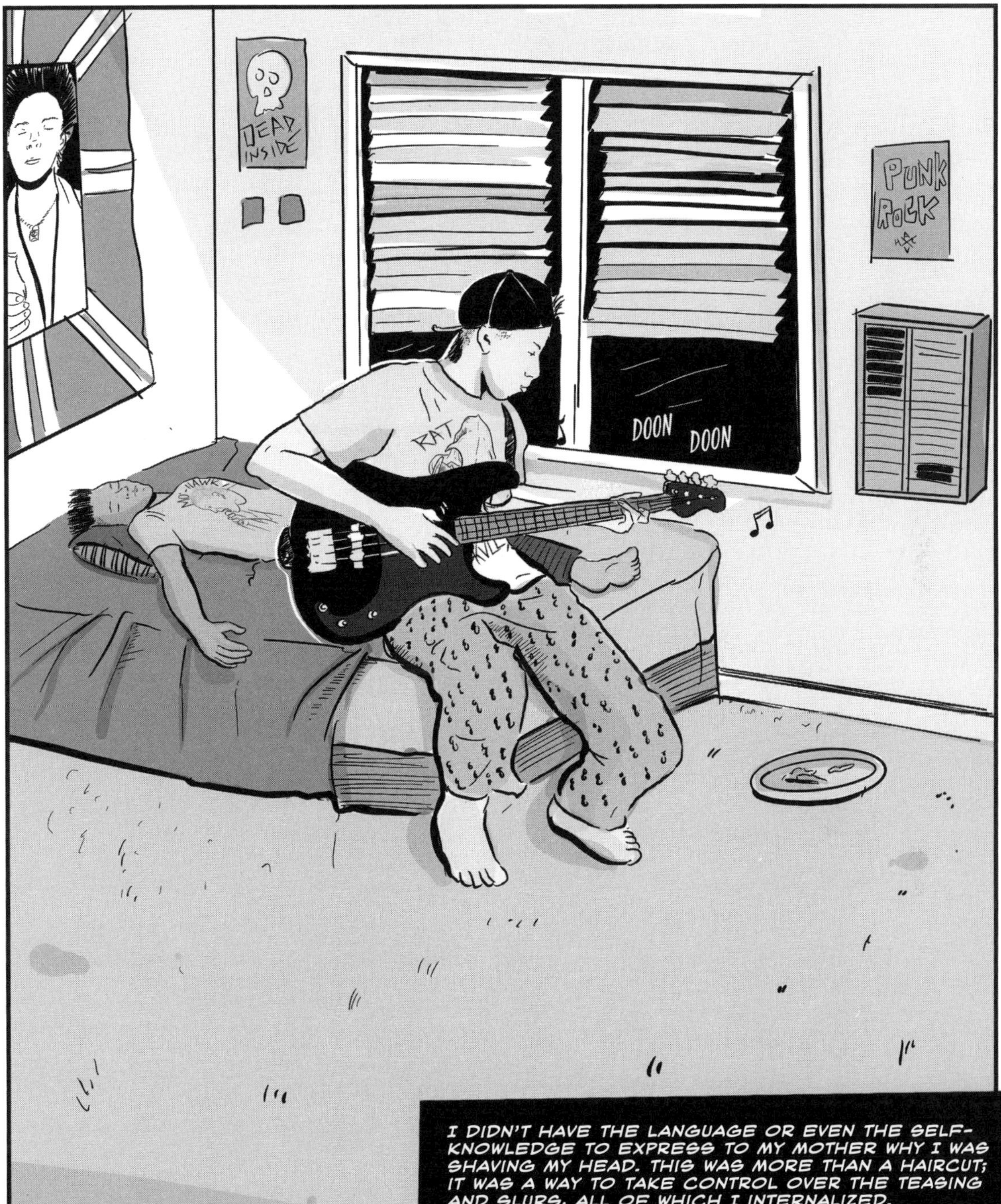
DEAD INSIDE
PUNK ROCK
RAT
DOON DOON
I DIDN'T HAVE THE LANGUAGE OR EVEN THE SELF-KNOWLEDGE TO EXPRESS TO MY MOTHER WHY I WAS SHAVING MY HEAD. THIS WAS MORE THAN A HAIRCUT; IT WAS A WAY TO TAKE CONTROL OVER THE TEASING AND SLURS, ALL OF WHICH I INTERNALIZED.
PUNK ROCK HELPED TO SET ME APART FROM ALL THE THINGS I HATED.

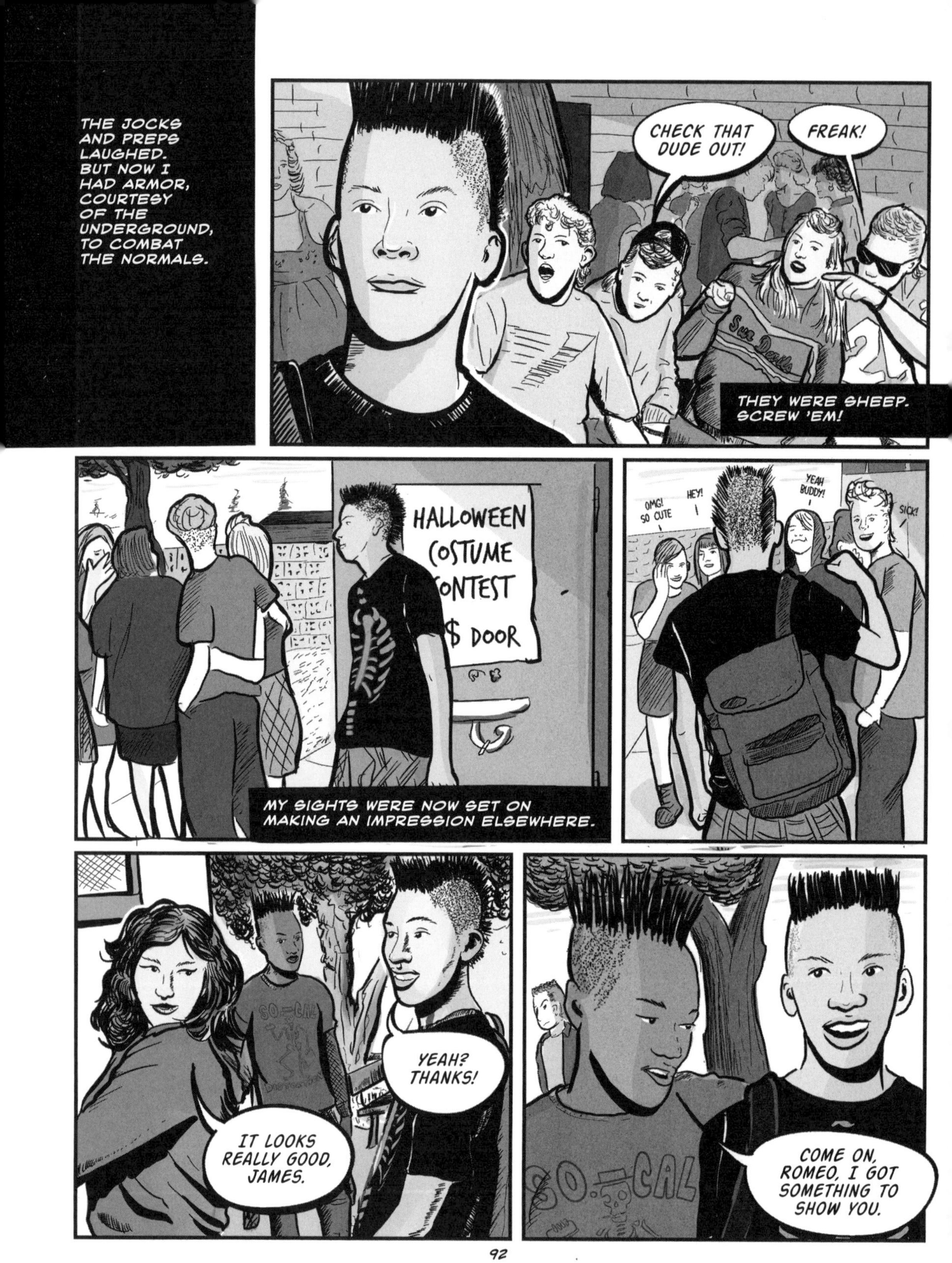
THE JOCKS AND PREPS LAUGHED. BUT NOW I HAD ARMOR, COURTESY OF THE UNDERGROUND, TO COMBAT THE NORMALS.
CHECK THAT DUDE OUT!
FREAK!
THEY WERE SHEEP. SCREW 'EM!
HALLOWEEN COSTUME CONTEST $ DOOR
MY SIGHTS WERE NOW SET ON MAKING AN IMPRESSION ELSEWHERE.
OMG! SO CUTE
HEY!
YEAH BUDDY!
SICK!
IT LOOKS REALLY GOOD, JAMES.
YEAH? THANKS!
SO-CAL
COME ON, ROMEO, I GOT SOMETHING TO SHOW YOU.

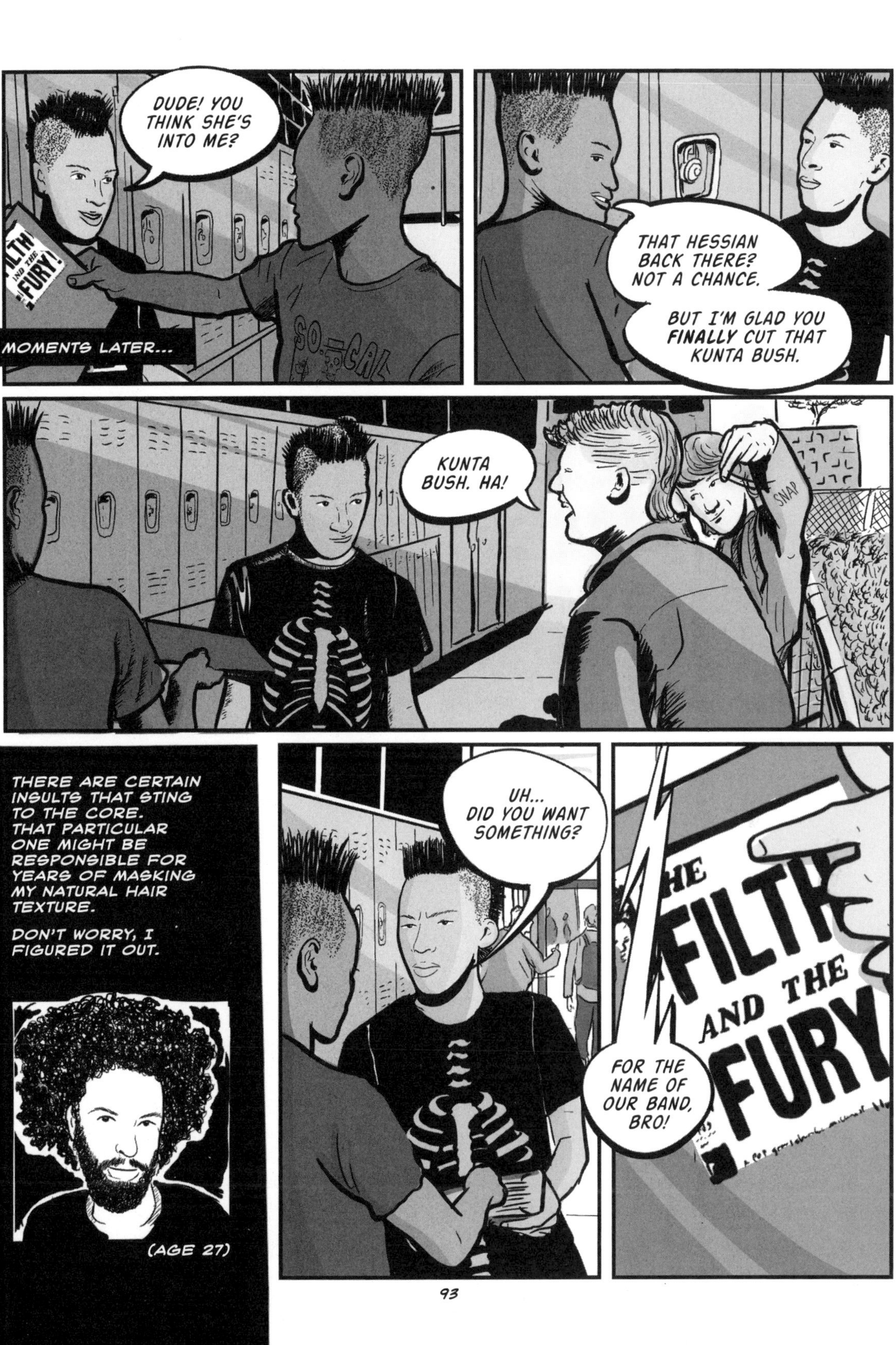
DUDE! YOU THINK SHE'S INTO ME?
MOMENTS LATER...
FILTH AND THE FURY!
SO-CAL
THAT HESSIAN BACK THERE? NOT A CHANCE.
BUT I'M GLAD YOU FINALLY CUT THAT KUNTA BUSH.
KUNTA BUSH. HA!
SNAP
THERE ARE CERTAIN INSULTS THAT STING TO THE CORE. THAT PARTICULAR ONE MIGHT BE RESPONSIBLE FOR YEARS OF MASKING MY NATURAL HAIR TEXTURE.
DON'T WORRY, I FIGURED IT OUT.
(AGE 27)
UH... DID YOU WANT SOMETHING?
THE FILTH AND THE FURY
FOR THE NAME OF OUR BAND, BRO!

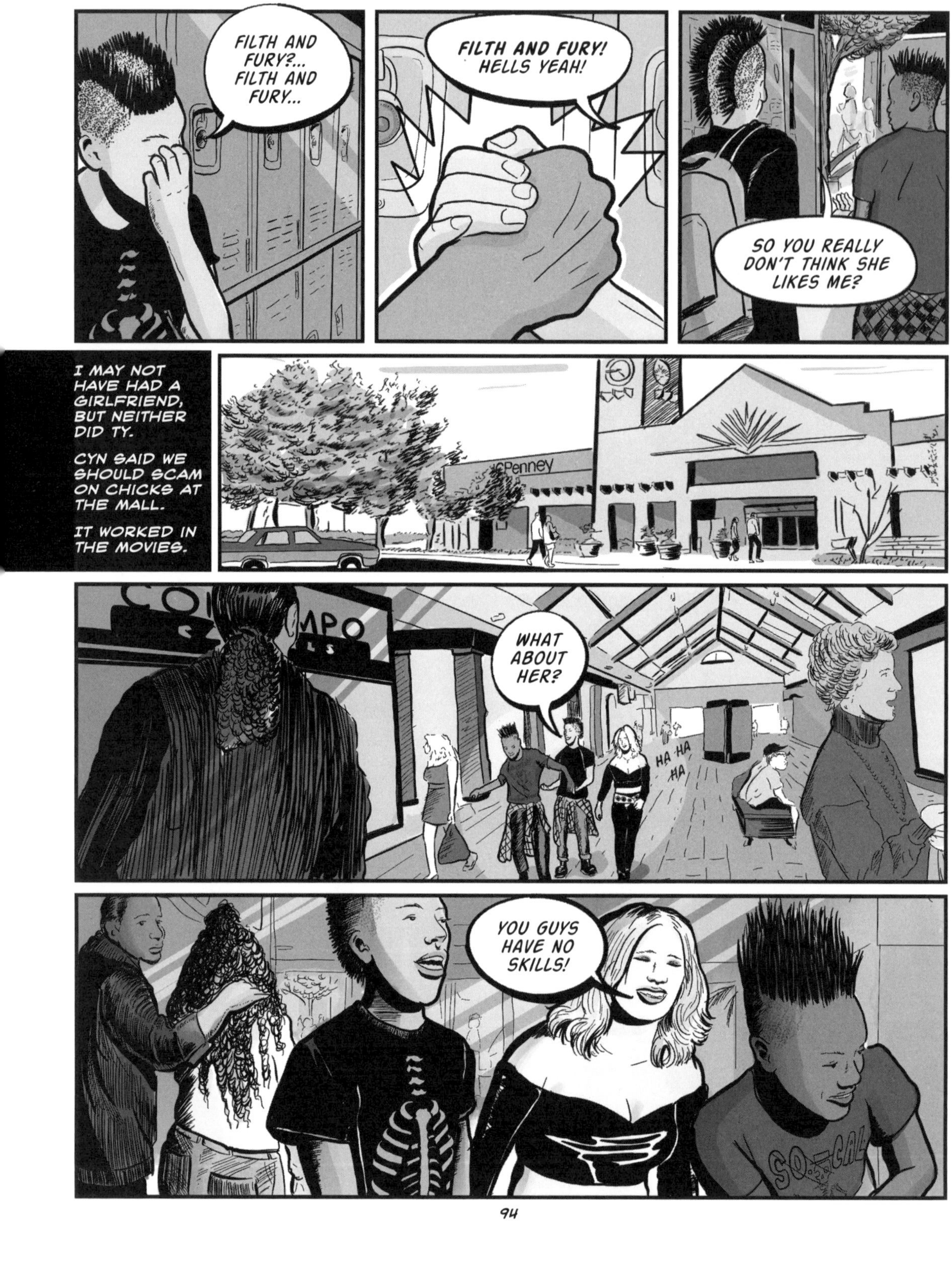
FILTH AND FURY?... FILTH AND FURY...
FILTH AND FURY! HELLS YEAH!
SO YOU REALLY DON'T THINK SHE LIKES ME?
I MAY NOT HAVE HAD A GIRLFRIEND, BUT NEITHER DID TY.
CYN SAID WE SHOULD SCAM ON CHICKS AT THE MALL.
IT WORKED IN THE MOVIES.
JCPenney
WHAT ABOUT HER?
HA HA HA
YOU GUYS HAVE NO SKILLS!
SO-CAL

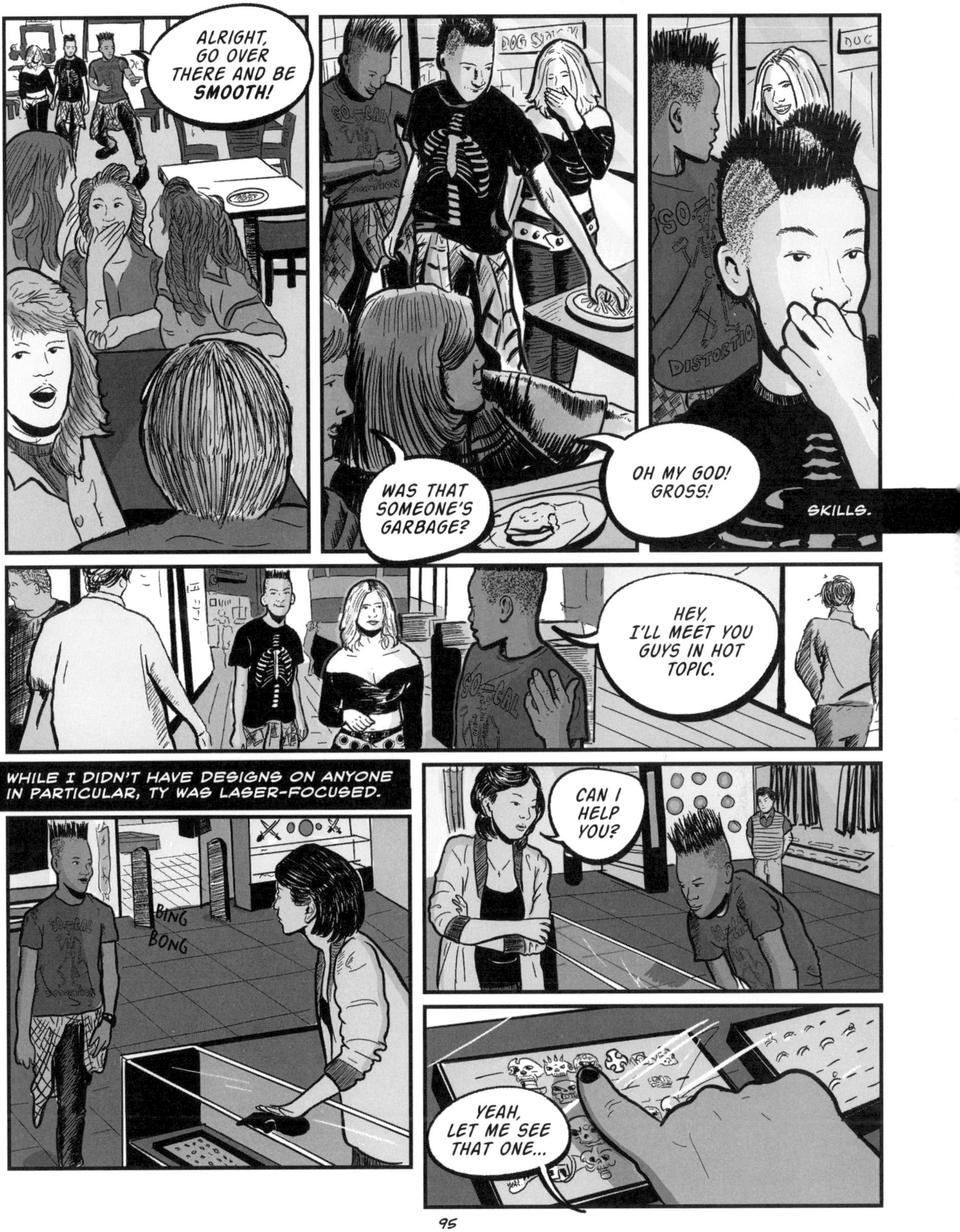
ALRIGHT, GO OVER THERE AND BE SMOOTH!
WAS THAT SOMEONE'S GARBAGE?
OH MY GOD! GROSS!
SKILLS.
HEY, I'LL MEET YOU GUYS IN HOT TOPIC.
WHILE I DIDN'T HAVE DESIGNS ON ANYONE IN PARTICULAR, TY WAS LASER-FOCUSED.
BING BONG
CAN I HELP YOU?
YEAH, LET ME SEE THAT ONE...

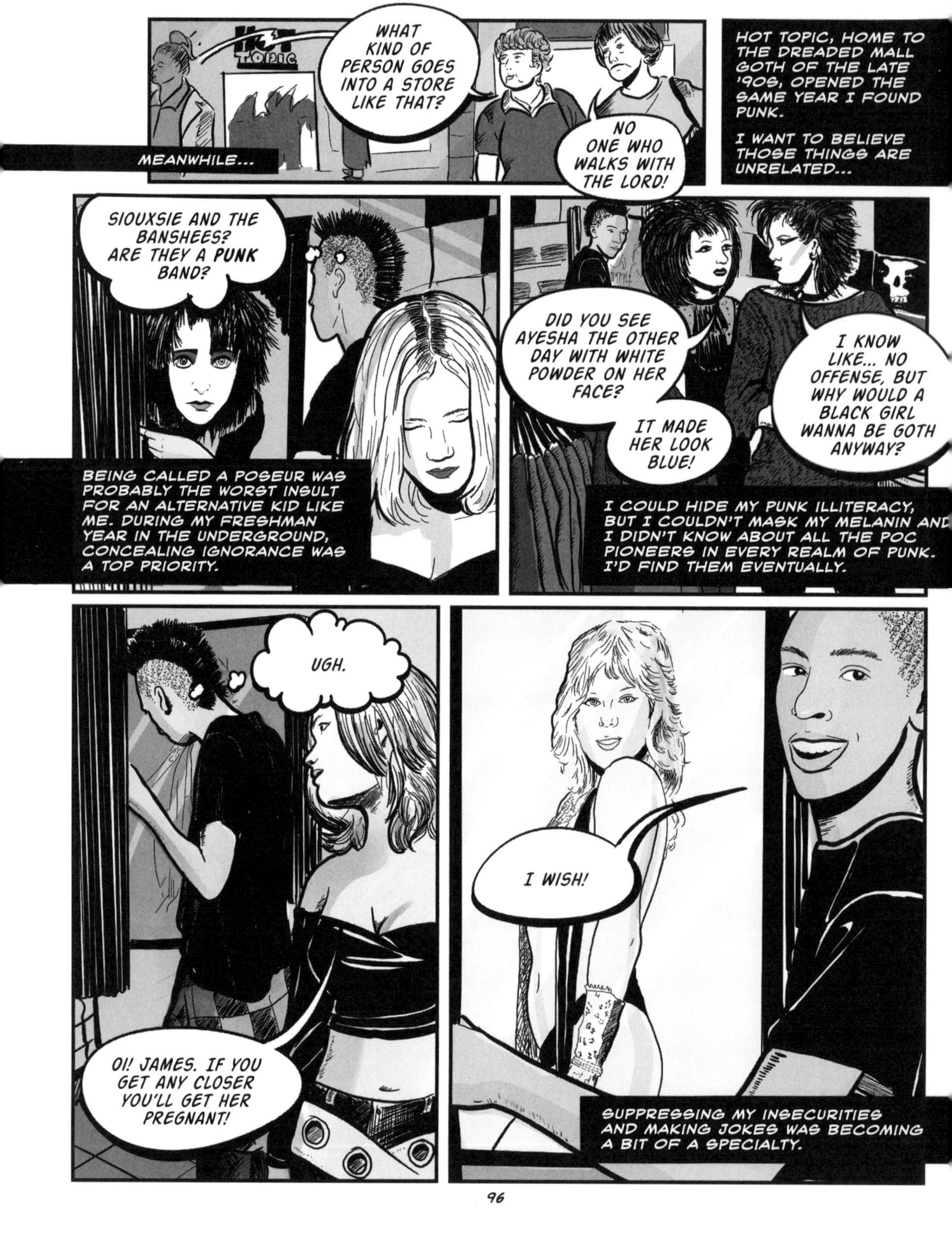
MEANWHILE...
WHAT KIND OF PERSON GOES INTO A STORE LIKE THAT?
NO ONE WHO WALKS WITH THE LORD!
HOT TOPIC, HOME TO THE DREADED MALL GOTH OF THE LATE '90S, OPENED THE SAME YEAR I FOUND PUNK.
I WANT TO BELIEVE THOSE THINGS ARE UNRELATED...
SIOUXSIE AND THE BANSHEES? ARE THEY A **PUNK** BAND?
BEING CALLED A POSEUR WAS PROBABLY THE WORST INSULT FOR AN ALTERNATIVE KID LIKE ME. DURING MY FRESHMAN YEAR IN THE UNDERGROUND, CONCEALING IGNORANCE WAS A TOP PRIORITY.
DID YOU SEE AYESHA THE OTHER DAY WITH WHITE POWDER ON HER FACE?
IT MADE HER LOOK BLUE!
I KNOW LIKE... NO OFFENSE, BUT WHY WOULD A BLACK GIRL WANNA BE GOTH ANYWAY?
I COULD HIDE MY PUNK ILLITERACY, BUT I COULDN'T MASK MY MELANIN AND I DIDN'T KNOW ABOUT ALL THE POC PIONEERS IN EVERY REALM OF PUNK. I'D FIND THEM EVENTUALLY.
UGH.
OI! JAMES. IF YOU GET ANY CLOSER YOU'LL GET HER PREGNANT!
I WISH!
SUPPRESSING MY INSECURITIES AND MAKING JOKES WAS BECOMING A BIT OF A SPECIALTY.

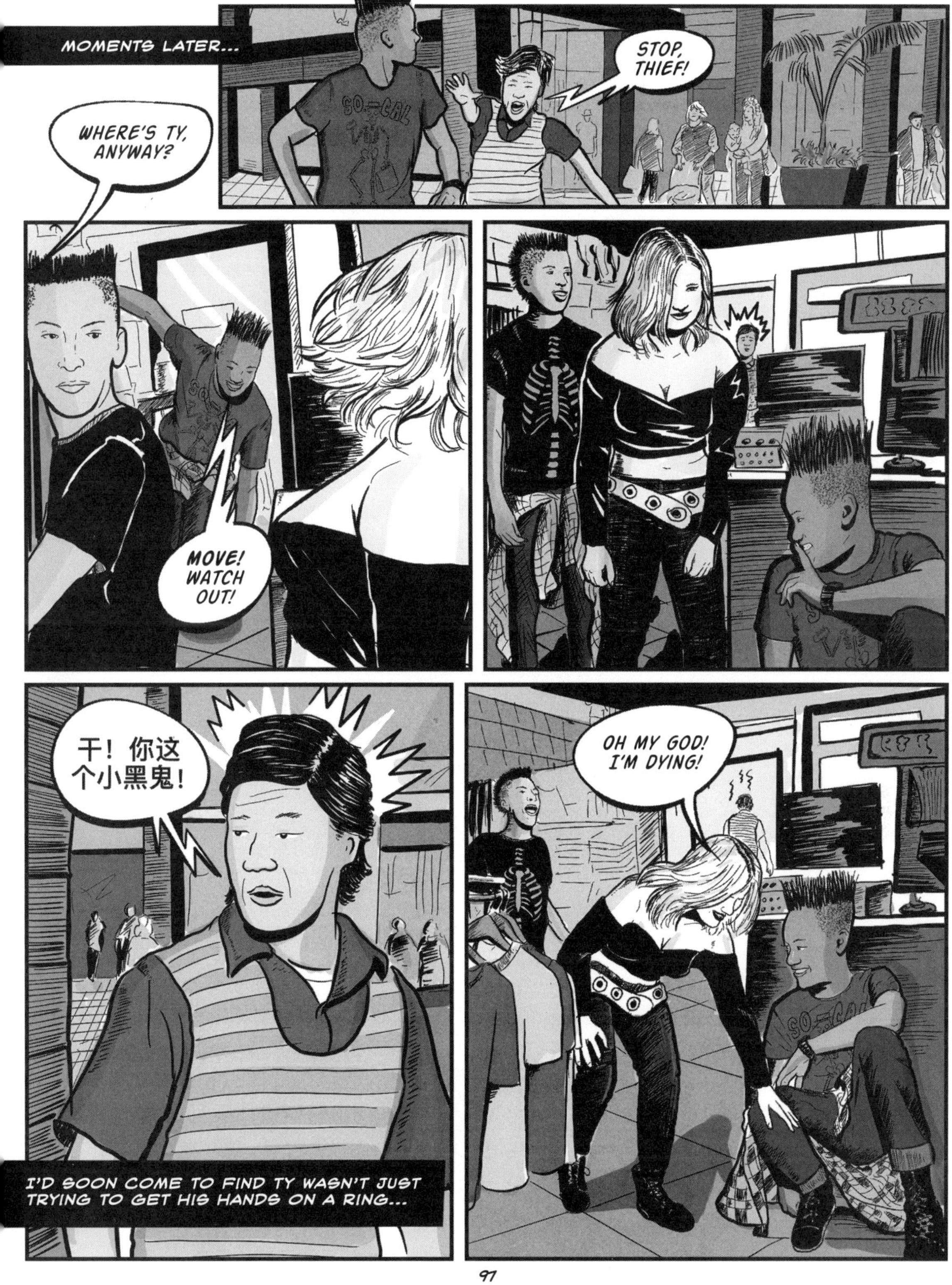
MOMENTS LATER...
STOP, THIEF!
WHERE'S TY, ANYWAY?
MOVE! WATCH OUT!
干！你这个小黑鬼！
OH MY GOD! I'M DYING!
I'D SOON COME TO FIND TY WASN'T JUST TRYING TO GET HIS HANDS ON A RING...

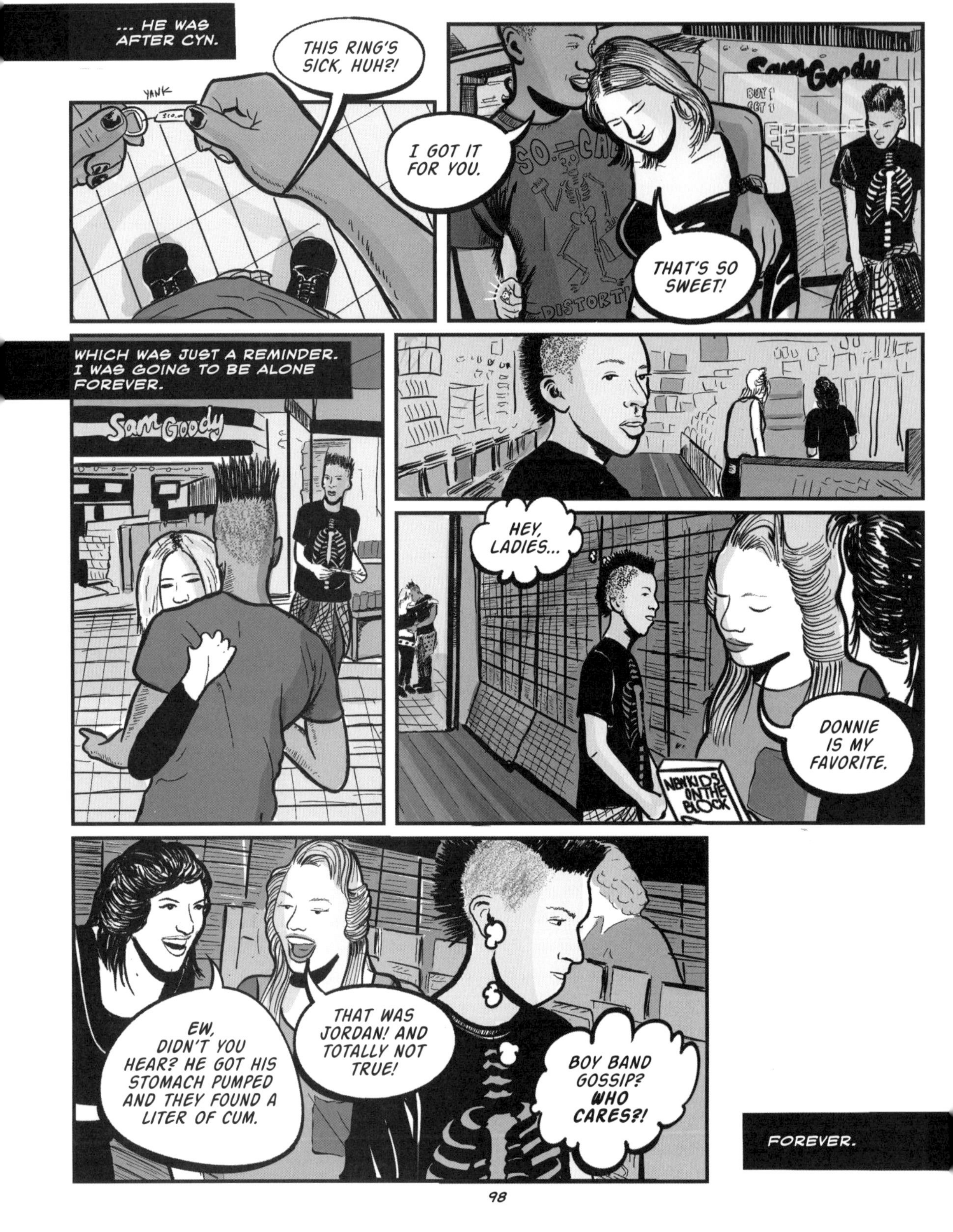
... HE WAS AFTER CYN.
YANK
THIS RING'S SICK, HUH?!
I GOT IT FOR YOU.
THAT'S SO SWEET!
Sam Goody
BUY 1 GET 1
WHICH WAS JUST A REMINDER. I WAS GOING TO BE ALONE FOREVER.
Sam Goody
HEY, LADIES...
DONNIE IS MY FAVORITE.
NEW KIDS ON THE BLOCK
EW, DIDN'T YOU HEAR? HE GOT HIS STOMACH PUMPED AND THEY FOUND A LITER OF CUM.
THAT WAS JORDAN! AND TOTALLY NOT TRUE!
BOY BAND GOSSIP? **WHO CARES?!**
FOREVER.

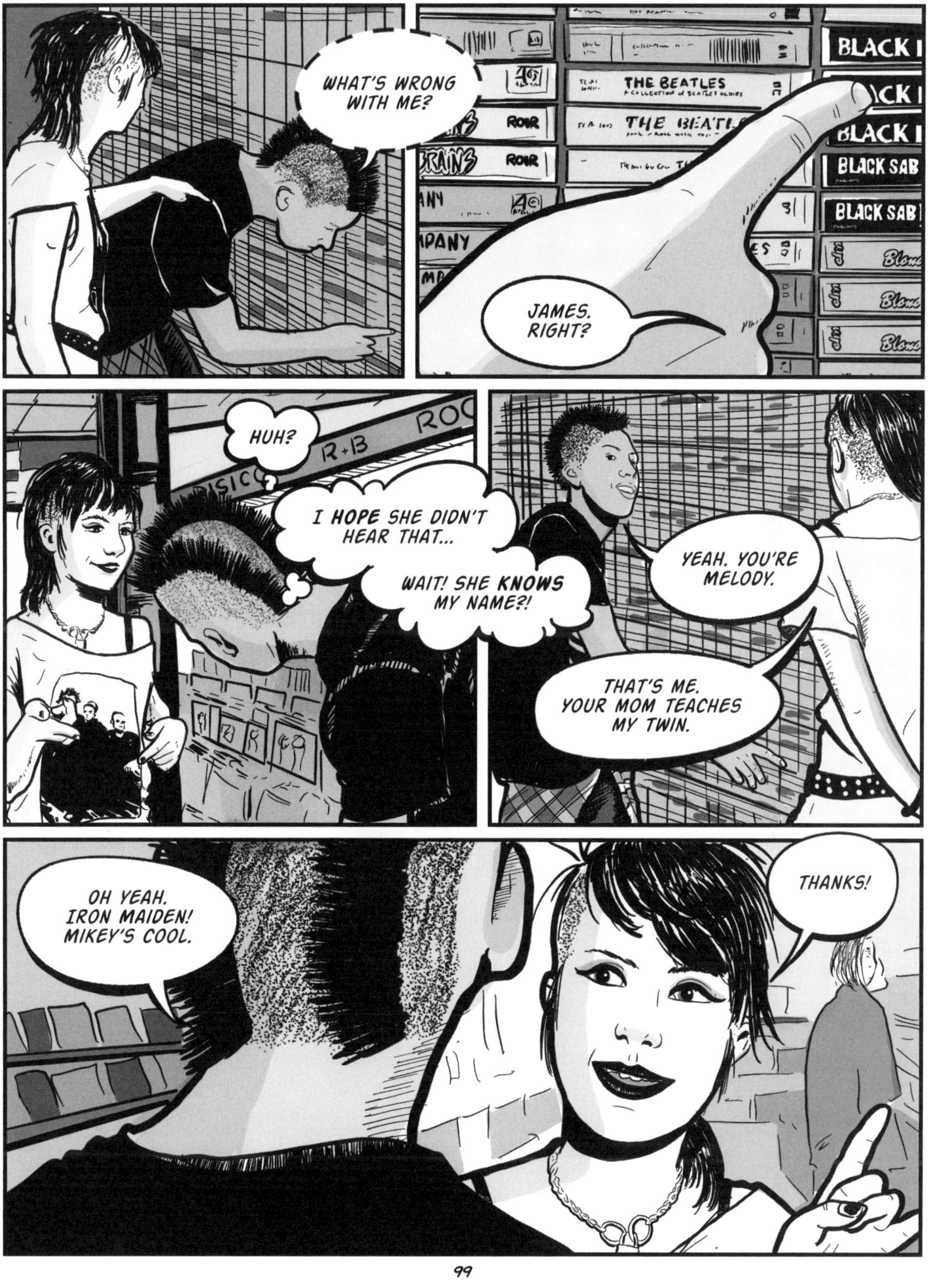
WHAT'S WRONG WITH ME?
THE BEATLES
THE BEATLES
BLACK
BLACK SAB
BLACK SAB
ROIR
ROIR
BRAINS
JAMES. RIGHT?
ROC
R+B
DISCO
HUH?
I HOPE SHE DIDN'T HEAR THAT...
WAIT! SHE KNOWS MY NAME?!
YEAH. YOU'RE MELODY.
THAT'S ME. YOUR MOM TEACHES MY TWIN.
OH YEAH. IRON MAIDEN! MIKEY'S COOL.
THANKS!

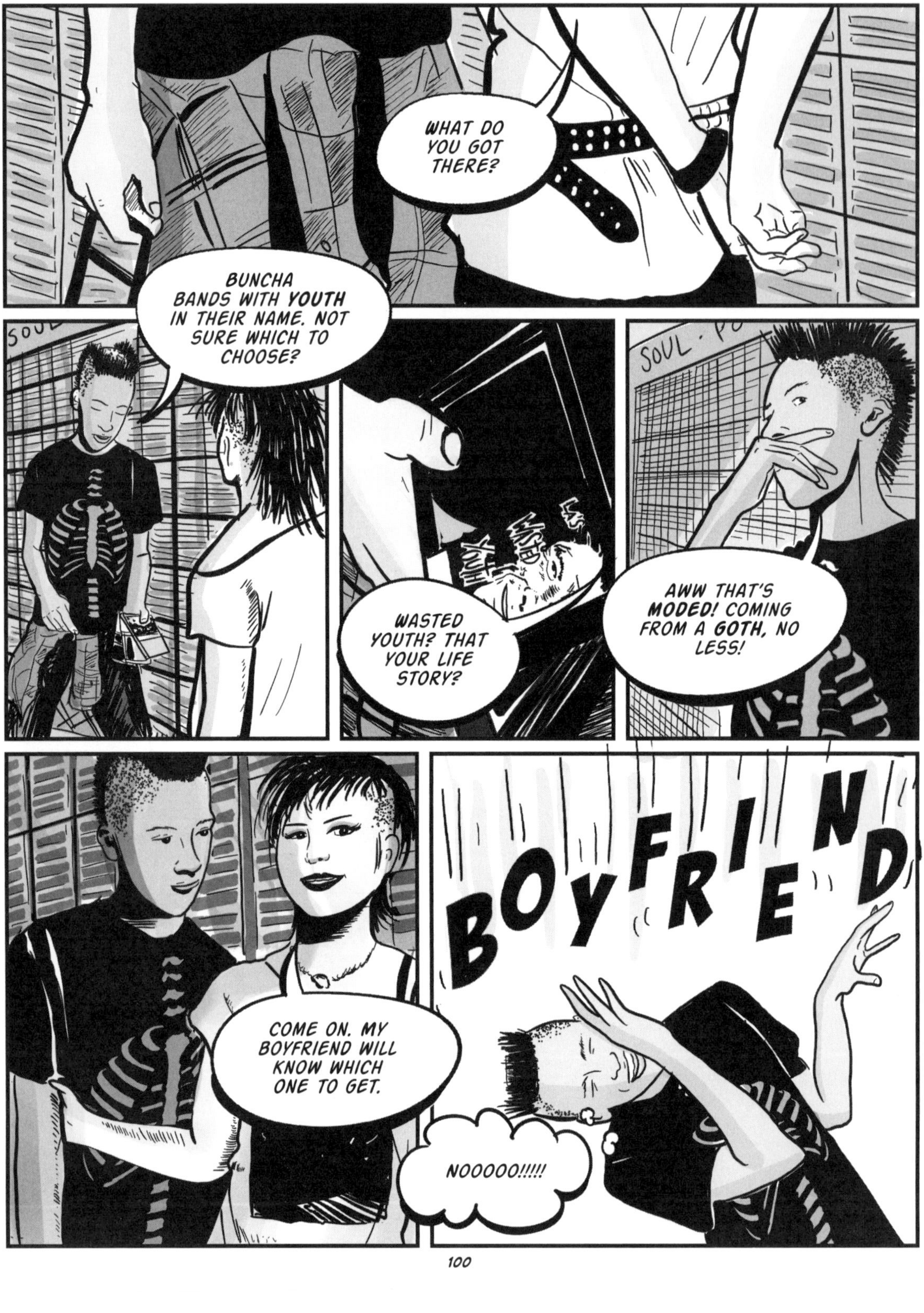
WHAT DO YOU GOT THERE?
BUNCHA BANDS WITH YOUTH IN THEIR NAME. NOT SURE WHICH TO CHOOSE?
WASTED YOUTH? THAT YOUR LIFE STORY?
AWW THAT'S MODED! COMING FROM A GOTH, NO LESS!
COME ON. MY BOYFRIEND WILL KNOW WHICH ONE TO GET.
BOYFRIEND
NOOOOO!!!!!

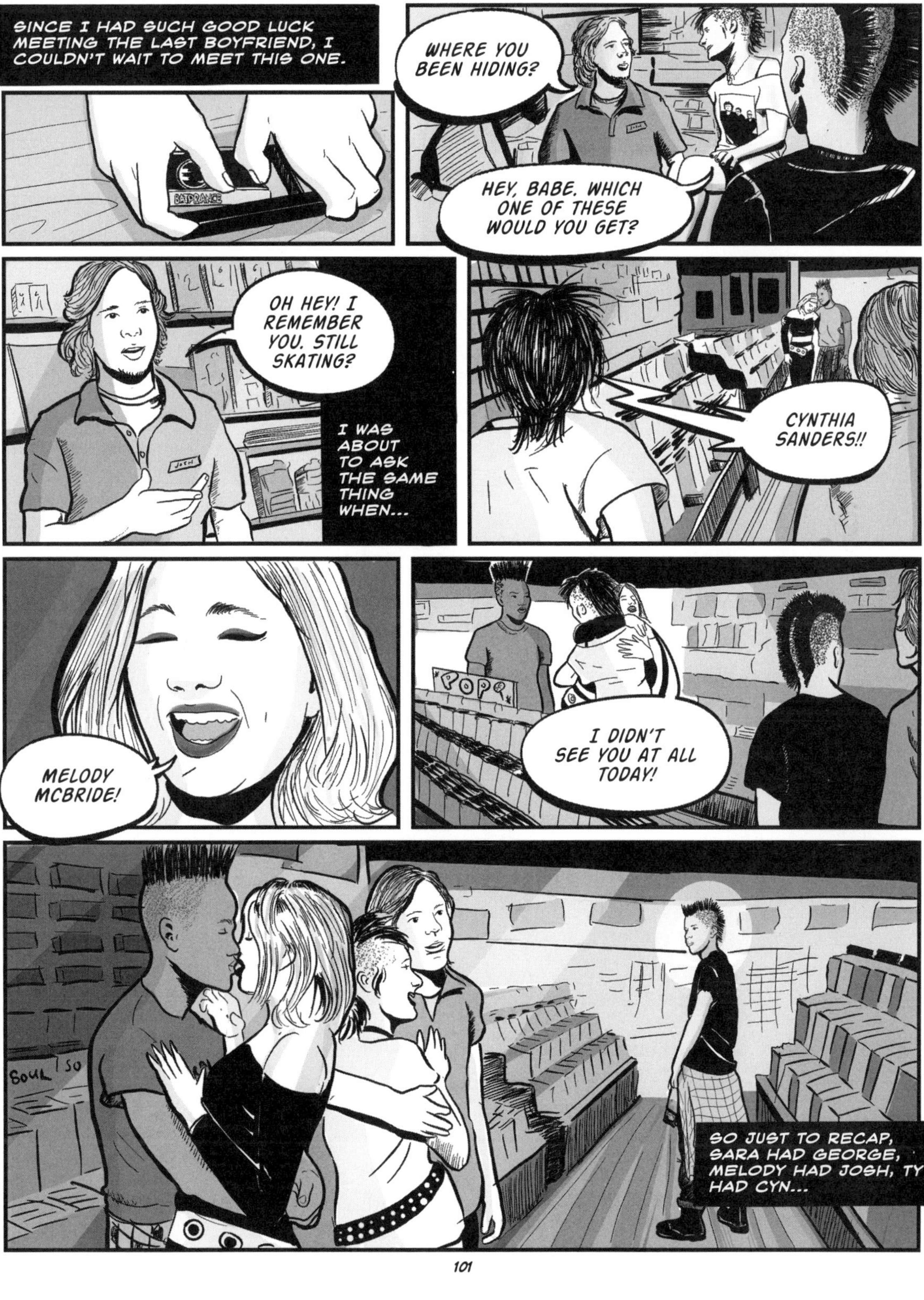
SINCE I HAD SUCH GOOD LUCK MEETING THE LAST BOYFRIEND, I COULDN'T WAIT TO MEET THIS ONE.
BATPRANCE
WHERE YOU BEEN HIDING?
HEY, BABE. WHICH ONE OF THESE WOULD YOU GET?
OH HEY! I REMEMBER YOU. STILL SKATING?
I WAS ABOUT TO ASK THE SAME THING WHEN...
CYNTHIA SANDERS!!
MELODY MCBRIDE!
POP
I DIDN'T SEE YOU AT ALL TODAY!
SOUL
SO JUST TO RECAP, SARA HAD GEORGE, MELODY HAD JOSH, TY HAD CYN...

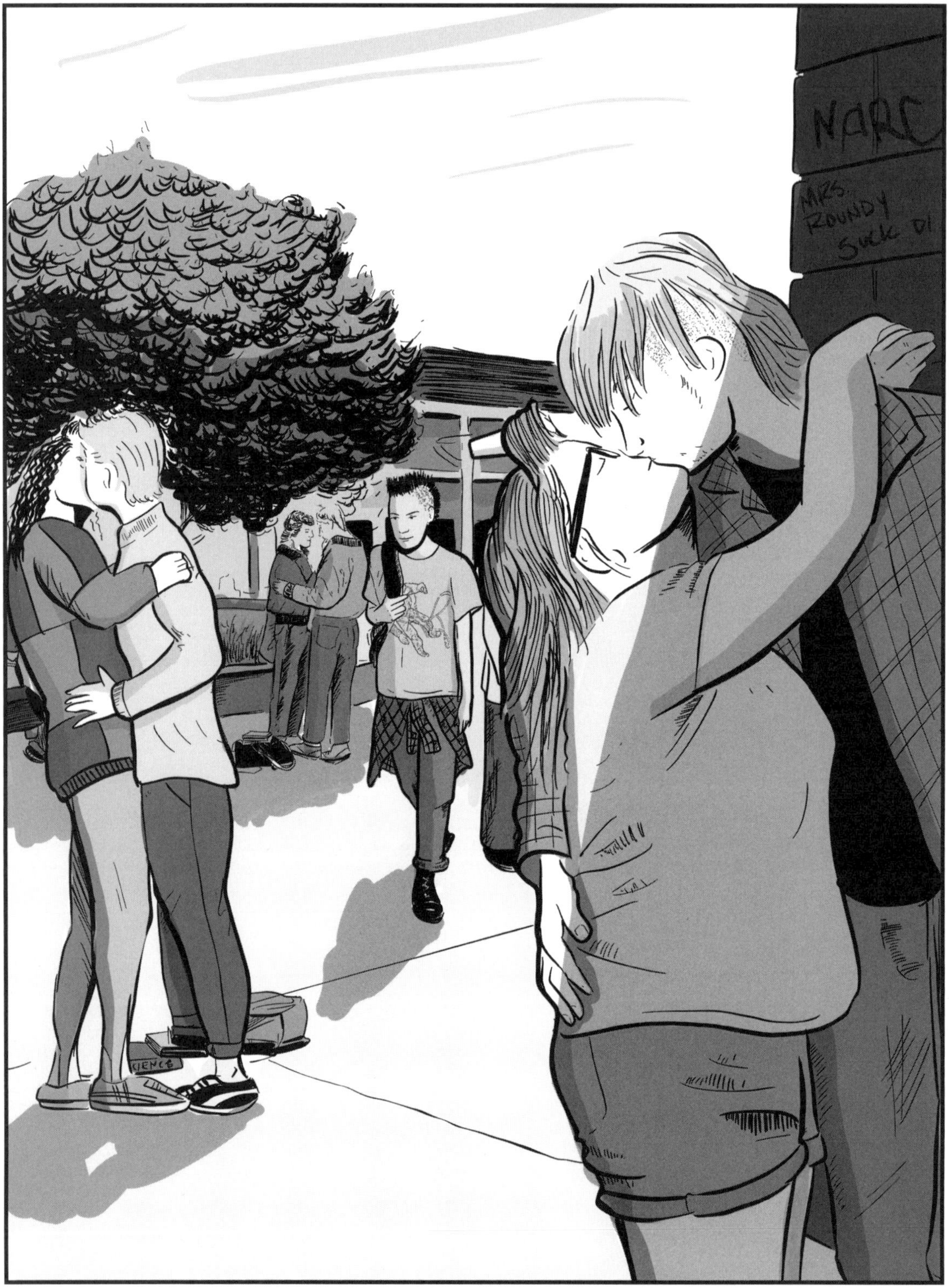
NARC
MRS. ROUNDY SUCK DI

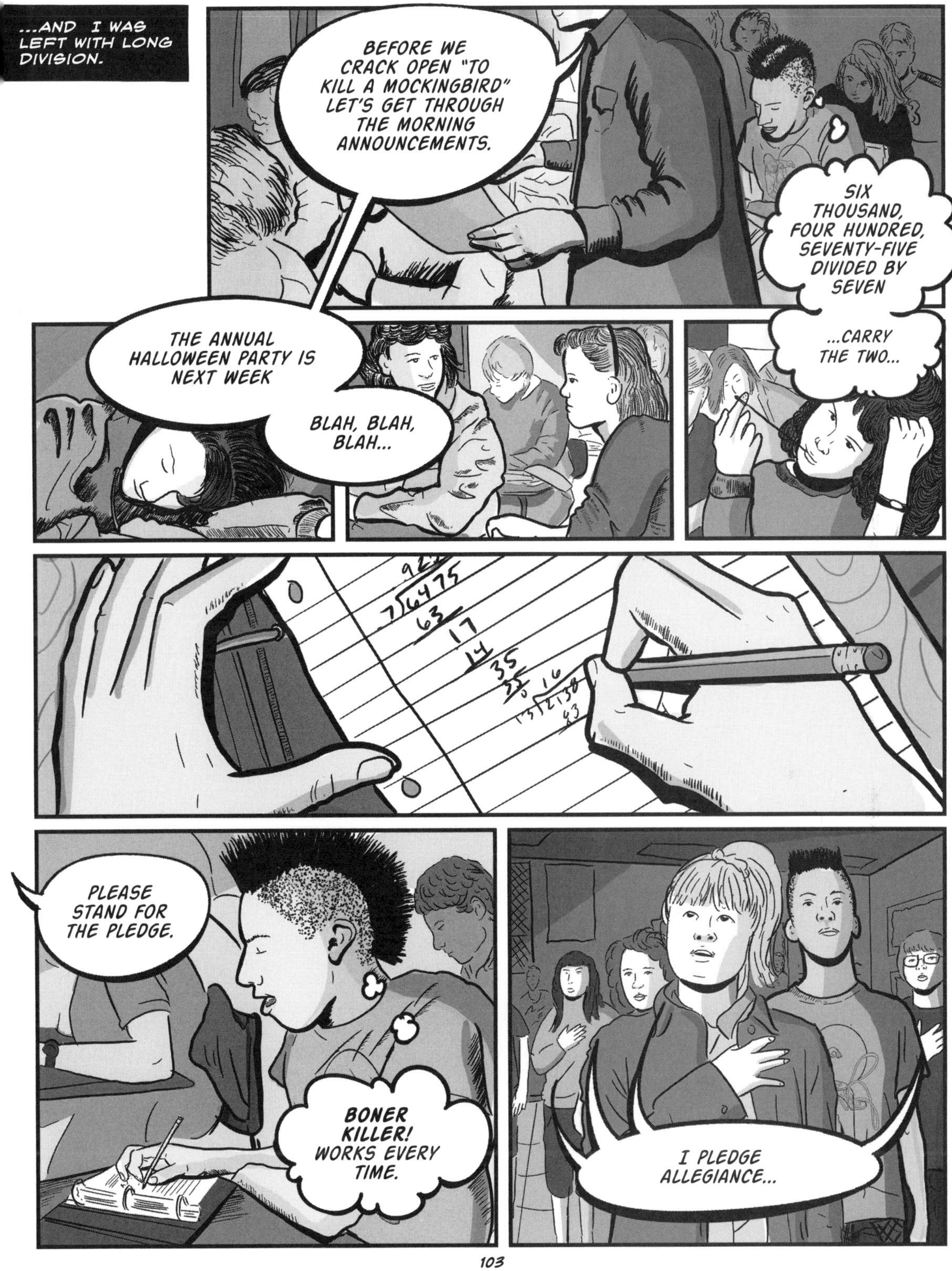
...AND I WAS LEFT WITH LONG DIVISION.
BEFORE WE CRACK OPEN "TO KILL A MOCKINGBIRD" LET'S GET THROUGH THE MORNING ANNOUNCEMENTS.
SIX THOUSAND, FOUR HUNDRED, SEVENTY-FIVE DIVIDED BY SEVEN
THE ANNUAL HALLOWEEN PARTY IS NEXT WEEK
BLAH, BLAH, BLAH...
...CARRY THE TWO...
PLEASE STAND FOR THE PLEDGE.
BONER KILLER! WORKS EVERY TIME.
I PLEDGE ALLEGIANCE...

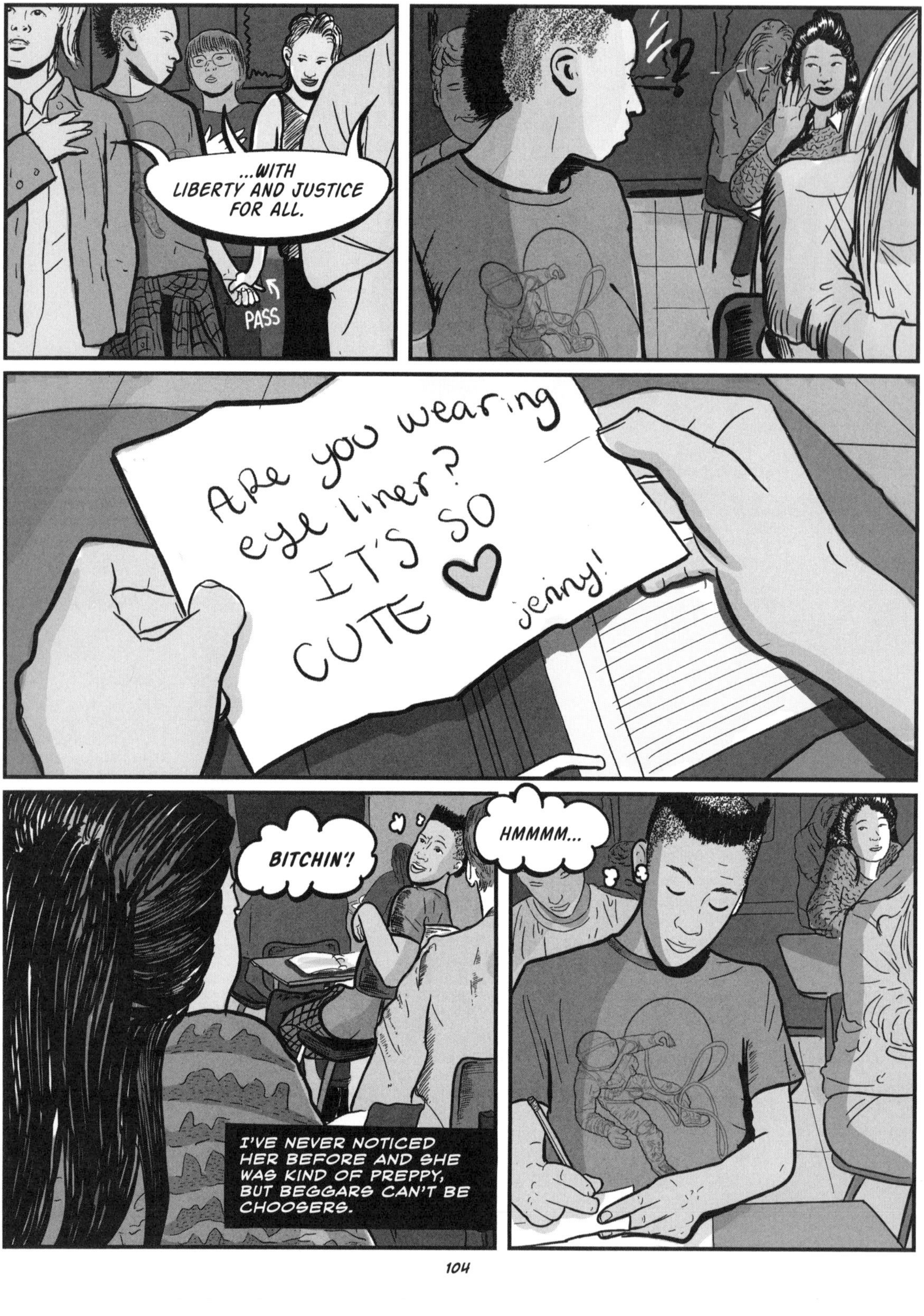
...WITH LIBERTY AND JUSTICE FOR ALL.
PASS
Are you wearing eye liner? IT'S SO CUTE
jenny!
BITCHIN'!
HMMMM...
I'VE NEVER NOTICED HER BEFORE AND SHE WAS KIND OF PREPPY, BUT BEGGARS CAN'T BE CHOOSERS.

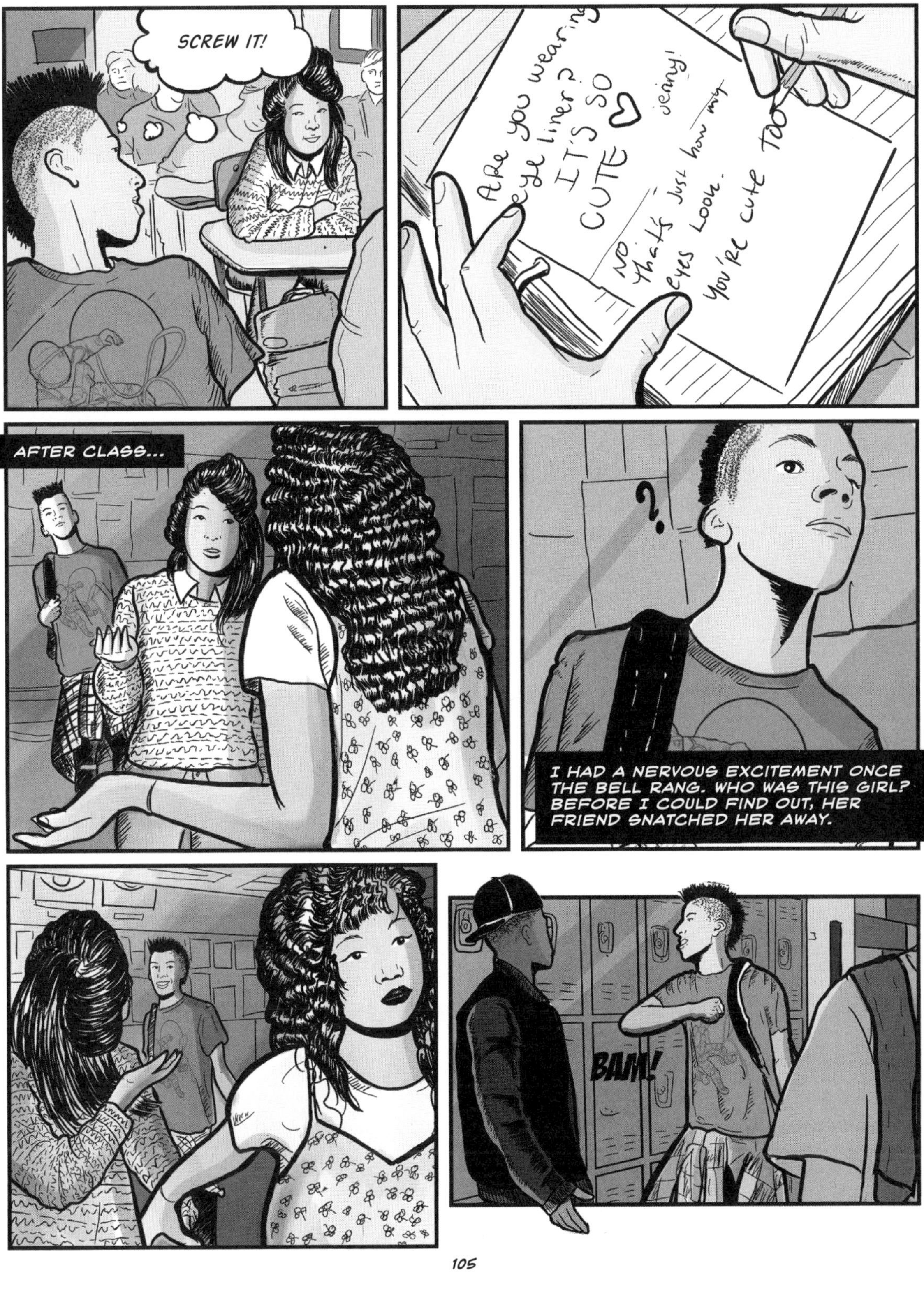
SCREW IT!
Are you wearing eye liner? IT'S SO CUTE ♥
jenny!
No that's just how my eyes look. You're cute TOO
AFTER CLASS...
?
I HAD A NERVOUS EXCITEMENT ONCE THE BELL RANG. WHO WAS THIS GIRL? BEFORE I COULD FIND OUT, HER FRIEND SNATCHED HER AWAY.
BAM!

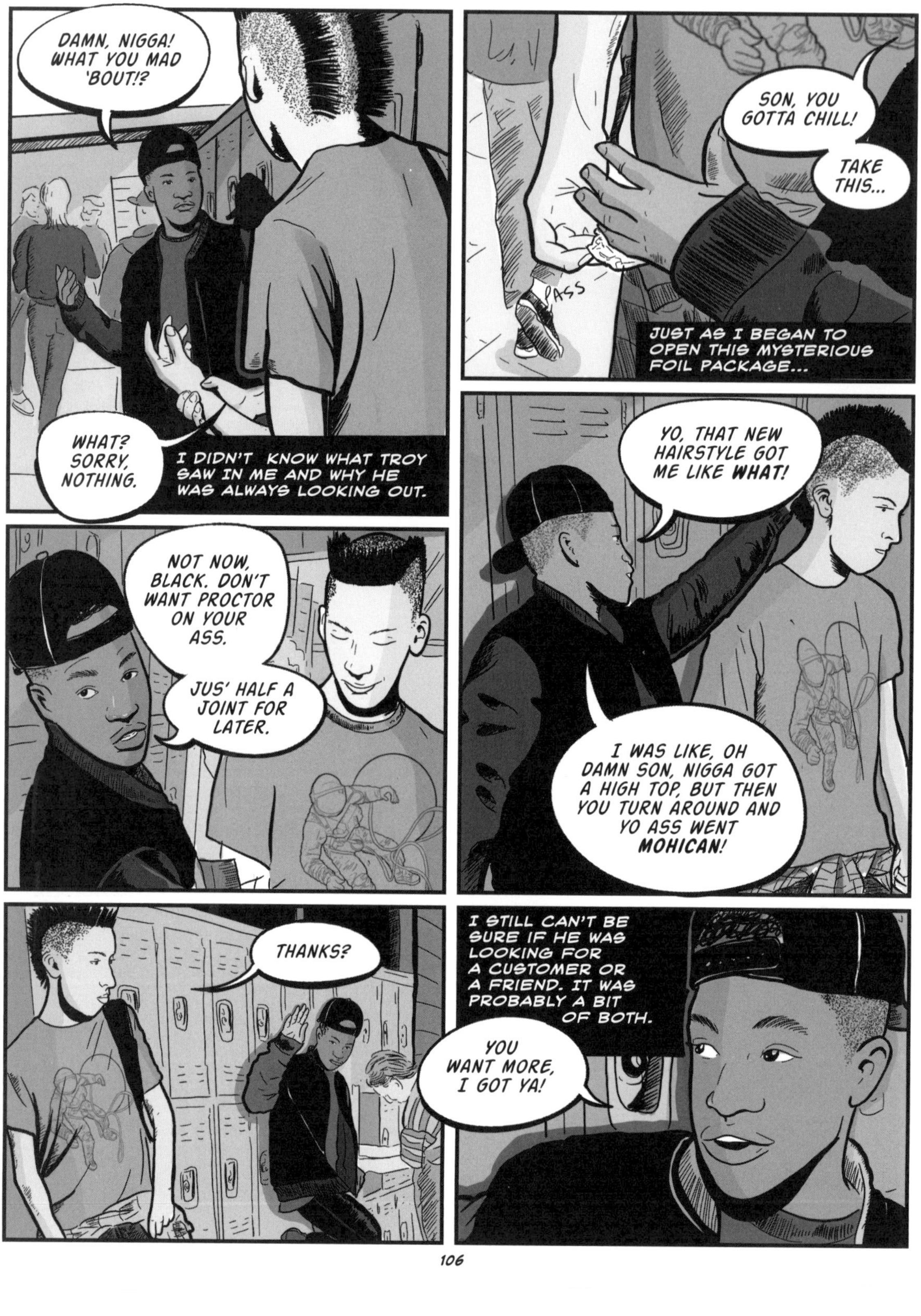
DAMN, NIGGA! WHAT YOU MAD 'BOUT!?
WHAT? SORRY, NOTHING.
I DIDN'T KNOW WHAT TROY SAW IN ME AND WHY HE WAS ALWAYS LOOKING OUT.
SON, YOU GOTTA CHILL!
TAKE THIS...
PASS
JUST AS I BEGAN TO OPEN THIS MYSTERIOUS FOIL PACKAGE...
NOT NOW, BLACK. DON'T WANT PROCTOR ON YOUR ASS.
JUS' HALF A JOINT FOR LATER.
YO, THAT NEW HAIRSTYLE GOT ME LIKE WHAT!
I WAS LIKE, OH DAMN SON, NIGGA GOT A HIGH TOP, BUT THEN YOU TURN AROUND AND YO ASS WENT MOHICAN!
THANKS?
I STILL CAN'T BE SURE IF HE WAS LOOKING FOR A CUSTOMER OR A FRIEND. IT WAS PROBABLY A BIT OF BOTH.
YOU WANT MORE, I GOT YA!

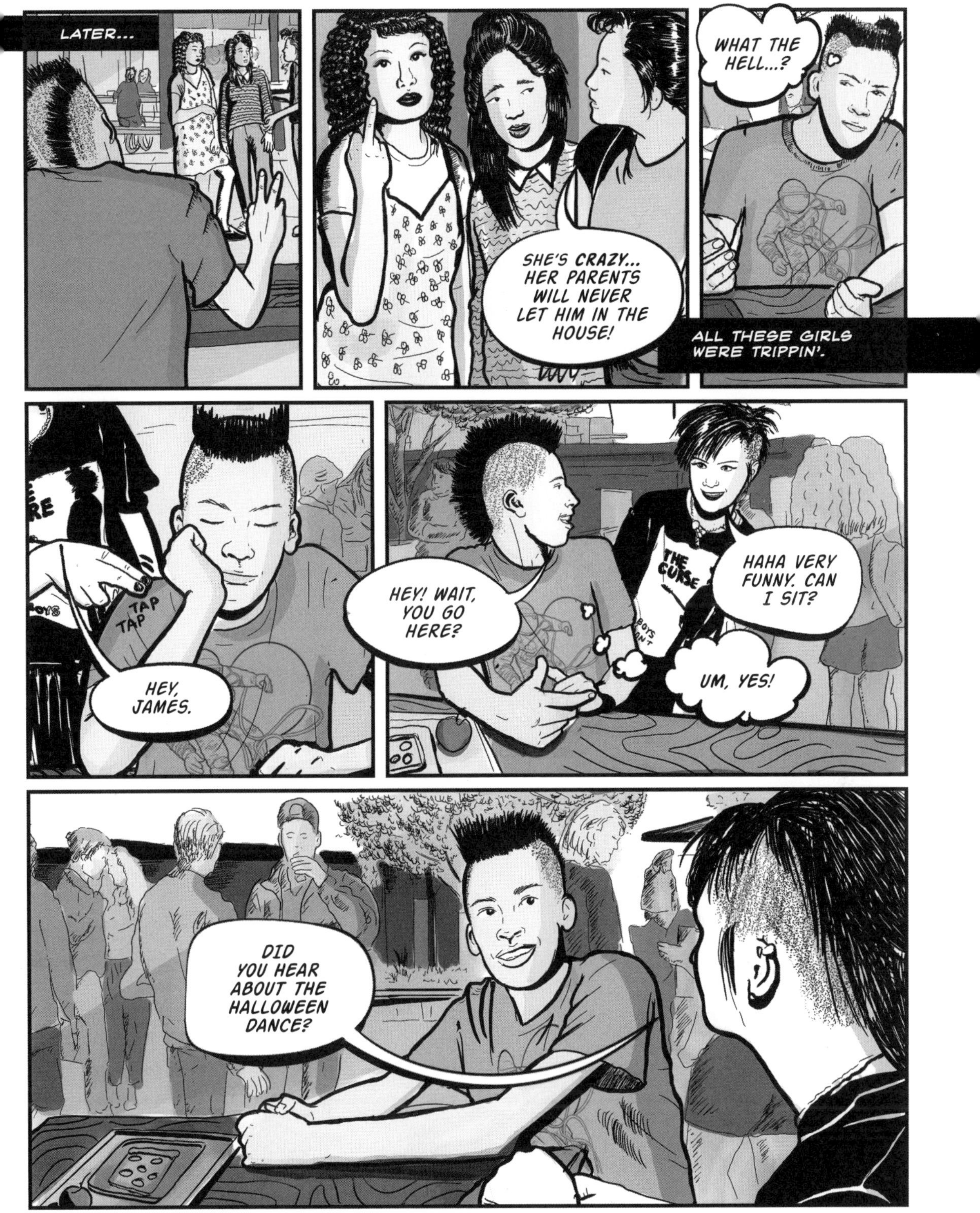
LATER...
WHAT THE HELL...?
SHE'S CRAZY... HER PARENTS WILL NEVER LET HIM IN THE HOUSE!
ALL THESE GIRLS WERE TRIPPIN'.
TAP TAP
HEY, JAMES.
HEY! WAIT, YOU GO HERE?
HAHA VERY FUNNY. CAN I SIT?
UM, YES!
DID YOU HEAR ABOUT THE HALLOWEEN DANCE?

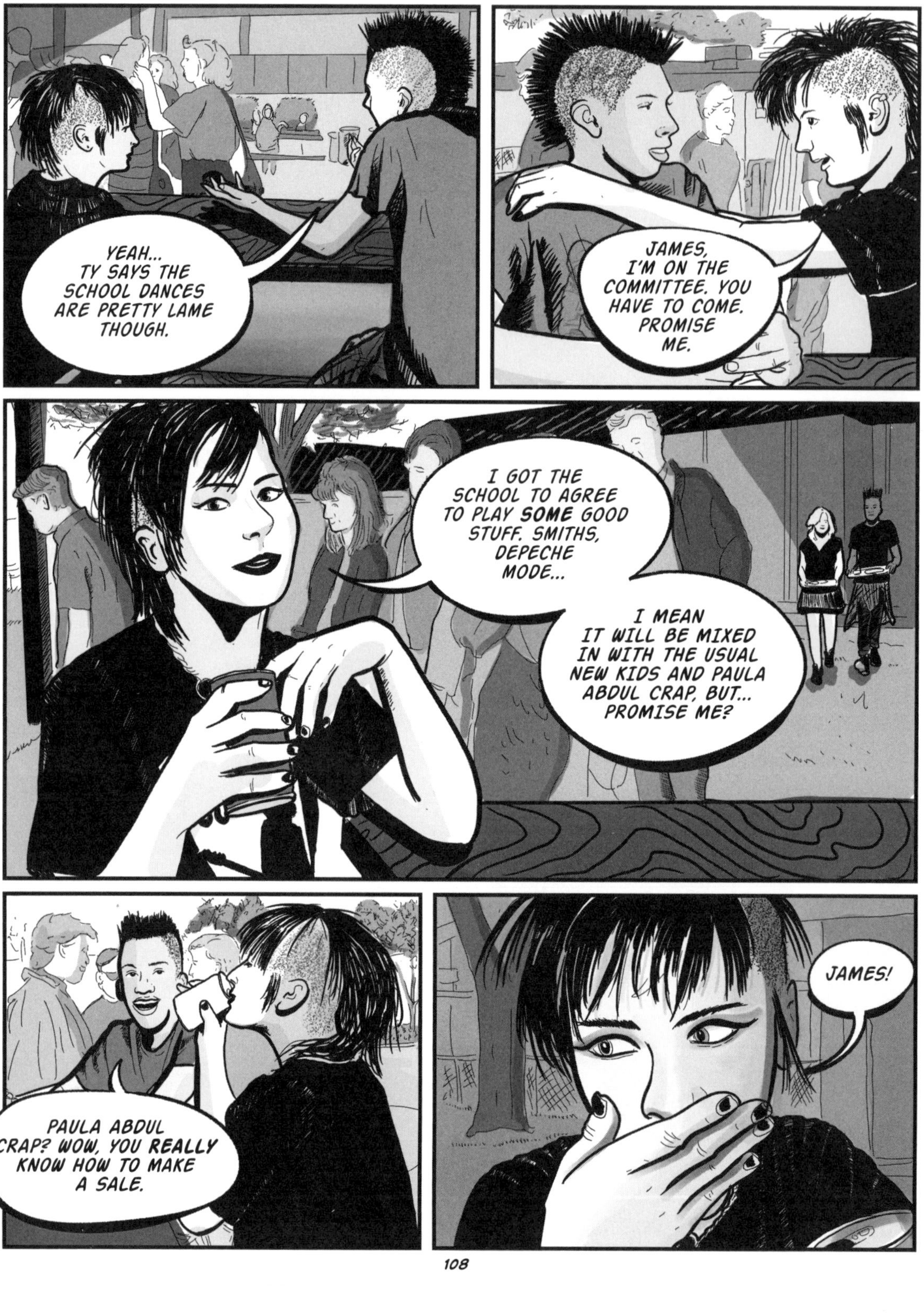
YEAH... TY SAYS THE SCHOOL DANCES ARE PRETTY LAME THOUGH.
JAMES, I'M ON THE COMMITTEE. YOU HAVE TO COME. PROMISE ME.
I GOT THE SCHOOL TO AGREE TO PLAY SOME GOOD STUFF. SMITHS, DEPECHE MODE...
I MEAN IT WILL BE MIXED IN WITH THE USUAL NEW KIDS AND PAULA ABDUL CRAP, BUT... PROMISE ME?
PAULA ABDUL CRAP? WOW, YOU REALLY KNOW HOW TO MAKE A SALE.
JAMES!

PLUS, YOU'LL GET TO SEE MY COSTUME. PROMISE ME?
OKAY, OKAY. I'M SOLD. SEE YOU IN THE PIT...
...YOU KNOW, IF JOSH WON'T MIND.
UGH, FORGET THAT LOSER. WE BROKE UP.
BUMMER.
YES!
WHAT UP, SUCKERS?
GUESS WE'RE GOING TO THE HALLOWEEN DANCE.

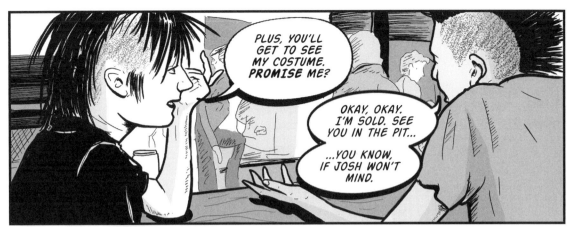

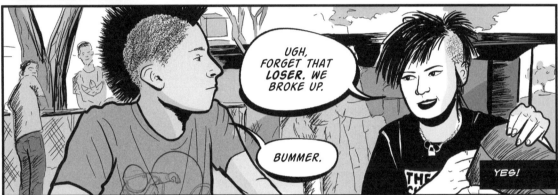

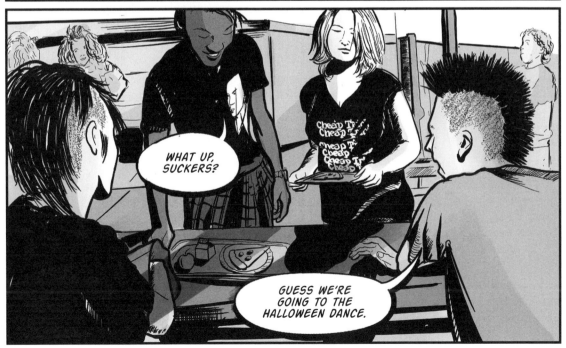

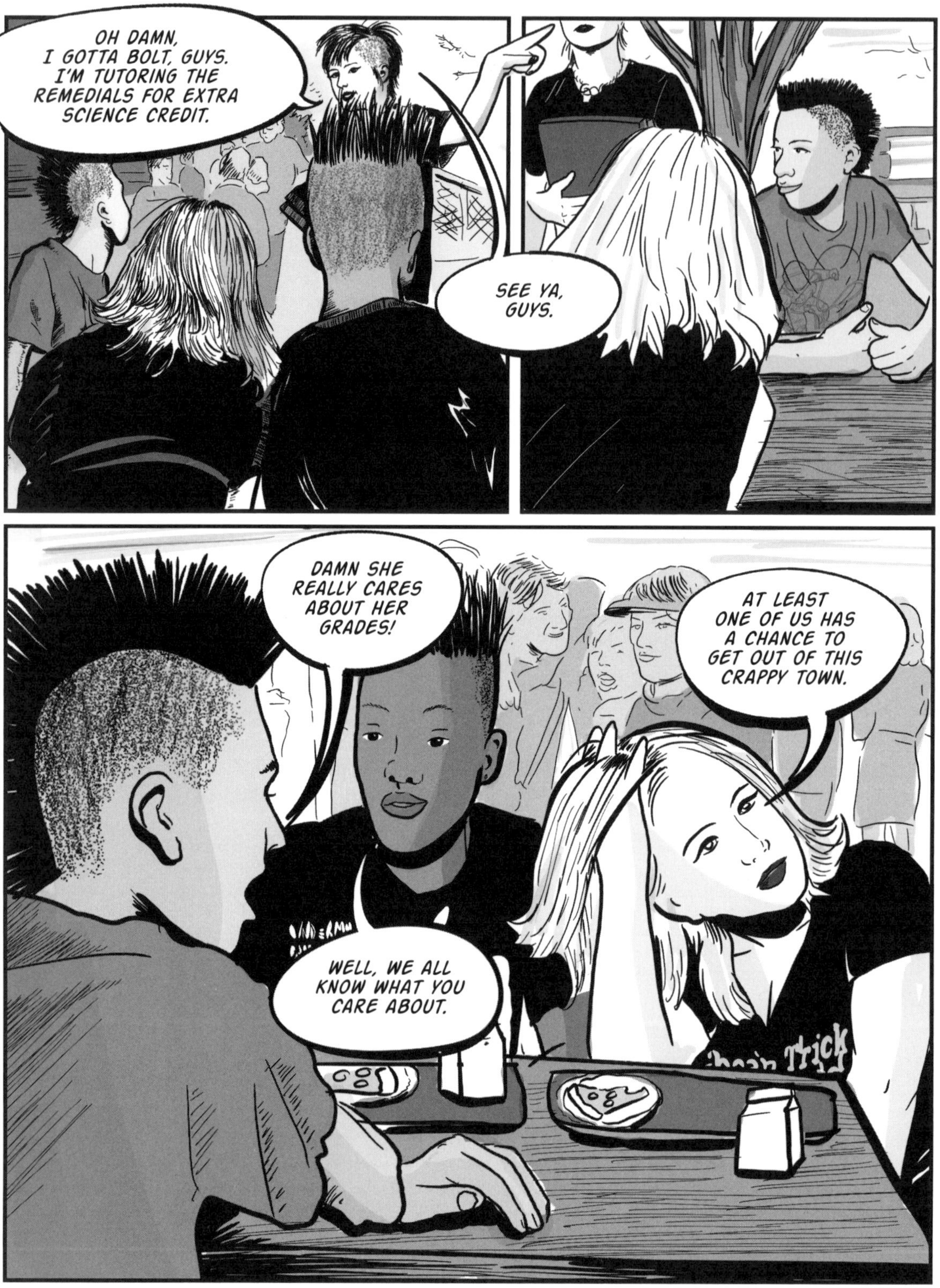
OH DAMN, I GOTTA BOLT, GUYS. I'M TUTORING THE REMEDIALS FOR EXTRA SCIENCE CREDIT.
SEE YA, GUYS.
DAMN SHE REALLY CARES ABOUT HER GRADES!
AT LEAST ONE OF US HAS A CHANCE TO GET OUT OF THIS CRAPPY TOWN.
WELL, WE ALL KNOW WHAT YOU CARE ABOUT.

CHAPTER 4
MY WAR

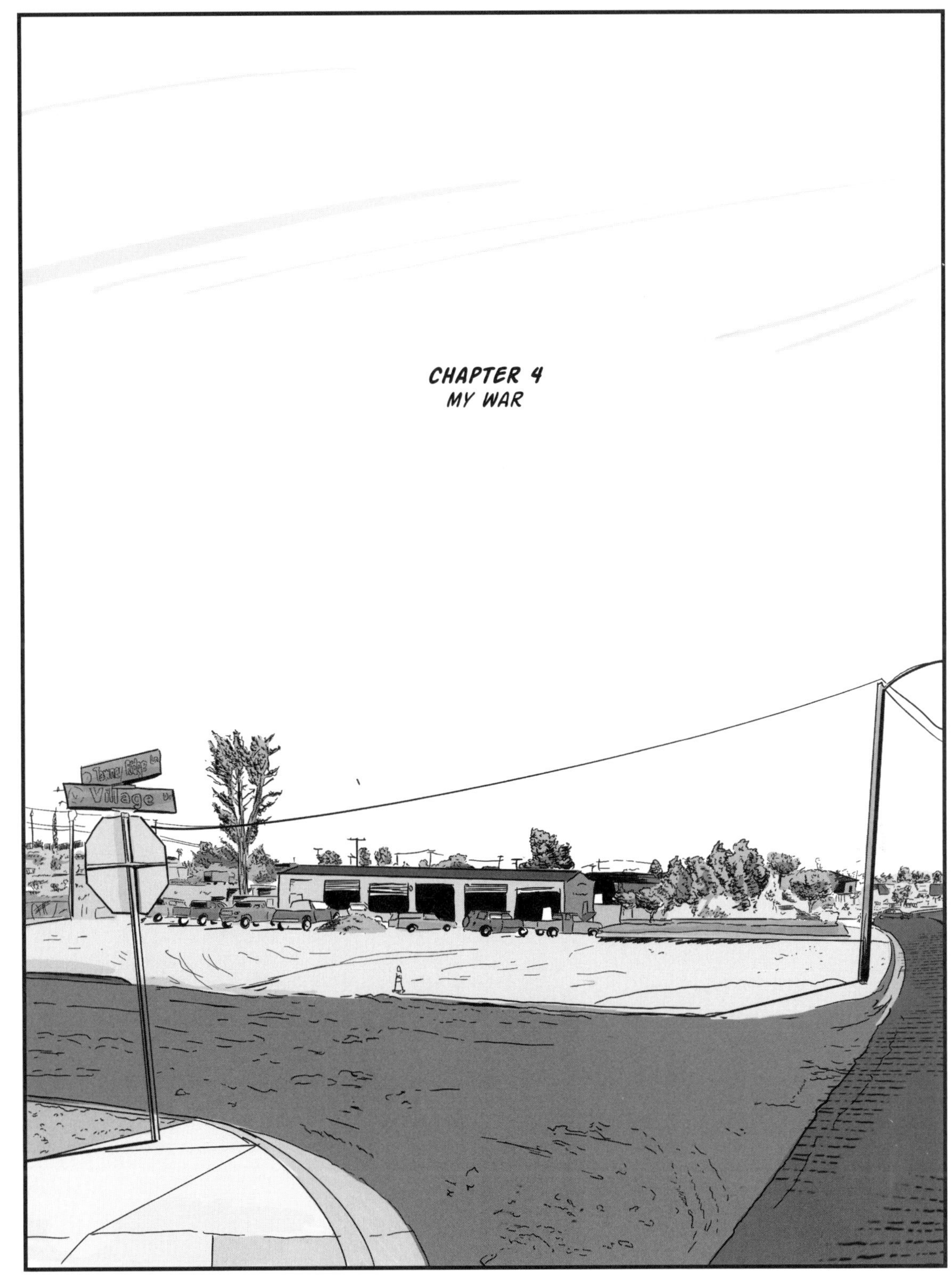
Village

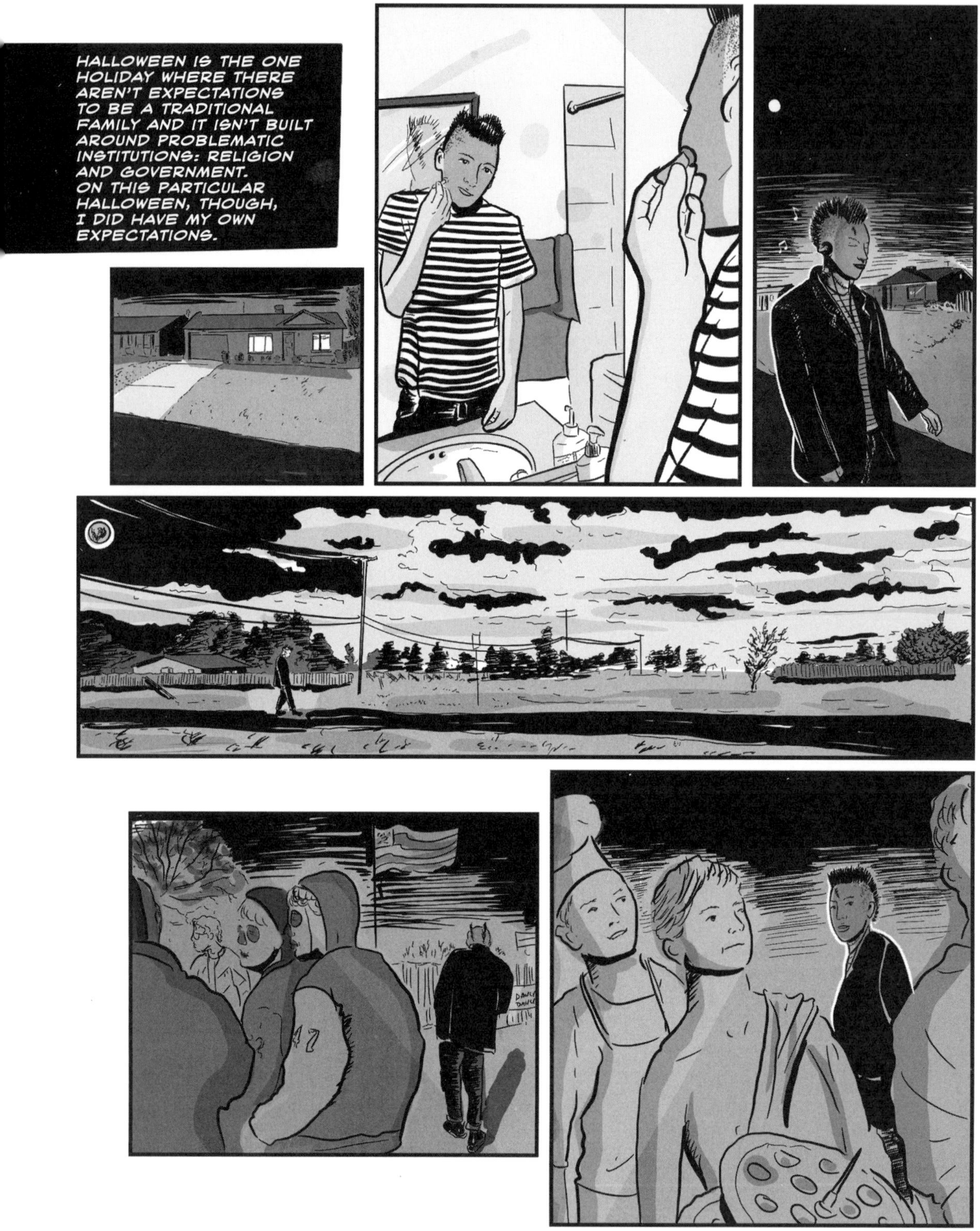
HALLOWEEN IS THE ONE HOLIDAY WHERE THERE AREN'T EXPECTATIONS TO BE A TRADITIONAL FAMILY AND IT ISN'T BUILT AROUND PROBLEMATIC INSTITUTIONS: RELIGION AND GOVERNMENT. ON THIS PARTICULAR HALLOWEEN, THOUGH, I DID HAVE MY OWN EXPECTATIONS.

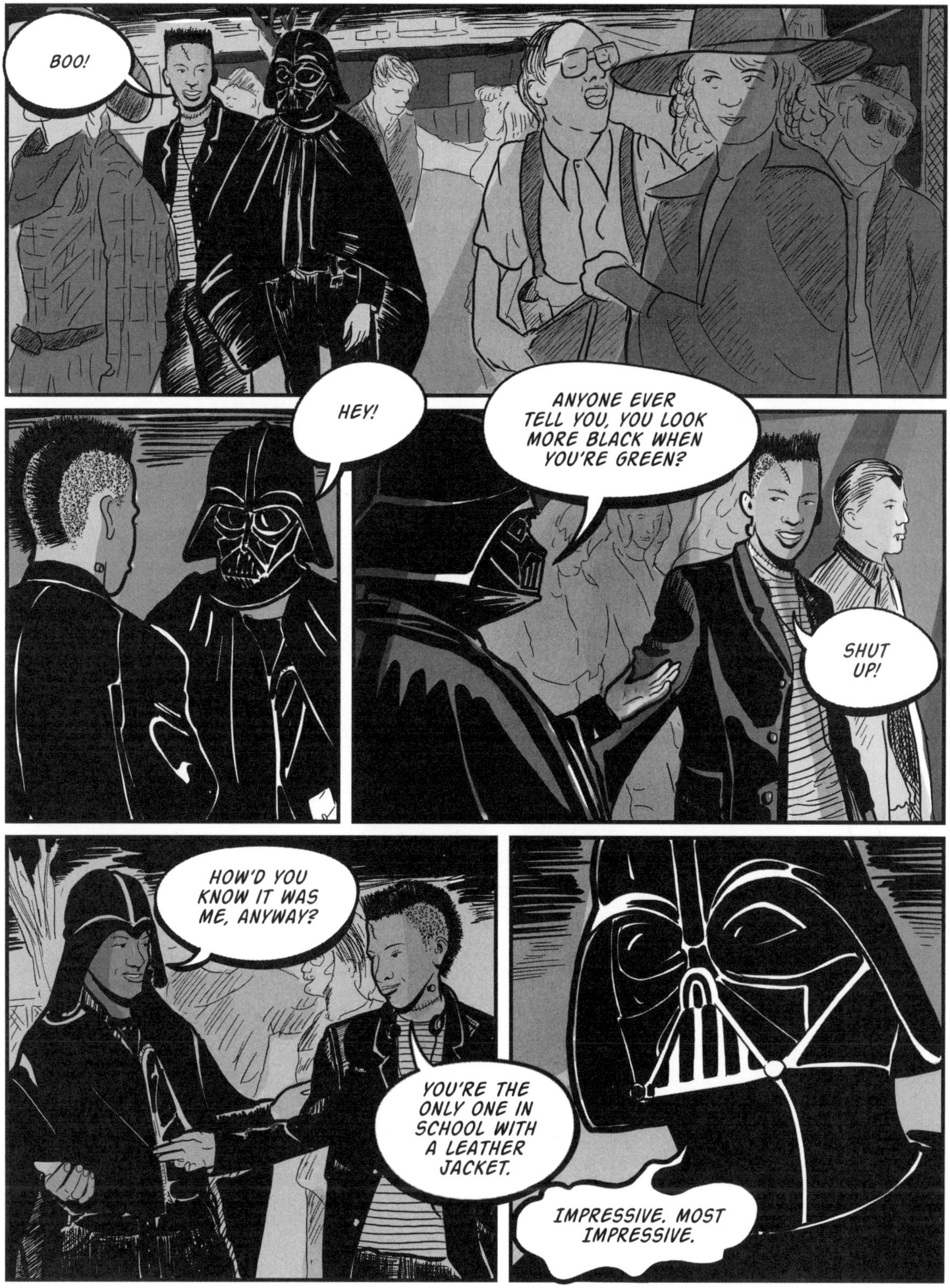
BOO!
HEY!
ANYONE EVER TELL YOU, YOU LOOK MORE BLACK WHEN YOU'RE GREEN?
SHUT UP!
HOW'D YOU KNOW IT WAS ME, ANYWAY?
YOU'RE THE ONLY ONE IN SCHOOL WITH A LEATHER JACKET.
IMPRESSIVE. MOST IMPRESSIVE.

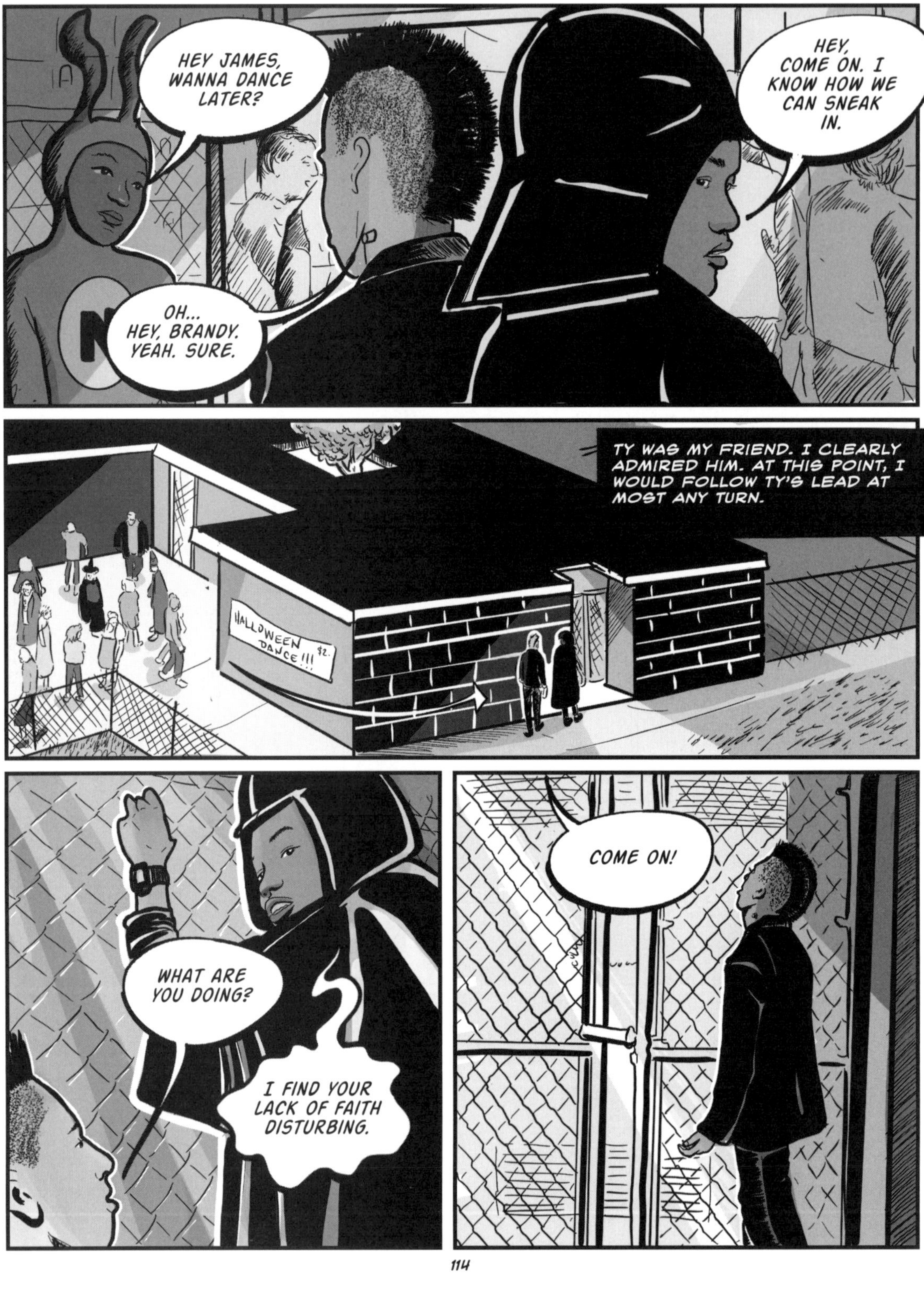
HEY JAMES, WANNA DANCE LATER?
OH... HEY, BRANDY. YEAH. SURE.
HEY, COME ON. I KNOW HOW WE CAN SNEAK IN.
TY WAS MY FRIEND. I CLEARLY ADMIRED HIM. AT THIS POINT, I WOULD FOLLOW TY'S LEAD AT MOST ANY TURN.
HALLOWEEN DANCE!!! $2.
WHAT ARE YOU DOING?
I FIND YOUR LACK OF FAITH DISTURBING.
COME ON!

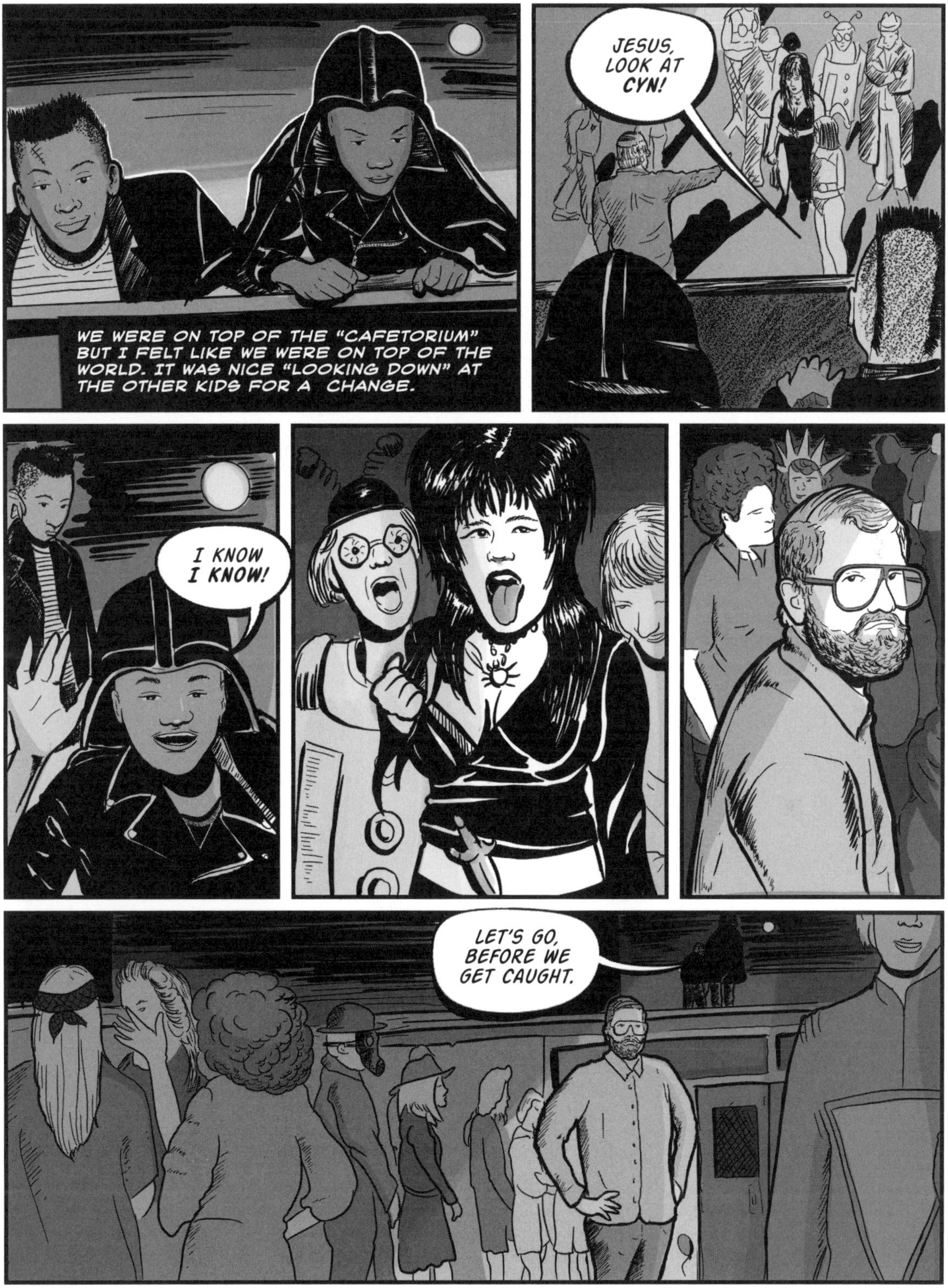
WE WERE ON TOP OF THE "CAFETORIUM" BUT I FELT LIKE WE WERE ON TOP OF THE WORLD. IT WAS NICE "LOOKING DOWN" AT THE OTHER KIDS FOR A CHANGE.
JESUS, LOOK AT CYN!
I KNOW I KNOW!
LET'S GO, BEFORE WE GET CAUGHT.

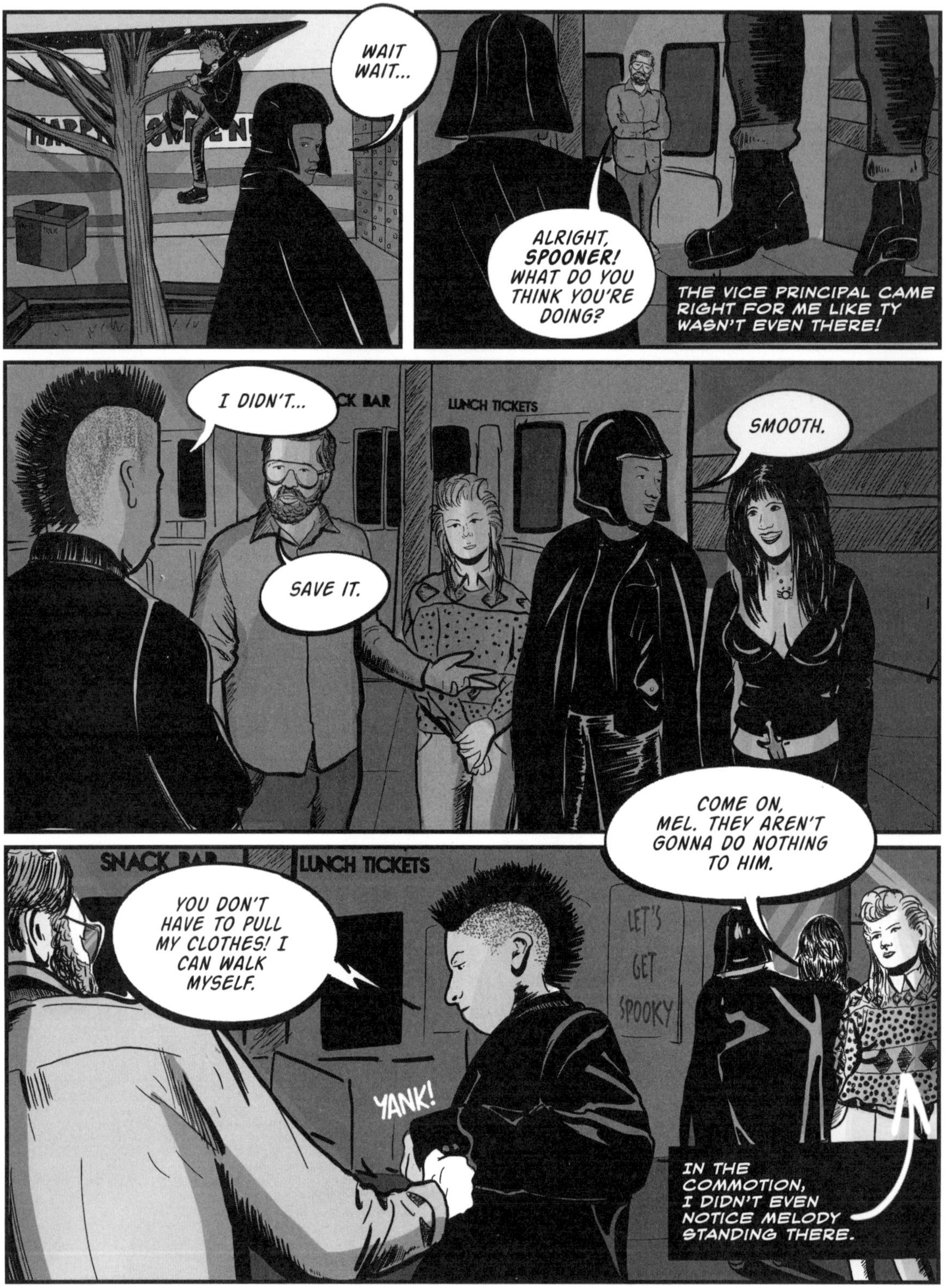
WAIT WAIT...
ALRIGHT, SPOONER! WHAT DO YOU THINK YOU'RE DOING?
THE VICE PRINCIPAL CAME RIGHT FOR ME LIKE TY WASN'T EVEN THERE!
SNACK BAR
LUNCH TICKETS
I DIDN'T...
SMOOTH.
SAVE IT.
SNACK BAR
LUNCH TICKETS
YOU DON'T HAVE TO PULL MY CLOTHES! I CAN WALK MYSELF.
COME ON, MEL. THEY AREN'T GONNA DO NOTHING TO HIM.
LET'S GET SPOOKY
YANK!
IN THE COMMOTION, I DIDN'T EVEN NOTICE MELODY STANDING THERE.

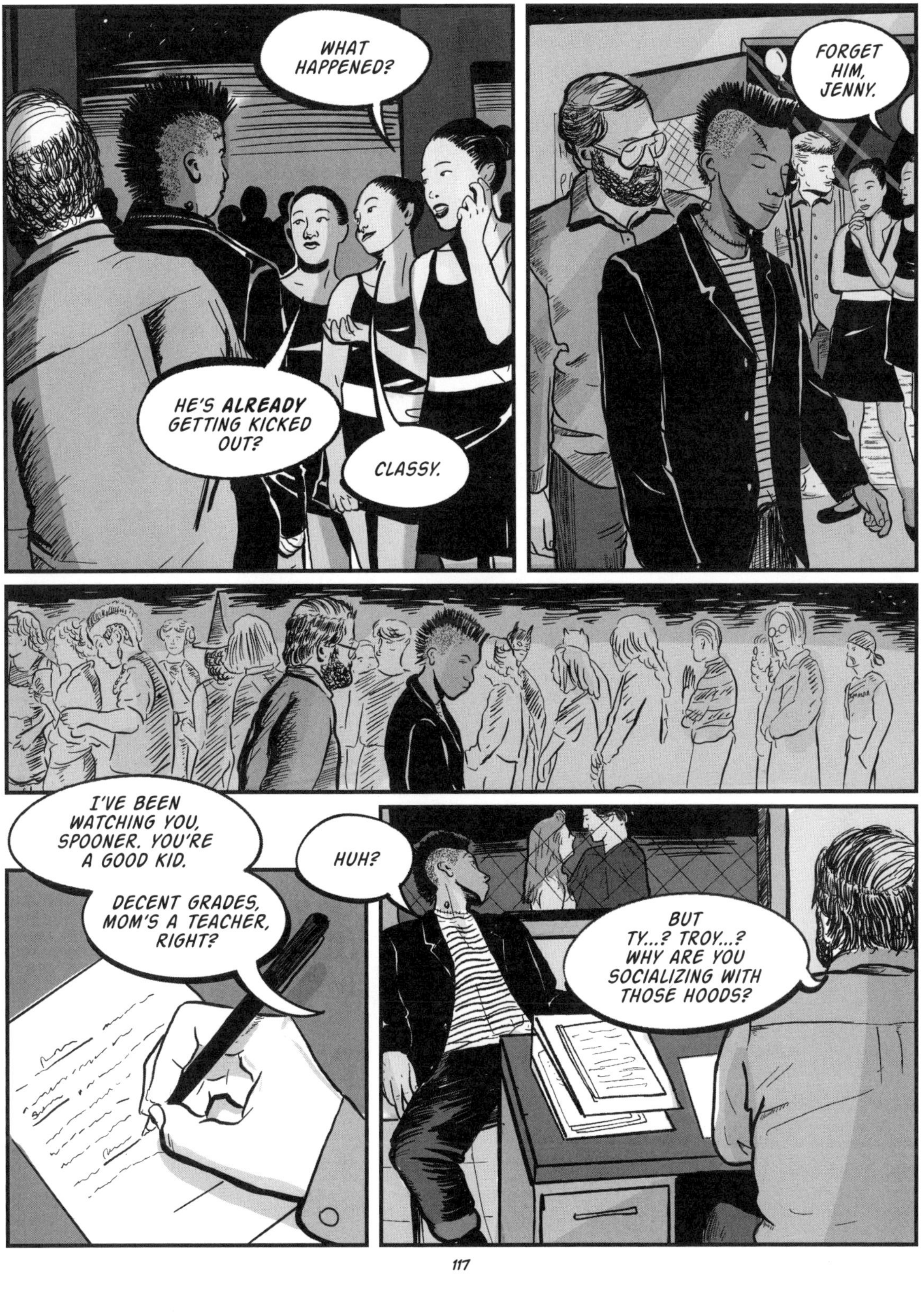
WHAT HAPPENED?
HE'S **ALREADY** GETTING KICKED OUT?
CLASSY.
FORGET HIM, JENNY.
I'VE BEEN WATCHING YOU, SPOONER. YOU'RE A GOOD KID.
DECENT GRADES, MOM'S A TEACHER, RIGHT?
HUH?
BUT TY...? TROY...? WHY ARE YOU SOCIALIZING WITH THOSE HOODS?

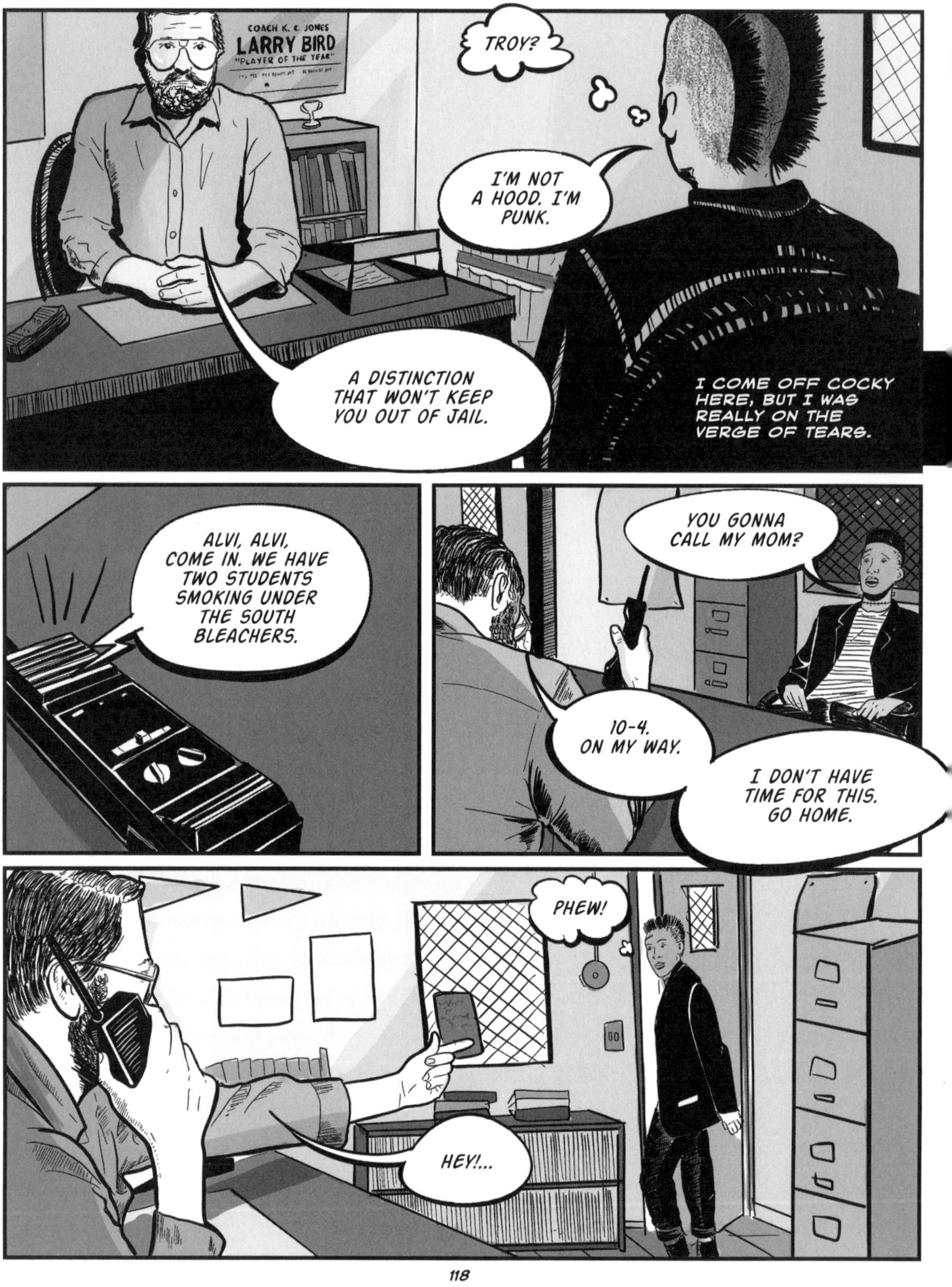
COACH K. C. JONES
LARRY BIRD
"PLAYER OF THE YEAR"
TROY?
I'M NOT A HOOD. I'M PUNK.
A DISTINCTION THAT WON'T KEEP YOU OUT OF JAIL.
I COME OFF COCKY HERE, BUT I WAS REALLY ON THE VERGE OF TEARS.
ALVI, ALVI, COME IN. WE HAVE TWO STUDENTS SMOKING UNDER THE SOUTH BLEACHERS.
YOU GONNA CALL MY MOM?
10-4. ON MY WAY.
I DON'T HAVE TIME FOR THIS. GO HOME.
PHEW!
HEY!...

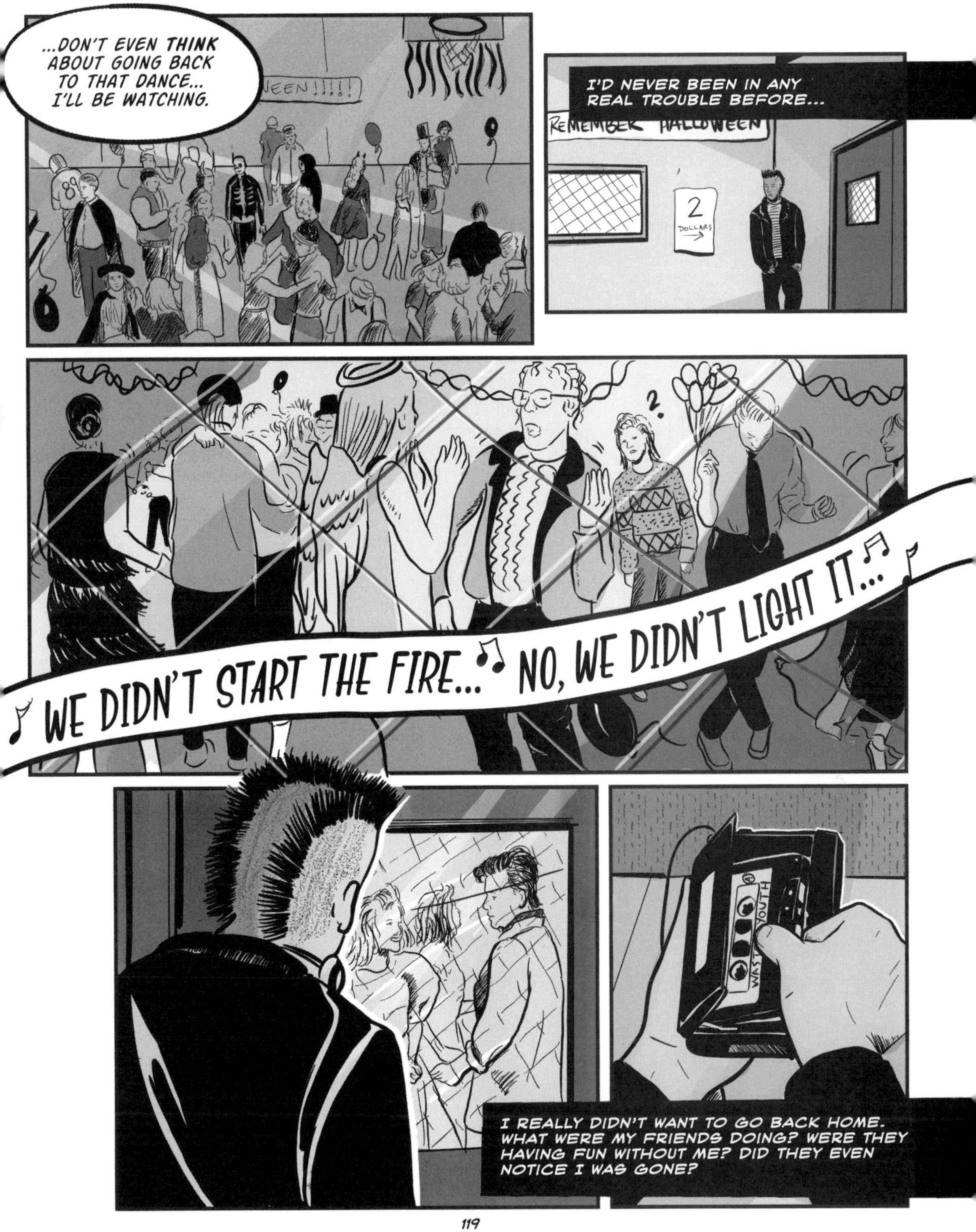

...DON'T EVEN THINK ABOUT GOING BACK TO THAT DANCE... I'LL BE WATCHING.
WEEN!!!!!
I'D NEVER BEEN IN ANY REAL TROUBLE BEFORE...
REMEMBER HALLOWEEN
2 DOLLARS
WE DIDN'T START THE FIRE... NO, WE DIDN'T LIGHT IT...
WASTE YOUTH
I REALLY DIDN'T WANT TO GO BACK HOME. WHAT WERE MY FRIENDS DOING? WERE THEY HAVING FUN WITHOUT ME? DID THEY EVEN NOTICE I WAS GONE?

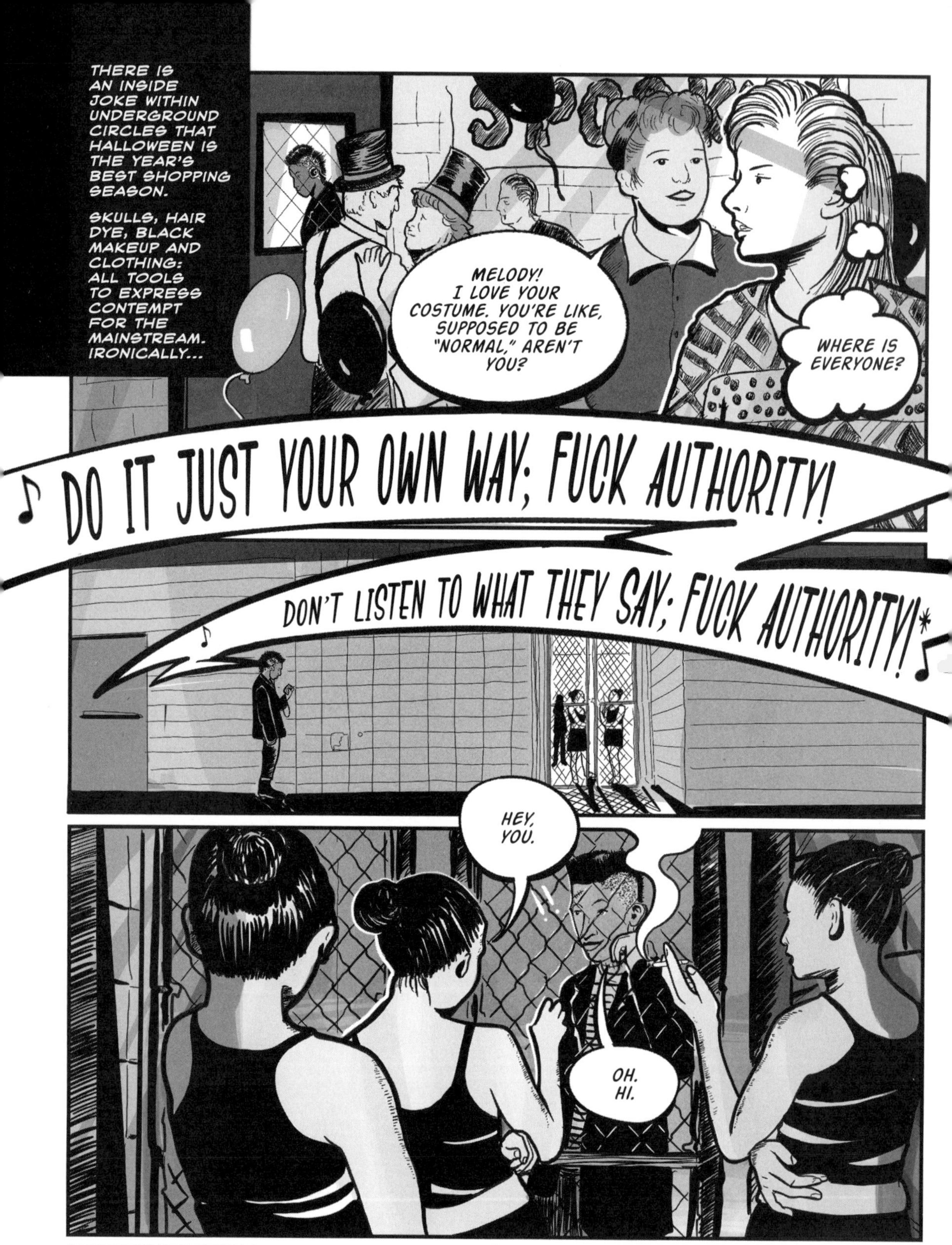
THERE IS AN INSIDE JOKE WITHIN UNDERGROUND CIRCLES THAT HALLOWEEN IS THE YEAR'S BEST SHOPPING SEASON.
SKULLS, HAIR DYE, BLACK MAKEUP AND CLOTHING: ALL TOOLS TO EXPRESS CONTEMPT FOR THE MAINSTREAM. IRONICALLY...
MELODY! I LOVE YOUR COSTUME. YOU'RE LIKE, SUPPOSED TO BE "NORMAL," AREN'T YOU?
WHERE IS EVERYONE?
♪ DO IT JUST YOUR OWN WAY; FUCK AUTHORITY!
♪ DON'T LISTEN TO WHAT THEY SAY; FUCK AUTHORITY!* ♪
HEY, YOU.
OH. HI.

*WASTED YOUTH "FUCK AUTHORITY"

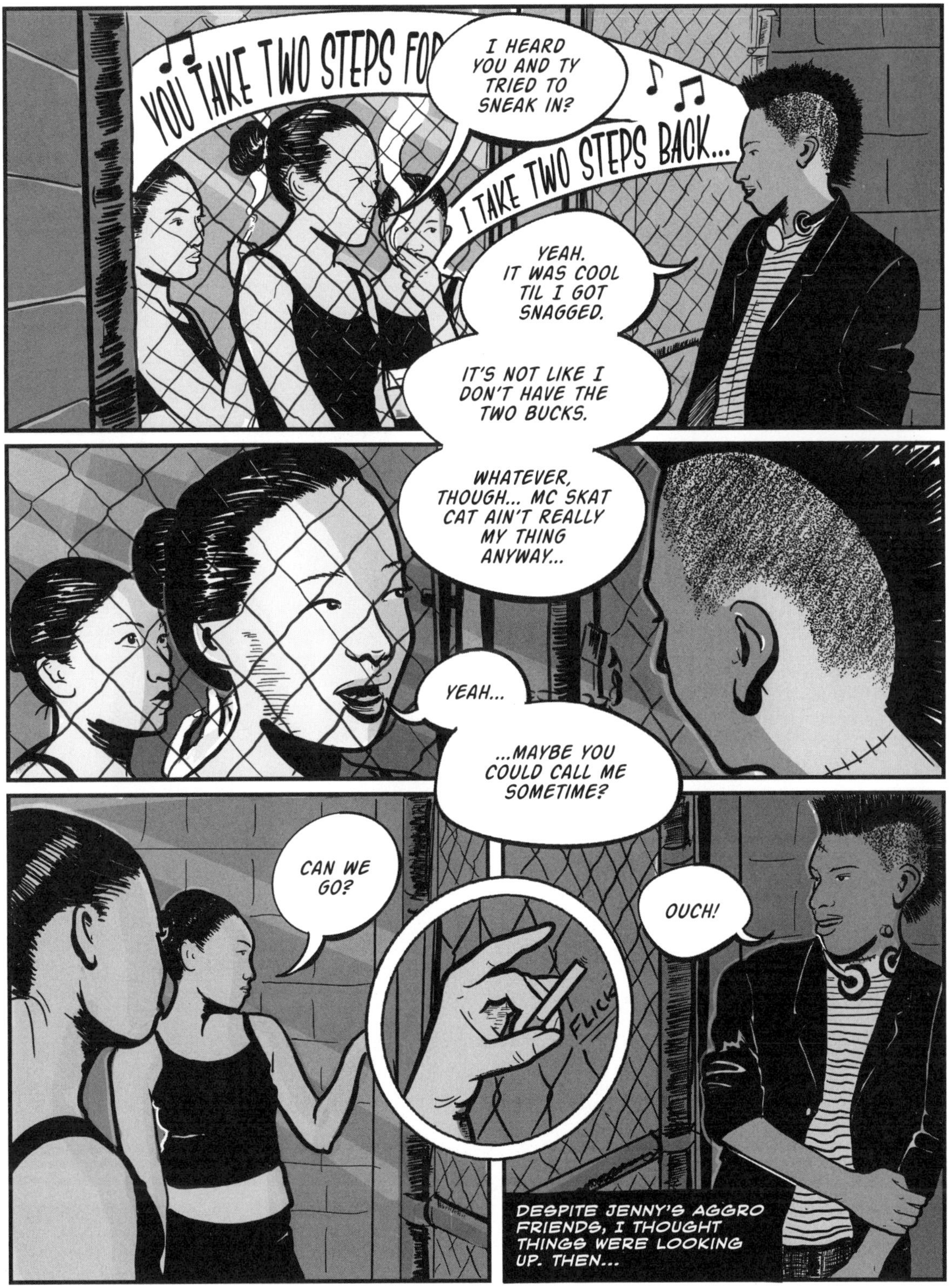
YOU TAKE TWO STEPS FOR
I HEARD YOU AND TY TRIED TO SNEAK IN?
I TAKE TWO STEPS BACK...
YEAH. IT WAS COOL TIL I GOT SNAGGED.
IT'S NOT LIKE I DON'T HAVE THE TWO BUCKS.
WHATEVER, THOUGH... MC SKAT CAT AIN'T REALLY MY THING ANYWAY...
YEAH...
...MAYBE YOU COULD CALL ME SOMETIME?
CAN WE GO?
FLICK
OUCH!
DESPITE JENNY'S AGGRO FRIENDS, I THOUGHT THINGS WERE LOOKING UP. THEN...

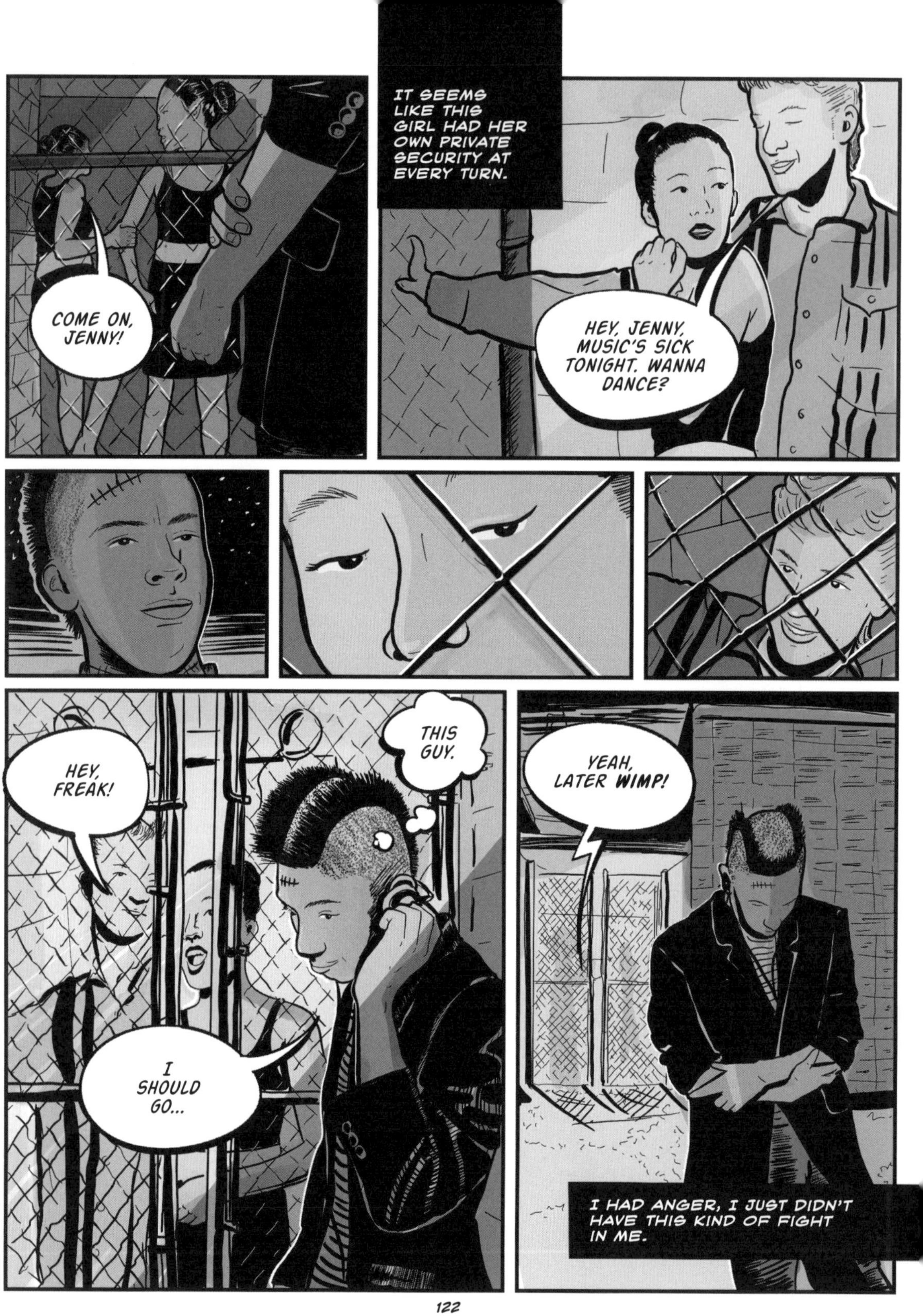
IT SEEMS LIKE THIS GIRL HAD HER OWN PRIVATE SECURITY AT EVERY TURN.
COME ON, JENNY!
HEY, JENNY, MUSIC'S SICK TONIGHT. WANNA DANCE?
HEY, FREAK!
THIS GUY.
I SHOULD GO...
YEAH, LATER WIMP!
I HAD ANGER, I JUST DIDN'T HAVE THIS KIND OF FIGHT IN ME.

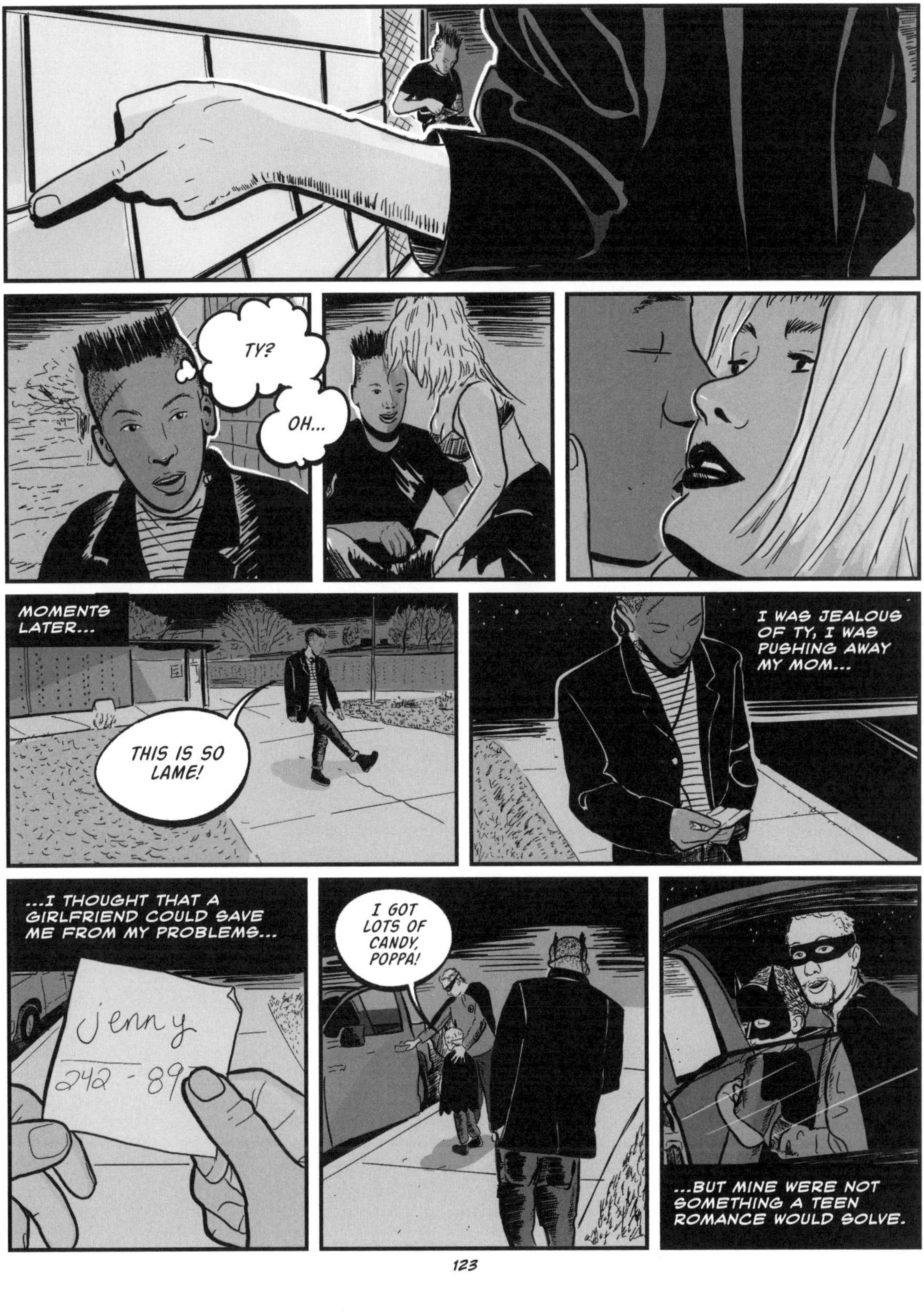
TY?
OH...
MOMENTS LATER...
THIS IS SO LAME!
I WAS JEALOUS OF TY, I WAS PUSHING AWAY MY MOM...
...I THOUGHT THAT A GIRLFRIEND COULD SAVE ME FROM MY PROBLEMS...
jenny
242 - 89
I GOT LOTS OF CANDY, POPPA!
...BUT MINE WERE NOT SOMETHING A TEEN ROMANCE WOULD SOLVE.

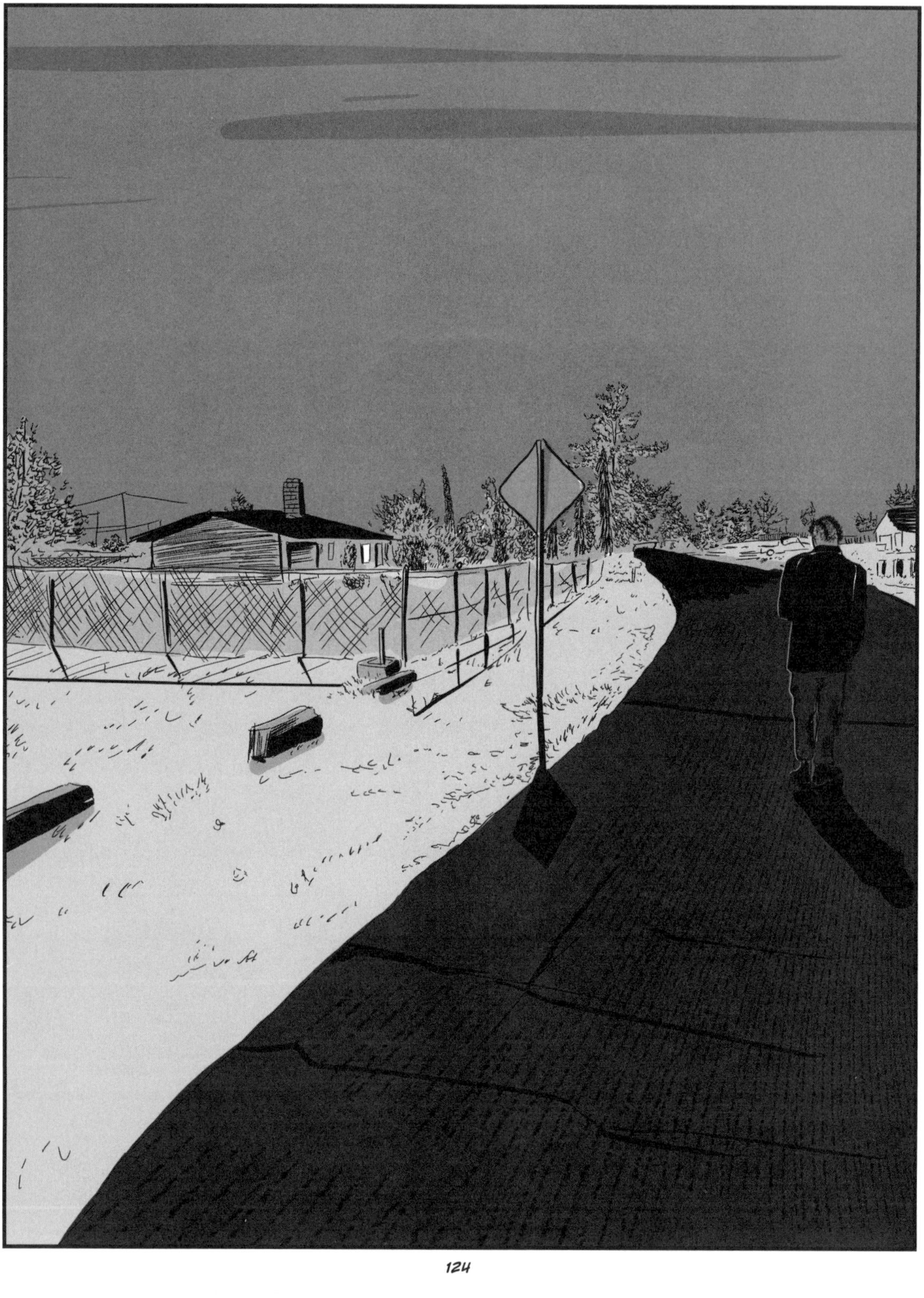

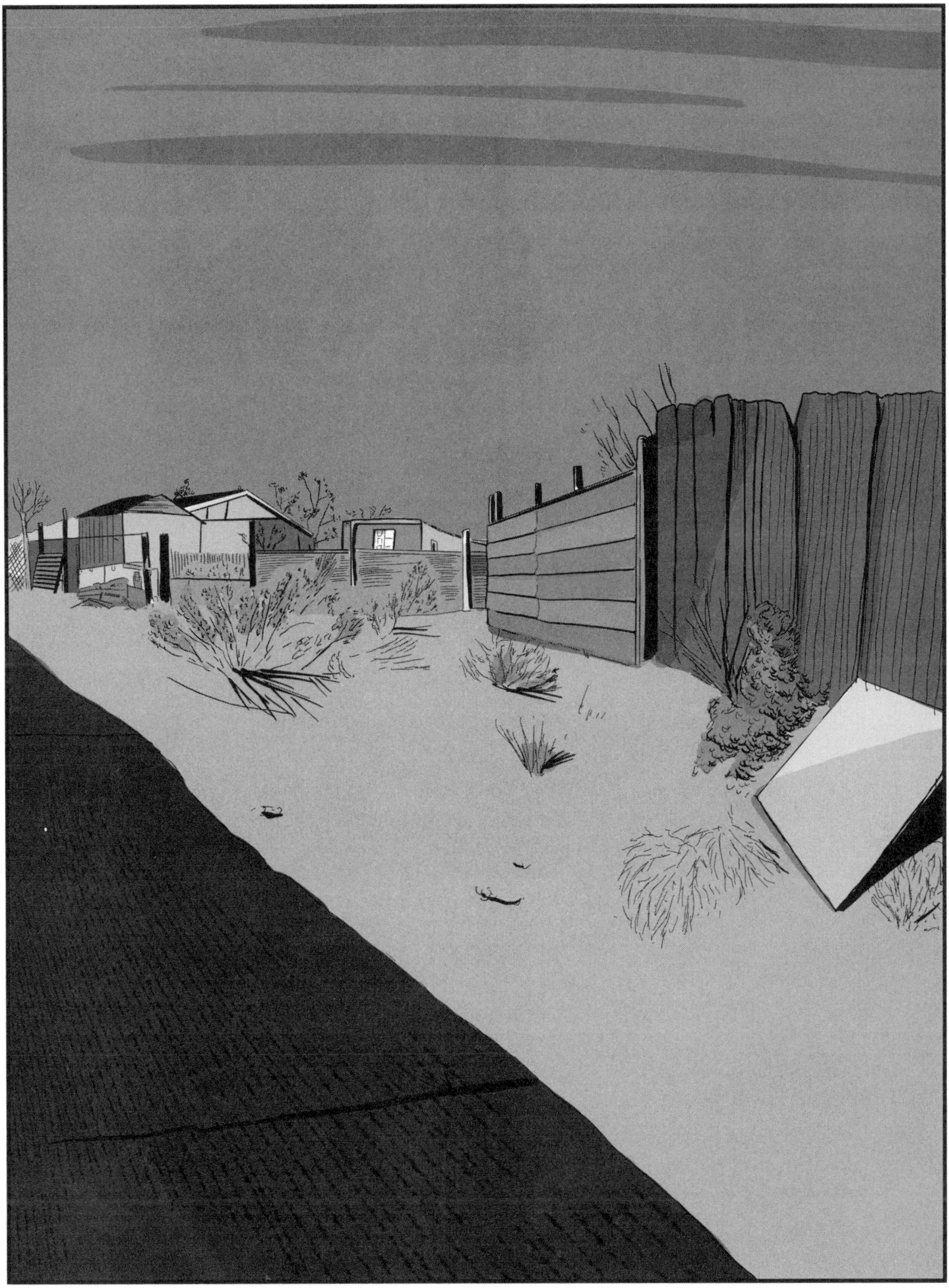

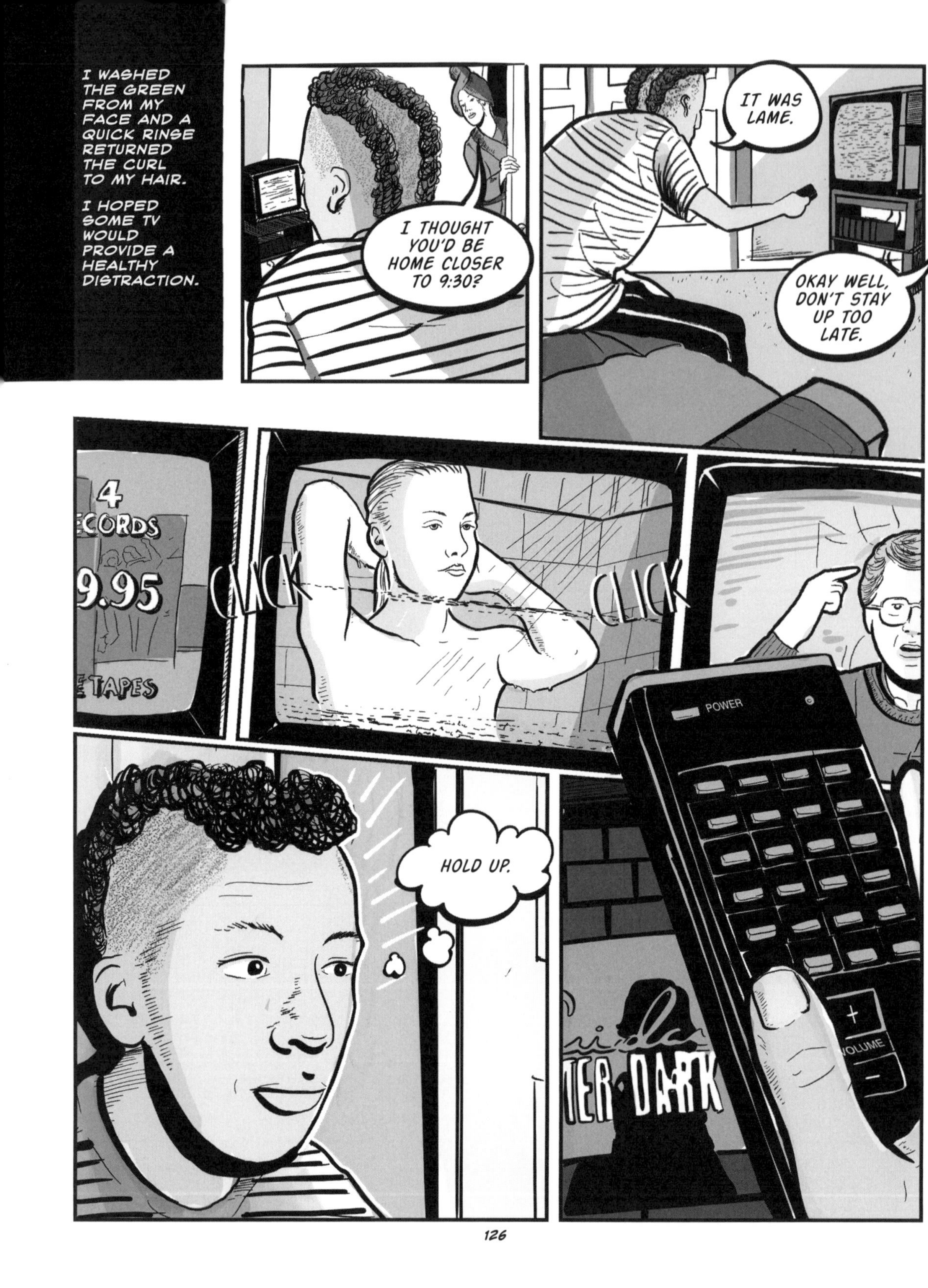
I WASHED THE GREEN FROM MY FACE AND A QUICK RINSE RETURNED THE CURL TO MY HAIR.
I HOPED SOME TV WOULD PROVIDE A HEALTHY DISTRACTION.
I THOUGHT YOU'D BE HOME CLOSER TO 9:30?
IT WAS LAME.
OKAY WELL, DON'T STAY UP TOO LATE.
4
9.95
CLICK
CLICK
POWER
HOLD UP.
VOLUME

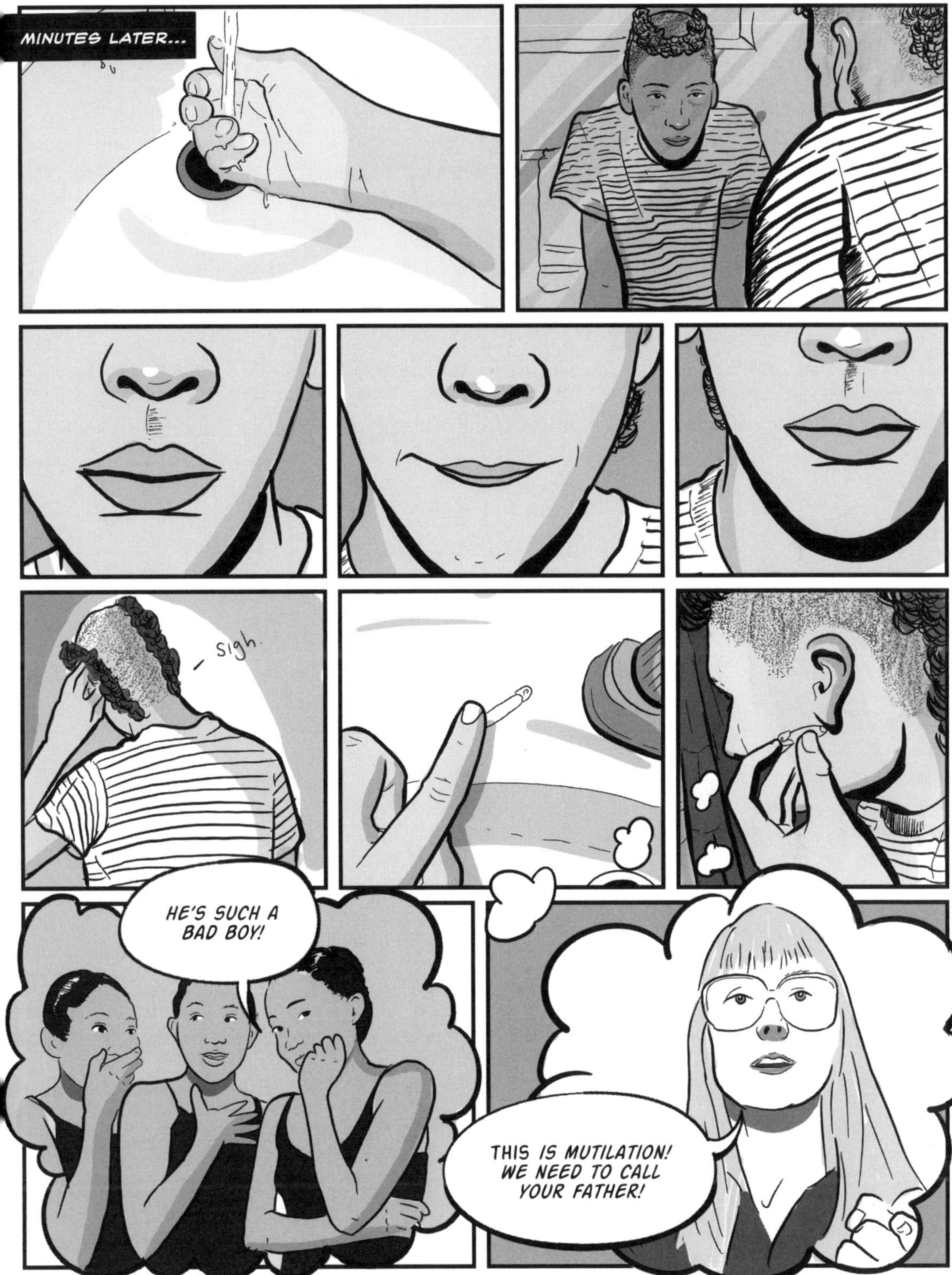
MINUTES LATER...
sigh.
HE'S SUCH A BAD BOY!
THIS IS MUTILATION! WE NEED TO CALL YOUR FATHER!

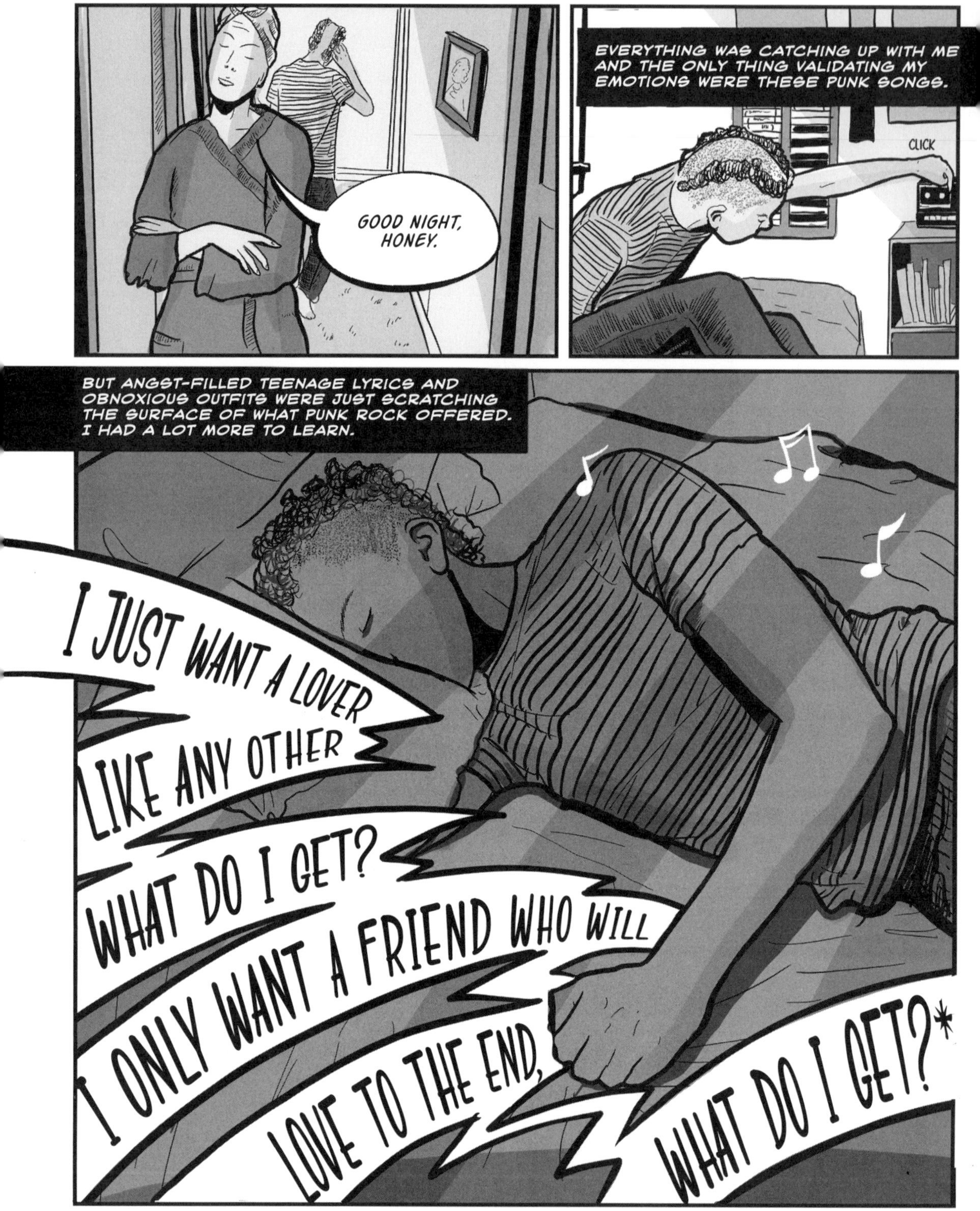
GOOD NIGHT, HONEY.
EVERYTHING WAS CATCHING UP WITH ME AND THE ONLY THING VALIDATING MY EMOTIONS WERE THESE PUNK SONGS.
CLICK
BUT ANGST-FILLED TEENAGE LYRICS AND OBNOXIOUS OUTFITS WERE JUST SCRATCHING THE SURFACE OF WHAT PUNK ROCK OFFERED. I HAD A LOT MORE TO LEARN.
I JUST WANT A LOVER
LIKE ANY OTHER
WHAT DO I GET?
I ONLY WANT A FRIEND WHO WILL
LOVE TO THE END,
WHAT DO I GET?*

*BUZZCOCKS "WHAT DO I GET?"

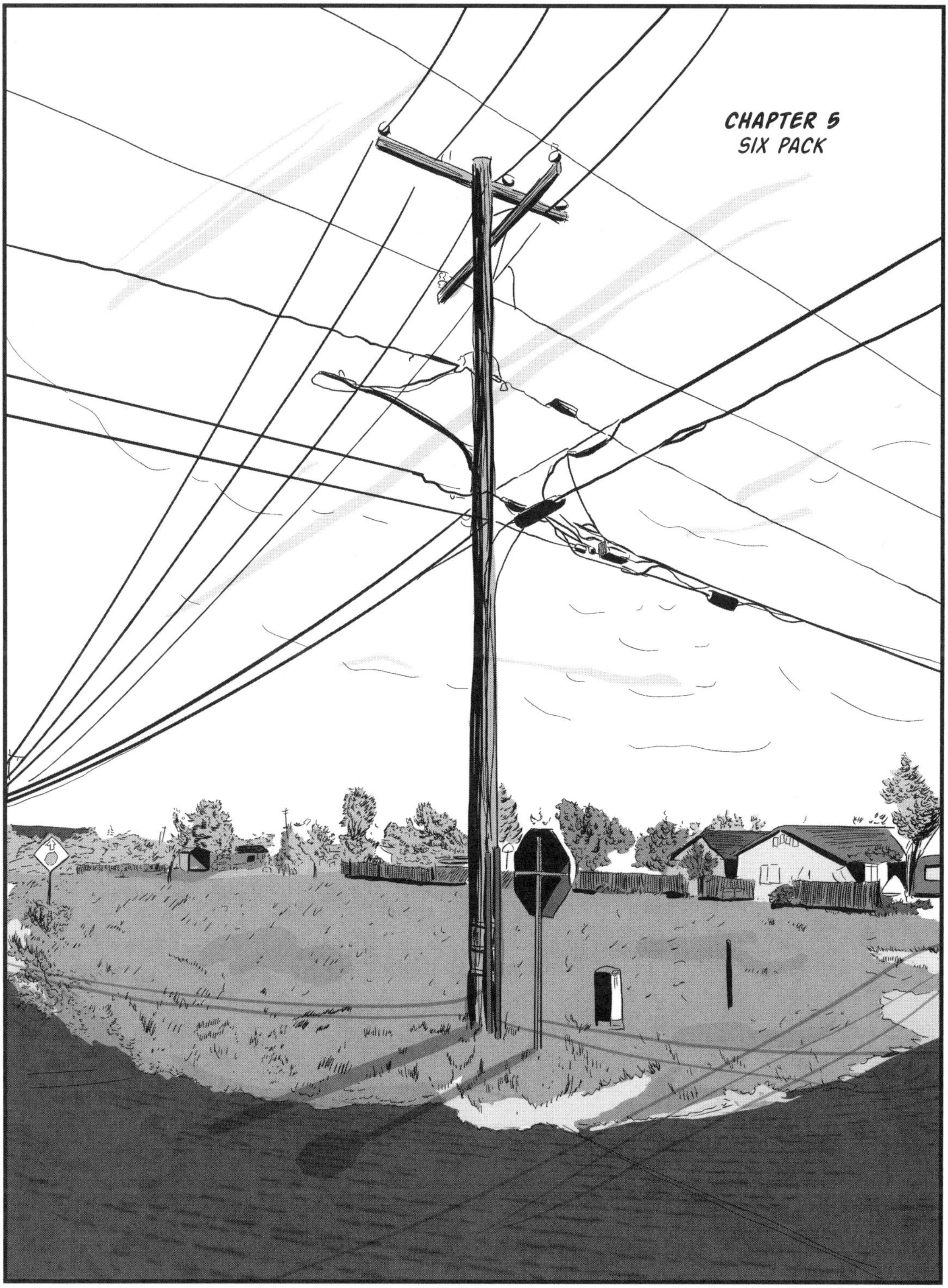
CHAPTER 5
SIX PACK

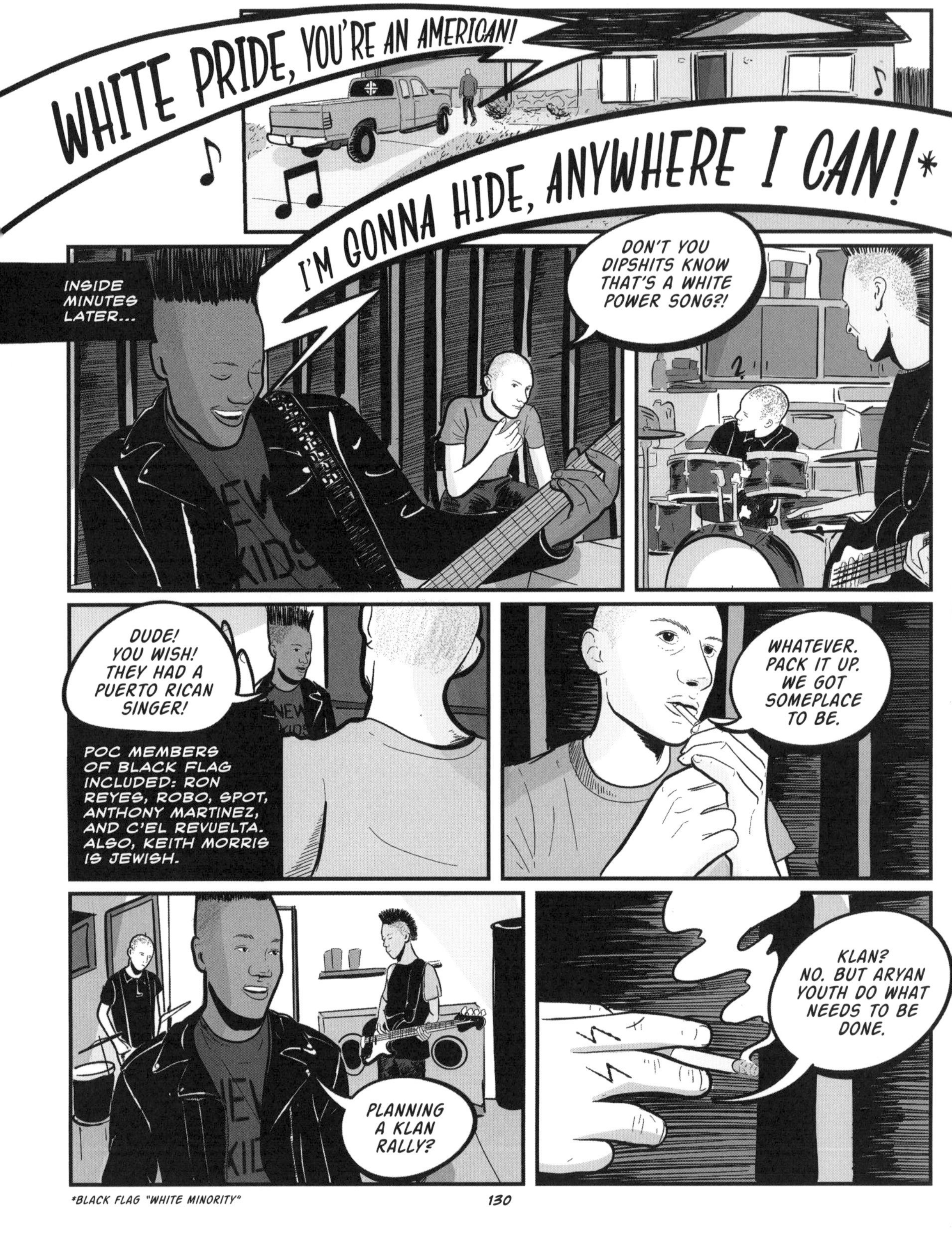

WHITE PRIDE, YOU'RE AN AMERICAN!
I'M GONNA HIDE, ANYWHERE I CAN!*
INSIDE MINUTES LATER...
DON'T YOU DIPSHITS KNOW THAT'S A WHITE POWER SONG?!
DUDE! YOU WISH! THEY HAD A PUERTO RICAN SINGER!
POC MEMBERS OF BLACK FLAG INCLUDED: RON REYES, ROBO, SPOT, ANTHONY MARTINEZ, AND C'EL REVUELTA. ALSO, KEITH MORRIS IS JEWISH.
WHATEVER. PACK IT UP. WE GOT SOMEPLACE TO BE.
PLANNING A KLAN RALLY?
KLAN? NO. BUT ARYAN YOUTH DO WHAT NEEDS TO BE DONE.

*BLACK FLAG "WHITE MINORITY"

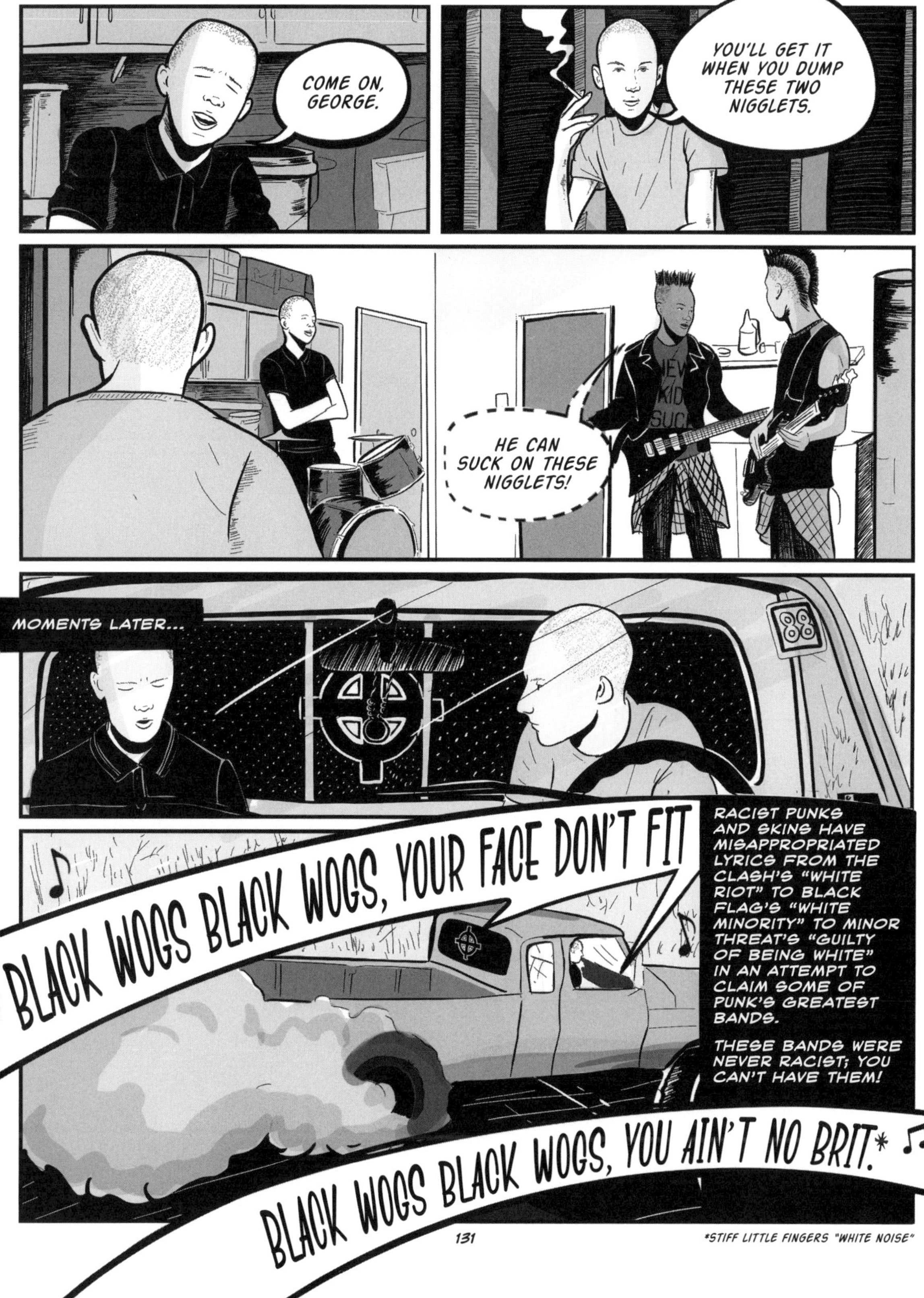
COME ON, GEORGE.
YOU'LL GET IT WHEN YOU DUMP THESE TWO NIGGLETS.
HE CAN SUCK ON THESE NIGGLETS!
NEW KIDS SUCK
MOMENTS LATER...
88
BLACK WOGS BLACK WOGS, YOUR FACE DON'T FIT
RACIST PUNKS AND SKINS HAVE MISAPPROPRIATED LYRICS FROM THE CLASH'S "WHITE RIOT" TO BLACK FLAG'S "WHITE MINORITY" TO MINOR THREAT'S "GUILTY OF BEING WHITE" IN AN ATTEMPT TO CLAIM SOME OF PUNK'S GREATEST BANDS.
THESE BANDS WERE NEVER RACIST; YOU CAN'T HAVE THEM!
BLACK WOGS BLACK WOGS, YOU AIN'T NO BRIT.*

*STIFF LITTLE FINGERS "WHITE NOISE"

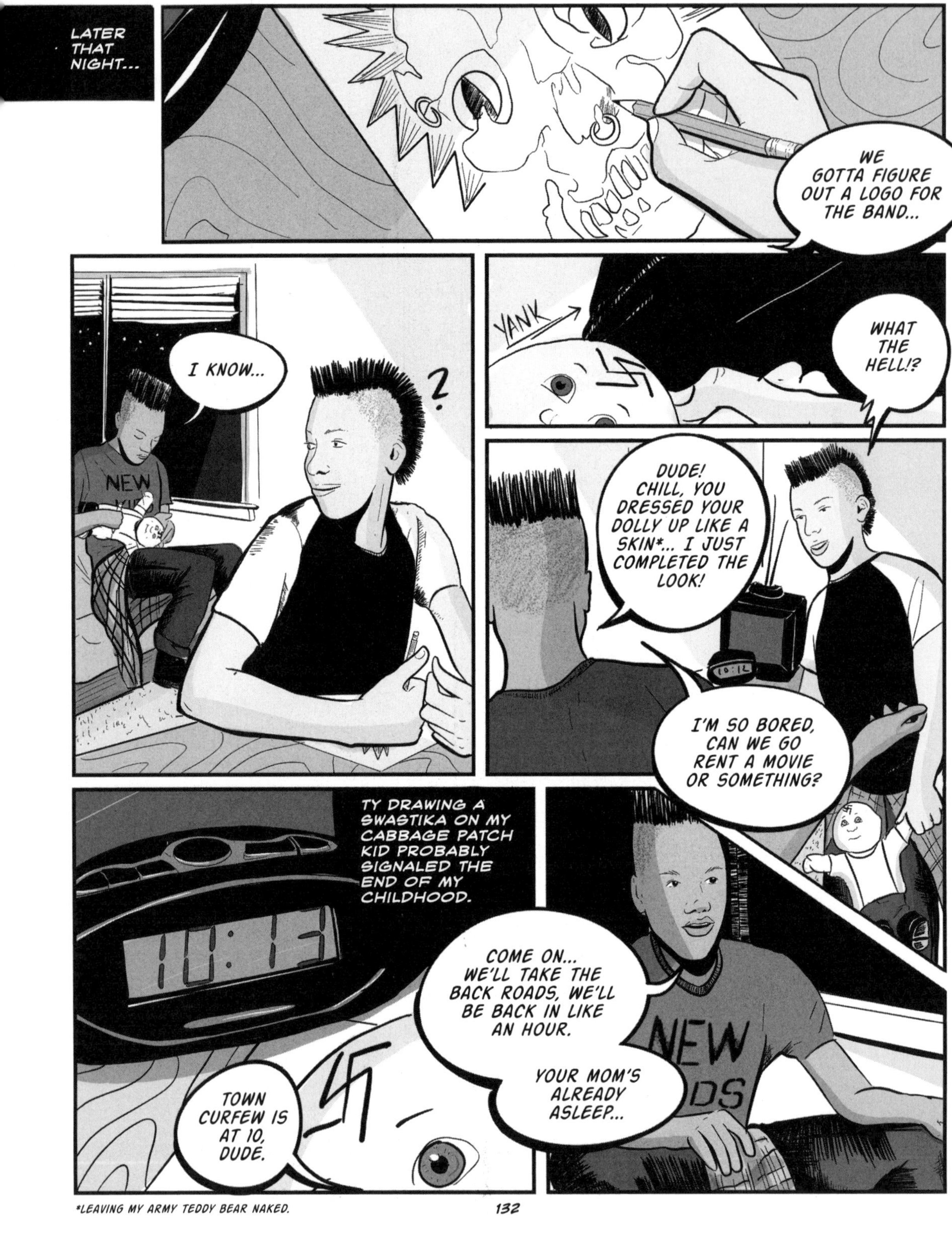
LATER THAT NIGHT...
WE GOTTA FIGURE OUT A LOGO FOR THE BAND...
I KNOW...
?
YANK
WHAT THE HELL!?
DUDE! CHILL, YOU DRESSED YOUR DOLLY UP LIKE A SKIN*... I JUST COMPLETED THE LOOK!
I'M SO BORED, CAN WE GO RENT A MOVIE OR SOMETHING?
TY DRAWING A SWASTIKA ON MY CABBAGE PATCH KID PROBABLY SIGNALED THE END OF MY CHILDHOOD.
10:13
COME ON... WE'LL TAKE THE BACK ROADS, WE'LL BE BACK IN LIKE AN HOUR.
YOUR MOM'S ALREADY ASLEEP...
TOWN CURFEW IS AT 10, DUDE.

*LEAVING MY ARMY TEDDY BEAR NAKED.

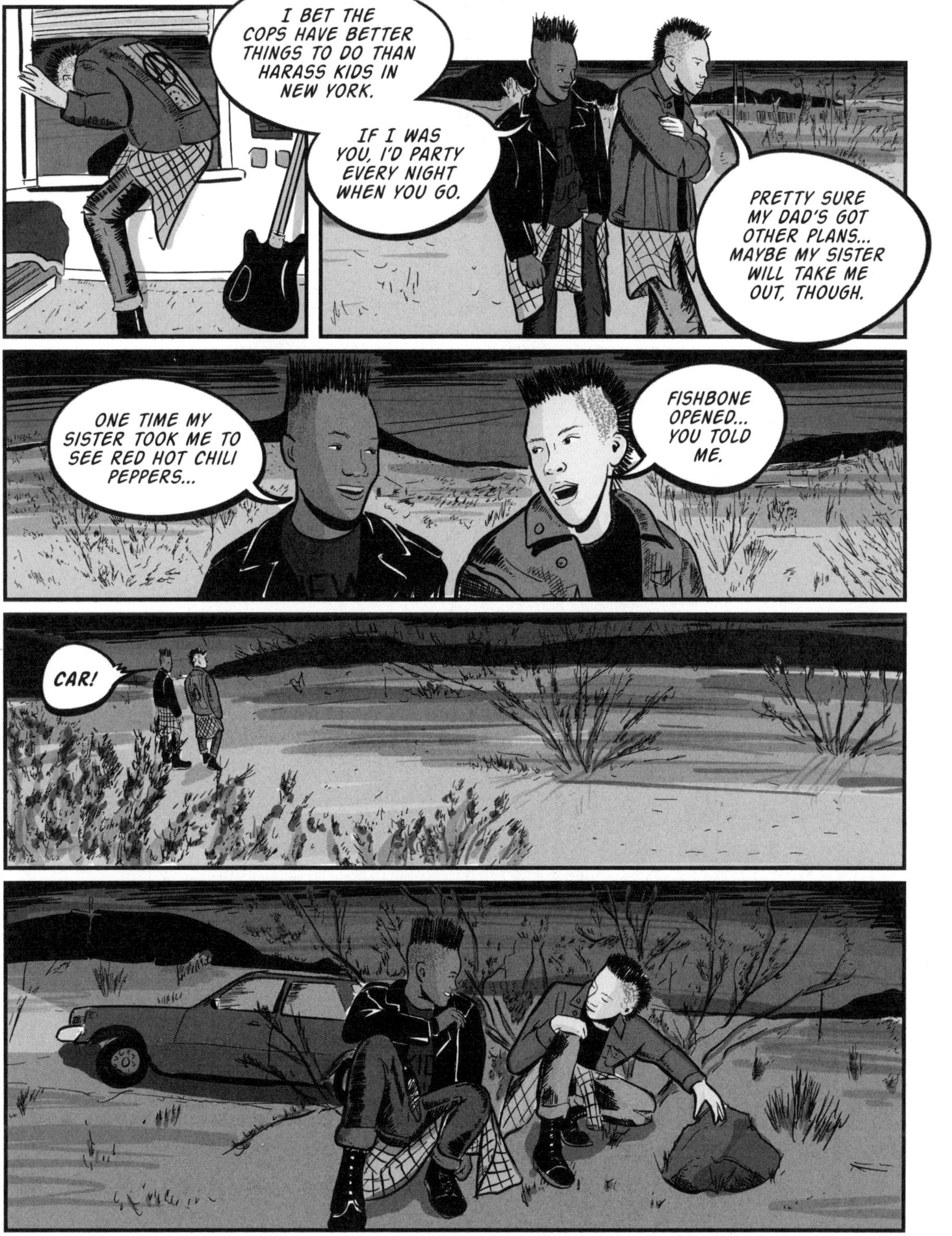
I BET THE COPS HAVE BETTER THINGS TO DO THAN HARASS KIDS IN NEW YORK.
IF I WAS YOU, I'D PARTY EVERY NIGHT WHEN YOU GO.
PRETTY SURE MY DAD'S GOT OTHER PLANS... MAYBE MY SISTER WILL TAKE ME OUT, THOUGH.
ONE TIME MY SISTER TOOK ME TO SEE RED HOT CHILI PEPPERS...
FISHBONE OPENED... YOU TOLD ME.
CAR!

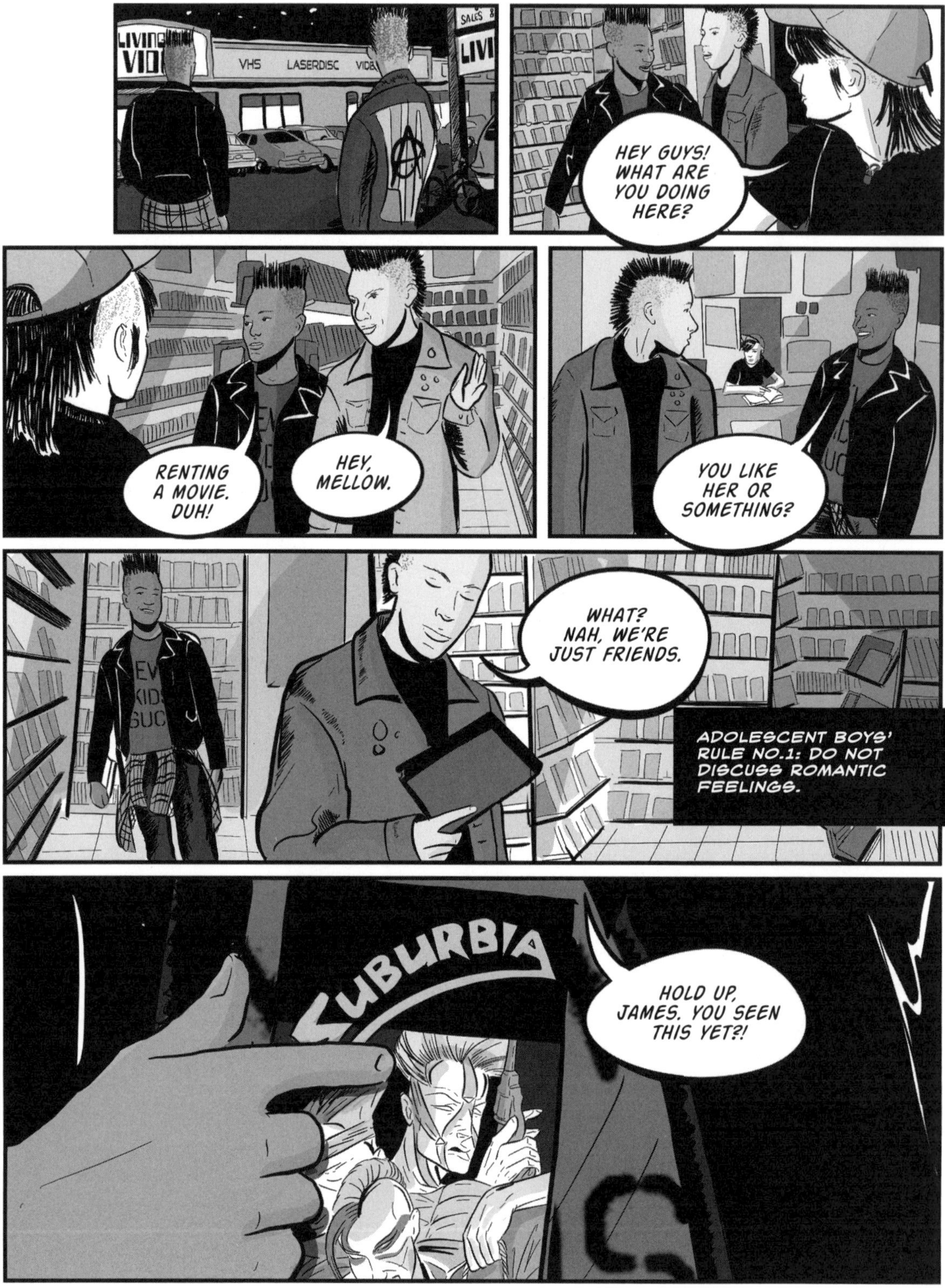
LIVING VID
VHS LASERDISC VIDE
SALES
LIVI
HEY GUYS! WHAT ARE YOU DOING HERE?
RENTING A MOVIE. DUH!
HEY, MELLOW.
YOU LIKE HER OR SOMETHING?
WHAT? NAH, WE'RE JUST FRIENDS.
ADOLESCENT BOYS' RULE NO.1: DO NOT DISCUSS ROMANTIC FEELINGS.
SUBURBIA
HOLD UP, JAMES. YOU SEEN THIS YET?!

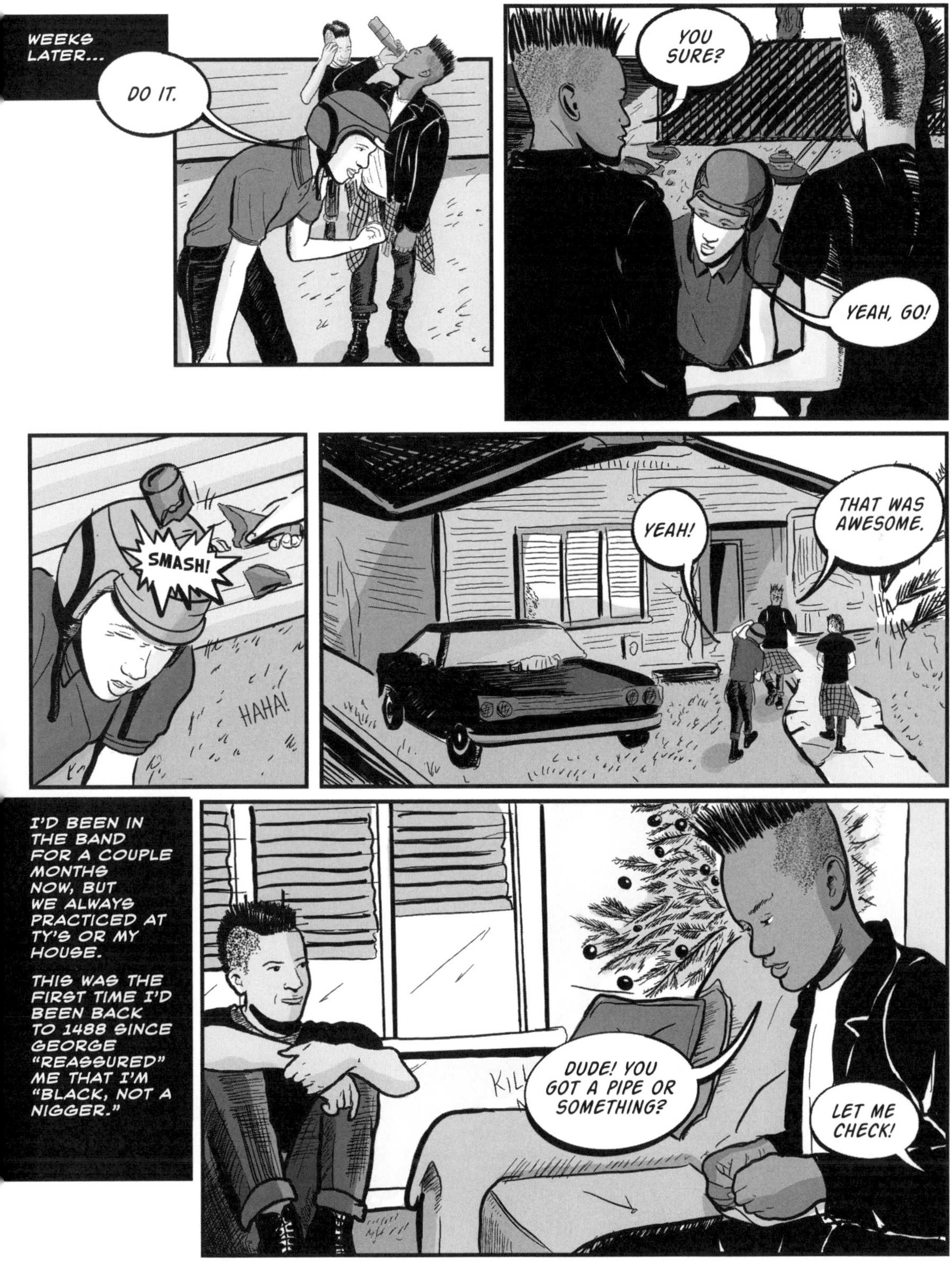
WEEKS LATER...
DO IT.
YOU SURE?
YEAH, GO!
SMASH!
HAHA!
YEAH!
THAT WAS AWESOME.
HA HA
I'D BEEN IN THE BAND FOR A COUPLE MONTHS NOW, BUT WE ALWAYS PRACTICED AT TY'S OR MY HOUSE.
THIS WAS THE FIRST TIME I'D BEEN BACK TO 1488 SINCE GEORGE "REASSURED" ME THAT I'M "BLACK, NOT A NIGGER."
DUDE! YOU GOT A PIPE OR SOMETHING?
LET ME CHECK!

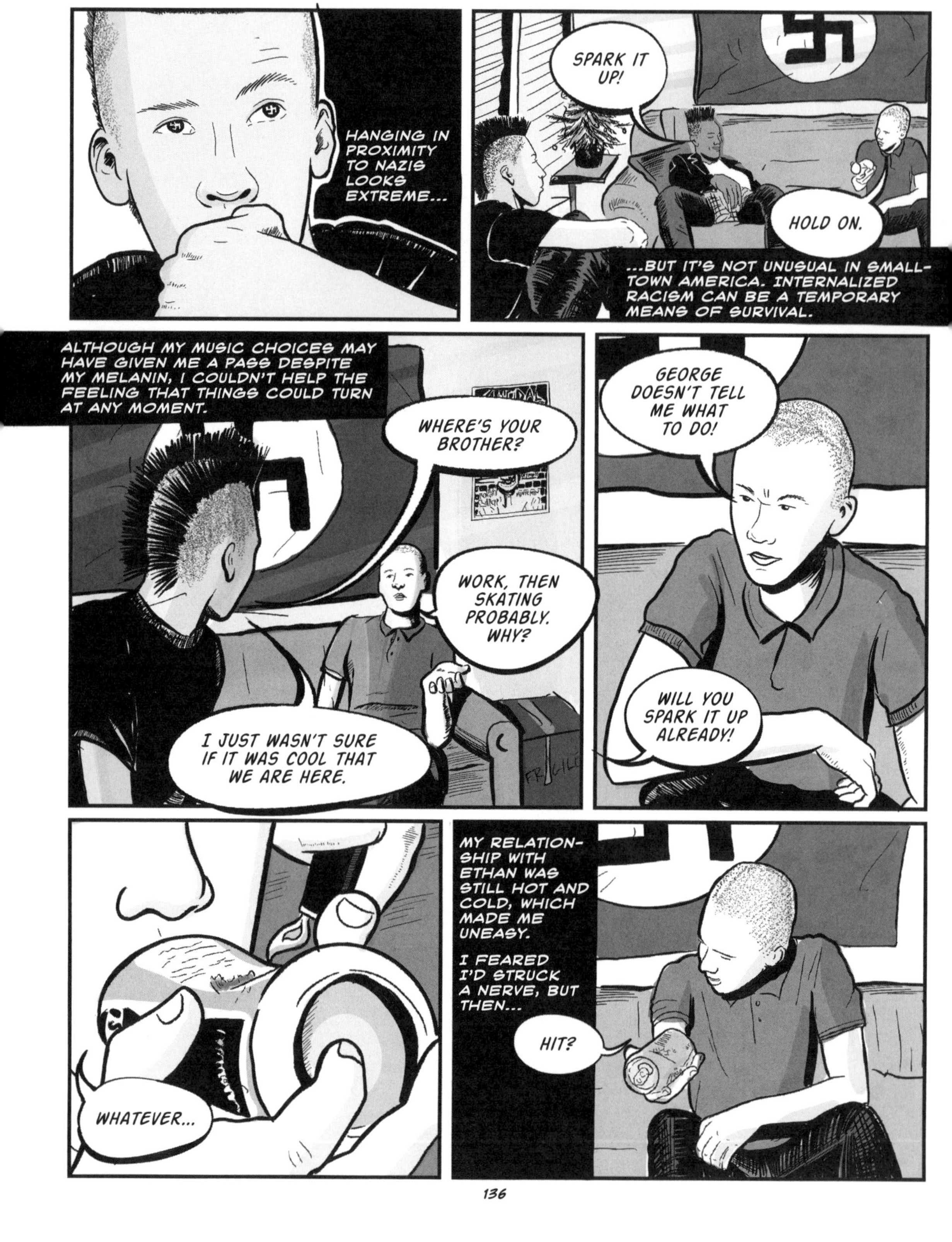
HANGING IN PROXIMITY TO NAZIS LOOKS EXTREME...
SPARK IT UP!
HOLD ON.
...BUT IT'S NOT UNUSUAL IN SMALL-TOWN AMERICA. INTERNALIZED RACISM CAN BE A TEMPORARY MEANS OF SURVIVAL.
ALTHOUGH MY MUSIC CHOICES MAY HAVE GIVEN ME A PASS DESPITE MY MELANIN, I COULDN'T HELP THE FEELING THAT THINGS COULD TURN AT ANY MOMENT.
WHERE'S YOUR BROTHER?
WORK, THEN SKATING PROBABLY. WHY?
I JUST WASN'T SURE IF IT WAS COOL THAT WE ARE HERE.
GEORGE DOESN'T TELL ME WHAT TO DO!
WILL YOU SPARK IT UP ALREADY!
WHATEVER...
MY RELATIONSHIP WITH ETHAN WAS STILL HOT AND COLD, WHICH MADE ME UNEASY.
I FEARED I'D STRUCK A NERVE, BUT THEN...
HIT?

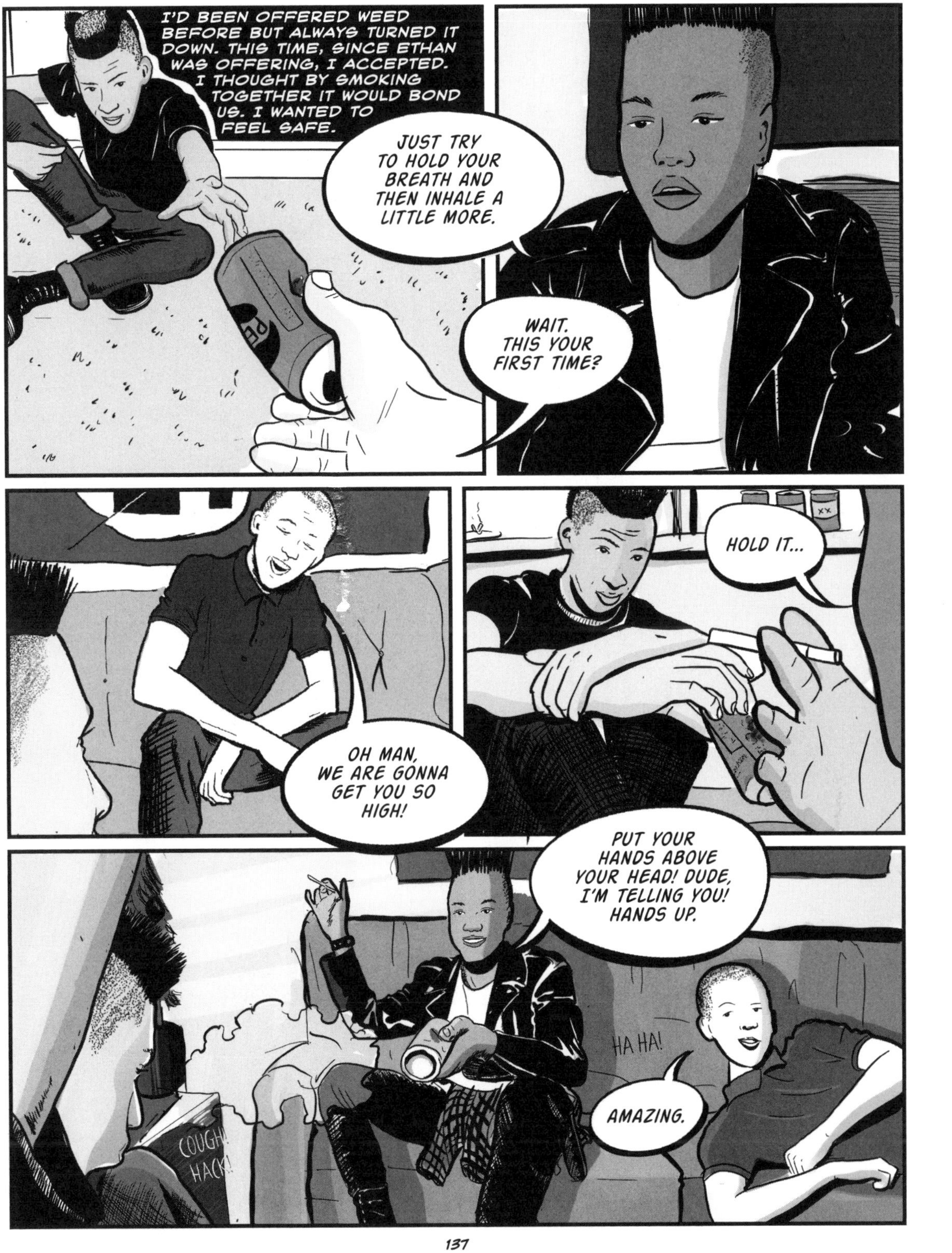
I'D BEEN OFFERED WEED BEFORE BUT ALWAYS TURNED IT DOWN. THIS TIME, SINCE ETHAN WAS OFFERING, I ACCEPTED. I THOUGHT BY SMOKING TOGETHER IT WOULD BOND US. I WANTED TO FEEL SAFE.
JUST TRY TO HOLD YOUR BREATH AND THEN INHALE A LITTLE MORE.
WAIT. THIS YOUR FIRST TIME?
OH MAN, WE ARE GONNA GET YOU SO HIGH!
HOLD IT...
PUT YOUR HANDS ABOVE YOUR HEAD! DUDE, I'M TELLING YOU! HANDS UP.
HA HA!
AMAZING.
COUGH! HACK!

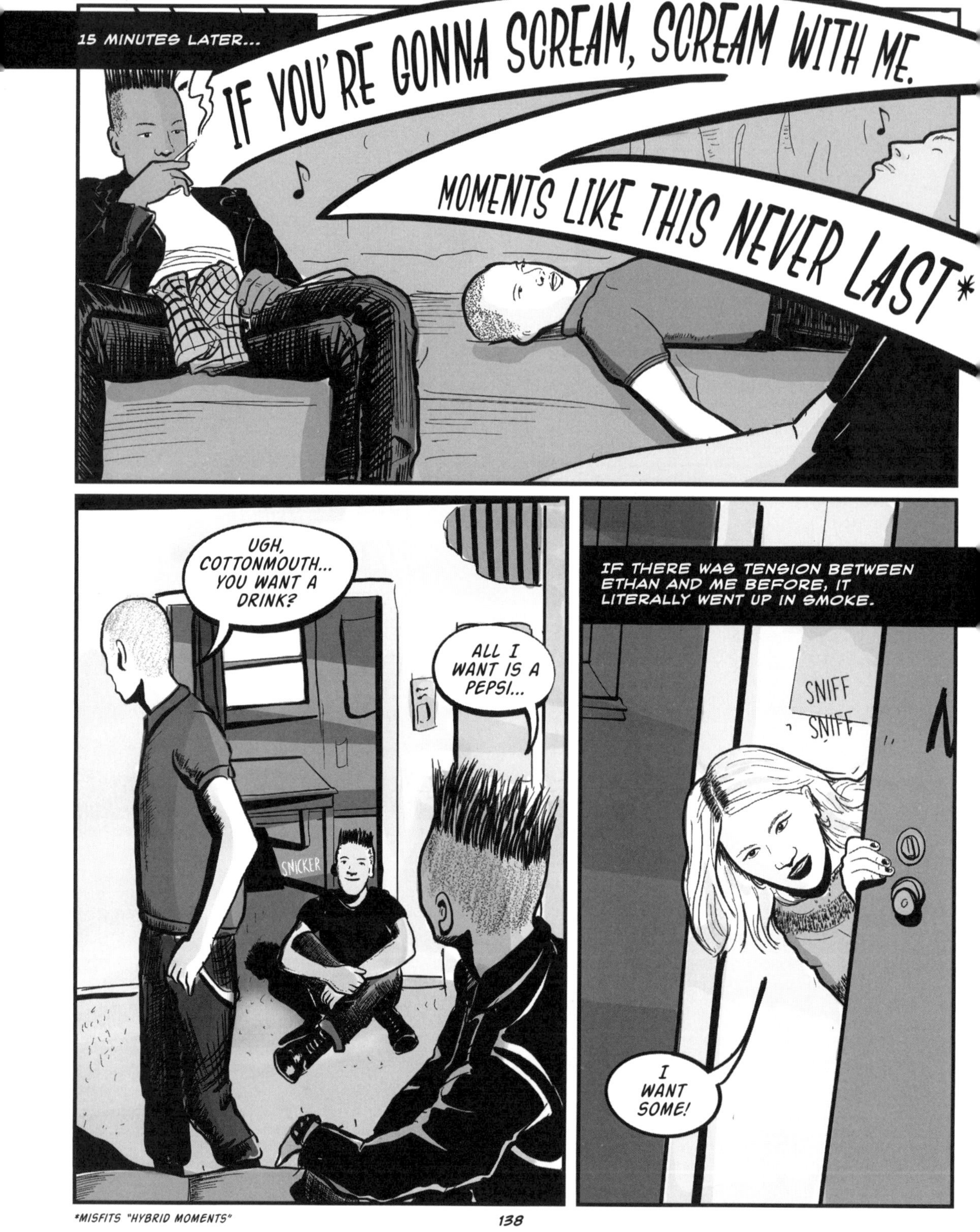
15 MINUTES LATER...
IF YOU'RE GONNA SCREAM, SCREAM WITH ME.
MOMENTS LIKE THIS NEVER LAST*
UGH, COTTONMOUTH... YOU WANT A DRINK?
ALL I WANT IS A PEPSI...
SNICKER
IF THERE WAS TENSION BETWEEN ETHAN AND ME BEFORE, IT LITERALLY WENT UP IN SMOKE.
SNIFF
SNIFF
I WANT SOME!

*MISFITS "HYBRID MOMENTS"

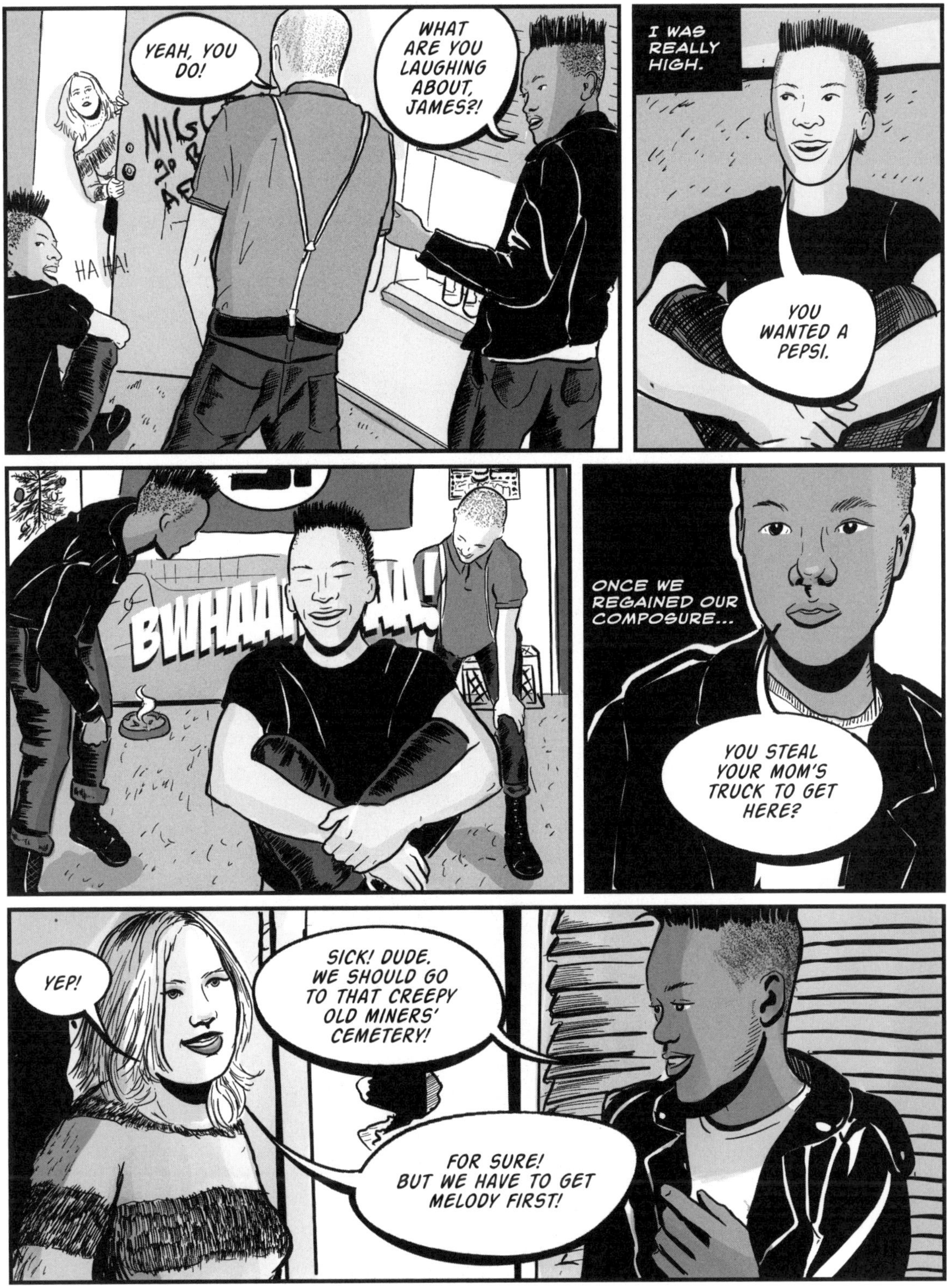
YEAH, YOU DO!
HA HA!
WHAT ARE YOU LAUGHING ABOUT, JAMES?!
I WAS REALLY HIGH.
YOU WANTED A PEPSI.
ONCE WE REGAINED OUR COMPOSURE...
YOU STEAL YOUR MOM'S TRUCK TO GET HERE?
YEP!
SICK! DUDE. WE SHOULD GO TO THAT CREEPY OLD MINERS' CEMETERY!
FOR SURE! BUT WE HAVE TO GET MELODY FIRST!

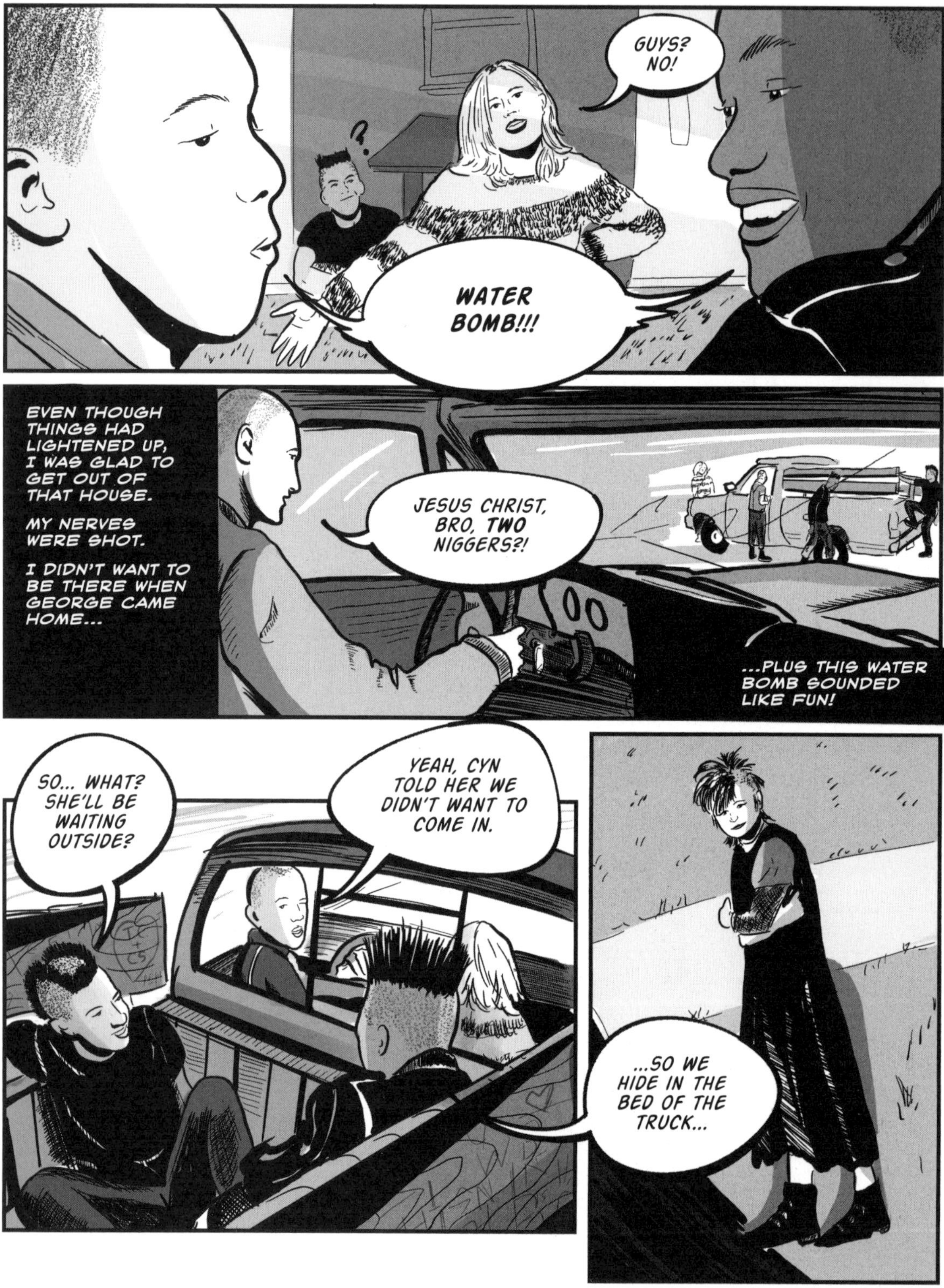
GUYS? NO!
WATER BOMB!!!
EVEN THOUGH THINGS HAD LIGHTENED UP, I WAS GLAD TO GET OUT OF THAT HOUSE.
MY NERVES WERE SHOT.
I DIDN'T WANT TO BE THERE WHEN GEORGE CAME HOME...
JESUS CHRIST, BRO, TWO NIGGERS?!
...PLUS THIS WATER BOMB SOUNDED LIKE FUN!
SO... WHAT? SHE'LL BE WAITING OUTSIDE?
YEAH, CYN TOLD HER WE DIDN'T WANT TO COME IN.
...SO WE HIDE IN THE BED OF THE TRUCK...

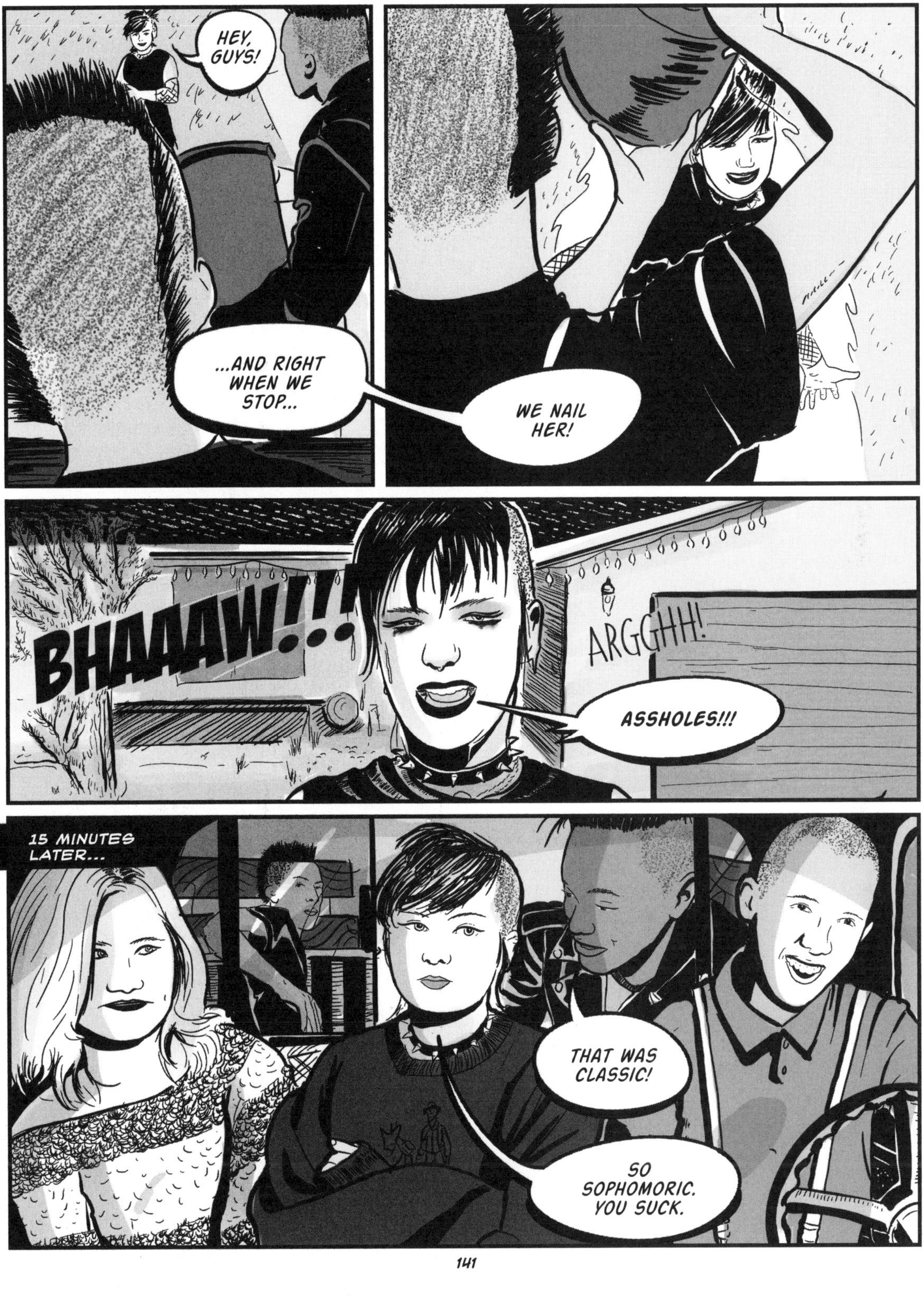
HEY, GUYS!
...AND RIGHT WHEN WE STOP...
WE NAIL HER!
BHAAAW!!!...
ARGGHH!
ASSHOLES!!!
15 MINUTES LATER...
THAT WAS CLASSIC!
SO SOPHOMORIC. YOU SUCK.

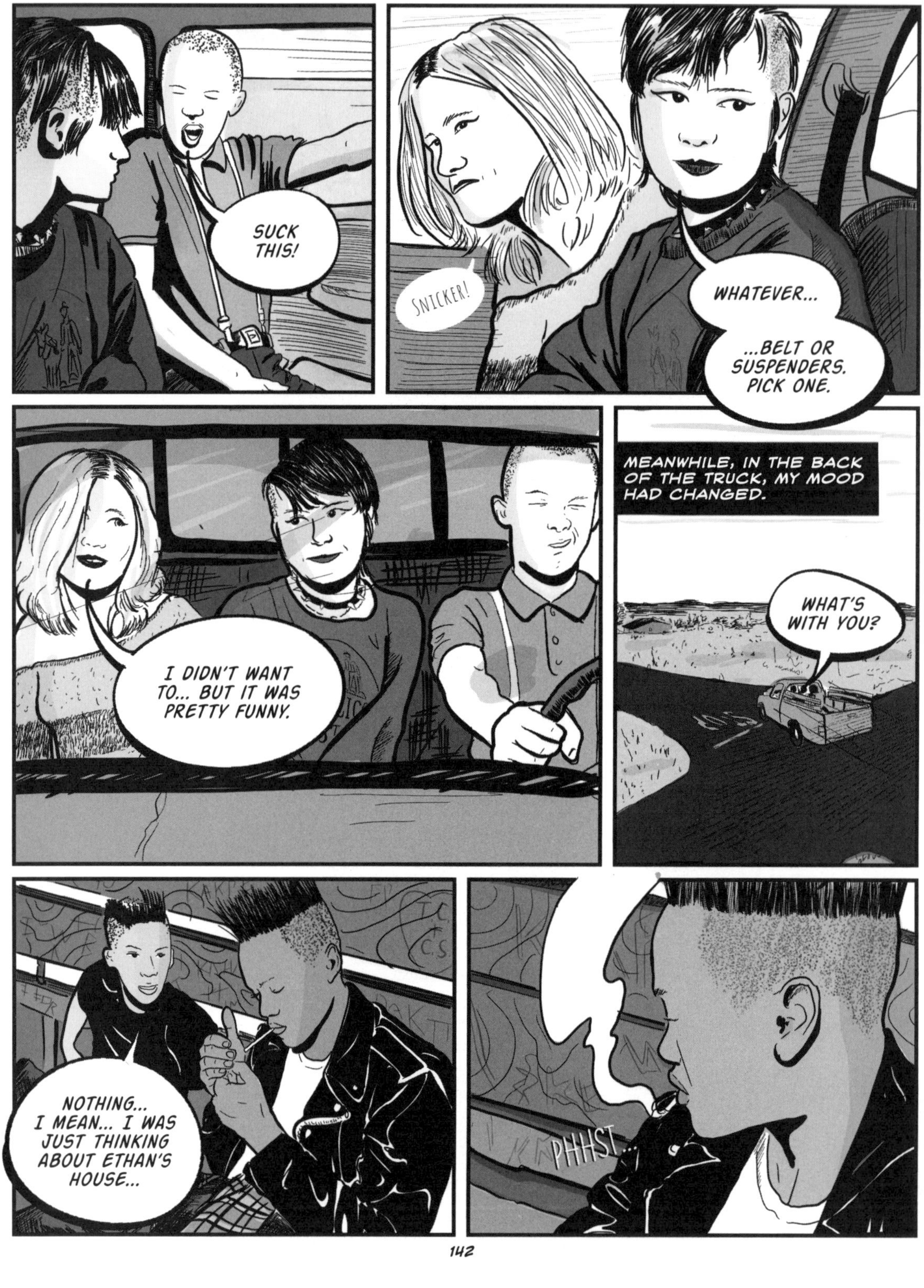
SUCK THIS!
SNICKER!
WHATEVER...
...BELT OR SUSPENDERS. PICK ONE.
I DIDN'T WANT TO... BUT IT WAS PRETTY FUNNY.
MEANWHILE, IN THE BACK OF THE TRUCK, MY MOOD HAD CHANGED.
WHAT'S WITH YOU?
NOTHING... I MEAN... I WAS JUST THINKING ABOUT ETHAN'S HOUSE...
PHHST...

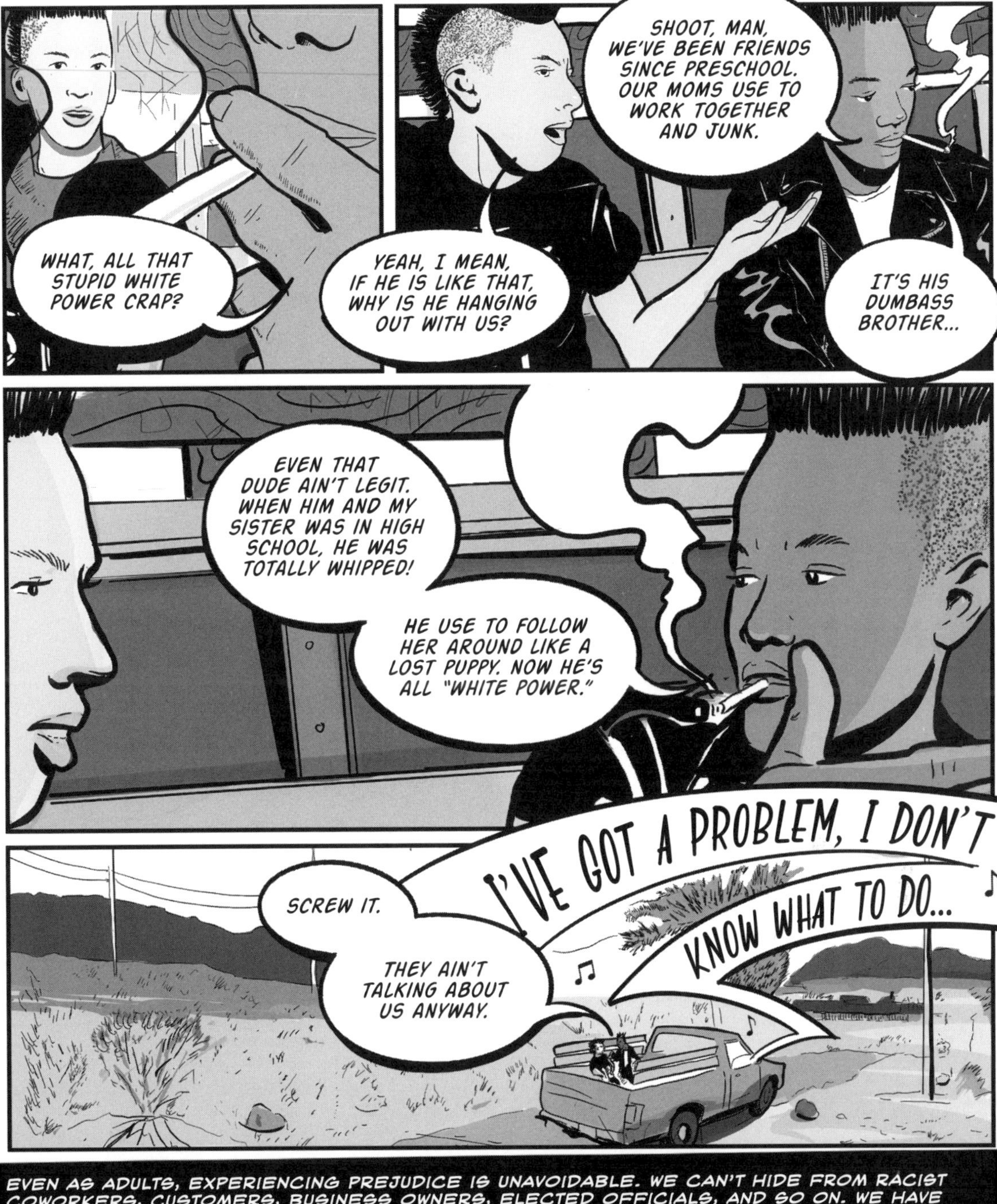
WHAT, ALL THAT STUPID WHITE POWER CRAP?
YEAH, I MEAN, IF HE IS LIKE THAT, WHY IS HE HANGING OUT WITH US?
SHOOT, MAN, WE'VE BEEN FRIENDS SINCE PRESCHOOL. OUR MOMS USE TO WORK TOGETHER AND JUNK.
IT'S HIS DUMBASS BROTHER...
EVEN THAT DUDE AIN'T LEGIT. WHEN HIM AND MY SISTER WAS IN HIGH SCHOOL, HE WAS TOTALLY WHIPPED!
HE USE TO FOLLOW HER AROUND LIKE A LOST PUPPY. NOW HE'S ALL "WHITE POWER."
SCREW IT.
THEY AIN'T TALKING ABOUT US ANYWAY.
I'VE GOT A PROBLEM, I DON'T KNOW WHAT TO DO...

EVEN AS ADULTS, EXPERIENCING PREJUDICE IS UNAVOIDABLE. WE CAN'T HIDE FROM RACIST COWORKERS, CUSTOMERS, BUSINESS OWNERS, ELECTED OFFICIALS, AND SO ON. WE HAVE ALWAYS HAD TO MAKE CHOICES AROUND WHEN WE SPEAK UP AND WHEN WE BITE OUR TONGUES.

THOUGH PART OF ME FEARED THIS WAS AN ELABORATE PRANK ENDING WITH MY CORPSE BEING DUMPED IN THE DESERT, I STAYED QUIET THE REST OF THE RIDE. IT HADN'T OCCURRED TO ME THAT MOST PEOPLE DON'T HAVE TO CONTEMPLATE THE POTENTIAL FOR HOMICIDE IN NEW FRIENDSHIPS.

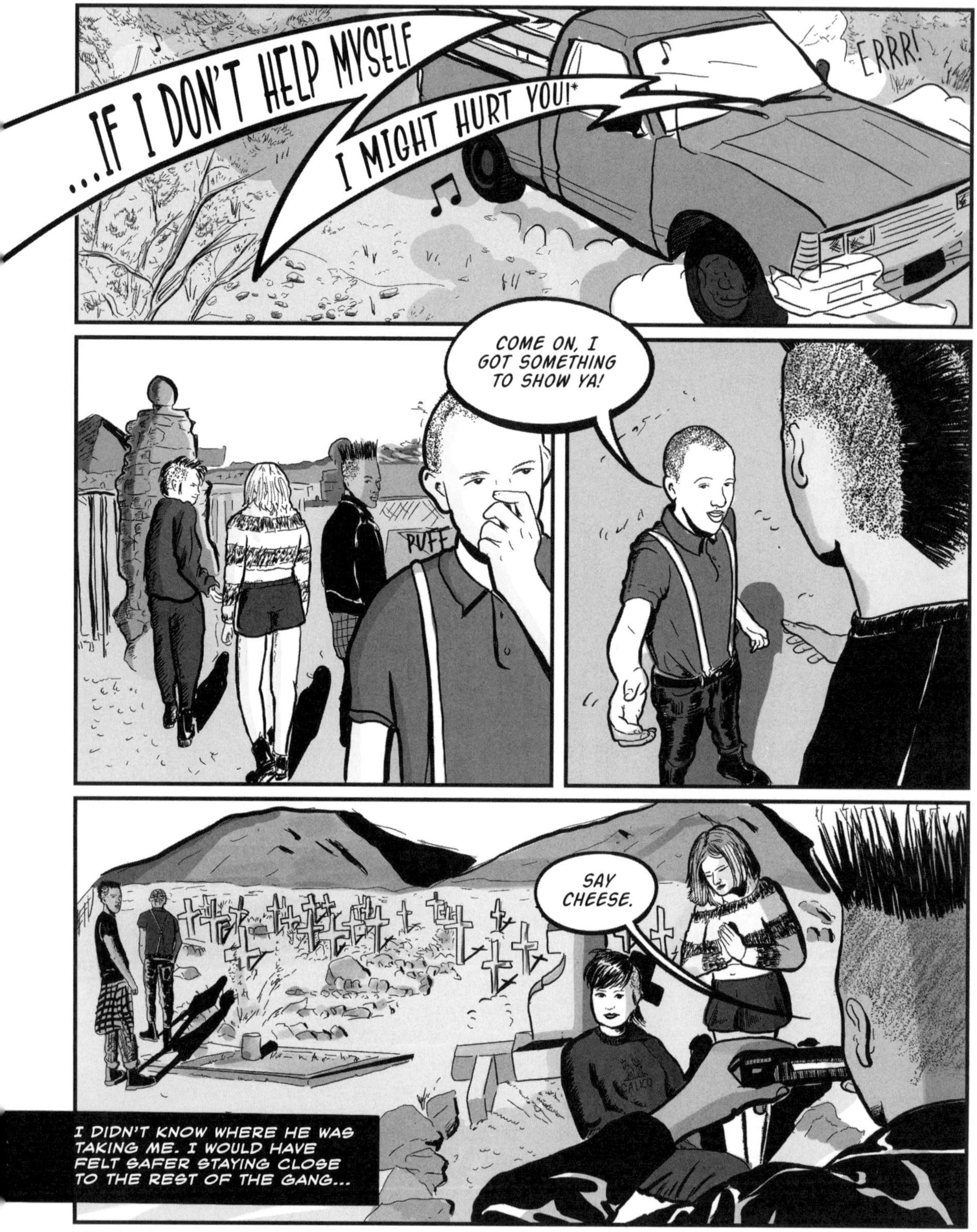
...IF I DON'T HELP MYSELF
I MIGHT HURT YOU!*
ERRR!
PUFF
COME ON, I GOT SOMETHING TO SHOW YA!
SAY CHEESE.
CALICO
I DIDN'T KNOW WHERE HE WAS TAKING ME. I WOULD HAVE FELT SAFER STAYING CLOSE TO THE REST OF THE GANG...

*THE MEATMEN "I'VE GOT A PROBLEM"

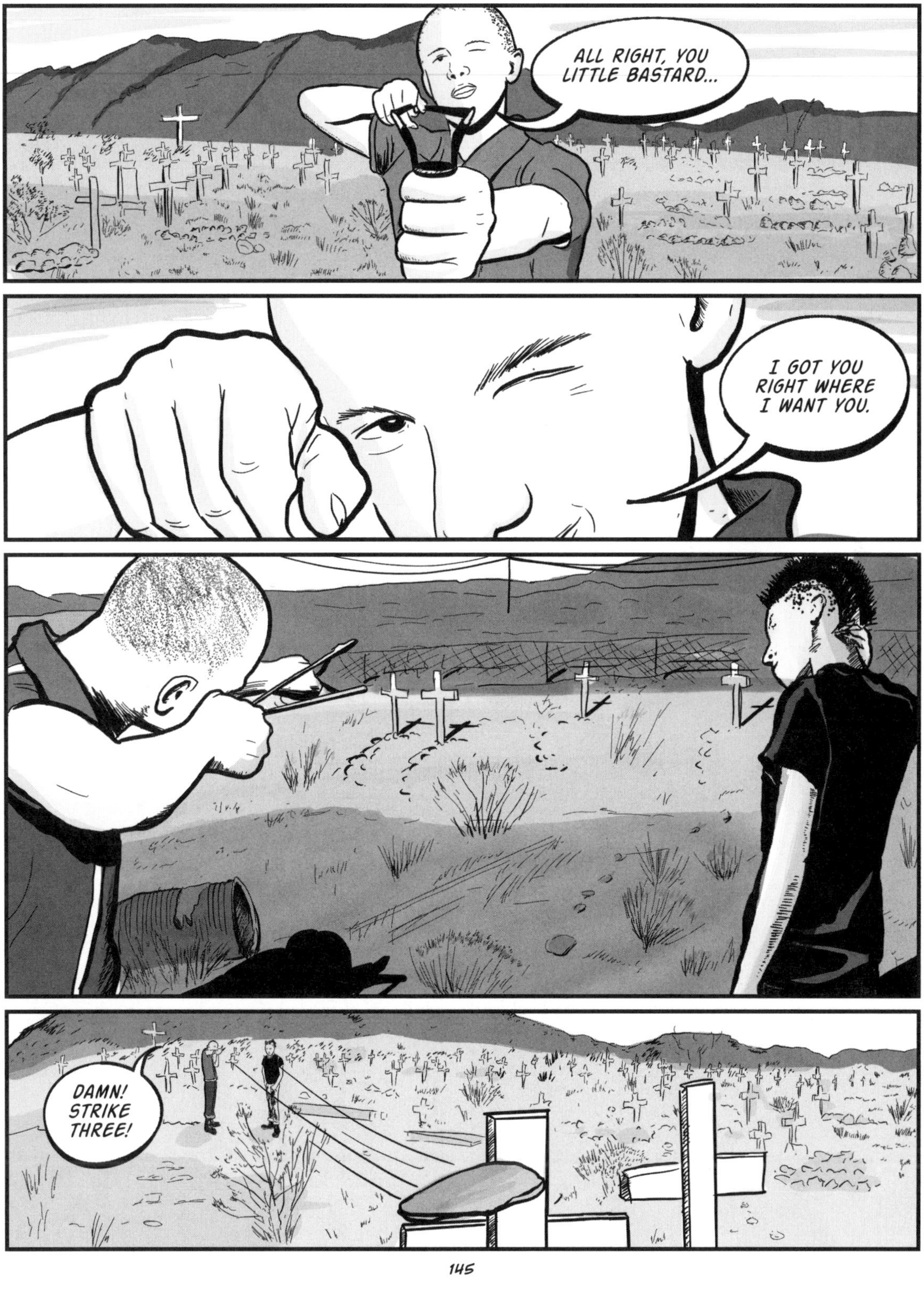
ALL RIGHT, YOU LITTLE BASTARD...
I GOT YOU RIGHT WHERE I WANT YOU.
DAMN! STRIKE THREE!

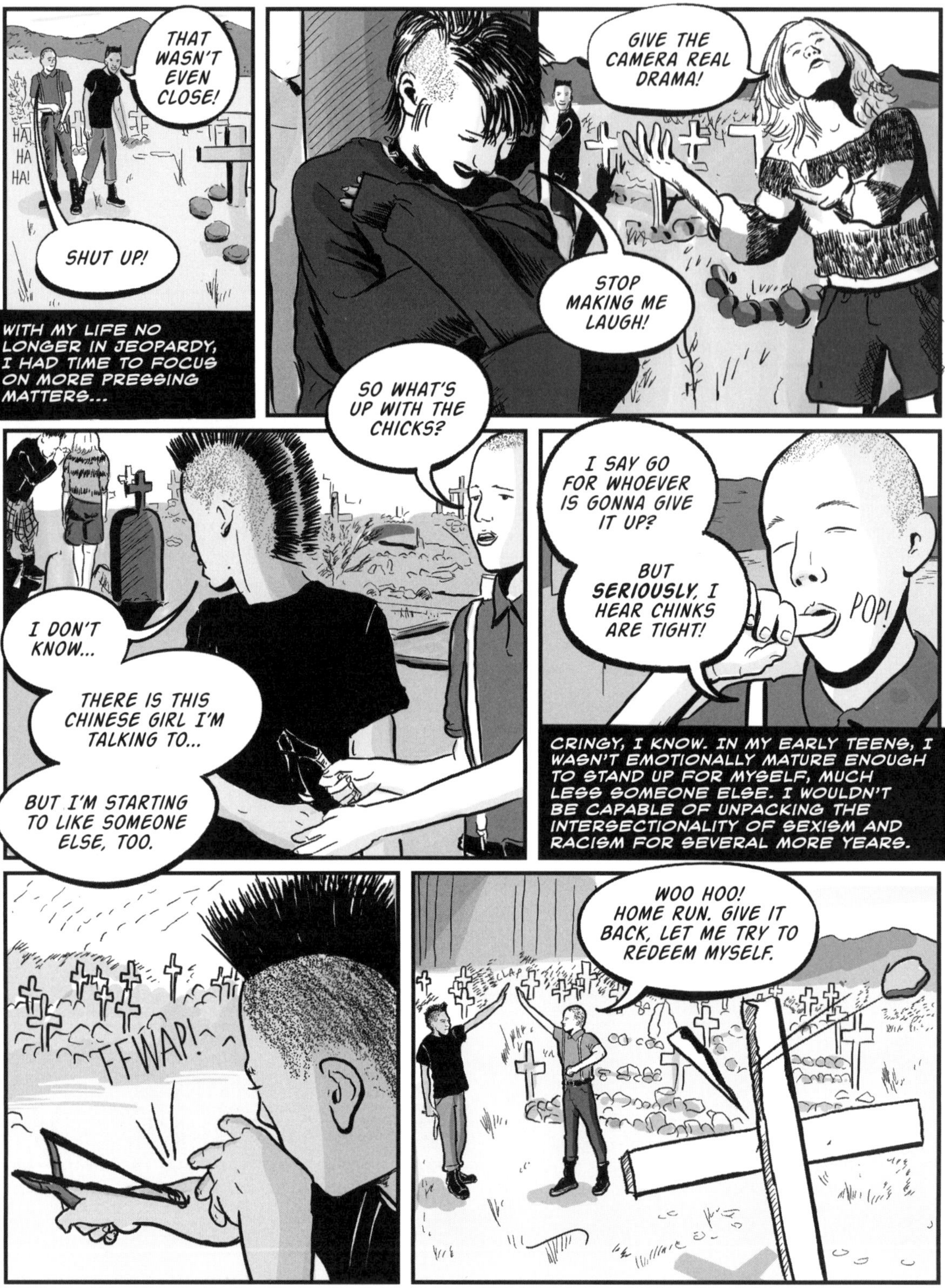

THAT WASN'T EVEN CLOSE!
HA HA HA!
SHUT UP!
WITH MY LIFE NO LONGER IN JEOPARDY, I HAD TIME TO FOCUS ON MORE PRESSING MATTERS...
GIVE THE CAMERA REAL DRAMA!
STOP MAKING ME LAUGH!
SO WHAT'S UP WITH THE CHICKS?
I DON'T KNOW...
THERE IS THIS CHINESE GIRL I'M TALKING TO...
BUT I'M STARTING TO LIKE SOMEONE ELSE, TOO.
I SAY GO FOR WHOEVER IS GONNA GIVE IT UP?
BUT SERIOUSLY, I HEAR CHINKS ARE TIGHT!
POP!
CRINGY, I KNOW. IN MY EARLY TEENS, I WASN'T EMOTIONALLY MATURE ENOUGH TO STAND UP FOR MYSELF, MUCH LESS SOMEONE ELSE. I WOULDN'T BE CAPABLE OF UNPACKING THE INTERSECTIONALITY OF SEXISM AND RACISM FOR SEVERAL MORE YEARS.
FFWAP!
CLAP
WOO HOO! HOME RUN. GIVE IT BACK, LET ME TRY TO REDEEM MYSELF.

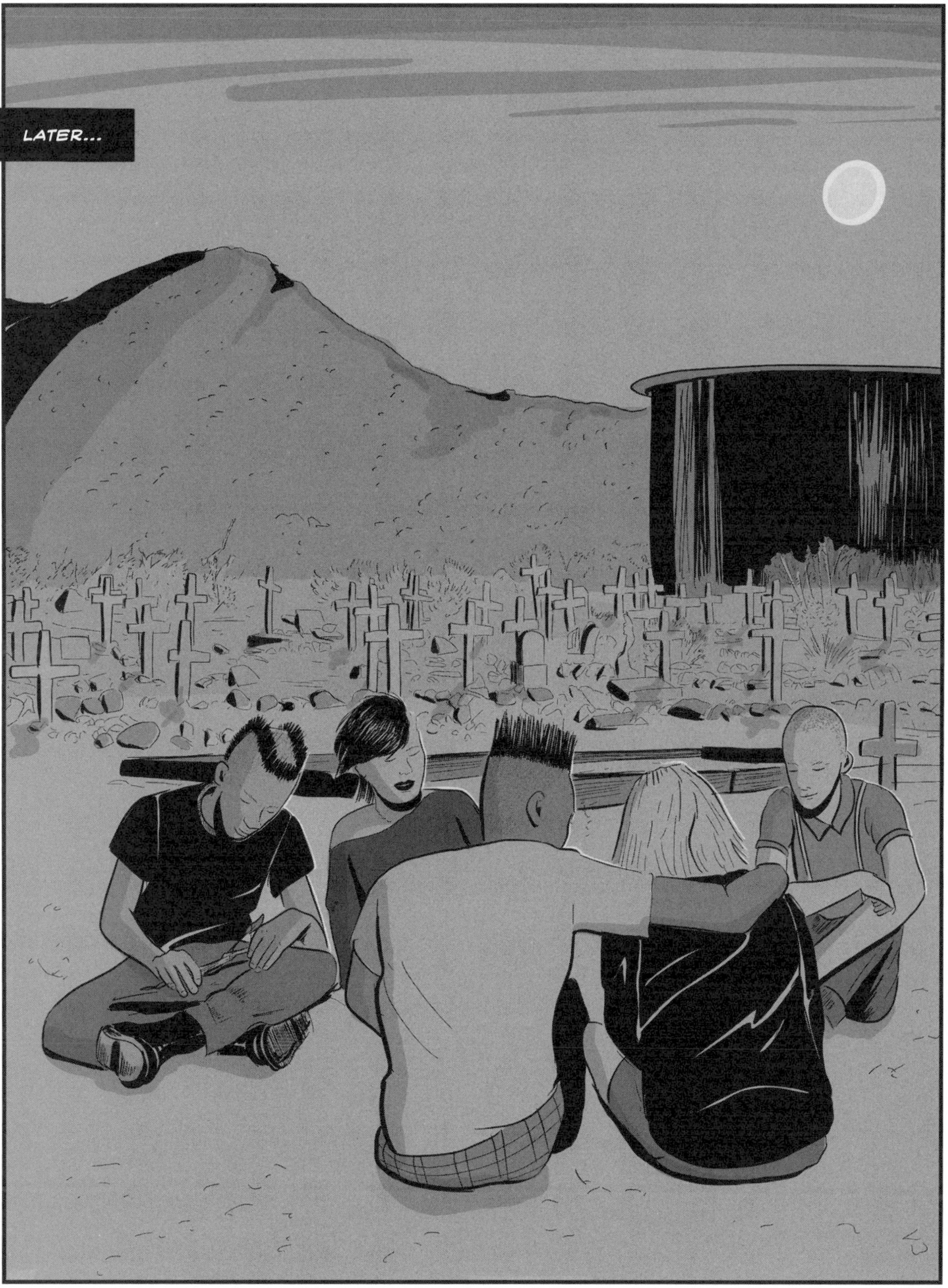
LATER...

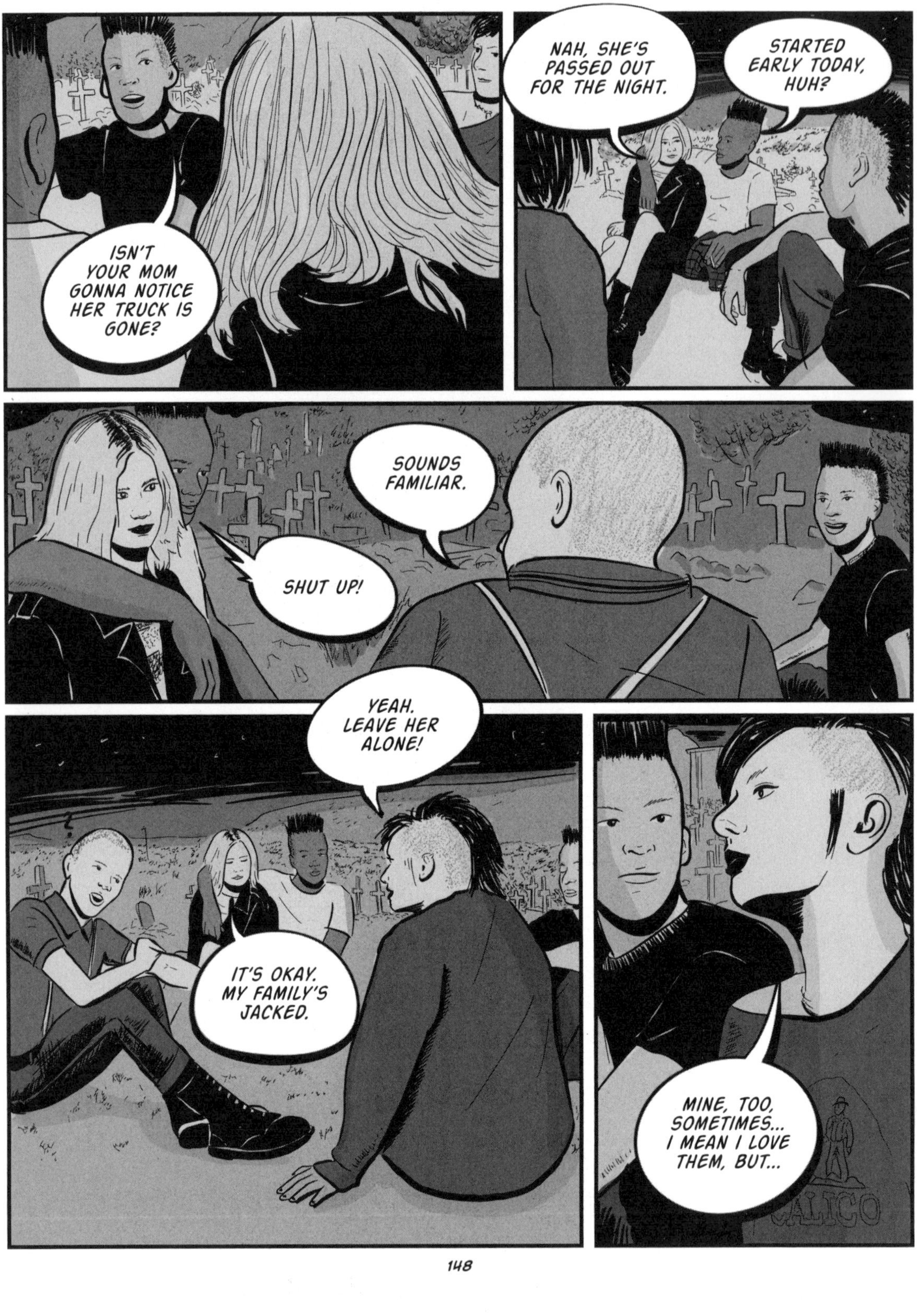
ISN'T YOUR MOM GONNA NOTICE HER TRUCK IS GONE?
NAH, SHE'S PASSED OUT FOR THE NIGHT.
STARTED EARLY TODAY, HUH?
SOUNDS FAMILIAR.
SHUT UP!
YEAH. LEAVE HER ALONE!
IT'S OKAY. MY FAMILY'S JACKED.
MINE, TOO, SOMETIMES... I MEAN I LOVE THEM, BUT...
CALICO

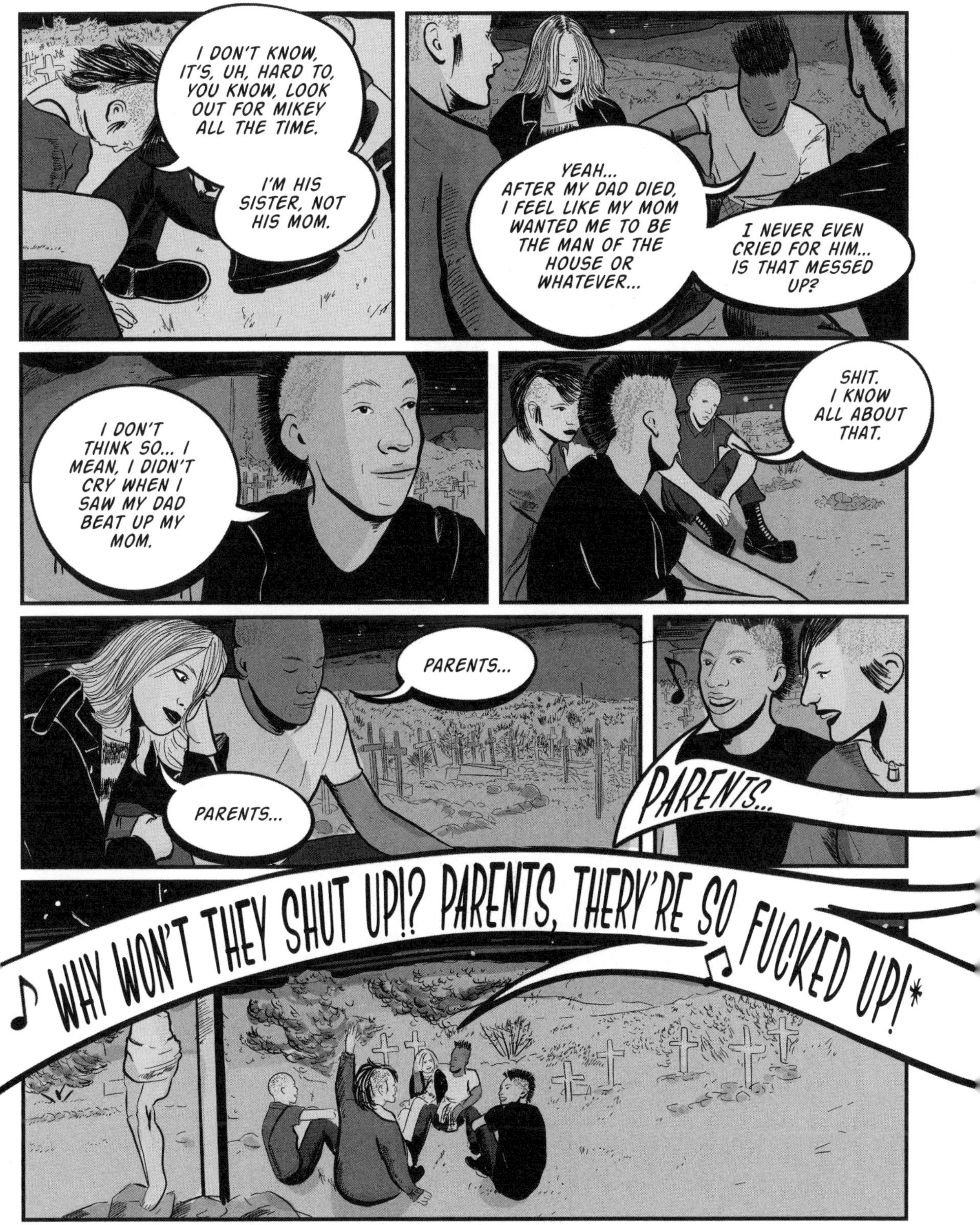

I DON'T KNOW, IT'S, UH, HARD TO, YOU KNOW, LOOK OUT FOR MIKEY ALL THE TIME.
I'M HIS SISTER, NOT HIS MOM.
YEAH... AFTER MY DAD DIED, I FEEL LIKE MY MOM WANTED ME TO BE THE MAN OF THE HOUSE OR WHATEVER...
I NEVER EVEN CRIED FOR HIM... IS THAT MESSED UP?
I DON'T THINK SO... I MEAN, I DIDN'T CRY WHEN I SAW MY DAD BEAT UP MY MOM.
SHIT. I KNOW ALL ABOUT THAT.
PARENTS...
PARENTS...
PARENTS...
♪ WHY WON'T THEY SHUT UP!? PARENTS, THERY'RE SO FUCKED UP!*

*DESCENDENTS "PARENTS"

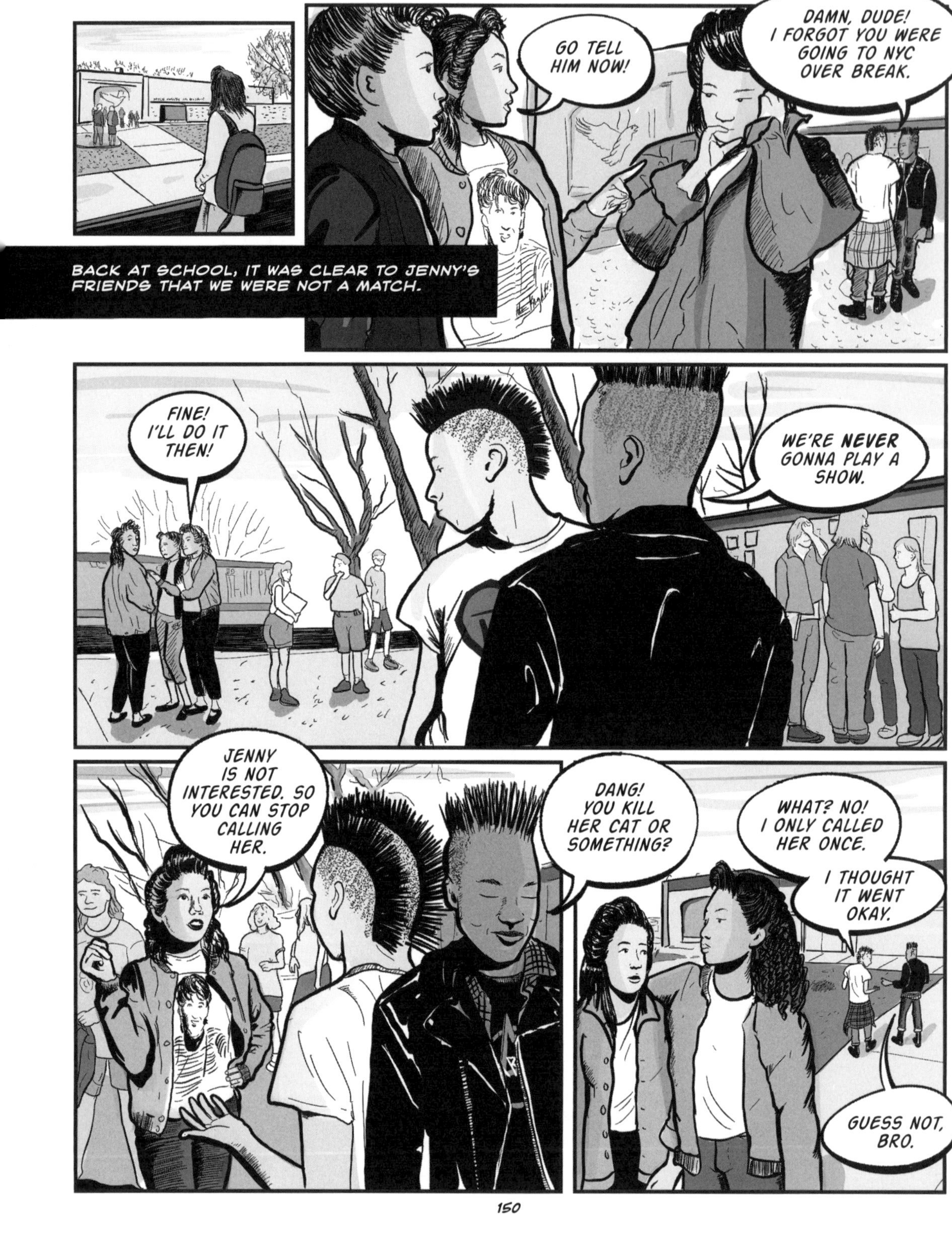
BACK AT SCHOOL, IT WAS CLEAR TO JENNY'S FRIENDS THAT WE WERE NOT A MATCH.
GO TELL HIM NOW!
DAMN, DUDE! I FORGOT YOU WERE GOING TO NYC OVER BREAK.
FINE! I'LL DO IT THEN!
WE'RE NEVER GONNA PLAY A SHOW.
JENNY IS NOT INTERESTED. SO YOU CAN STOP CALLING HER.
DANG! YOU KILL HER CAT OR SOMETHING?
WHAT? NO! I ONLY CALLED HER ONCE.
I THOUGHT IT WENT OKAY.
GUESS NOT, BRO.

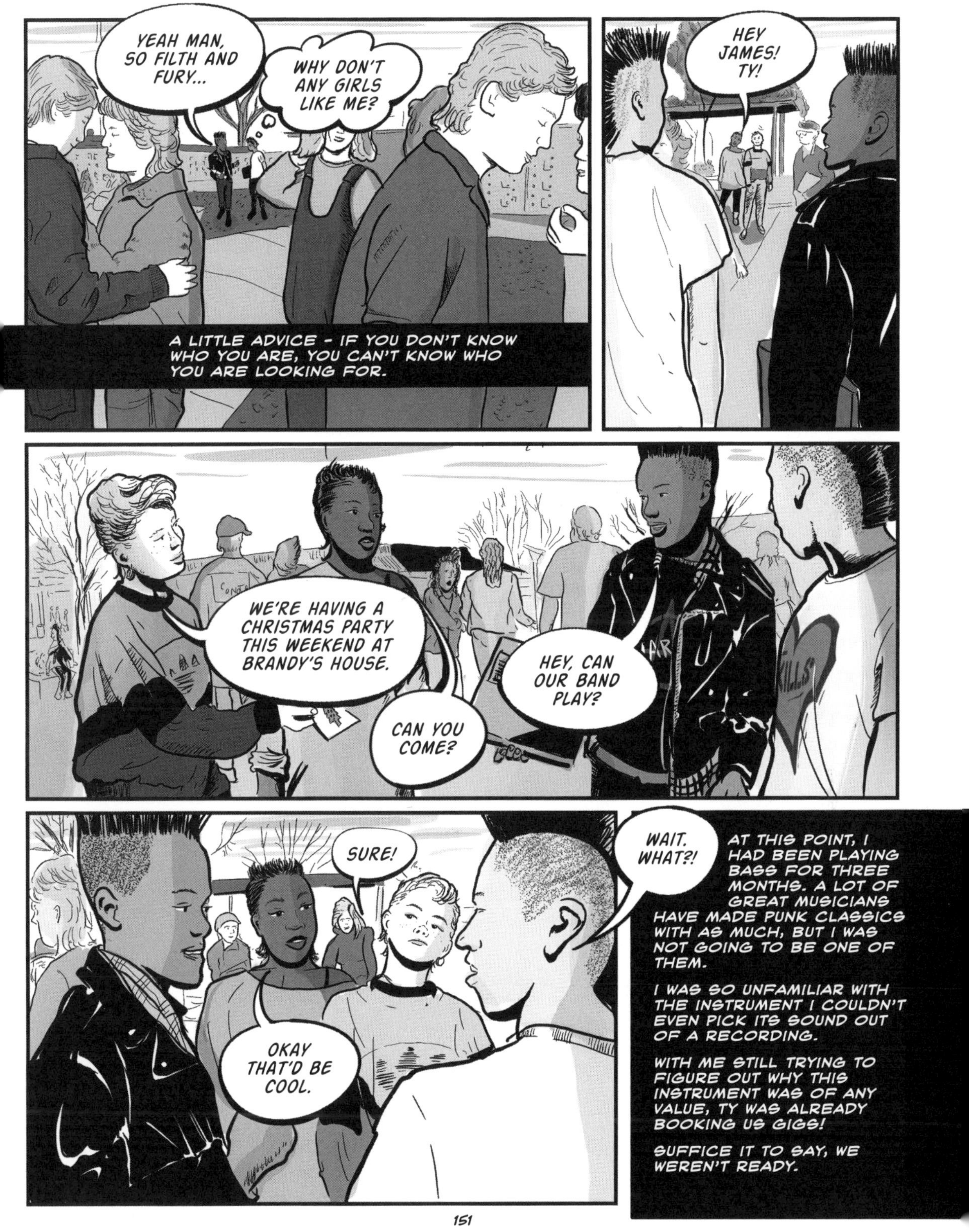
YEAH MAN, SO FILTH AND FURY...
WHY DON'T ANY GIRLS LIKE ME?
A LITTLE ADVICE - IF YOU DON'T KNOW WHO YOU ARE, YOU CAN'T KNOW WHO YOU ARE LOOKING FOR.
HEY JAMES! TY!
WE'RE HAVING A CHRISTMAS PARTY THIS WEEKEND AT BRANDY'S HOUSE.
CAN YOU COME?
HEY, CAN OUR BAND PLAY?
SURE!
OKAY THAT'D BE COOL.
WAIT. WHAT?!
AT THIS POINT, I HAD BEEN PLAYING BASS FOR THREE MONTHS. A LOT OF GREAT MUSICIANS HAVE MADE PUNK CLASSICS WITH AS MUCH, BUT I WAS NOT GOING TO BE ONE OF THEM.
I WAS SO UNFAMILIAR WITH THE INSTRUMENT I COULDN'T EVEN PICK ITS SOUND OUT OF A RECORDING.
WITH ME STILL TRYING TO FIGURE OUT WHY THIS INSTRUMENT WAS OF ANY VALUE, TY WAS ALREADY BOOKING US GIGS!
SUFFICE IT TO SAY, WE WEREN'T READY.

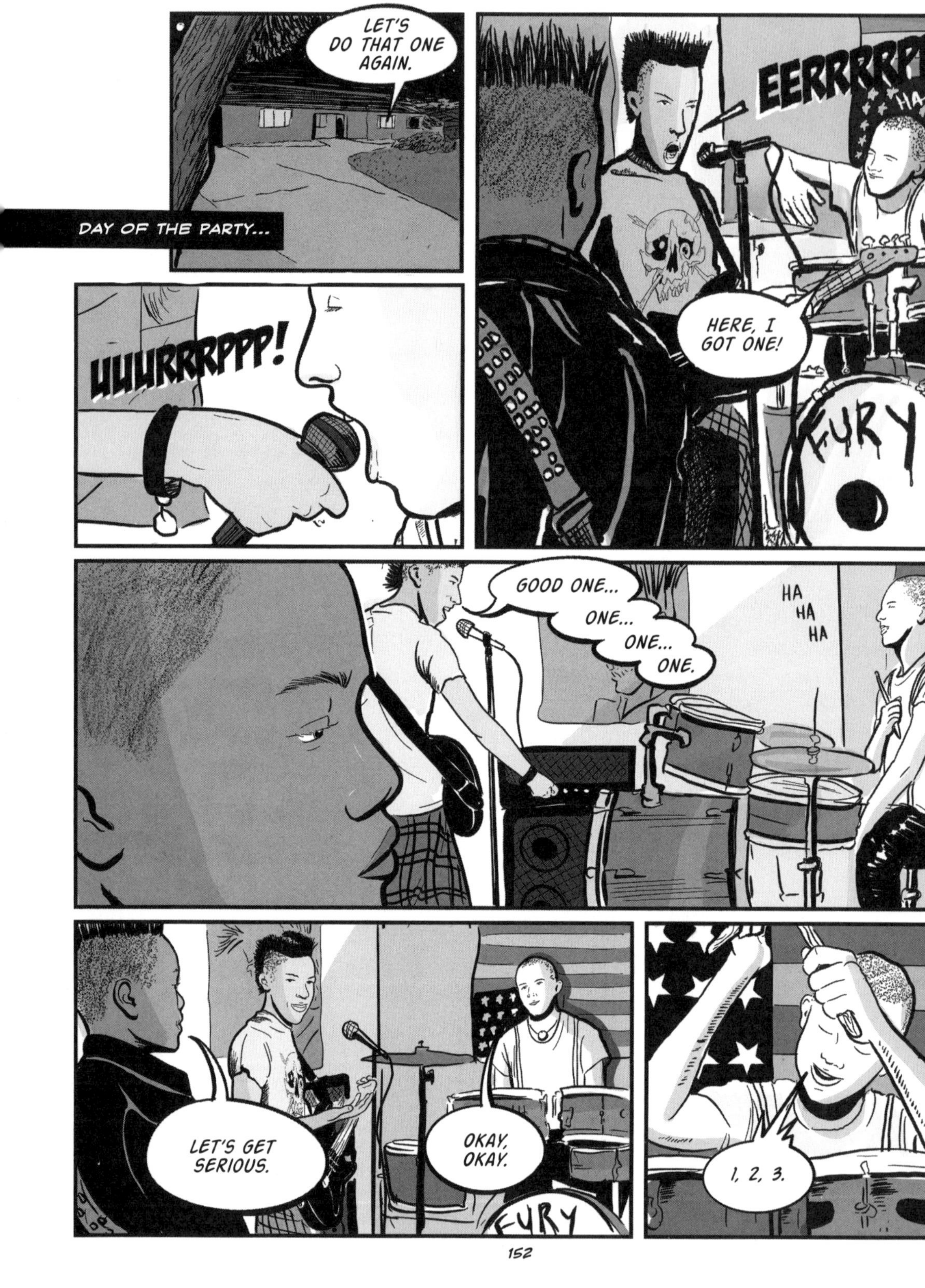

LET'S DO THAT ONE AGAIN.
DAY OF THE PARTY...
UUURRRPPP!
EERRRRPP!
HA! HA! HA!
HERE, I GOT ONE!
FURY
GOOD ONE... ONE... ONE... ONE.
HA HA HA
LET'S GET SERIOUS.
OKAY, OKAY.
FURY
1, 2, 3.

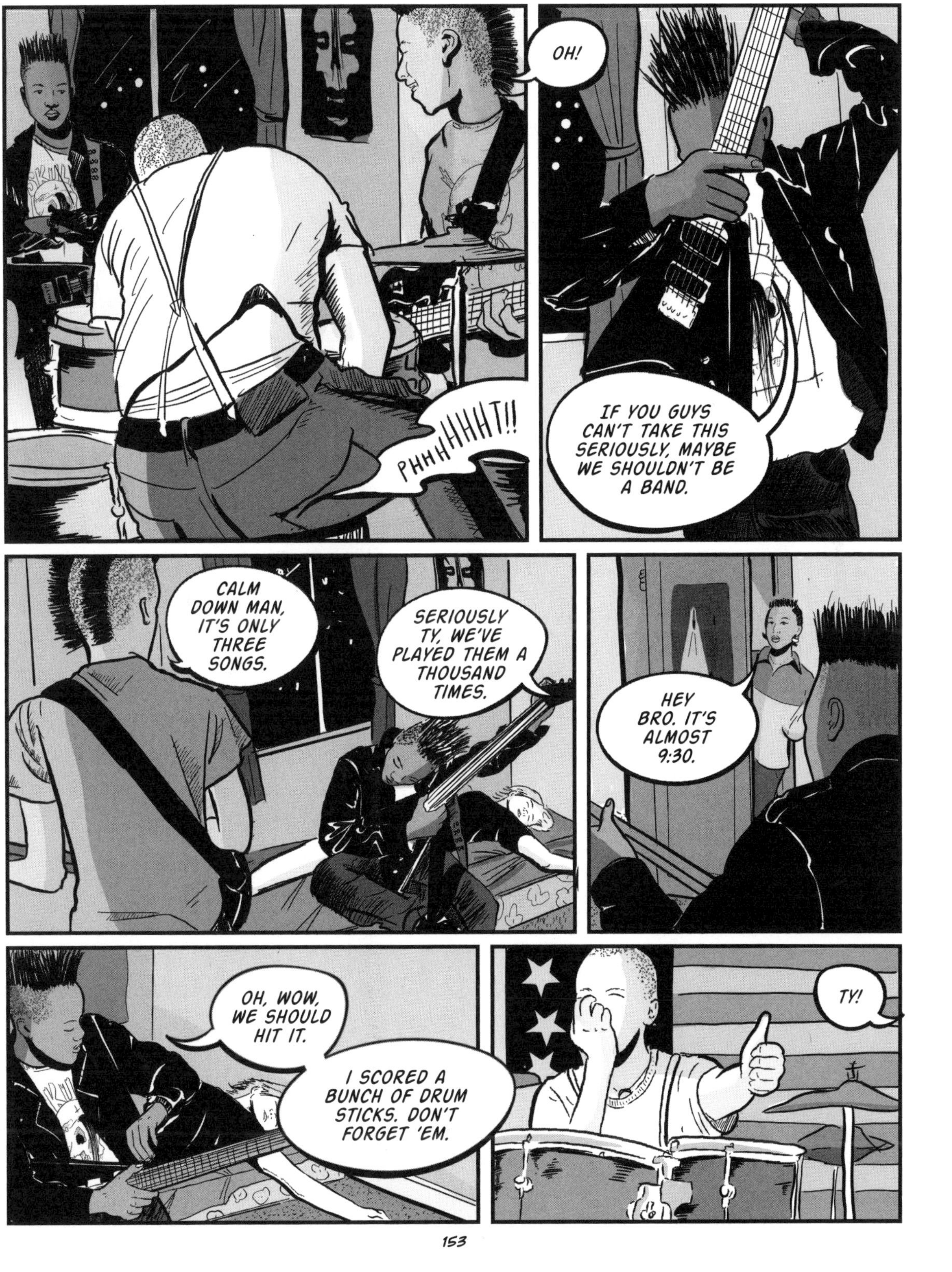
OH!
PHHHHHHT!!
IF YOU GUYS CAN'T TAKE THIS SERIOUSLY, MAYBE WE SHOULDN'T BE A BAND.
CALM DOWN MAN, IT'S ONLY THREE SONGS.
SERIOUSLY TY, WE'VE PLAYED THEM A THOUSAND TIMES.
HEY BRO. IT'S ALMOST 9:30.
OH, WOW, WE SHOULD HIT IT.
I SCORED A BUNCH OF DRUM STICKS. DON'T FORGET 'EM.
TY!

RICKS MUSIC
WILL YOU GIVE THAT GIRL HER DIGNITY AND COVER HER UP?
WHAT DIGNITY?
NEVER MIND
FURY
MAN! SHUT UP!
LATER...
SHE'S ALREADY WASTED.
WHAT'D SHE TAKE, ANYWAY?
WHO THE HELL KNOWS? PEOPLE ARE ALWAYS GIVING HER STUFF.
THEM D'S COME WITH "PERKS."
HA HA

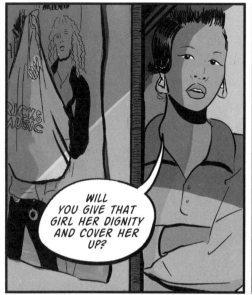

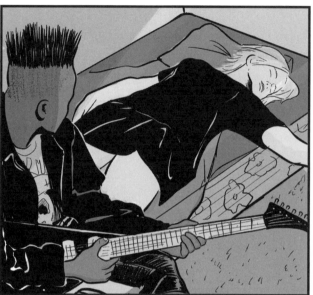

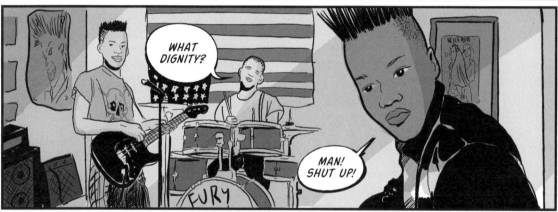

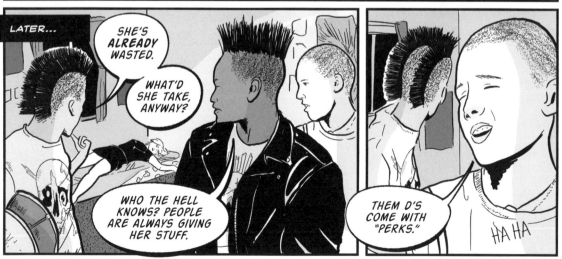

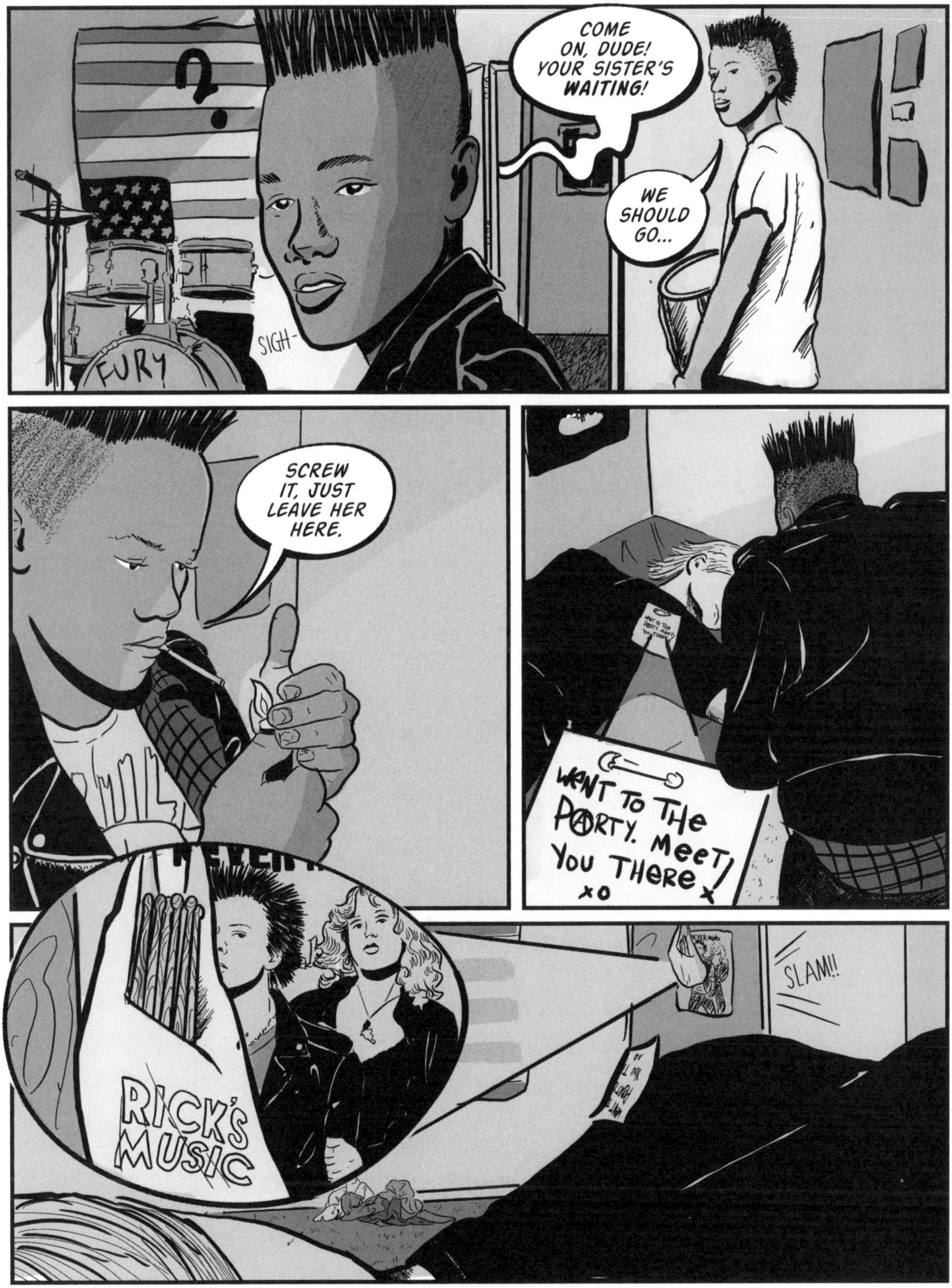
COME ON, DUDE! YOUR SISTER'S WAITING!
WE SHOULD GO...
FURY
SIGH-
SCREW IT, JUST LEAVE HER HERE.
WENT TO THE PARTY. MEET YOU THERE
xo
RICK'S MUSIC
SLAM!!

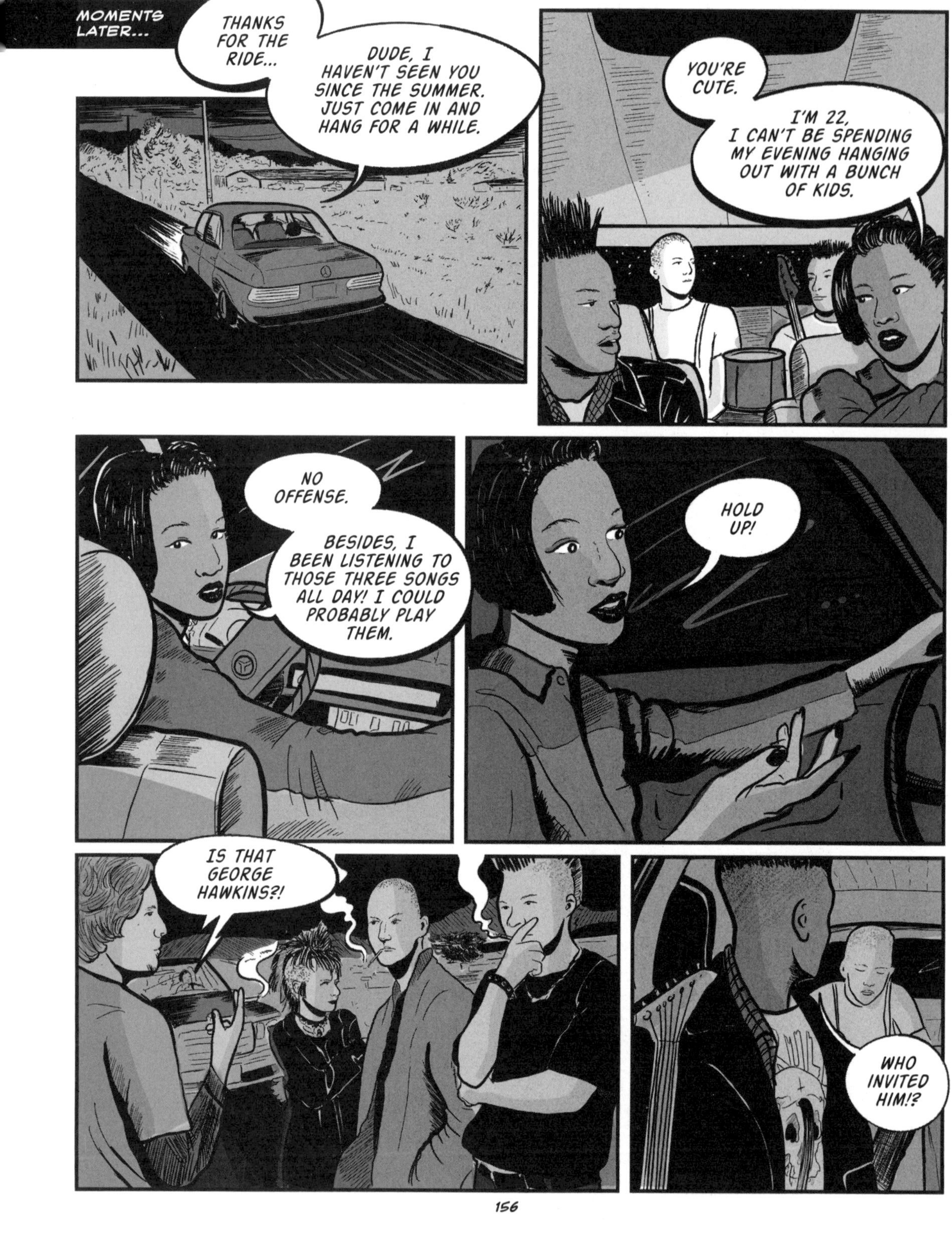
MOMENTS LATER...
THANKS FOR THE RIDE...
DUDE, I HAVEN'T SEEN YOU SINCE THE SUMMER. JUST COME IN AND HANG FOR A WHILE.
YOU'RE CUTE.
I'M 22, I CAN'T BE SPENDING MY EVENING HANGING OUT WITH A BUNCH OF KIDS.
NO OFFENSE.
BESIDES, I BEEN LISTENING TO THOSE THREE SONGS ALL DAY! I COULD PROBABLY PLAY THEM.
HOLD UP!
IS THAT GEORGE HAWKINS?!
WHO INVITED HIM!?

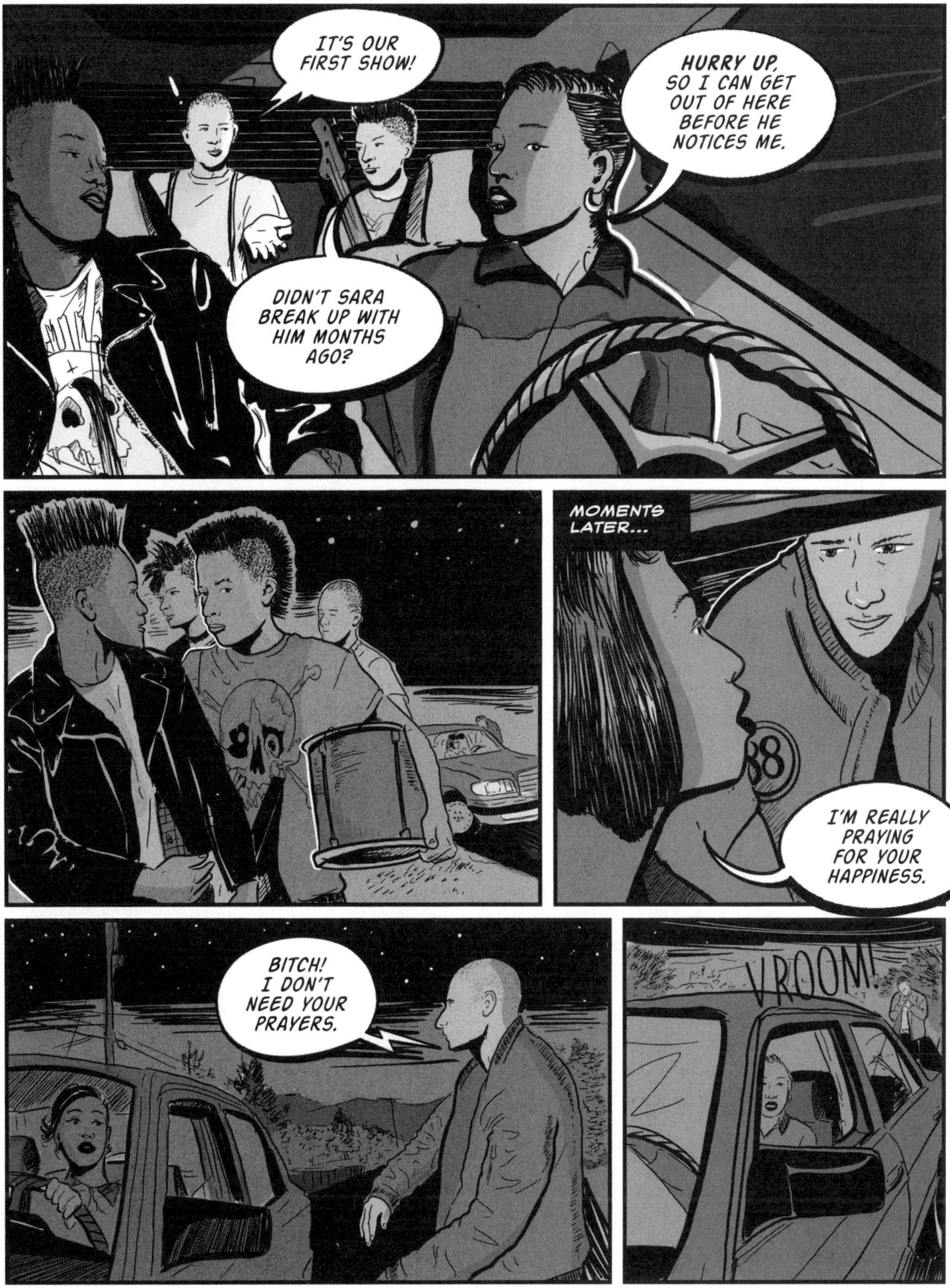
IT'S OUR FIRST SHOW!
HURRY UP, SO I CAN GET OUT OF HERE BEFORE HE NOTICES ME.
DIDN'T SARA BREAK UP WITH HIM MONTHS AGO?
MOMENTS LATER...
I'M REALLY PRAYING FOR YOUR HAPPINESS.
BITCH! I DON'T NEED YOUR PRAYERS.
VROOM!

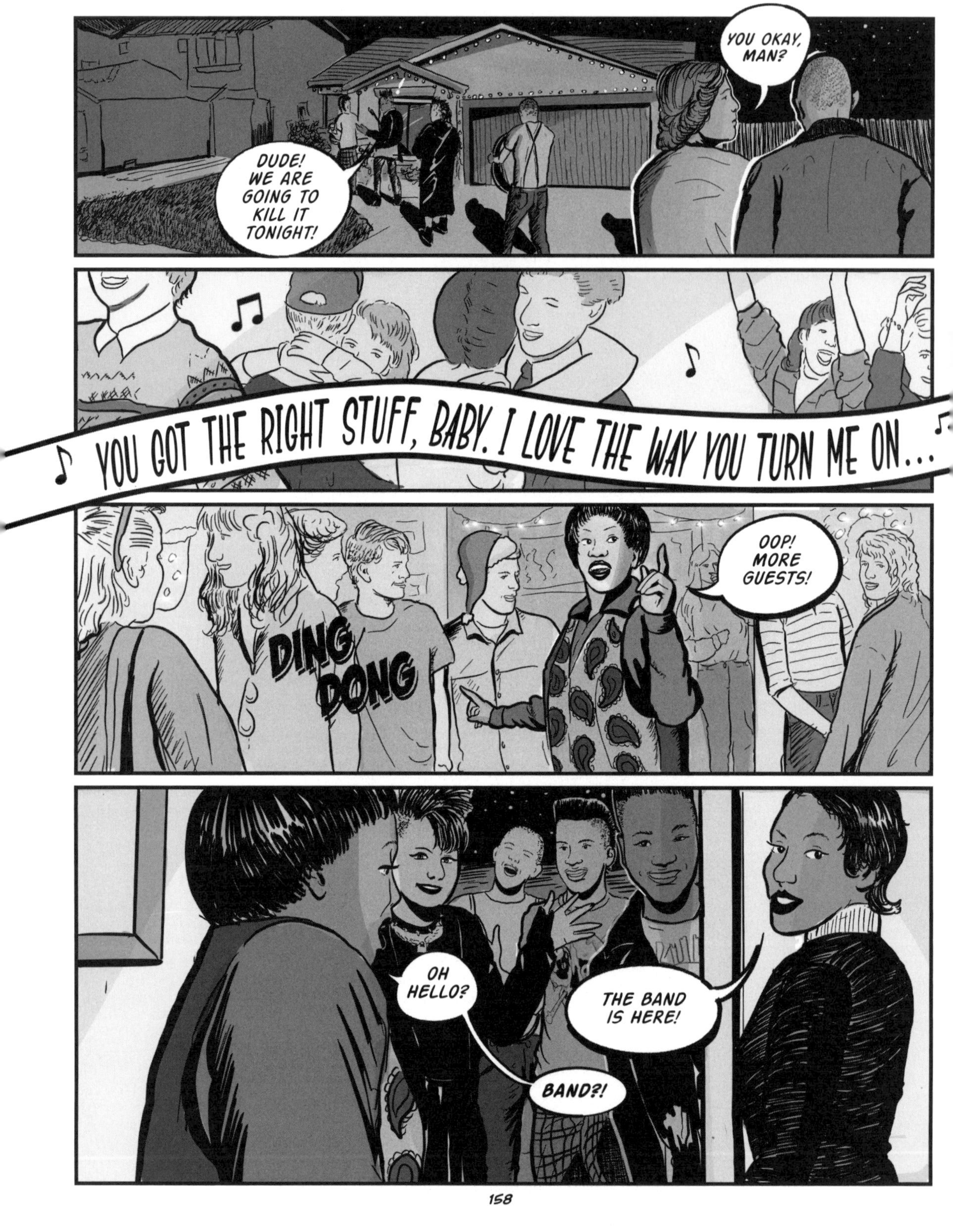
DUDE! WE ARE GOING TO KILL IT TONIGHT!
YOU OKAY, MAN?
♪ YOU GOT THE RIGHT STUFF, BABY. I LOVE THE WAY YOU TURN ME ON... ♪
DING DONG
OOP! MORE GUESTS!
OH HELLO?
THE BAND IS HERE!
BAND?!

YOU REMEMBER JAMES... FROM MR. ILLMAN'S CLASS A COUPLE YEARS BACK?

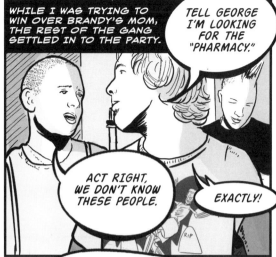

WHILE I WAS TRYING TO WIN OVER BRANDY'S MOM, THE REST OF THE GANG SETTLED IN TO THE PARTY.

TELL GEORGE I'M LOOKING FOR THE "PHARMACY."

ACT RIGHT, WE DON'T KNOW THESE PEOPLE.

EXACTLY!

UM... WHAT KIND OF BAND IS THIS?

HEY... UM... HI.

MOM!

UM, MR. LATHAN SAID HE NEEDS MORE PIZZA BITES FROM THE GARAGE FREEZER.

ON IT, THANK YOU, SARA.

WHAT IS GEORGE DOING HERE?!

WHO ARE THOSE OTHER KIDS?

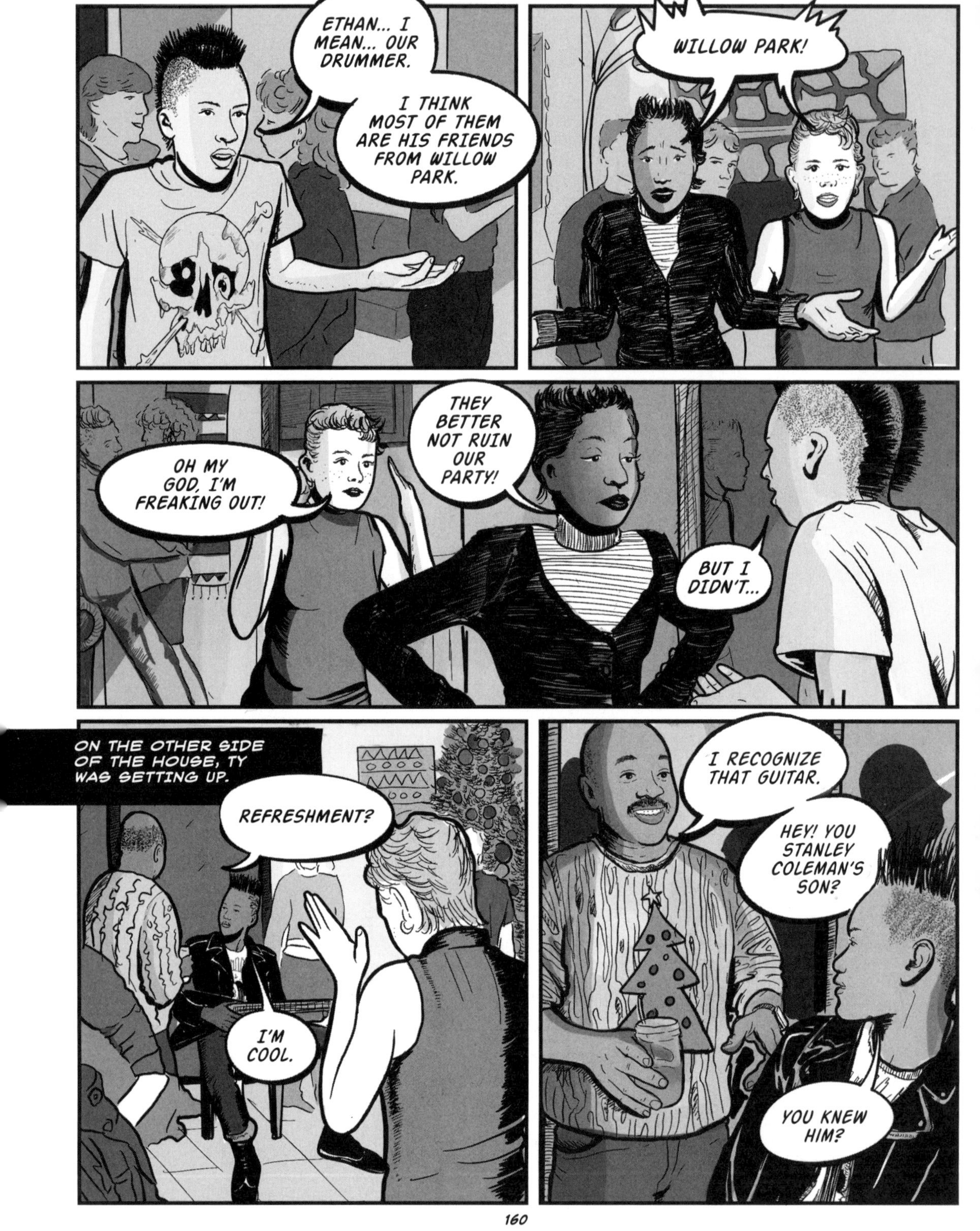

ETHAN... I MEAN... OUR DRUMMER.
I THINK MOST OF THEM ARE HIS FRIENDS FROM WILLOW PARK.
WILLOW PARK!
OH MY GOD, I'M FREAKING OUT!
THEY BETTER NOT RUIN OUR PARTY!
BUT I DIDN'T...
ON THE OTHER SIDE OF THE HOUSE, TY WAS SETTING UP.
REFRESHMENT?
I'M COOL.
I RECOGNIZE THAT GUITAR.
HEY! YOU STANLEY COLEMAN'S SON?
YOU KNEW HIM?

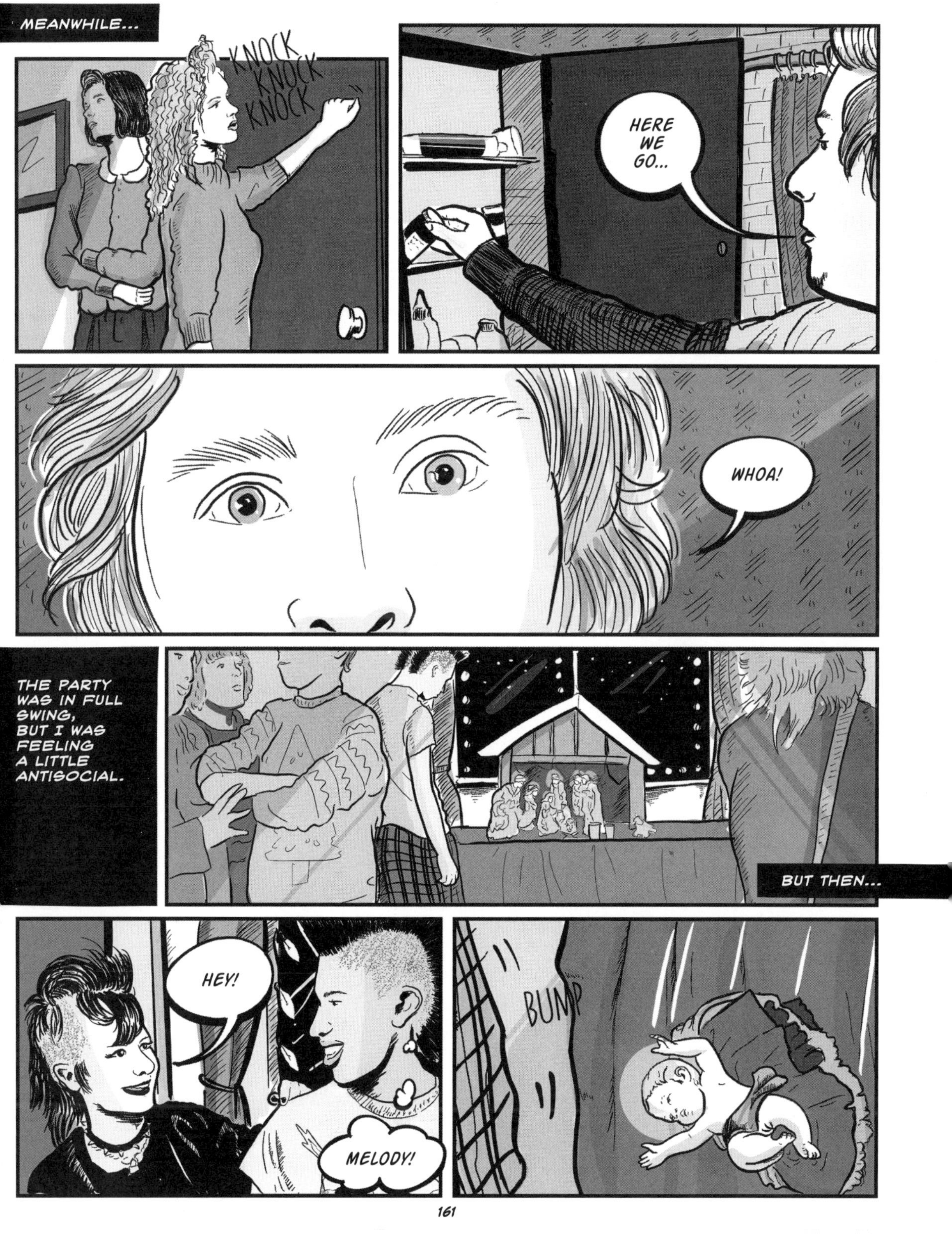
MEANWHILE...
KNOCK KNOCK KNOCK
HERE WE GO...
WHOA!
THE PARTY WAS IN FULL SWING, BUT I WAS FEELING A LITTLE ANTISOCIAL.
BUT THEN...
HEY!
MELODY!
BUMP

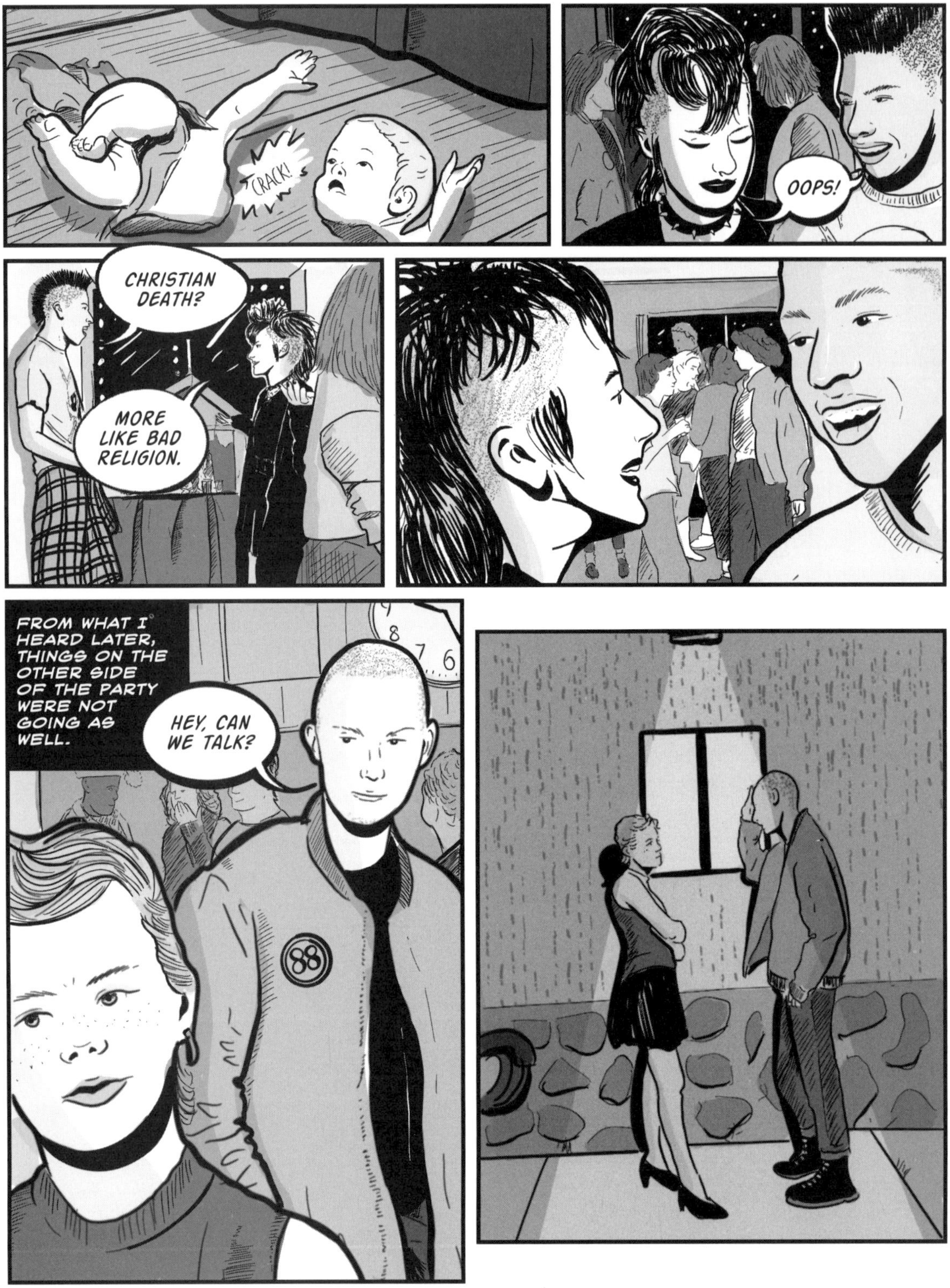
CRACK!
OOPS!
CHRISTIAN DEATH?
MORE LIKE BAD RELIGION.
FROM WHAT I HEARD LATER, THINGS ON THE OTHER SIDE OF THE PARTY WERE NOT GOING AS WELL.
HEY, CAN WE TALK?
88

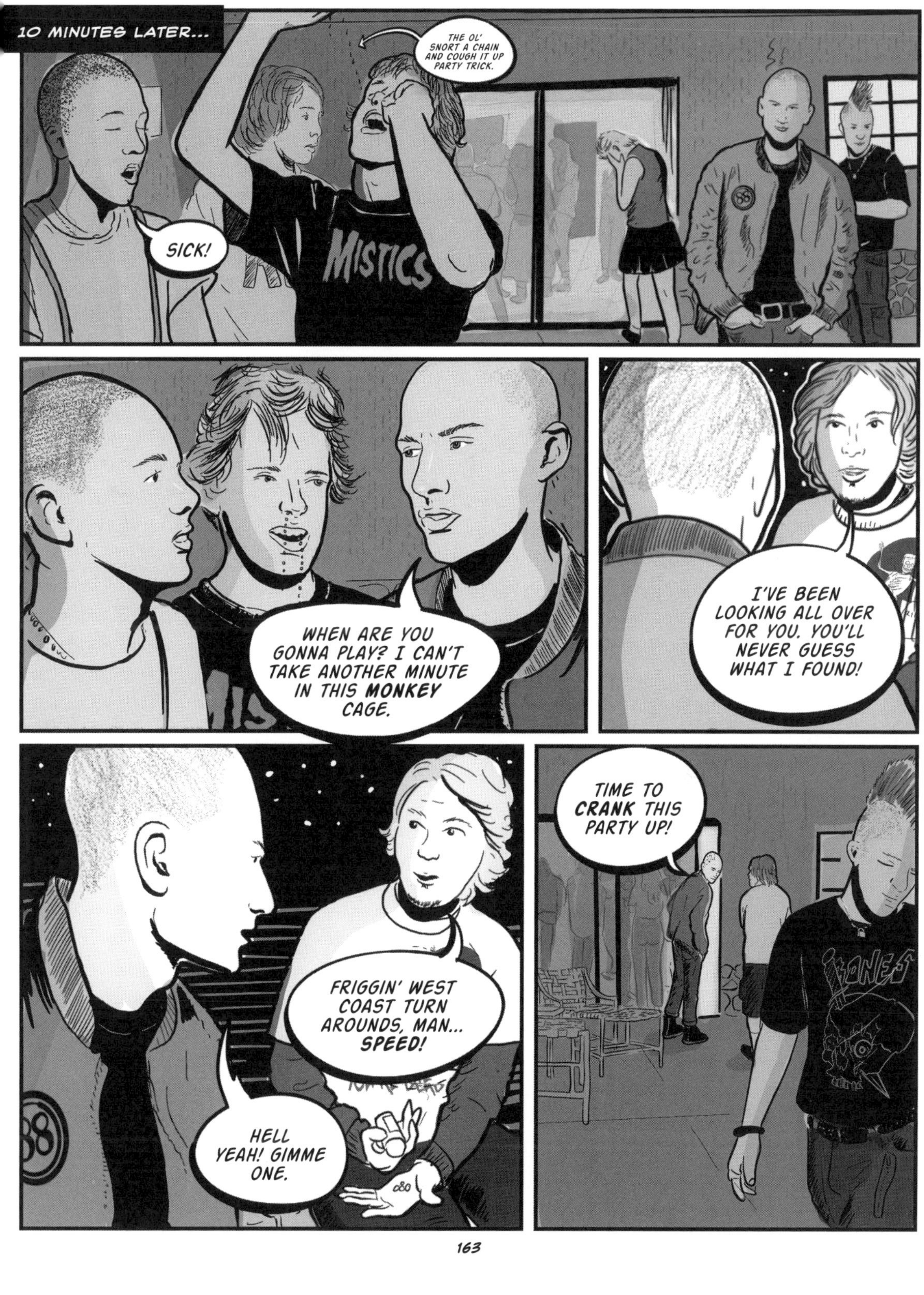
10 MINUTES LATER...
THE OL' SNORT A CHAIN AND COUGH IT UP PARTY TRICK.
SICK!
MISTICS
WHEN ARE YOU GONNA PLAY? I CAN'T TAKE ANOTHER MINUTE IN THIS MONKEY CAGE.
I'VE BEEN LOOKING ALL OVER FOR YOU. YOU'LL NEVER GUESS WHAT I FOUND!
FRIGGIN' WEST COAST TURN AROUNDS, MAN... SPEED!
HELL YEAH! GIMME ONE.
TIME TO CRANK THIS PARTY UP!

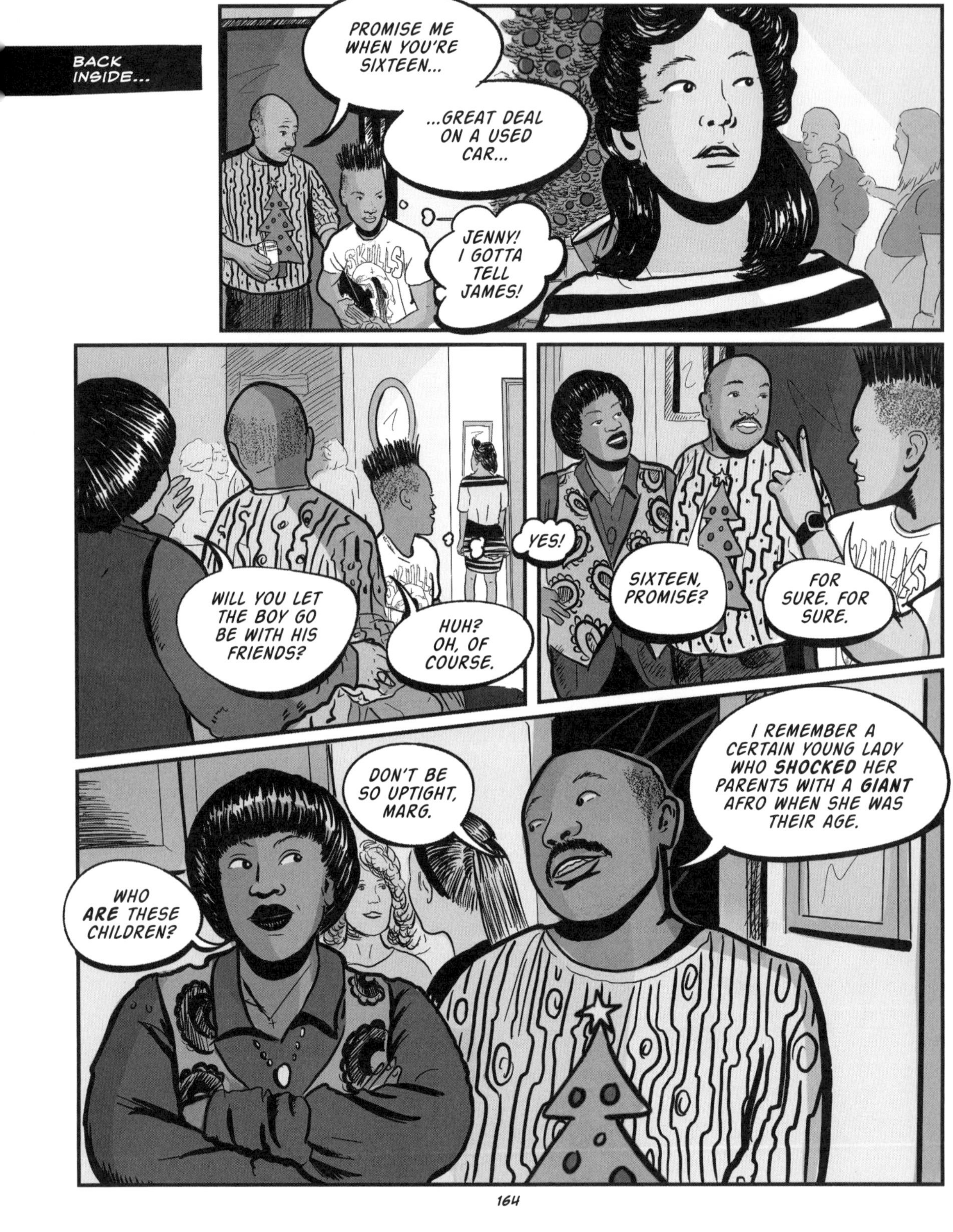

BACK INSIDE...
PROMISE ME WHEN YOU'RE SIXTEEN...
...GREAT DEAL ON A USED CAR...
JENNY! I GOTTA TELL JAMES!
WILL YOU LET THE BOY GO BE WITH HIS FRIENDS?
HUH? OH, OF COURSE.
YES!
SIXTEEN, PROMISE?
FOR SURE. FOR SURE.
DON'T BE SO UPTIGHT, MARG.
I REMEMBER A CERTAIN YOUNG LADY WHO SHOCKED HER PARENTS WITH A GIANT AFRO WHEN SHE WAS THEIR AGE.
WHO ARE THESE CHILDREN?

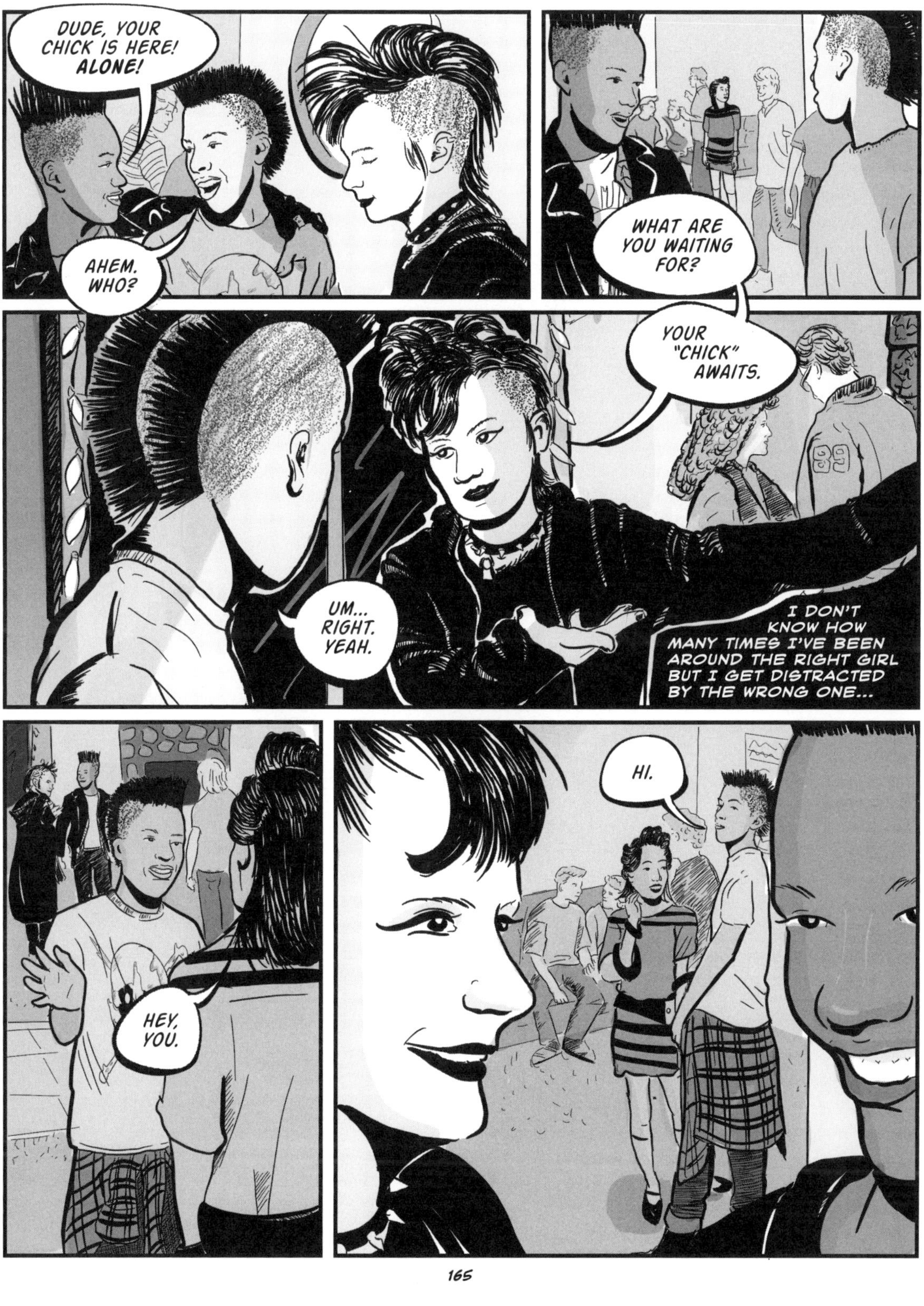
DUDE, YOUR CHICK IS HERE! ALONE!
AHEM. WHO?
WHAT ARE YOU WAITING FOR?
YOUR "CHICK" AWAITS.
UM... RIGHT. YEAH.
I DON'T KNOW HOW MANY TIMES I'VE BEEN AROUND THE RIGHT GIRL BUT I GET DISTRACTED BY THE WRONG ONE...
HEY, YOU.
HI.

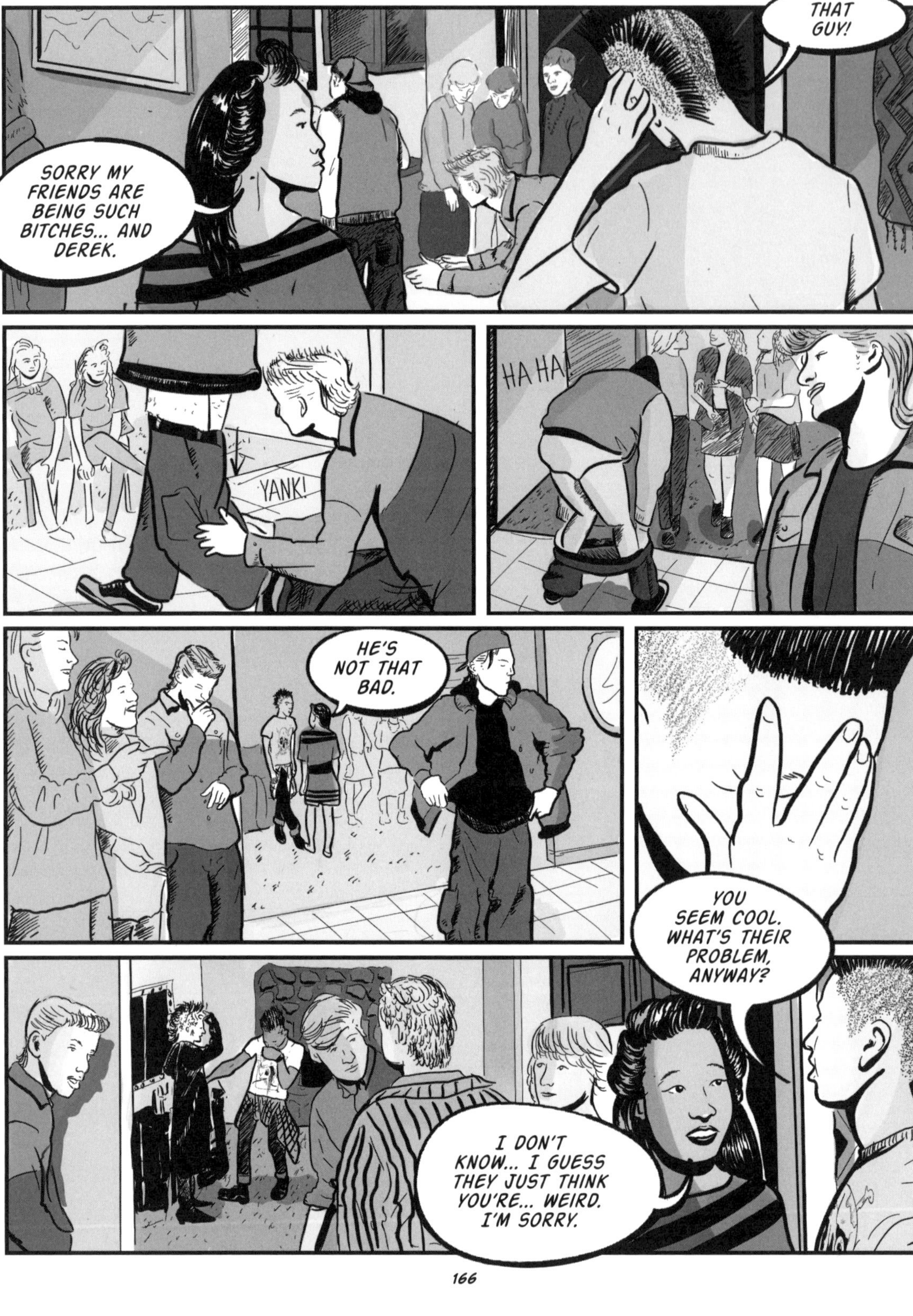
THAT GUY!
SORRY MY FRIENDS ARE BEING SUCH BITCHES... AND DEREK.
YANK!
HA HA!
HE'S NOT THAT BAD.
YOU SEEM COOL. WHAT'S THEIR PROBLEM, ANYWAY?
I DON'T KNOW... I GUESS THEY JUST THINK YOU'RE... WEIRD. I'M SORRY.

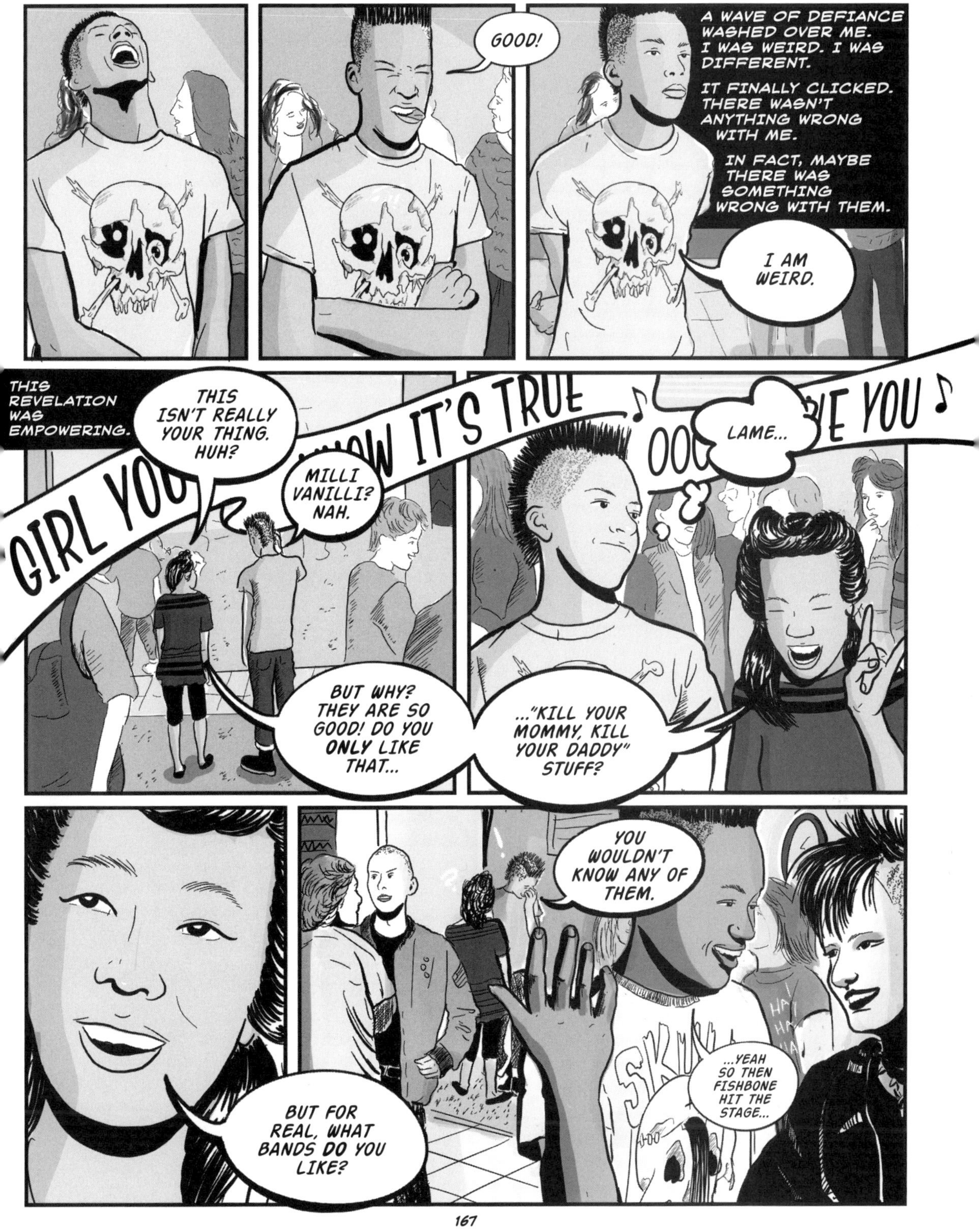
GOOD!
A WAVE OF DEFIANCE WASHED OVER ME. I WAS WEIRD. I WAS DIFFERENT.
IT FINALLY CLICKED. THERE WASN'T ANYTHING WRONG WITH ME.
IN FACT, MAYBE THERE WAS SOMETHING WRONG WITH THEM.
I AM WEIRD.
THIS REVELATION WAS EMPOWERING.
THIS ISN'T REALLY YOUR THING. HUH?
MILLI VANILLI? NAH.
GIRL YOU
KNOW IT'S TRUE ♪
OOO
VE YOU ♪
LAME...
BUT WHY? THEY ARE SO GOOD! DO YOU ONLY LIKE THAT...
..."KILL YOUR MOMMY, KILL YOUR DADDY" STUFF?
BUT FOR REAL, WHAT BANDS DO YOU LIKE?
YOU WOULDN'T KNOW ANY OF THEM.
...YEAH SO THEN FISHBONE HIT THE STAGE...

DUDE, YOU GUYS GONNA PLAY OR WHAT?
IF I HEAR ONE MORE OF THESE GODDAMN NEW KIDS ON THE BLOCK SONGS...
HOW CAN YOU NOT LIKE NEW KIDS ON THE BLOCK?
YEAH, DUDE, ARE YOU GOING TO PLAY?
PINCH
THIS IS THE FACE DEREK MAKES WHEN HE'S TRYING TO BE INTIMIDATING.
WHAT A DICK.
GUESS IT'S TIME TO BE WEIRD.
GUESS SO, FREAK!
I WAS SO DISTRACTED BY DEREK'S STUPID FACE THAT I TOTALLY MISSED JOSH AND GEORGE DEVISING A SCHEME.

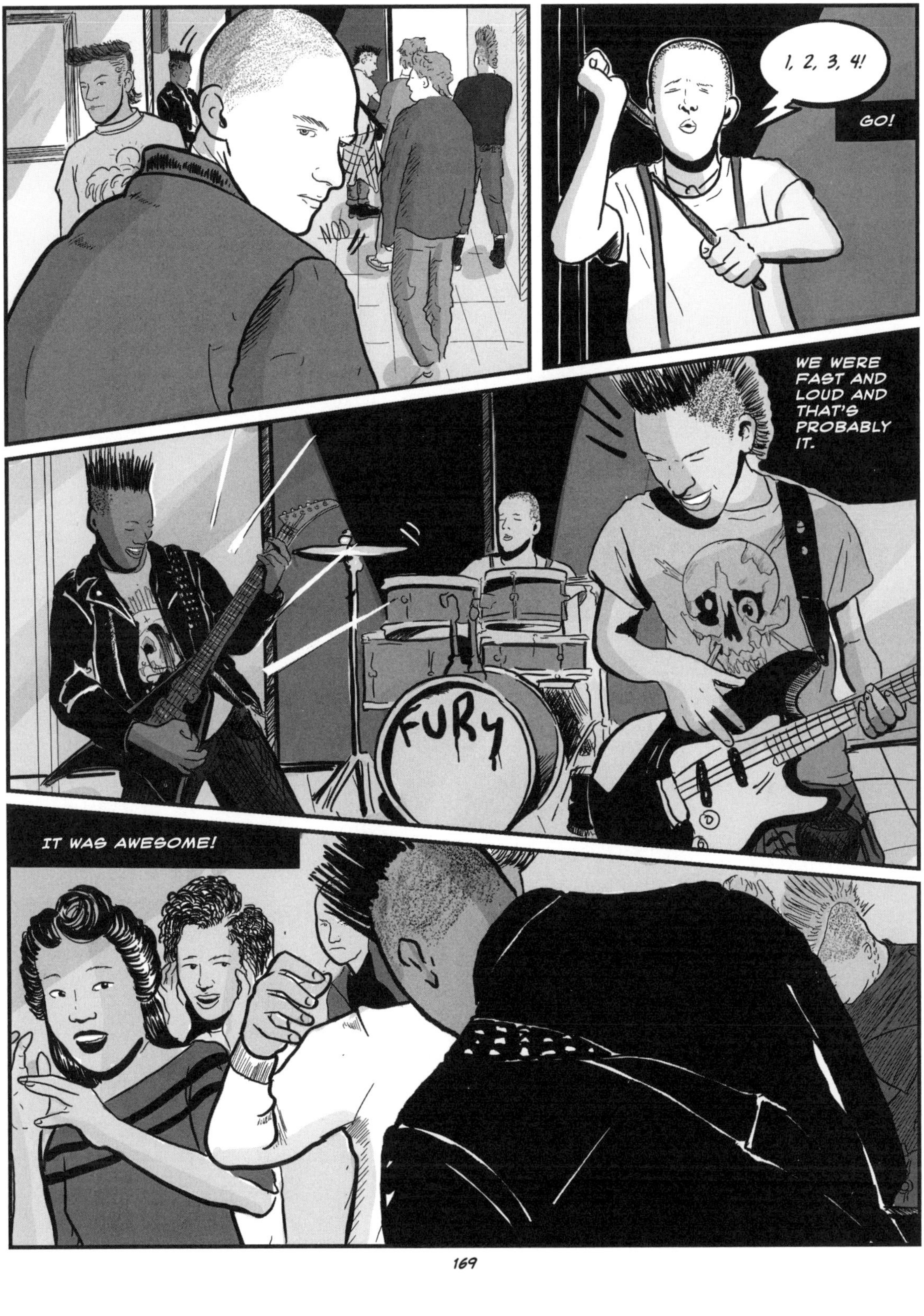
NOD
1, 2, 3, 4!
GO!
WE WERE FAST AND LOUD AND THAT'S PROBABLY IT.
FURY
IT WAS AWESOME!

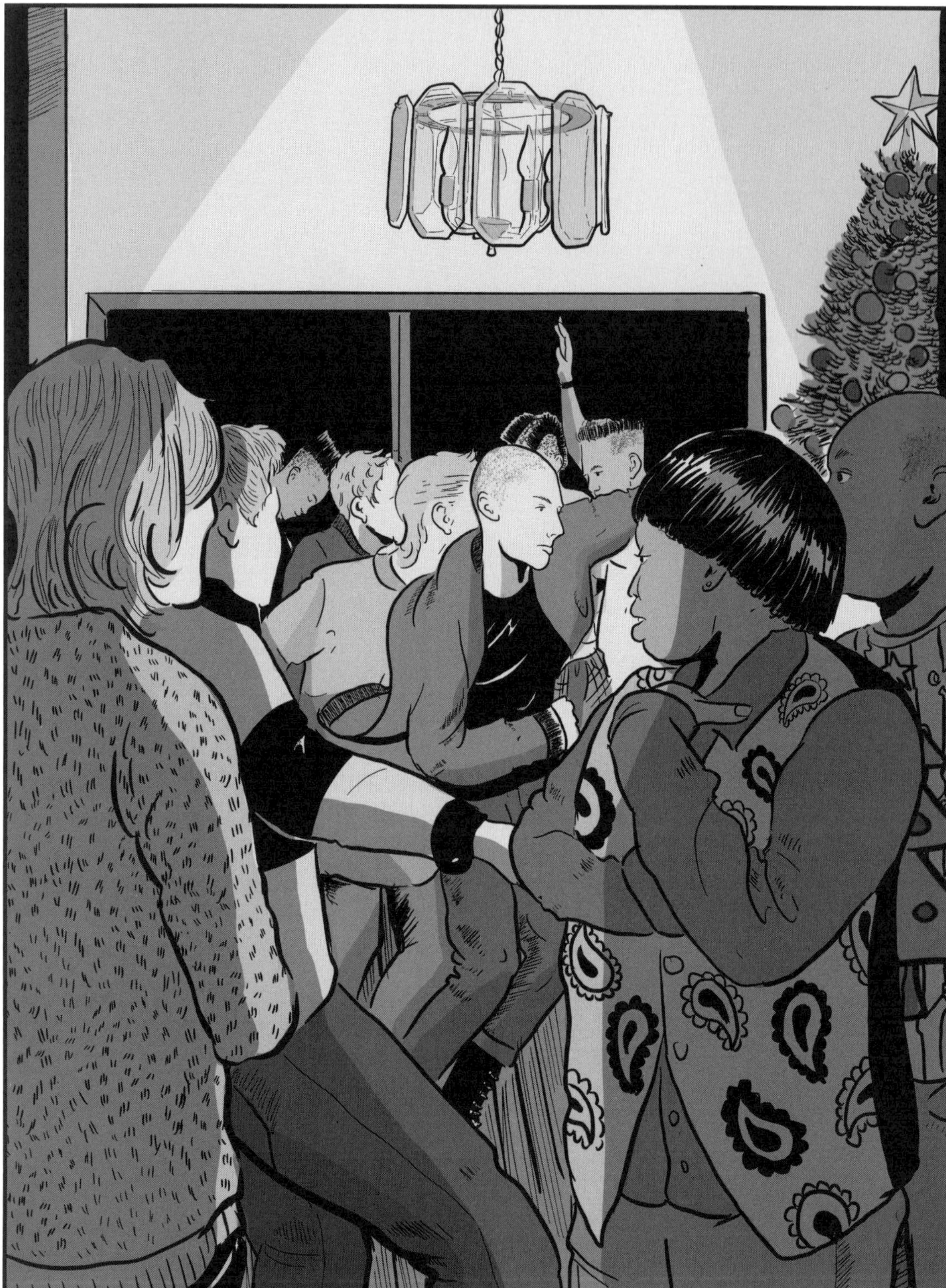

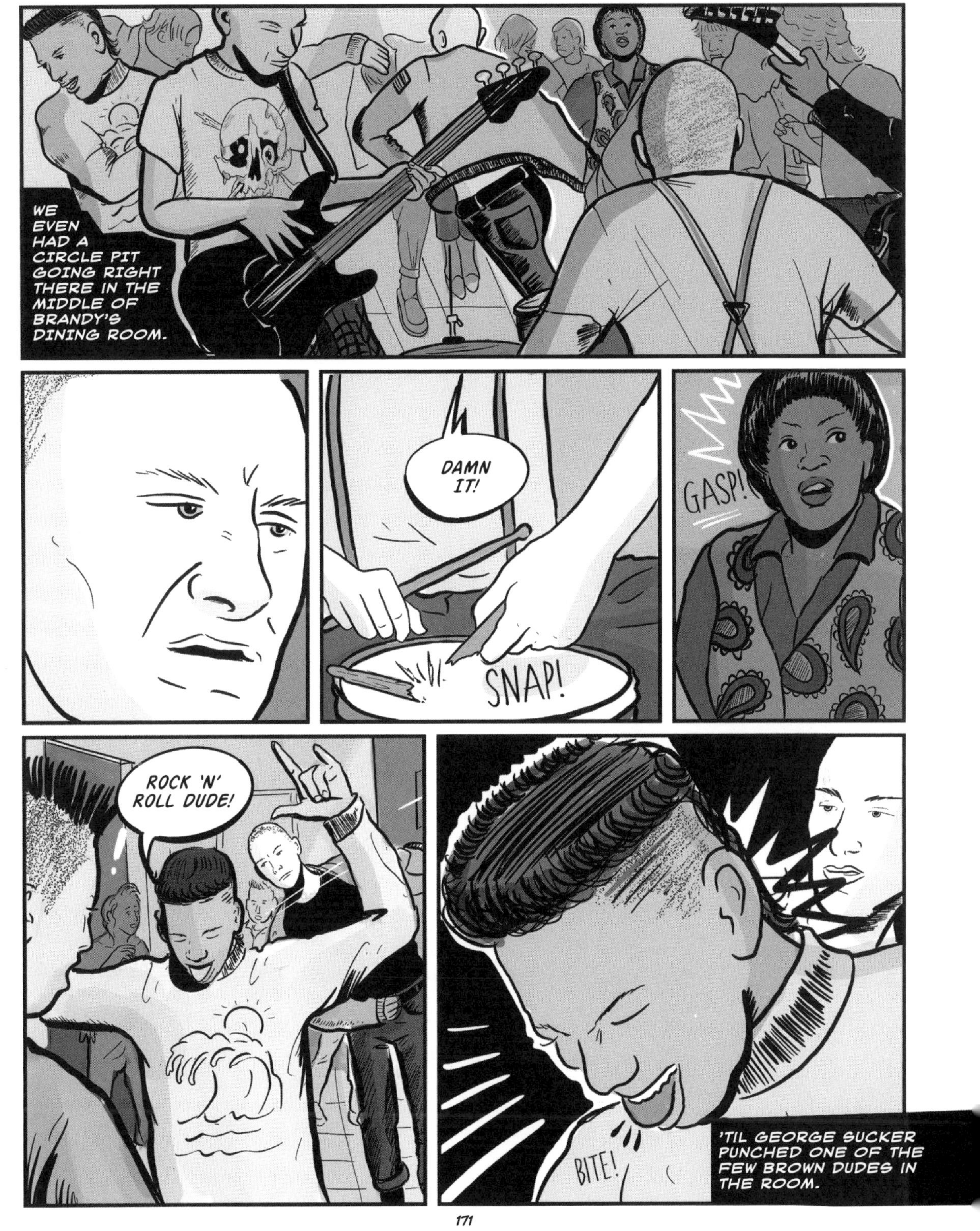

WE EVEN HAD A CIRCLE PIT GOING RIGHT THERE IN THE MIDDLE OF BRANDY'S DINING ROOM.
DAMN IT!
SNAP!
GASP!
ROCK 'N' ROLL DUDE!
BITE!
'TIL GEORGE SUCKER PUNCHED ONE OF THE FEW BROWN DUDES IN THE ROOM.

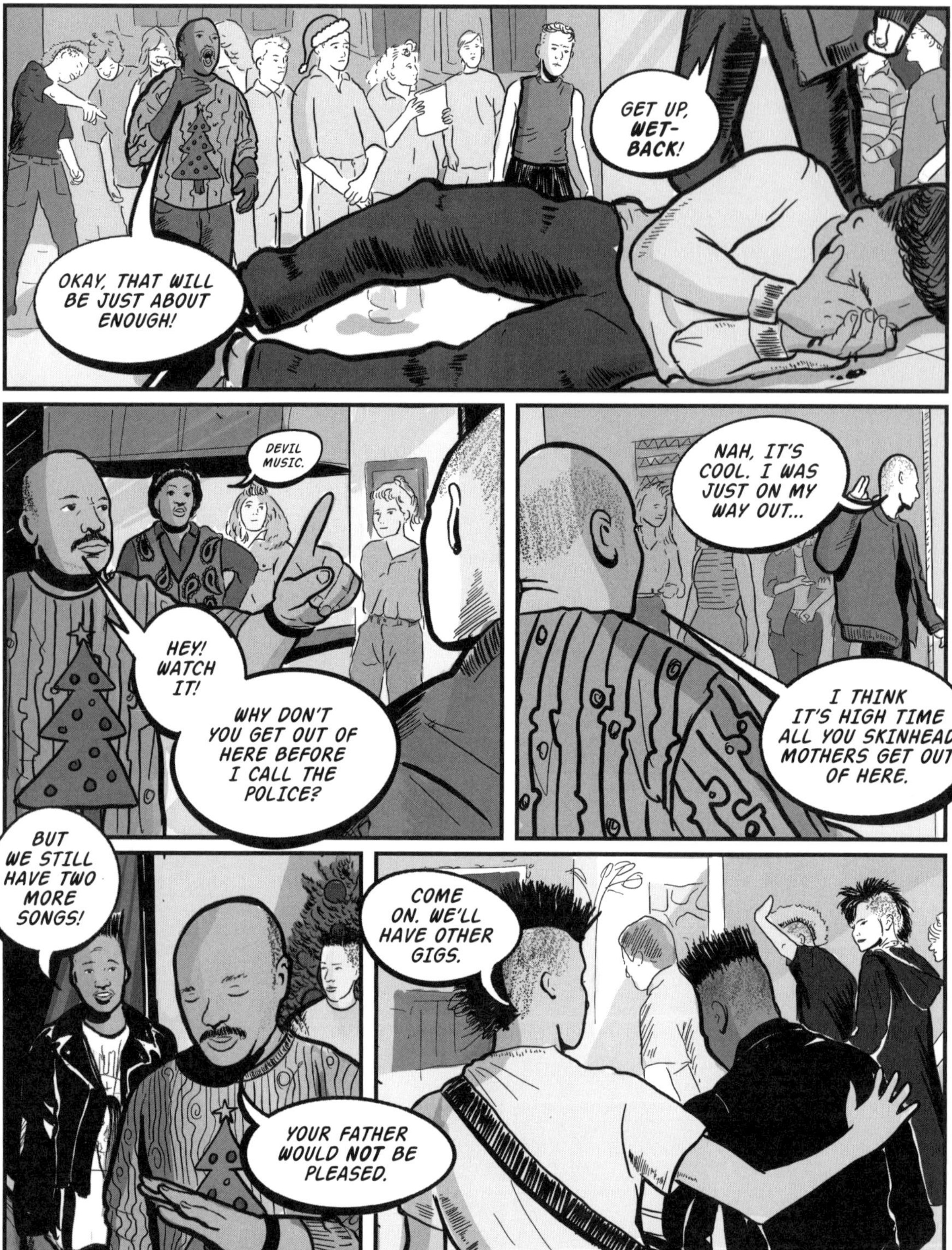
GET UP, WET-BACK!
OKAY, THAT WILL BE JUST ABOUT ENOUGH!
DEVIL MUSIC.
HEY! WATCH IT!
WHY DON'T YOU GET OUT OF HERE BEFORE I CALL THE POLICE?
NAH, IT'S COOL. I WAS JUST ON MY WAY OUT...
I THINK IT'S HIGH TIME ALL YOU SKINHEAD MOTHERS GET OUT OF HERE.
BUT WE STILL HAVE TWO MORE SONGS!
YOUR FATHER WOULD NOT BE PLEASED.
COME ON. WE'LL HAVE OTHER GIGS.

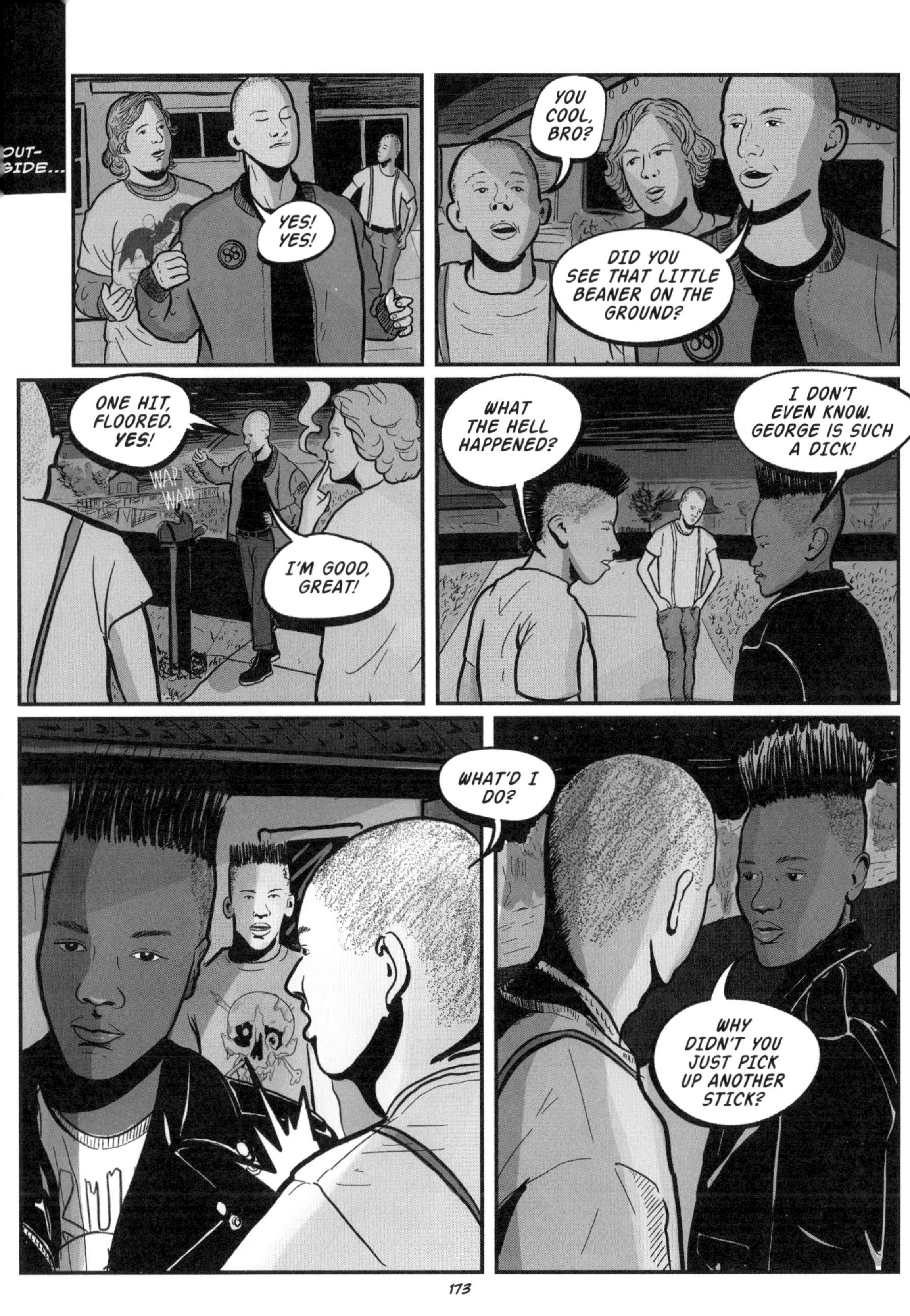
OUT-
SIDE...
YES!
YES!
YOU
COOL,
BRO?
DID YOU
SEE THAT LITTLE
BEANER ON THE
GROUND?
ONE HIT,
FLOORED.
YES!
WAP!
WAP!
I'M GOOD,
GREAT!
WHAT
THE HELL
HAPPENED?
I DON'T
EVEN KNOW.
GEORGE IS SUCH
A DICK!
WHAT'D I
DO?
WHY
DIDN'T YOU
JUST PICK
UP ANOTHER
STICK?

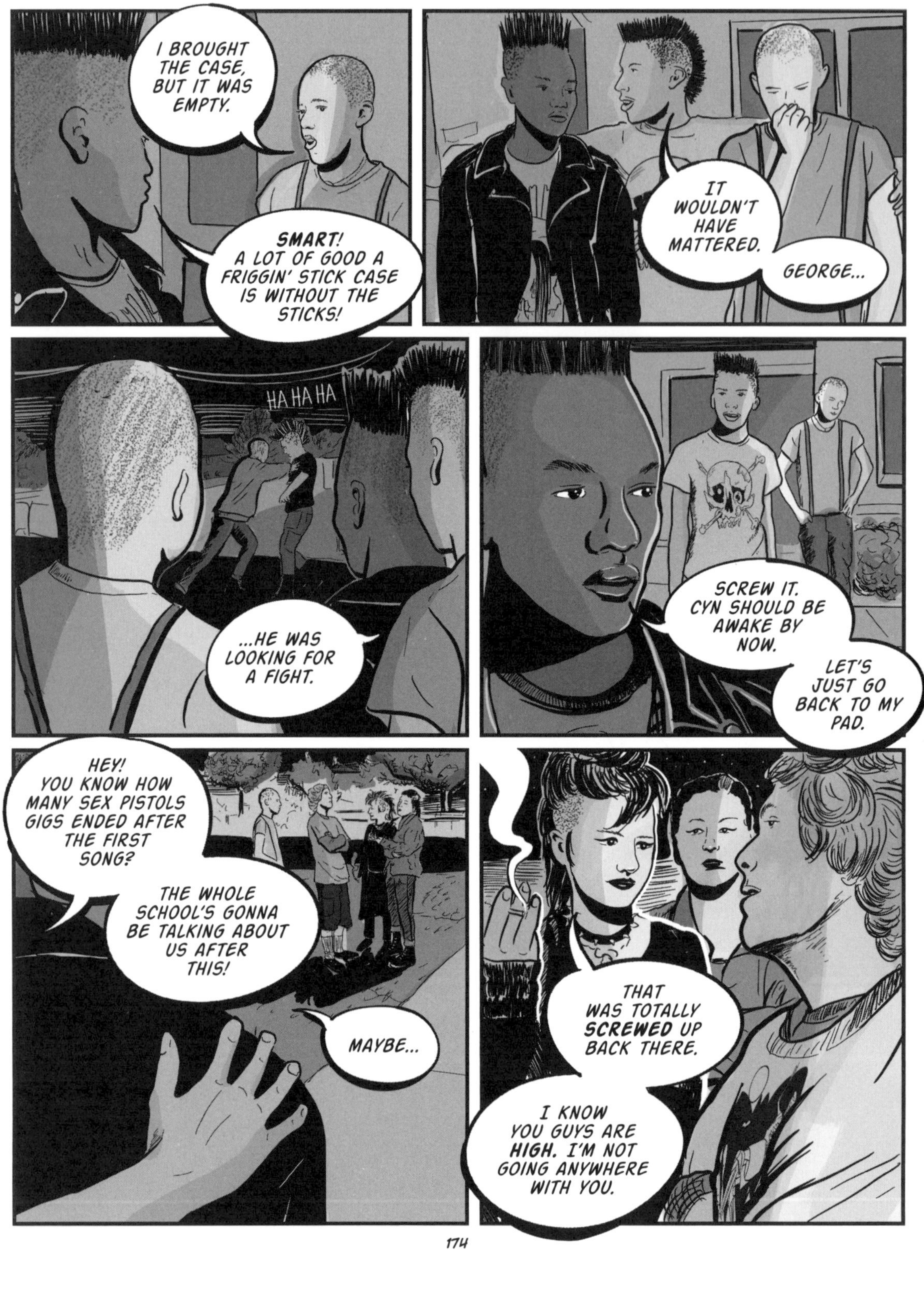

I BROUGHT THE CASE, BUT IT WAS EMPTY.
SMART! A LOT OF GOOD A FRIGGIN' STICK CASE IS WITHOUT THE STICKS!
IT WOULDN'T HAVE MATTERED.
GEORGE...
HA HA HA
...HE WAS LOOKING FOR A FIGHT.
SCREW IT. CYN SHOULD BE AWAKE BY NOW.
LET'S JUST GO BACK TO MY PAD.
HEY! YOU KNOW HOW MANY SEX PISTOLS GIGS ENDED AFTER THE FIRST SONG?
THE WHOLE SCHOOL'S GONNA BE TALKING ABOUT US AFTER THIS!
MAYBE...
THAT WAS TOTALLY **SCREWED** UP BACK THERE.
I KNOW YOU GUYS ARE **HIGH.** I'M NOT GOING ANYWHERE WITH YOU.

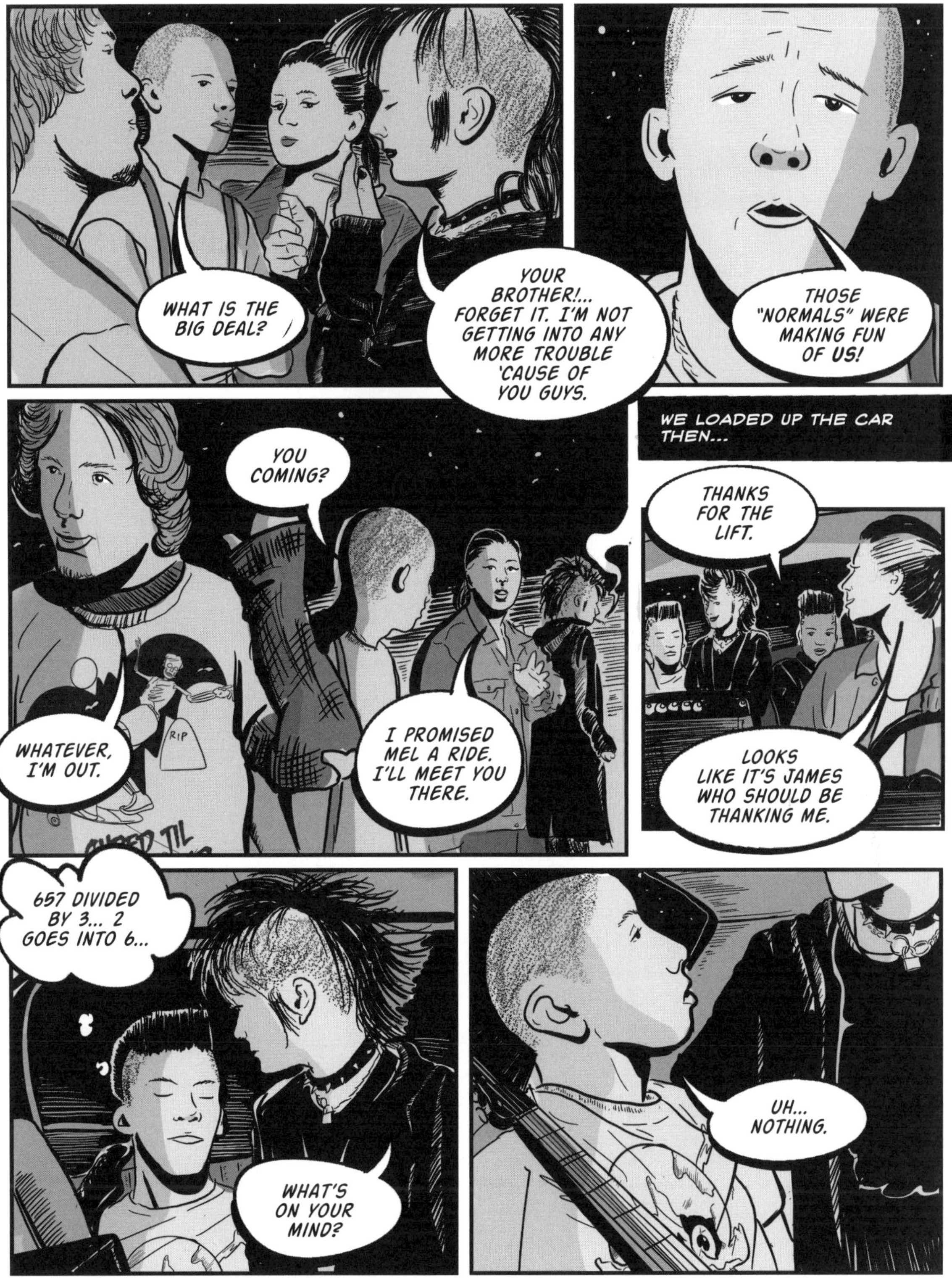

WHAT IS THE BIG DEAL?
YOUR BROTHER!... FORGET IT. I'M NOT GETTING INTO ANY MORE TROUBLE 'CAUSE OF YOU GUYS.
THOSE "NORMALS" WERE MAKING FUN OF US!
YOU COMING?
WHATEVER, I'M OUT.
I PROMISED MEL A RIDE. I'LL MEET YOU THERE.
WE LOADED UP THE CAR THEN...
THANKS FOR THE LIFT.
LOOKS LIKE IT'S JAMES WHO SHOULD BE THANKING ME.
657 DIVIDED BY 3... 2 GOES INTO 6...
WHAT'S ON YOUR MIND?
UH... NOTHING.

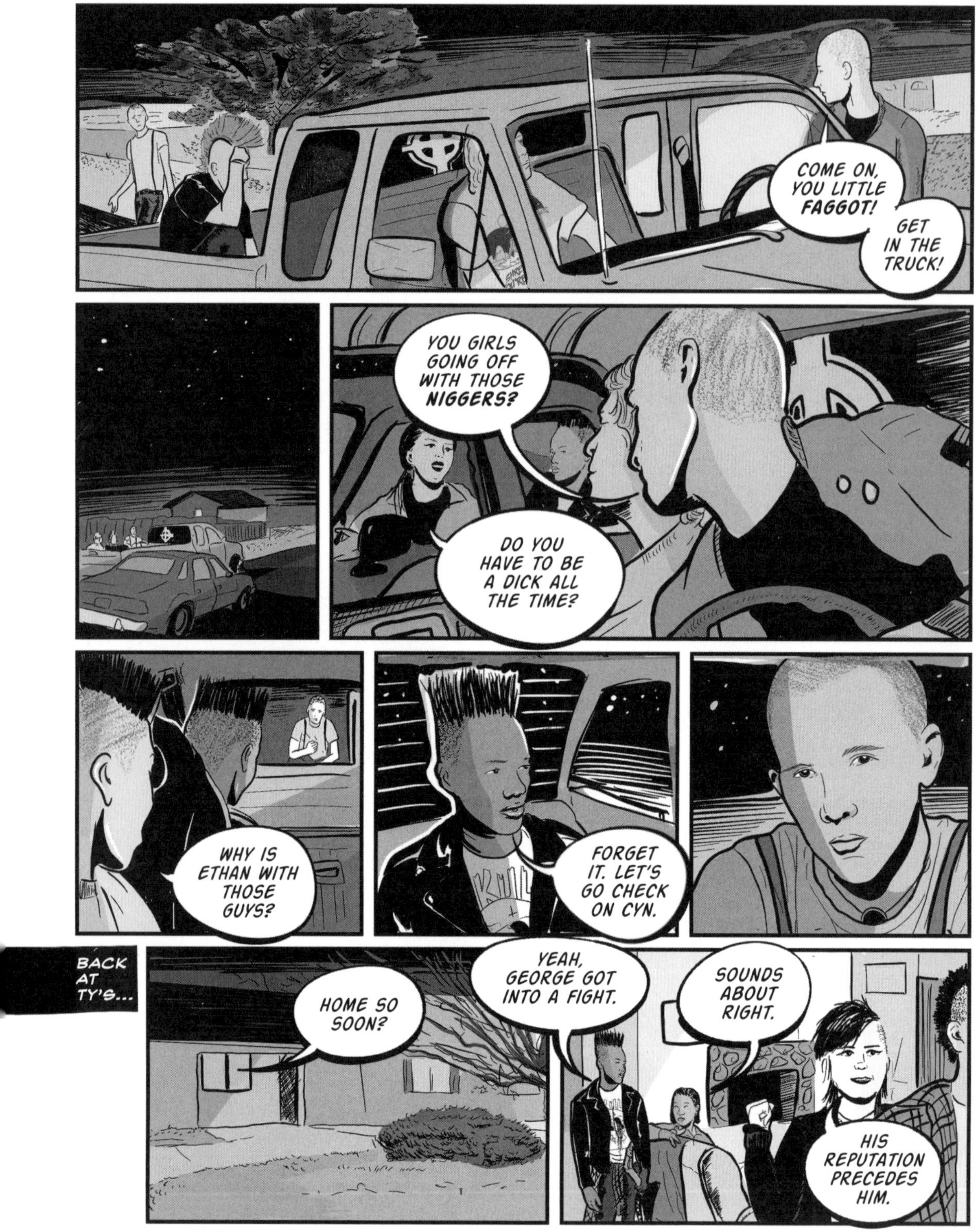
COME ON, YOU LITTLE FAGGOT!
GET IN THE TRUCK!
YOU GIRLS GOING OFF WITH THOSE NIGGERS?
DO YOU HAVE TO BE A DICK ALL THE TIME?
WHY IS ETHAN WITH THOSE GUYS?
FORGET IT. LET'S GO CHECK ON CYN.
BACK AT TY'S...
HOME SO SOON?
YEAH, GEORGE GOT INTO A FIGHT.
SOUNDS ABOUT RIGHT.
HIS REPUTATION PRECEDES HIM.

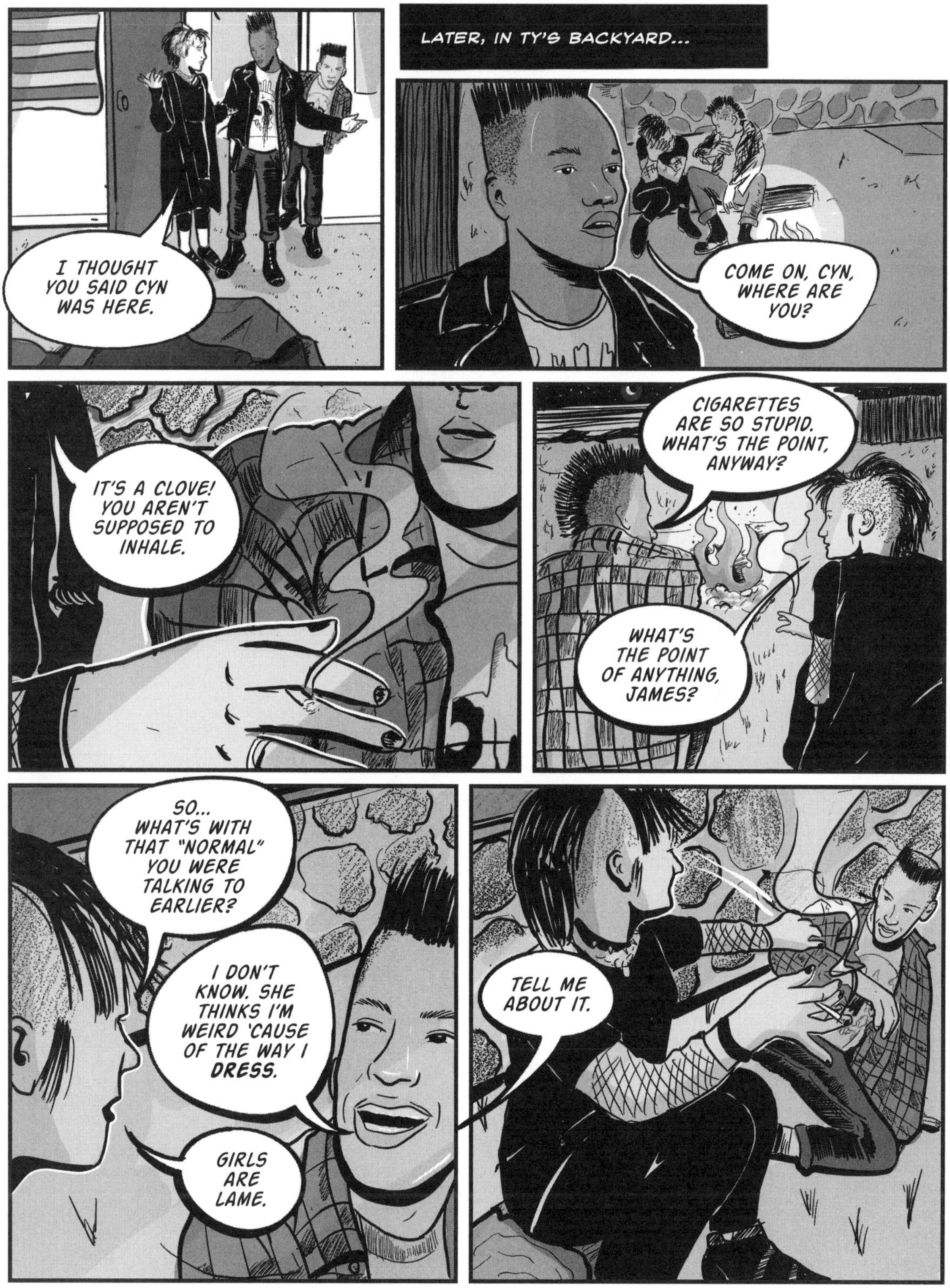

I THOUGHT YOU SAID CYN WAS HERE.
LATER, IN TY'S BACKYARD...
COME ON, CYN, WHERE ARE YOU?
IT'S A CLOVE! YOU AREN'T SUPPOSED TO INHALE.
CIGARETTES ARE SO STUPID. WHAT'S THE POINT, ANYWAY?
WHAT'S THE POINT OF ANYTHING, JAMES?
SO... WHAT'S WITH THAT "NORMAL" YOU WERE TALKING TO EARLIER?
I DON'T KNOW. SHE THINKS I'M WEIRD 'CAUSE OF THE WAY I DRESS.
GIRLS ARE LAME.
TELL ME ABOUT IT.

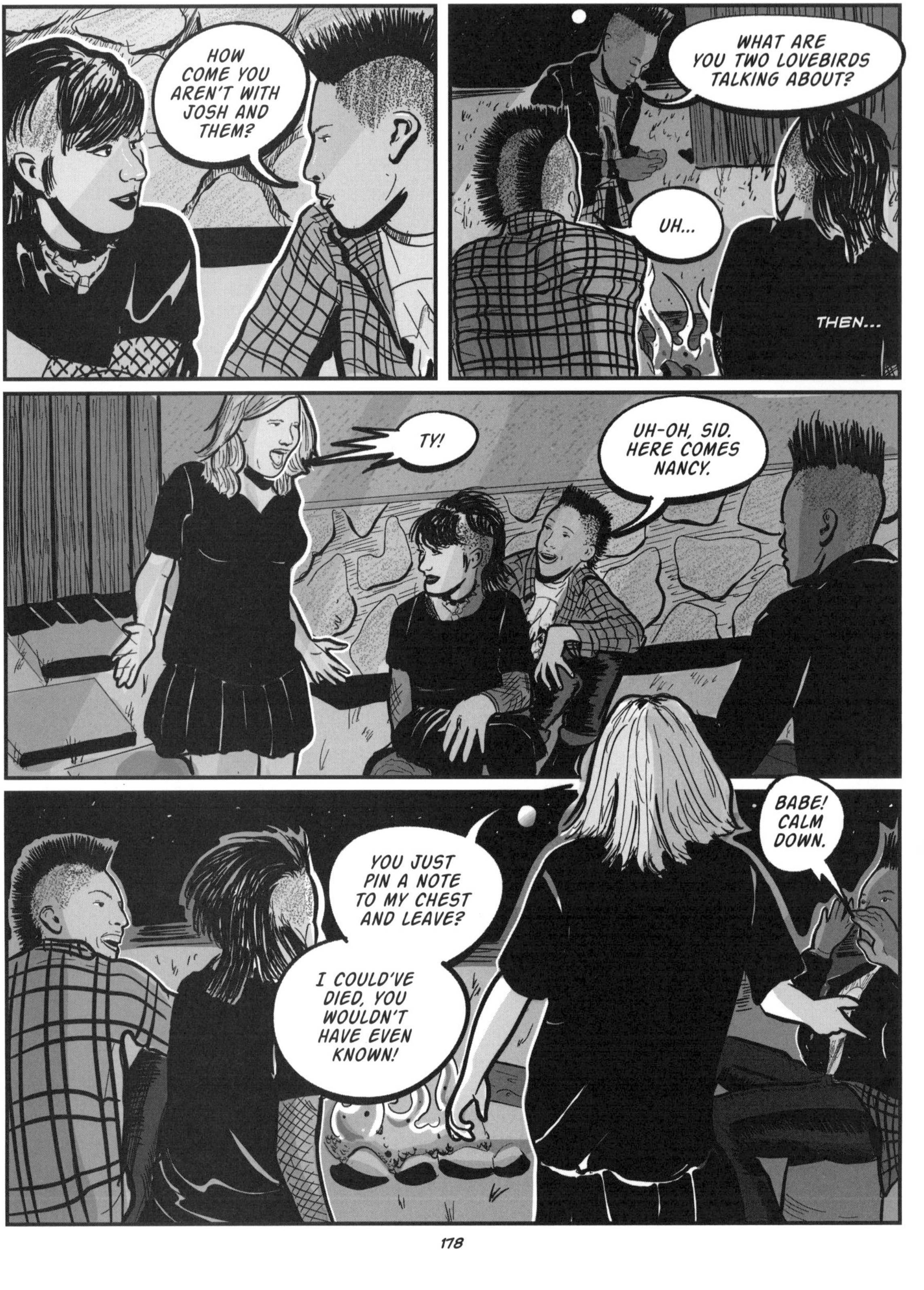
HOW COME YOU AREN'T WITH JOSH AND THEM?
WHAT ARE YOU TWO LOVEBIRDS TALKING ABOUT?
UH...
THEN...
TY!
UH-OH, SID. HERE COMES NANCY.
YOU JUST PIN A NOTE TO MY CHEST AND LEAVE?
I COULD'VE DIED, YOU WOULDN'T HAVE EVEN KNOWN!
BABE! CALM DOWN.

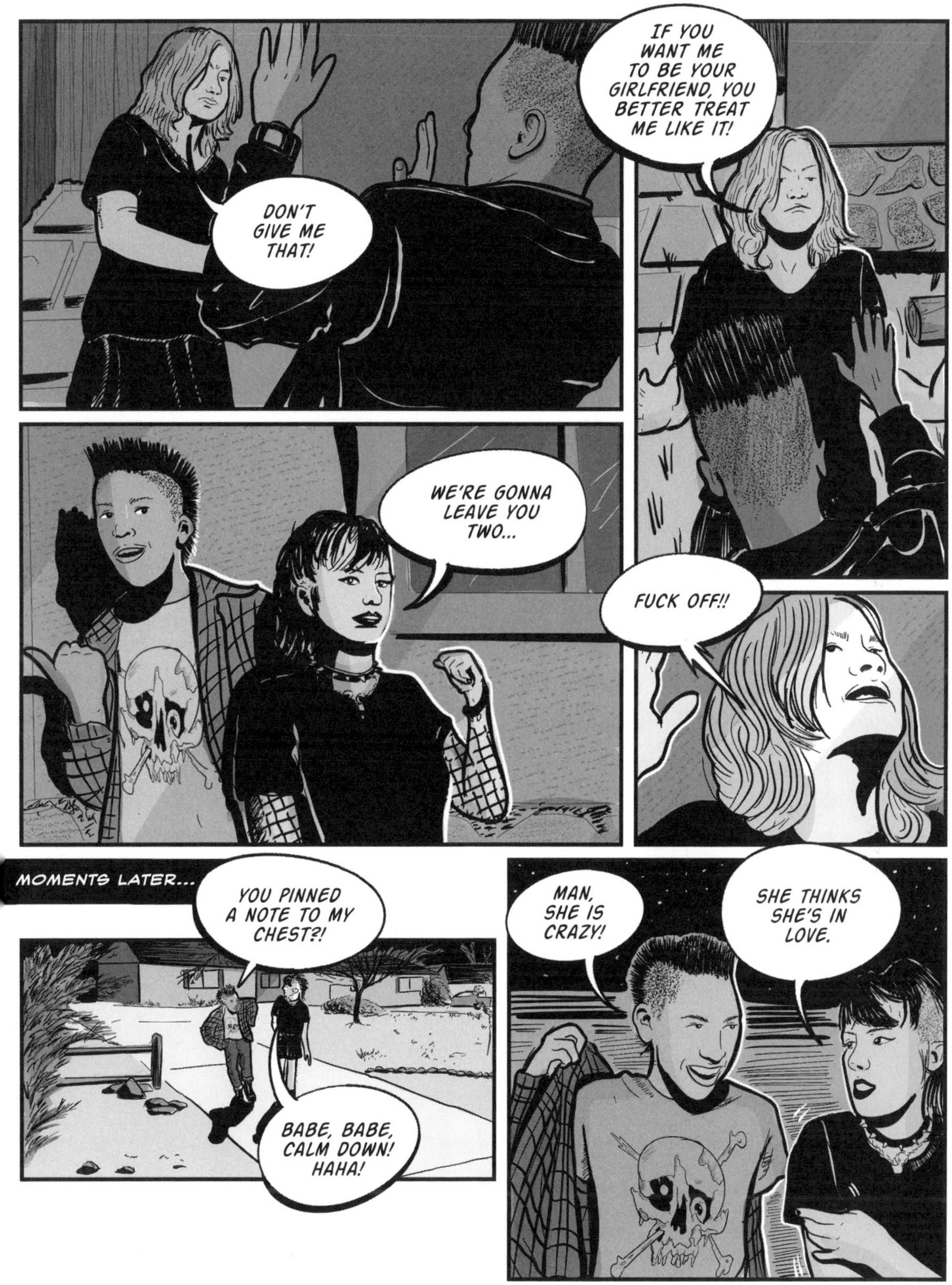
DON'T GIVE ME THAT!
IF YOU WANT ME TO BE YOUR GIRLFRIEND, YOU BETTER TREAT ME LIKE IT!
WE'RE GONNA LEAVE YOU TWO...
FUCK OFF!!
MOMENTS LATER...
YOU PINNED A NOTE TO MY CHEST?!
BABE, BABE, CALM DOWN! HAHA!
MAN, SHE IS CRAZY!
SHE THINKS SHE'S IN LOVE.

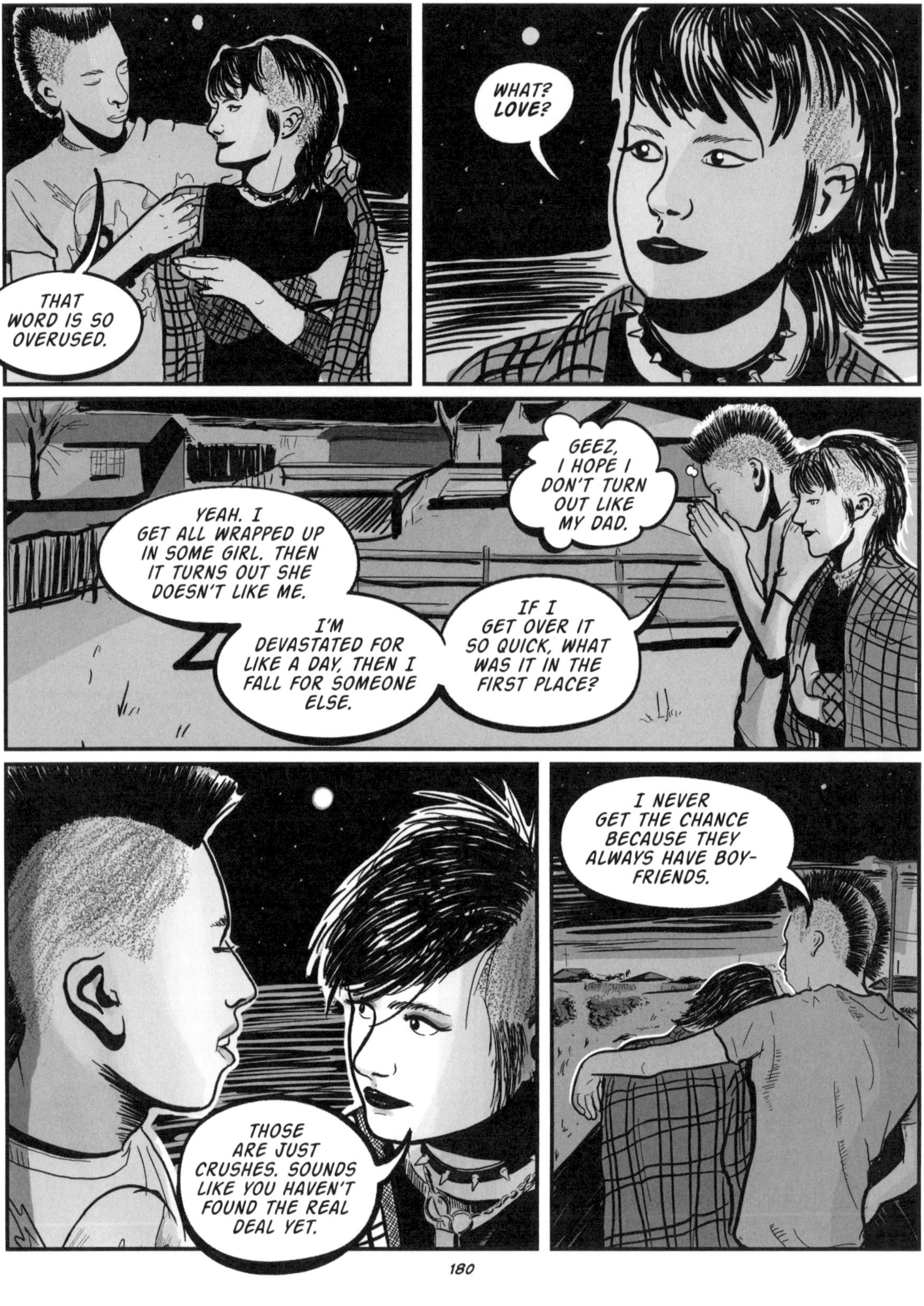
THAT WORD IS SO OVERUSED.
WHAT? LOVE?
YEAH. I GET ALL WRAPPED UP IN SOME GIRL. THEN IT TURNS OUT SHE DOESN'T LIKE ME.
I'M DEVASTATED FOR LIKE A DAY, THEN I FALL FOR SOMEONE ELSE.
IF I GET OVER IT SO QUICK, WHAT WAS IT IN THE FIRST PLACE?
GEEZ, I HOPE I DON'T TURN OUT LIKE MY DAD.
THOSE ARE JUST CRUSHES. SOUNDS LIKE YOU HAVEN'T FOUND THE REAL DEAL YET.
I NEVER GET THE CHANCE BECAUSE THEY ALWAYS HAVE BOY-FRIENDS.

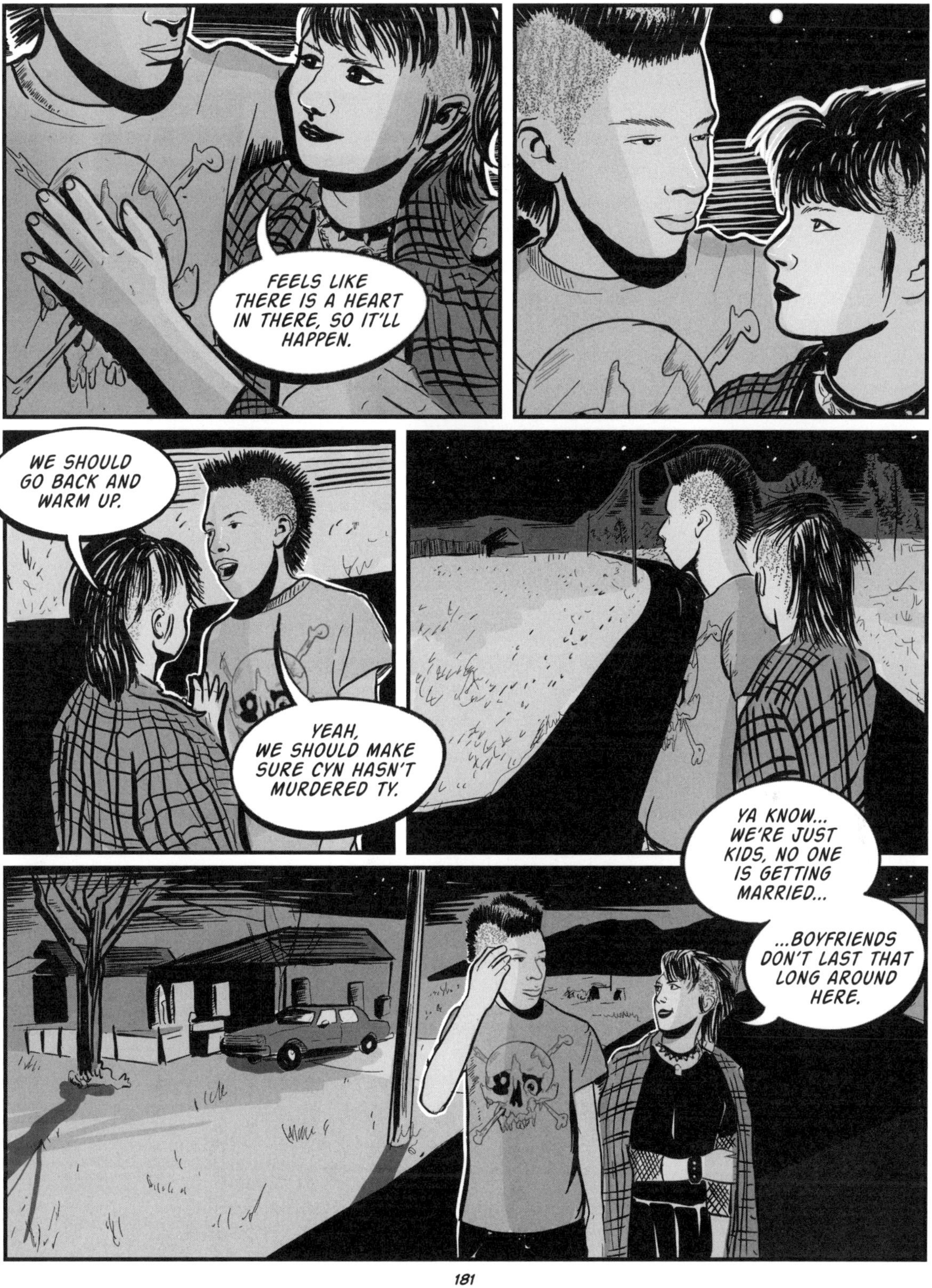
FEELS LIKE THERE IS A HEART IN THERE, SO IT'LL HAPPEN.
WE SHOULD GO BACK AND WARM UP.
YEAH, WE SHOULD MAKE SURE CYN HASN'T MURDERED TY.
YA KNOW... WE'RE JUST KIDS, NO ONE IS GETTING MARRIED...
...BOYFRIENDS DON'T LAST THAT LONG AROUND HERE.

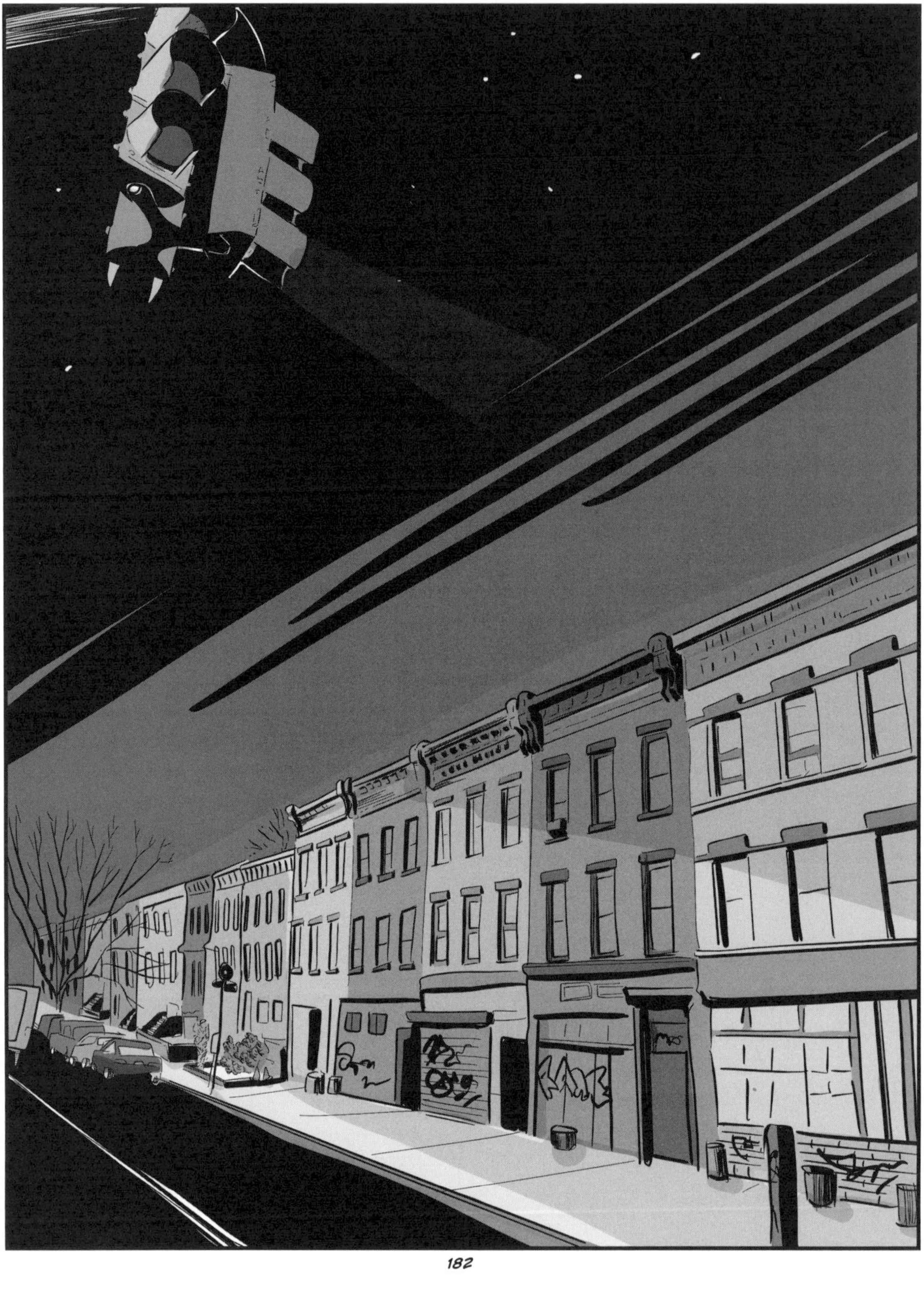

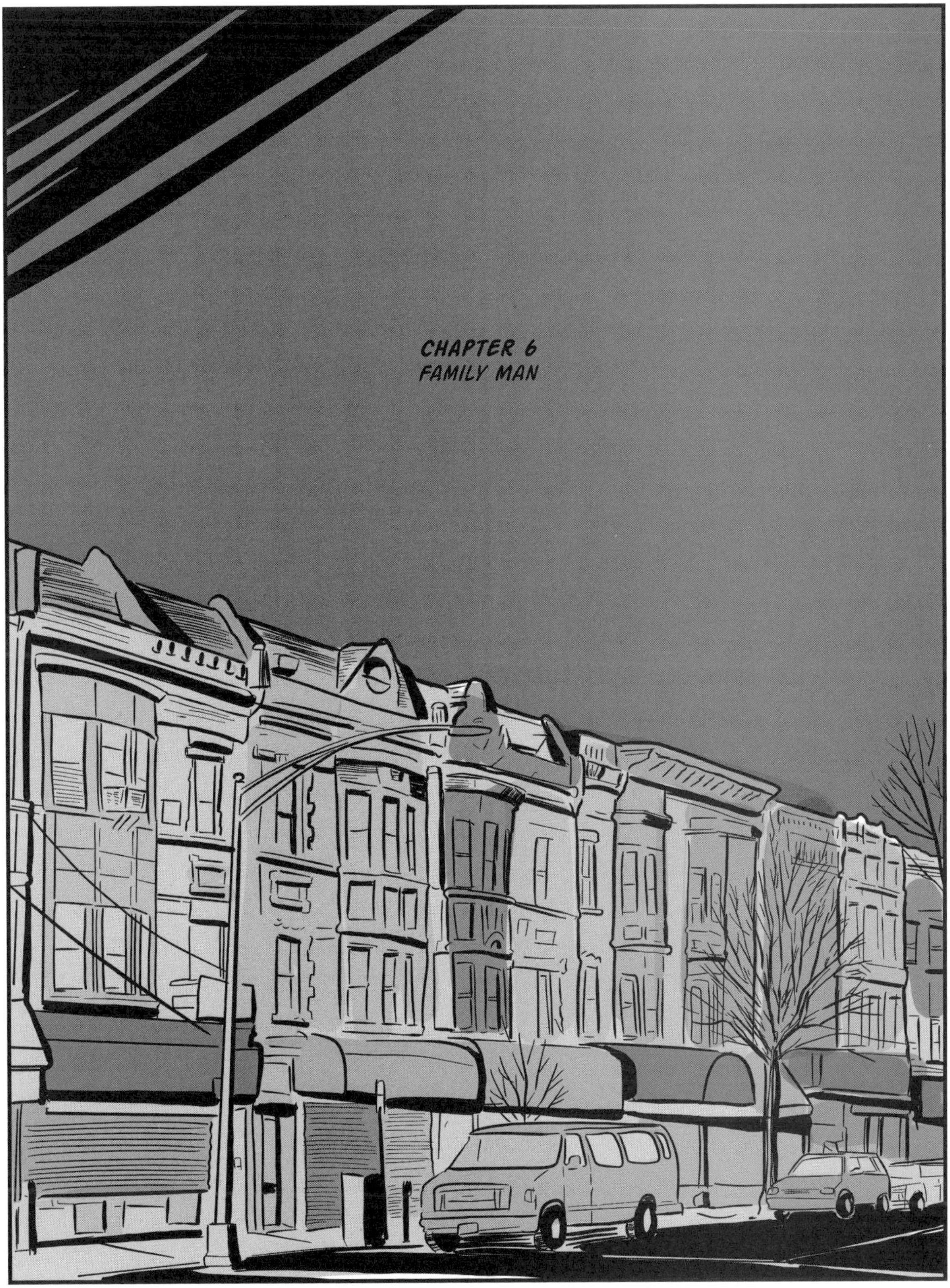
CHAPTER 6
FAMILY MAN

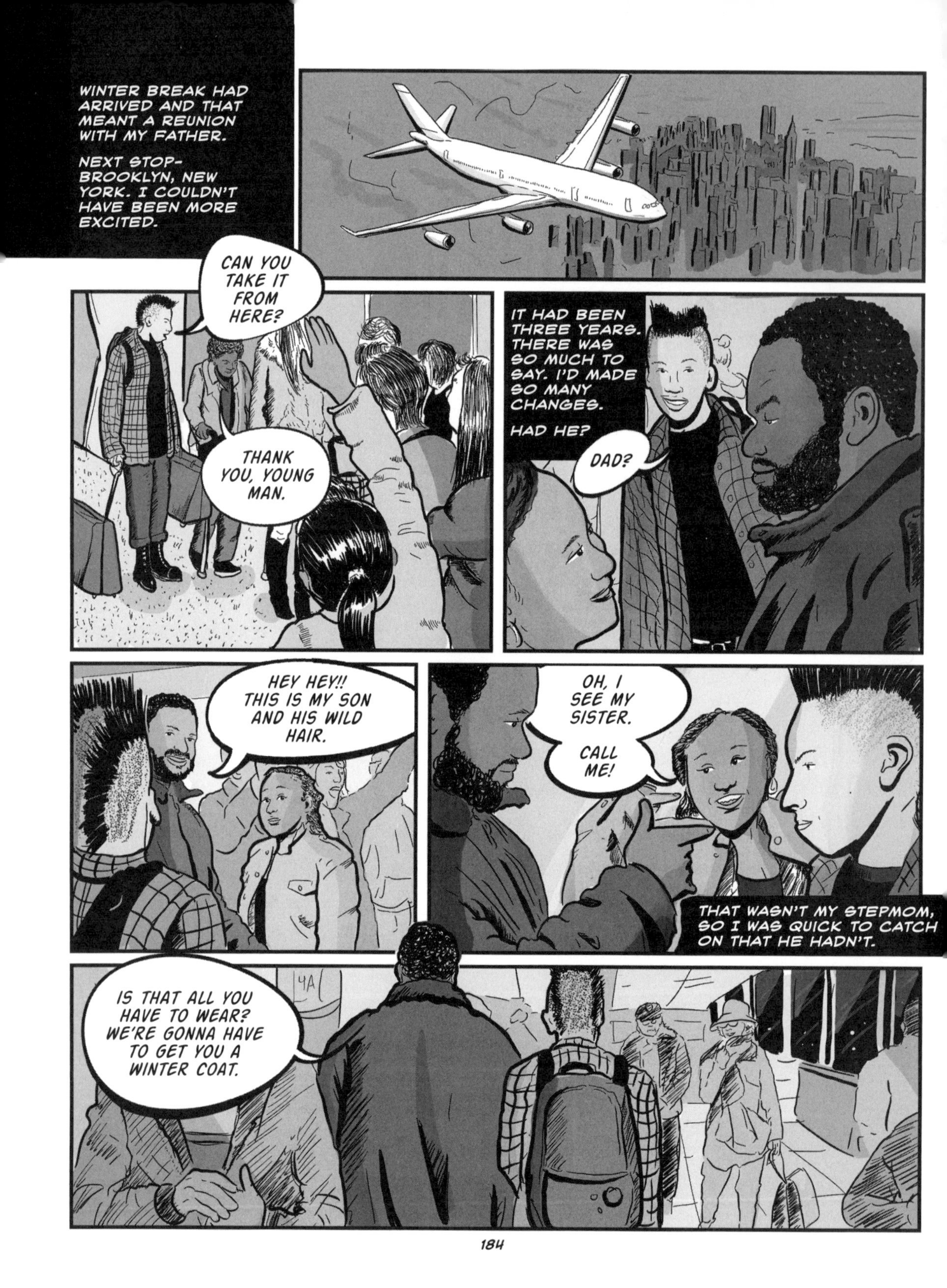
WINTER BREAK HAD ARRIVED AND THAT MEANT A REUNION WITH MY FATHER.
NEXT STOP- BROOKLYN, NEW YORK. I COULDN'T HAVE BEEN MORE EXCITED.
CAN YOU TAKE IT FROM HERE?
THANK YOU, YOUNG MAN.
IT HAD BEEN THREE YEARS. THERE WAS SO MUCH TO SAY. I'D MADE SO MANY CHANGES.
HAD HE?
DAD?
HEY HEY!! THIS IS MY SON AND HIS WILD HAIR.
OH, I SEE MY SISTER.
CALL ME!
THAT WASN'T MY STEPMOM, SO I WAS QUICK TO CATCH ON THAT HE HADN'T.
IS THAT ALL YOU HAVE TO WEAR? WE'RE GONNA HAVE TO GET YOU A WINTER COAT.

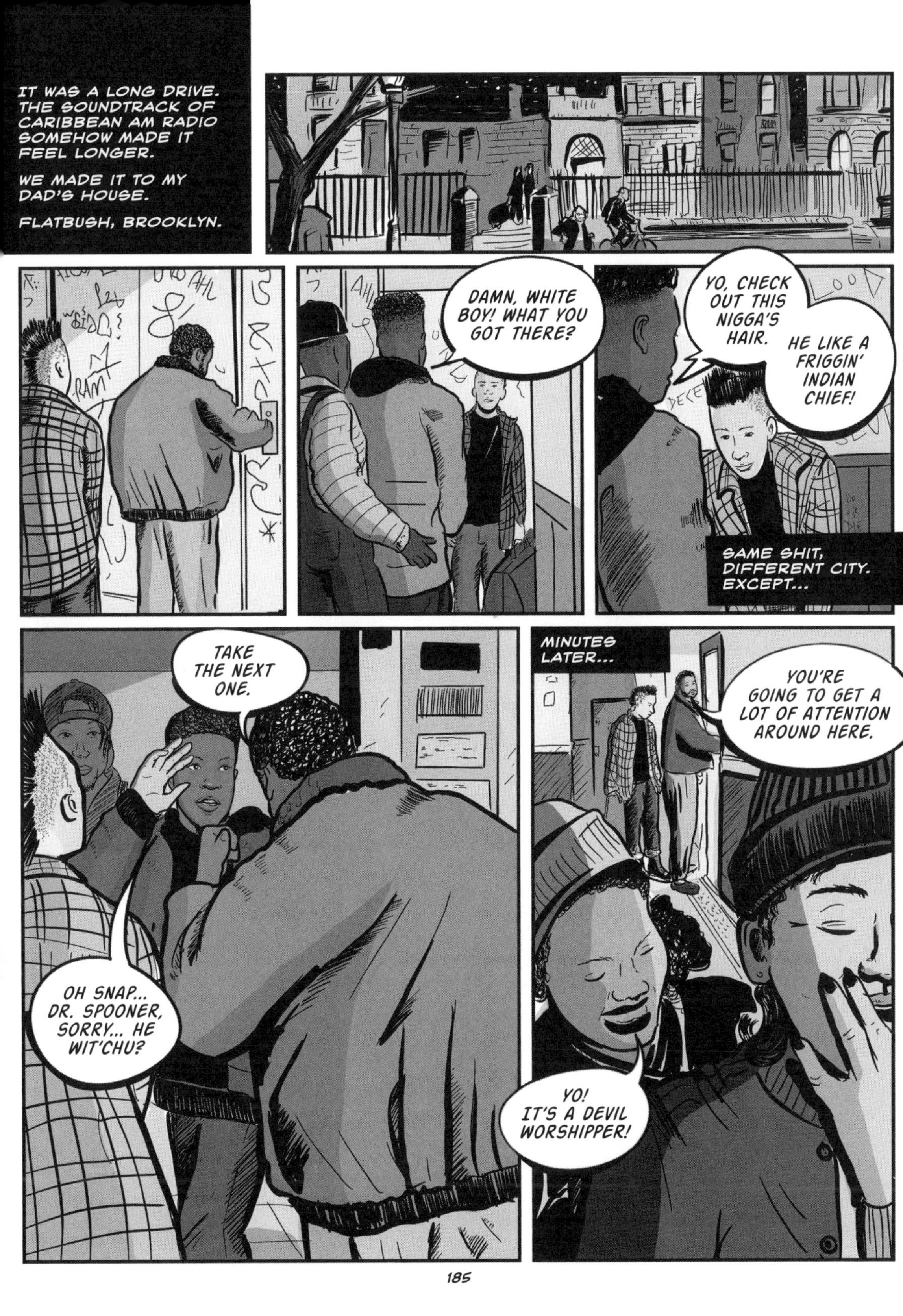
IT WAS A LONG DRIVE. THE SOUNDTRACK OF CARIBBEAN AM RADIO SOMEHOW MADE IT FEEL LONGER.
WE MADE IT TO MY DAD'S HOUSE.
FLATBUSH, BROOKLYN.
DAMN, WHITE BOY! WHAT YOU GOT THERE?
YO, CHECK OUT THIS NIGGA'S HAIR.
HE LIKE A FRIGGIN' INDIAN CHIEF!
SAME SHIT, DIFFERENT CITY. EXCEPT...
TAKE THE NEXT ONE.
OH SNAP... DR. SPOONER, SORRY... HE WIT'CHU?
MINUTES LATER...
YOU'RE GOING TO GET A LOT OF ATTENTION AROUND HERE.
YO! IT'S A DEVIL WORSHIPPER!

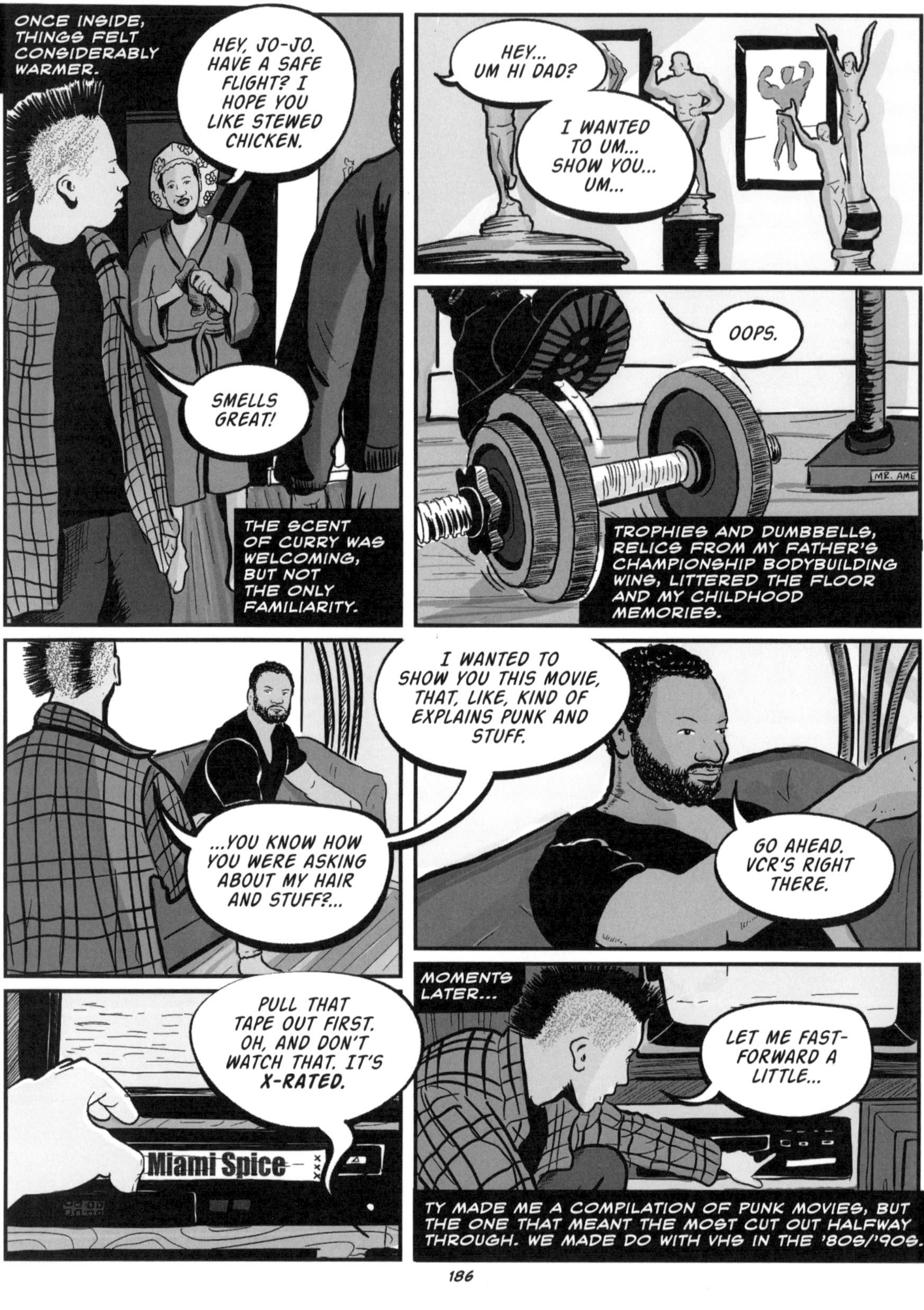

ONCE INSIDE, THINGS FELT CONSIDERABLY WARMER.
HEY, JO-JO. HAVE A SAFE FLIGHT? I HOPE YOU LIKE STEWED CHICKEN.
SMELLS GREAT!
THE SCENT OF CURRY WAS WELCOMING, BUT NOT THE ONLY FAMILIARITY.
HEY... UM HI DAD?
I WANTED TO UM... SHOW YOU... UM...
OOPS.
MR. AME
TROPHIES AND DUMBBELLS, RELICS FROM MY FATHER'S CHAMPIONSHIP BODYBUILDING WINS, LITTERED THE FLOOR AND MY CHILDHOOD MEMORIES.
I WANTED TO SHOW YOU THIS MOVIE, THAT, LIKE, KIND OF EXPLAINS PUNK AND STUFF.
...YOU KNOW HOW YOU WERE ASKING ABOUT MY HAIR AND STUFF?...
GO AHEAD. VCR'S RIGHT THERE.
PULL THAT TAPE OUT FIRST. OH, AND DON'T WATCH THAT. IT'S X-RATED.
Miami Spice
XXX
MOMENTS LATER...
LET ME FAST-FORWARD A LITTLE...
TY MADE ME A COMPILATION OF PUNK MOVIES, BUT THE ONE THAT MEANT THE MOST CUT OUT HALFWAY THROUGH. WE MADE DO WITH VHS IN THE '80S/'90S.

GIVE ME A MINUTE.

A DISAPPOINTING 10 MINUTES LATER...

ALRIGHT.

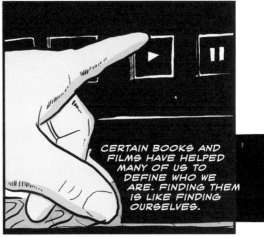

CERTAIN BOOKS AND FILMS HAVE HELPED MANY OF US TO DEFINE WHO WE ARE. FINDING THEM IS LIKE FINDING OURSELVES.

"FOR AN INCREASING AMOUNT OF KIDS, PUNKS AND NON-PUNKS, THE ALL-AMERICAN DREAM JUST ISN'T VIABLE."*

HOW DO THESE GUYS MAKE MONEY?

IT'S NOT ABOUT THE MONEY...

...WHICH IS WHY IT'S PAINFUL TO SEE OUR CULTURE CO-OPTED FOR PROFIT.

187 *FROM ANOTHER STATE OF MIND *DIR. ADAM SMALL AND PETER STUART, 1984*

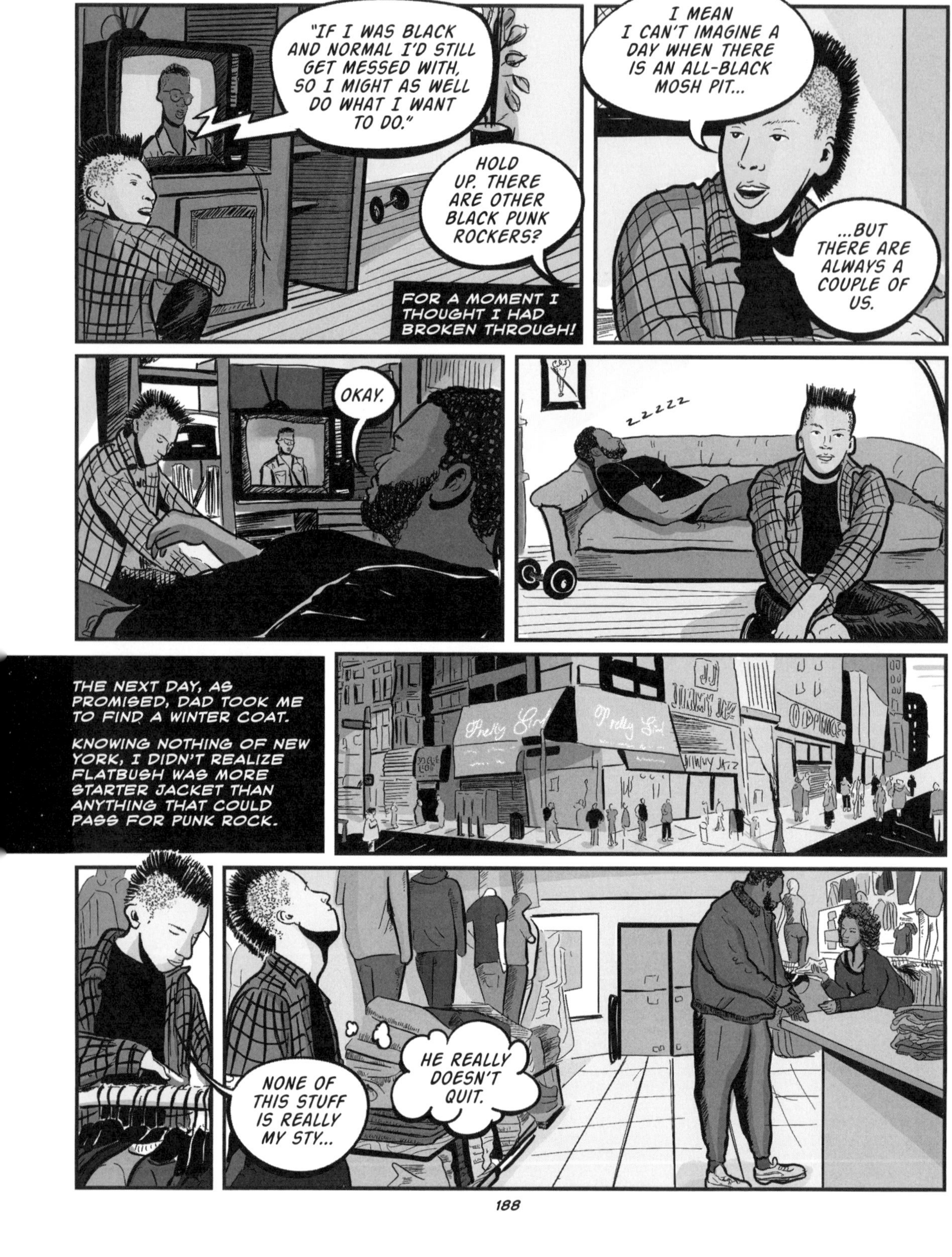
"IF I WAS BLACK AND NORMAL I'D STILL GET MESSED WITH, SO I MIGHT AS WELL DO WHAT I WANT TO DO."
HOLD UP. THERE ARE OTHER BLACK PUNK ROCKERS?
FOR A MOMENT I THOUGHT I HAD BROKEN THROUGH!
I MEAN I CAN'T IMAGINE A DAY WHEN THERE IS AN ALL-BLACK MOSH PIT...
...BUT THERE ARE ALWAYS A COUPLE OF US.
OKAY.
ZZZZZ
THE NEXT DAY, AS PROMISED, DAD TOOK ME TO FIND A WINTER COAT.
KNOWING NOTHING OF NEW YORK, I DIDN'T REALIZE FLATBUSH WAS MORE STARTER JACKET THAN ANYTHING THAT COULD PASS FOR PUNK ROCK.
NONE OF THIS STUFF IS REALLY MY STY...
HE REALLY DOESN'T QUIT.

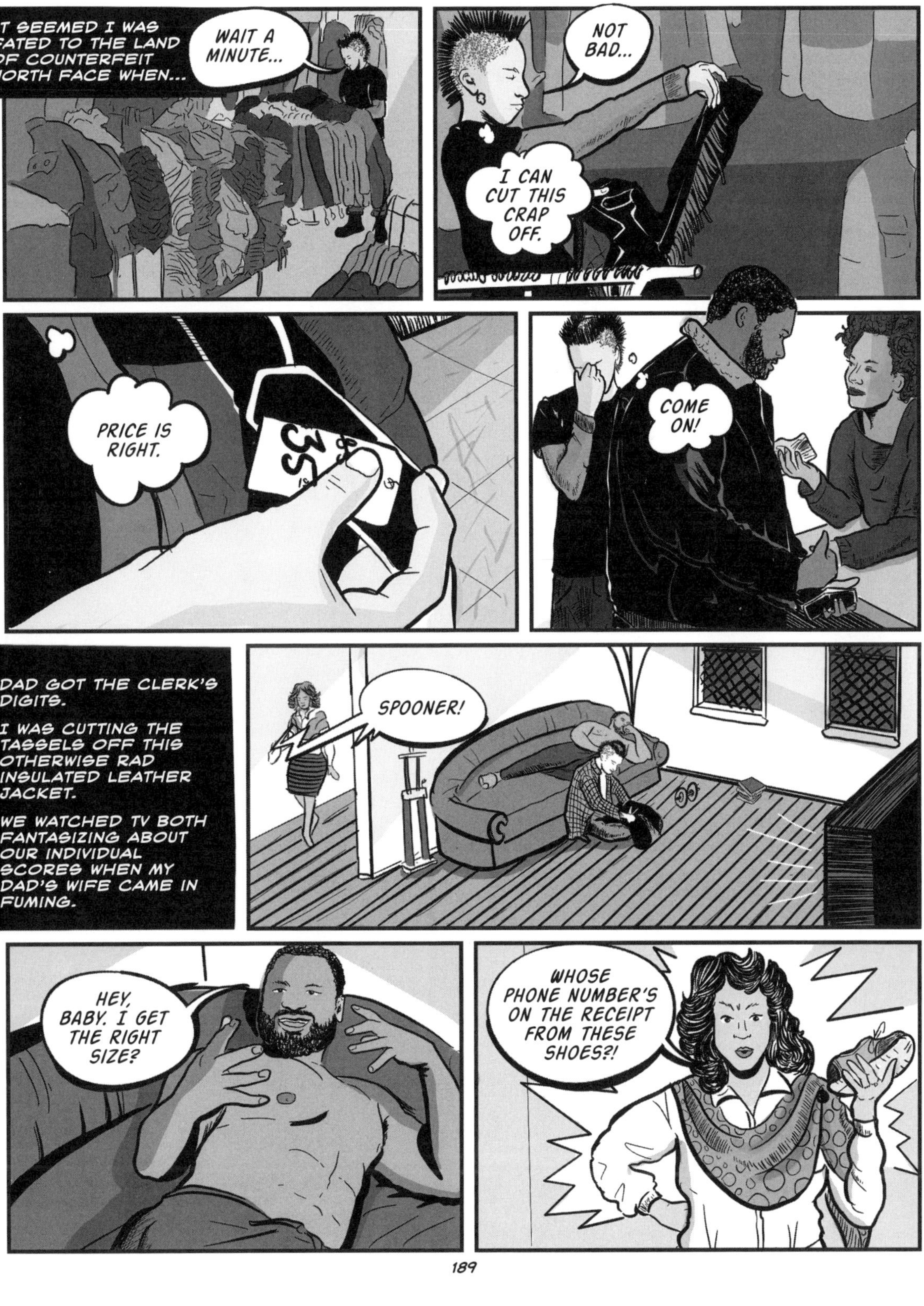
IT SEEMED I WAS FATED TO THE LAND OF COUNTERFEIT NORTH FACE WHEN...
WAIT A MINUTE...
NOT BAD...
I CAN CUT THIS CRAP OFF.
PRICE IS RIGHT.
COME ON!
DAD GOT THE CLERK'S DIGITS.
I WAS CUTTING THE TASSELS OFF THIS OTHERWISE RAD INSULATED LEATHER JACKET.
WE WATCHED TV BOTH FANTASIZING ABOUT OUR INDIVIDUAL SCORES WHEN MY DAD'S WIFE CAME IN FUMING.
SPOONER!
HEY, BABY. I GET THE RIGHT SIZE?
WHOSE PHONE NUMBER'S ON THE RECEIPT FROM THESE SHOES?!

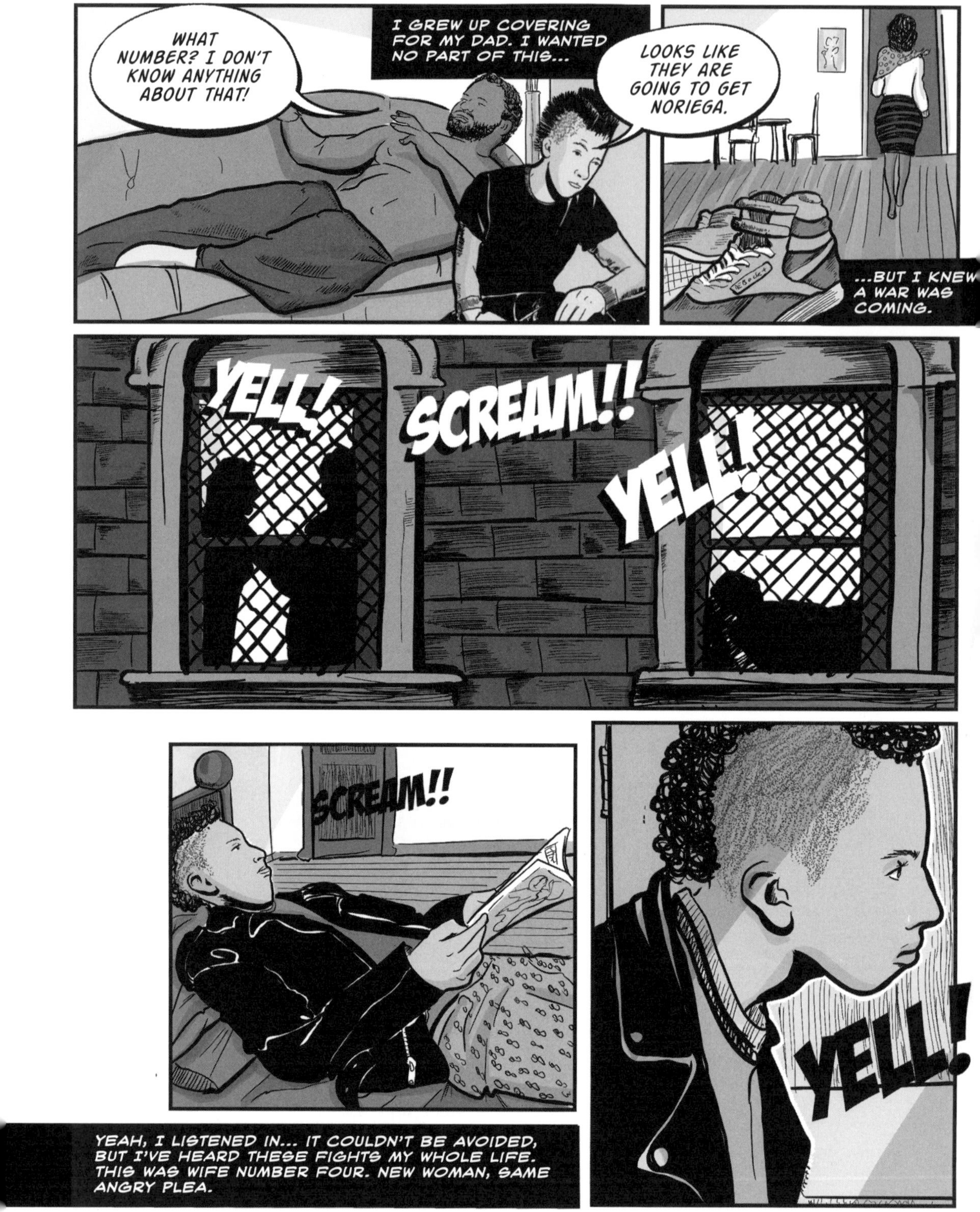
WHAT NUMBER? I DON'T KNOW ANYTHING ABOUT THAT!
I GREW UP COVERING FOR MY DAD. I WANTED NO PART OF THIS...
LOOKS LIKE THEY ARE GOING TO GET NORIEGA.
...BUT I KNEW A WAR WAS COMING.
YELL!
SCREAM!!
YELL!
SCREAM!!
YEAH, I LISTENED IN... IT COULDN'T BE AVOIDED, BUT I'VE HEARD THESE FIGHTS MY WHOLE LIFE. THIS WAS WIFE NUMBER FOUR. NEW WOMAN, SAME ANGRY PLEA.
YELL!

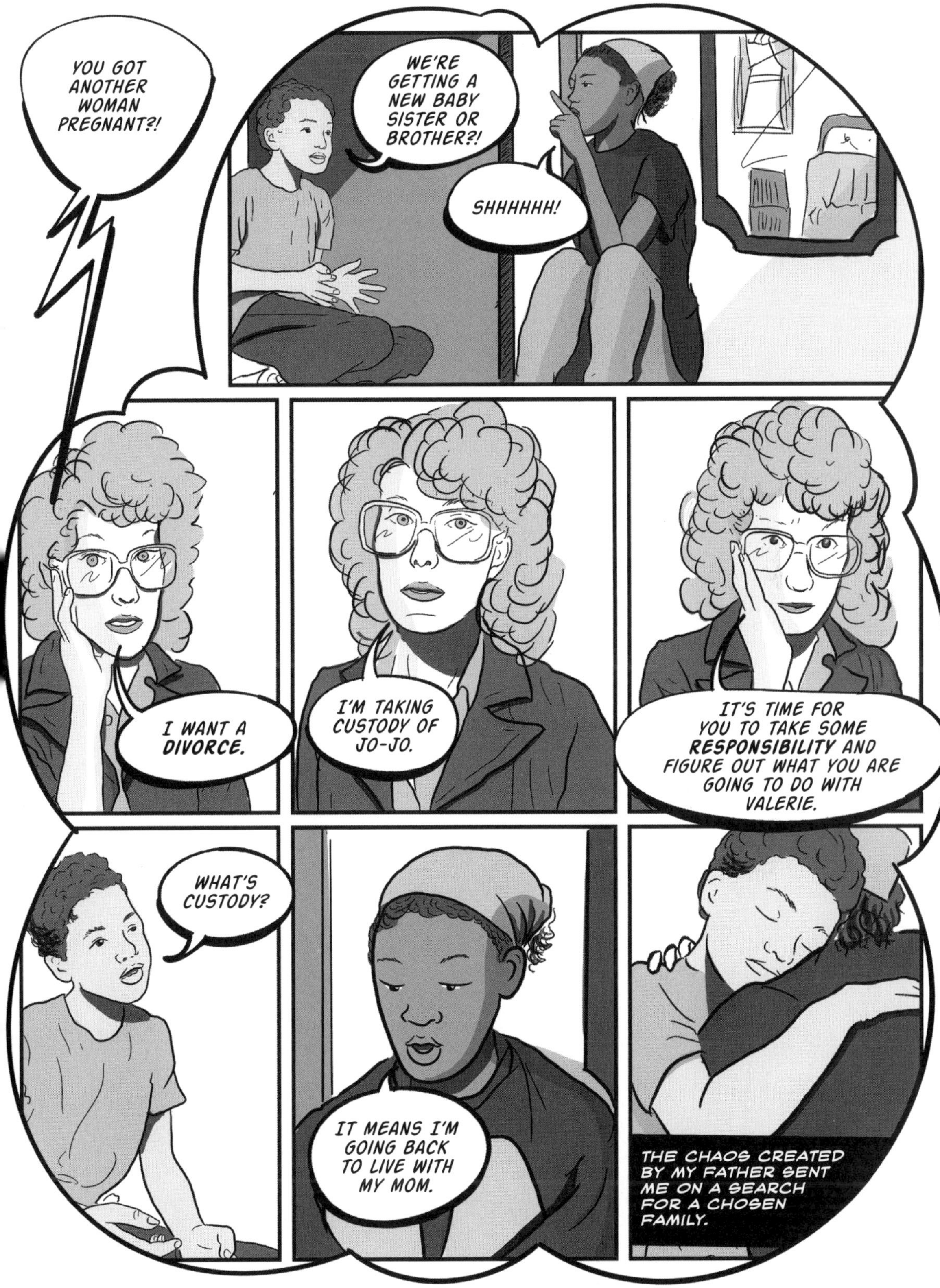

YOU GOT ANOTHER WOMAN PREGNANT?!
WE'RE GETTING A NEW BABY SISTER OR BROTHER?!
SHHHHHH!
I WANT A DIVORCE.
I'M TAKING CUSTODY OF JO-JO.
IT'S TIME FOR YOU TO TAKE SOME RESPONSIBILITY AND FIGURE OUT WHAT YOU ARE GOING TO DO WITH VALERIE.
WHAT'S CUSTODY?
IT MEANS I'M GOING BACK TO LIVE WITH MY MOM.
THE CHAOS CREATED BY MY FATHER SENT ME ON A SEARCH FOR A CHOSEN FAMILY.

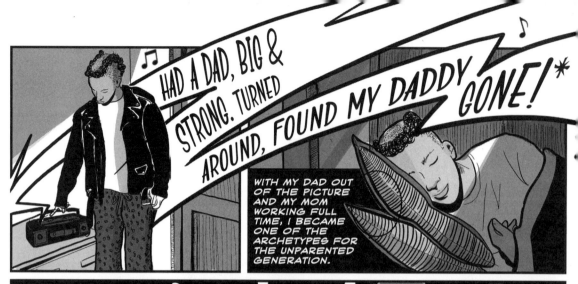

HAD A DAD, BIG & STRONG. TURNED AROUND, FOUND MY DADDY GONE!*

WITH MY DAD OUT OF THE PICTURE AND MY MOM WORKING FULL TIME, I BECAME ONE OF THE ARCHETYPES FOR THE UNPARENTED GENERATION.

JO-JO! YOUR MOTHER!

HELLO?

MERRY CHRISTMAS!

*JANE'S ADDICTION "HAD A DAD"

YOU TOO, MOM.

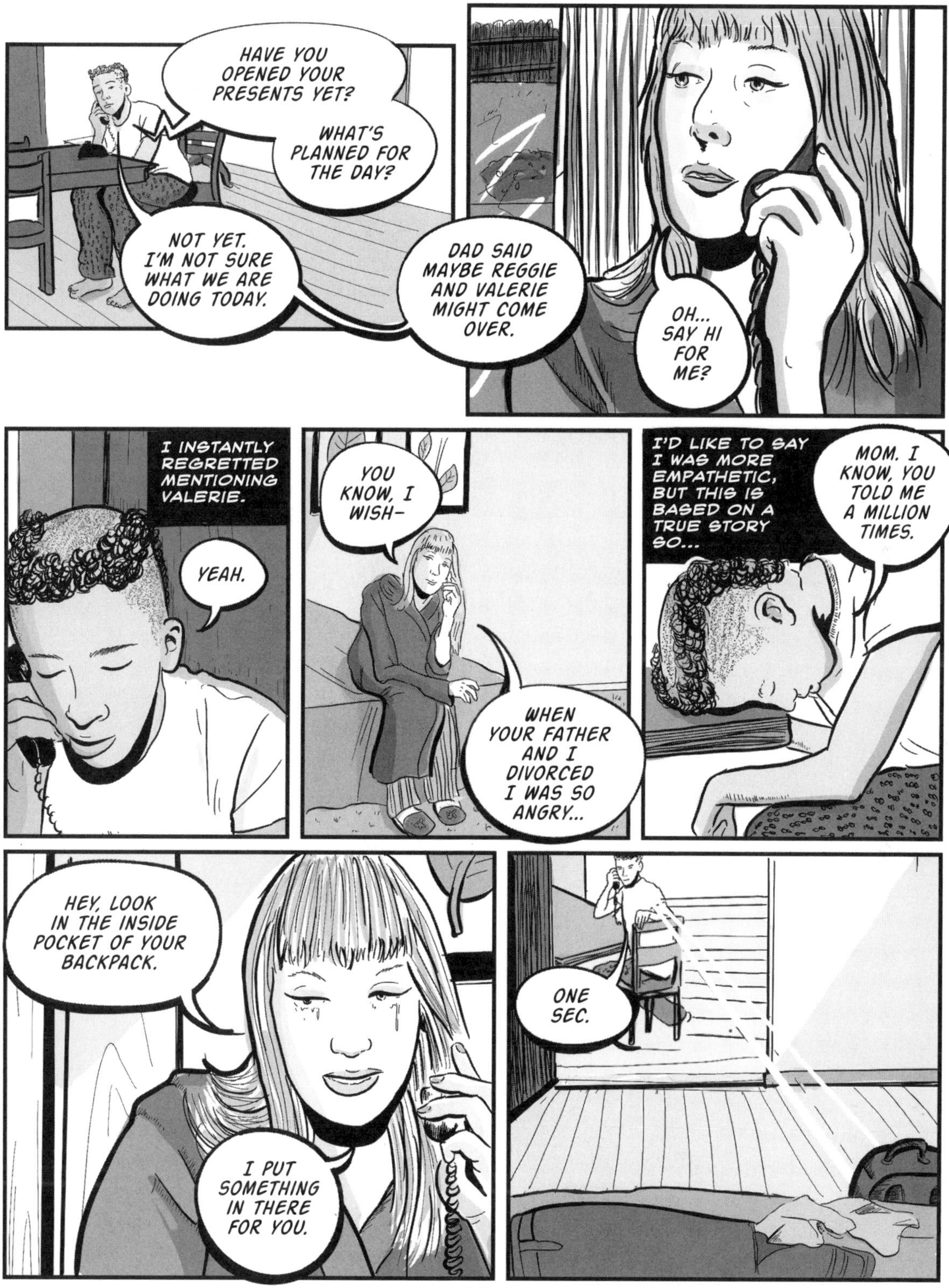
HAVE YOU OPENED YOUR PRESENTS YET?
WHAT'S PLANNED FOR THE DAY?
NOT YET. I'M NOT SURE WHAT WE ARE DOING TODAY.
DAD SAID MAYBE REGGIE AND VALERIE MIGHT COME OVER.
OH... SAY HI FOR ME?
I INSTANTLY REGRETTED MENTIONING VALERIE.
YEAH.
YOU KNOW, I WISH–
WHEN YOUR FATHER AND I DIVORCED I WAS SO ANGRY...
I'D LIKE TO SAY I WAS MORE EMPATHETIC, BUT THIS IS BASED ON A TRUE STORY SO...
MOM. I KNOW, YOU TOLD ME A MILLION TIMES.
HEY, LOOK IN THE INSIDE POCKET OF YOUR BACKPACK.
I PUT SOMETHING IN THERE FOR YOU.
ONE SEC.

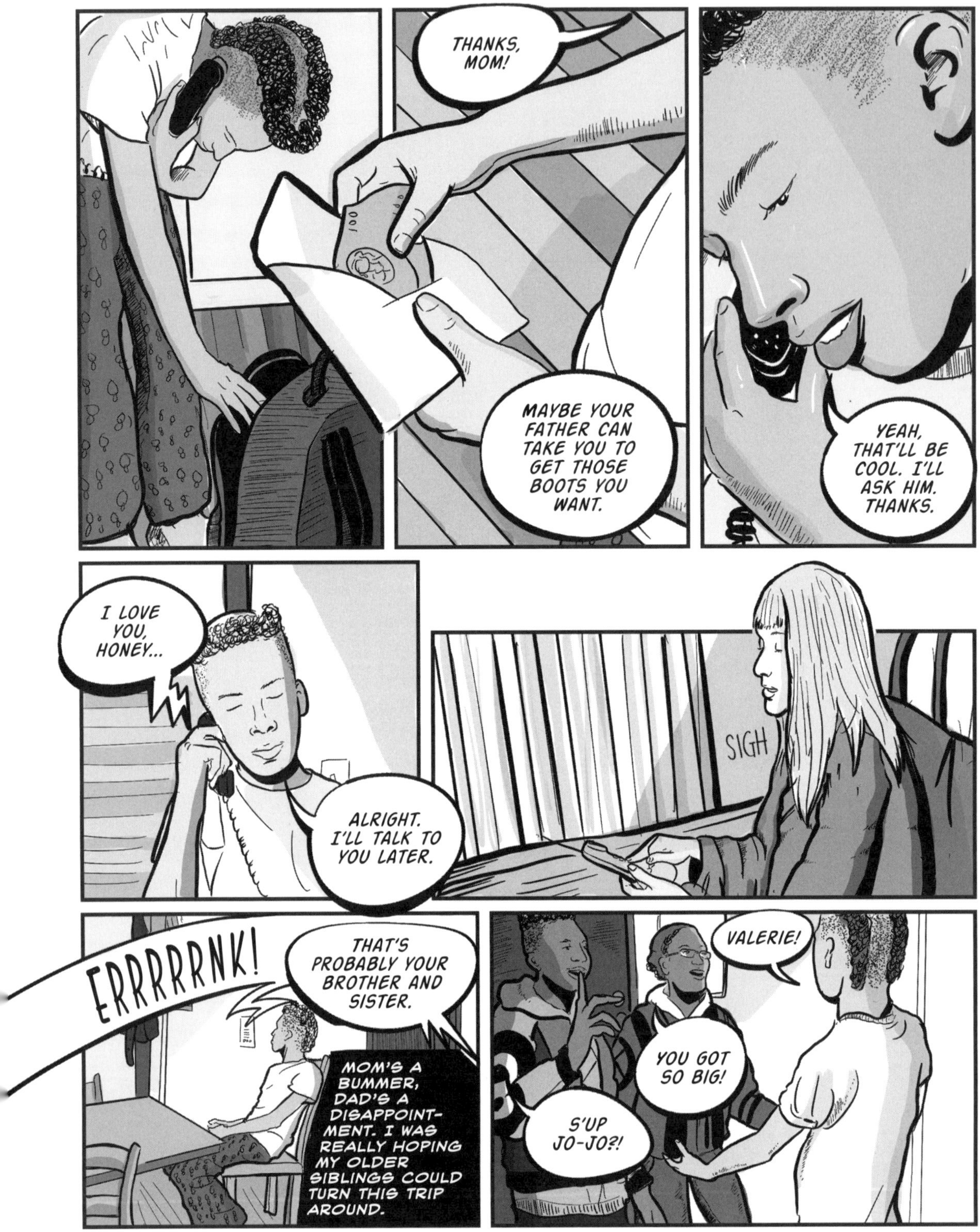
THANKS, MOM!
MAYBE YOUR FATHER CAN TAKE YOU TO GET THOSE BOOTS YOU WANT.
YEAH, THAT'LL BE COOL. I'LL ASK HIM. THANKS.
I LOVE YOU, HONEY...
ALRIGHT. I'LL TALK TO YOU LATER.
SIGH
ERRRRRNK!
THAT'S PROBABLY YOUR BROTHER AND SISTER.
MOM'S A BUMMER, DAD'S A DISAPPOINT-MENT. I WAS REALLY HOPING MY OLDER SIBLINGS COULD TURN THIS TRIP AROUND.
VALERIE!
YOU GOT SO BIG!
S'UP JO-JO?!

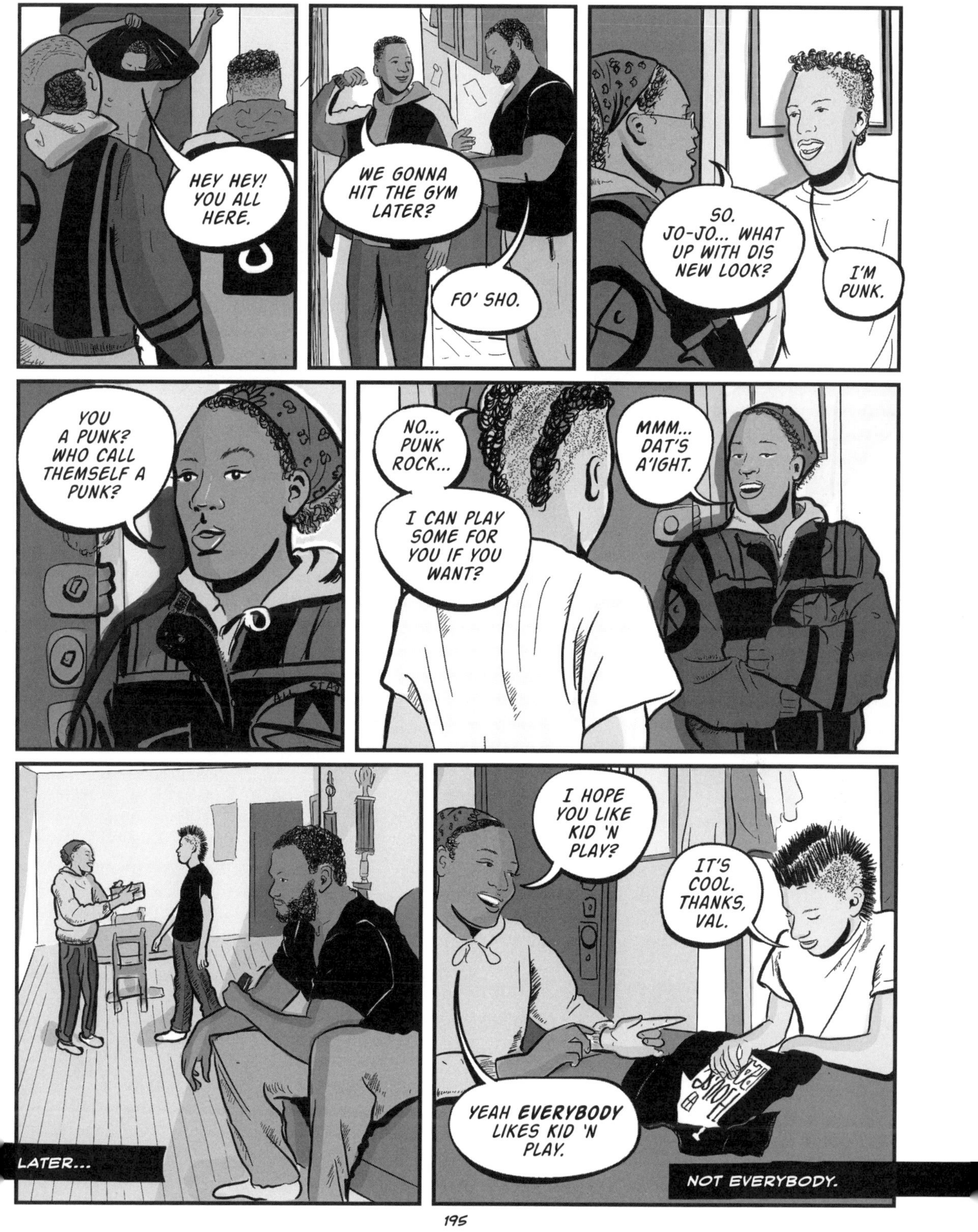
HEY HEY! YOU ALL HERE.
WE GONNA HIT THE GYM LATER?
FO' SHO.
SO. JO-JO... WHAT UP WITH DIS NEW LOOK?
I'M PUNK.
YOU A PUNK? WHO CALL THEMSELF A PUNK?
NO... PUNK ROCK...
I CAN PLAY SOME FOR YOU IF YOU WANT?
MMM... DAT'S A'IGHT.
LATER...
I HOPE YOU LIKE KID 'N PLAY?
IT'S COOL. THANKS, VAL.
YEAH **EVERYBODY** LIKES KID 'N PLAY.
NOT EVERYBODY.

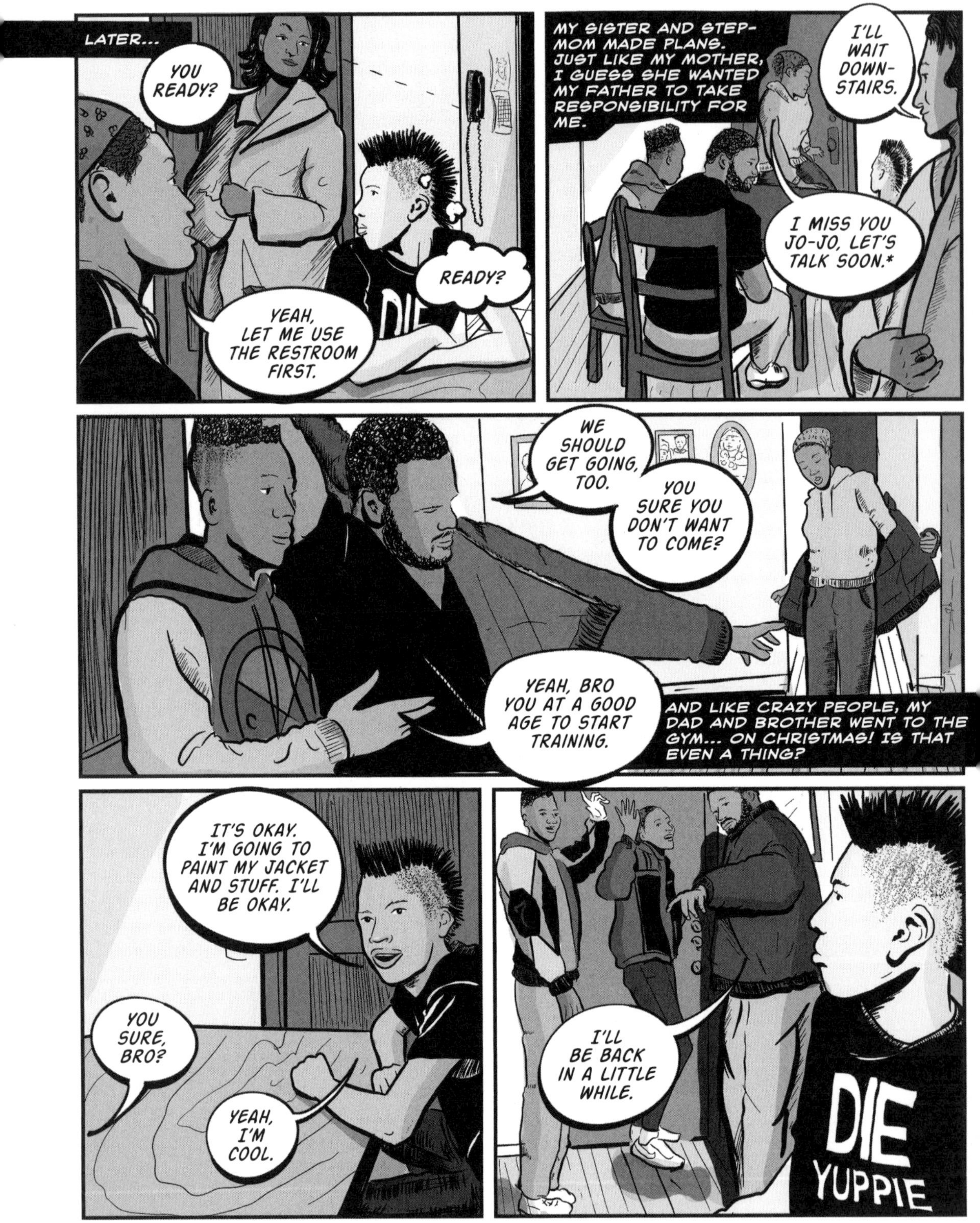
LATER...
YOU READY?
READY?
YEAH, LET ME USE THE RESTROOM FIRST.
MY SISTER AND STEP-MOM MADE PLANS. JUST LIKE MY MOTHER, I GUESS SHE WANTED MY FATHER TO TAKE RESPONSIBILITY FOR ME.
I'LL WAIT DOWN-STAIRS.
I MISS YOU JO-JO, LET'S TALK SOON.*
WE SHOULD GET GOING, TOO.
YOU SURE YOU DON'T WANT TO COME?
YEAH, BRO YOU AT A GOOD AGE TO START TRAINING.
AND LIKE CRAZY PEOPLE, MY DAD AND BROTHER WENT TO THE GYM... ON CHRISTMAS! IS THAT EVEN A THING?
IT'S OKAY. I'M GOING TO PAINT MY JACKET AND STUFF. I'LL BE OKAY.
YOU SURE, BRO?
YEAH, I'M COOL.
I'LL BE BACK IN A LITTLE WHILE.
DIE YUPPIE

*WE DIDN'T TALK FOR ANOTHER FIVE YEARS

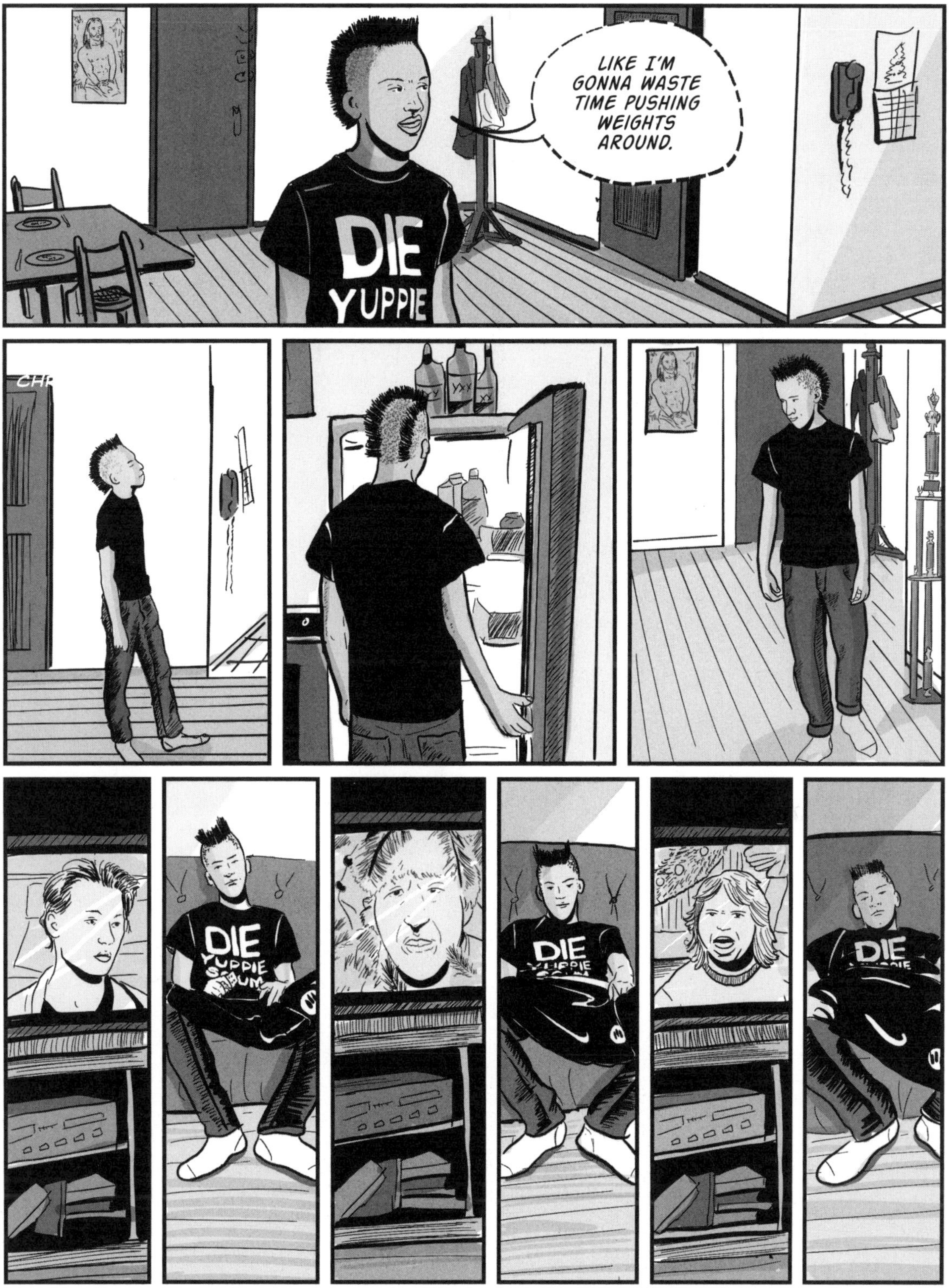
DIE
YUPPIE
LIKE I'M GONNA WASTE TIME PUSHING WEIGHTS AROUND.

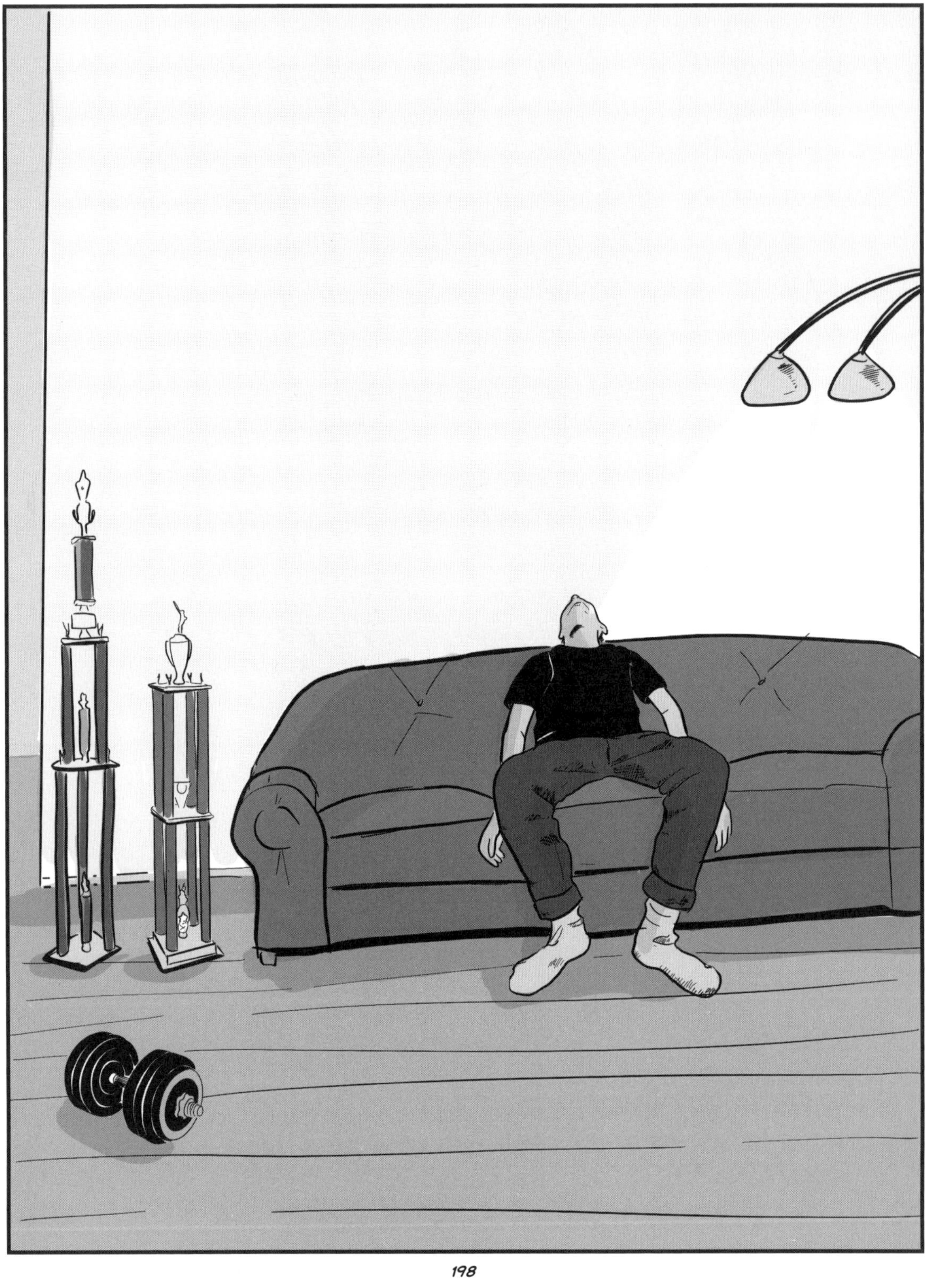

PISSSS

MR. AMERICA DAI

WHOOSH

BZZZZZ

HMMMM

DIE
YUPPIE
SCUM

SCREW
IT!

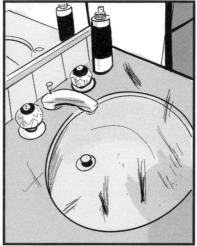

HELLS
YEAH!

DIE

199

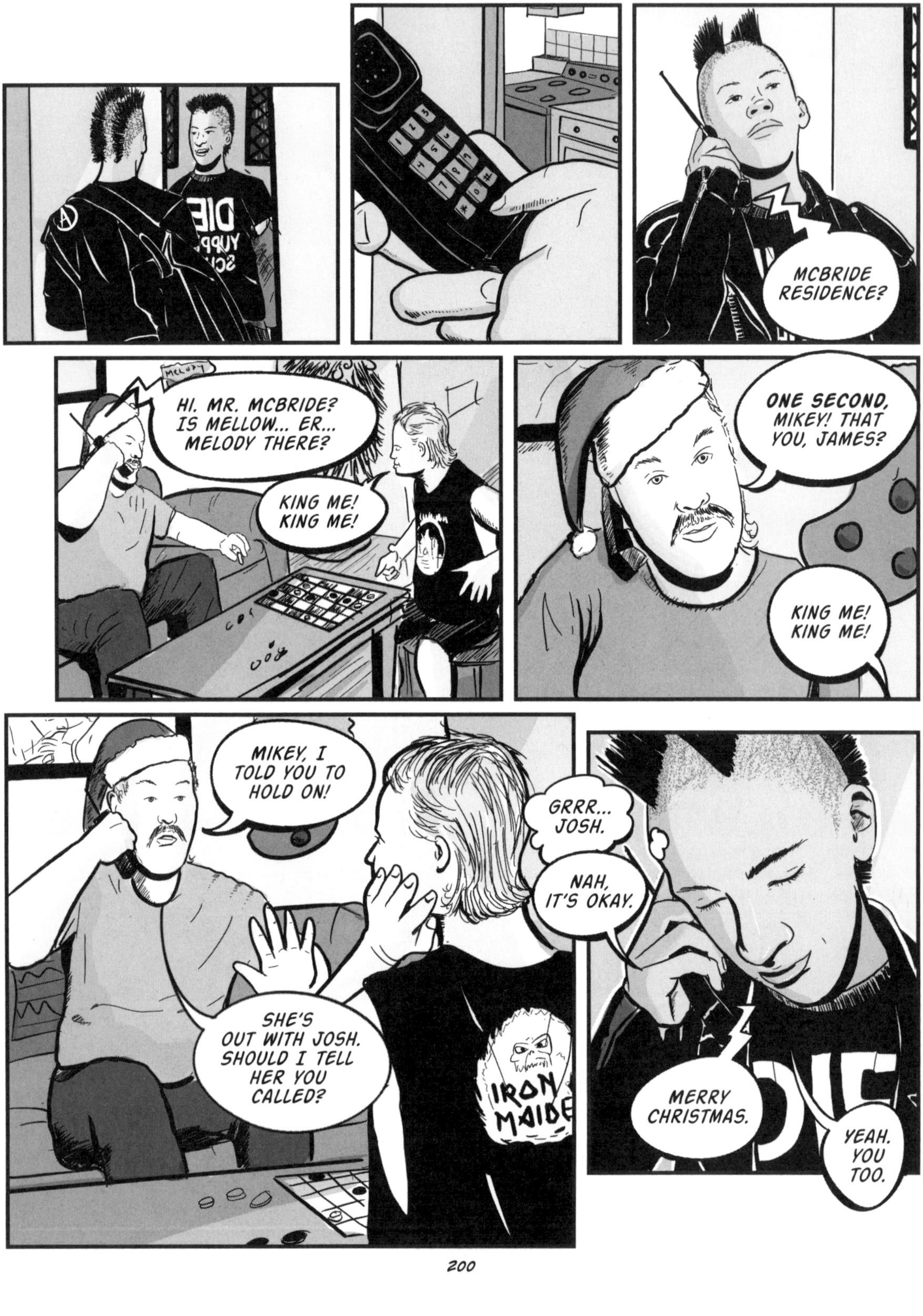
MCBRIDE RESIDENCE?
HI. MR. MCBRIDE? IS MELLOW... ER... MELODY THERE?
KING ME! KING ME!
ONE SECOND, MIKEY! THAT YOU, JAMES?
KING ME! KING ME!
MIKEY, I TOLD YOU TO HOLD ON!
GRRR... JOSH.
NAH, IT'S OKAY.
SHE'S OUT WITH JOSH. SHOULD I TELL HER YOU CALLED?
IRON MAIDE
MERRY CHRISTMAS.
YEAH. YOU TOO.

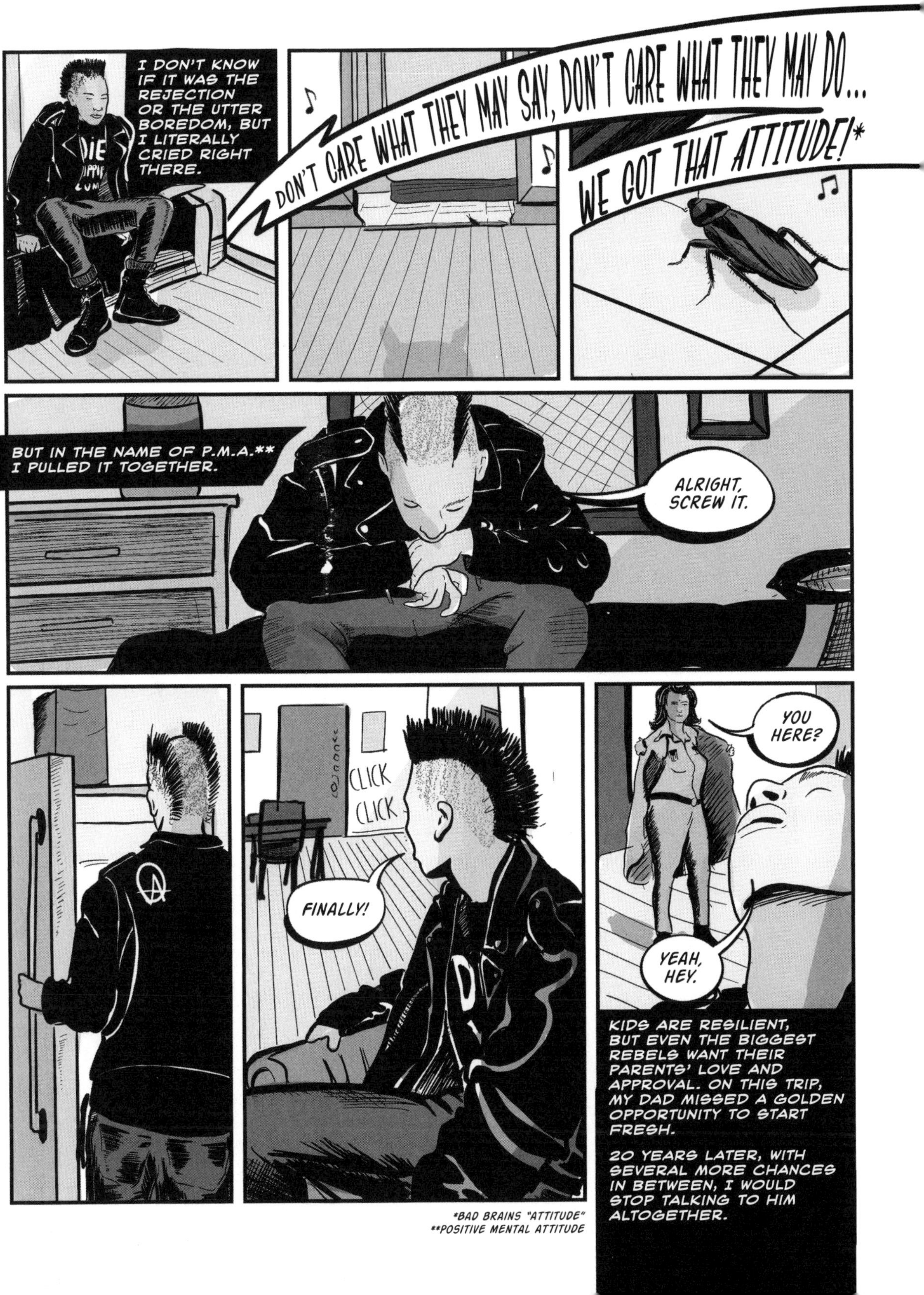
I DON'T KNOW IF IT WAS THE REJECTION OR THE UTTER BOREDOM, BUT I LITERALLY CRIED RIGHT THERE.
DON'T CARE WHAT THEY MAY SAY, DON'T CARE WHAT THEY MAY DO...
WE GOT THAT ATTITUDE!*
BUT IN THE NAME OF P.M.A.** I PULLED IT TOGETHER.
ALRIGHT, SCREW IT.
CLICK CLICK
FINALLY!
YOU HERE?
YEAH, HEY.
KIDS ARE RESILIENT, BUT EVEN THE BIGGEST REBELS WANT THEIR PARENTS' LOVE AND APPROVAL. ON THIS TRIP, MY DAD MISSED A GOLDEN OPPORTUNITY TO START FRESH.
20 YEARS LATER, WITH SEVERAL MORE CHANCES IN BETWEEN, I WOULD STOP TALKING TO HIM ALTOGETHER.

*BAD BRAINS "ATTITUDE"
**POSITIVE MENTAL ATTITUDE

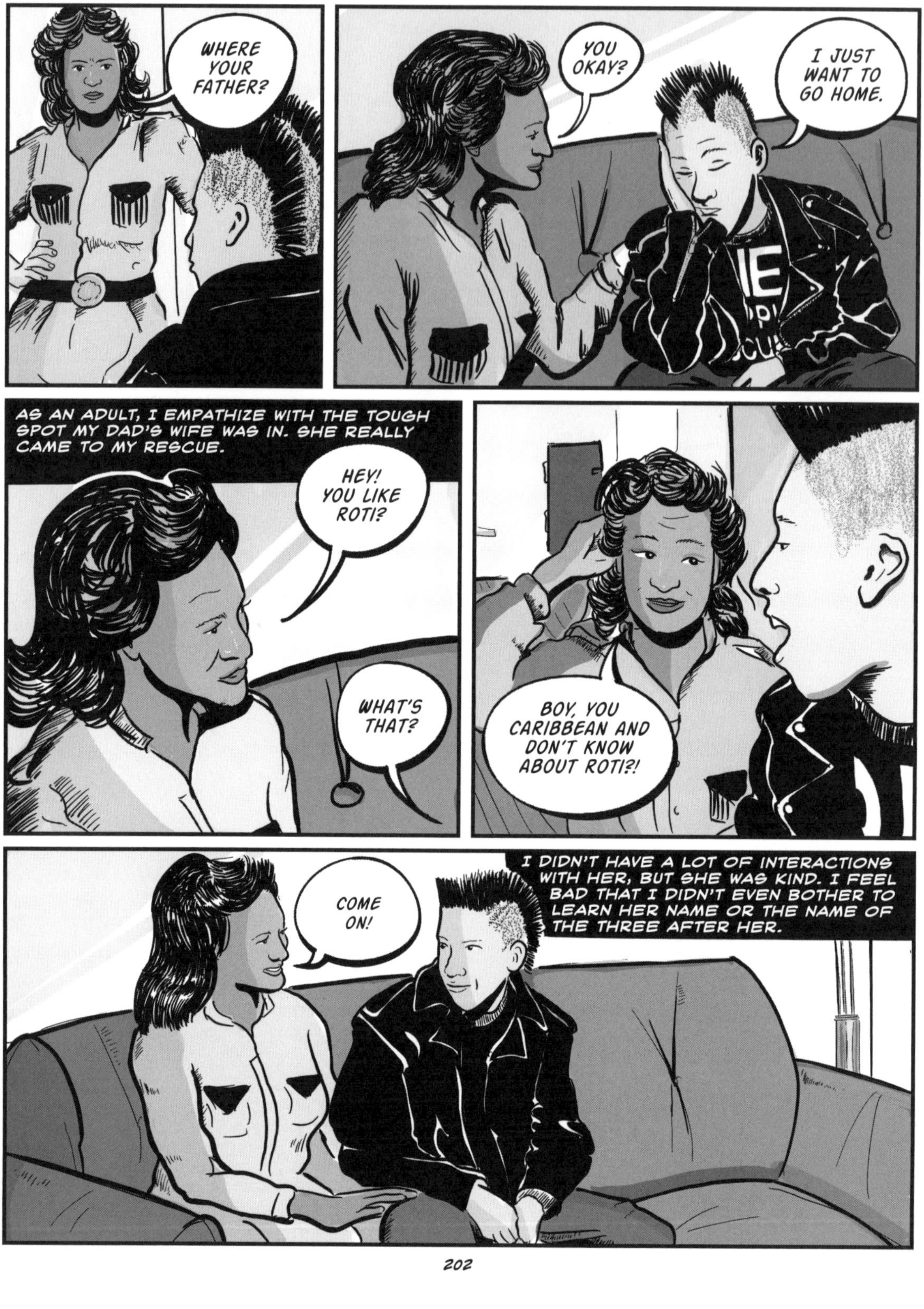

WHERE YOUR FATHER?
YOU OKAY?
I JUST WANT TO GO HOME.
AS AN ADULT, I EMPATHIZE WITH THE TOUGH SPOT MY DAD'S WIFE WAS IN. SHE REALLY CAME TO MY RESCUE.
HEY! YOU LIKE ROTI?
WHAT'S THAT?
BOY, YOU CARIBBEAN AND DON'T KNOW ABOUT ROTI?!
COME ON!
I DIDN'T HAVE A LOT OF INTERACTIONS WITH HER, BUT SHE WAS KIND. I FEEL BAD THAT I DIDN'T EVEN BOTHER TO LEARN HER NAME OR THE NAME OF THE THREE AFTER HER.

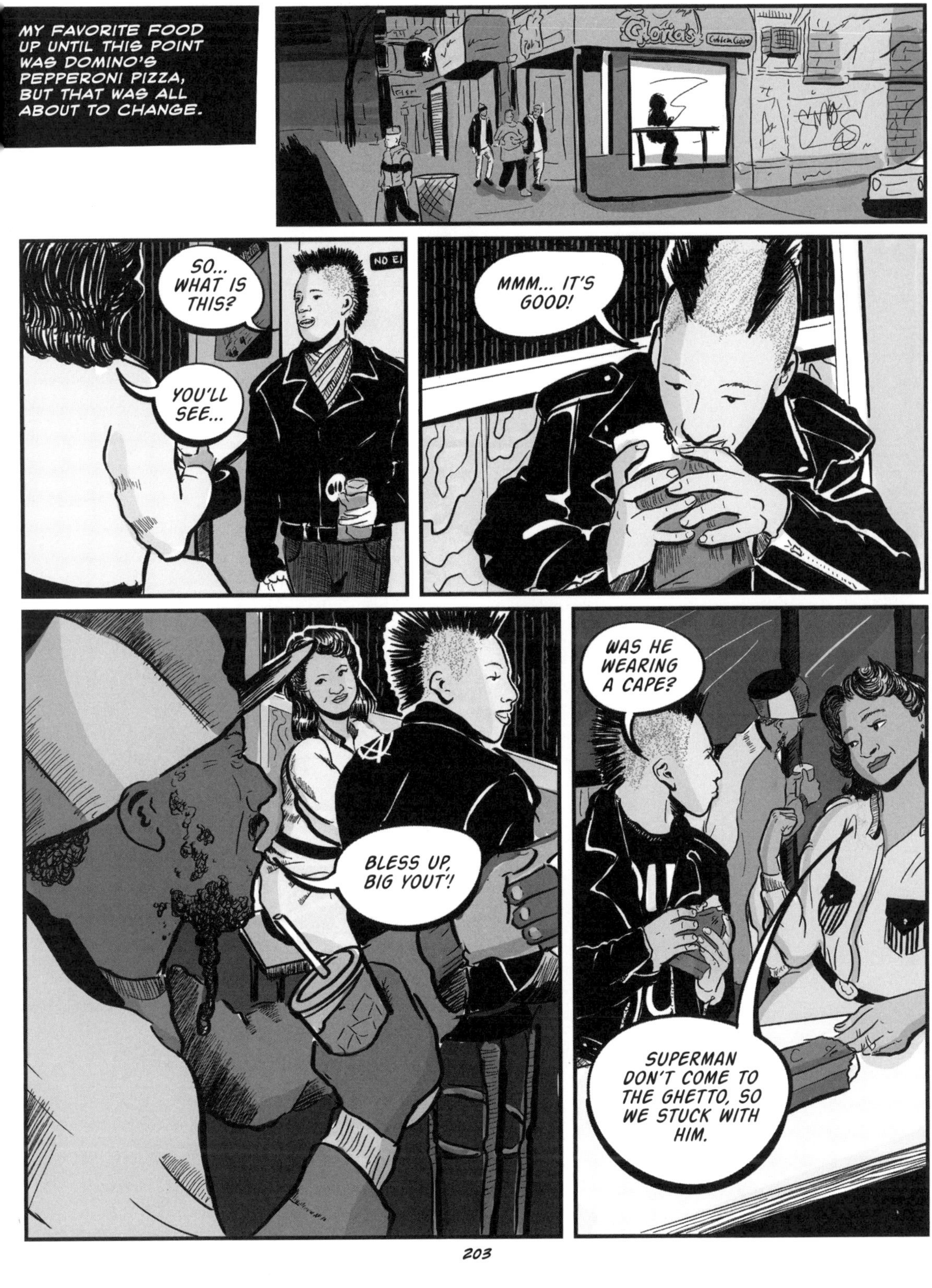
MY FAVORITE FOOD UP UNTIL THIS POINT WAS DOMINO'S PEPPERONI PIZZA, BUT THAT WAS ALL ABOUT TO CHANGE.
SO... WHAT IS THIS?
YOU'LL SEE...
MMM... IT'S GOOD!
BLESS UP, BIG YOUT'!
WAS HE WEARING A CAPE?
SUPERMAN DON'T COME TO THE GHETTO, SO WE STUCK WITH HIM.

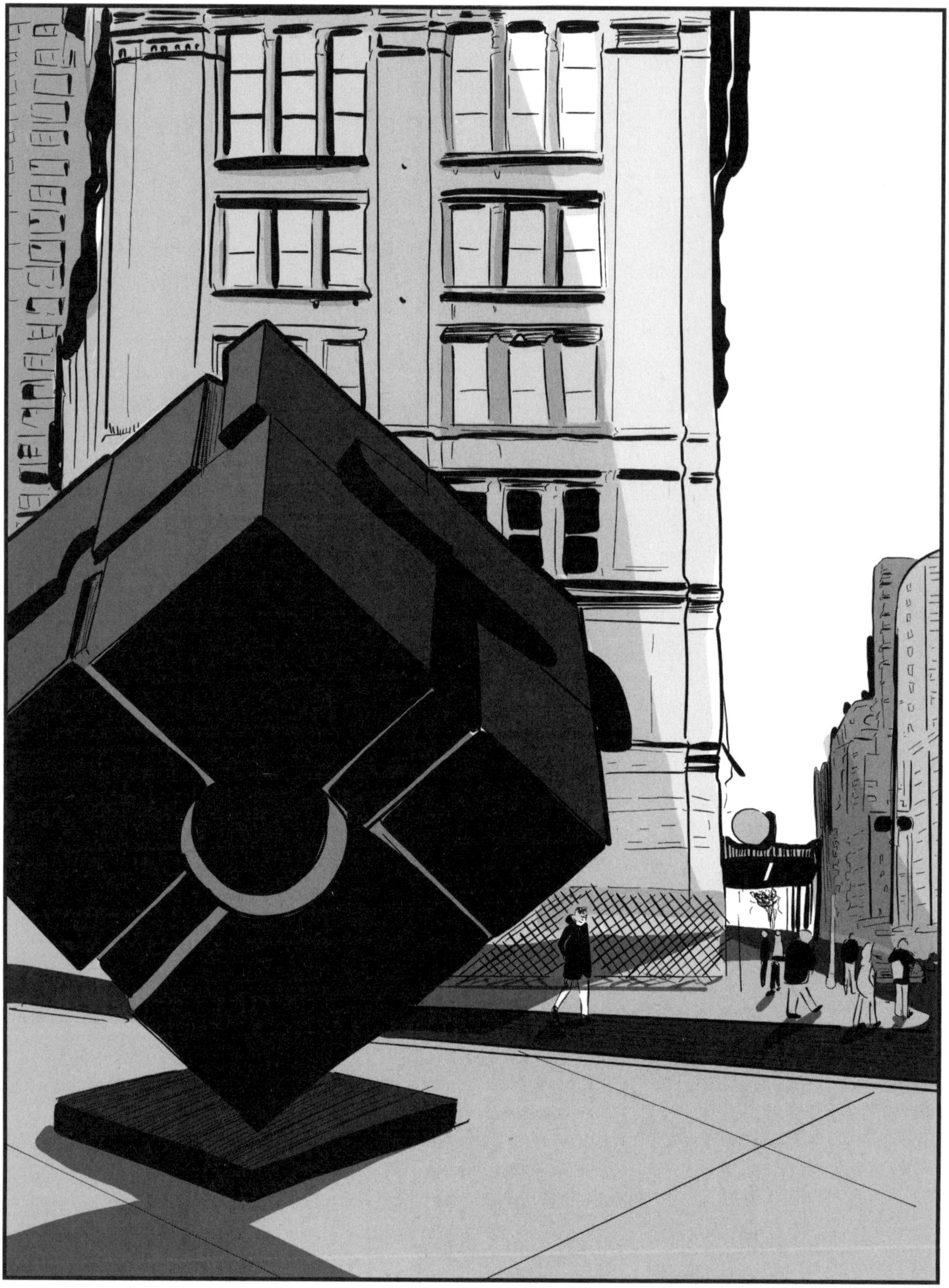

CHAPTER 7
...UNLESS AND UNTIL I CAN STICK ALL OF YOU

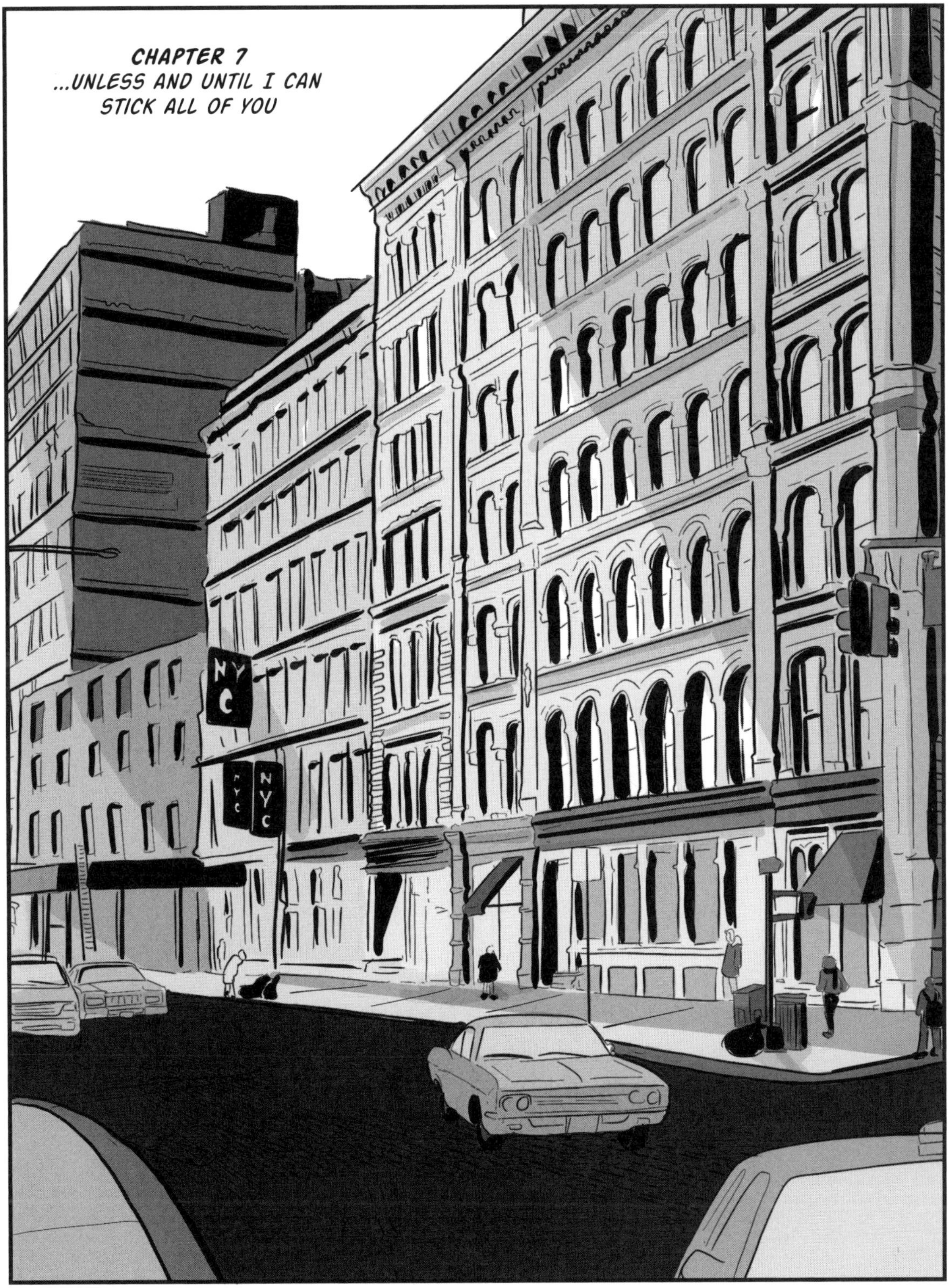
NYC
NYC
NYC

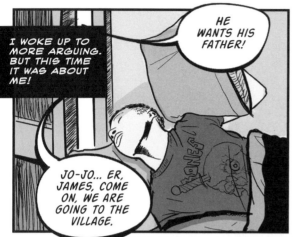

I WOKE UP TO MORE ARGUING. BUT THIS TIME IT WAS ABOUT ME!

HE WANTS HIS FATHER!

JO-JO... ER, JAMES, COME ON, WE ARE GOING TO THE VILLAGE.

THE VILLAGE!

MY STEP-MOM MADE MY DAD STEP UP!

AND AN HOUR LATER WE WERE ROLLING INTO THE LOWER EAST SIDE.

THOSE ARE THE BOOTS I WANT!

SURE YOU DON'T WANT A PAIR OF SNEAKERS?

I COULDN'T EXPECT HIM TO GET IT... STILL, I WISHED HE DID.

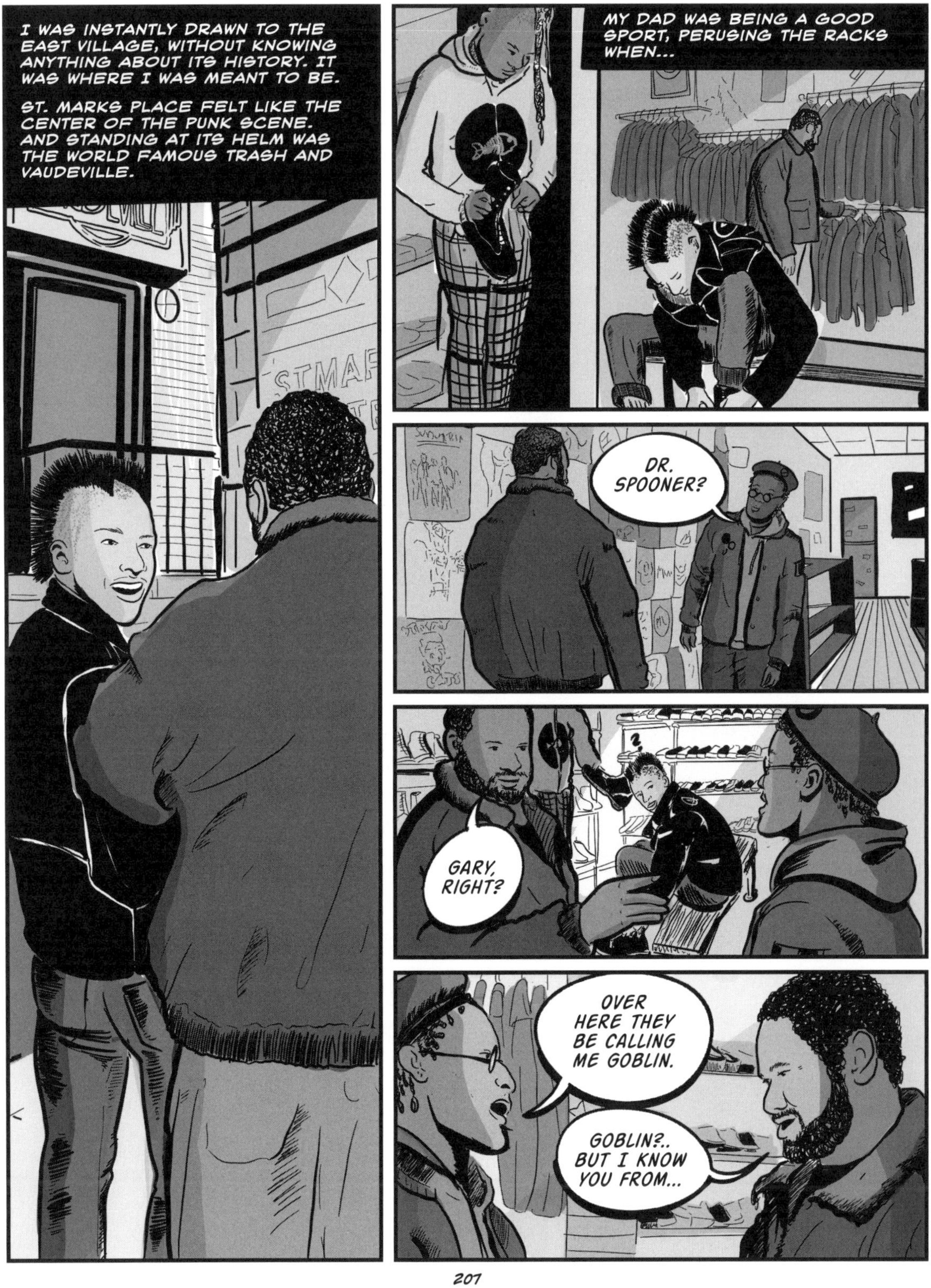
I WAS INSTANTLY DRAWN TO THE EAST VILLAGE, WITHOUT KNOWING ANYTHING ABOUT ITS HISTORY. IT WAS WHERE I WAS MEANT TO BE.
ST. MARKS PLACE FELT LIKE THE CENTER OF THE PUNK SCENE. AND STANDING AT ITS HELM WAS THE WORLD FAMOUS TRASH AND VAUDEVILLE.
MY DAD WAS BEING A GOOD SPORT, PERUSING THE RACKS WHEN...
DR. SPOONER?
GARY, RIGHT?
OVER HERE THEY BE CALLING ME GOBLIN.
GOBLIN?.. BUT I KNOW YOU FROM...

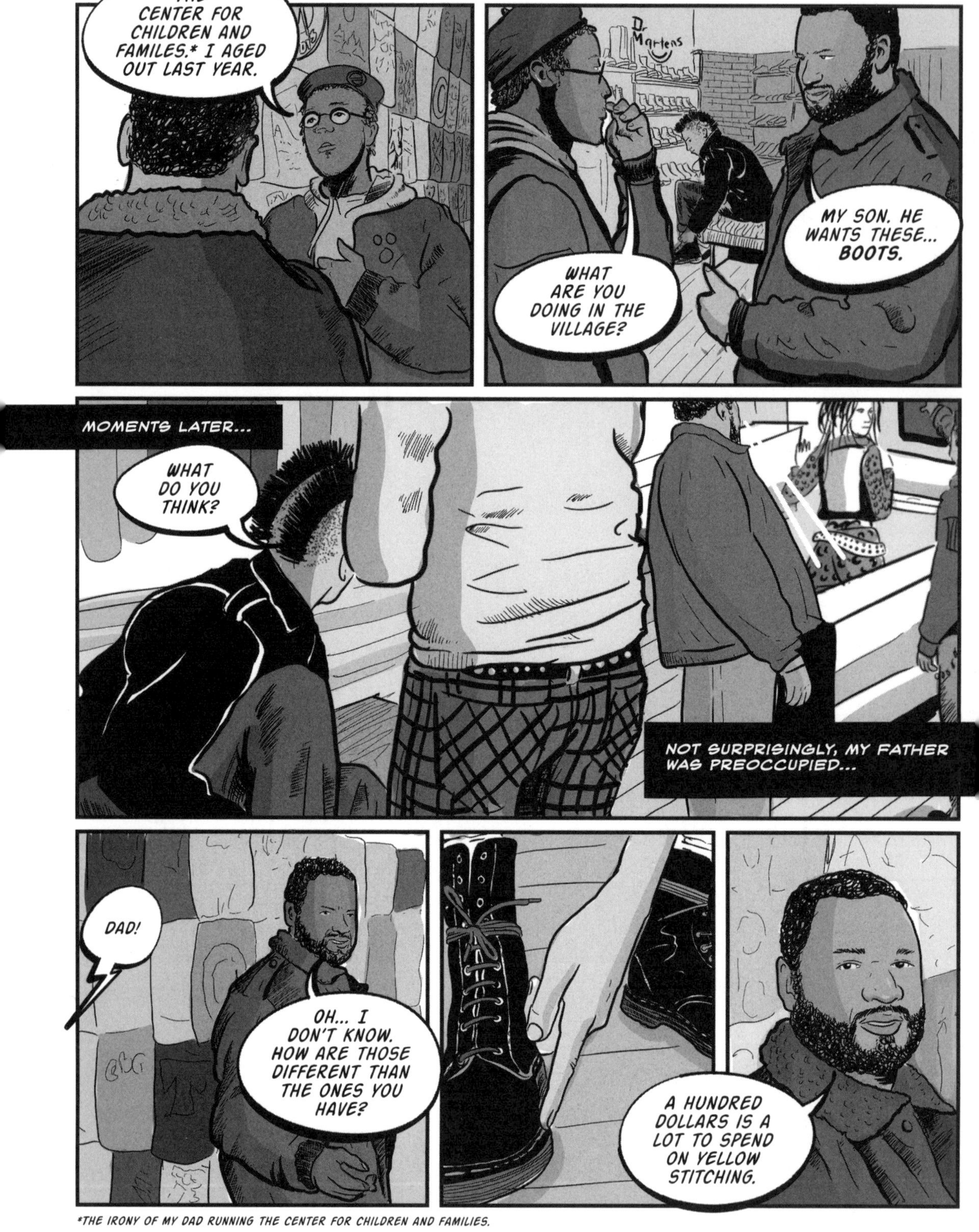

THE CENTER FOR CHILDREN AND FAMILES.* I AGED OUT LAST YEAR.
Dr Martens
WHAT ARE YOU DOING IN THE VILLAGE?
MY SON. HE WANTS THESE... BOOTS.
MOMENTS LATER...
WHAT DO YOU THINK?
NOT SURPRISINGLY, MY FATHER WAS PREOCCUPIED...
DAD!
OH... I DON'T KNOW. HOW ARE THOSE DIFFERENT THAN THE ONES YOU HAVE?
A HUNDRED DOLLARS IS A LOT TO SPEND ON YELLOW STITCHING.

*THE IRONY OF MY DAD RUNNING THE CENTER FOR CHILDREN AND FAMILIES.

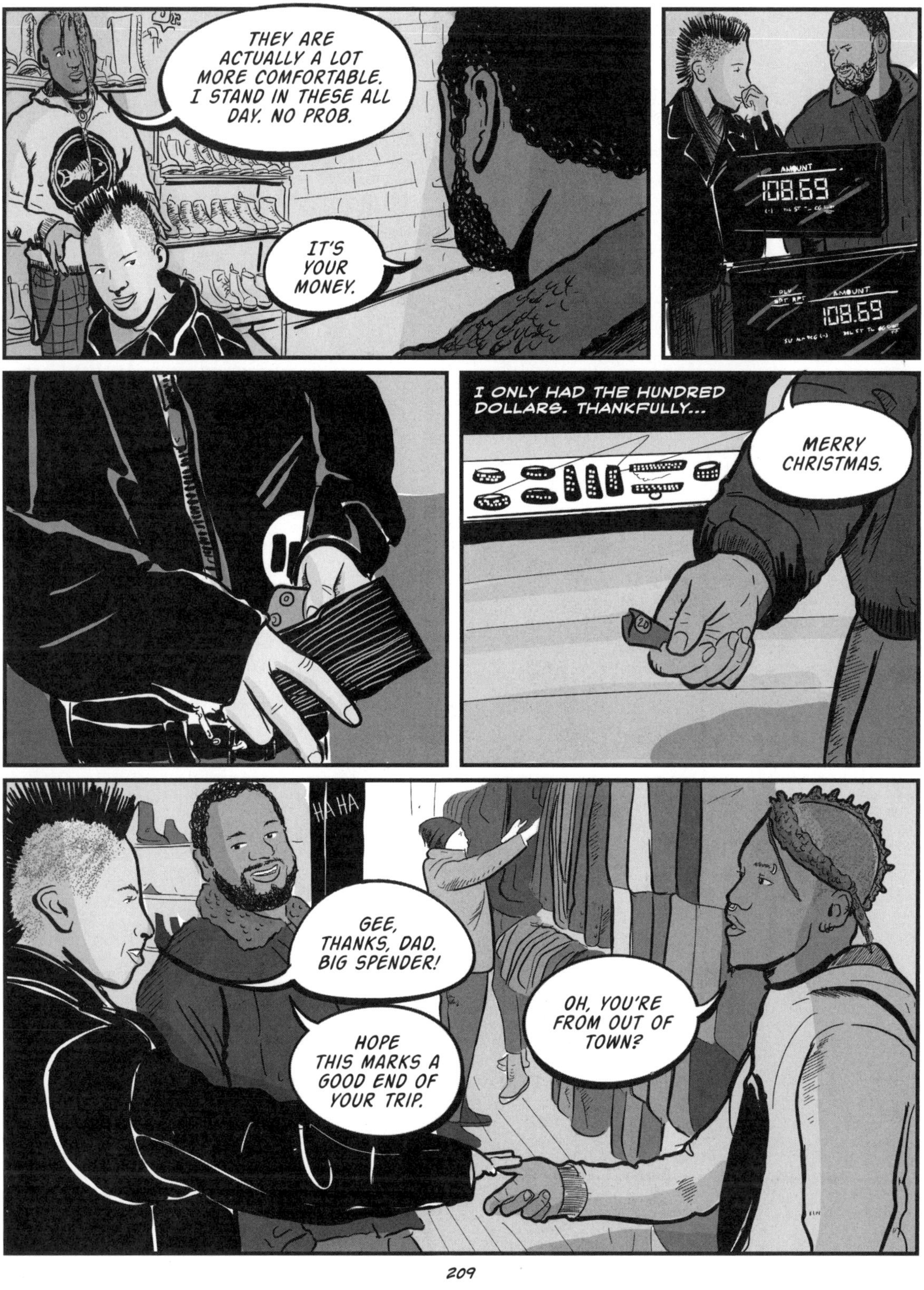
THEY ARE ACTUALLY A LOT MORE COMFORTABLE. I STAND IN THESE ALL DAY. NO PROB.
IT'S YOUR MONEY.
AMOUNT
108.69
AMOUNT
108.69
I ONLY HAD THE HUNDRED DOLLARS. THANKFULLY...
MERRY CHRISTMAS.
HA HA
GEE, THANKS, DAD. BIG SPENDER!
HOPE THIS MARKS A GOOD END OF YOUR TRIP.
OH, YOU'RE FROM OUT OF TOWN?

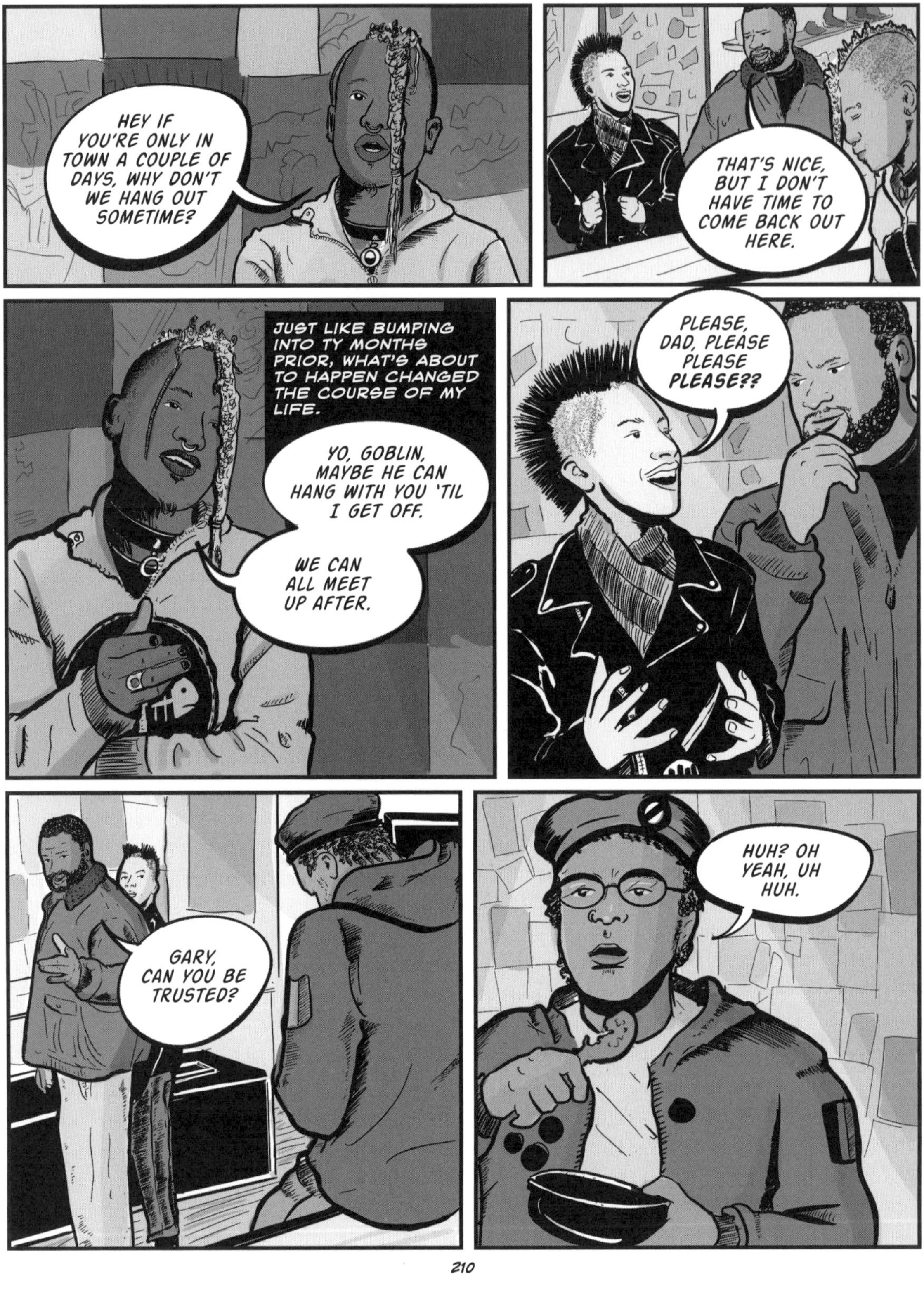
HEY IF YOU'RE ONLY IN TOWN A COUPLE OF DAYS, WHY DON'T WE HANG OUT SOMETIME?
THAT'S NICE, BUT I DON'T HAVE TIME TO COME BACK OUT HERE.
JUST LIKE BUMPING INTO TY MONTHS PRIOR, WHAT'S ABOUT TO HAPPEN CHANGED THE COURSE OF MY LIFE.
YO, GOBLIN, MAYBE HE CAN HANG WITH YOU 'TIL I GET OFF.
WE CAN ALL MEET UP AFTER.
PLEASE, DAD, PLEASE PLEASE PLEASE??
GARY, CAN YOU BE TRUSTED?
HUH? OH YEAH, UH HUH.

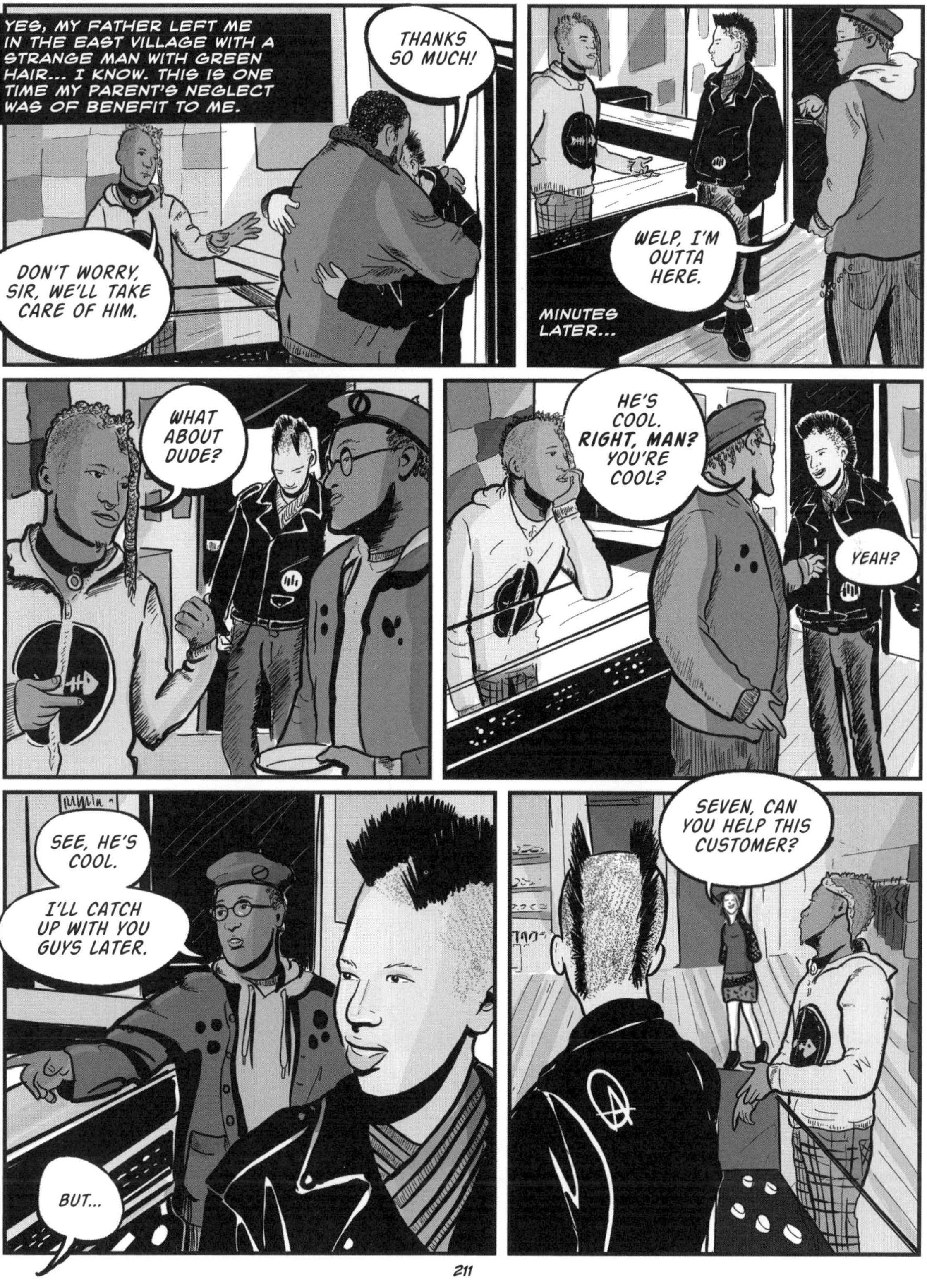
YES, MY FATHER LEFT ME IN THE EAST VILLAGE WITH A STRANGE MAN WITH GREEN HAIR... I KNOW. THIS IS ONE TIME MY PARENT'S NEGLECT WAS OF BENEFIT TO ME.
THANKS SO MUCH!
DON'T WORRY, SIR, WE'LL TAKE CARE OF HIM.
WELP, I'M OUTTA HERE.
MINUTES LATER...
WHAT ABOUT DUDE?
HE'S COOL. RIGHT, MAN? YOU'RE COOL?
YEAH?
SEE, HE'S COOL.
I'LL CATCH UP WITH YOU GUYS LATER.
BUT...
SEVEN, CAN YOU HELP THIS CUSTOMER?

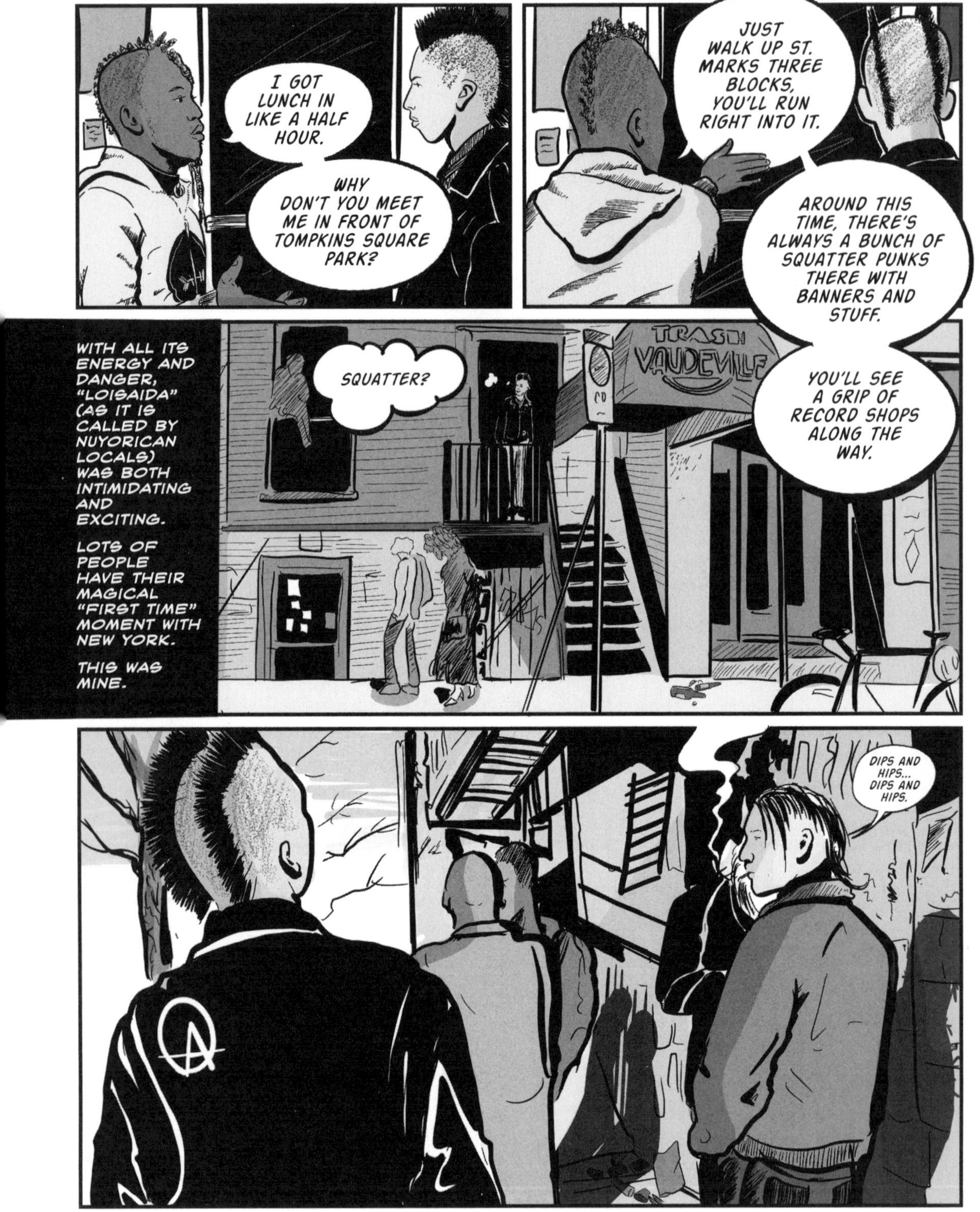
I GOT LUNCH IN LIKE A HALF HOUR.
WHY DON'T YOU MEET ME IN FRONT OF TOMPKINS SQUARE PARK?
JUST WALK UP ST. MARKS THREE BLOCKS, YOU'LL RUN RIGHT INTO IT.
AROUND THIS TIME, THERE'S ALWAYS A BUNCH OF SQUATTER PUNKS THERE WITH BANNERS AND STUFF.
WITH ALL ITS ENERGY AND DANGER, "LOISAIDA" (AS IT IS CALLED BY NUYORICAN LOCALS) WAS BOTH INTIMIDATING AND EXCITING.
LOTS OF PEOPLE HAVE THEIR MAGICAL "FIRST TIME" MOMENT WITH NEW YORK.
THIS WAS MINE.
SQUATTER?
TRASH VAUDEVILLE
YOU'LL SEE A GRIP OF RECORD SHOPS ALONG THE WAY.
DIPS AND HIPS... DIPS AND HIPS.

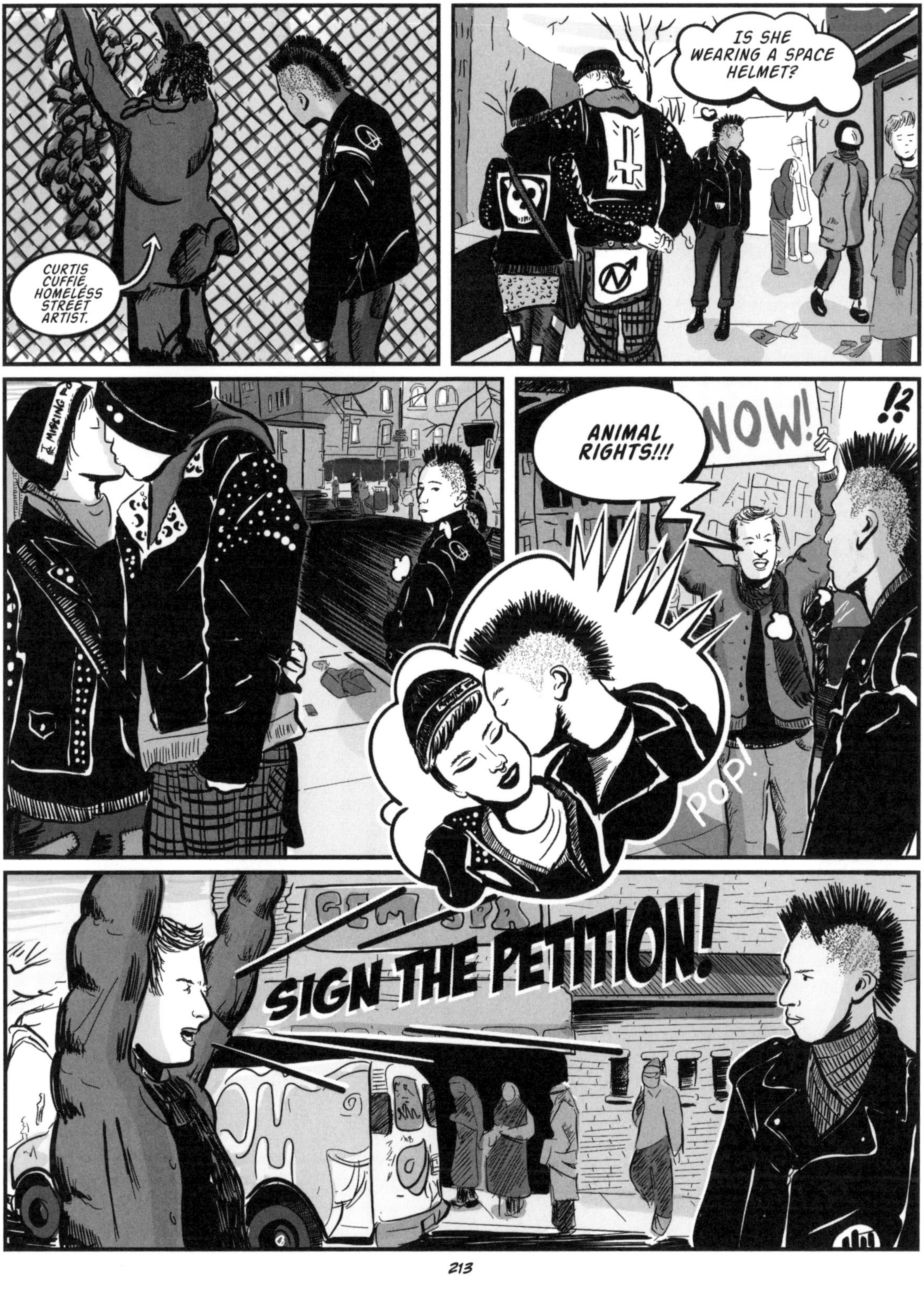
CURTIS CUFFIE, HOMELESS STREET ARTIST.
IS SHE WEARING A SPACE HELMET?
NOW!
ANIMAL RIGHTS!!!
POP!
SIGN THE PETITION!

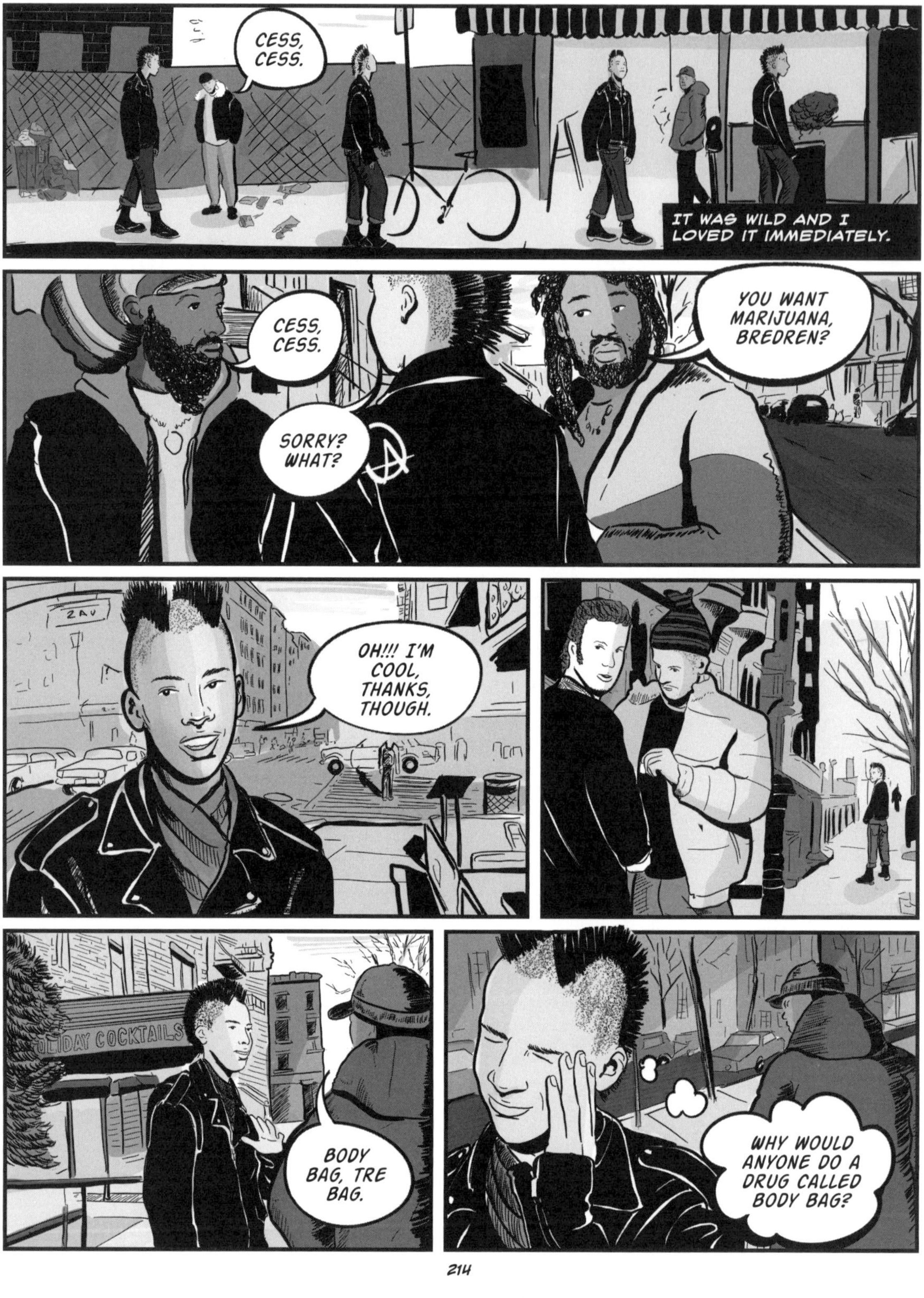
CESS, CESS.
IT WAS WILD AND I LOVED IT IMMEDIATELY.
CESS, CESS.
YOU WANT MARIJUANA, BREDREN?
SORRY? WHAT?
OH!!! I'M COOL, THANKS, THOUGH.
BODY BAG, TRE BAG.
WHY WOULD ANYONE DO A DRUG CALLED BODY BAG?

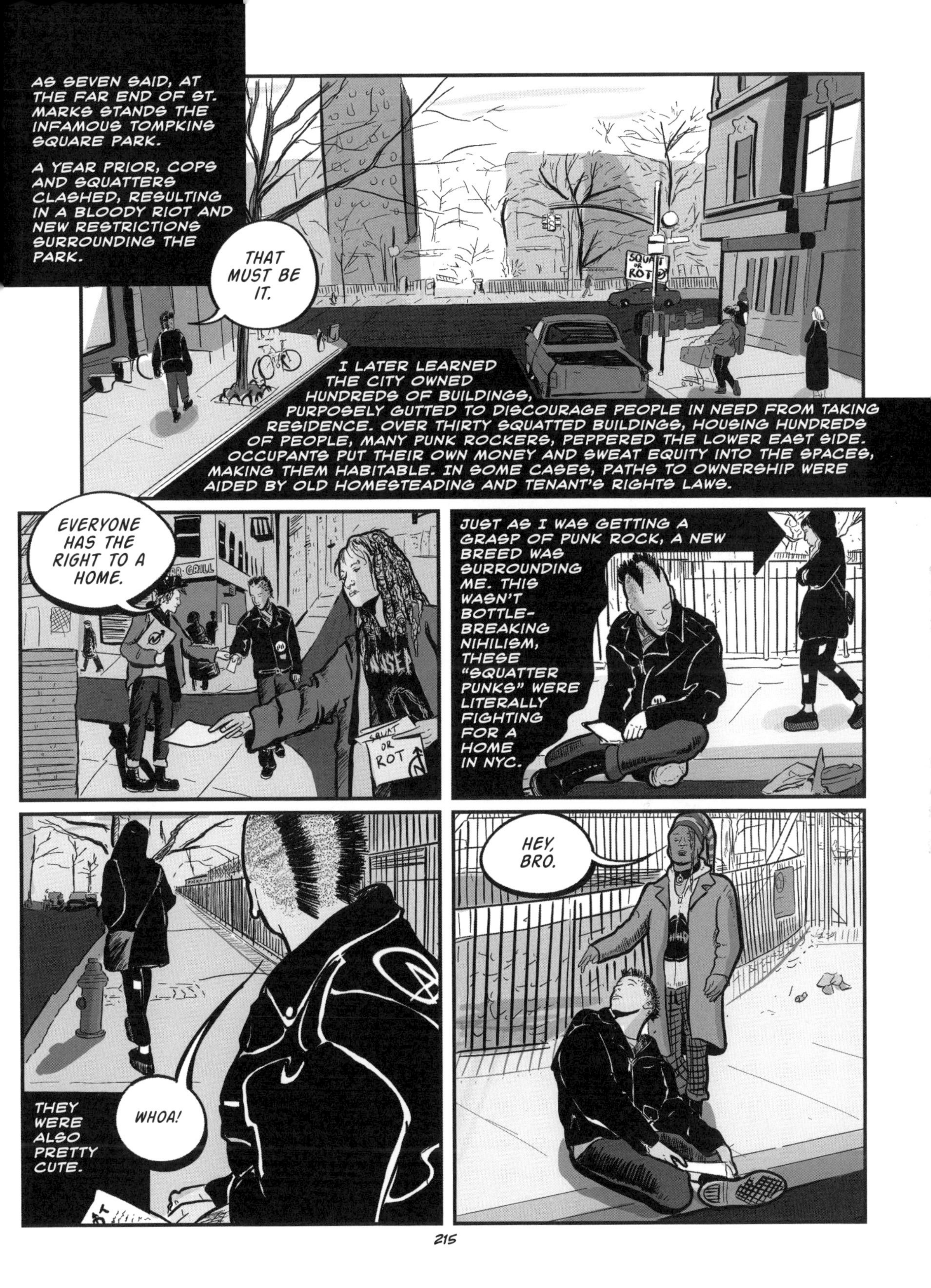

AS SEVEN SAID, AT THE FAR END OF ST. MARKS STANDS THE INFAMOUS TOMPKINS SQUARE PARK.
A YEAR PRIOR, COPS AND SQUATTERS CLASHED, RESULTING IN A BLOODY RIOT AND NEW RESTRICTIONS SURROUNDING THE PARK.
THAT MUST BE IT.
SQUAT OR ROT
I LATER LEARNED THE CITY OWNED HUNDREDS OF BUILDINGS, PURPOSELY GUTTED TO DISCOURAGE PEOPLE IN NEED FROM TAKING RESIDENCE. OVER THIRTY SQUATTED BUILDINGS, HOUSING HUNDREDS OF PEOPLE, MANY PUNK ROCKERS, PEPPERED THE LOWER EAST SIDE. OCCUPANTS PUT THEIR OWN MONEY AND SWEAT EQUITY INTO THE SPACES, MAKING THEM HABITABLE. IN SOME CASES, PATHS TO OWNERSHIP WERE AIDED BY OLD HOMESTEADING AND TENANT'S RIGHTS LAWS.
EVERYONE HAS THE RIGHT TO A HOME.
BAR-GRILL
SQUAT OR ROT
JUST AS I WAS GETTING A GRASP OF PUNK ROCK, A NEW BREED WAS SURROUNDING ME. THIS WASN'T BOTTLE-BREAKING NIHILISM, THESE "SQUATTER PUNKS" WERE LITERALLY FIGHTING FOR A HOME IN NYC.
THEY WERE ALSO PRETTY CUTE.
WHOA!
HEY, BRO.

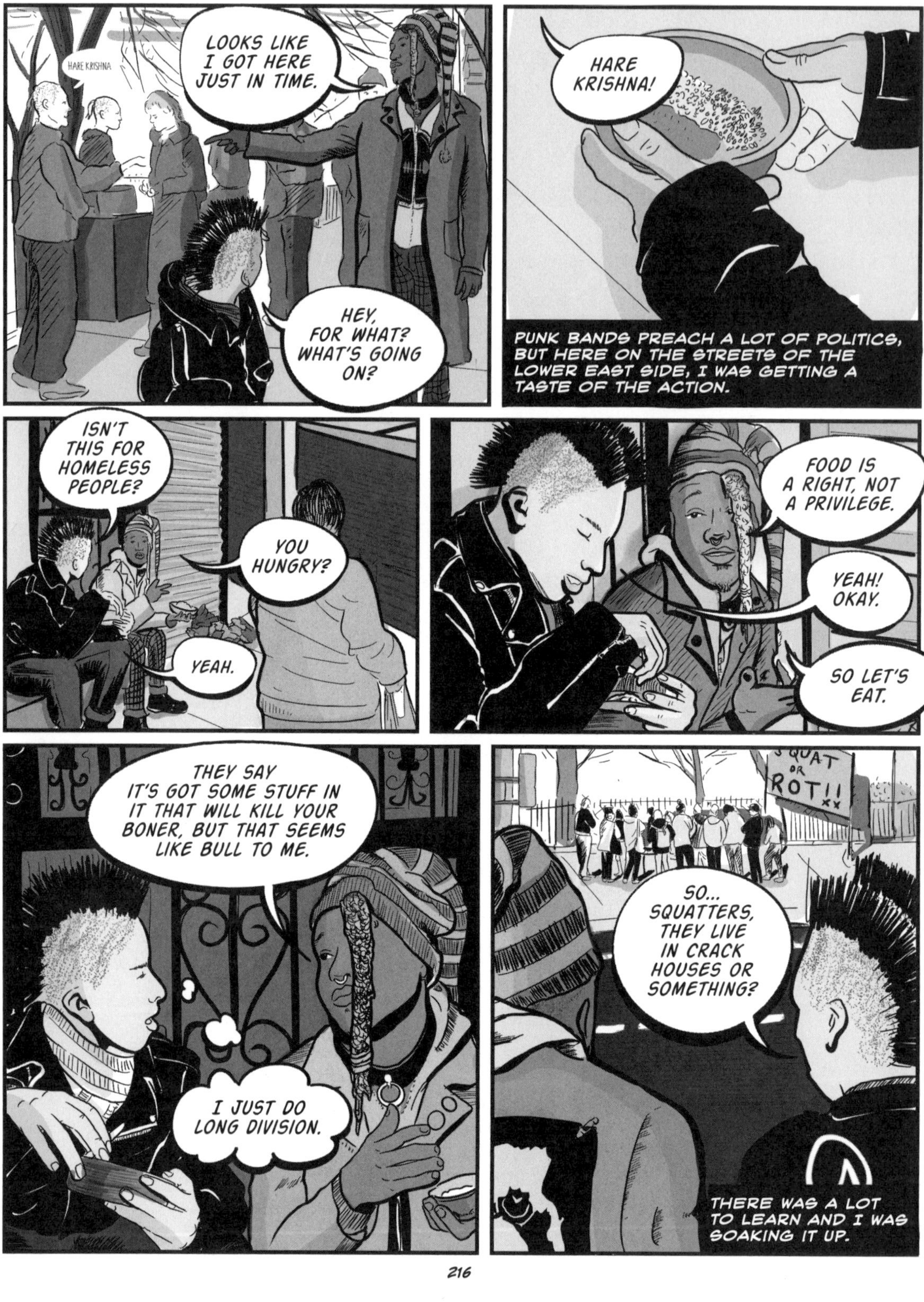

HARE KRISHNA
LOOKS LIKE I GOT HERE JUST IN TIME.
HEY, FOR WHAT? WHAT'S GOING ON?
HARE KRISHNA!
PUNK BANDS PREACH A LOT OF POLITICS, BUT HERE ON THE STREETS OF THE LOWER EAST SIDE, I WAS GETTING A TASTE OF THE ACTION.
ISN'T THIS FOR HOMELESS PEOPLE?
YOU HUNGRY?
YEAH.
FOOD IS A RIGHT, NOT A PRIVILEGE.
YEAH! OKAY.
SO LET'S EAT.
THEY SAY IT'S GOT SOME STUFF IN IT THAT WILL KILL YOUR BONER, BUT THAT SEEMS LIKE BULL TO ME.
I JUST DO LONG DIVISION.
SQUAT OR ROT!!
SO... SQUATTERS, THEY LIVE IN CRACK HOUSES OR SOMETHING?
THERE WAS A LOT TO LEARN AND I WAS SOAKING IT UP.

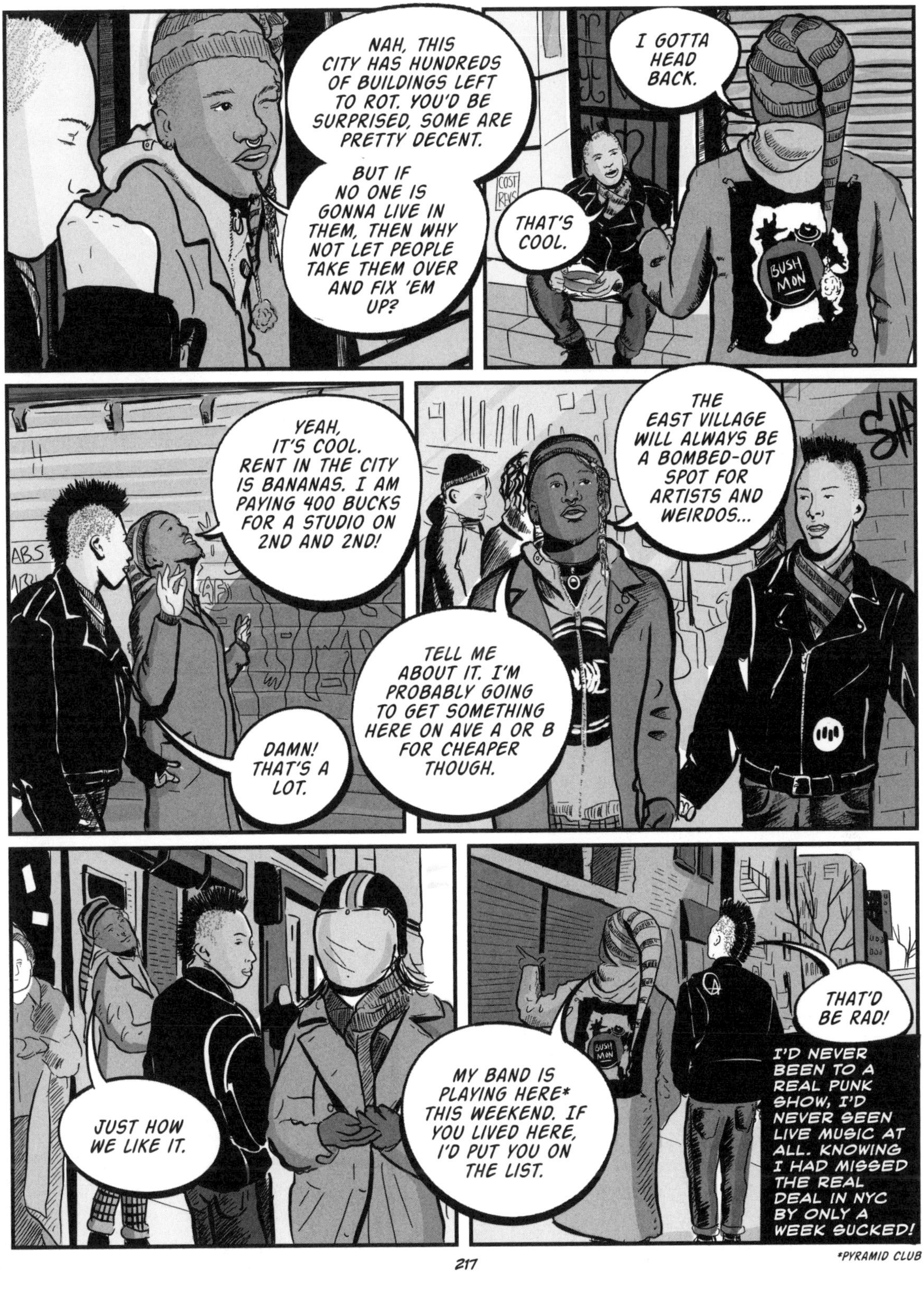
NAH, THIS CITY HAS HUNDREDS OF BUILDINGS LEFT TO ROT. YOU'D BE SURPRISED, SOME ARE PRETTY DECENT.
BUT IF NO ONE IS GONNA LIVE IN THEM, THEN WHY NOT LET PEOPLE TAKE THEM OVER AND FIX 'EM UP?
I GOTTA HEAD BACK.
THAT'S COOL.
BUSH MON
YEAH, IT'S COOL. RENT IN THE CITY IS BANANAS. I AM PAYING 400 BUCKS FOR A STUDIO ON 2ND AND 2ND!
DAMN! THAT'S A LOT.
THE EAST VILLAGE WILL ALWAYS BE A BOMBED-OUT SPOT FOR ARTISTS AND WEIRDOS...
TELL ME ABOUT IT. I'M PROBABLY GOING TO GET SOMETHING HERE ON AVE A OR B FOR CHEAPER THOUGH.
JUST HOW WE LIKE IT.
MY BAND IS PLAYING HERE* THIS WEEKEND. IF YOU LIVED HERE, I'D PUT YOU ON THE LIST.
THAT'D BE RAD!
I'D NEVER BEEN TO A REAL PUNK SHOW, I'D NEVER SEEN LIVE MUSIC AT ALL. KNOWING I HAD MISSED THE REAL DEAL IN NYC BY ONLY A WEEK SUCKED!

*PYRAMID CLUB

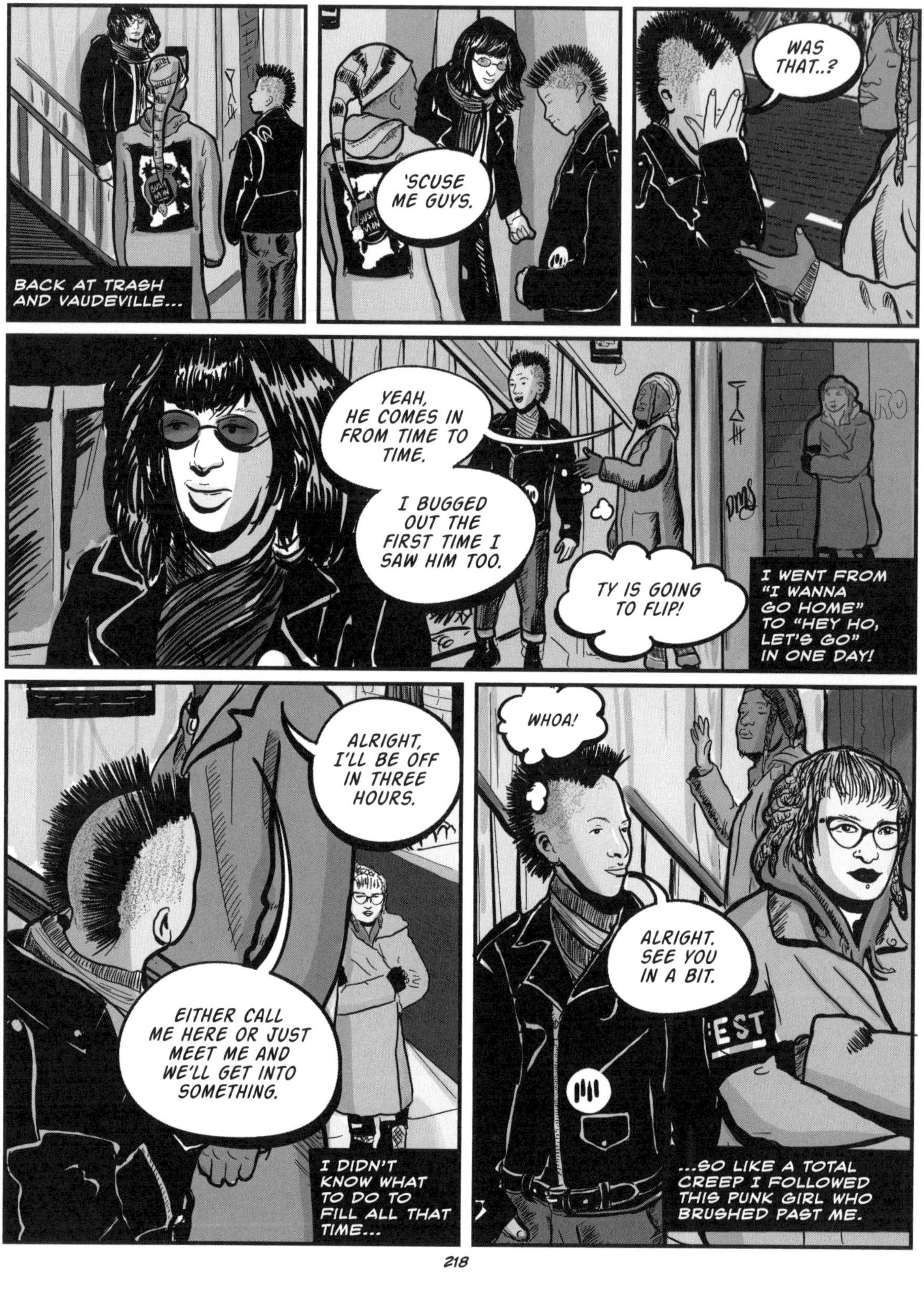

BACK AT TRASH AND VAUDEVILLE...
'SCUSE ME GUYS.
WAS THAT..?
YEAH, HE COMES IN FROM TIME TO TIME.
I BUGGED OUT THE FIRST TIME I SAW HIM TOO.
TY IS GOING TO FLIP!
I WENT FROM "I WANNA GO HOME" TO "HEY HO, LET'S GO" IN ONE DAY!
ALRIGHT, I'LL BE OFF IN THREE HOURS.
EITHER CALL ME HERE OR JUST MEET ME AND WE'LL GET INTO SOMETHING.
I DIDN'T KNOW WHAT TO DO TO FILL ALL THAT TIME...
WHOA!
ALRIGHT. SEE YOU IN A BIT.
...SO LIKE A TOTAL CREEP I FOLLOWED THIS PUNK GIRL WHO BRUSHED PAST ME.

WHAT IS SHE DOING?

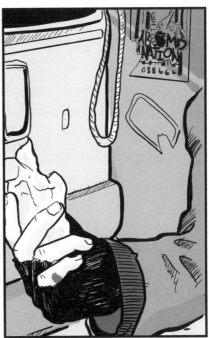

EVENTUALLY I FIGURED OUT THAT SHE HAD STUFFED NAPKINS INTO THE PAY PHONE SO PEOPLE COULDN'T GET THEIR CHANGE. THEN WHEN SHE PULLED IT OUT...

...VEGAS SLOTS!

AND I KEPT FOLLOWING.

I'M SUCH A FREAK, WHAT AM I EVEN DOING?

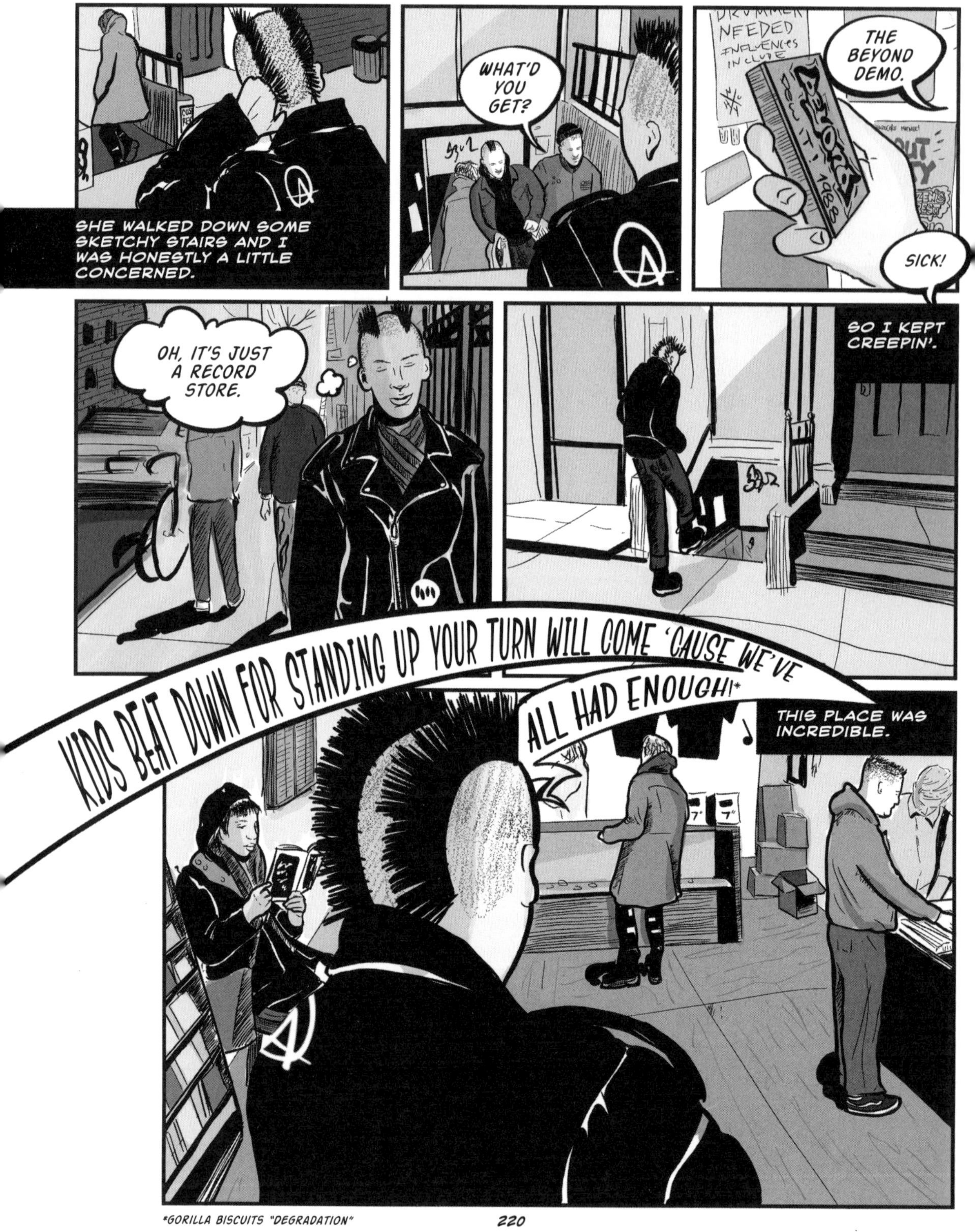

SHE WALKED DOWN SOME SKETCHY STAIRS AND I WAS HONESTLY A LITTLE CONCERNED.
WHAT'D YOU GET?
THE BEYOND DEMO.
SICK!
OH, IT'S JUST A RECORD STORE.
SO I KEPT CREEPIN'.
KIDS BEAT DOWN FOR STANDING UP YOUR TURN WILL COME 'CAUSE WE'VE ALL HAD ENOUGH!*
THIS PLACE WAS INCREDIBLE.

*GORILLA BISCUITS "DEGRADATION"

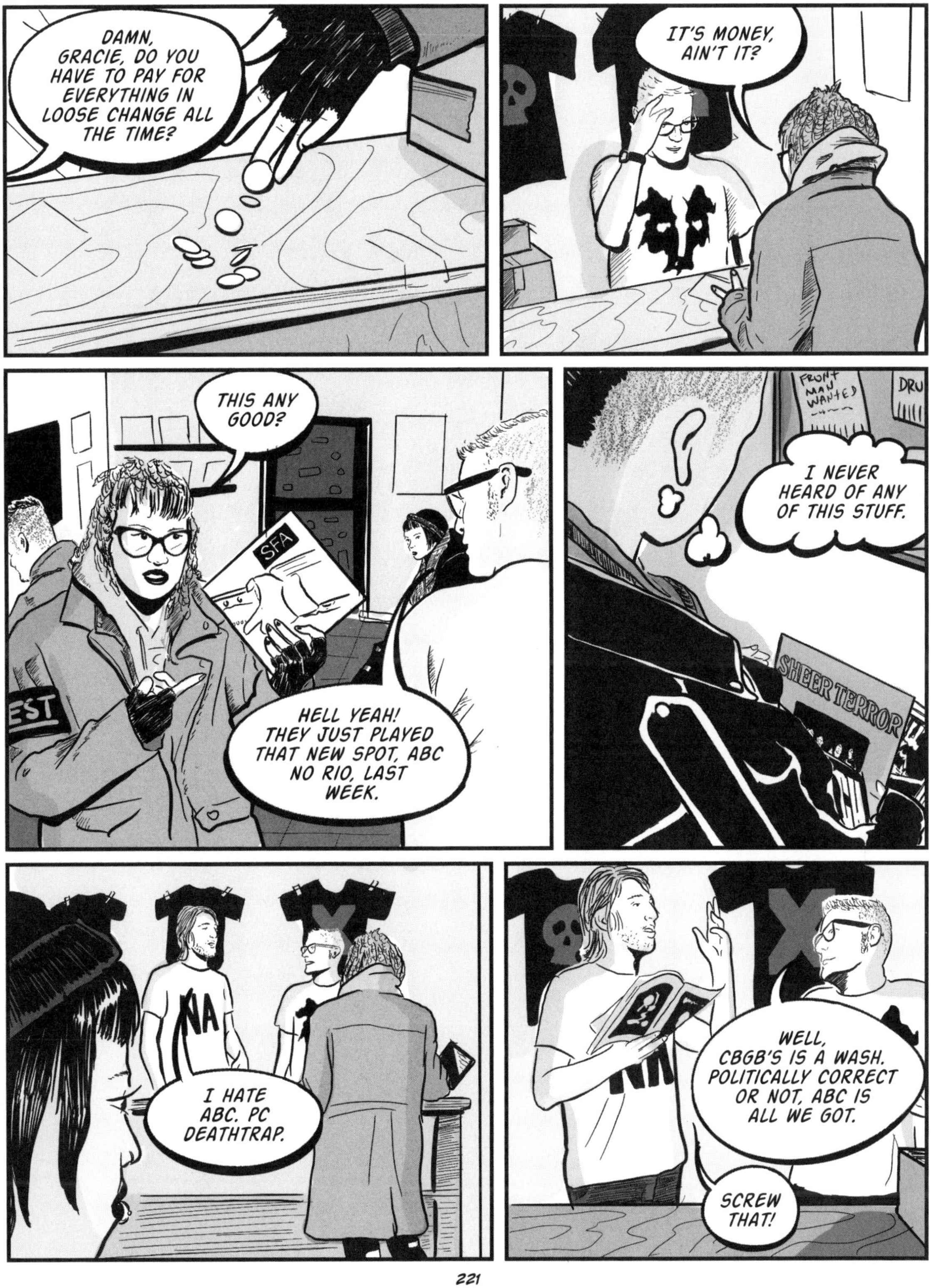
DAMN, GRACIE, DO YOU HAVE TO PAY FOR EVERYTHING IN LOOSE CHANGE ALL THE TIME?
IT'S MONEY, AIN'T IT?
THIS ANY GOOD?
SFA
HELL YEAH! THEY JUST PLAYED THAT NEW SPOT, ABC NO RIO, LAST WEEK.
FRONT MAN WANTED
I NEVER HEARD OF ANY OF THIS STUFF.
SHEER TERROR
I HATE ABC. PC DEATHTRAP.
WELL, CBGB'S IS A WASH. POLITICALLY CORRECT OR NOT, ABC IS ALL WE GOT.
SCREW THAT!

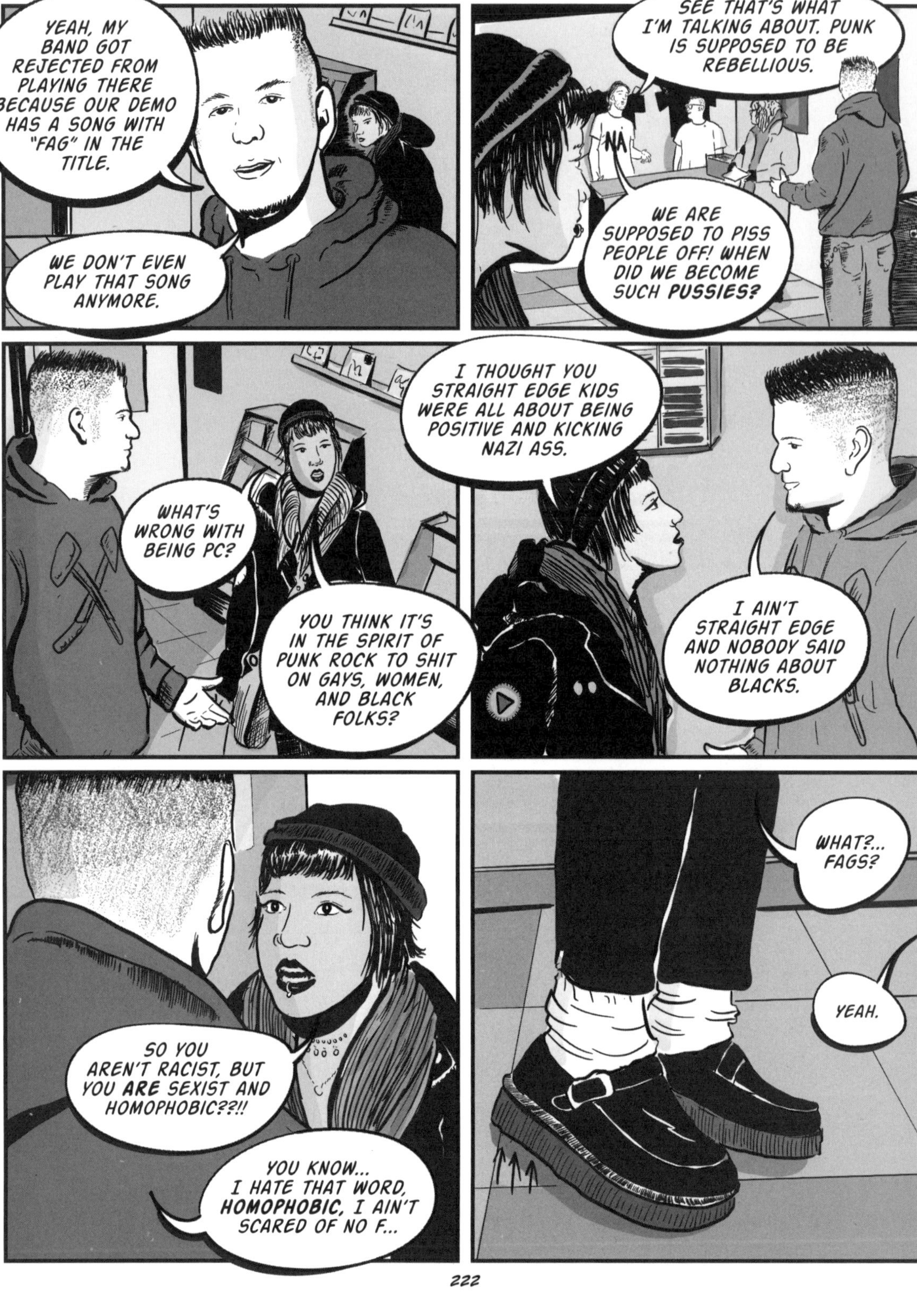
YEAH, MY BAND GOT REJECTED FROM PLAYING THERE BECAUSE OUR DEMO HAS A SONG WITH "FAG" IN THE TITLE.
WE DON'T EVEN PLAY THAT SONG ANYMORE.
SEE THAT'S WHAT I'M TALKING ABOUT. PUNK IS SUPPOSED TO BE REBELLIOUS.
NA
WE ARE SUPPOSED TO PISS PEOPLE OFF! WHEN DID WE BECOME SUCH PUSSIES?
WHAT'S WRONG WITH BEING PC?
YOU THINK IT'S IN THE SPIRIT OF PUNK ROCK TO SHIT ON GAYS, WOMEN, AND BLACK FOLKS?
I THOUGHT YOU STRAIGHT EDGE KIDS WERE ALL ABOUT BEING POSITIVE AND KICKING NAZI ASS.
I AIN'T STRAIGHT EDGE AND NOBODY SAID NOTHING ABOUT BLACKS.
SO YOU AREN'T RACIST, BUT YOU ARE SEXIST AND HOMOPHOBIC??!!
YOU KNOW... I HATE THAT WORD, HOMOPHOBIC, I AIN'T SCARED OF NO F...
WHAT?... FAGS?
YEAH.

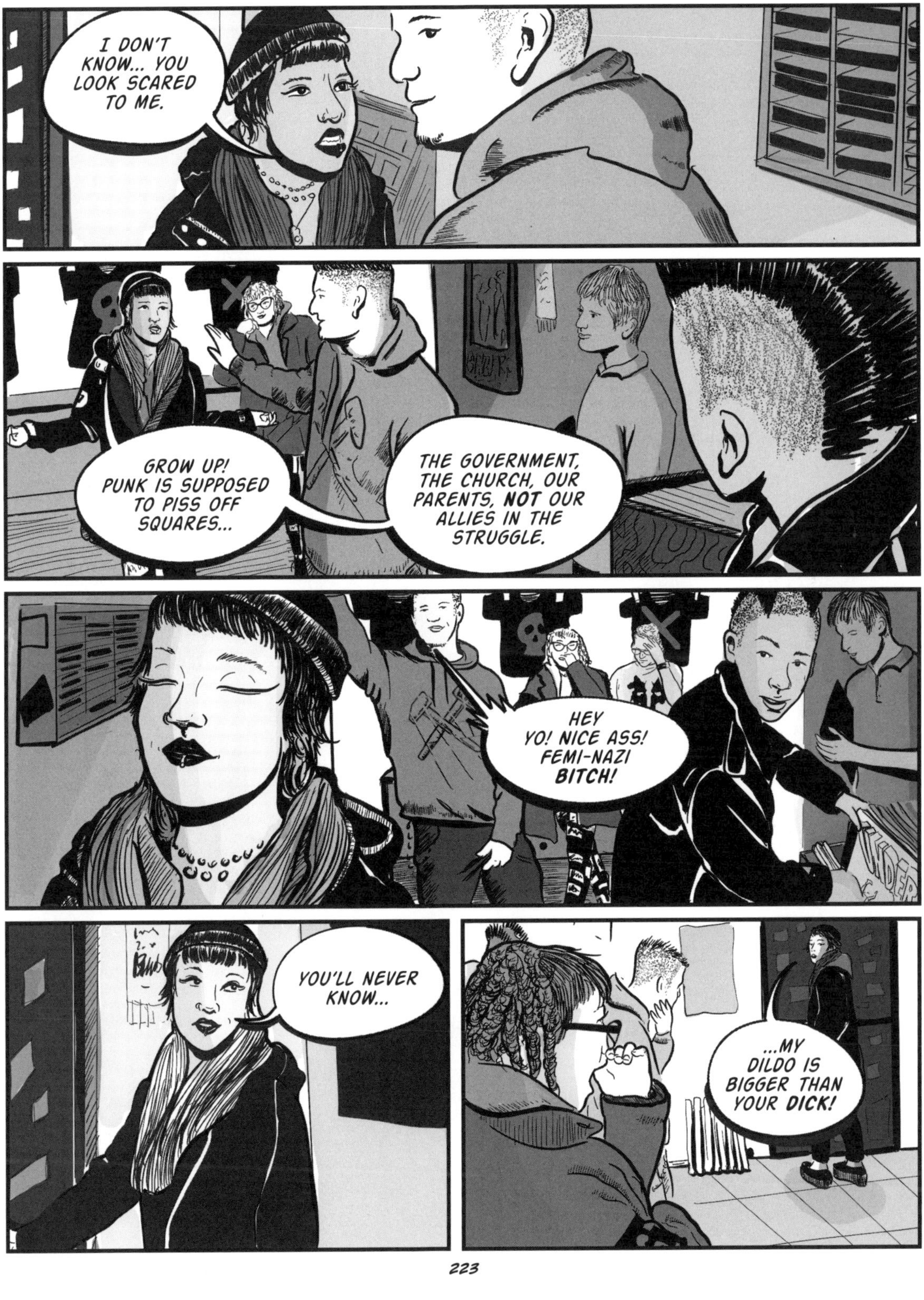
I DON'T KNOW... YOU LOOK SCARED TO ME.
GROW UP! PUNK IS SUPPOSED TO PISS OFF SQUARES...
THE GOVERNMENT, THE CHURCH, OUR PARENTS, **NOT** OUR ALLIES IN THE STRUGGLE.
HEY YO! NICE ASS! FEMI-NAZI **BITCH!**
YOU'LL NEVER KNOW...
...MY DILDO IS BIGGER THAN YOUR **DICK!**

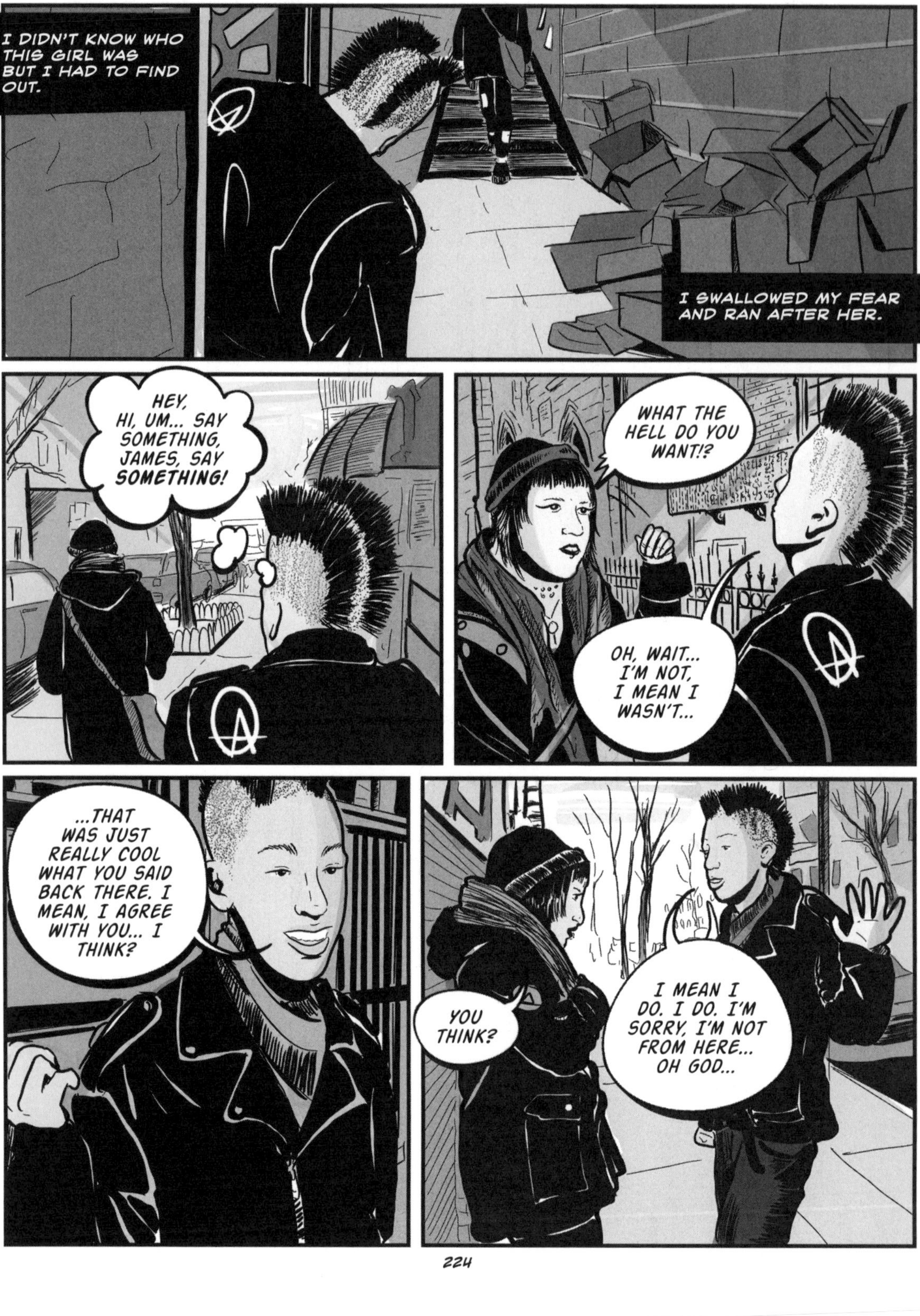
I DIDN'T KNOW WHO THIS GIRL WAS BUT I HAD TO FIND OUT.
I SWALLOWED MY FEAR AND RAN AFTER HER.
HEY, HI, UM... SAY SOMETHING, JAMES, SAY SOMETHING!
WHAT THE HELL DO YOU WANT!?
OH, WAIT... I'M NOT, I MEAN I WASN'T...
...THAT WAS JUST REALLY COOL WHAT YOU SAID BACK THERE. I MEAN, I AGREE WITH YOU... I THINK?
YOU THINK?
I MEAN I DO. I DO. I'M SORRY, I'M NOT FROM HERE... OH GOD...

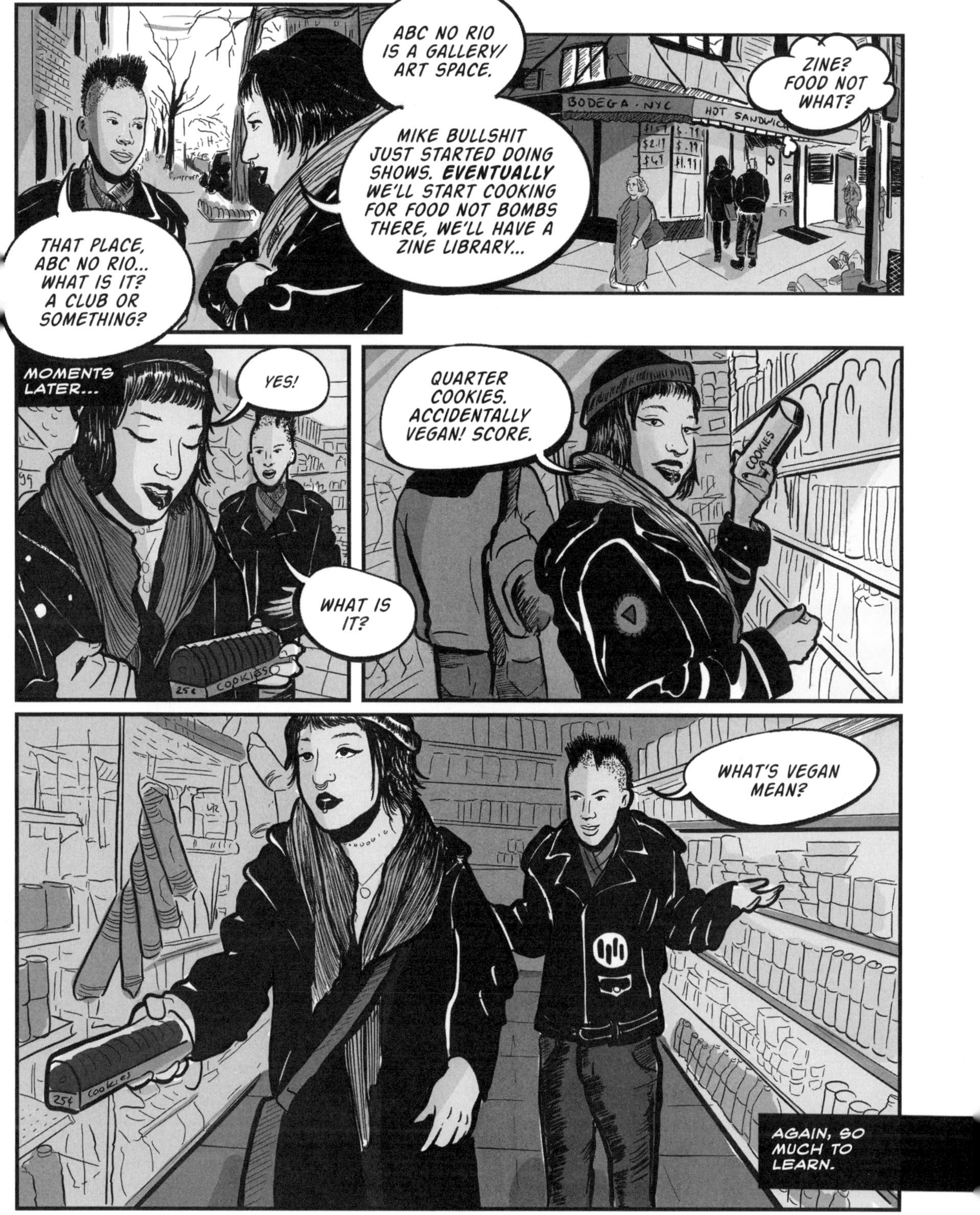
THAT PLACE, ABC NO RIO... WHAT IS IT? A CLUB OR SOMETHING?
ABC NO RIO IS A GALLERY/ ART SPACE.
MIKE BULLSHIT JUST STARTED DOING SHOWS. **EVENTUALLY** WE'LL START COOKING FOR FOOD NOT BOMBS THERE, WE'LL HAVE A ZINE LIBRARY...
BODEGA · NYC
HOT SANDWICH
ZINE? FOOD NOT WHAT?
MOMENTS LATER...
YES!
WHAT IS IT?
COOKIES
25¢
QUARTER COOKIES. ACCIDENTALLY VEGAN! SCORE.
COOKIES
WHAT'S VEGAN MEAN?
25¢ cookies
AGAIN, SO MUCH TO LEARN.

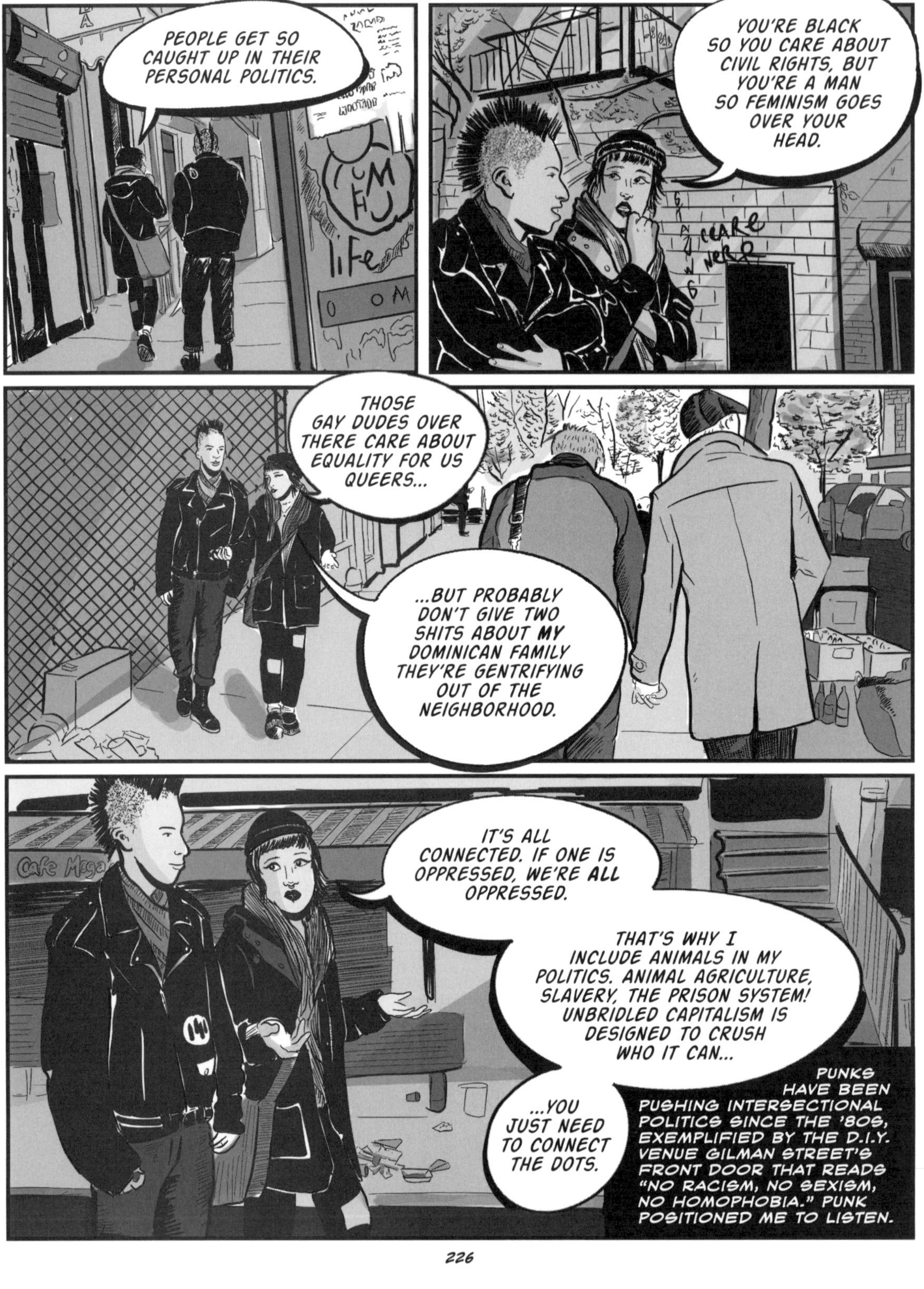
PEOPLE GET SO CAUGHT UP IN THEIR PERSONAL POLITICS.
YOU'RE BLACK SO YOU CARE ABOUT CIVIL RIGHTS, BUT YOU'RE A MAN SO FEMINISM GOES OVER YOUR HEAD.
THOSE GAY DUDES OVER THERE CARE ABOUT EQUALITY FOR US QUEERS...
...BUT PROBABLY DON'T GIVE TWO SHITS ABOUT MY DOMINICAN FAMILY THEY'RE GENTRIFYING OUT OF THE NEIGHBORHOOD.
Cafe Mega
IT'S ALL CONNECTED. IF ONE IS OPPRESSED, WE'RE ALL OPPRESSED.
THAT'S WHY I INCLUDE ANIMALS IN MY POLITICS. ANIMAL AGRICULTURE, SLAVERY, THE PRISON SYSTEM! UNBRIDLED CAPITALISM IS DESIGNED TO CRUSH WHO IT CAN...
...YOU JUST NEED TO CONNECT THE DOTS.
PUNKS HAVE BEEN PUSHING INTERSECTIONAL POLITICS SINCE THE '80S, EXEMPLIFIED BY THE D.I.Y. VENUE GILMAN STREET'S FRONT DOOR THAT READS "NO RACISM, NO SEXISM, NO HOMOPHOBIA." PUNK POSITIONED ME TO LISTEN.

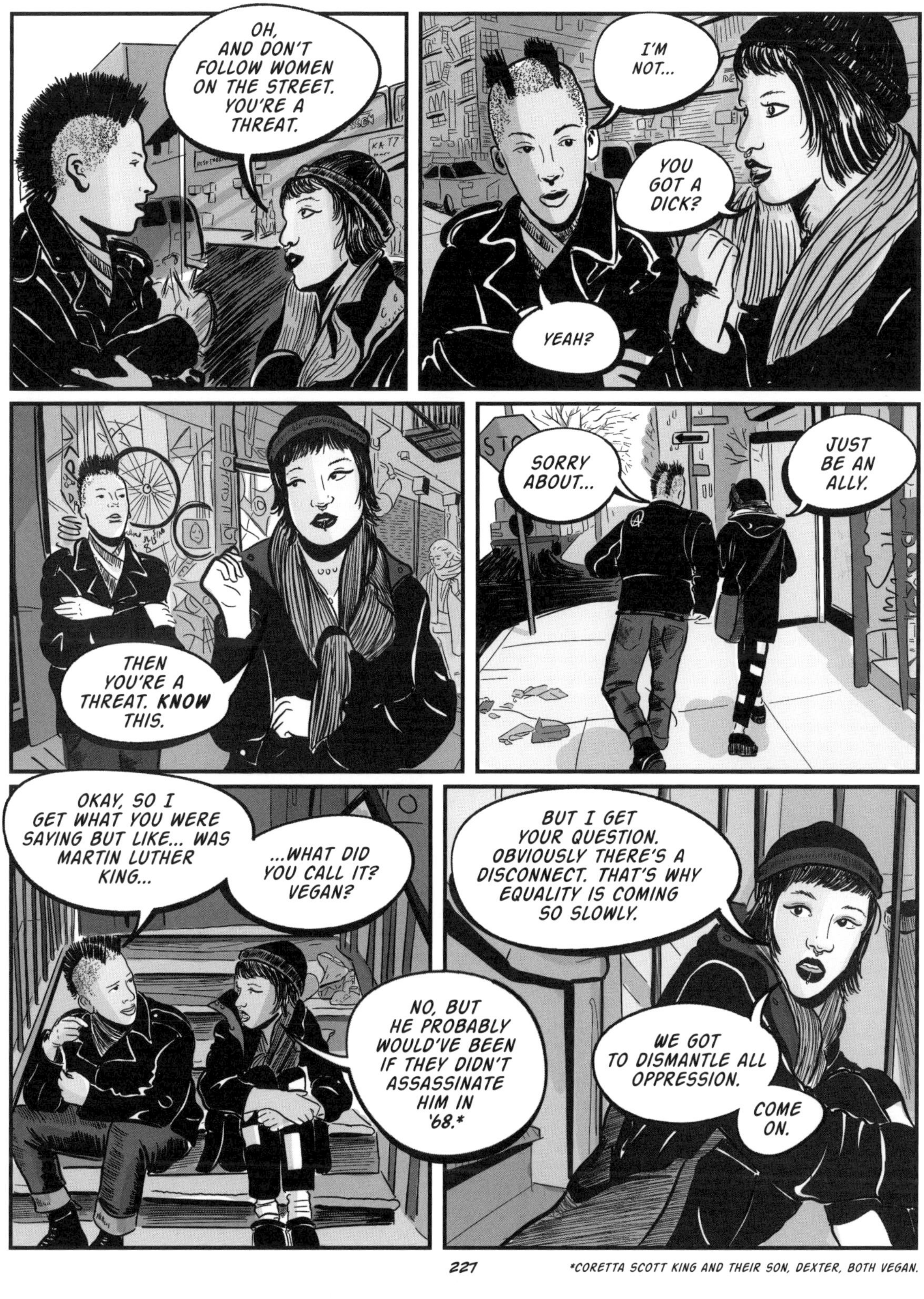
OH, AND DON'T FOLLOW WOMEN ON THE STREET. YOU'RE A THREAT.
I'M NOT...
YOU GOT A DICK?
YEAH?
THEN YOU'RE A THREAT. **KNOW** THIS.
SORRY ABOUT...
JUST BE AN ALLY.
OKAY, SO I GET WHAT YOU WERE SAYING BUT LIKE... WAS MARTIN LUTHER KING...
...WHAT DID YOU CALL IT? VEGAN?
NO, BUT HE PROBABLY WOULD'VE BEEN IF THEY DIDN'T ASSASSINATE HIM IN '68.*
BUT I GET YOUR QUESTION. OBVIOUSLY THERE'S A DISCONNECT. THAT'S WHY EQUALITY IS COMING SO SLOWLY.
WE GOT TO DISMANTLE ALL OPPRESSION.
COME ON.

*CORETTA SCOTT KING AND THEIR SON, DEXTER, BOTH VEGAN.

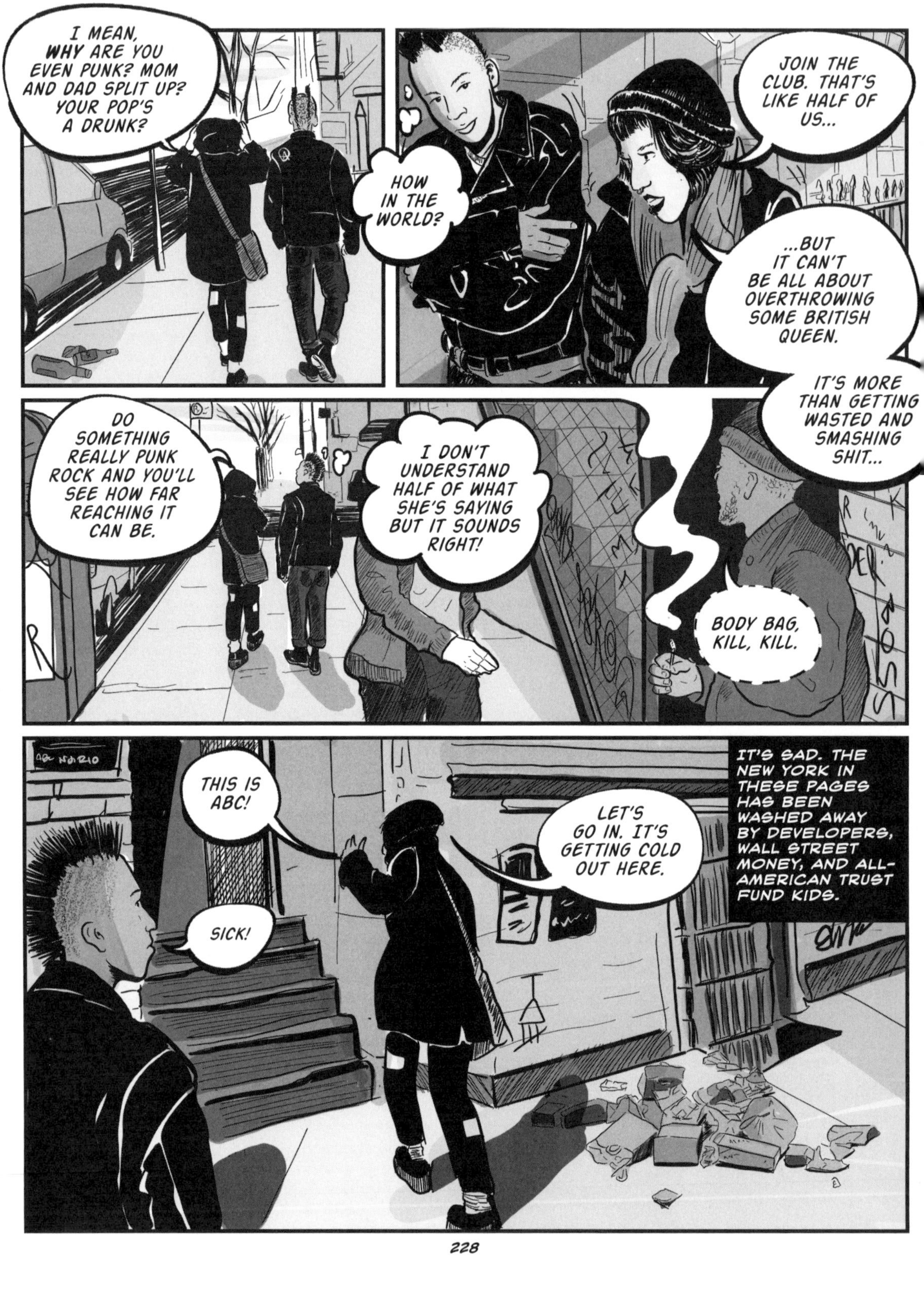
I MEAN, WHY ARE YOU EVEN PUNK? MOM AND DAD SPLIT UP? YOUR POP'S A DRUNK?
JOIN THE CLUB. THAT'S LIKE HALF OF US...
HOW IN THE WORLD?
...BUT IT CAN'T BE ALL ABOUT OVERTHROWING SOME BRITISH QUEEN.
IT'S MORE THAN GETTING WASTED AND SMASHING SHIT...
DO SOMETHING REALLY PUNK ROCK AND YOU'LL SEE HOW FAR REACHING IT CAN BE.
I DON'T UNDERSTAND HALF OF WHAT SHE'S SAYING BUT IT SOUNDS RIGHT!
BODY BAG, KILL, KILL.
THIS IS ABC!
LET'S GO IN. IT'S GETTING COLD OUT HERE.
SICK!
IT'S SAD. THE NEW YORK IN THESE PAGES HAS BEEN WASHED AWAY BY DEVELOPERS, WALL STREET MONEY, AND ALL-AMERICAN TRUST FUND KIDS.

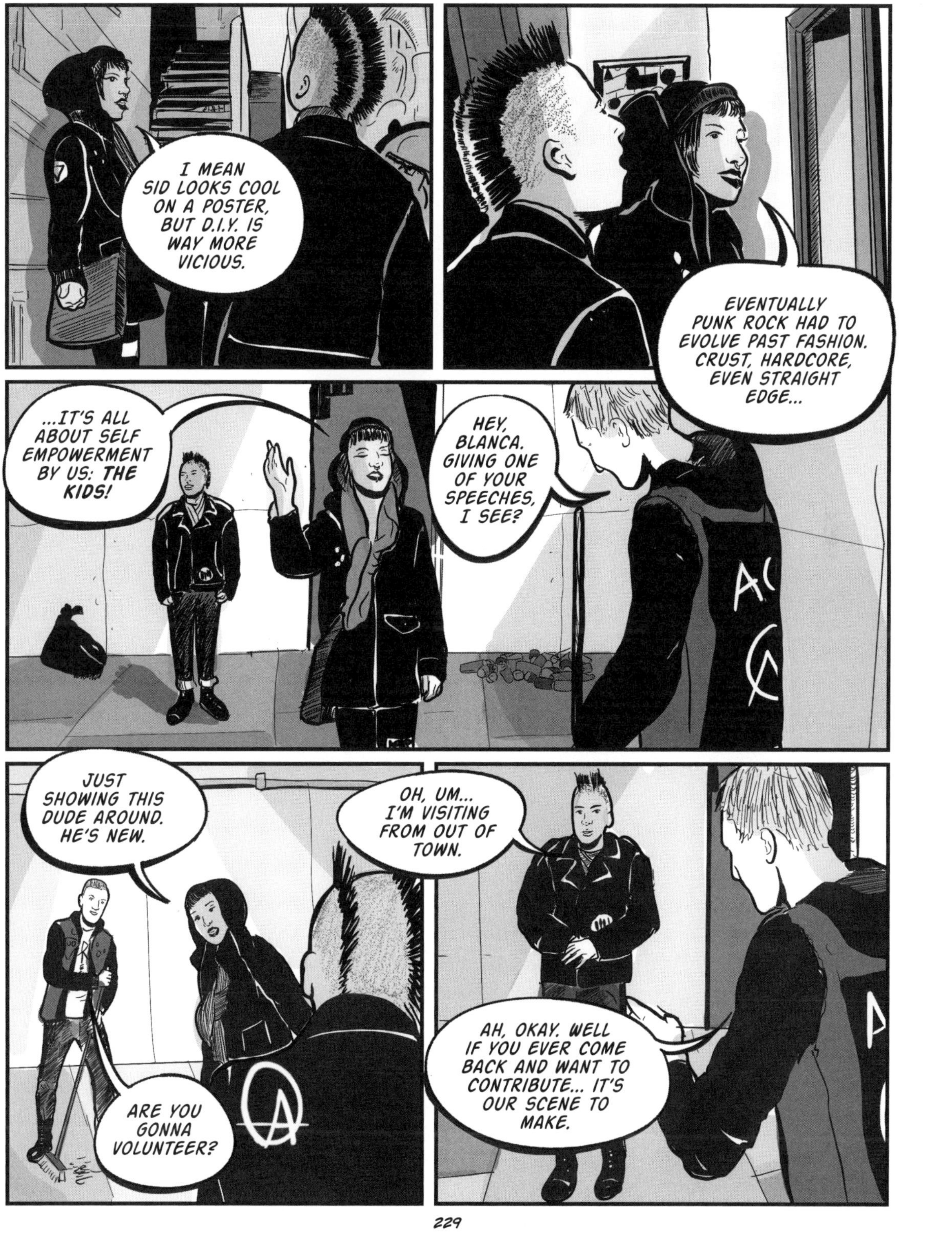
I MEAN SID LOOKS COOL ON A POSTER, BUT D.I.Y. IS WAY MORE VICIOUS.
EVENTUALLY PUNK ROCK HAD TO EVOLVE PAST FASHION. CRUST, HARDCORE, EVEN STRAIGHT EDGE...
...IT'S ALL ABOUT SELF EMPOWERMENT BY US: **THE KIDS!**
HEY, BLANCA. GIVING ONE OF YOUR SPEECHES, I SEE?
JUST SHOWING THIS DUDE AROUND. HE'S NEW.
ARE YOU GONNA VOLUNTEER?
OH, UM... I'M VISITING FROM OUT OF TOWN.
AH, OKAY. WELL IF YOU EVER COME BACK AND WANT TO CONTRIBUTE... IT'S OUR SCENE TO MAKE.

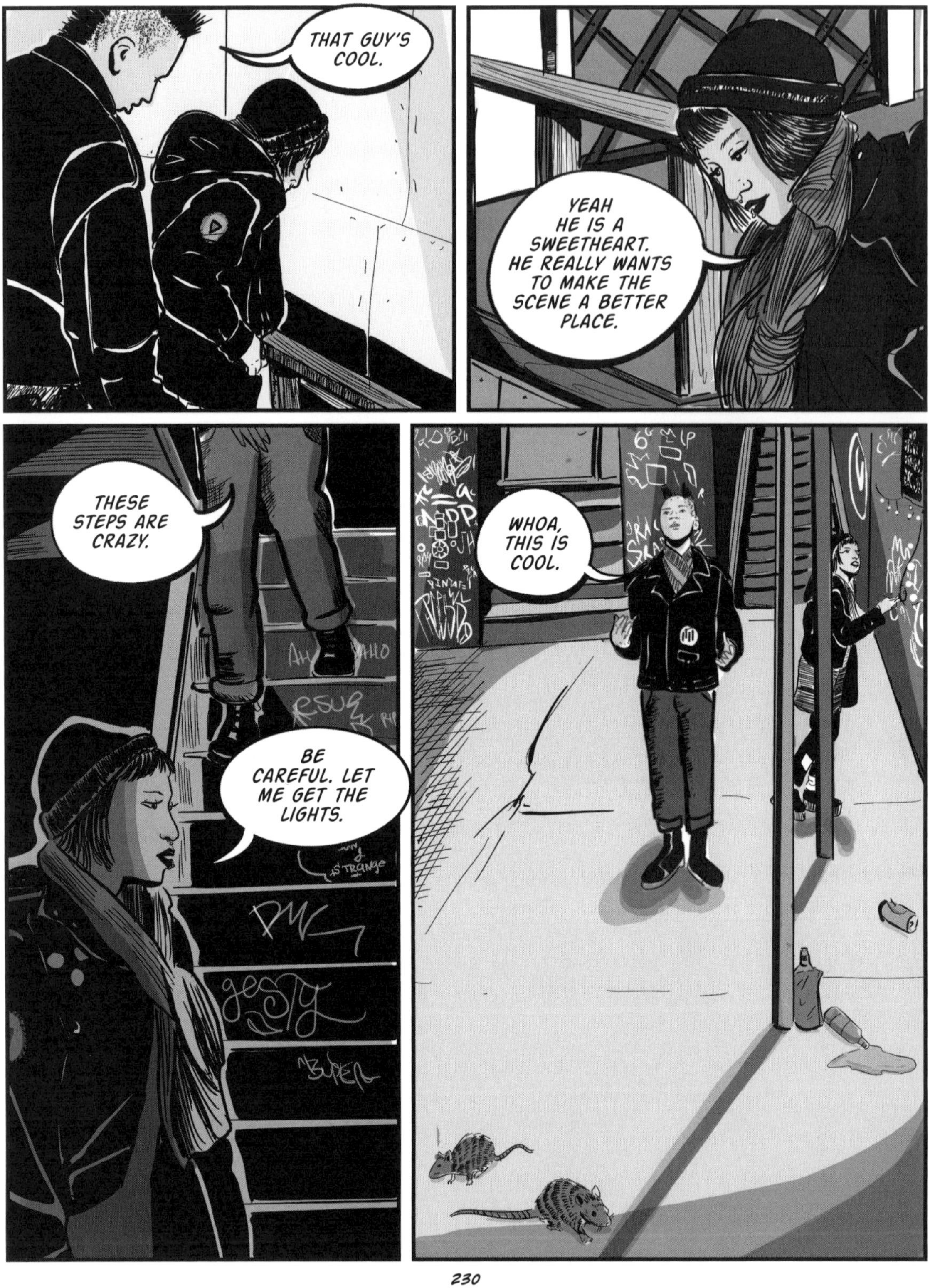

THAT GUY'S COOL.
YEAH HE IS A SWEETHEART. HE REALLY WANTS TO MAKE THE SCENE A BETTER PLACE.
THESE STEPS ARE CRAZY.
BE CAREFUL. LET ME GET THE LIGHTS.
WHOA, THIS IS COOL.

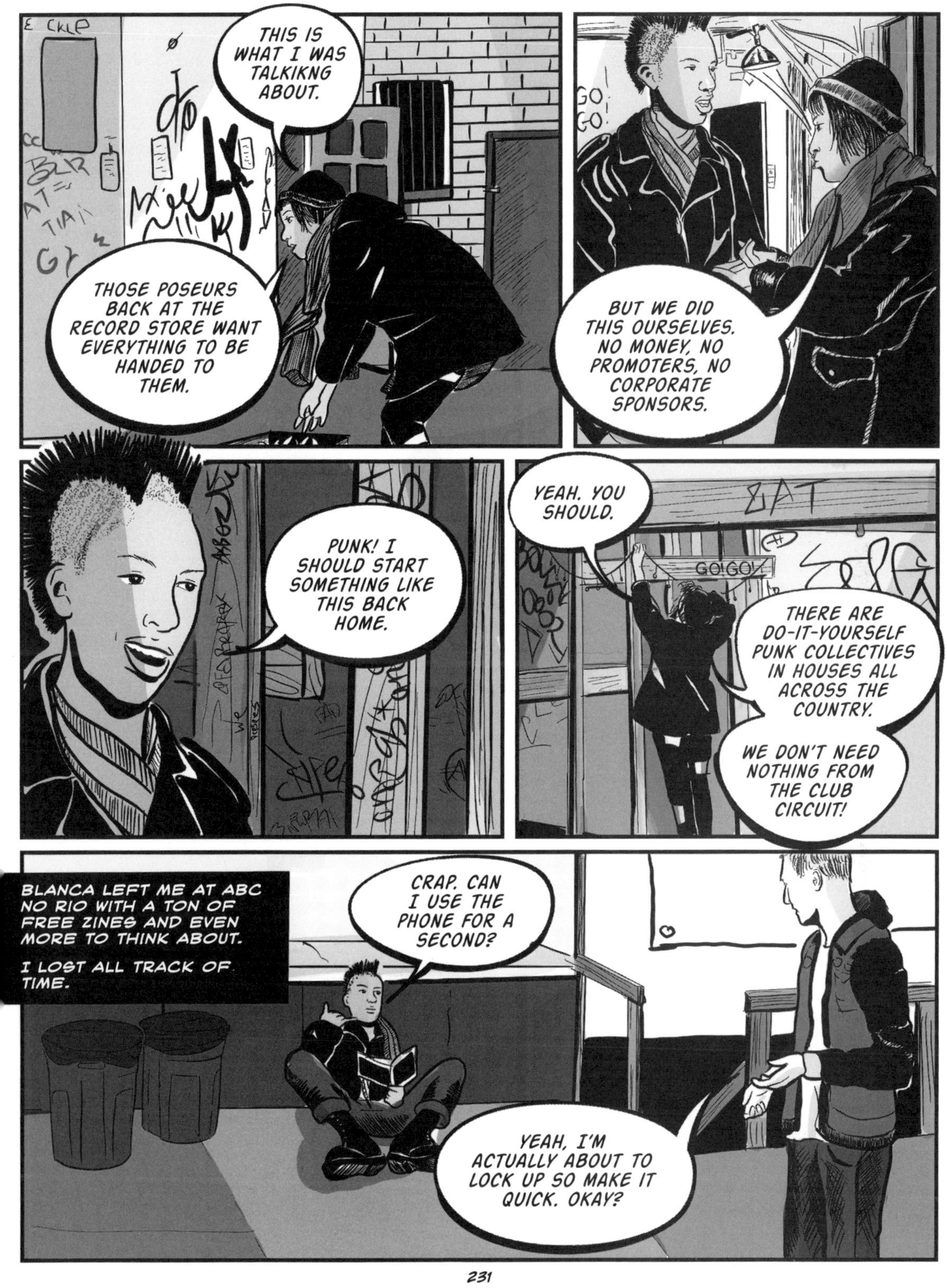
THIS IS WHAT I WAS TALKIKNG ABOUT.
THOSE POSEURS BACK AT THE RECORD STORE WANT EVERYTHING TO BE HANDED TO THEM.
GO! GO!
BUT WE DID THIS OURSELVES. NO MONEY, NO PROMOTERS, NO CORPORATE SPONSORS.
PUNK! I SHOULD START SOMETHING LIKE THIS BACK HOME.
YEAH. YOU SHOULD.
GO!GO!
THERE ARE DO-IT-YOURSELF PUNK COLLECTIVES IN HOUSES ALL ACROSS THE COUNTRY.
WE DON'T NEED NOTHING FROM THE CLUB CIRCUIT!
BLANCA LEFT ME AT ABC NO RIO WITH A TON OF FREE ZINES AND EVEN MORE TO THINK ABOUT.
I LOST ALL TRACK OF TIME.
CRAP. CAN I USE THE PHONE FOR A SECOND?
YEAH, I'M ACTUALLY ABOUT TO LOCK UP SO MAKE IT QUICK. OKAY?

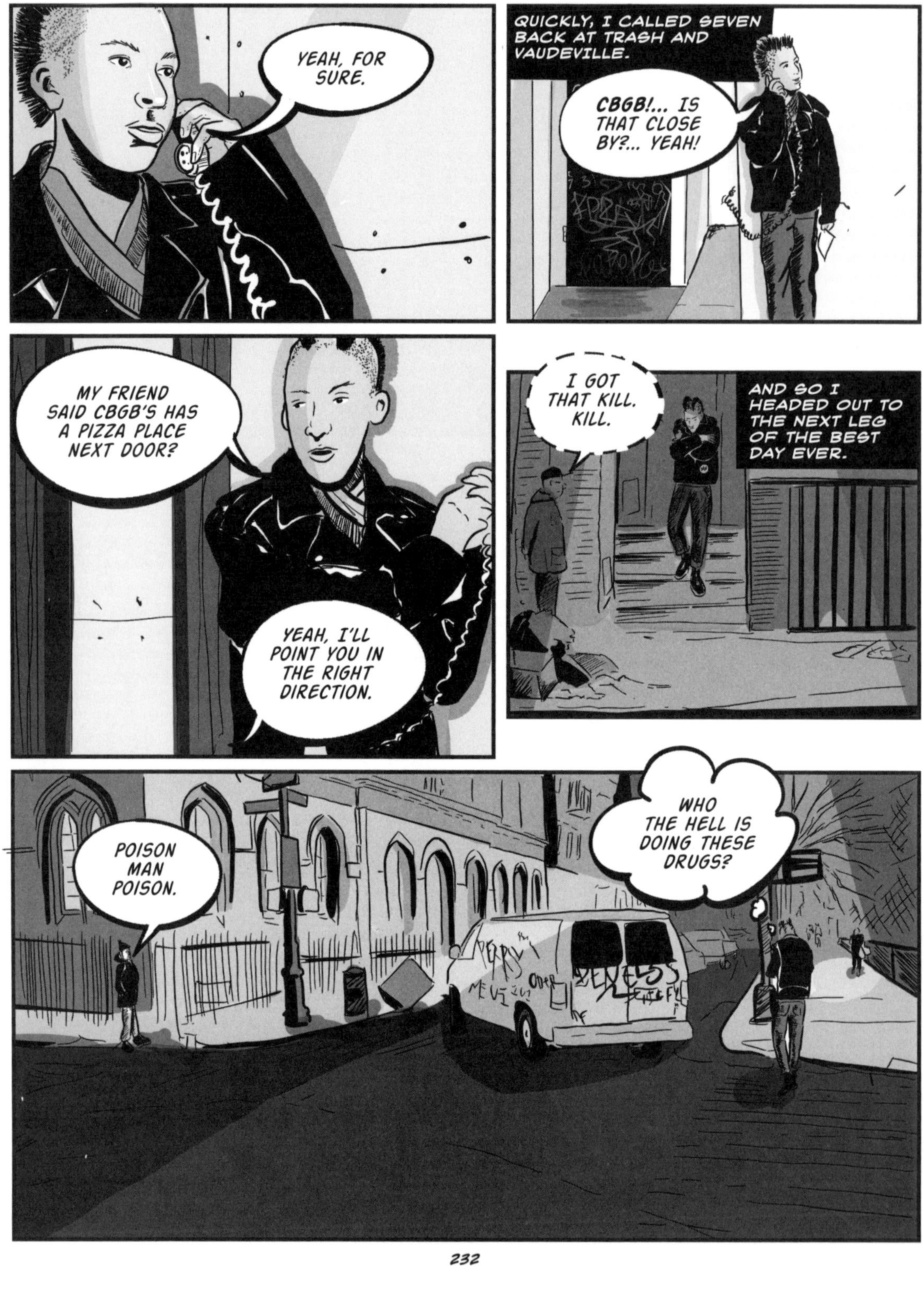
YEAH, FOR SURE.
QUICKLY, I CALLED SEVEN BACK AT TRASH AND VAUDEVILLE.
CBGB!... IS THAT CLOSE BY?... YEAH!
MY FRIEND SAID CBGB'S HAS A PIZZA PLACE NEXT DOOR?
YEAH, I'LL POINT YOU IN THE RIGHT DIRECTION.
I GOT THAT KILL. KILL.
AND SO I HEADED OUT TO THE NEXT LEG OF THE BEST DAY EVER.
POISON MAN POISON.
WHO THE HELL IS DOING THESE DRUGS?

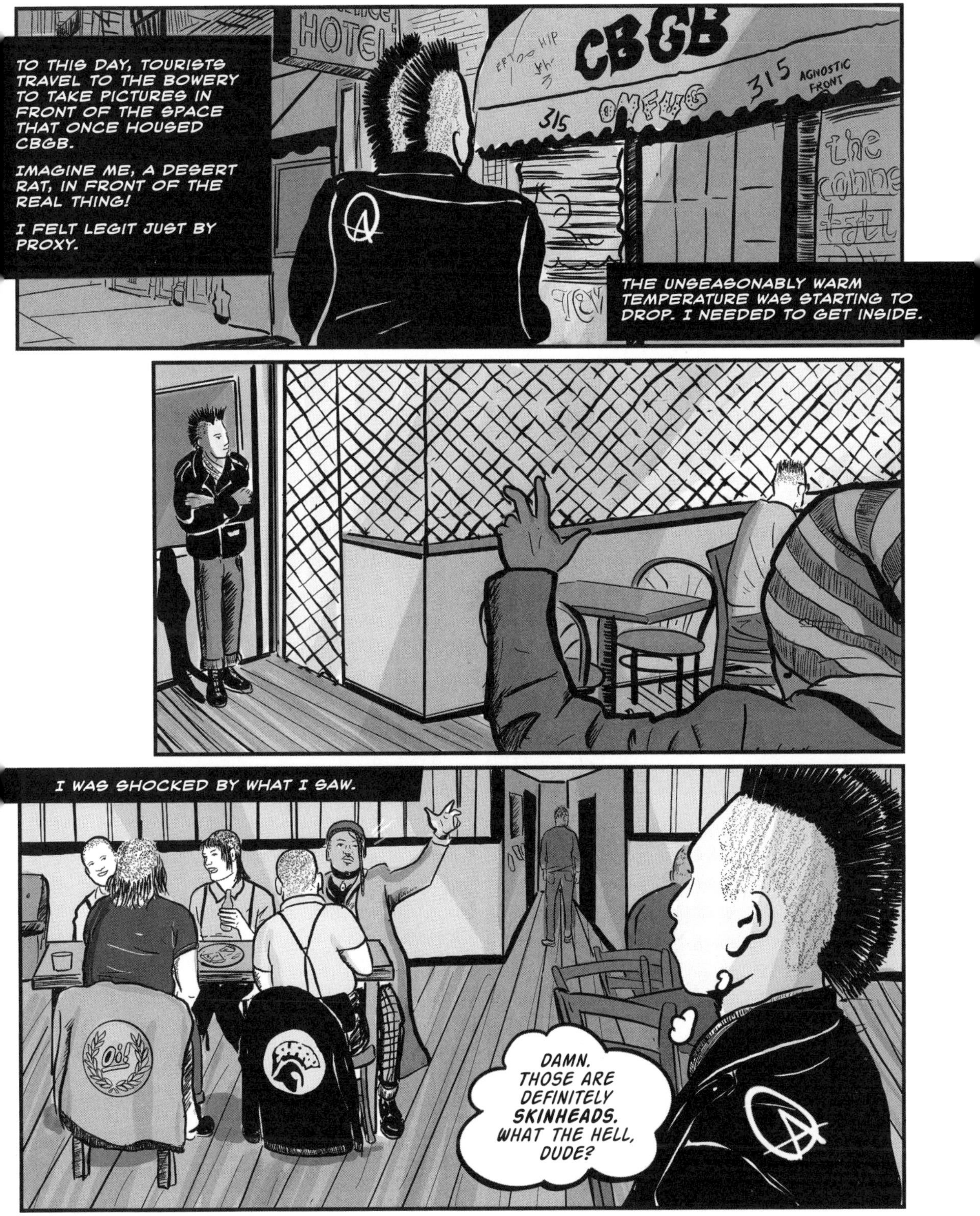
TO THIS DAY, TOURISTS TRAVEL TO THE BOWERY TO TAKE PICTURES IN FRONT OF THE SPACE THAT ONCE HOUSED CBGB.
IMAGINE ME, A DESERT RAT, IN FRONT OF THE REAL THING!
I FELT LEGIT JUST BY PROXY.
HOTEL
CBGB
315
OMFUG
AGNOSTIC FRONT
THE UNSEASONABLY WARM TEMPERATURE WAS STARTING TO DROP. I NEEDED TO GET INSIDE.
I WAS SHOCKED BY WHAT I SAW.
Oi!
DAMN. THOSE ARE DEFINITELY **SKINHEADS.** WHAT THE HELL, DUDE?

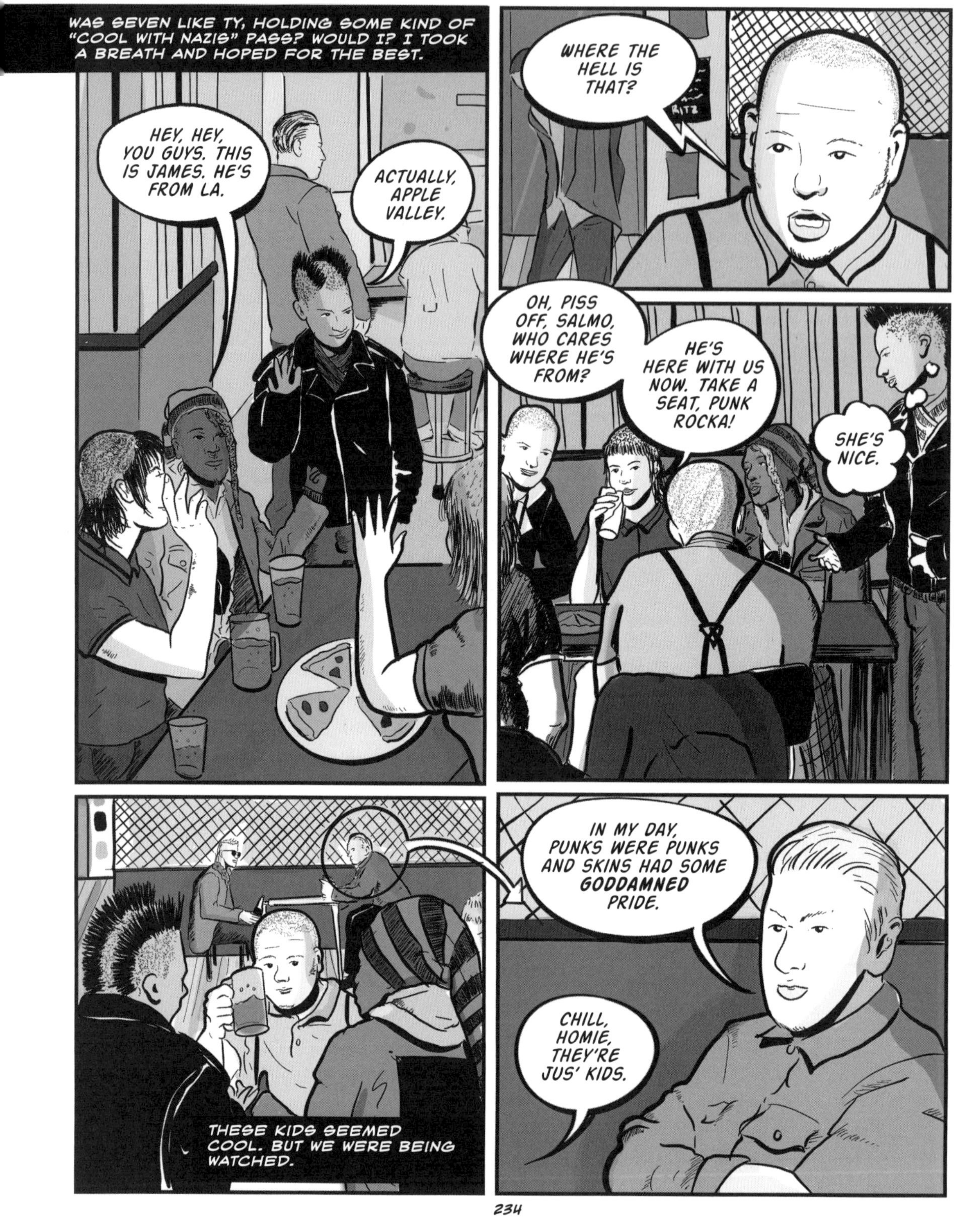

WAS SEVEN LIKE TY, HOLDING SOME KIND OF "COOL WITH NAZIS" PASS? WOULD I? I TOOK A BREATH AND HOPED FOR THE BEST.
HEY, HEY, YOU GUYS. THIS IS JAMES. HE'S FROM LA.
ACTUALLY, APPLE VALLEY.
WHERE THE HELL IS THAT?
RITZ
OH, PISS OFF, SALMO, WHO CARES WHERE HE'S FROM?
HE'S HERE WITH US NOW. TAKE A SEAT, PUNK ROCKA!
SHE'S NICE.
THESE KIDS SEEMED COOL. BUT WE WERE BEING WATCHED.
IN MY DAY, PUNKS WERE PUNKS AND SKINS HAD SOME **GODDAMNED** PRIDE.
CHILL, HOMIE, THEY'RE JUS' KIDS.

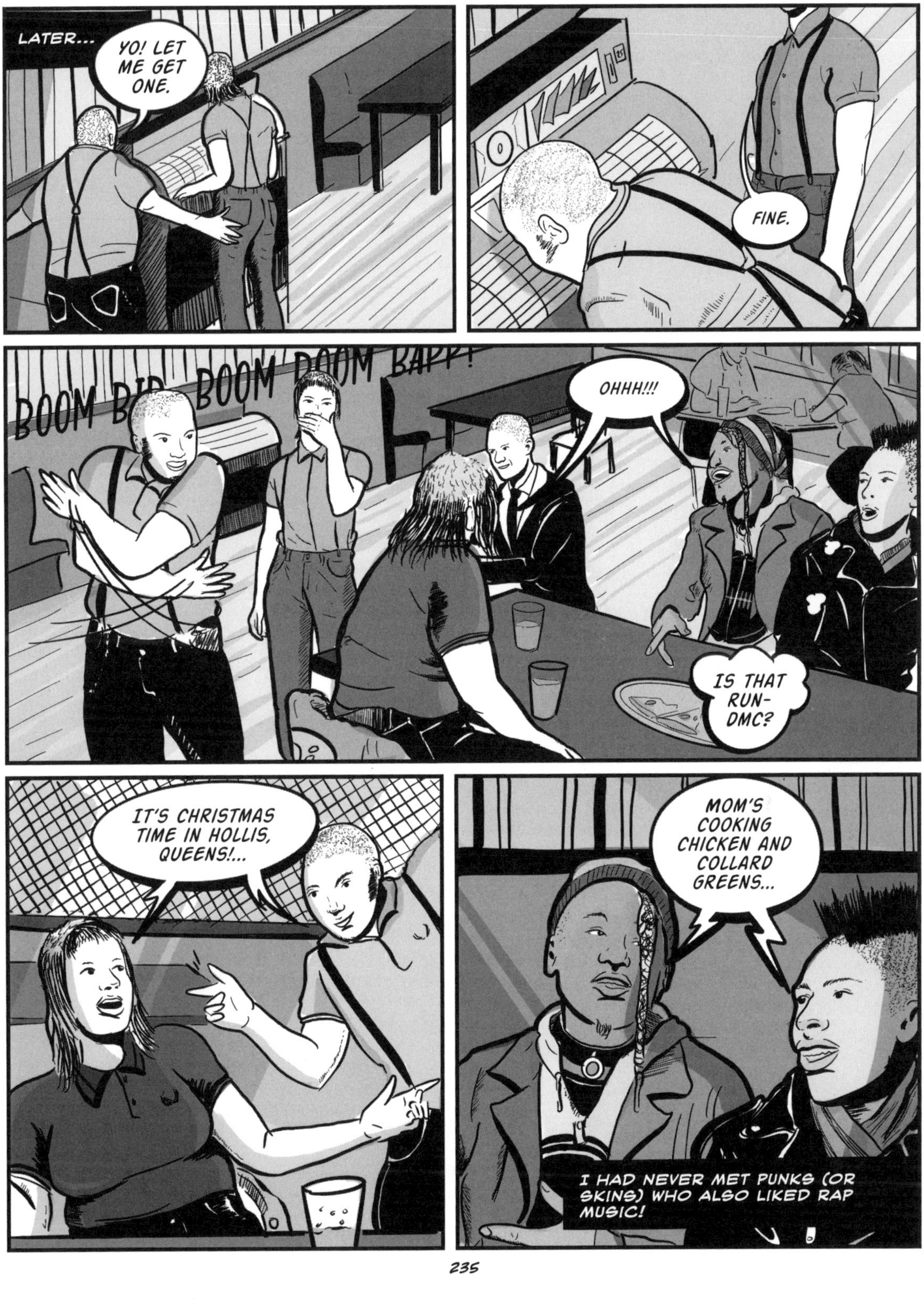

LATER...
YO! LET ME GET ONE.
FINE.
BOOM BIP BOOM BOOM BAPP!
OHHH!!!
IS THAT RUN-DMC?
IT'S CHRISTMAS TIME IN HOLLIS, QUEENS!...
MOM'S COOKING CHICKEN AND COLLARD GREENS...
I HAD NEVER MET PUNKS (OR SKINS) WHO ALSO LIKED RAP MUSIC!

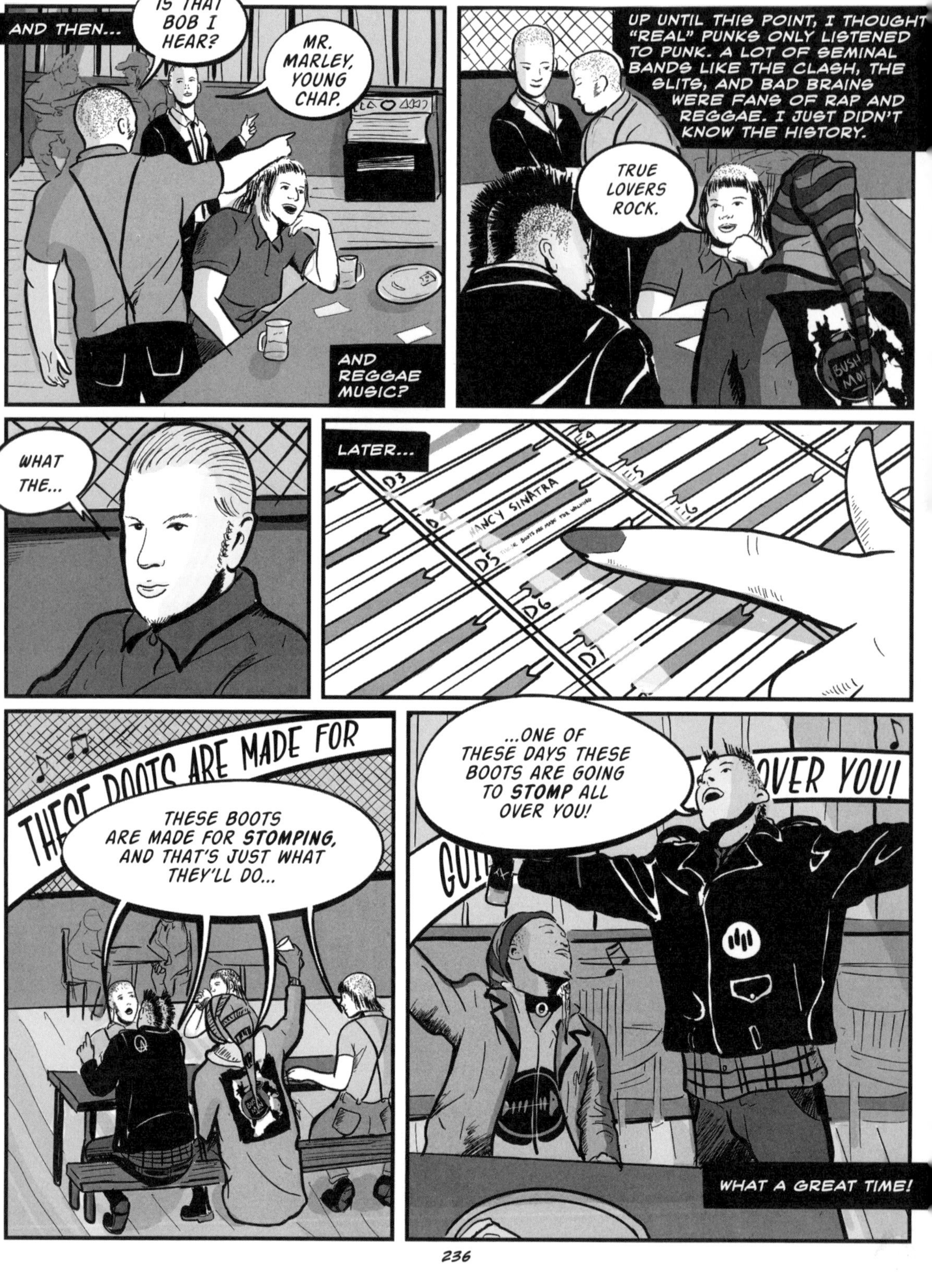
AND THEN...
IS THAT BOB I HEAR?
MR. MARLEY, YOUNG CHAP.
AND REGGAE MUSIC?
UP UNTIL THIS POINT, I THOUGHT "REAL" PUNKS ONLY LISTENED TO PUNK. A LOT OF SEMINAL BANDS LIKE THE CLASH, THE SLITS, AND BAD BRAINS WERE FANS OF RAP AND REGGAE. I JUST DIDN'T KNOW THE HISTORY.
TRUE LOVERS ROCK.
WHAT THE...
LATER...
D3
D4
NANCY SINATRA
D5
D6
D7
THESE BOOTS ARE MADE FOR
THESE BOOTS ARE MADE FOR STOMPING, AND THAT'S JUST WHAT THEY'LL DO...
...ONE OF THESE DAYS THESE BOOTS ARE GOING TO STOMP ALL OVER YOU!
OVER YOU!
WHAT A GREAT TIME!

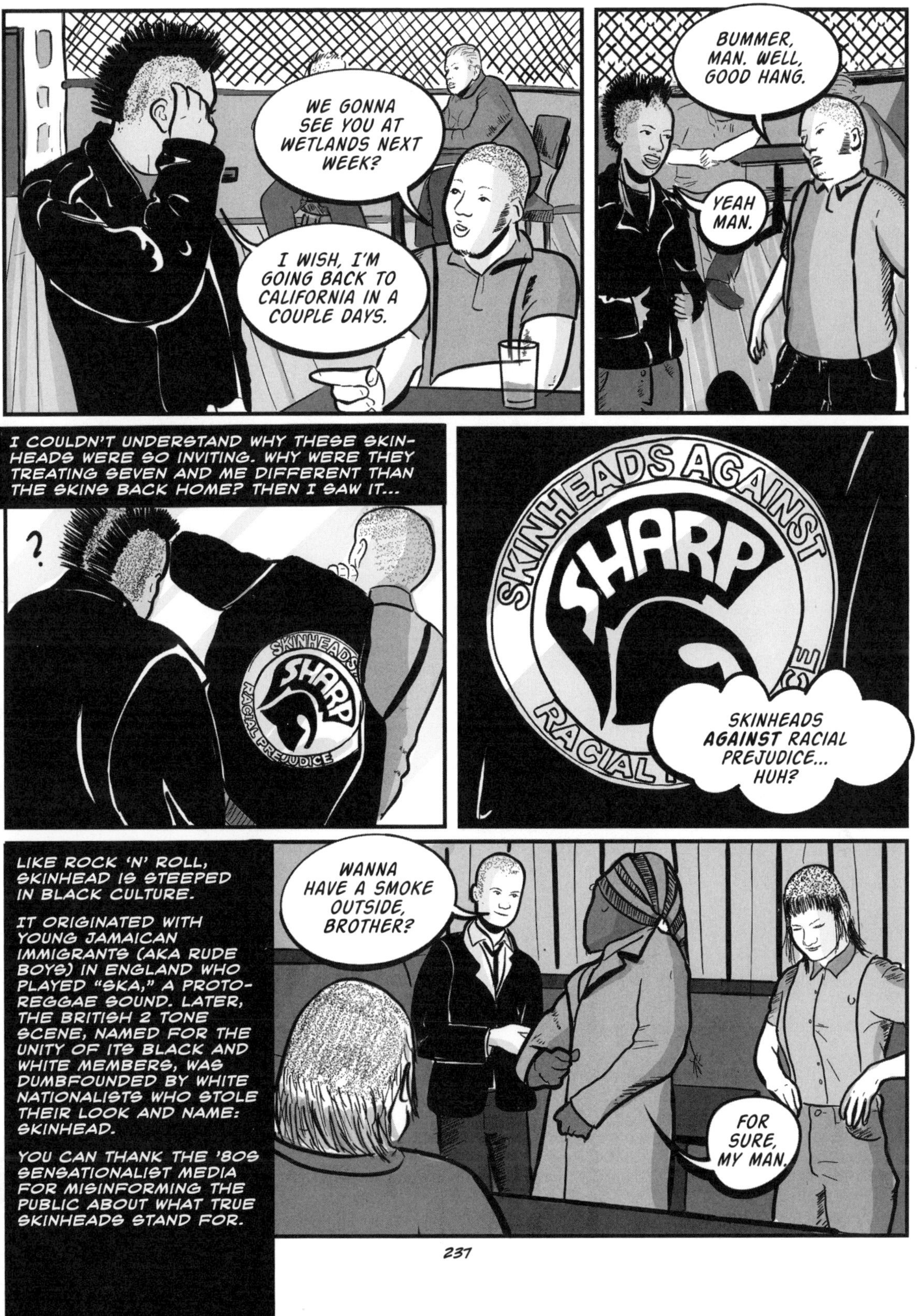
WE GONNA SEE YOU AT WETLANDS NEXT WEEK?
I WISH, I'M GOING BACK TO CALIFORNIA IN A COUPLE DAYS.
BUMMER, MAN. WELL, GOOD HANG.
YEAH MAN.
I COULDN'T UNDERSTAND WHY THESE SKINHEADS WERE SO INVITING. WHY WERE THEY TREATING SEVEN AND ME DIFFERENT THAN THE SKINS BACK HOME? THEN I SAW IT...
?
SKINHEADS SHARP RACIAL PREJUDICE
SKINHEADS AGAINST SHARP RACIAL
SKINHEADS **AGAINST** RACIAL PREJUDICE... HUH?
LIKE ROCK 'N' ROLL, SKINHEAD IS STEEPED IN BLACK CULTURE.
IT ORIGINATED WITH YOUNG JAMAICAN IMMIGRANTS (AKA RUDE BOYS) IN ENGLAND WHO PLAYED "SKA," A PROTO-REGGAE SOUND. LATER, THE BRITISH 2 TONE SCENE, NAMED FOR THE UNITY OF ITS BLACK AND WHITE MEMBERS, WAS DUMBFOUNDED BY WHITE NATIONALISTS WHO STOLE THEIR LOOK AND NAME: SKINHEAD.
YOU CAN THANK THE '80S SENSATIONALIST MEDIA FOR MISINFORMING THE PUBLIC ABOUT WHAT TRUE SKINHEADS STAND FOR.
WANNA HAVE A SMOKE OUTSIDE, BROTHER?
FOR SURE, MY MAN.

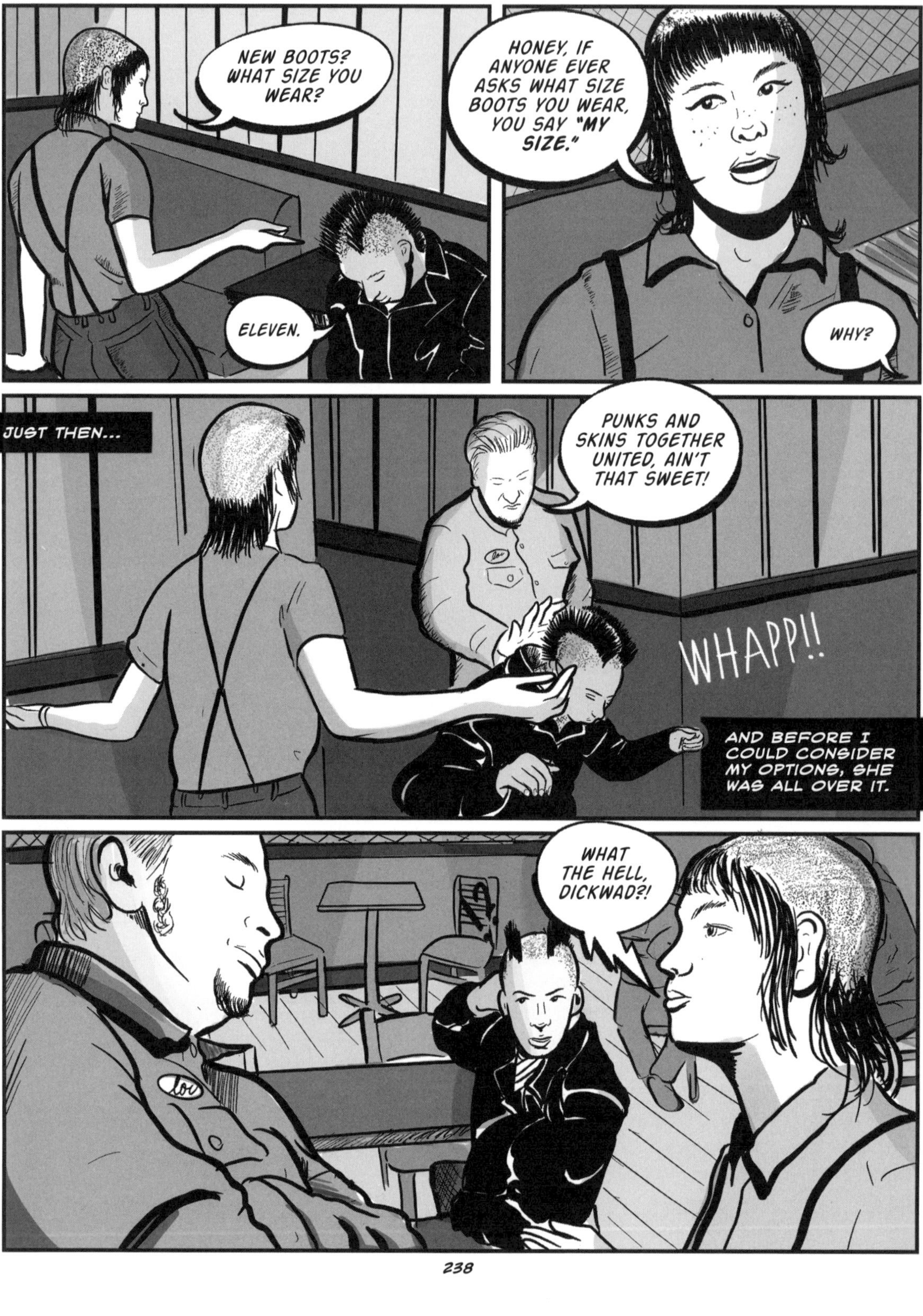

NEW BOOTS? WHAT SIZE YOU WEAR?
ELEVEN.
HONEY, IF ANYONE EVER ASKS WHAT SIZE BOOTS YOU WEAR, YOU SAY "MY SIZE."
WHY?
JUST THEN...
PUNKS AND SKINS TOGETHER UNITED, AIN'T THAT SWEET!
WHAPP!!
AND BEFORE I COULD CONSIDER MY OPTIONS, SHE WAS ALL OVER IT.
WHAT THE HELL, DICKWAD?!

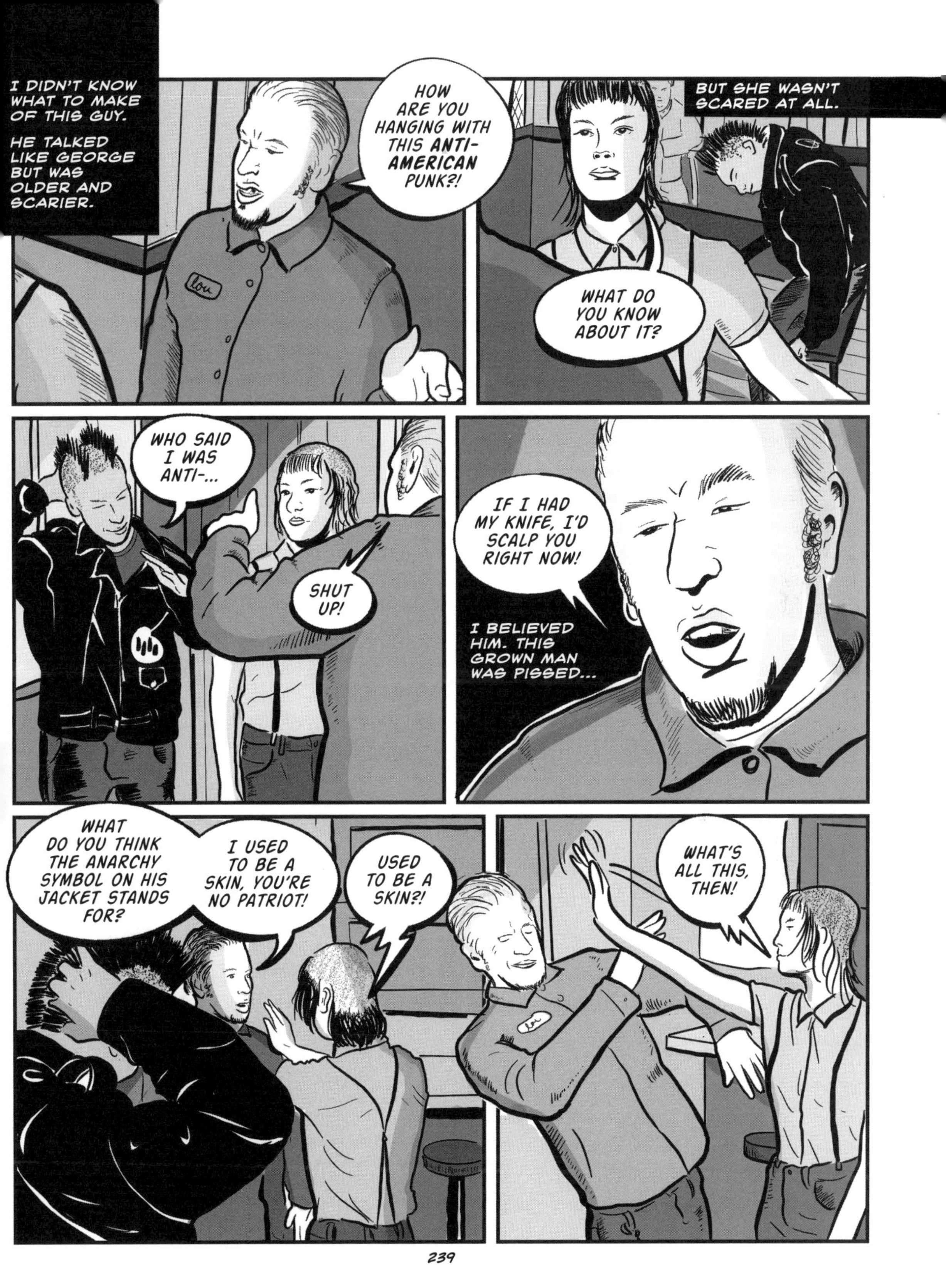

I DIDN'T KNOW WHAT TO MAKE OF THIS GUY.
HE TALKED LIKE GEORGE BUT WAS OLDER AND SCARIER.
HOW ARE YOU HANGING WITH THIS ANTI-AMERICAN PUNK?!
BUT SHE WASN'T SCARED AT ALL.
WHAT DO YOU KNOW ABOUT IT?
WHO SAID I WAS ANTI-...
SHUT UP!
IF I HAD MY KNIFE, I'D SCALP YOU RIGHT NOW!
I BELIEVED HIM. THIS GROWN MAN WAS PISSED...
WHAT DO YOU THINK THE ANARCHY SYMBOL ON HIS JACKET STANDS FOR?
I USED TO BE A SKIN, YOU'RE NO PATRIOT!
USED TO BE A SKIN?!
WHAT'S ALL THIS, THEN!

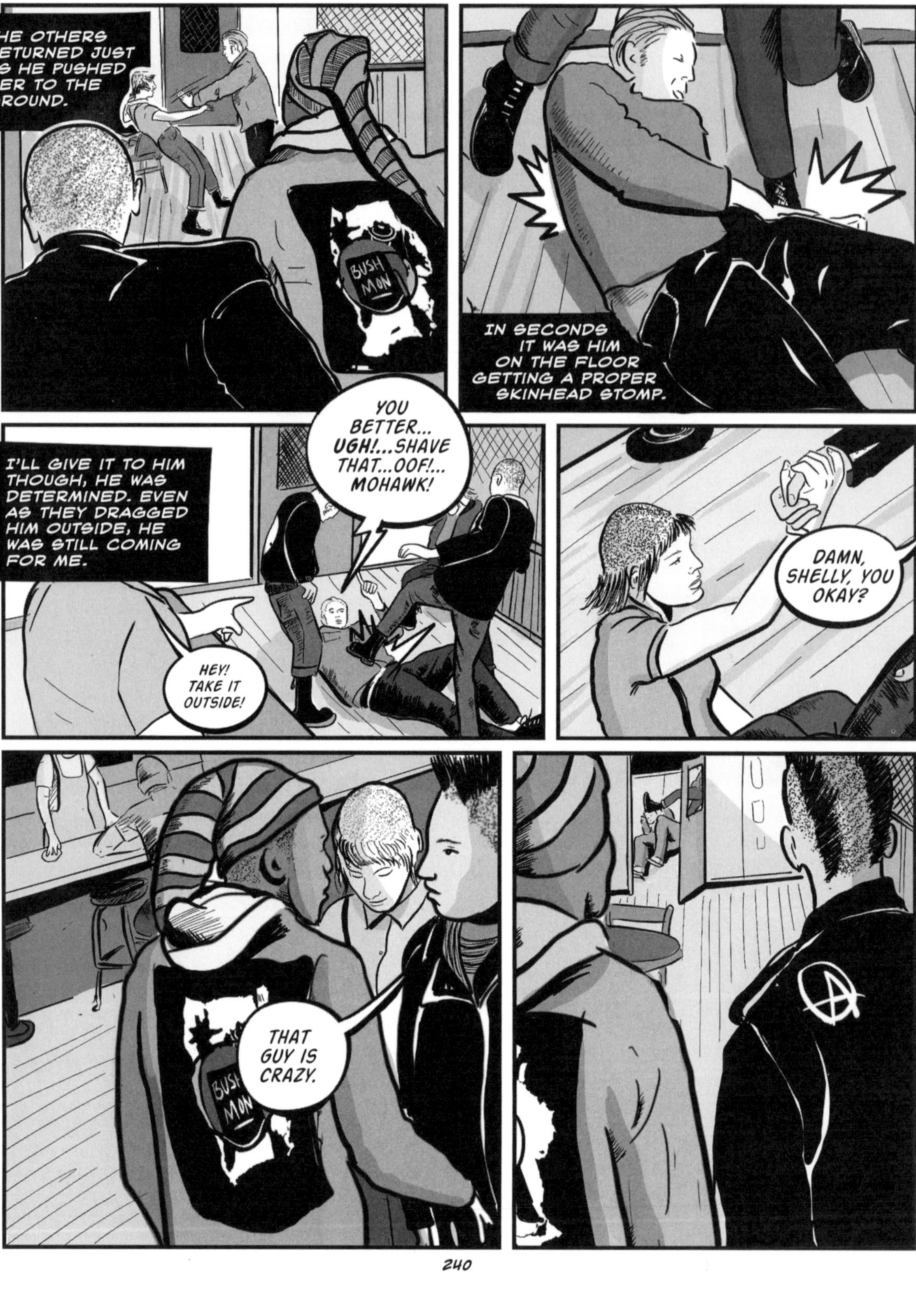
THE OTHERS RETURNED JUST AS HE PUSHED HER TO THE GROUND.
BUSH MON
IN SECONDS IT WAS HIM ON THE FLOOR GETTING A PROPER SKINHEAD STOMP.
I'LL GIVE IT TO HIM THOUGH, HE WAS DETERMINED. EVEN AS THEY DRAGGED HIM OUTSIDE, HE WAS STILL COMING FOR ME.
YOU BETTER... UGH!...SHAVE THAT...OOF!... MOHAWK!
HEY! TAKE IT OUTSIDE!
DAMN, SHELLY, YOU OKAY?
BUSH MON
THAT GUY IS CRAZY.

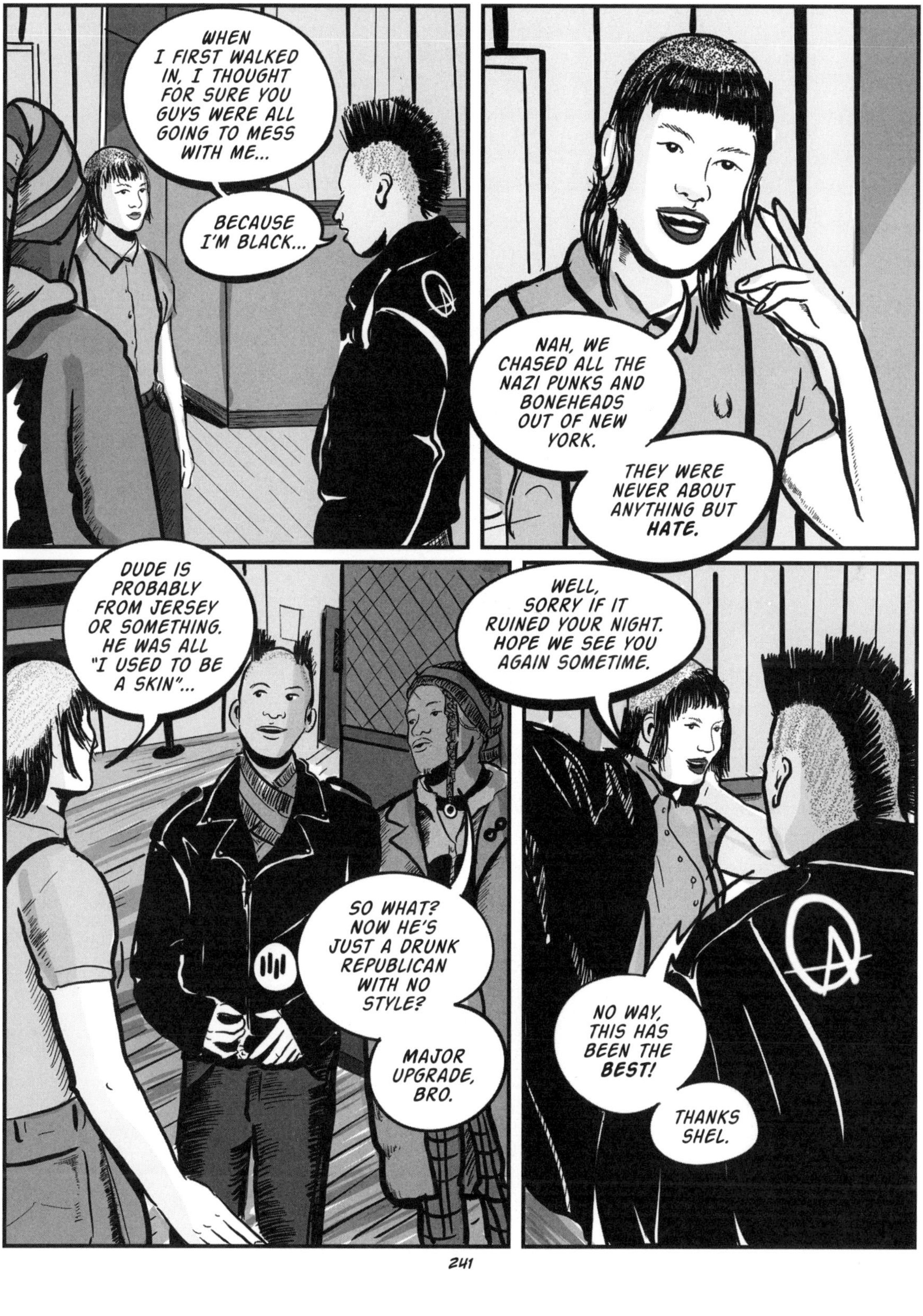
WHEN I FIRST WALKED IN, I THOUGHT FOR SURE YOU GUYS WERE ALL GOING TO MESS WITH ME...
BECAUSE I'M BLACK...
NAH, WE CHASED ALL THE NAZI PUNKS AND BONEHEADS OUT OF NEW YORK.
THEY WERE NEVER ABOUT ANYTHING BUT HATE.
DUDE IS PROBABLY FROM JERSEY OR SOMETHING. HE WAS ALL "I USED TO BE A SKIN"...
SO WHAT? NOW HE'S JUST A DRUNK REPUBLICAN WITH NO STYLE?
MAJOR UPGRADE, BRO.
WELL, SORRY IF IT RUINED YOUR NIGHT. HOPE WE SEE YOU AGAIN SOMETIME.
NO WAY, THIS HAS BEEN THE BEST!
THANKS SHEL.

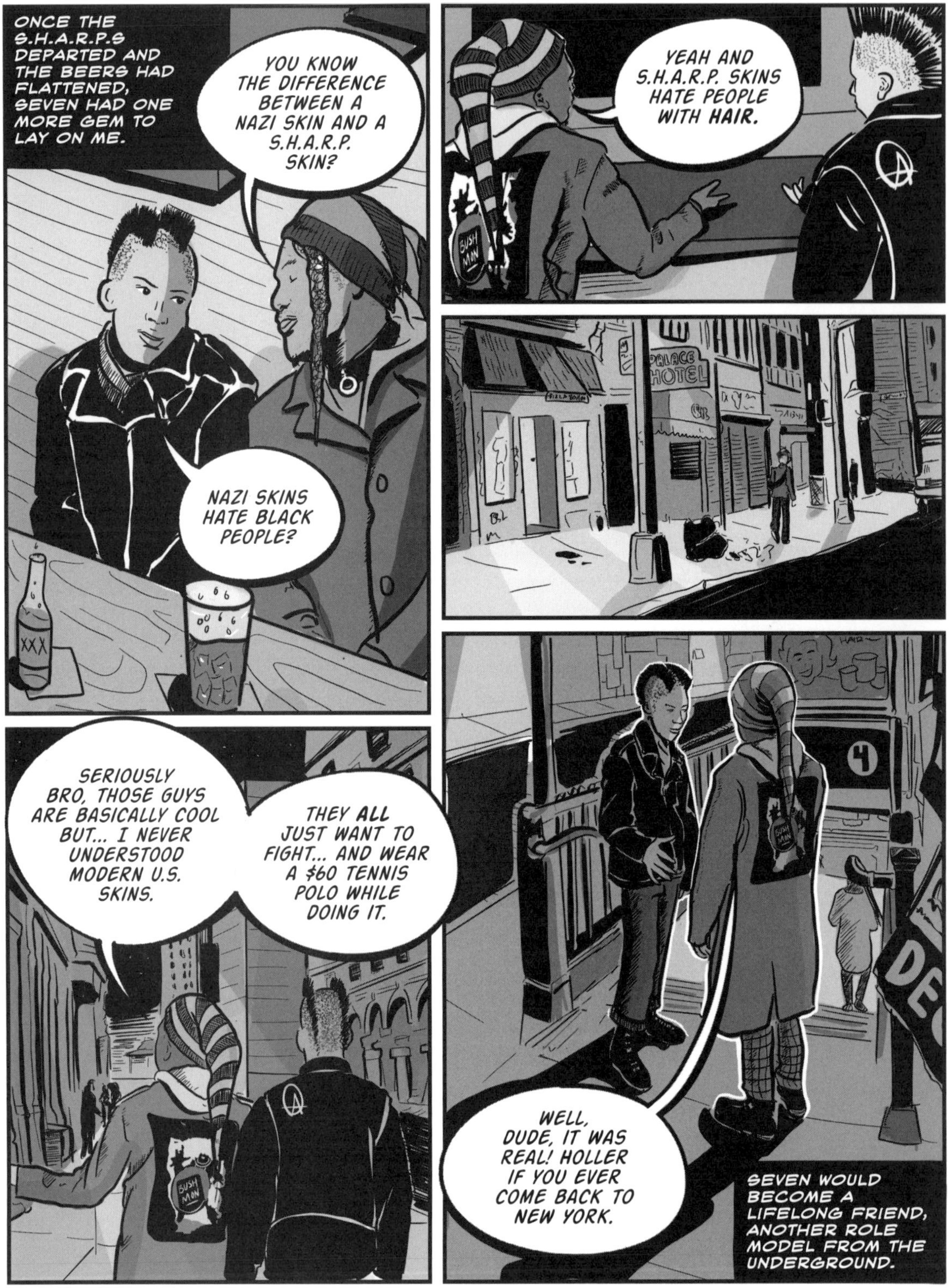

ONCE THE S.H.A.R.P.S DEPARTED AND THE BEERS HAD FLATTENED, SEVEN HAD ONE MORE GEM TO LAY ON ME.
YOU KNOW THE DIFFERENCE BETWEEN A NAZI SKIN AND A S.H.A.R.P. SKIN?
NAZI SKINS HATE BLACK PEOPLE?
YEAH AND S.H.A.R.P. SKINS HATE PEOPLE WITH HAIR.
PALACE HOTEL
SERIOUSLY BRO, THOSE GUYS ARE BASICALLY COOL BUT... I NEVER UNDERSTOOD MODERN U.S. SKINS.
THEY ALL JUST WANT TO FIGHT... AND WEAR A $60 TENNIS POLO WHILE DOING IT.
WELL, DUDE, IT WAS REAL! HOLLER IF YOU EVER COME BACK TO NEW YORK.
SEVEN WOULD BECOME A LIFELONG FRIEND, ANOTHER ROLE MODEL FROM THE UNDERGROUND.

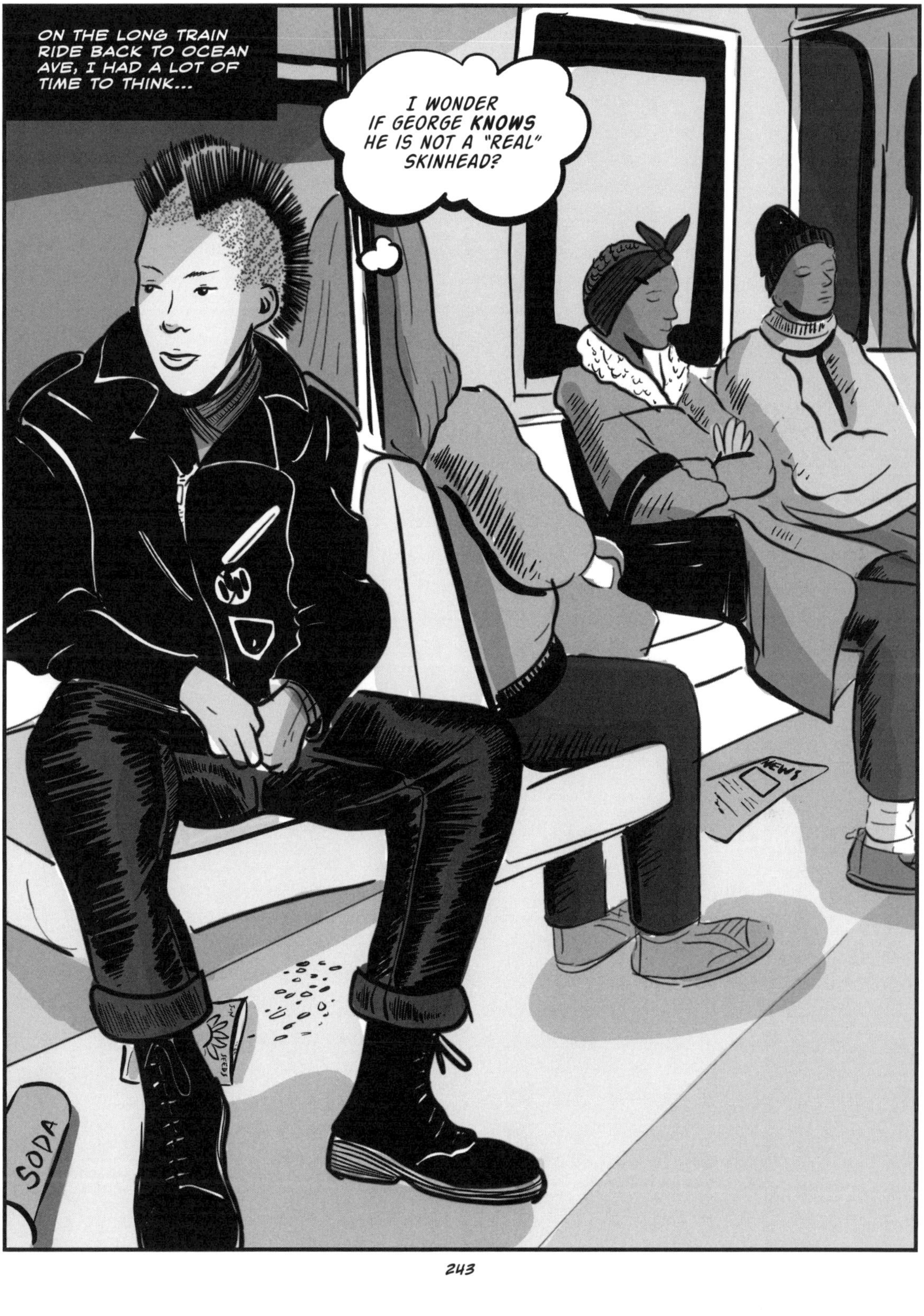
ON THE LONG TRAIN RIDE BACK TO OCEAN AVE, I HAD A LOT OF TIME TO THINK...
I WONDER IF GEORGE KNOWS HE IS NOT A "REAL" SKINHEAD?
NEWS
SEEDS
SODA

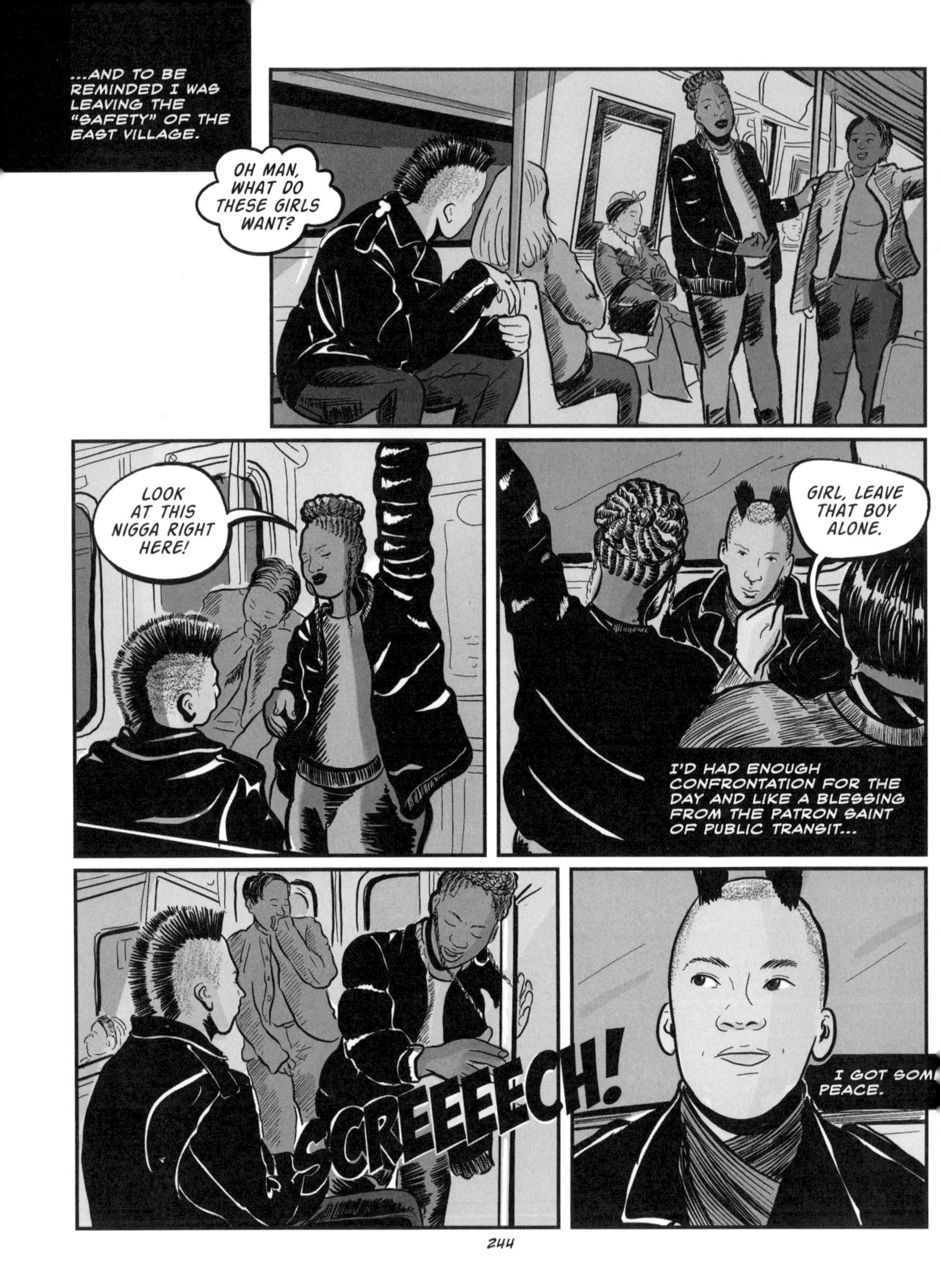
...AND TO BE REMINDED I WAS LEAVING THE "SAFETY" OF THE EAST VILLAGE.
OH MAN, WHAT DO THESE GIRLS WANT?
LOOK AT THIS NIGGA RIGHT HERE!
GIRL, LEAVE THAT BOY ALONE.
I'D HAD ENOUGH CONFRONTATION FOR THE DAY AND LIKE A BLESSING FROM THE PATRON SAINT OF PUBLIC TRANSIT...
SCREEEECH!
I GOT SOM
PEACE.

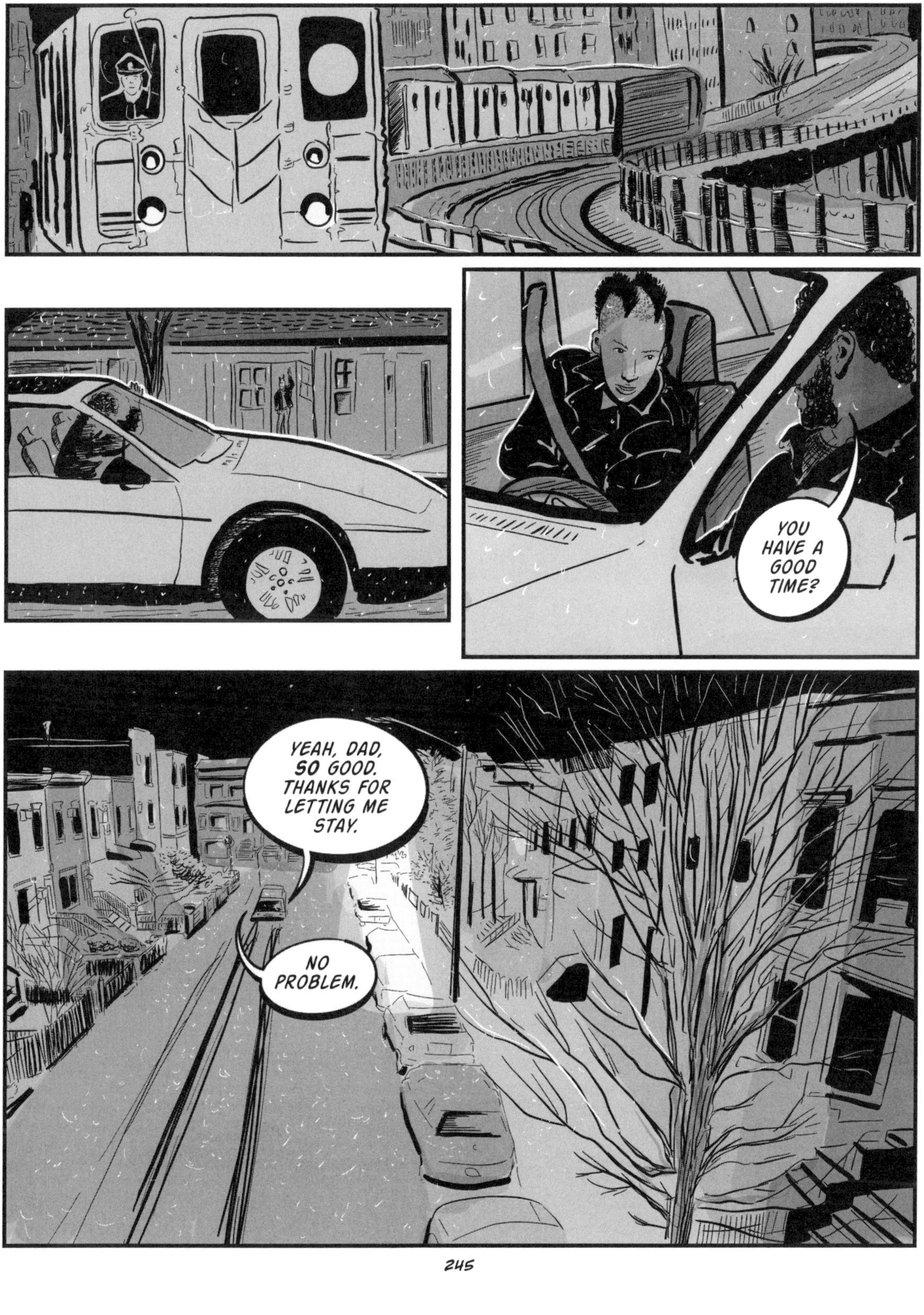
YOU HAVE A GOOD TIME?
YEAH, DAD, SO GOOD. THANKS FOR LETTING ME STAY.
NO PROBLEM.

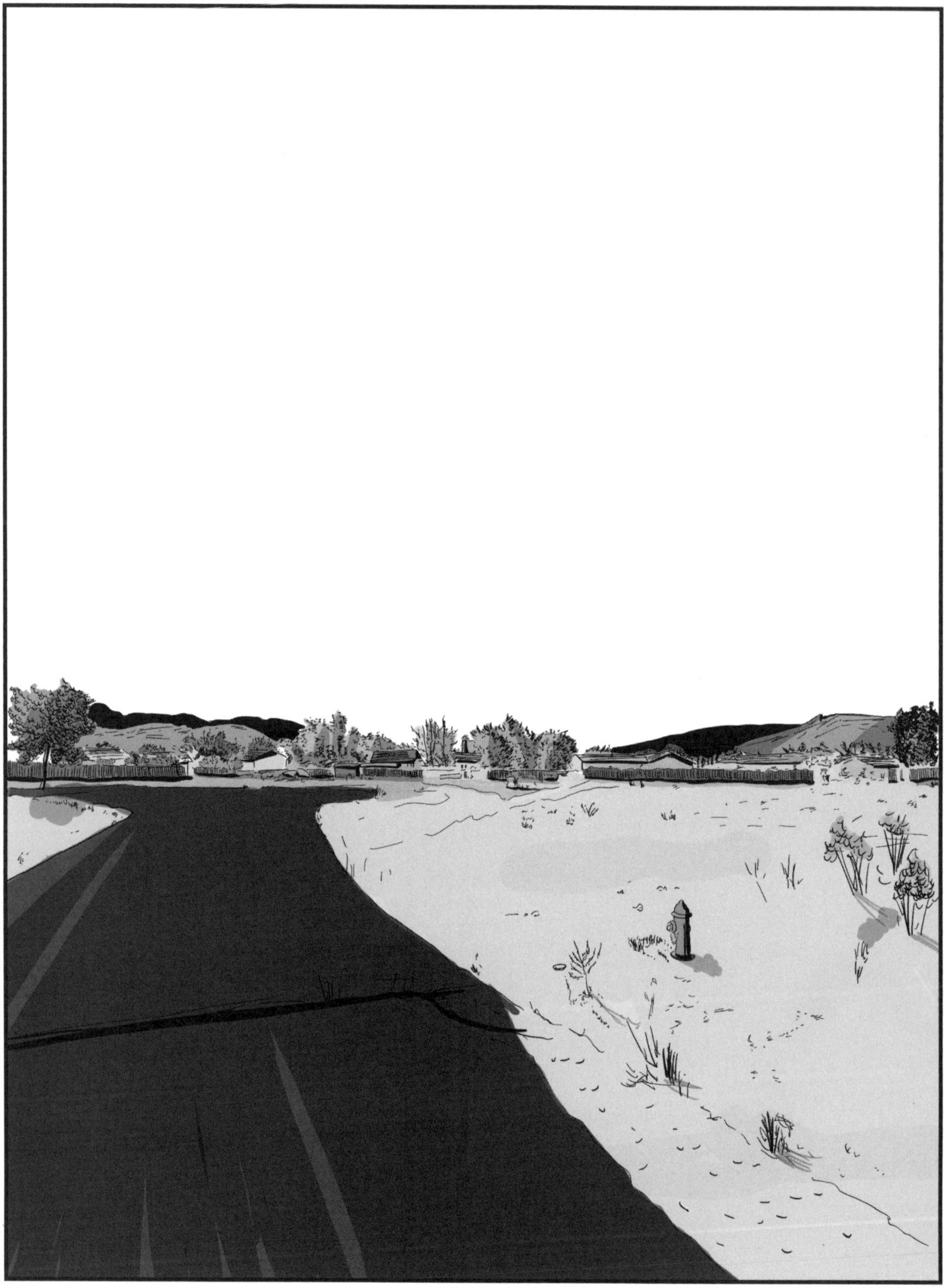

CHAPTER 8
I'M THE ONE

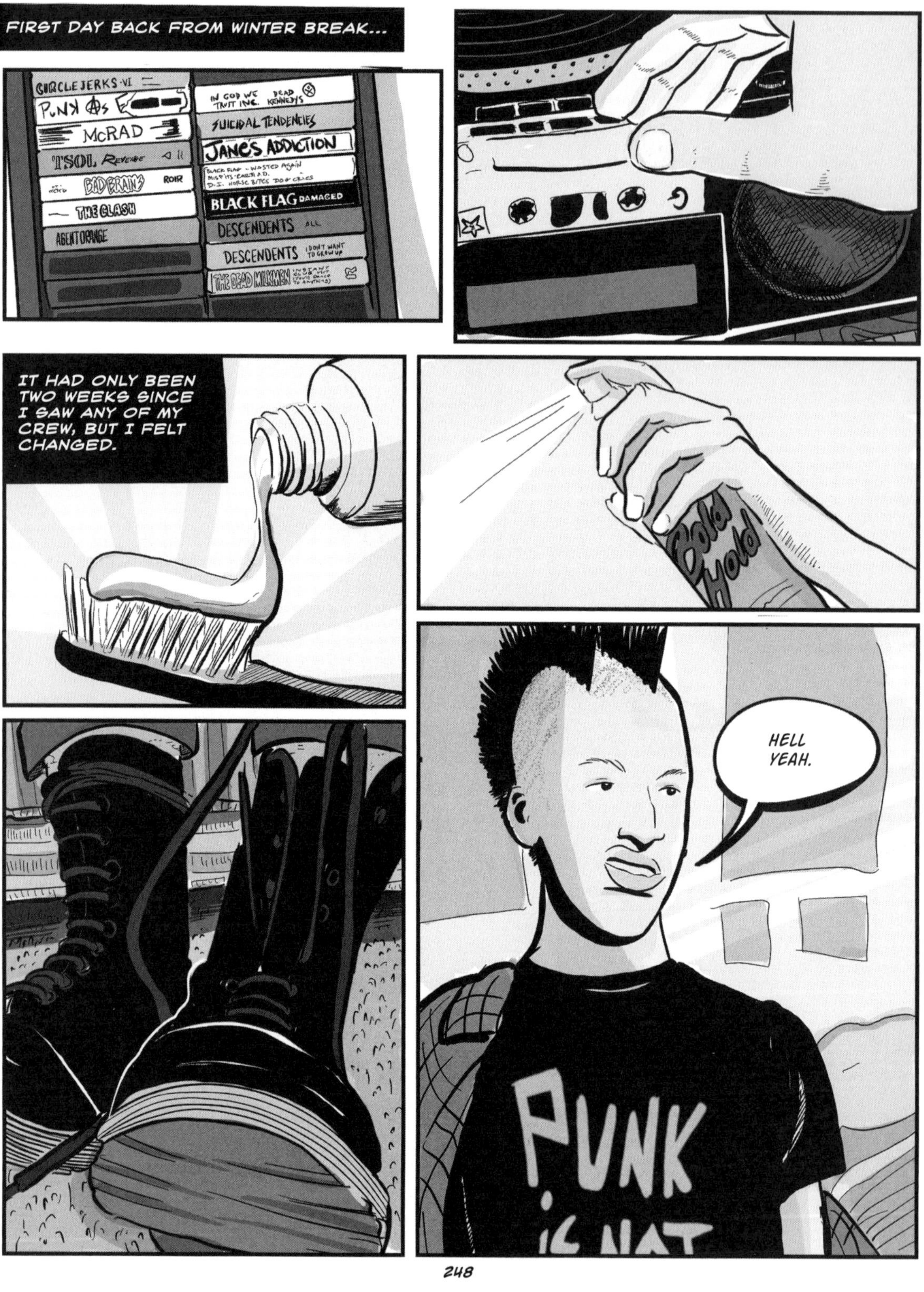
FIRST DAY BACK FROM WINTER BREAK...
CIRCLE JERKS VI
MCRAD
TSOL Revenge
BAD BRAINS ROIR
THE CLASH
AGENT ORANGE
IN GOD WE TRUST INC. DEAD KENNEDYS
SUICIDAL TENDENCIES
JANE'S ADDICTION
BLACK FLAG DAMAGED
DESCENDENTS ALL
DESCENDENTS I DON'T WANT TO GROW UP
THE DEAD MILKMEN
IT HAD ONLY BEEN TWO WEEKS SINCE I SAW ANY OF MY CREW, BUT I FELT CHANGED.
Bold Hold
HELL YEAH.
PUNK

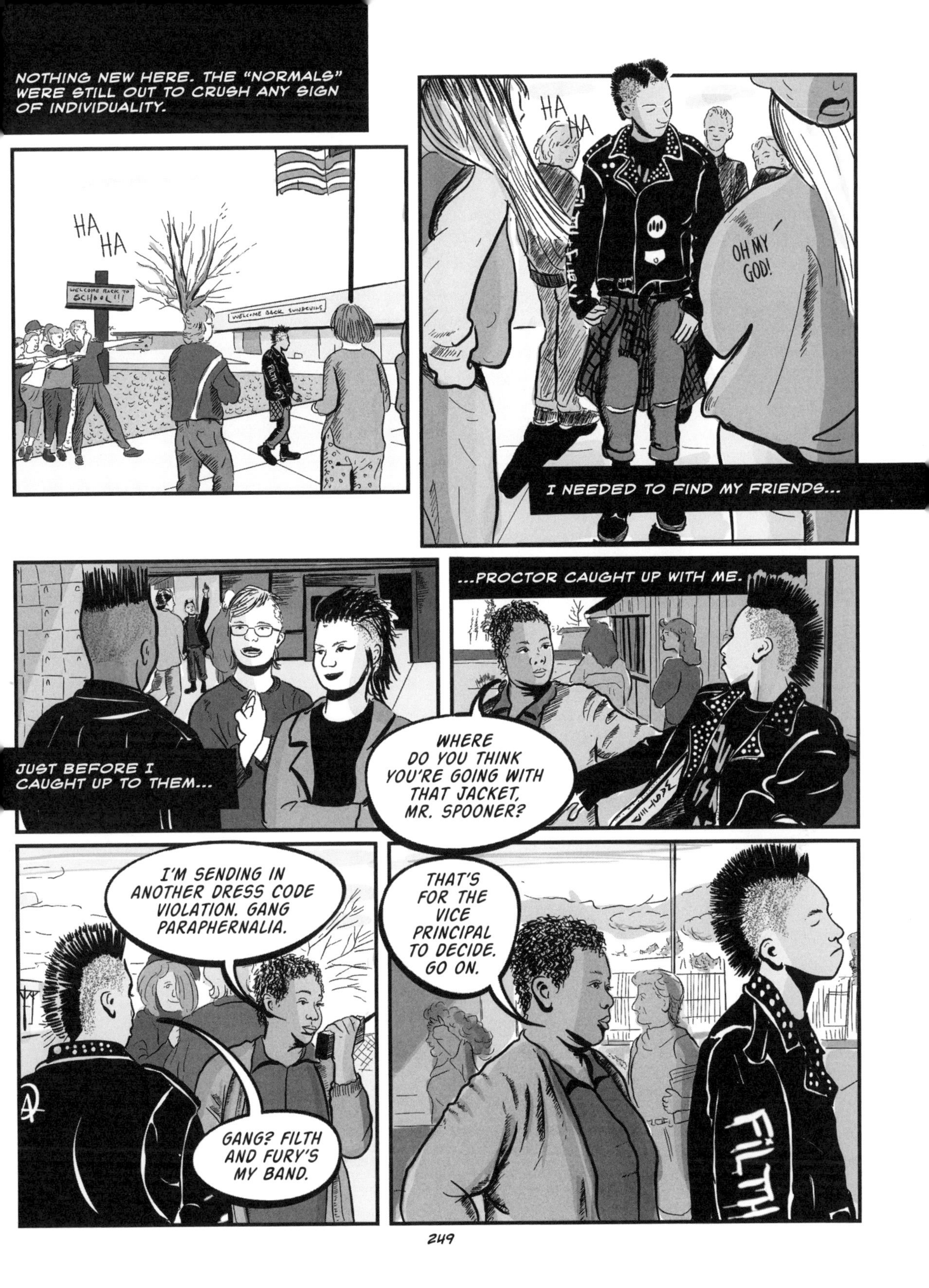

NOTHING NEW HERE. THE "NORMALS" WERE STILL OUT TO CRUSH ANY SIGN OF INDIVIDUALITY.
HA HA
WELCOME BACK TO SCHOOL!!!
WELCOME BACK SUNDEVILS
HA HA
OH MY GOD!
I NEEDED TO FIND MY FRIENDS...
JUST BEFORE I CAUGHT UP TO THEM...
...PROCTOR CAUGHT UP WITH ME.
WHERE DO YOU THINK YOU'RE GOING WITH THAT JACKET, MR. SPOONER?
I'M SENDING IN ANOTHER DRESS CODE VIOLATION. GANG PARAPHERNALIA.
GANG? FILTH AND FURY'S MY BAND.
THAT'S FOR THE VICE PRINCIPAL TO DECIDE. GO ON.
FILTH

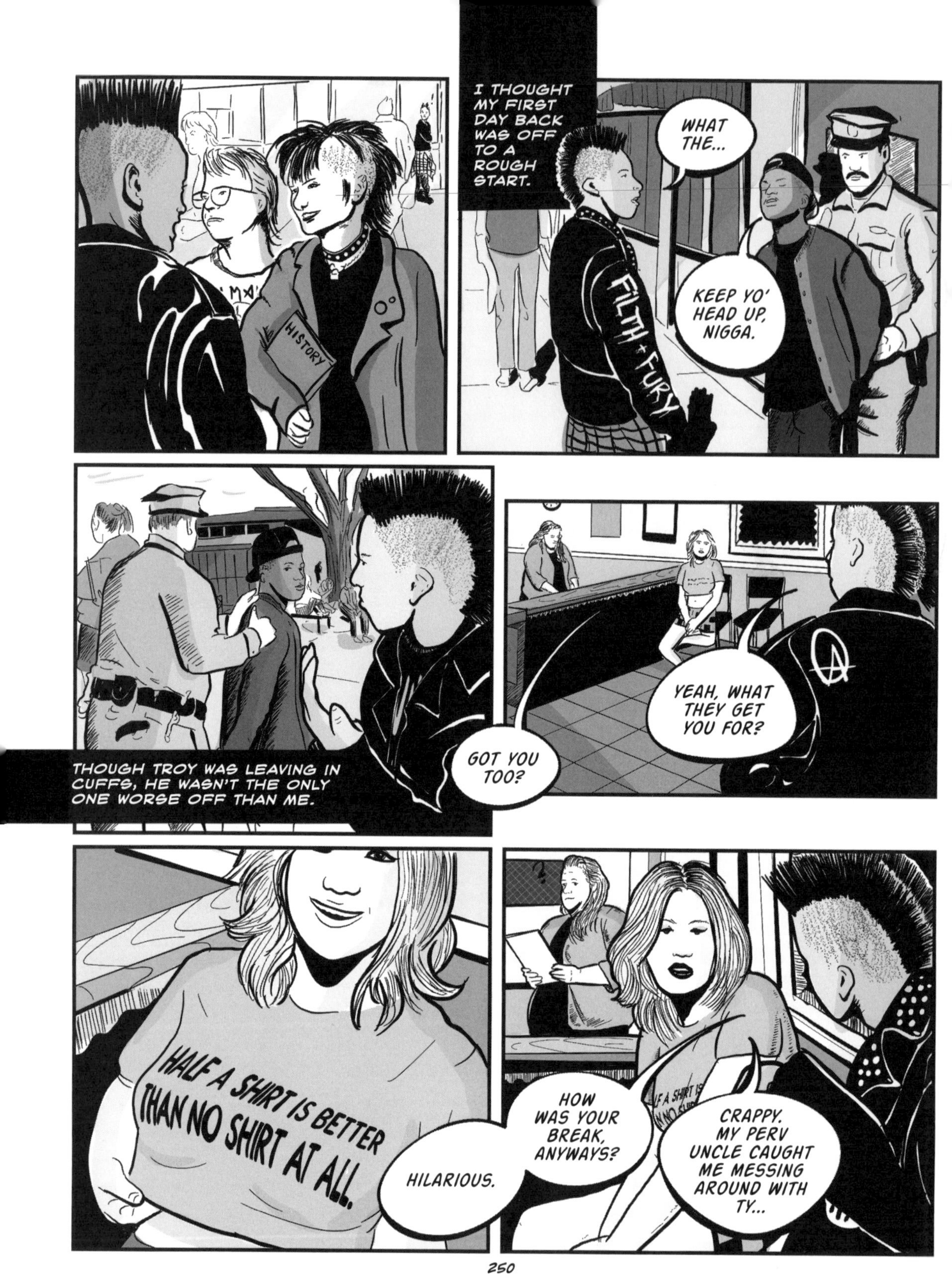
HISTORY
I THOUGHT MY FIRST DAY BACK WAS OFF TO A ROUGH START.
WHAT THE...
KEEP YO' HEAD UP, NIGGA.
FILTH + FURY
THOUGH TROY WAS LEAVING IN CUFFS, HE WASN'T THE ONLY ONE WORSE OFF THAN ME.
GOT YOU TOO?
YEAH, WHAT THEY GET YOU FOR?
HALF A SHIRT IS BETTER THAN NO SHIRT AT ALL.
HILARIOUS.
HOW WAS YOUR BREAK, ANYWAYS?
CRAPPY. MY PERV UNCLE CAUGHT ME MESSING AROUND WITH TY...

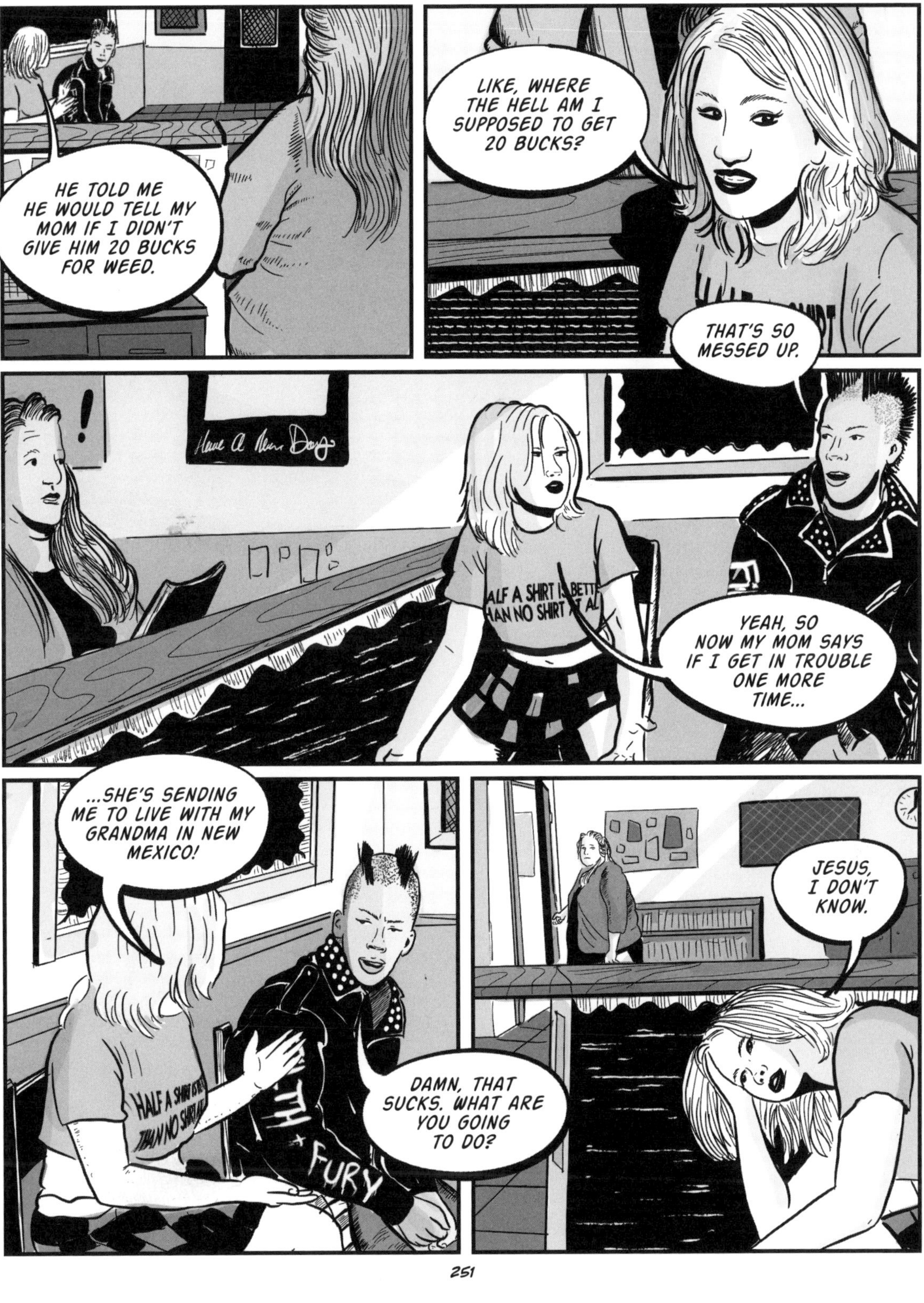
HE TOLD ME HE WOULD TELL MY MOM IF I DIDN'T GIVE HIM 20 BUCKS FOR WEED.
LIKE, WHERE THE HELL AM I SUPPOSED TO GET 20 BUCKS?
THAT'S SO MESSED UP.
Have A Nice Day
HALF A SHIRT IS BETTE
HAN NO SHIRT AT AL
YEAH, SO NOW MY MOM SAYS IF I GET IN TROUBLE ONE MORE TIME...
...SHE'S SENDING ME TO LIVE WITH MY GRANDMA IN NEW MEXICO!
DAMN, THAT SUCKS. WHAT ARE YOU GOING TO DO?
FURY
JESUS, I DON'T KNOW.

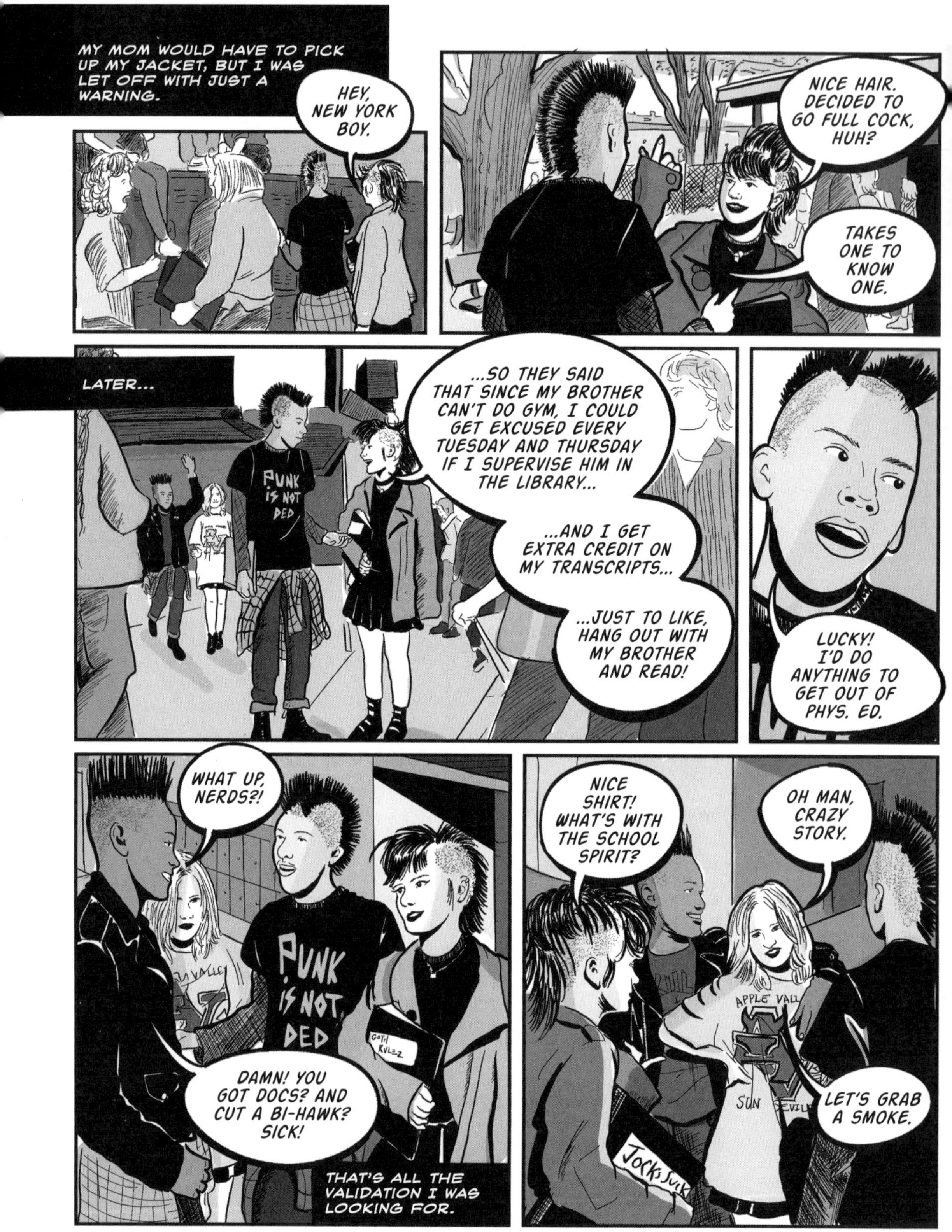
MY MOM WOULD HAVE TO PICK UP MY JACKET, BUT I WAS LET OFF WITH JUST A WARNING.
HEY, NEW YORK BOY.
NICE HAIR. DECIDED TO GO FULL COCK, HUH?
TAKES ONE TO KNOW ONE.
LATER...
PUNK IS NOT DED
...SO THEY SAID THAT SINCE MY BROTHER CAN'T DO GYM, I COULD GET EXCUSED EVERY TUESDAY AND THURSDAY IF I SUPERVISE HIM IN THE LIBRARY...
...AND I GET EXTRA CREDIT ON MY TRANSCRIPTS...
...JUST TO LIKE, HANG OUT WITH MY BROTHER AND READ!
LUCKY! I'D DO ANYTHING TO GET OUT OF PHYS. ED.
WHAT UP, NERDS?!
PUNK IS NOT DED
GOTH RVLEZ
DAMN! YOU GOT DOCS? AND CUT A BI-HAWK? SICK!
THAT'S ALL THE VALIDATION I WAS LOOKING FOR.
NICE SHIRT! WHAT'S WITH THE SCHOOL SPIRIT?
OH MAN, CRAZY STORY.
APPLE VALL
SUN DEVIL
LET'S GRAB A SMOKE.
JOCKS SUCK

SO I GOT BUSTED FOR MY HALF-TOP, YOU KNOW?

SO I WENT IN THERE ALL BOO-HOO CRYING AND JUNK TO MR. ALVI.

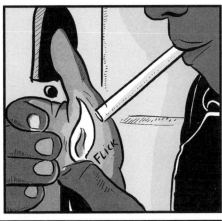

FLICK

I TOLD HIM THIS SOB STORY ABOUT HOW I HAD TO WEAR THIS SHIRT BECAUSE WE COULDN'T AFFORD DETERGENT THIS MONTH.

BWAAH!

YEAH, SO THEN, HE TELLS ME I HAVE TO WEAR THIS CORNY-ASS SHIRT TODAY AND THEN...

APPLE VALLEY

...GAVE ME TEN BUCKS TO BUY DETERGENT!

NO WAY! YOU SCAMMED MR. ALVI?!

PUNK

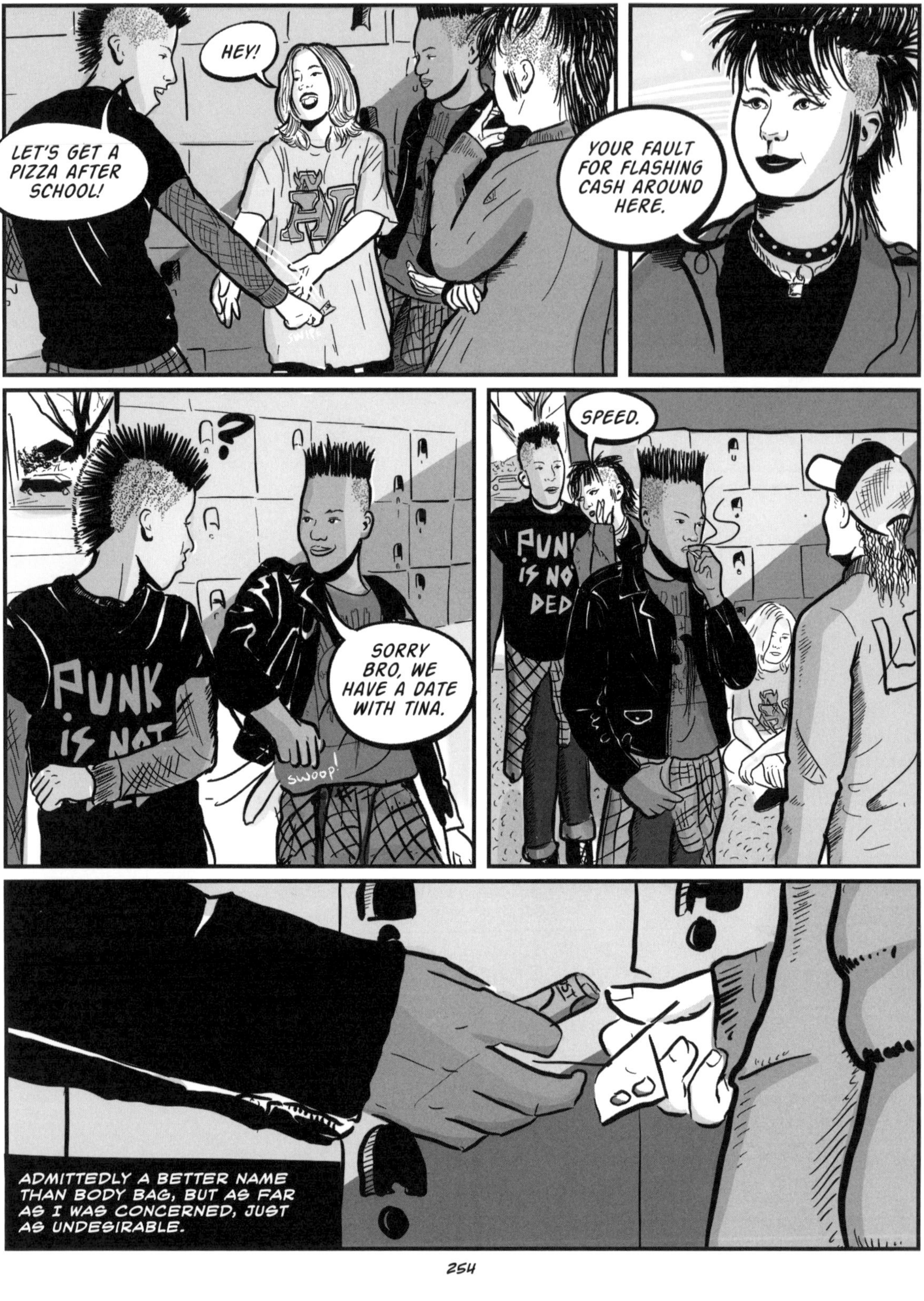
LET'S GET A PIZZA AFTER SCHOOL!
HEY!
SWIPE
YOUR FAULT FOR FLASHING CASH AROUND HERE.
PUNK IS NOT
SORRY BRO, WE HAVE A DATE WITH TINA.
SWOOP!
SPEED.
PUNK IS NOT DED
ADMITTEDLY A BETTER NAME THAN BODY BAG, BUT AS FAR AS I WAS CONCERNED, JUST AS UNDESIRABLE.

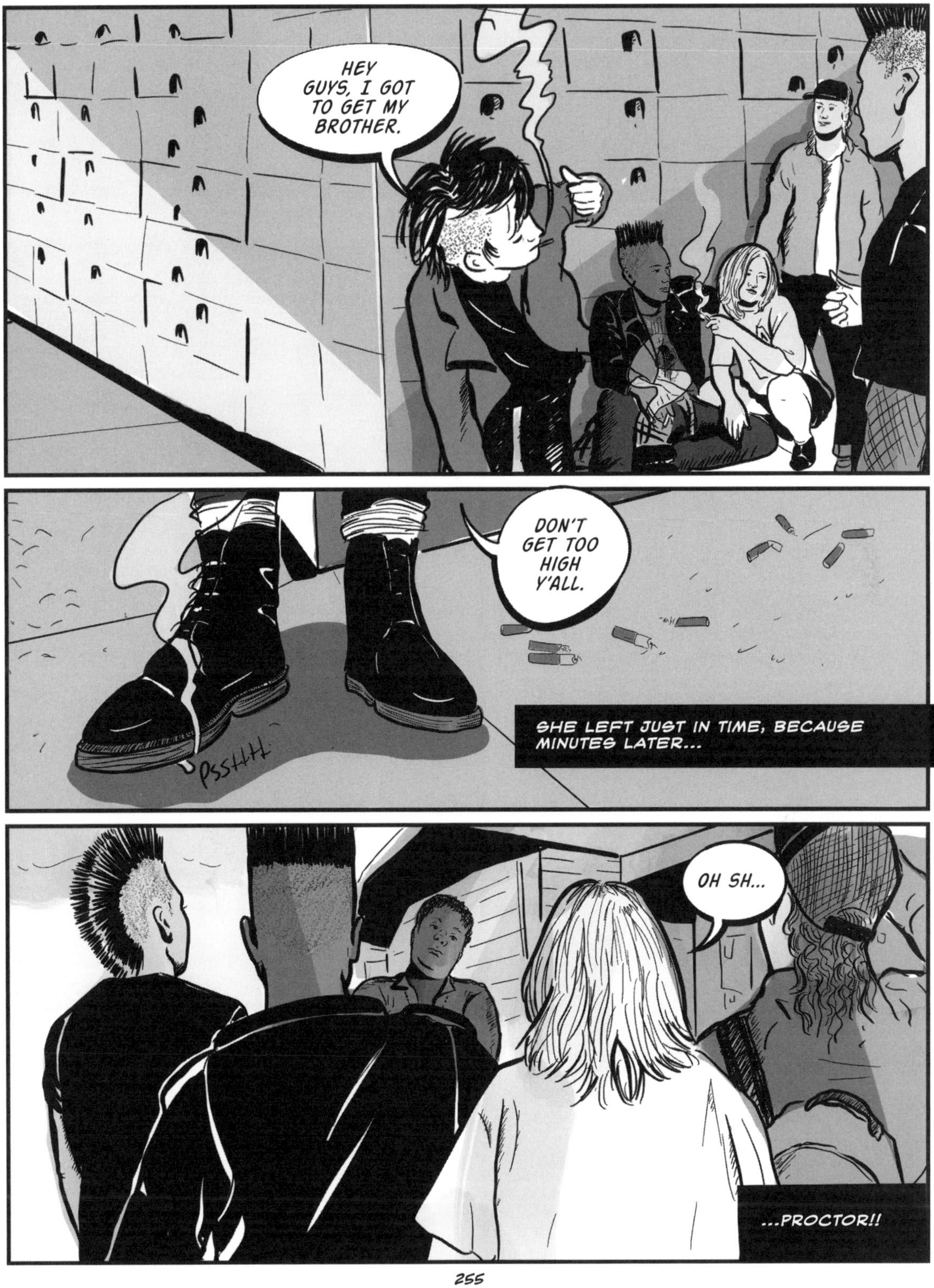

HEY GUYS, I GOT TO GET MY BROTHER.
DON'T GET TOO HIGH Y'ALL.
PSSHHH
SHE LEFT JUST IN TIME, BECAUSE MINUTES LATER...
OH SH...
...PROCTOR!!

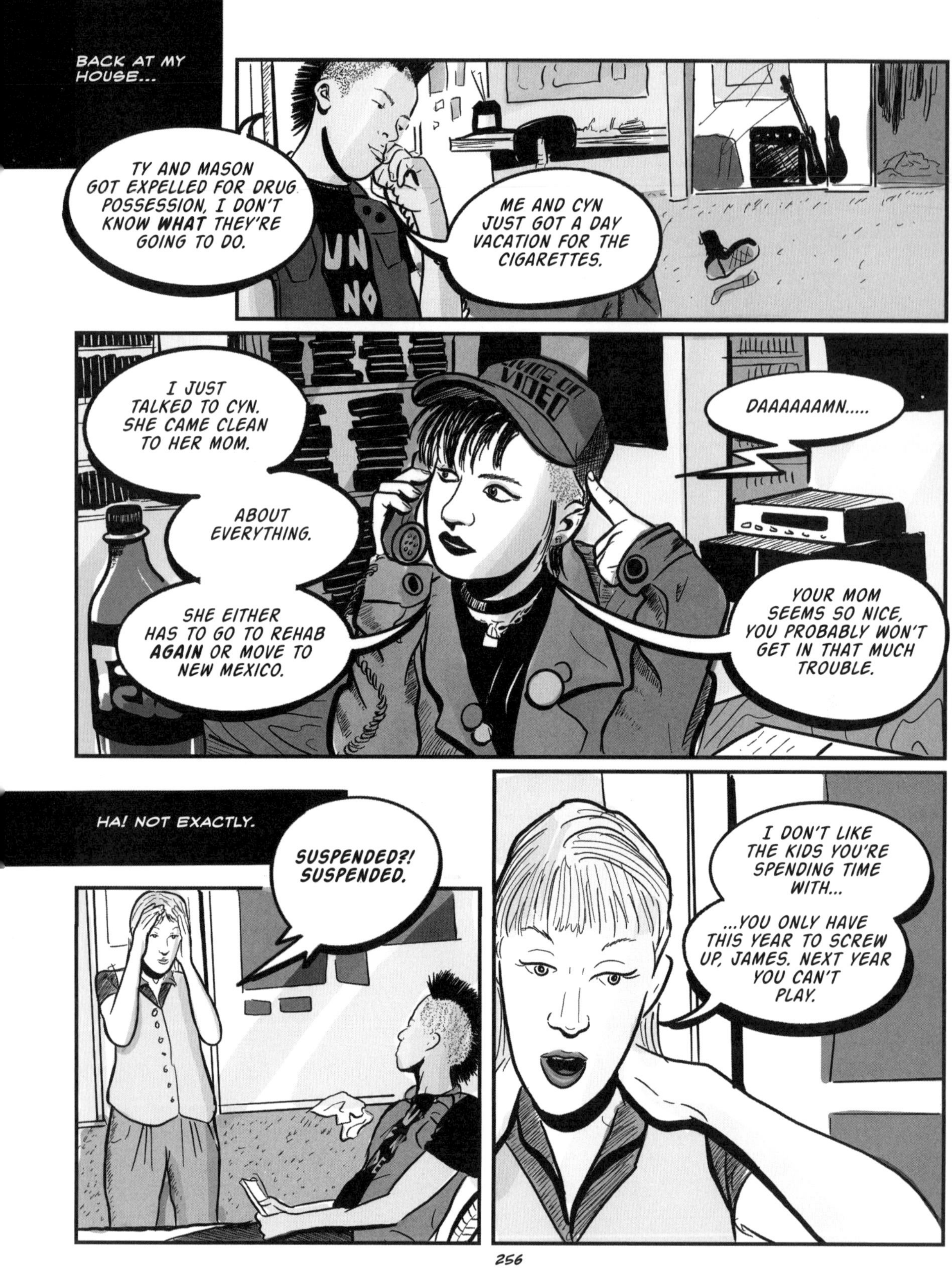

BACK AT MY HOUSE...
TY AND MASON GOT EXPELLED FOR DRUG POSSESSION, I DON'T KNOW WHAT THEY'RE GOING TO DO.
ME AND CYN JUST GOT A DAY VACATION FOR THE CIGARETTES.
I JUST TALKED TO CYN. SHE CAME CLEAN TO HER MOM.
ABOUT EVERYTHING.
SHE EITHER HAS TO GO TO REHAB AGAIN OR MOVE TO NEW MEXICO.
DAAAAAAMN.....
YOUR MOM SEEMS SO NICE, YOU PROBABLY WON'T GET IN THAT MUCH TROUBLE.
HA! NOT EXACTLY.
SUSPENDED?! SUSPENDED.
I DON'T LIKE THE KIDS YOU'RE SPENDING TIME WITH...
...YOU ONLY HAVE THIS YEAR TO SCREW UP, JAMES. NEXT YEAR YOU CAN'T PLAY.

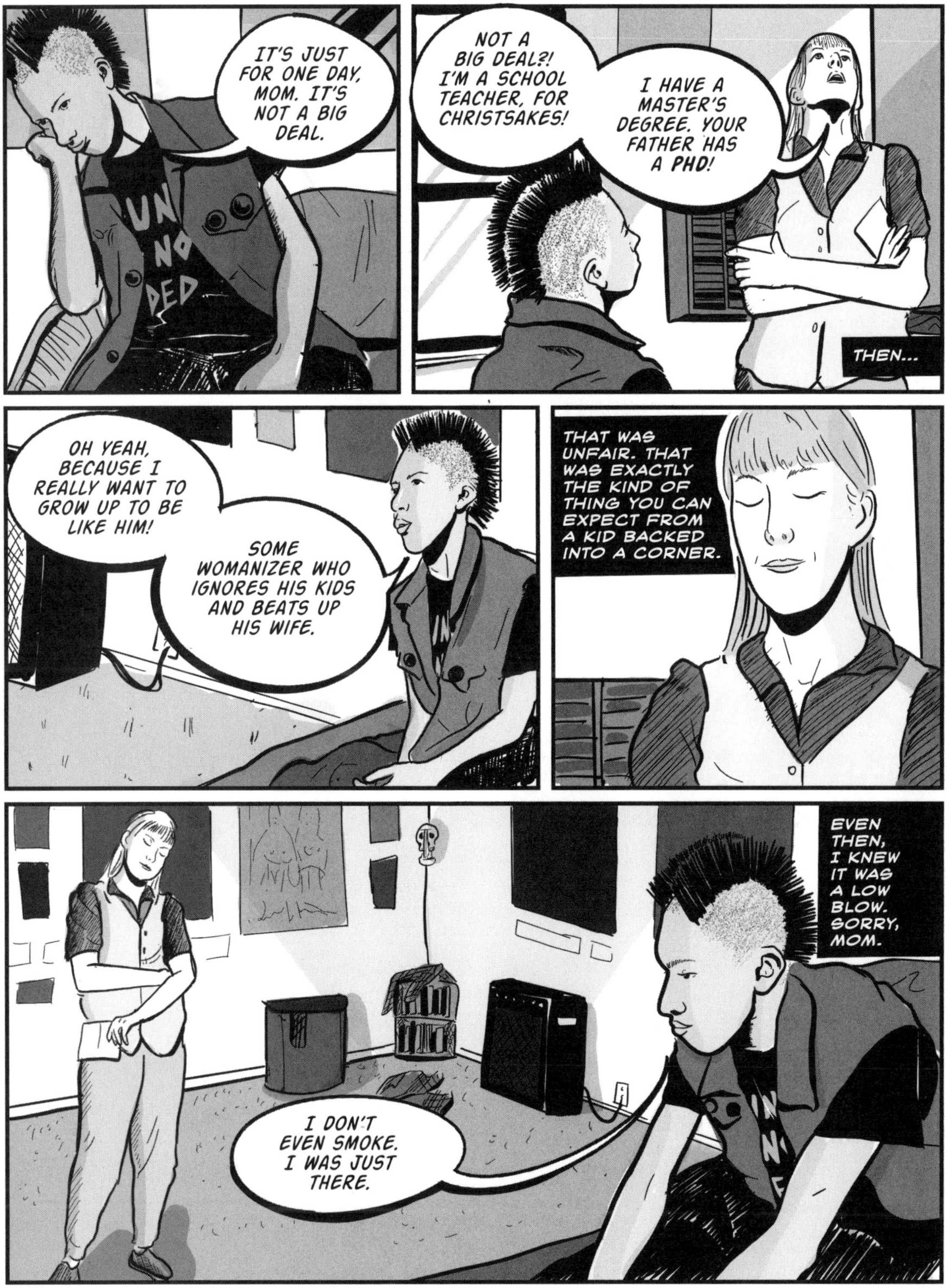
IT'S JUST FOR ONE DAY, MOM. IT'S NOT A BIG DEAL.
NOT A BIG DEAL?! I'M A SCHOOL TEACHER, FOR CHRISTSAKES!
I HAVE A MASTER'S DEGREE. YOUR FATHER HAS A PHD!
THEN...
OH YEAH, BECAUSE I REALLY WANT TO GROW UP TO BE LIKE HIM!
SOME WOMANIZER WHO IGNORES HIS KIDS AND BEATS UP HIS WIFE.
THAT WAS UNFAIR. THAT WAS EXACTLY THE KIND OF THING YOU CAN EXPECT FROM A KID BACKED INTO A CORNER.
EVEN THEN, I KNEW IT WAS A LOW BLOW. SORRY, MOM.
I DON'T EVEN SMOKE. I WAS JUST THERE.

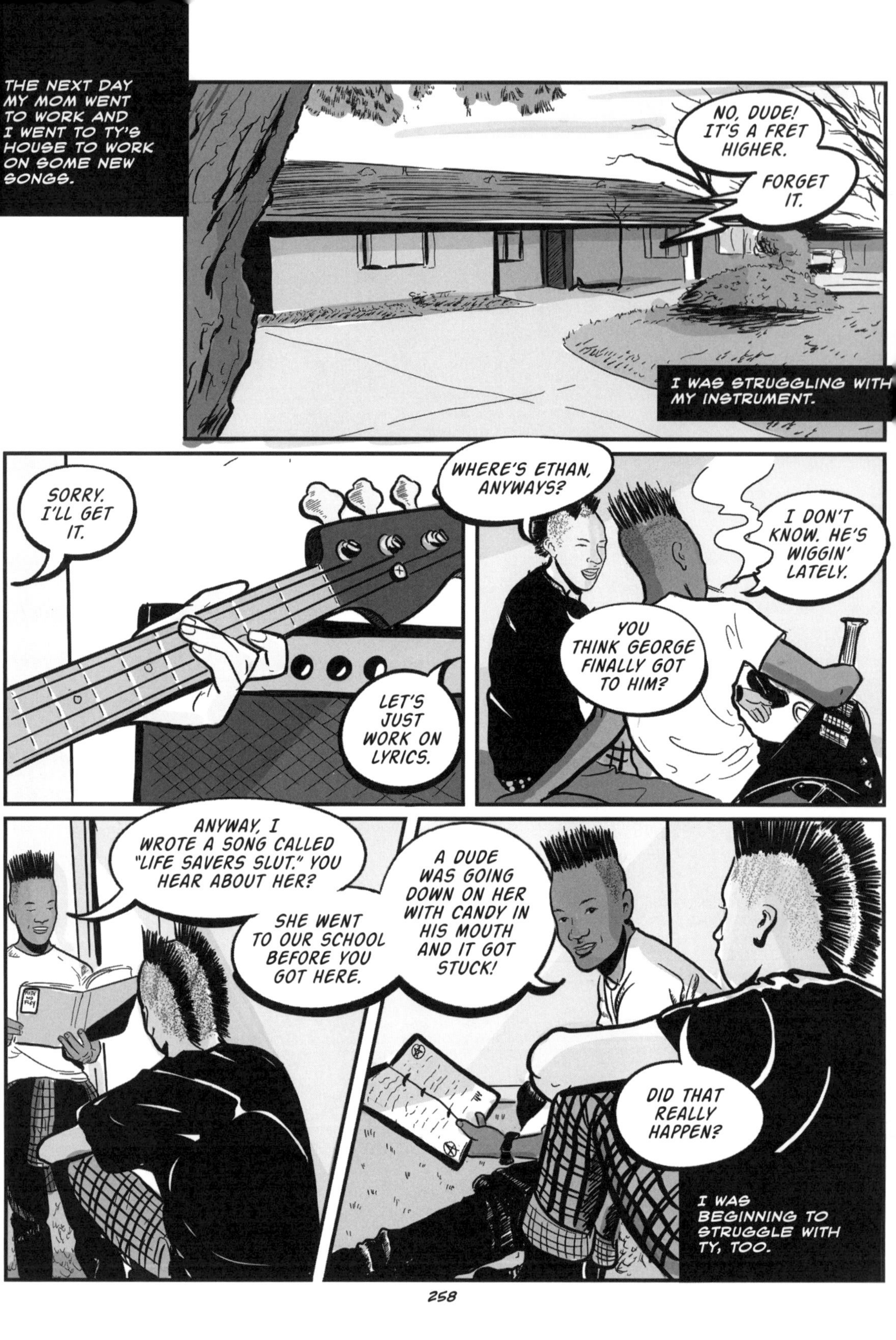
THE NEXT DAY MY MOM WENT TO WORK AND I WENT TO TY'S HOUSE TO WORK ON SOME NEW SONGS.
NO, DUDE! IT'S A FRET HIGHER.
FORGET IT.
I WAS STRUGGLING WITH MY INSTRUMENT.
SORRY. I'LL GET IT.
LET'S JUST WORK ON LYRICS.
WHERE'S ETHAN, ANYWAYS?
I DON'T KNOW. HE'S WIGGIN' LATELY.
YOU THINK GEORGE FINALLY GOT TO HIM?
ANYWAY, I WROTE A SONG CALLED "LIFE SAVERS SLUT." YOU HEAR ABOUT HER?
SHE WENT TO OUR SCHOOL BEFORE YOU GOT HERE.
A DUDE WAS GOING DOWN ON HER WITH CANDY IN HIS MOUTH AND IT GOT STUCK!
DID THAT REALLY HAPPEN?
I WAS BEGINNING TO STRUGGLE WITH TY, TOO.

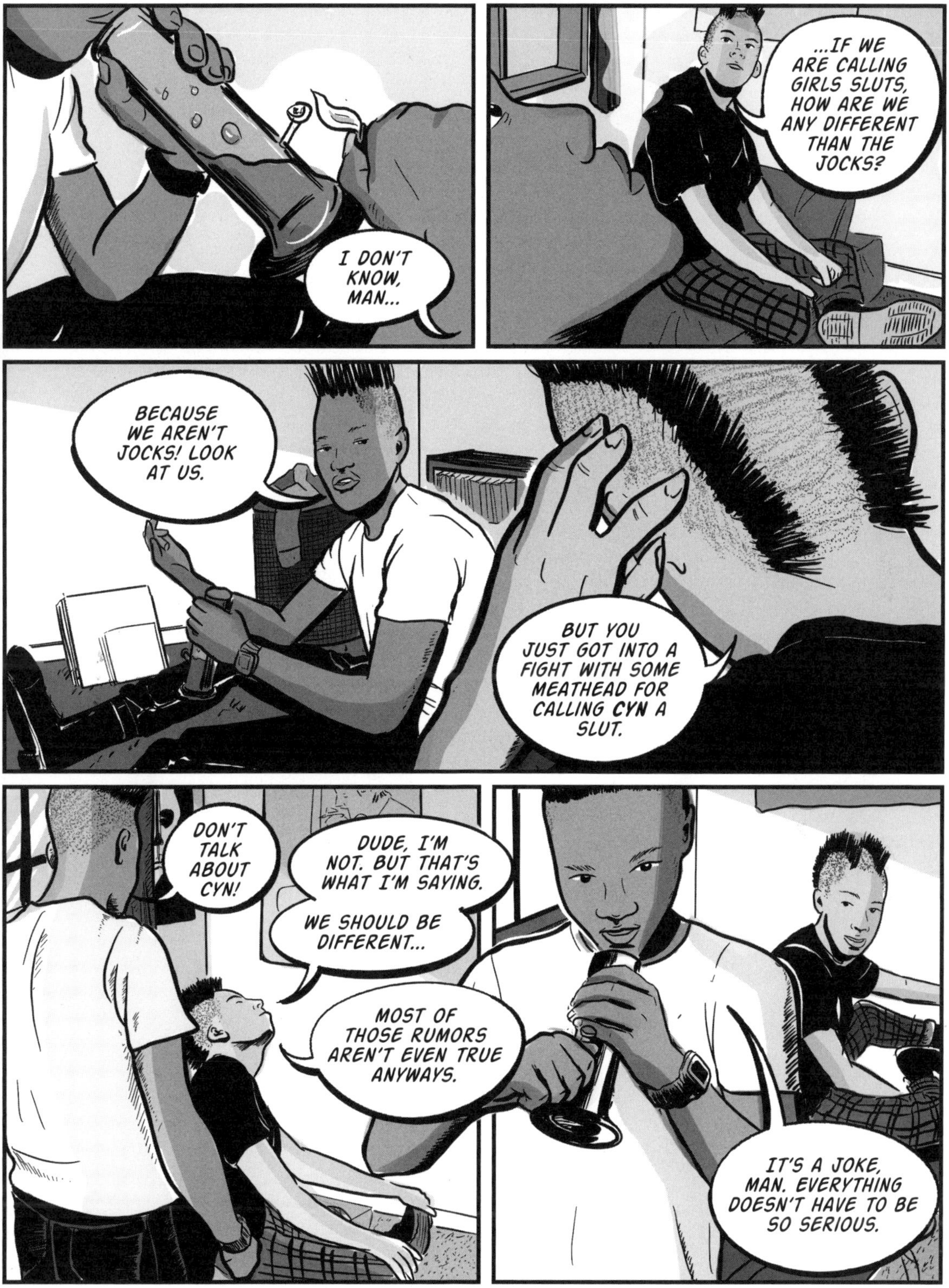
I DON'T KNOW, MAN...
...IF WE ARE CALLING GIRLS SLUTS, HOW ARE WE ANY DIFFERENT THAN THE JOCKS?
BECAUSE WE AREN'T JOCKS! LOOK AT US.
BUT YOU JUST GOT INTO A FIGHT WITH SOME MEATHEAD FOR CALLING CYN A SLUT.
DON'T TALK ABOUT CYN!
DUDE, I'M NOT. BUT THAT'S WHAT I'M SAYING.
WE SHOULD BE DIFFERENT...
MOST OF THOSE RUMORS AREN'T EVEN TRUE ANYWAYS.
IT'S A JOKE, MAN. EVERYTHING DOESN'T HAVE TO BE SO SERIOUS.

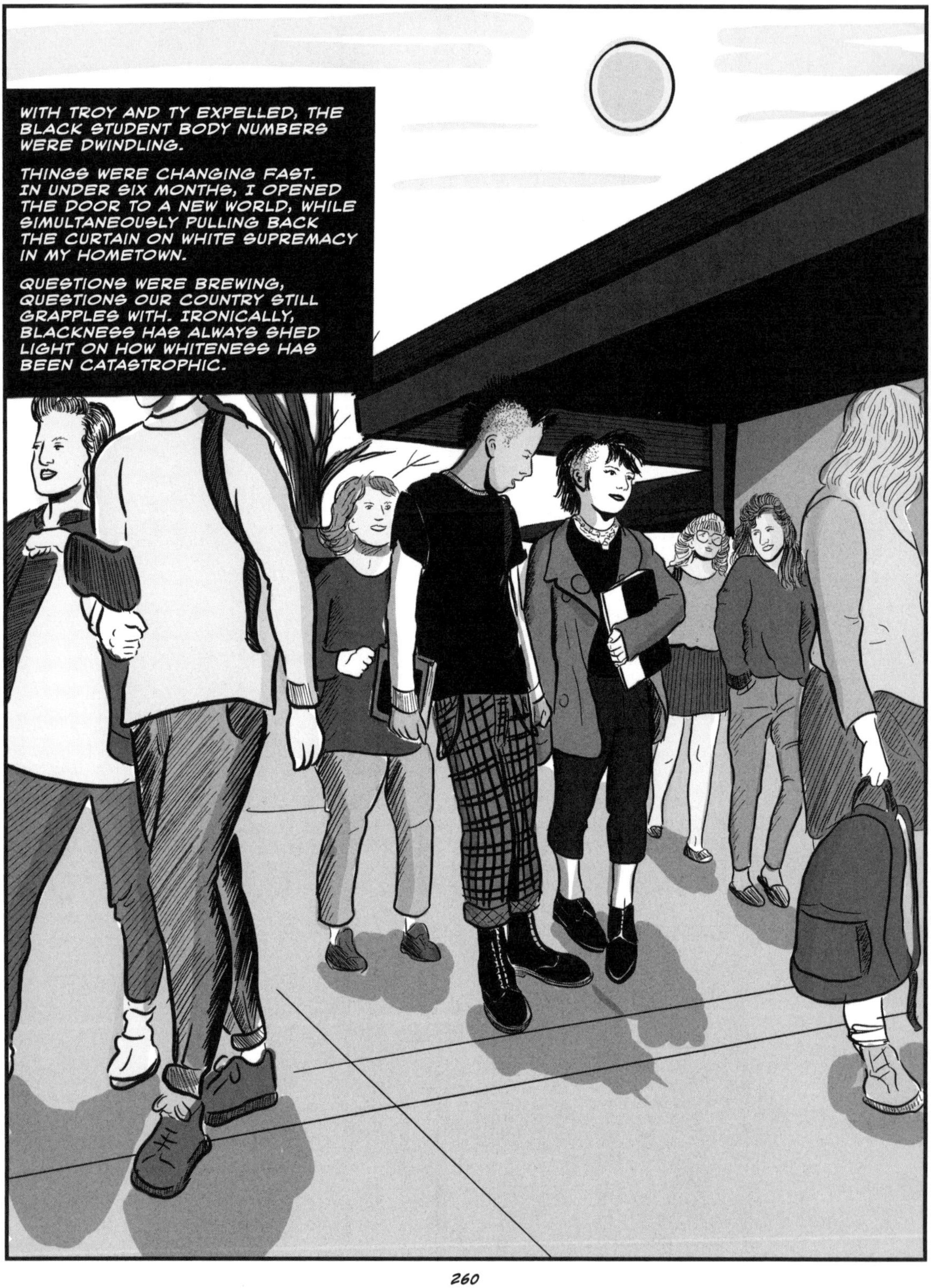
WITH TROY AND TY EXPELLED, THE BLACK STUDENT BODY NUMBERS WERE DWINDLING.
THINGS WERE CHANGING FAST. IN UNDER SIX MONTHS, I OPENED THE DOOR TO A NEW WORLD, WHILE SIMULTANEOUSLY PULLING BACK THE CURTAIN ON WHITE SUPREMACY IN MY HOMETOWN.
QUESTIONS WERE BREWING, QUESTIONS OUR COUNTRY STILL GRAPPLES WITH. IRONICALLY, BLACKNESS HAS ALWAYS SHED LIGHT ON HOW WHITENESS HAS BEEN CATASTROPHIC.

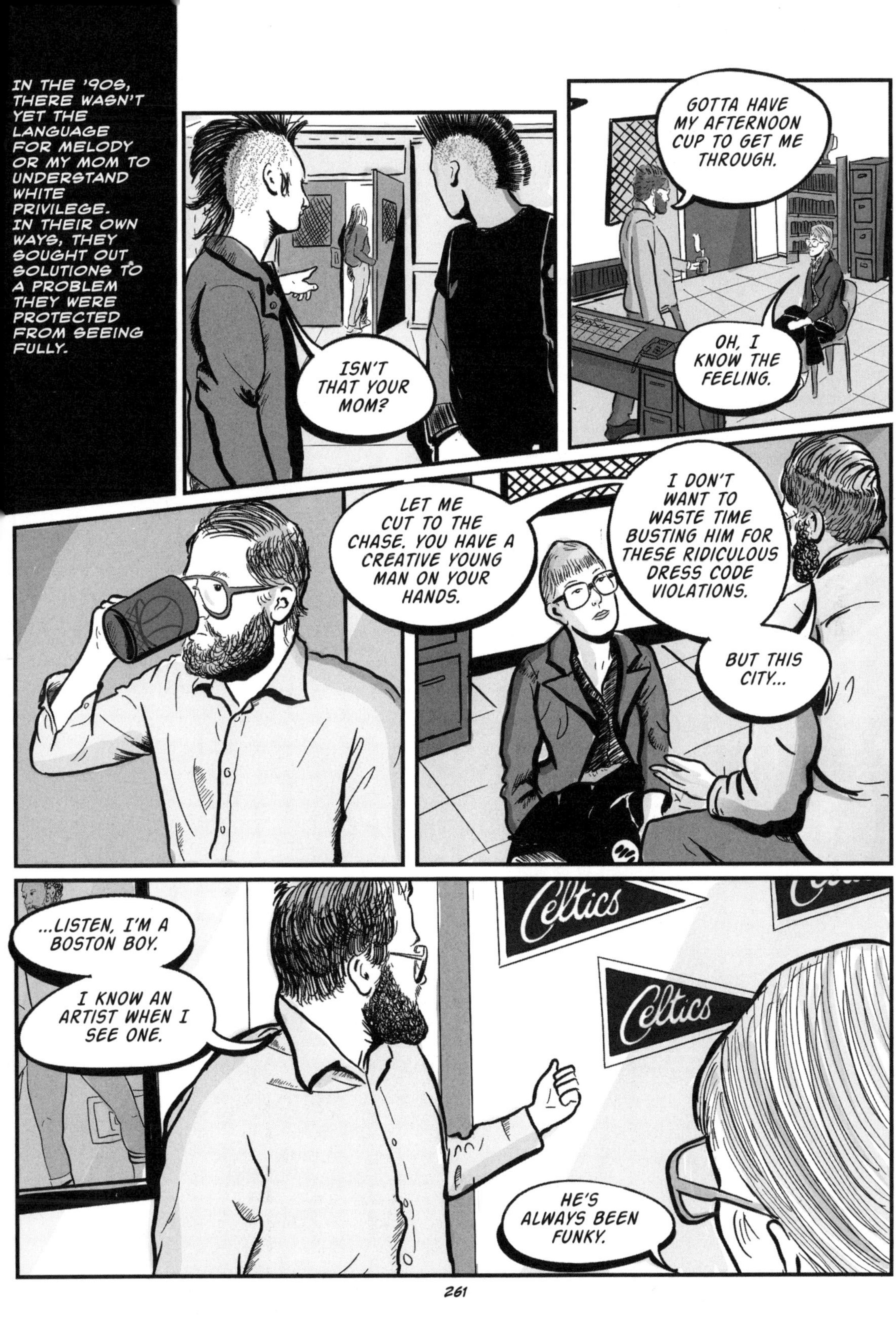

IN THE '90S, THERE WASN'T YET THE LANGUAGE FOR MELODY OR MY MOM TO UNDERSTAND WHITE PRIVILEGE. IN THEIR OWN WAYS, THEY SOUGHT OUT SOLUTIONS TO A PROBLEM THEY WERE PROTECTED FROM SEEING FULLY.
ISN'T THAT YOUR MOM?
GOTTA HAVE MY AFTERNOON CUP TO GET ME THROUGH.
OH, I KNOW THE FEELING.
LET ME CUT TO THE CHASE. YOU HAVE A CREATIVE YOUNG MAN ON YOUR HANDS.
I DON'T WANT TO WASTE TIME BUSTING HIM FOR THESE RIDICULOUS DRESS CODE VIOLATIONS.
BUT THIS CITY...
...LISTEN, I'M A BOSTON BOY.
I KNOW AN ARTIST WHEN I SEE ONE.
Celtics
Celtics
HE'S ALWAYS BEEN FUNKY.

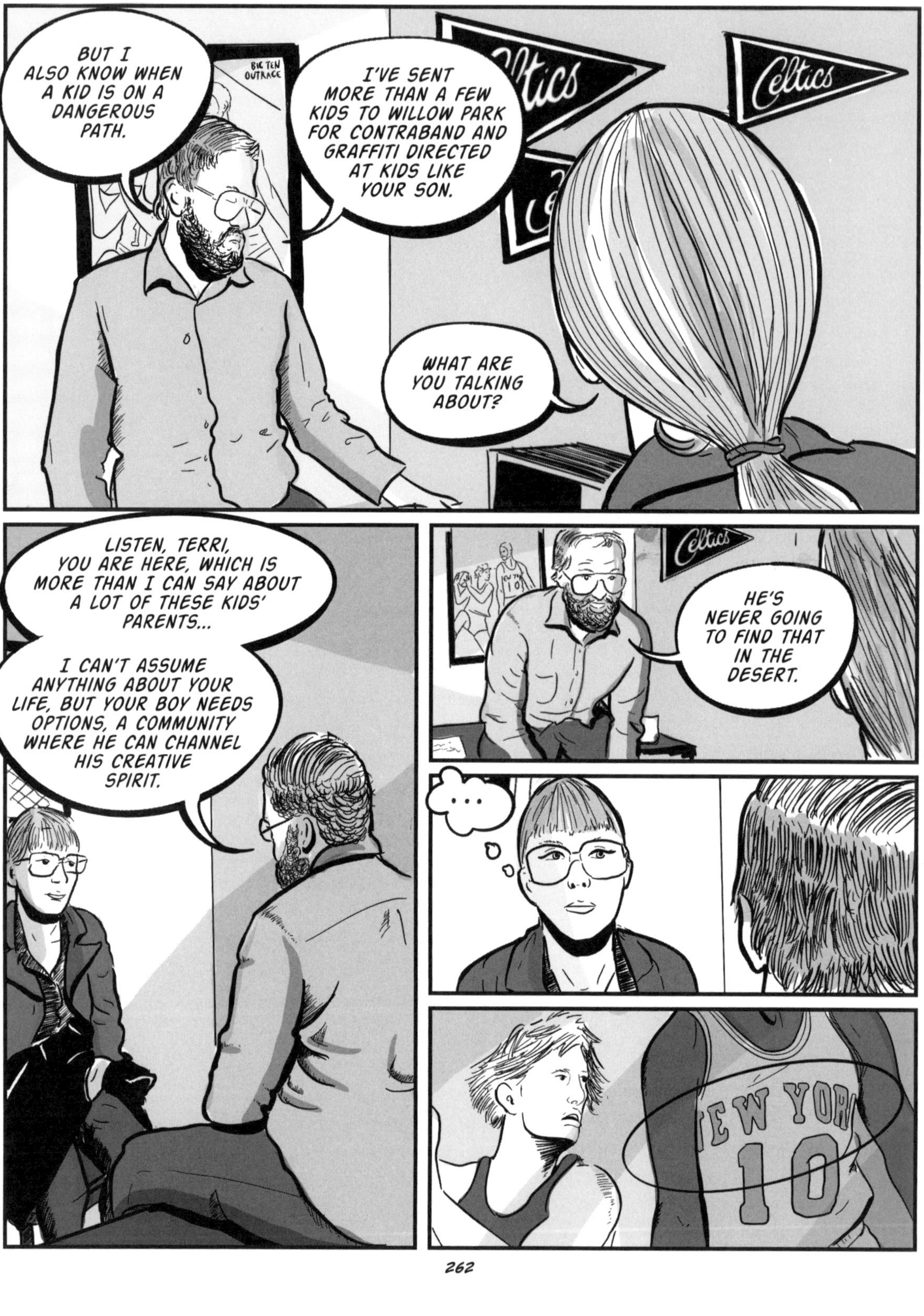
BUT I ALSO KNOW WHEN A KID IS ON A DANGEROUS PATH.
I'VE SENT MORE THAN A FEW KIDS TO WILLOW PARK FOR CONTRABAND AND GRAFFITI DIRECTED AT KIDS LIKE YOUR SON.
WHAT ARE YOU TALKING ABOUT?
LISTEN, TERRI, YOU ARE HERE, WHICH IS MORE THAN I CAN SAY ABOUT A LOT OF THESE KIDS' PARENTS...
I CAN'T ASSUME ANYTHING ABOUT YOUR LIFE, BUT YOUR BOY NEEDS OPTIONS, A COMMUNITY WHERE HE CAN CHANNEL HIS CREATIVE SPIRIT.
HE'S NEVER GOING TO FIND THAT IN THE DESERT.
...
NEW YORK
10

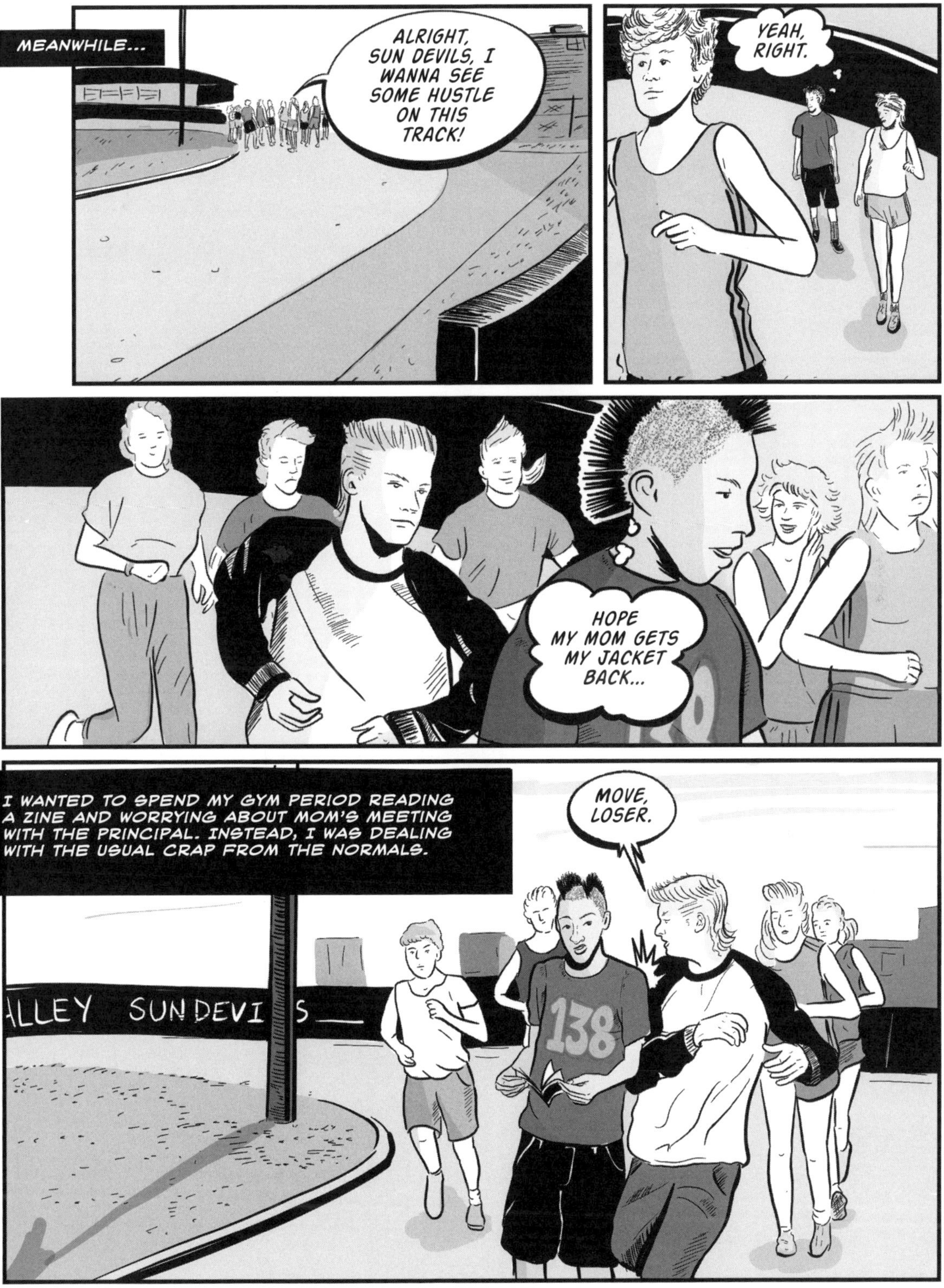
MEANWHILE...
ALRIGHT, SUN DEVILS, I WANNA SEE SOME HUSTLE ON THIS TRACK!
YEAH, RIGHT.
HOPE MY MOM GETS MY JACKET BACK...
I WANTED TO SPEND MY GYM PERIOD READING A ZINE AND WORRYING ABOUT MOM'S MEETING WITH THE PRINCIPAL. INSTEAD, I WAS DEALING WITH THE USUAL CRAP FROM THE NORMALS.
MOVE, LOSER.
ALLEY SUNDEVI S
138

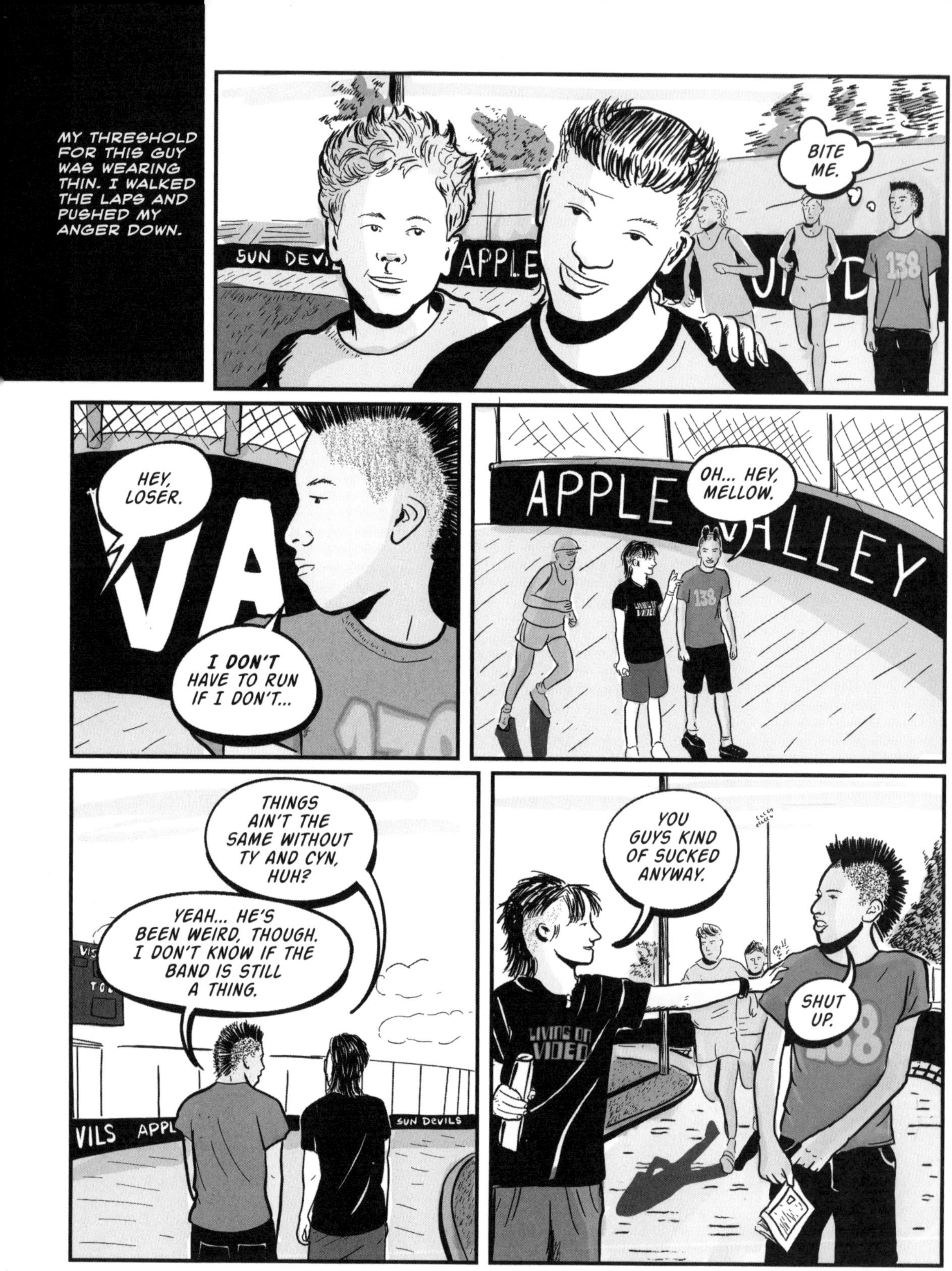
MY THRESHOLD FOR THIS GUY WAS WEARING THIN. I WALKED THE LAPS AND PUSHED MY ANGER DOWN.
SUN DEVI
APPLE
138
BITE ME.
HEY, LOSER.
I DON'T HAVE TO RUN IF I DON'T...
APPLE VALLEY
OH... HEY, MELLOW.
THINGS AIN'T THE SAME WITHOUT TY AND CYN, HUH?
YEAH... HE'S BEEN WEIRD, THOUGH. I DON'T KNOW IF THE BAND IS STILL A THING.
VILS APPL
SUN DEVILS
YOU GUYS KIND OF SUCKED ANYWAY.
LIVING ON VIDEO
SHUT UP.

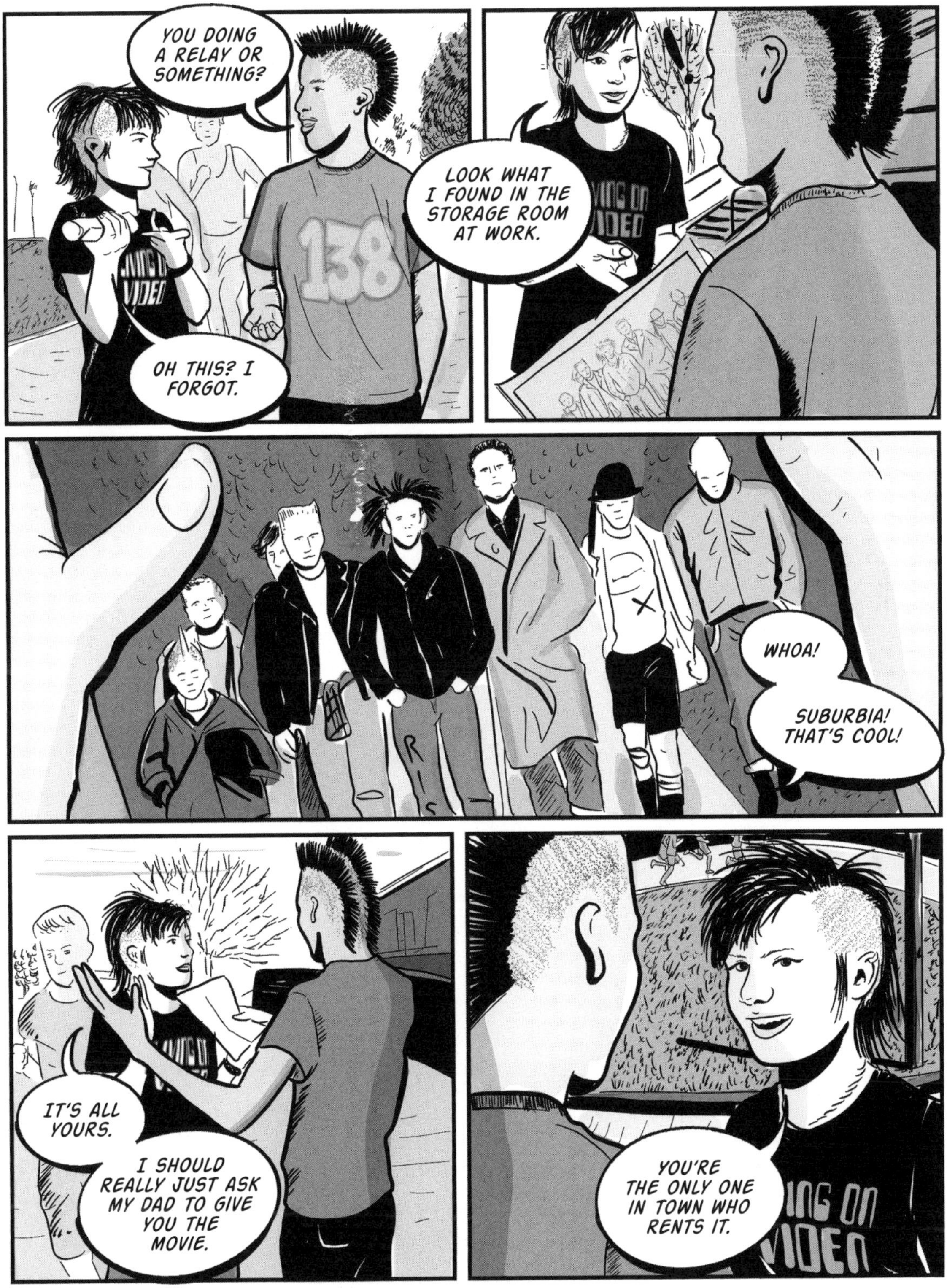
YOU DOING A RELAY OR SOMETHING?
OH THIS? I FORGOT.
LOOK WHAT I FOUND IN THE STORAGE ROOM AT WORK.
WHOA!
SUBURBIA! THAT'S COOL!
IT'S ALL YOURS.
I SHOULD REALLY JUST ASK MY DAD TO GIVE YOU THE MOVIE.
YOU'RE THE ONLY ONE IN TOWN WHO RENTS IT.

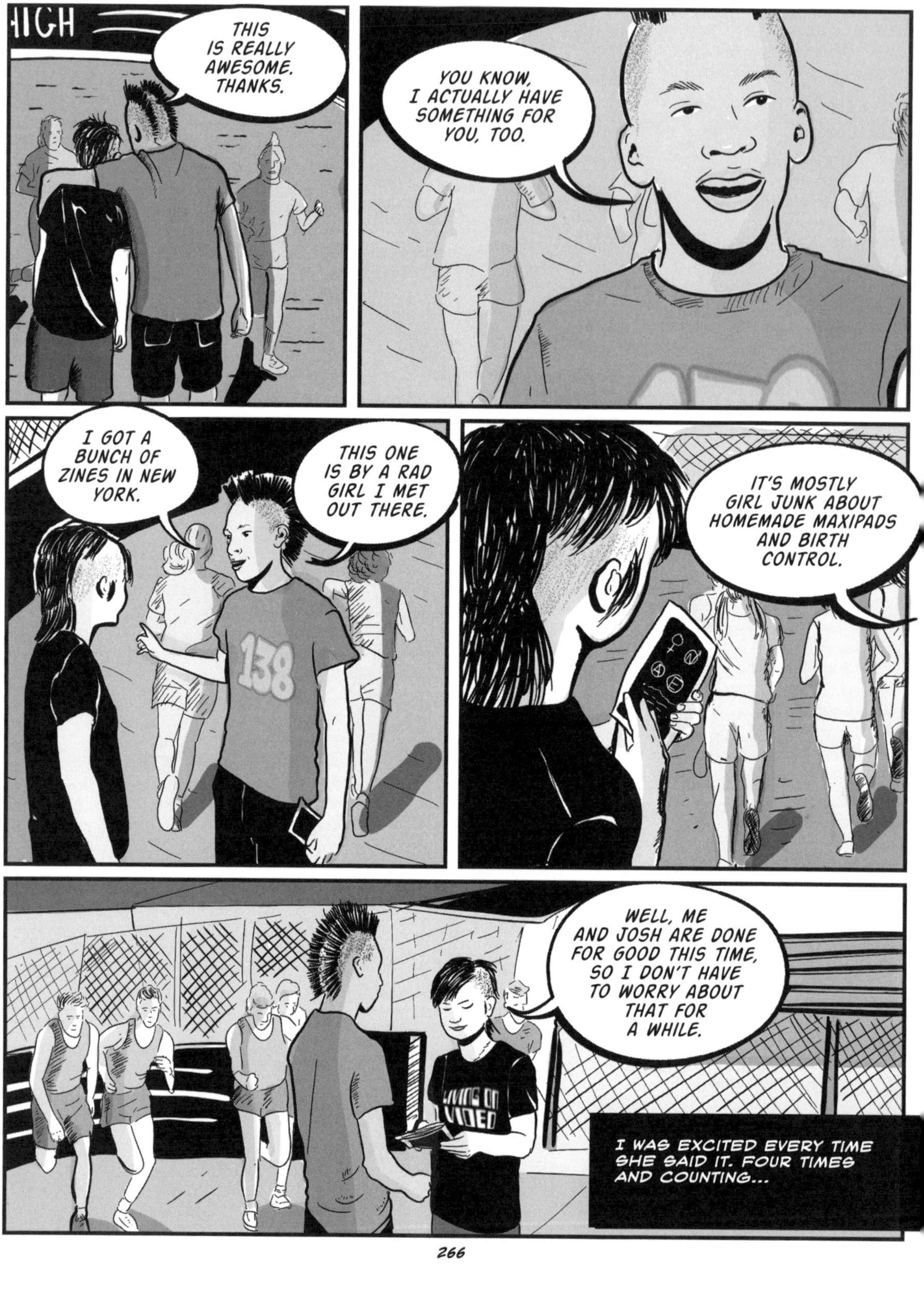
HIGH
THIS IS REALLY AWESOME. THANKS.
YOU KNOW, I ACTUALLY HAVE SOMETHING FOR YOU, TOO.
I GOT A BUNCH OF ZINES IN NEW YORK.
THIS ONE IS BY A RAD GIRL I MET OUT THERE.
138
IT'S MOSTLY GIRL JUNK ABOUT HOMEMADE MAXIPADS AND BIRTH CONTROL.
WELL, ME AND JOSH ARE DONE FOR GOOD THIS TIME, SO I DON'T HAVE TO WORRY ABOUT THAT FOR A WHILE.
LIVING ON VIDEO
I WAS EXCITED EVERY TIME SHE SAID IT. FOUR TIMES AND COUNTING...

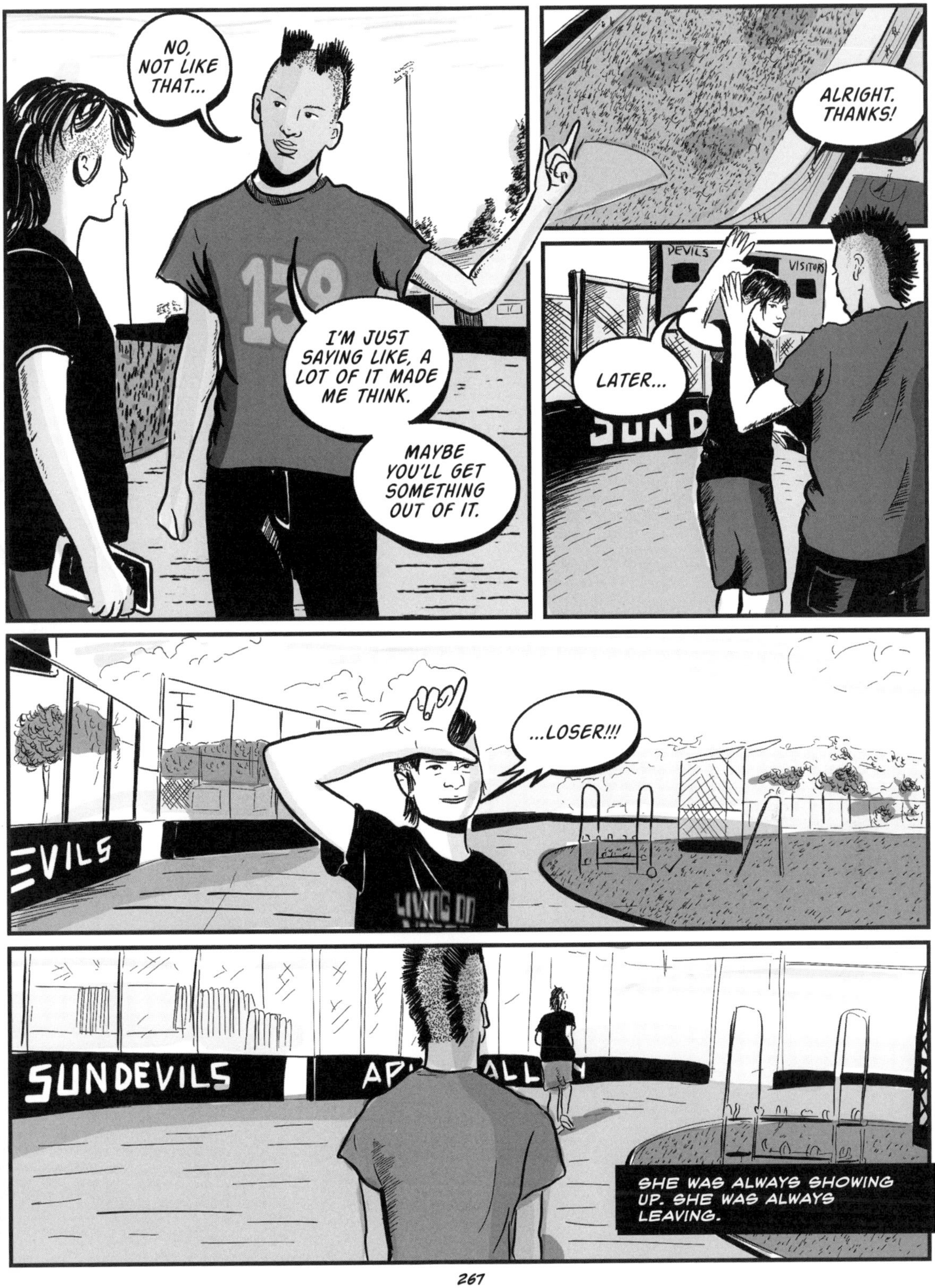

NO, NOT LIKE THAT...
I'M JUST SAYING LIKE, A LOT OF IT MADE ME THINK.
MAYBE YOU'LL GET SOMETHING OUT OF IT.
ALRIGHT. THANKS!
DEVILS
VISITORS
LATER...
SUN D
...LOSER!!!
EVILS
SUNDEVILS
SHE WAS ALWAYS SHOWING UP. SHE WAS ALWAYS LEAVING.

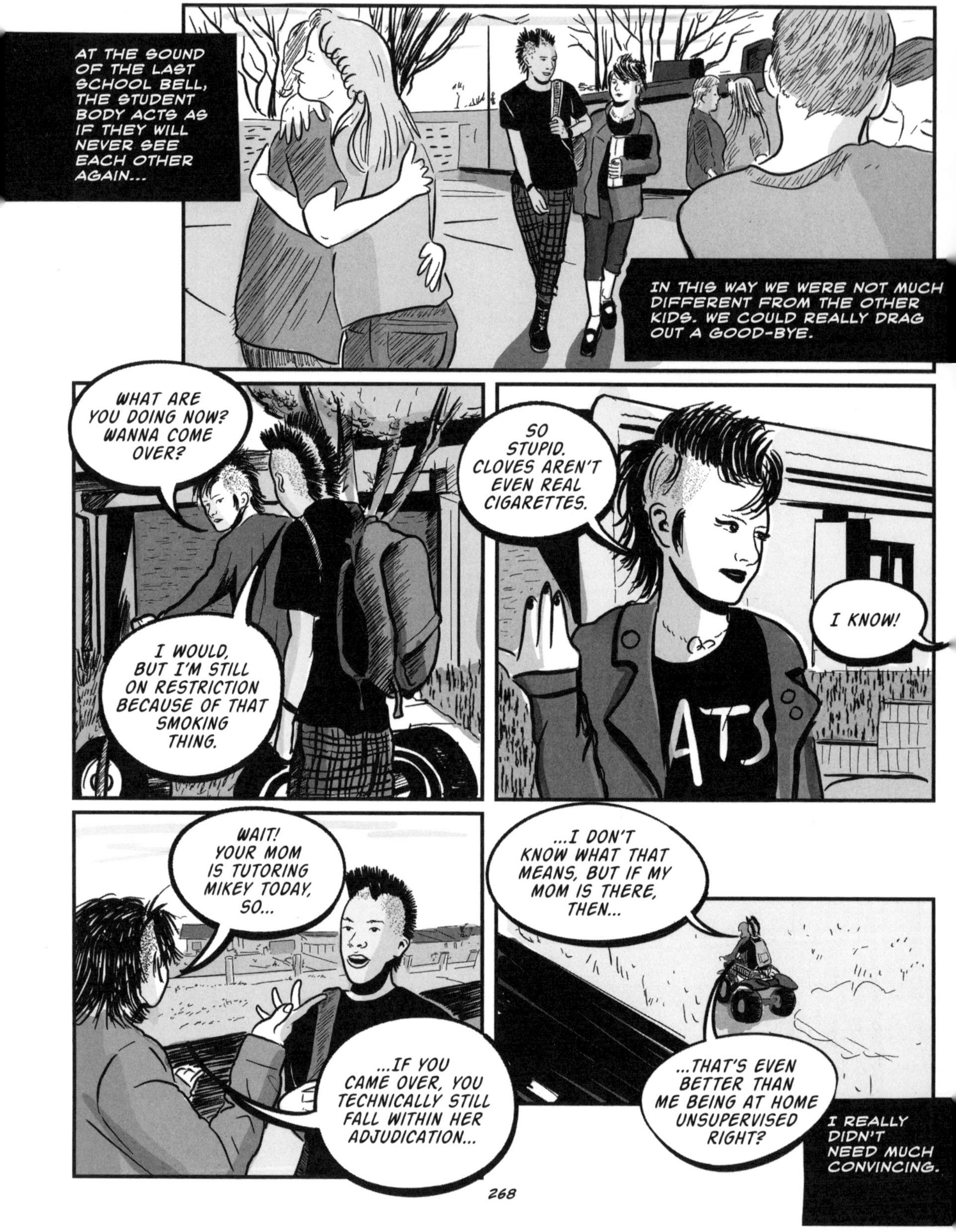
AT THE SOUND OF THE LAST SCHOOL BELL, THE STUDENT BODY ACTS AS IF THEY WILL NEVER SEE EACH OTHER AGAIN...
IN THIS WAY WE WERE NOT MUCH DIFFERENT FROM THE OTHER KIDS. WE COULD REALLY DRAG OUT A GOOD-BYE.
WHAT ARE YOU DOING NOW? WANNA COME OVER?
I WOULD, BUT I'M STILL ON RESTRICTION BECAUSE OF THAT SMOKING THING.
SO STUPID. CLOVES AREN'T EVEN REAL CIGARETTES.
I KNOW!
WAIT! YOUR MOM IS TUTORING MIKEY TODAY, SO...
...IF YOU CAME OVER, YOU TECHNICALLY STILL FALL WITHIN HER ADJUDICATION...
...I DON'T KNOW WHAT THAT MEANS, BUT IF MY MOM IS THERE, THEN...
...THAT'S EVEN BETTER THAN ME BEING AT HOME UNSUPERVISED RIGHT?
I REALLY DIDN'T NEED MUCH CONVINCING.

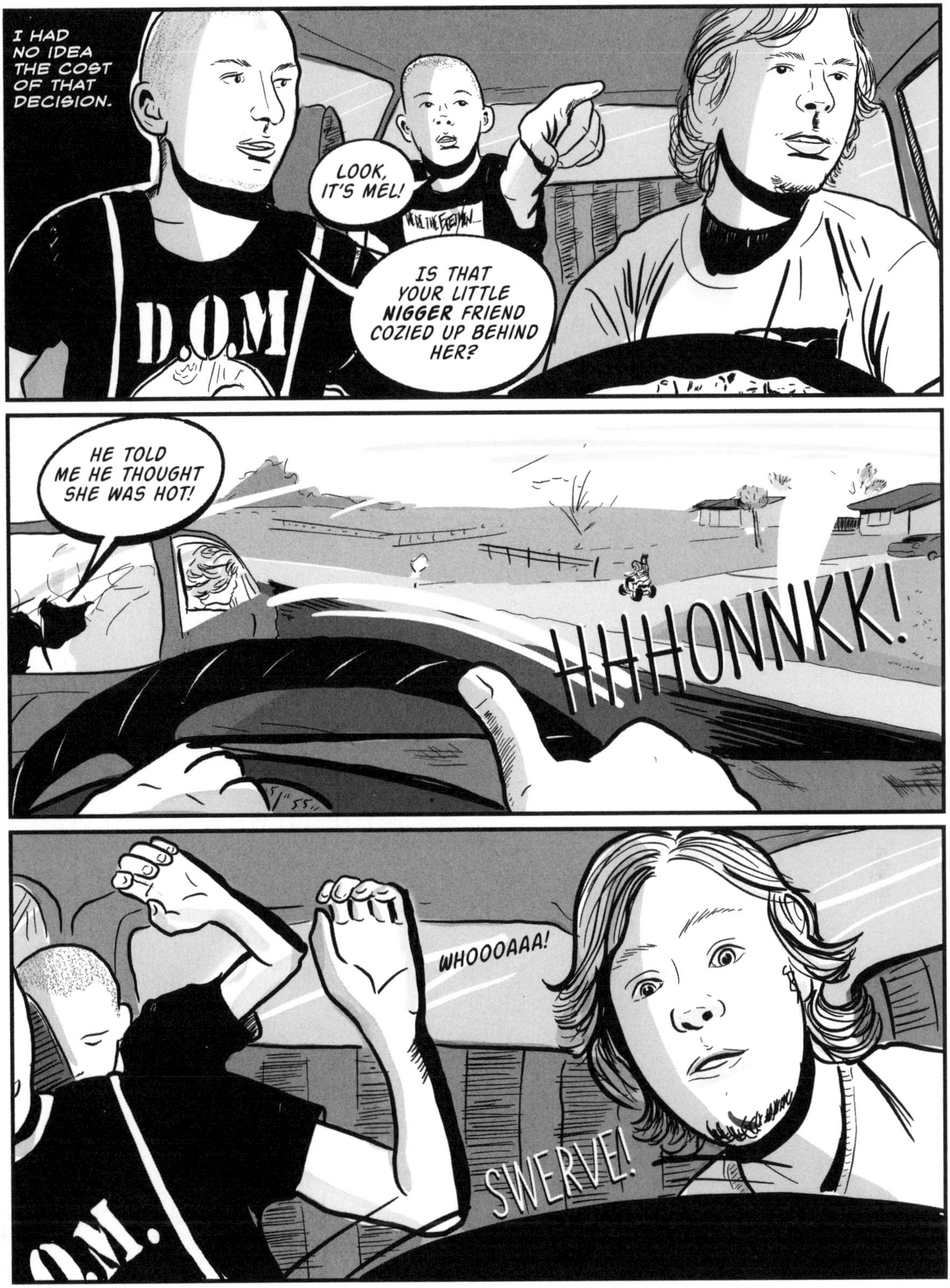
I HAD NO IDEA THE COST OF THAT DECISION.
LOOK, IT'S MEL!
IS THAT YOUR LITTLE NIGGER FRIEND COZIED UP BEHIND HER?
D.O.M
HE TOLD ME HE THOUGHT SHE WAS HOT!
HHHONNKK!
WHOOOAAA!
SWERVE!

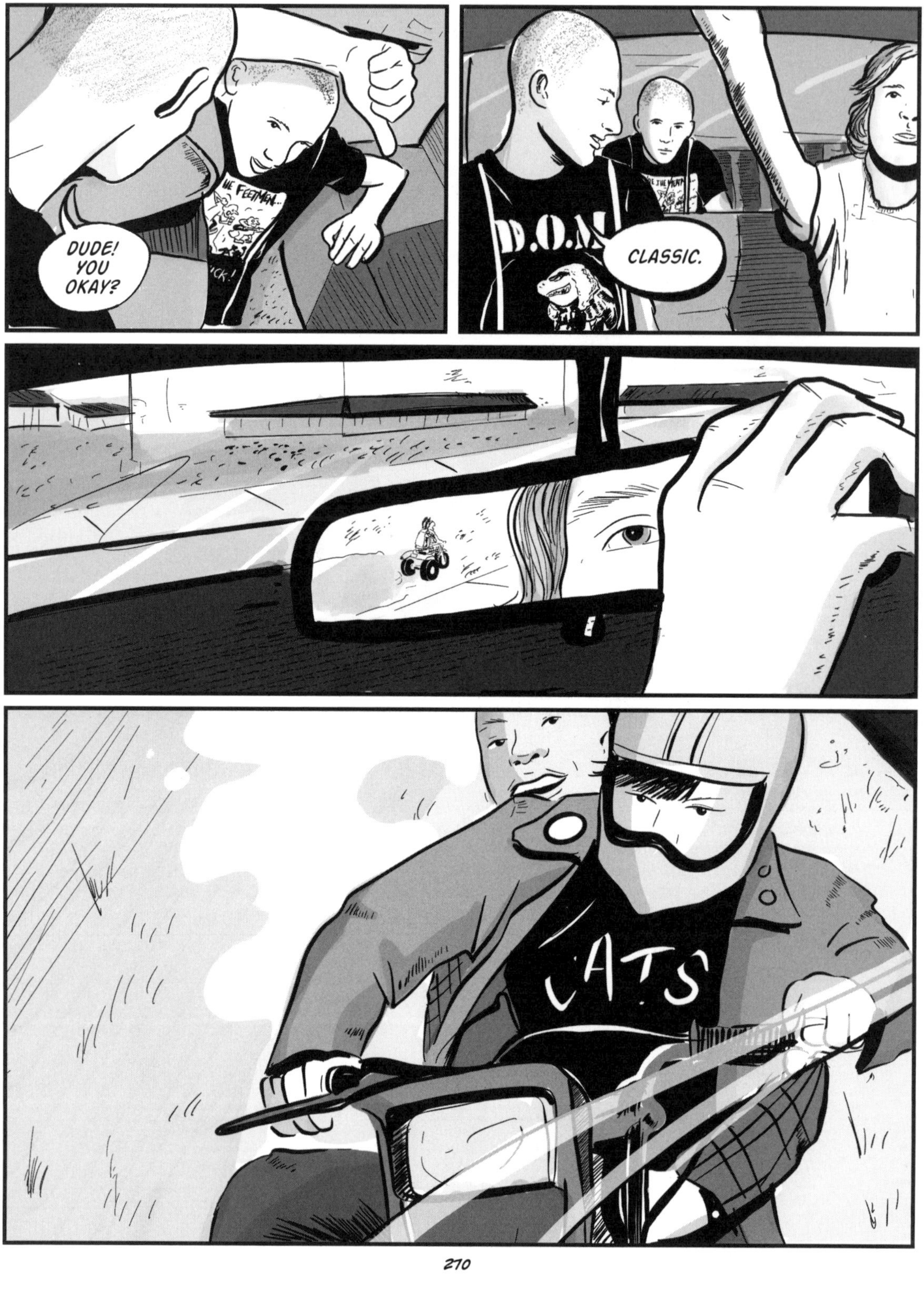
THE FEETMEN...
DUDE! YOU OKAY?
D.O.A.
CLASSIC.
CATS

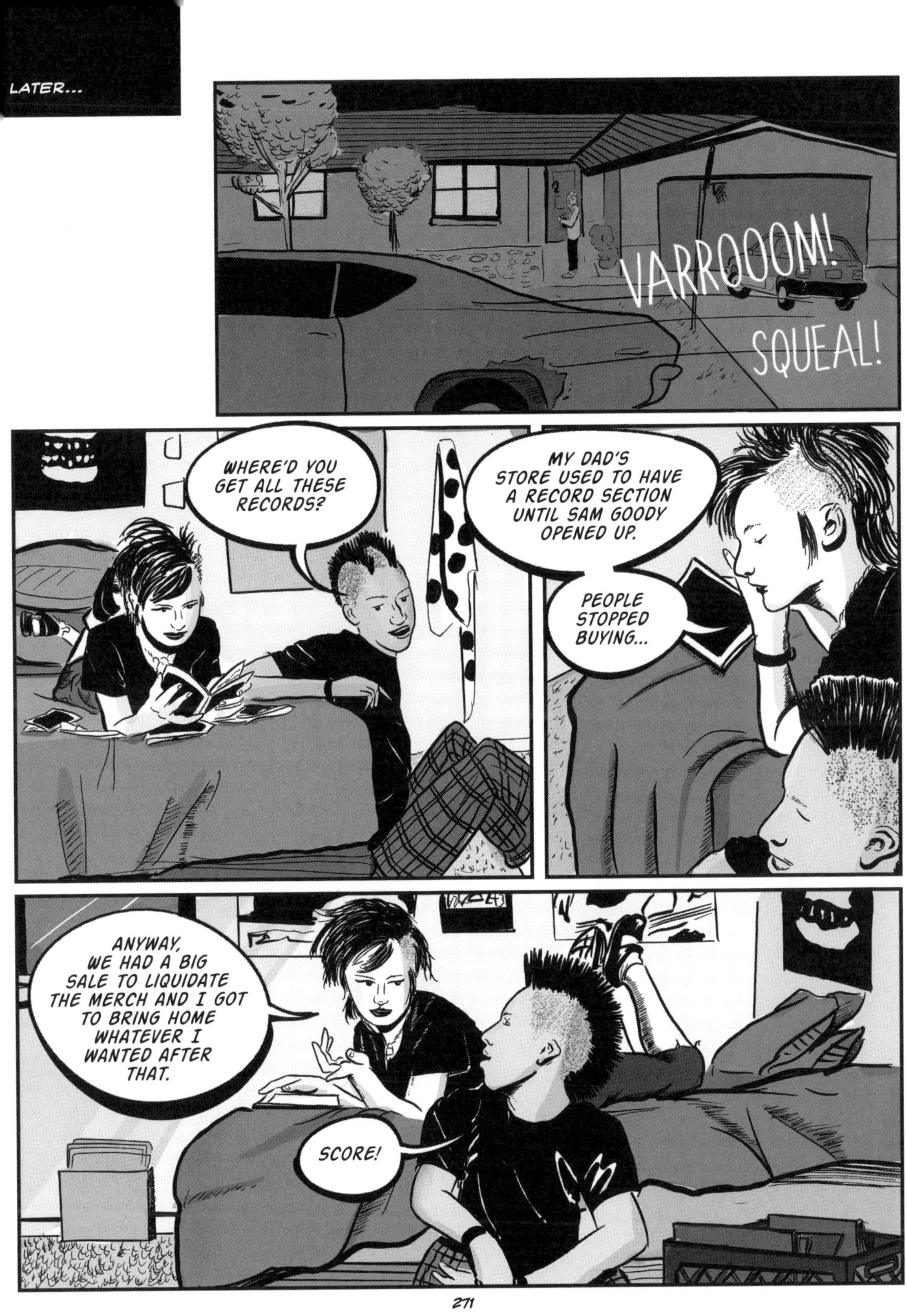
LATER...
VARROOOM!
SQUEAL!
WHERE'D YOU GET ALL THESE RECORDS?
MY DAD'S STORE USED TO HAVE A RECORD SECTION UNTIL SAM GOODY OPENED UP.
PEOPLE STOPPED BUYING...
ANYWAY, WE HAD A BIG SALE TO LIQUIDATE THE MERCH AND I GOT TO BRING HOME WHATEVER I WANTED AFTER THAT.
SCORE!

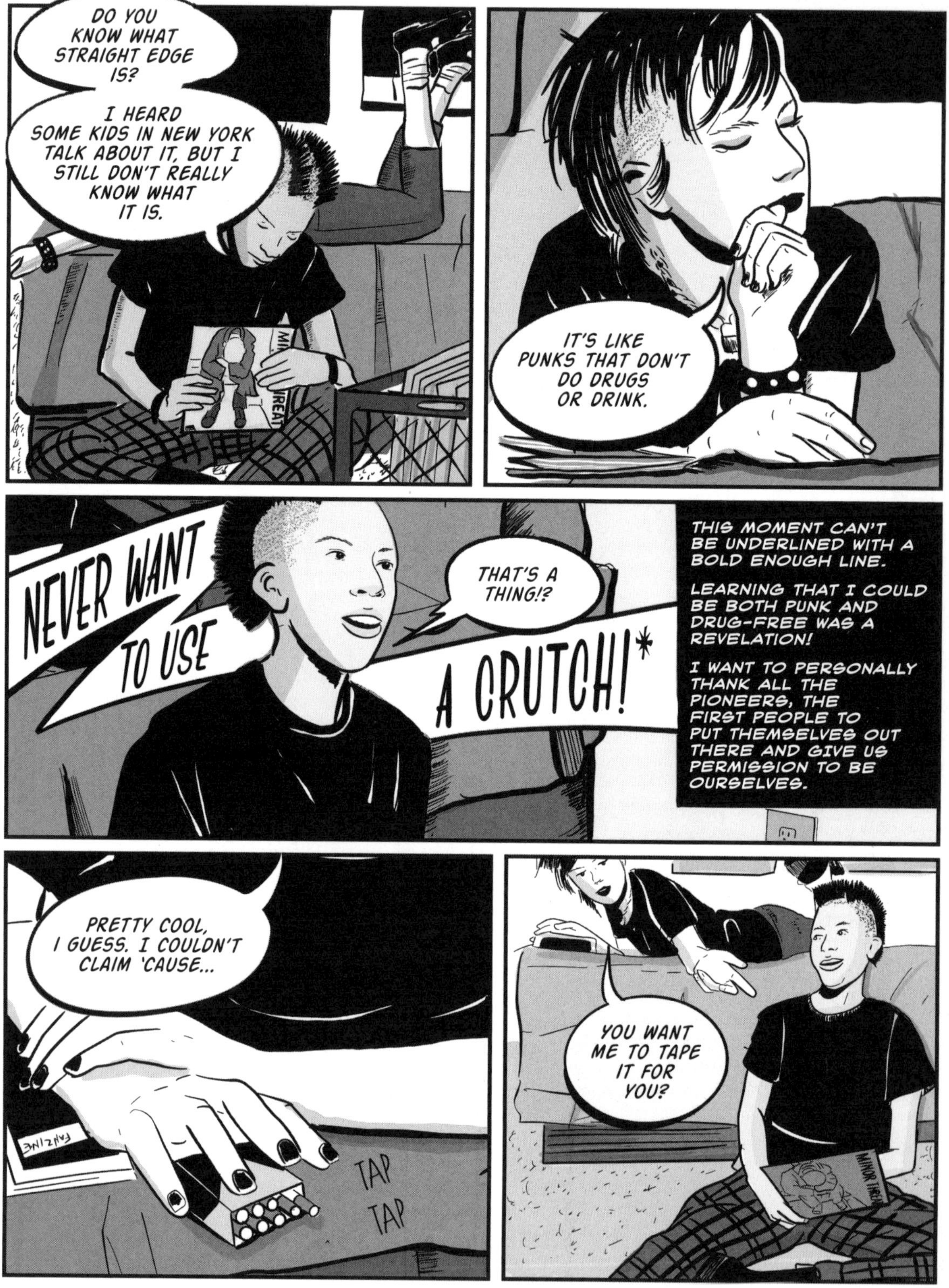
DO YOU KNOW WHAT STRAIGHT EDGE IS?
I HEARD SOME KIDS IN NEW YORK TALK ABOUT IT, BUT I STILL DON'T REALLY KNOW WHAT IT IS.
IT'S LIKE PUNKS THAT DON'T DO DRUGS OR DRINK.
NEVER WANT TO USE A CRUTCH!*
THAT'S A THING!?
THIS MOMENT CAN'T BE UNDERLINED WITH A BOLD ENOUGH LINE.
LEARNING THAT I COULD BE BOTH PUNK AND DRUG-FREE WAS A REVELATION!
I WANT TO PERSONALLY THANK ALL THE PIONEERS, THE FIRST PEOPLE TO PUT THEMSELVES OUT THERE AND GIVE US PERMISSION TO BE OURSELVES.
PRETTY COOL, I GUESS. I COULDN'T CLAIM 'CAUSE...
TAP
TAP
YOU WANT ME TO TAPE IT FOR YOU?

*MINOR THREAT "STRAIGHT EDGE"

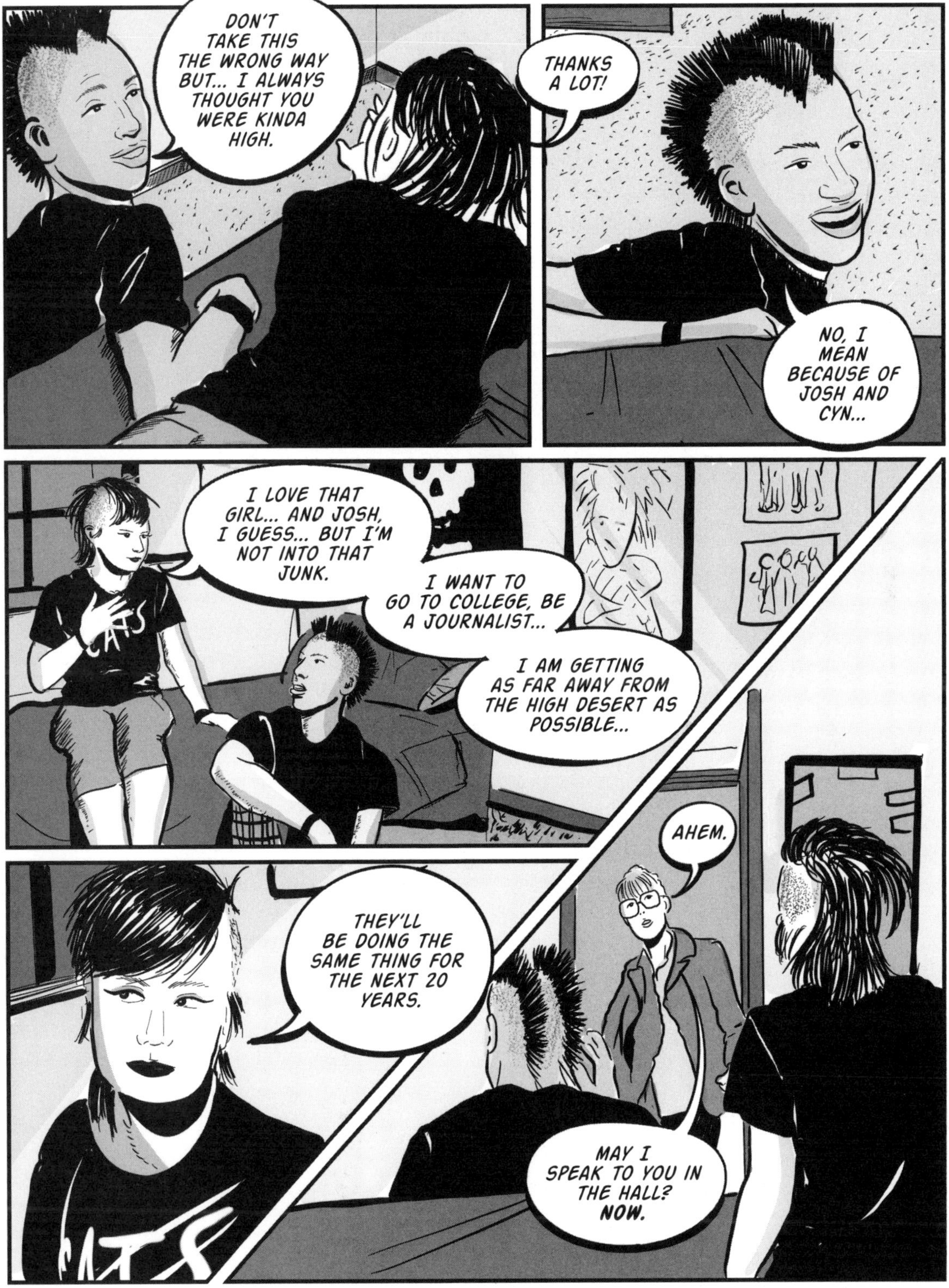
DON'T TAKE THIS THE WRONG WAY BUT... I ALWAYS THOUGHT YOU WERE KINDA HIGH.
THANKS A LOT!
NO, I MEAN BECAUSE OF JOSH AND CYN...
I LOVE THAT GIRL... AND JOSH, I GUESS... BUT I'M NOT INTO THAT JUNK.
I WANT TO GO TO COLLEGE, BE A JOURNALIST...
I AM GETTING AS FAR AWAY FROM THE HIGH DESERT AS POSSIBLE...
THEY'LL BE DOING THE SAME THING FOR THE NEXT 20 YEARS.
AHEM.
MAY I SPEAK TO YOU IN THE HALL? **NOW.**

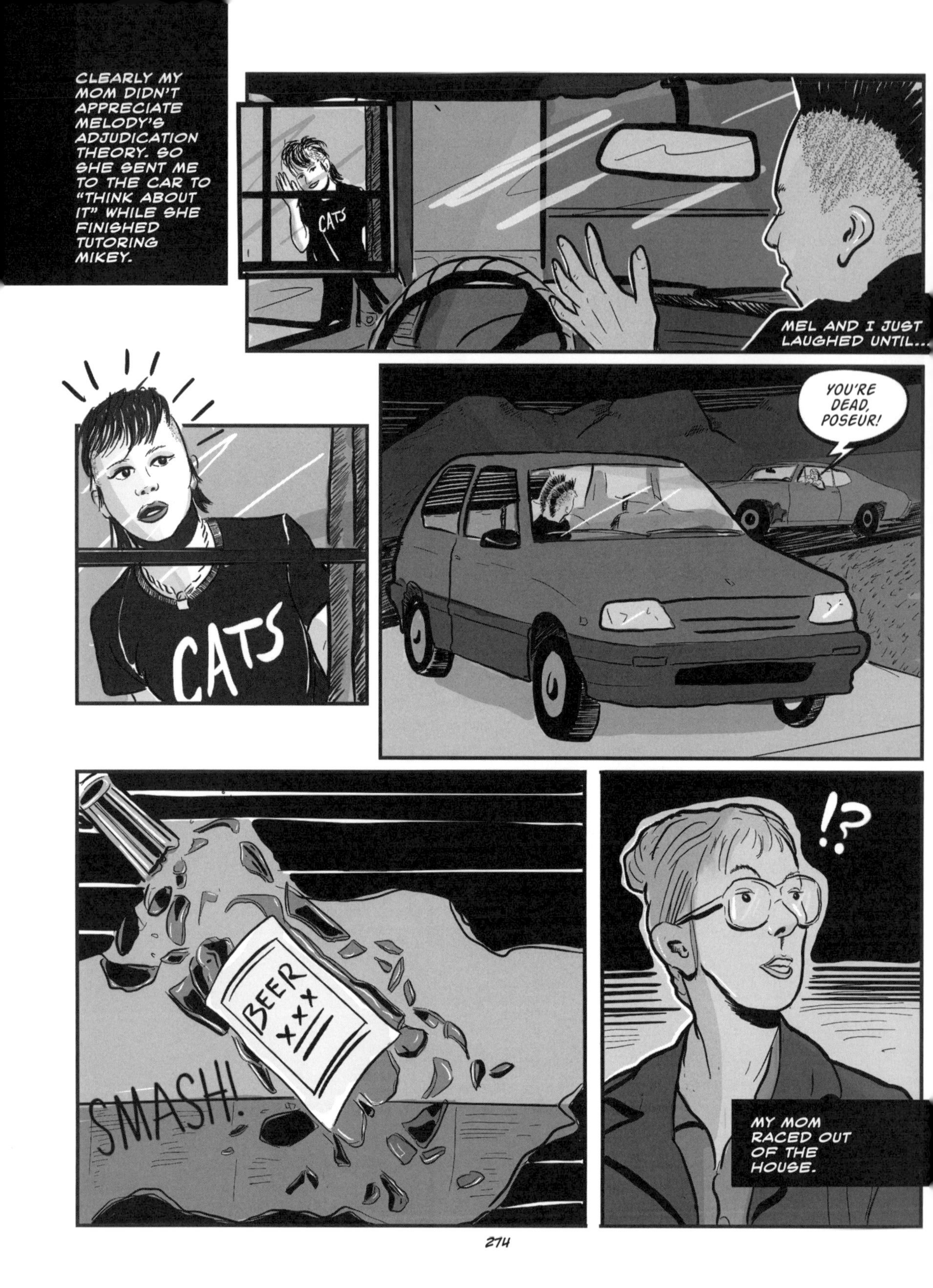

CLEARLY MY MOM DIDN'T APPRECIATE MELODY'S ADJUDICATION THEORY. SO SHE SENT ME TO THE CAR TO "THINK ABOUT IT" WHILE SHE FINISHED TUTORING MIKEY.
CATS
MEL AND I JUST LAUGHED UNTIL...
CATS
YOU'RE DEAD, POSEUR!
BEER XXX
SMASH!
!?
MY MOM RACED OUT OF THE HOUSE.

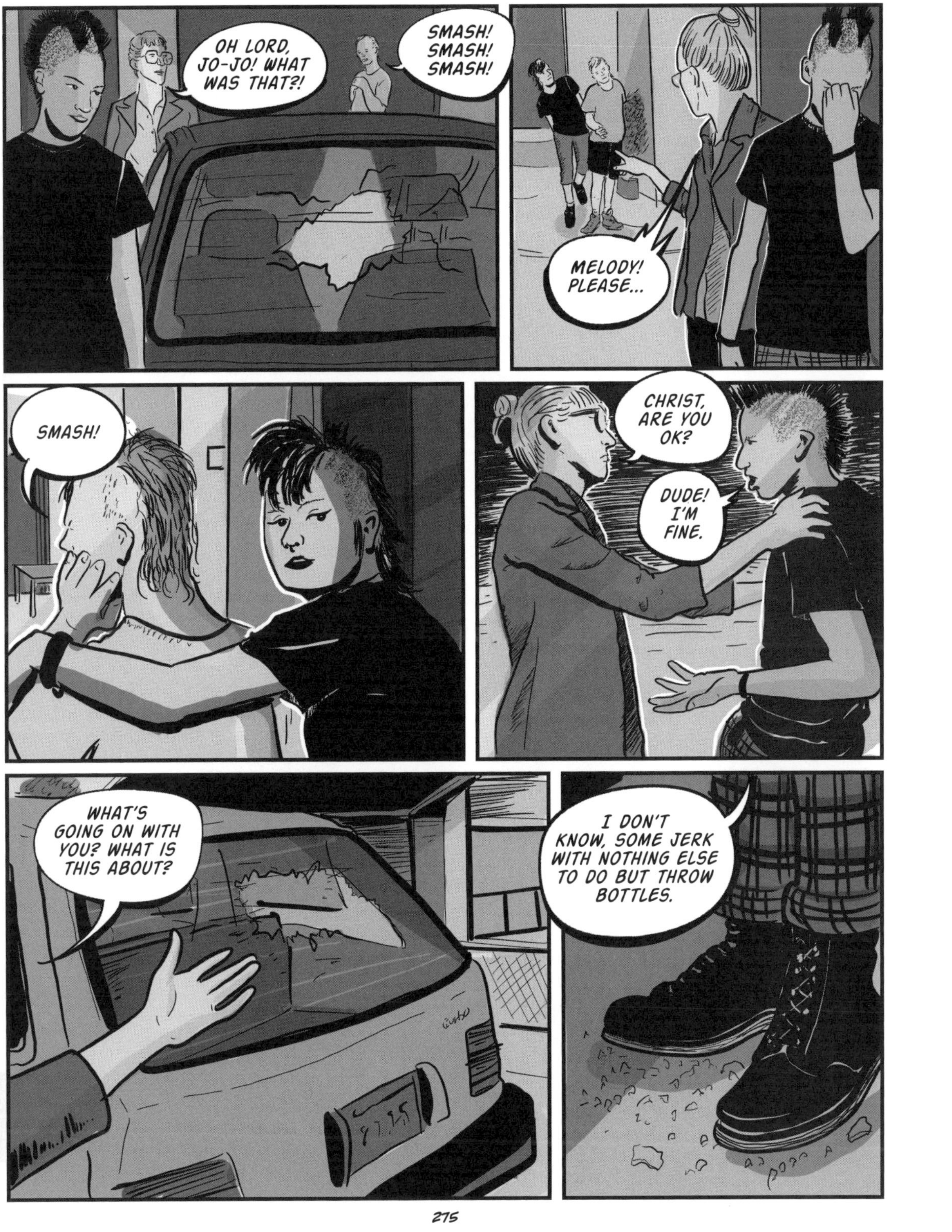
OH LORD, JO-JO! WHAT WAS THAT?!
SMASH! SMASH! SMASH!
MELODY! PLEASE...
SMASH!
CHRIST, ARE YOU OK?
DUDE! I'M FINE.
WHAT'S GOING ON WITH YOU? WHAT IS THIS ABOUT?
I DON'T KNOW, SOME JERK WITH NOTHING ELSE TO DO BUT THROW BOTTLES.

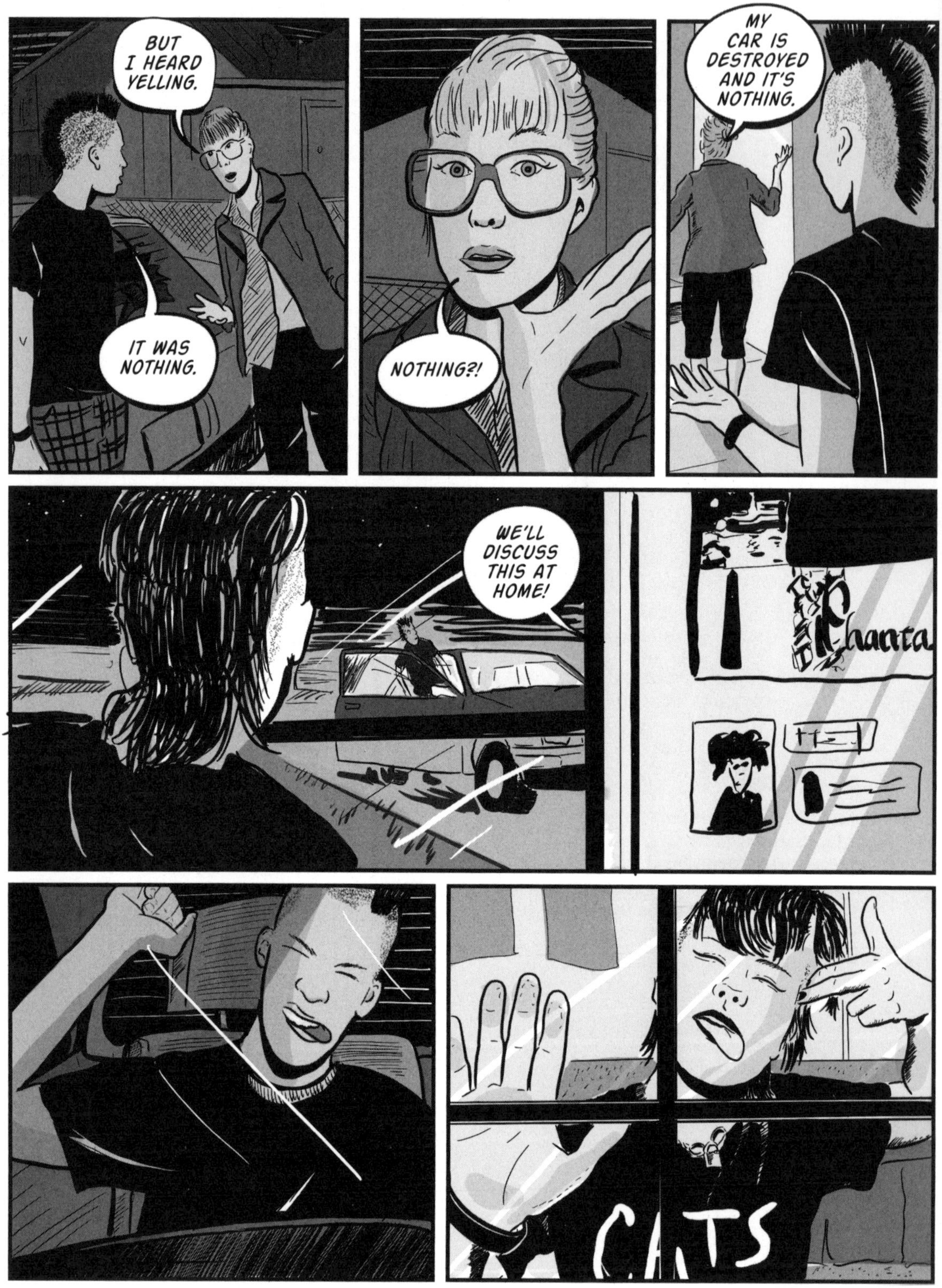
BUT I HEARD YELLING.
IT WAS NOTHING.
NOTHING?!
MY CAR IS DESTROYED AND IT'S NOTHING.
WE'LL DISCUSS THIS AT HOME!
CATS

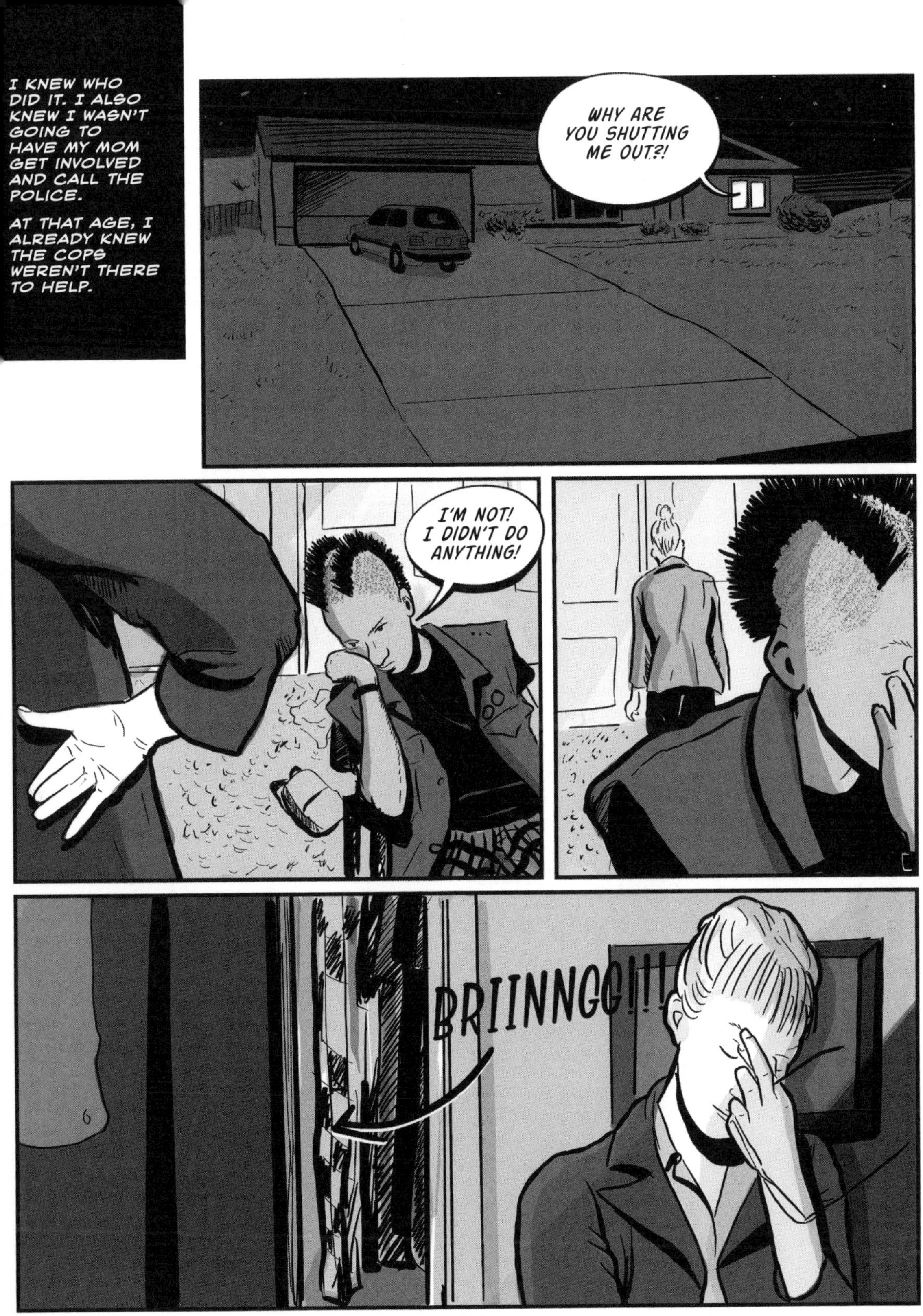
I KNEW WHO DID IT. I ALSO KNEW I WASN'T GOING TO HAVE MY MOM GET INVOLVED AND CALL THE POLICE.
AT THAT AGE, I ALREADY KNEW THE COPS WEREN'T THERE TO HELP.
WHY ARE YOU SHUTTING ME OUT?!
I'M NOT! I DIDN'T DO ANYTHING!
BRIINNGG!!!

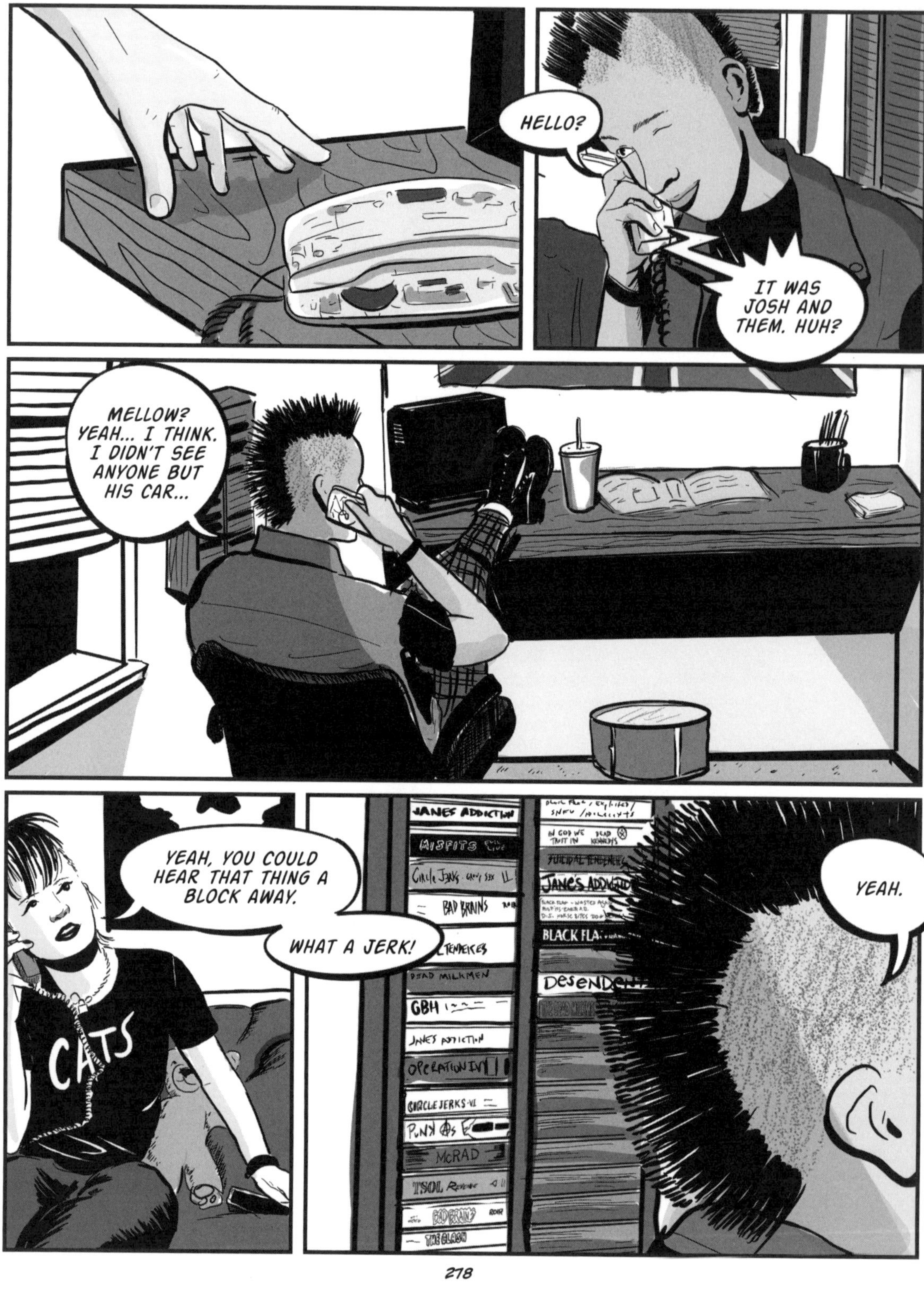
HELLO?
IT WAS JOSH AND THEM. HUH?
MELLOW? YEAH... I THINK. I DIDN'T SEE ANYONE BUT HIS CAR...
YEAH, YOU COULD HEAR THAT THING A BLOCK AWAY.
WHAT A JERK!
YEAH.
CATS
JANES ADDICTION
MISFITS
BAD BRAINS
DEAD MILKMEN
GBH
JANES ADDICTION
OPERATION IVY
McRAD
TSOL
THE CLASH
BLACK FLAG

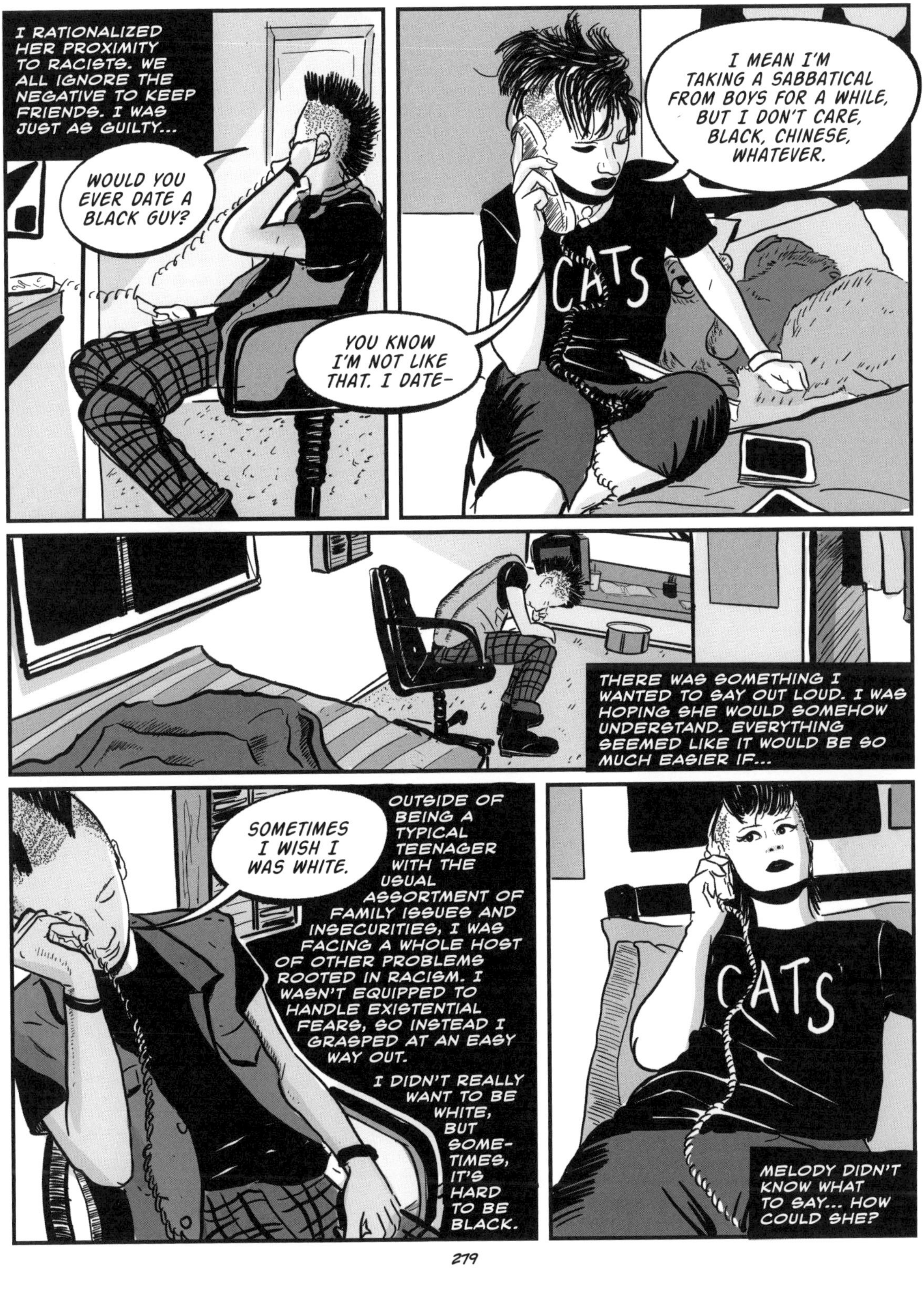
I RATIONALIZED HER PROXIMITY TO RACISTS. WE ALL IGNORE THE NEGATIVE TO KEEP FRIENDS. I WAS JUST AS GUILTY...
WOULD YOU EVER DATE A BLACK GUY?
YOU KNOW I'M NOT LIKE THAT. I DATE-
I MEAN I'M TAKING A SABBATICAL FROM BOYS FOR A WHILE, BUT I DON'T CARE, BLACK, CHINESE, WHATEVER.
CATS
THERE WAS SOMETHING I WANTED TO SAY OUT LOUD. I WAS HOPING SHE WOULD SOMEHOW UNDERSTAND. EVERYTHING SEEMED LIKE IT WOULD BE SO MUCH EASIER IF...
SOMETIMES I WISH I WAS WHITE.
OUTSIDE OF BEING A TYPICAL TEENAGER WITH THE USUAL ASSORTMENT OF FAMILY ISSUES AND INSECURITIES, I WAS FACING A WHOLE HOST OF OTHER PROBLEMS ROOTED IN RACISM. I WASN'T EQUIPPED TO HANDLE EXISTENTIAL FEARS, SO INSTEAD I GRASPED AT AN EASY WAY OUT.
I DIDN'T REALLY WANT TO BE WHITE, BUT SOMETIMES, IT'S HARD TO BE BLACK.
CATS
MELODY DIDN'T KNOW WHAT TO SAY... HOW COULD SHE?

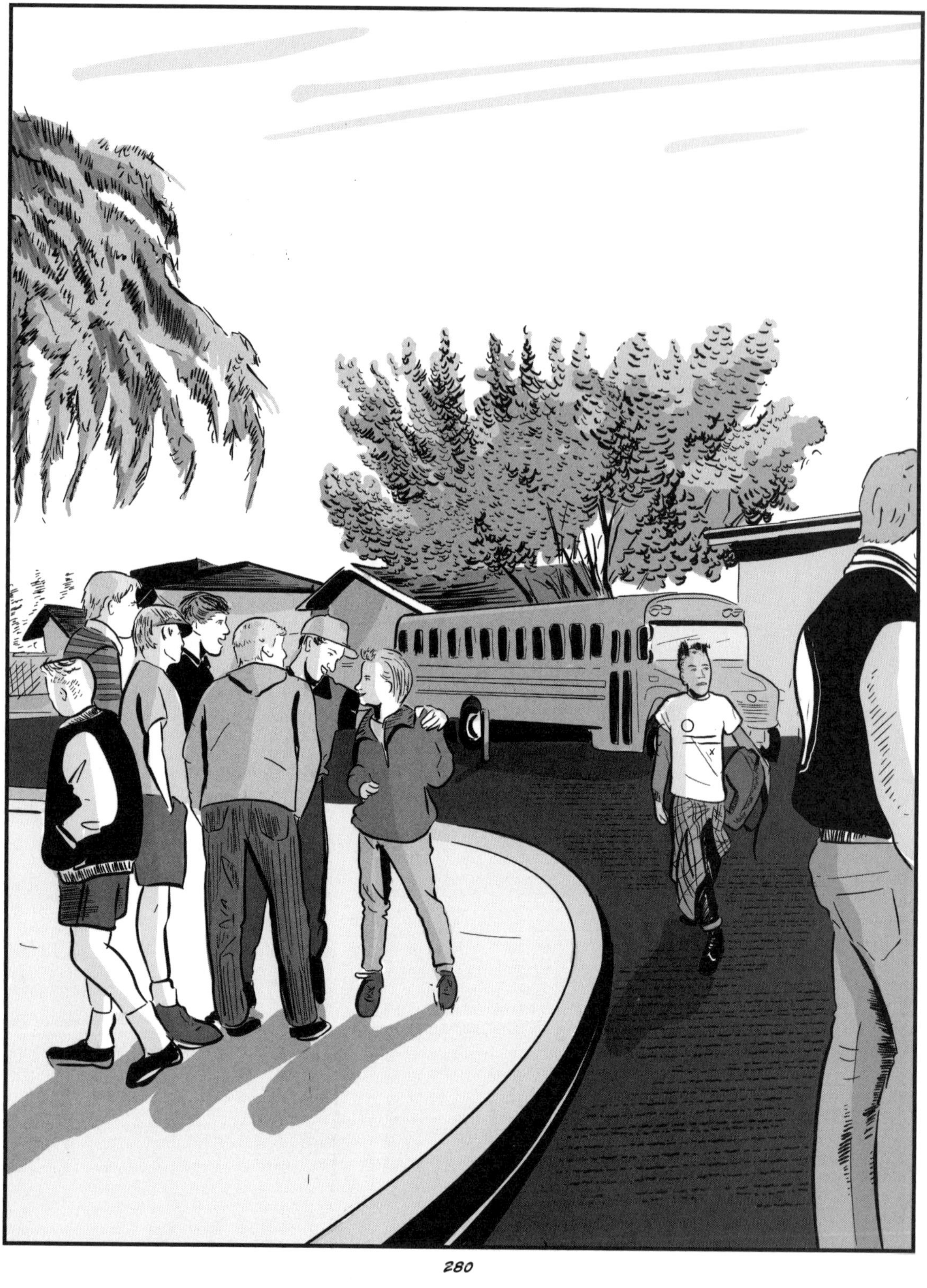

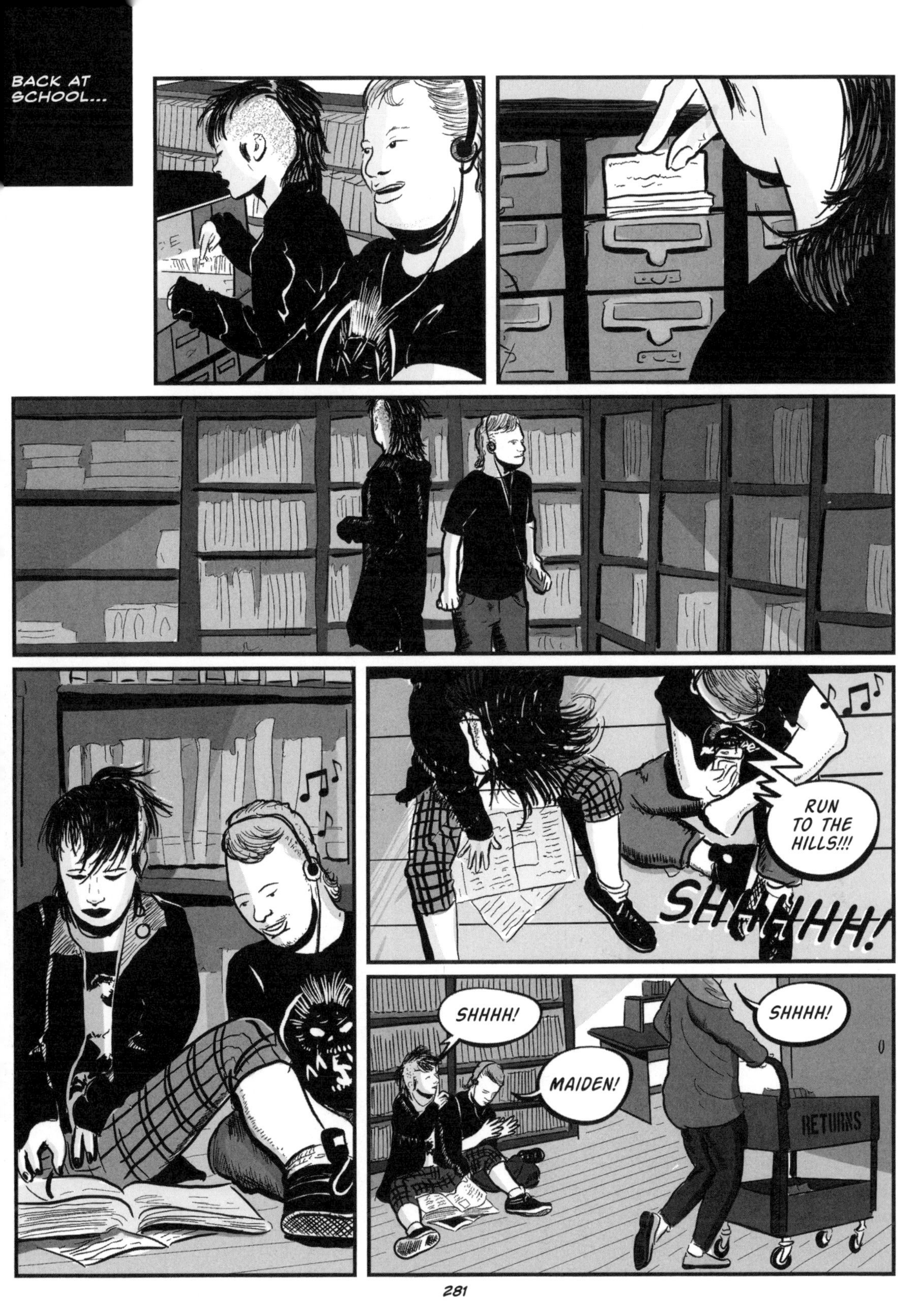
BACK AT SCHOOL...
RUN TO THE HILLS!!!
SHHHHH!
SHHHH!
MAIDEN!
SHHHH!
RETURNS

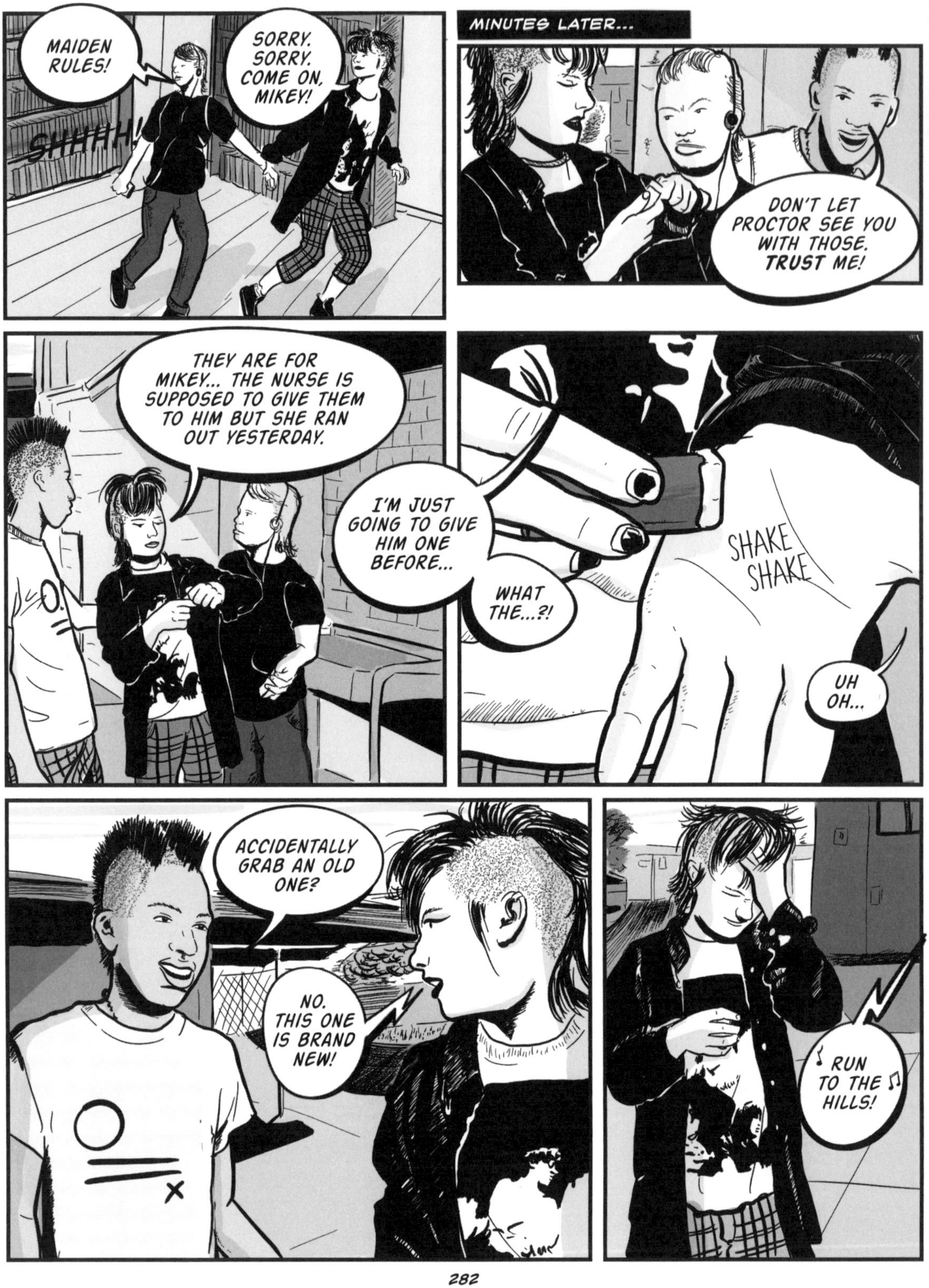
MAIDEN RULES!
SHHHH!
SORRY. SORRY. COME ON, MIKEY!
MINUTES LATER...
DON'T LET PROCTOR SEE YOU WITH THOSE. TRUST ME!
THEY ARE FOR MIKEY... THE NURSE IS SUPPOSED TO GIVE THEM TO HIM BUT SHE RAN OUT YESTERDAY.
I'M JUST GOING TO GIVE HIM ONE BEFORE...
WHAT THE...?!
SHAKE SHAKE
UH OH...
ACCIDENTALLY GRAB AN OLD ONE?
NO. THIS ONE IS BRAND NEW!
RUN TO THE HILLS!

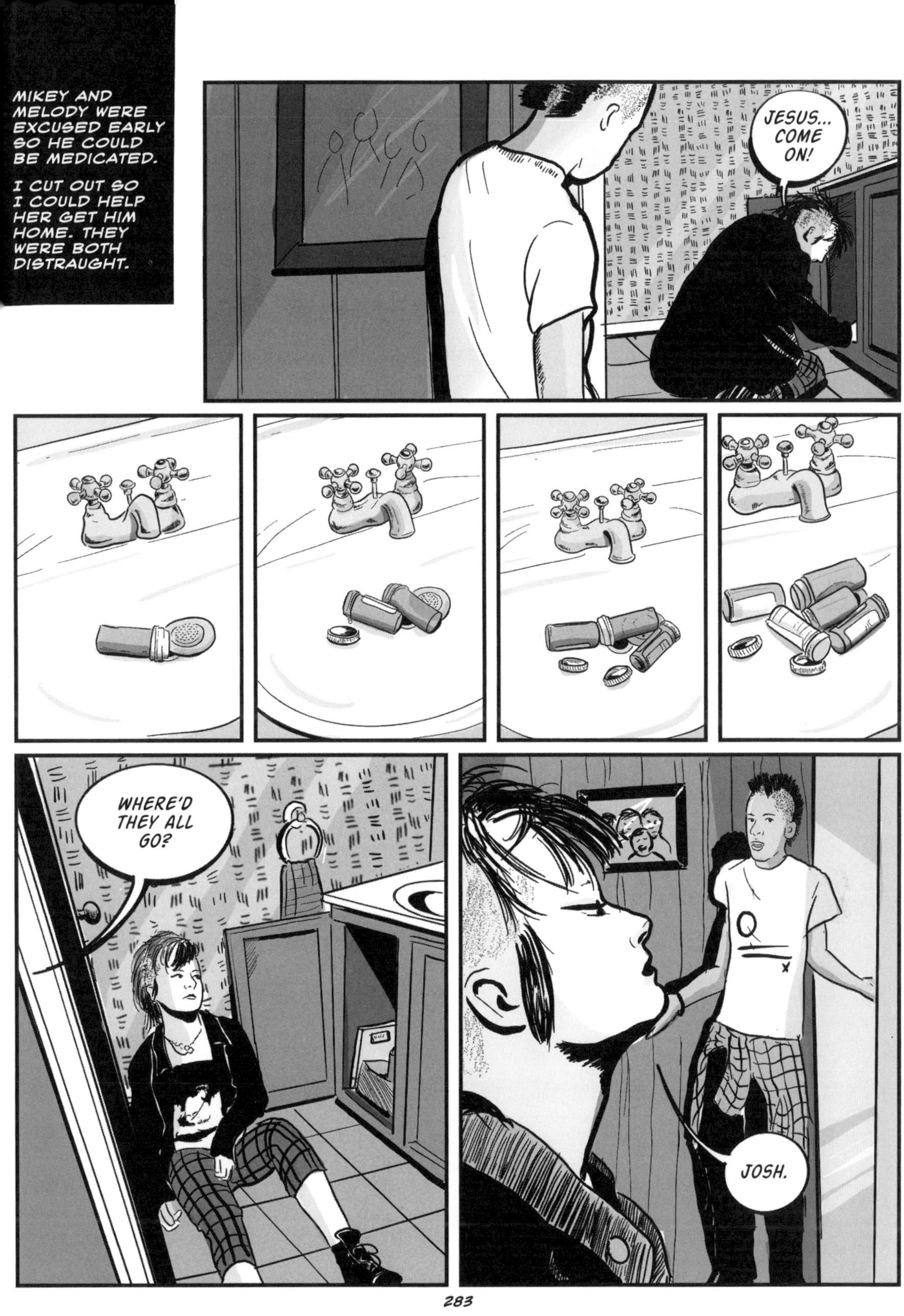
MIKEY AND MELODY WERE EXCUSED EARLY SO HE COULD BE MEDICATED.
I CUT OUT SO I COULD HELP HER GET HIM HOME. THEY WERE BOTH DISTRAUGHT.
JESUS... COME ON!
WHERE'D THEY ALL GO?
JOSH.

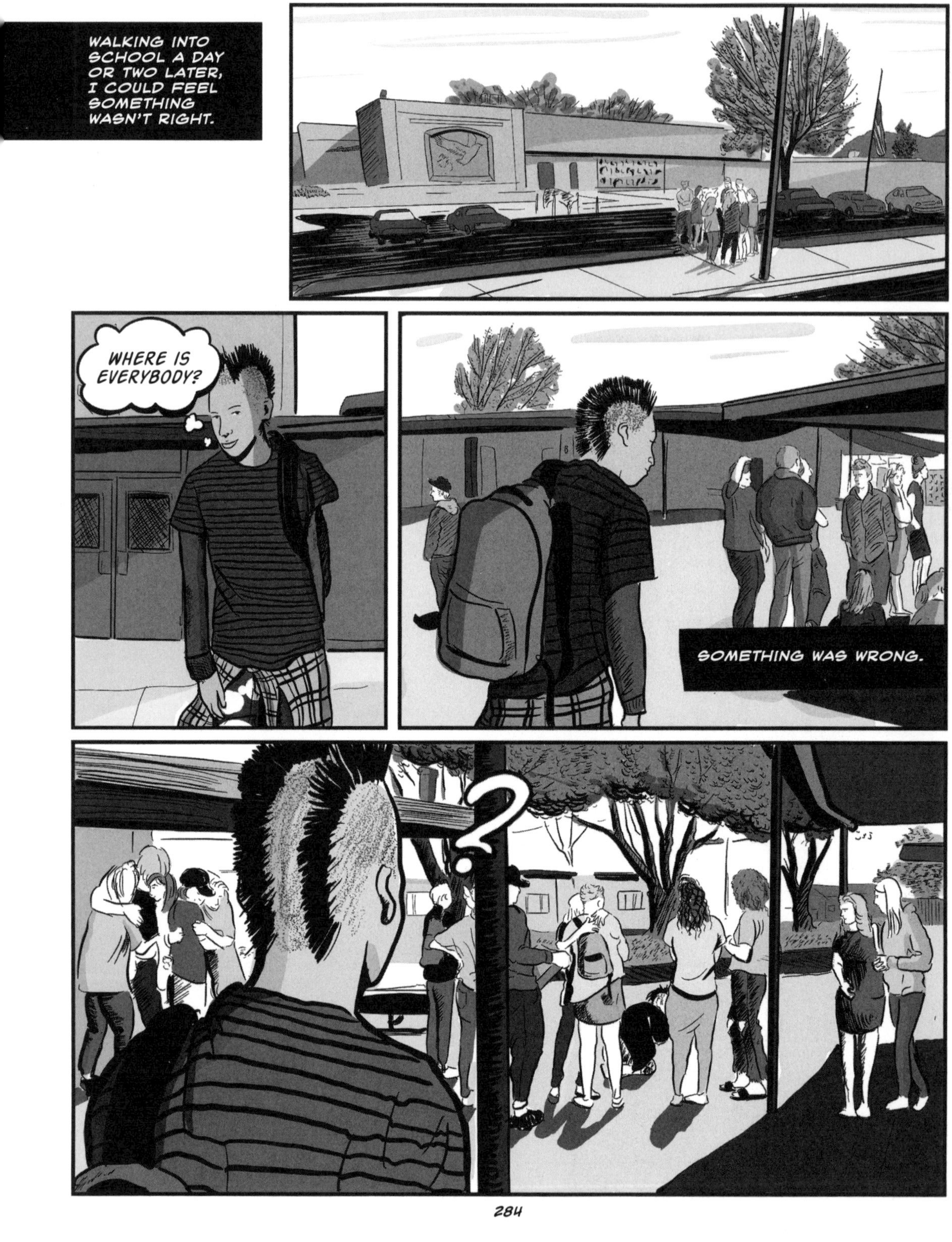
WALKING INTO SCHOOL A DAY OR TWO LATER, I COULD FEEL SOMETHING WASN'T RIGHT.
WHERE IS EVERYBODY?
SOMETHING WAS WRONG.
?

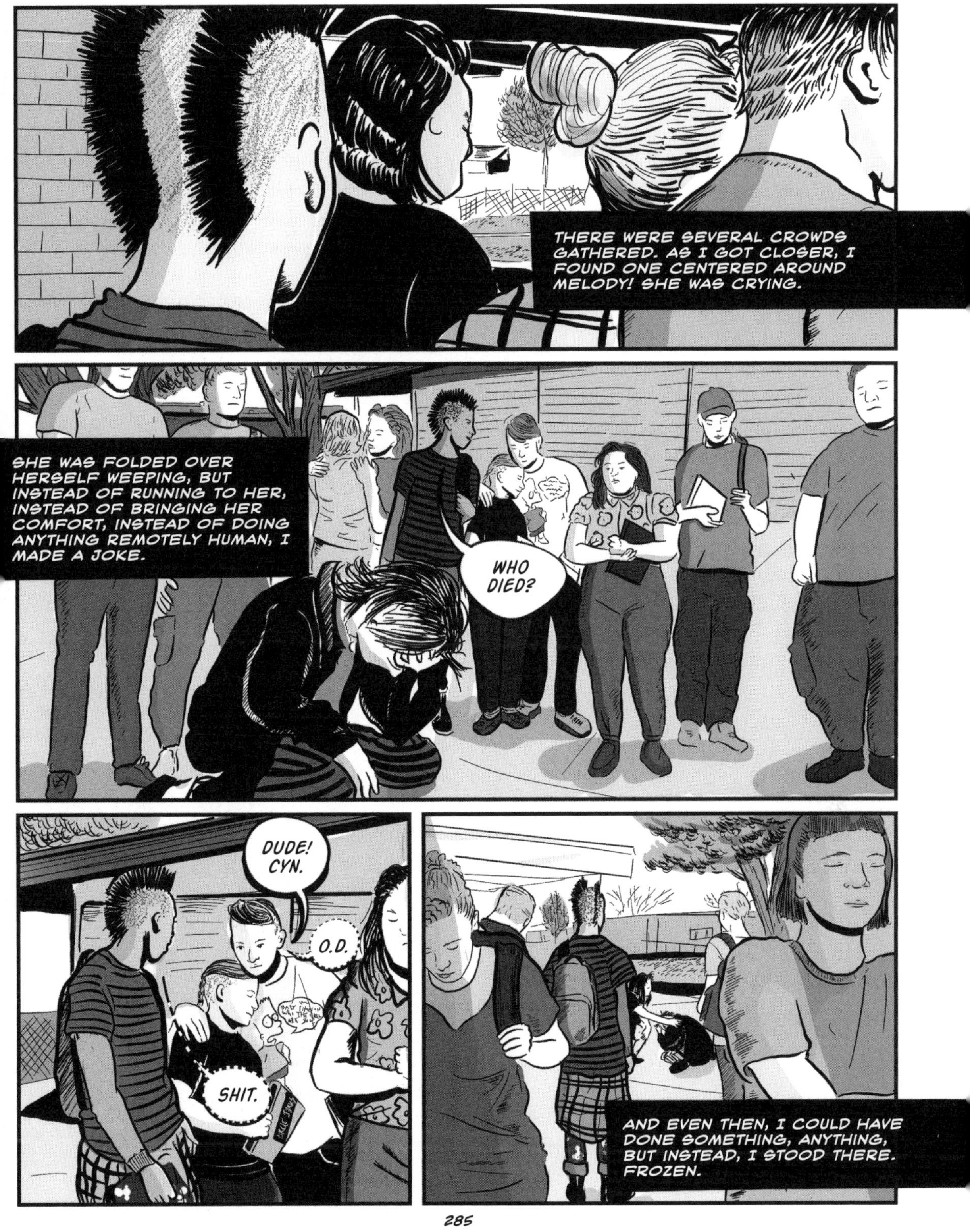
THERE WERE SEVERAL CROWDS GATHERED. AS I GOT CLOSER, I FOUND ONE CENTERED AROUND MELODY! SHE WAS CRYING.
SHE WAS FOLDED OVER HERSELF WEEPING, BUT INSTEAD OF RUNNING TO HER, INSTEAD OF BRINGING HER COMFORT, INSTEAD OF DOING ANYTHING REMOTELY HUMAN, I MADE A JOKE.
WHO DIED?
DUDE! CYN.
O.D.
SHIT.
AND EVEN THEN, I COULD HAVE DONE SOMETHING, ANYTHING, BUT INSTEAD, I STOOD THERE. FROZEN.

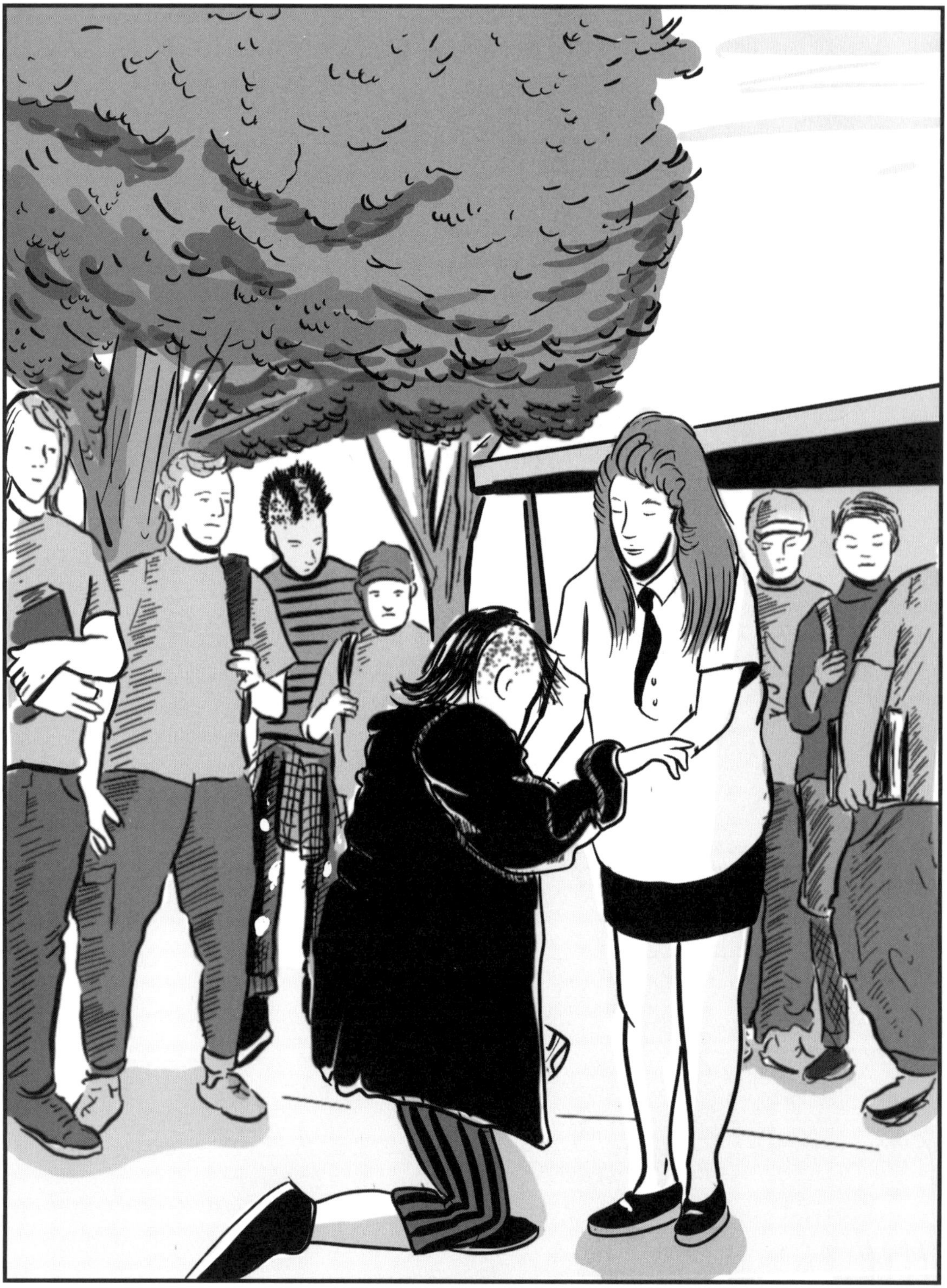

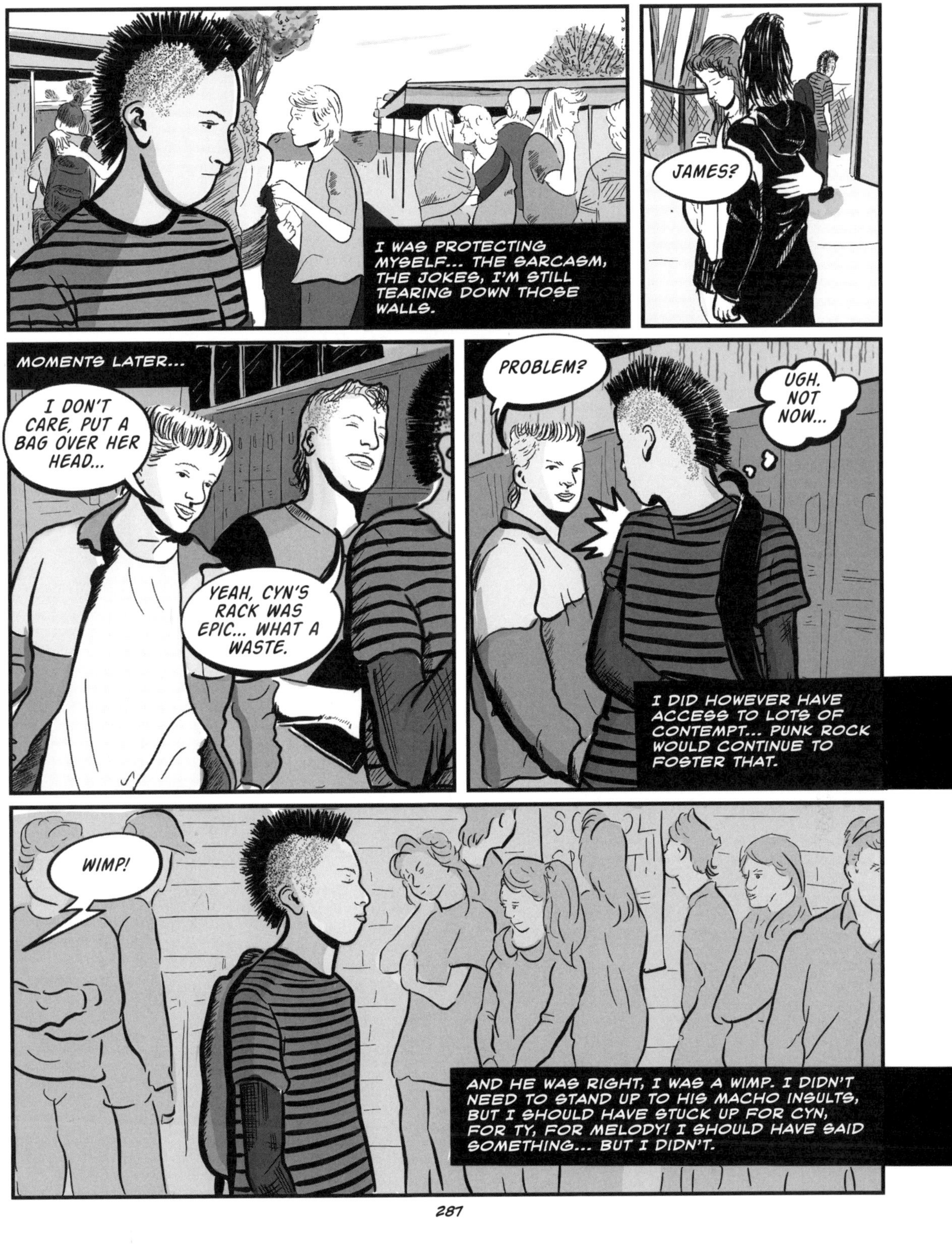
I WAS PROTECTING MYSELF... THE SARCASM, THE JOKES, I'M STILL TEARING DOWN THOSE WALLS.
JAMES?
MOMENTS LATER...
I DON'T CARE, PUT A BAG OVER HER HEAD...
YEAH, CYN'S RACK WAS EPIC... WHAT A WASTE.
PROBLEM?
UGH. NOT NOW...
I DID HOWEVER HAVE ACCESS TO LOTS OF CONTEMPT... PUNK ROCK WOULD CONTINUE TO FOSTER THAT.
WIMP!
AND HE WAS RIGHT, I WAS A WIMP. I DIDN'T NEED TO STAND UP TO HIS MACHO INSULTS, BUT I SHOULD HAVE STUCK UP FOR CYN, FOR TY, FOR MELODY! I SHOULD HAVE SAID SOMETHING... BUT I DIDN'T.

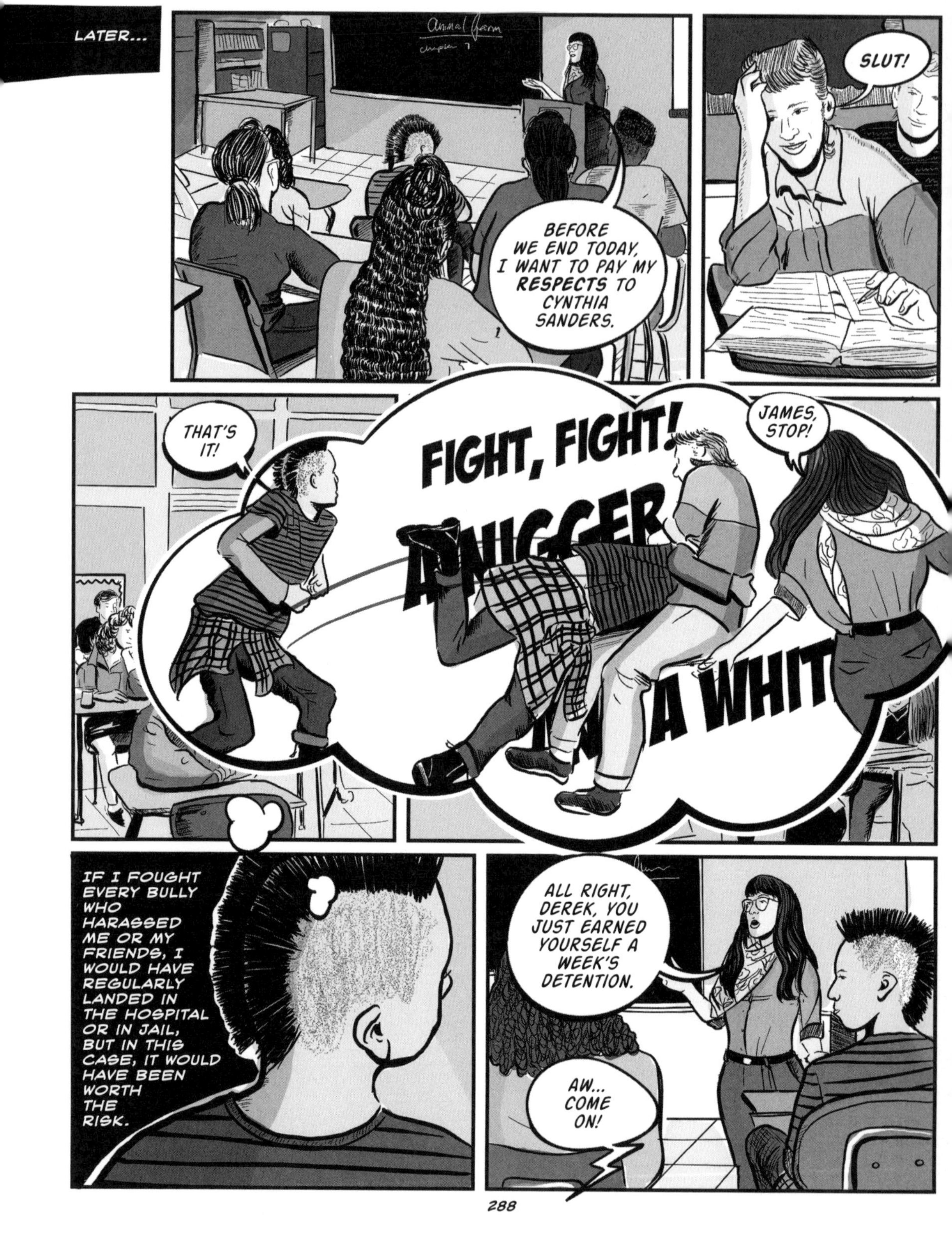
LATER...
Animal farm
chapter 7
BEFORE WE END TODAY, I WANT TO PAY MY RESPECTS TO CYNTHIA SANDERS.
SLUT!
THAT'S IT!
FIGHT, FIGHT!
A NIGGER
A WHIT
JAMES, STOP!
IF I FOUGHT EVERY BULLY WHO HARASSED ME OR MY FRIENDS, I WOULD HAVE REGULARLY LANDED IN THE HOSPITAL OR IN JAIL, BUT IN THIS CASE, IT WOULD HAVE BEEN WORTH THE RISK.
ALL RIGHT, DEREK, YOU JUST EARNED YOURSELF A WEEK'S DETENTION.
AW... COME ON!

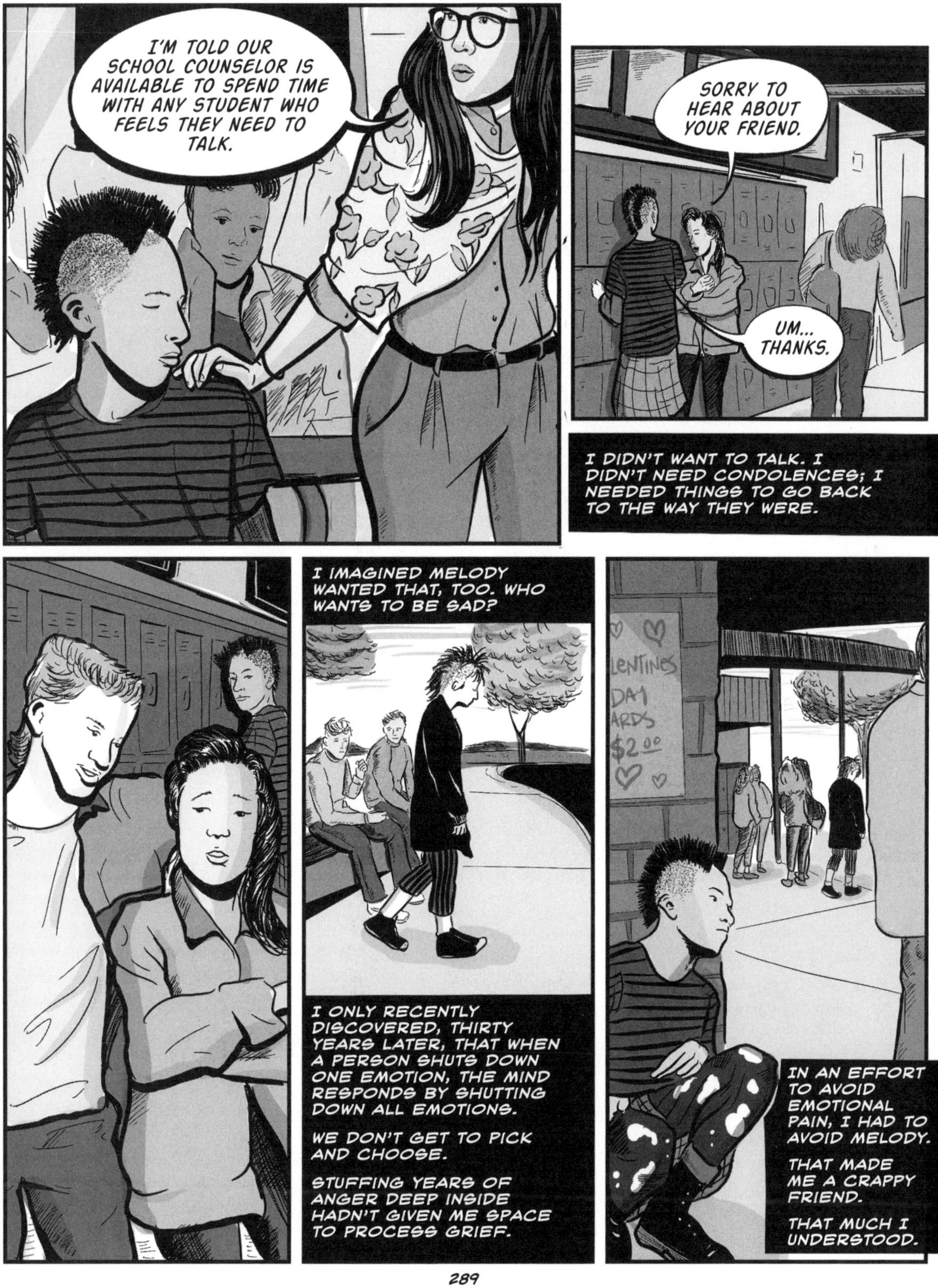

I'M TOLD OUR SCHOOL COUNSELOR IS AVAILABLE TO SPEND TIME WITH ANY STUDENT WHO FEELS THEY NEED TO TALK.
SORRY TO HEAR ABOUT YOUR FRIEND.
UM... THANKS.
I DIDN'T WANT TO TALK. I DIDN'T NEED CONDOLENCES; I NEEDED THINGS TO GO BACK TO THE WAY THEY WERE.
I IMAGINED MELODY WANTED THAT, TOO. WHO WANTS TO BE SAD?
I ONLY RECENTLY DISCOVERED, THIRTY YEARS LATER, THAT WHEN A PERSON SHUTS DOWN ONE EMOTION, THE MIND RESPONDS BY SHUTTING DOWN ALL EMOTIONS.
WE DON'T GET TO PICK AND CHOOSE.
STUFFING YEARS OF ANGER DEEP INSIDE HADN'T GIVEN ME SPACE TO PROCESS GRIEF.
IN AN EFFORT TO AVOID EMOTIONAL PAIN, I HAD TO AVOID MELODY.
THAT MADE ME A CRAPPY FRIEND.
THAT MUCH I UNDERSTOOD.

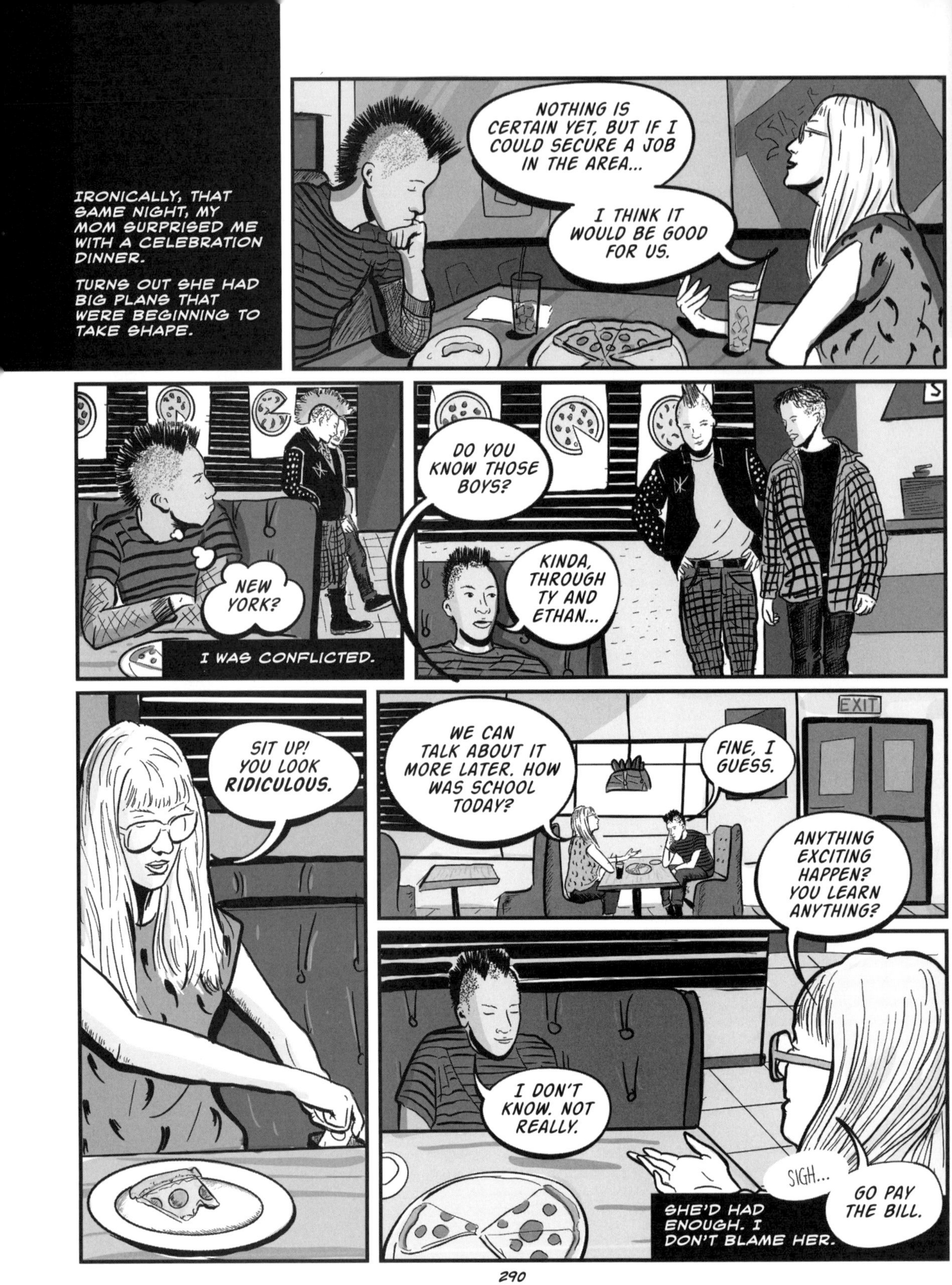
IRONICALLY, THAT SAME NIGHT, MY MOM SURPRISED ME WITH A CELEBRATION DINNER.
TURNS OUT SHE HAD BIG PLANS THAT WERE BEGINNING TO TAKE SHAPE.
NOTHING IS CERTAIN YET, BUT IF I COULD SECURE A JOB IN THE AREA...
I THINK IT WOULD BE GOOD FOR US.
NEW YORK?
I WAS CONFLICTED.
DO YOU KNOW THOSE BOYS?
KINDA, THROUGH TY AND ETHAN...
SIT UP! YOU LOOK **RIDICULOUS.**
WE CAN TALK ABOUT IT MORE LATER. HOW WAS SCHOOL TODAY?
FINE, I GUESS.
ANYTHING EXCITING HAPPEN? YOU LEARN ANYTHING?
I DON'T KNOW. NOT REALLY.
SIGH...
GO PAY THE BILL.
SHE'D HAD ENOUGH. I DON'T BLAME HER.

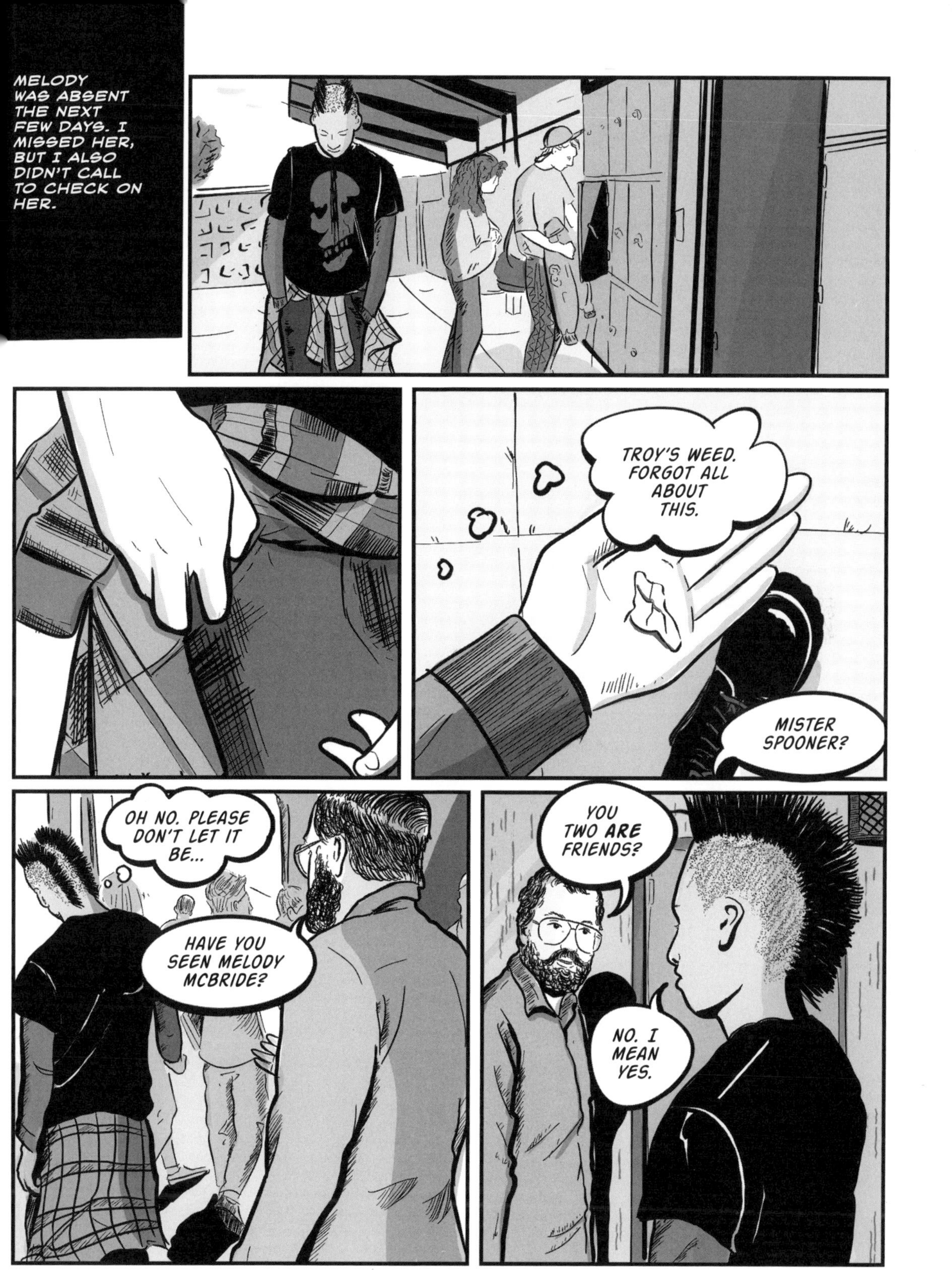
MELODY WAS ABSENT THE NEXT FEW DAYS. I MISSED HER, BUT I ALSO DIDN'T CALL TO CHECK ON HER.
TROY'S WEED. FORGOT ALL ABOUT THIS.
MISTER SPOONER?
OH NO. PLEASE DON'T LET IT BE...
HAVE YOU SEEN MELODY MCBRIDE?
YOU TWO ARE FRIENDS?
NO. I MEAN YES.

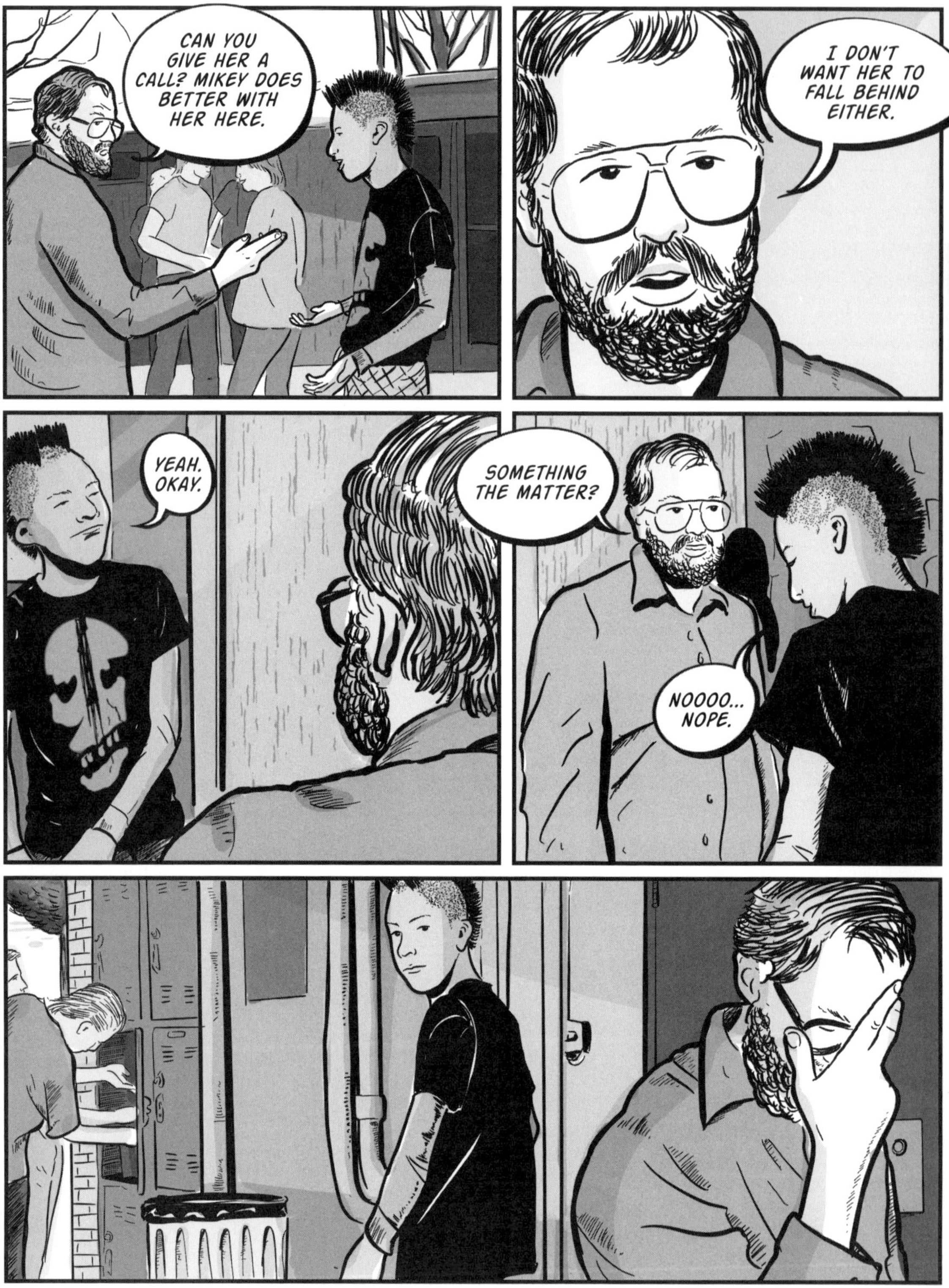
CAN YOU GIVE HER A CALL? MIKEY DOES BETTER WITH HER HERE.
I DON'T WANT HER TO FALL BEHIND EITHER.
YEAH. OKAY.
SOMETHING THE MATTER?
NOOOO... NOPE.

EVEN THOUGH MY INTERACTIONS WITH CYN WERE LIMITED, SHE WAS IMPORTANT TO A LOT OF MY FRIENDS. I KNEW EVENTUALLY I WOULD HAVE TO DEAL WITH HOW I TOTALLY GHOSTED THEM WHEN THEY NEEDED ME MOST.

LET ME GO GET HIM.

MOM? CAN'T YOU WAIT 'TIL I SAY COME IN?

SORRY...

HONEY, WHY DIDN'T YOU TELL ME ONE OF YOUR LITTLE FRIENDS DIED?

HUH? HOW...

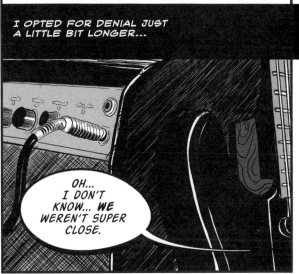

I OPTED FOR DENIAL JUST A LITTLE BIT LONGER...

OH... I DON'T KNOW... WE WEREN'T SUPER CLOSE.

293

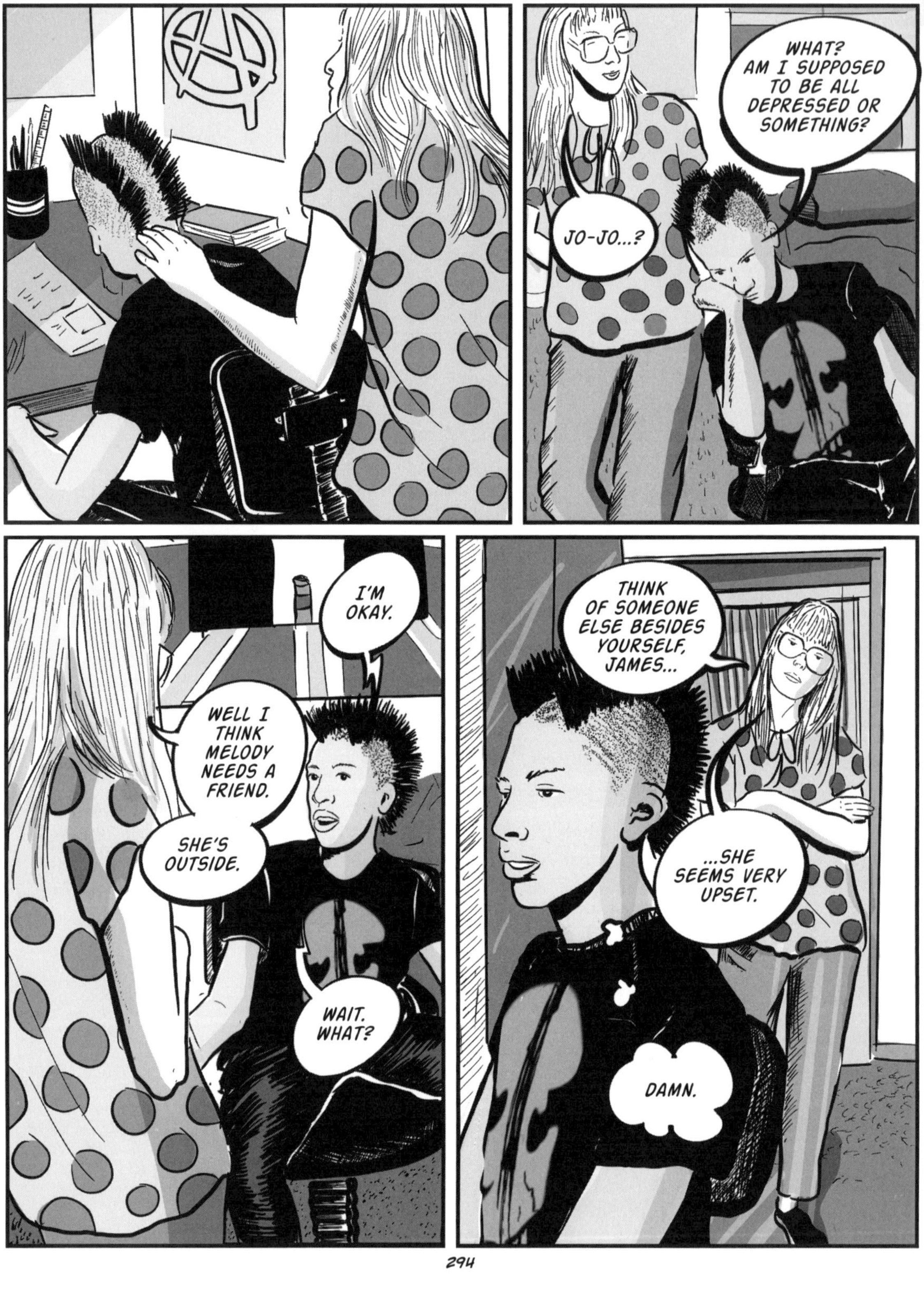
WHAT? AM I SUPPOSED TO BE ALL DEPRESSED OR SOMETHING?
JO-JO...?
I'M OKAY.
WELL I THINK MELODY NEEDS A FRIEND.
SHE'S OUTSIDE.
WAIT. WHAT?
THINK OF SOMEONE ELSE BESIDES YOURSELF, JAMES...
...SHE SEEMS VERY UPSET.
DAMN.

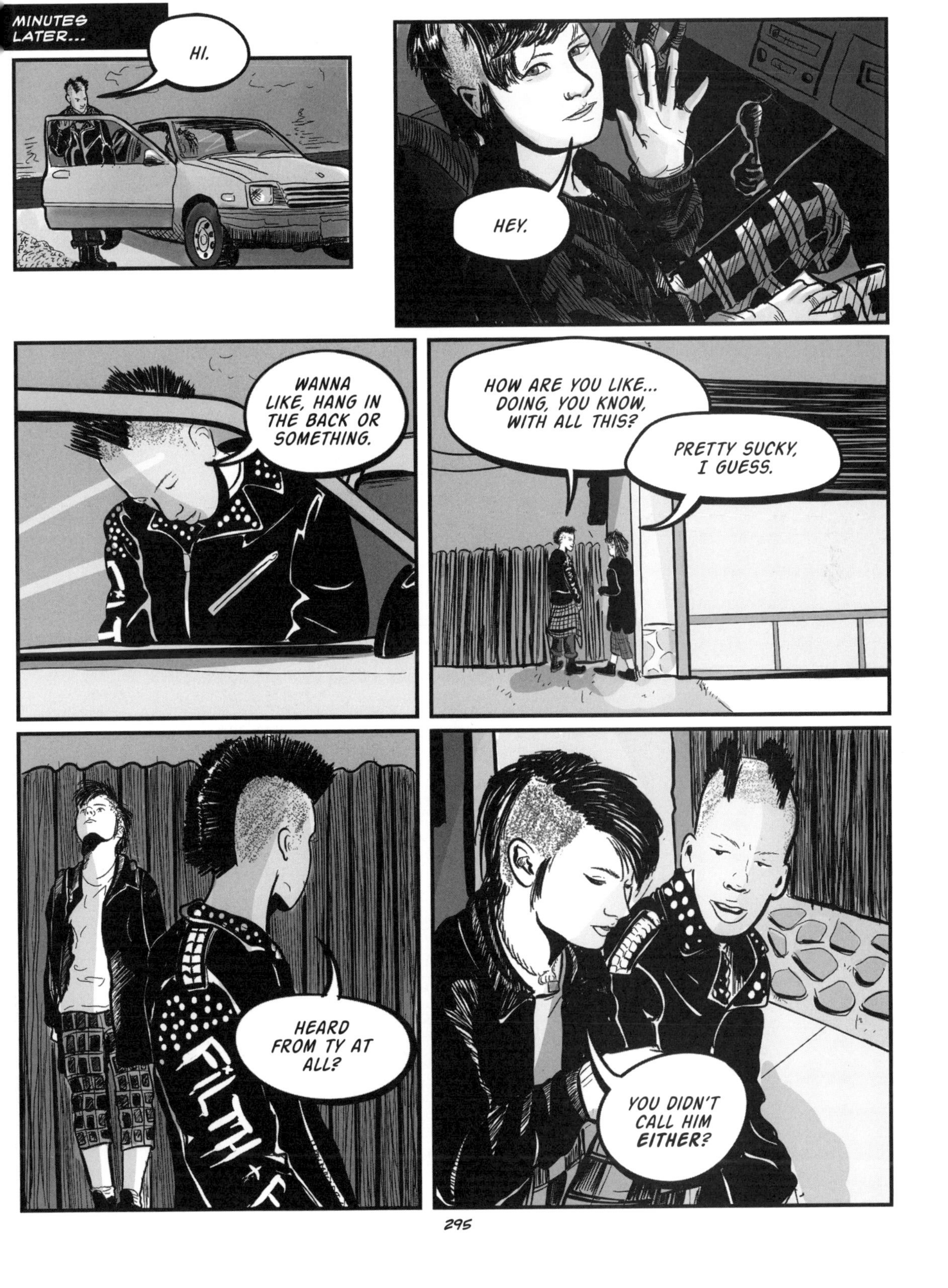
MINUTES LATER...
HI.
HEY.
WANNA LIKE, HANG IN THE BACK OR SOMETHING.
HOW ARE YOU LIKE... DOING, YOU KNOW, WITH ALL THIS?
PRETTY SUCKY, I GUESS.
HEARD FROM TY AT ALL?
YOU DIDN'T CALL HIM EITHER?

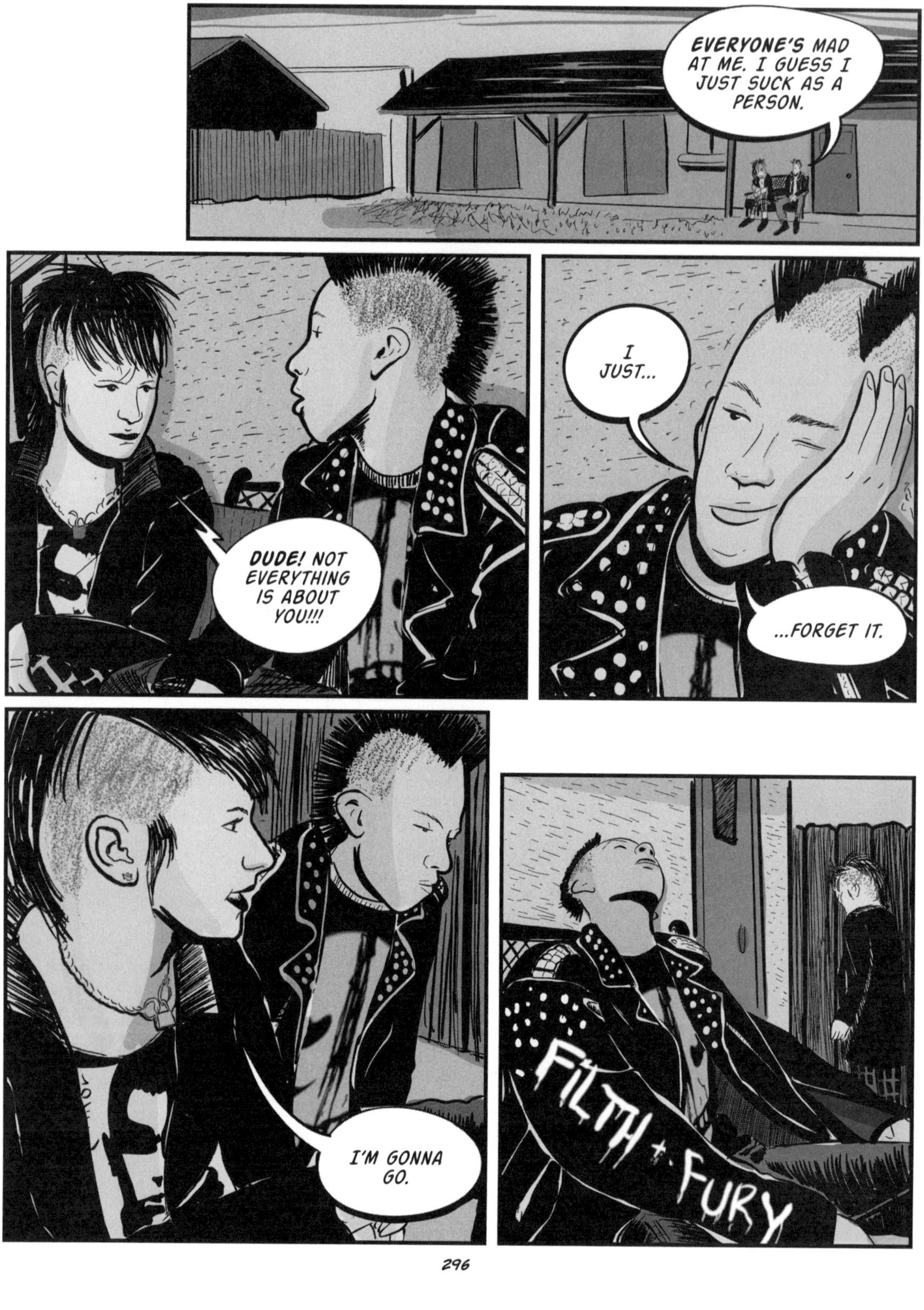
EVERYONE'S MAD AT ME. I GUESS I JUST SUCK AS A PERSON.
DUDE! NOT EVERYTHING IS ABOUT YOU!!!
I JUST...
...FORGET IT.
I'M GONNA GO.
FILTH + FURY

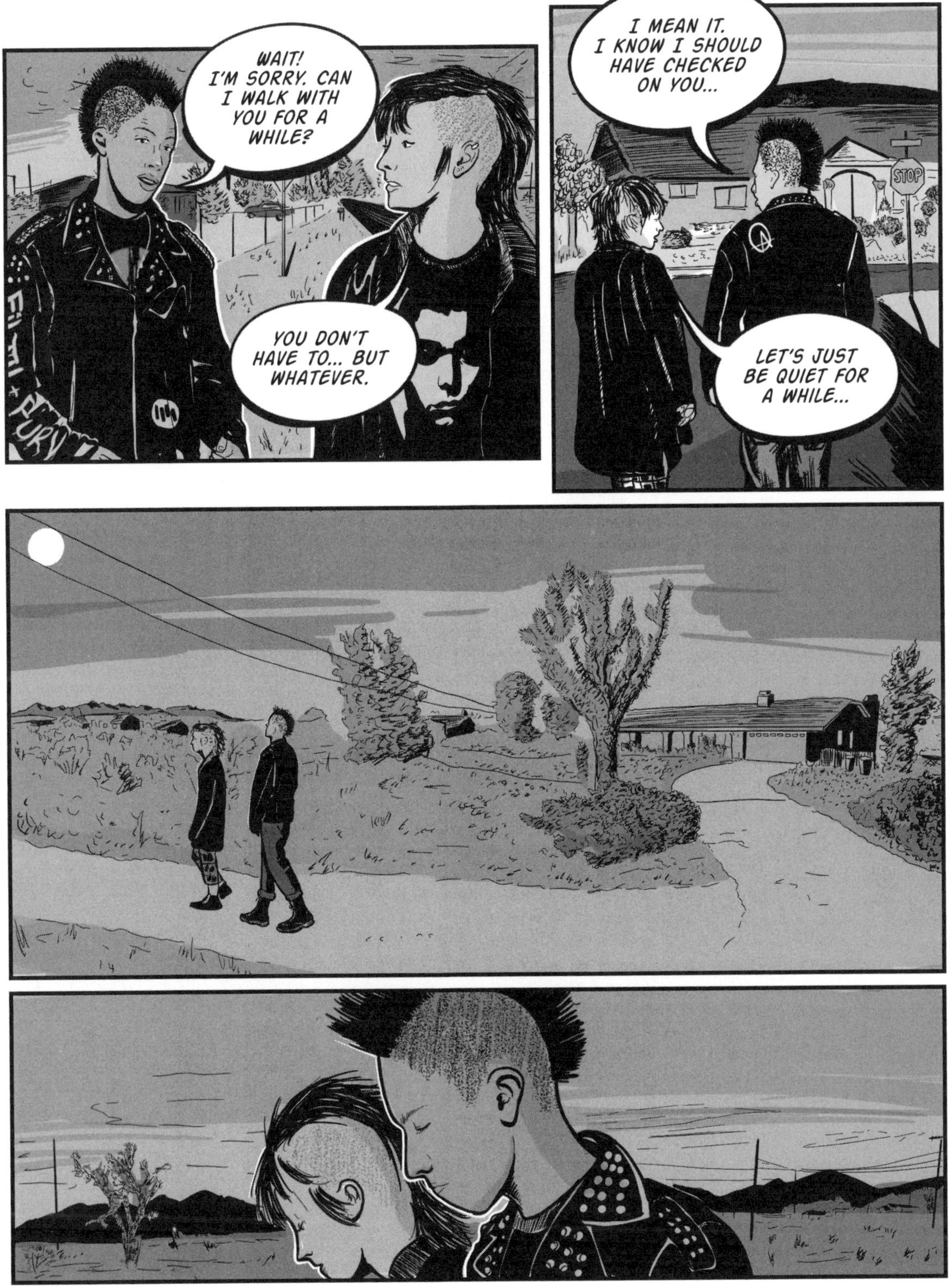
WAIT! I'M SORRY. CAN I WALK WITH YOU FOR A WHILE?
YOU DON'T HAVE TO... BUT WHATEVER.
I MEAN IT. I KNOW I SHOULD HAVE CHECKED ON YOU...
LET'S JUST BE QUIET FOR A WHILE...
STOP

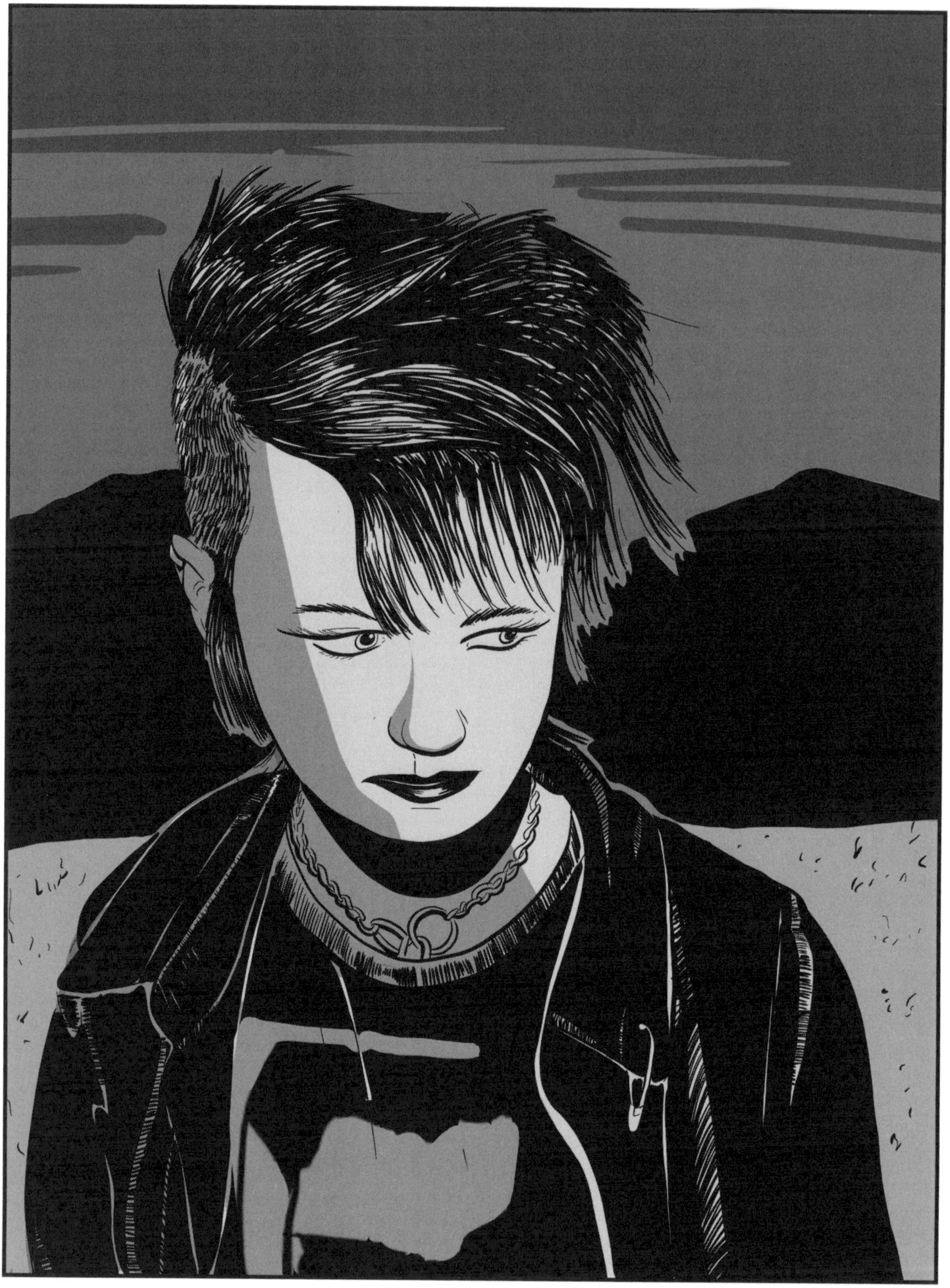

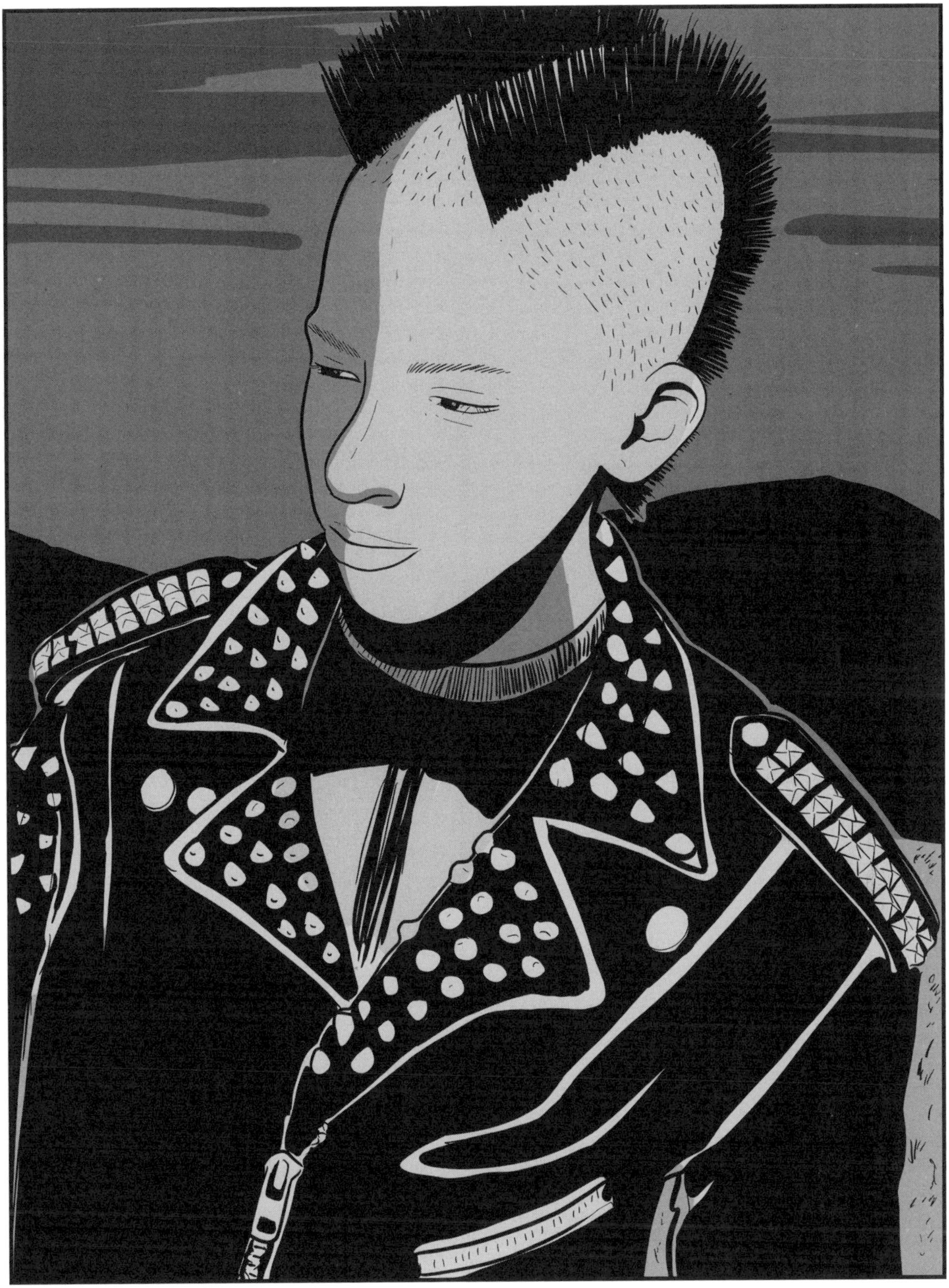

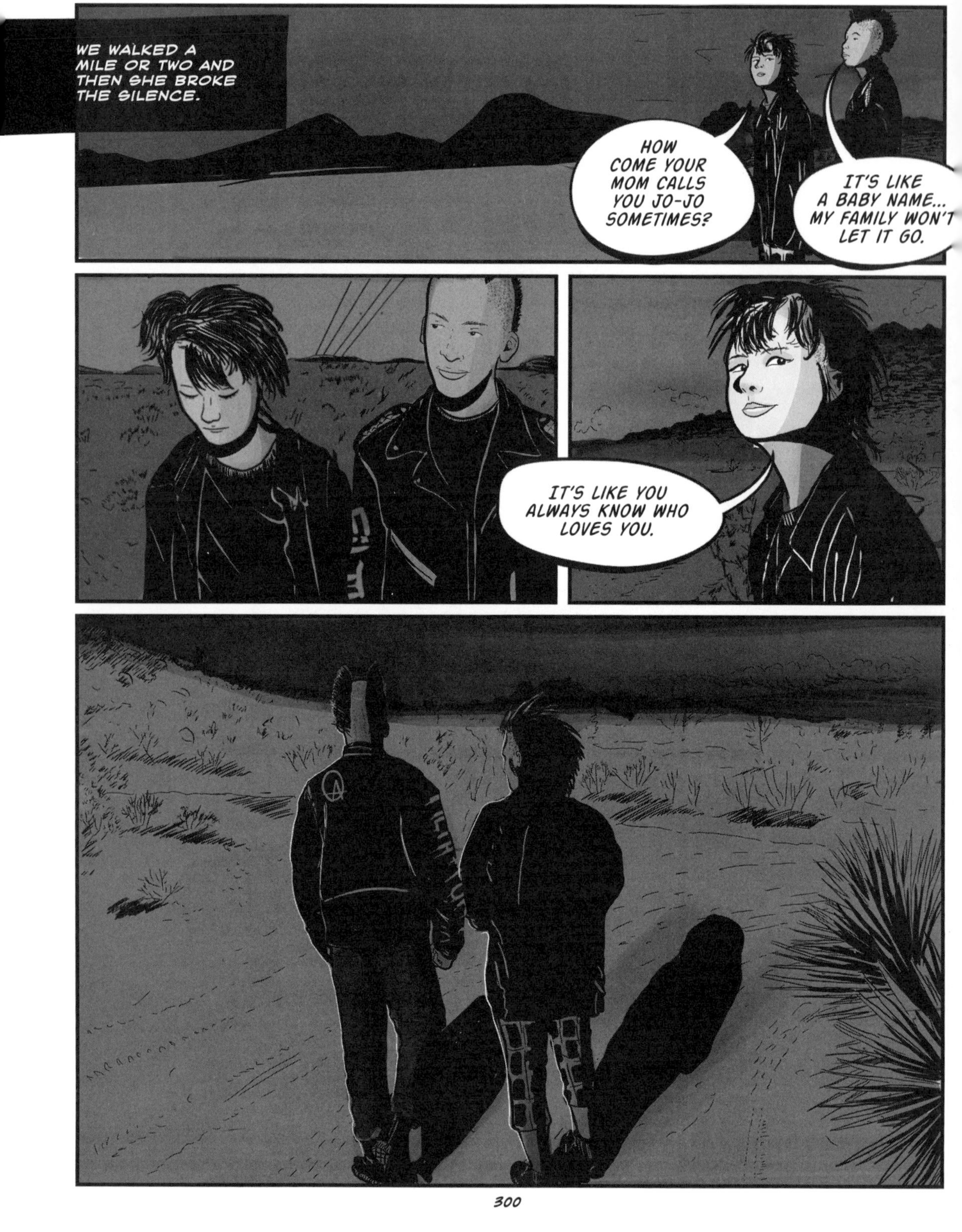
WE WALKED A MILE OR TWO AND THEN SHE BROKE THE SILENCE.
HOW COME YOUR MOM CALLS YOU JO-JO SOMETIMES?
IT'S LIKE A BABY NAME... MY FAMILY WON'T LET IT GO.
IT'S LIKE YOU ALWAYS KNOW WHO LOVES YOU.

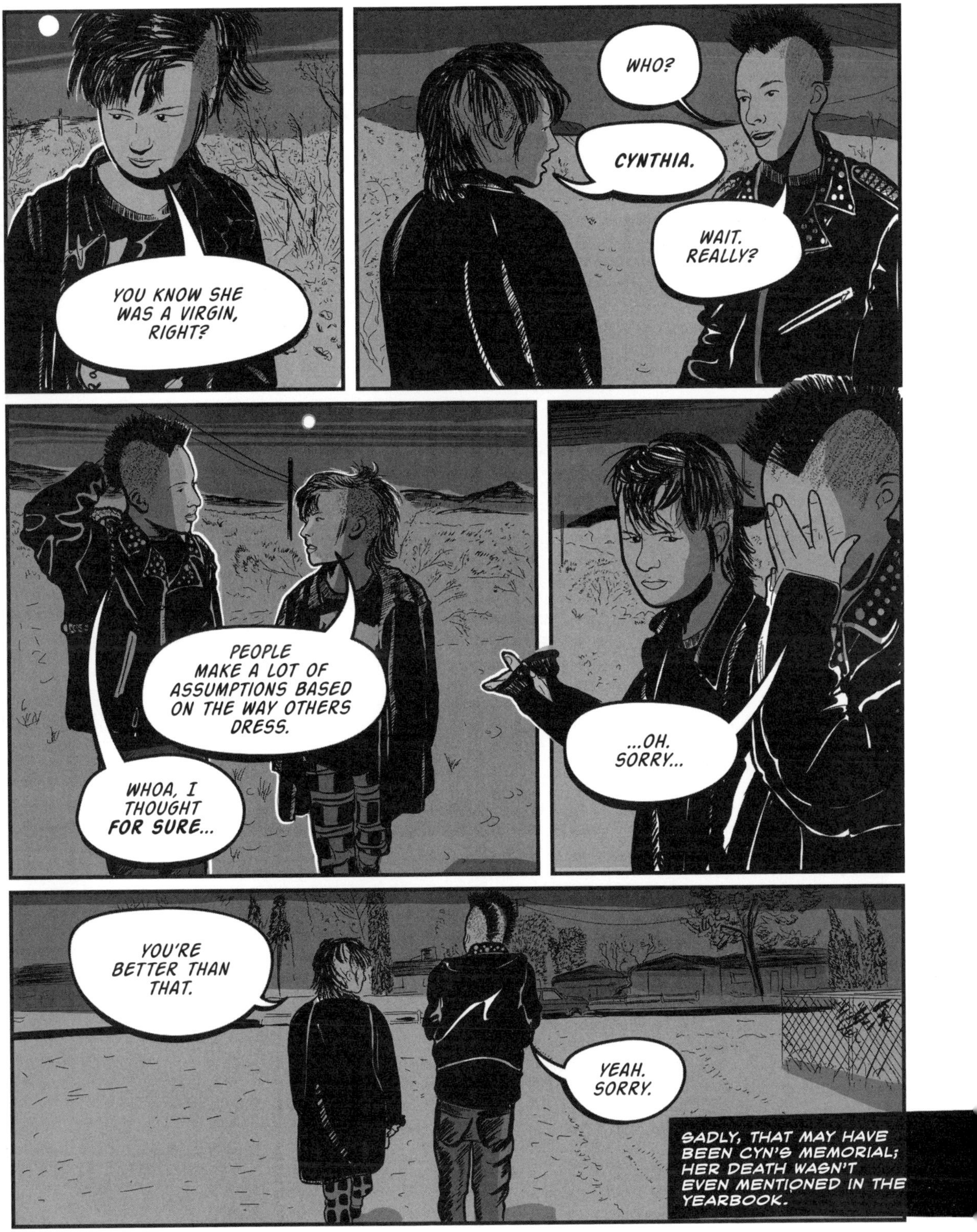
YOU KNOW SHE WAS A VIRGIN, RIGHT?
WHO?
CYNTHIA.
WAIT. REALLY?
PEOPLE MAKE A LOT OF ASSUMPTIONS BASED ON THE WAY OTHERS DRESS.
WHOA, I THOUGHT FOR SURE...
...OH. SORRY...
YOU'RE BETTER THAN THAT.
YEAH. SORRY.
SADLY, THAT MAY HAVE BEEN CYN'S MEMORIAL; HER DEATH WASN'T EVEN MENTIONED IN THE YEARBOOK.

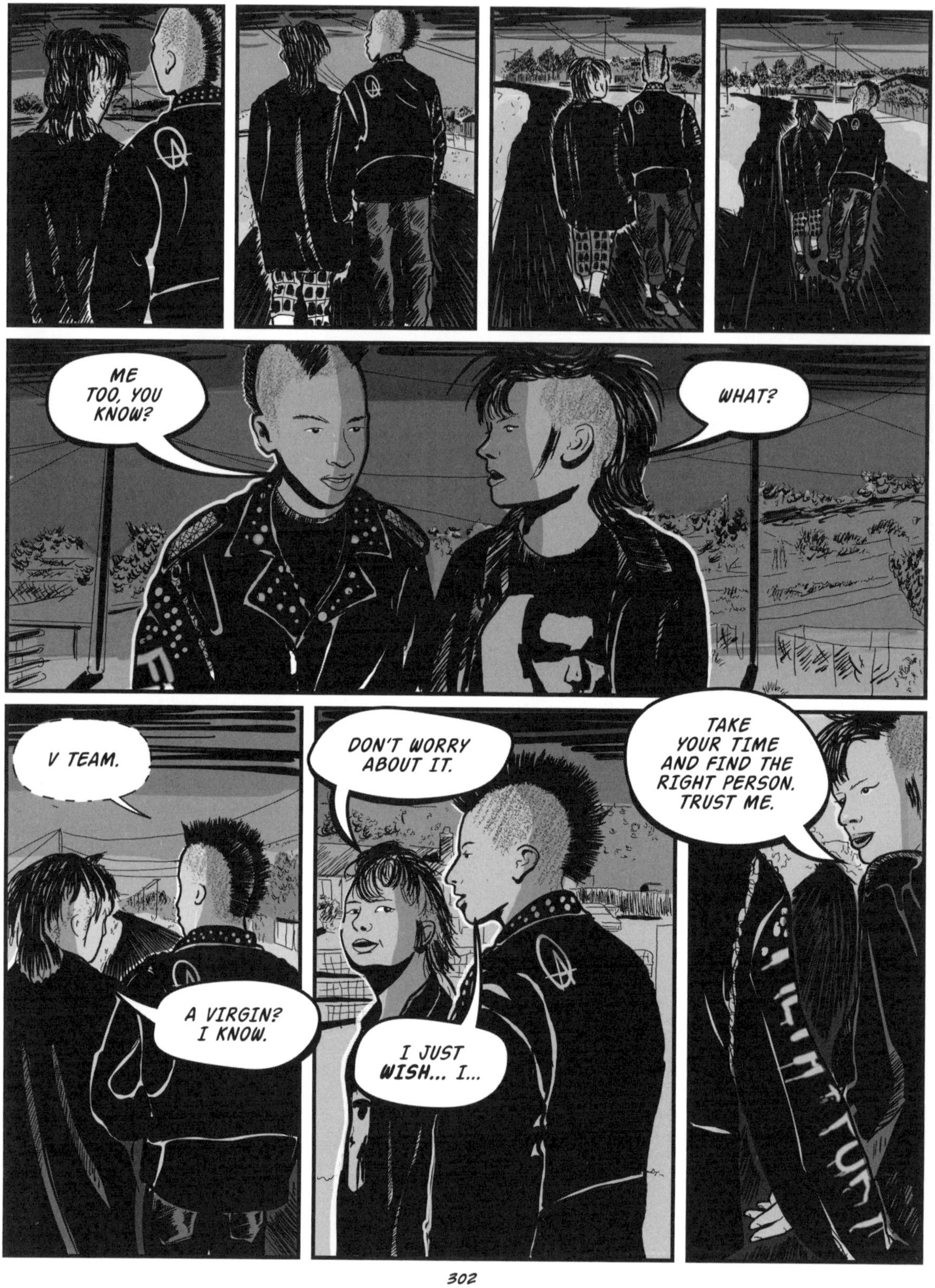
ME TOO, YOU KNOW?
WHAT?
V TEAM.
A VIRGIN? I KNOW.
DON'T WORRY ABOUT IT.
I JUST WISH... I...
TAKE YOUR TIME AND FIND THE RIGHT PERSON. TRUST ME.

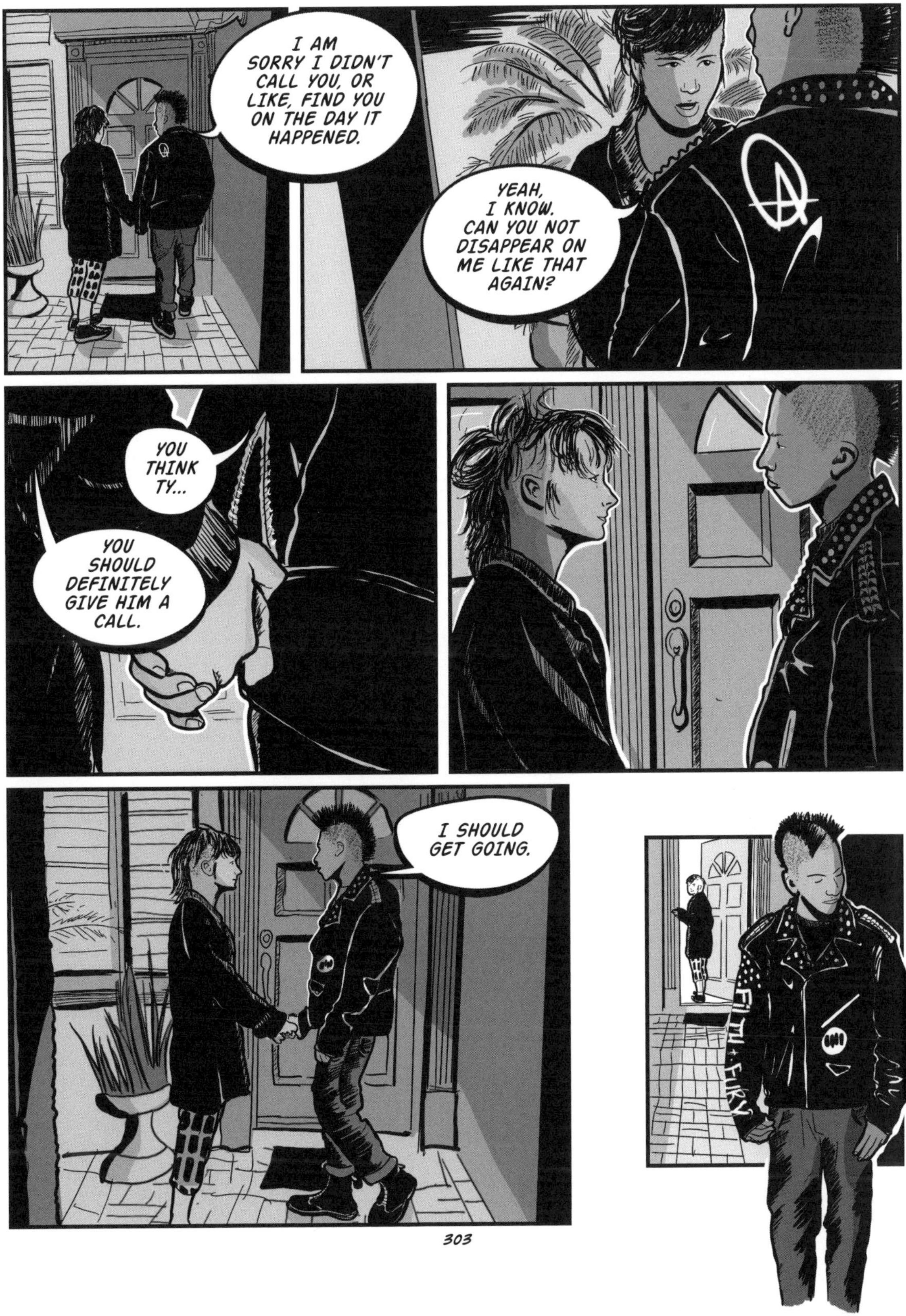
I AM SORRY I DIDN'T CALL YOU, OR LIKE, FIND YOU ON THE DAY IT HAPPENED.
YEAH, I KNOW. CAN YOU NOT DISAPPEAR ON ME LIKE THAT AGAIN?
YOU THINK TY...
YOU SHOULD DEFINITELY GIVE HIM A CALL.
I SHOULD GET GOING.
FILTH + FURY

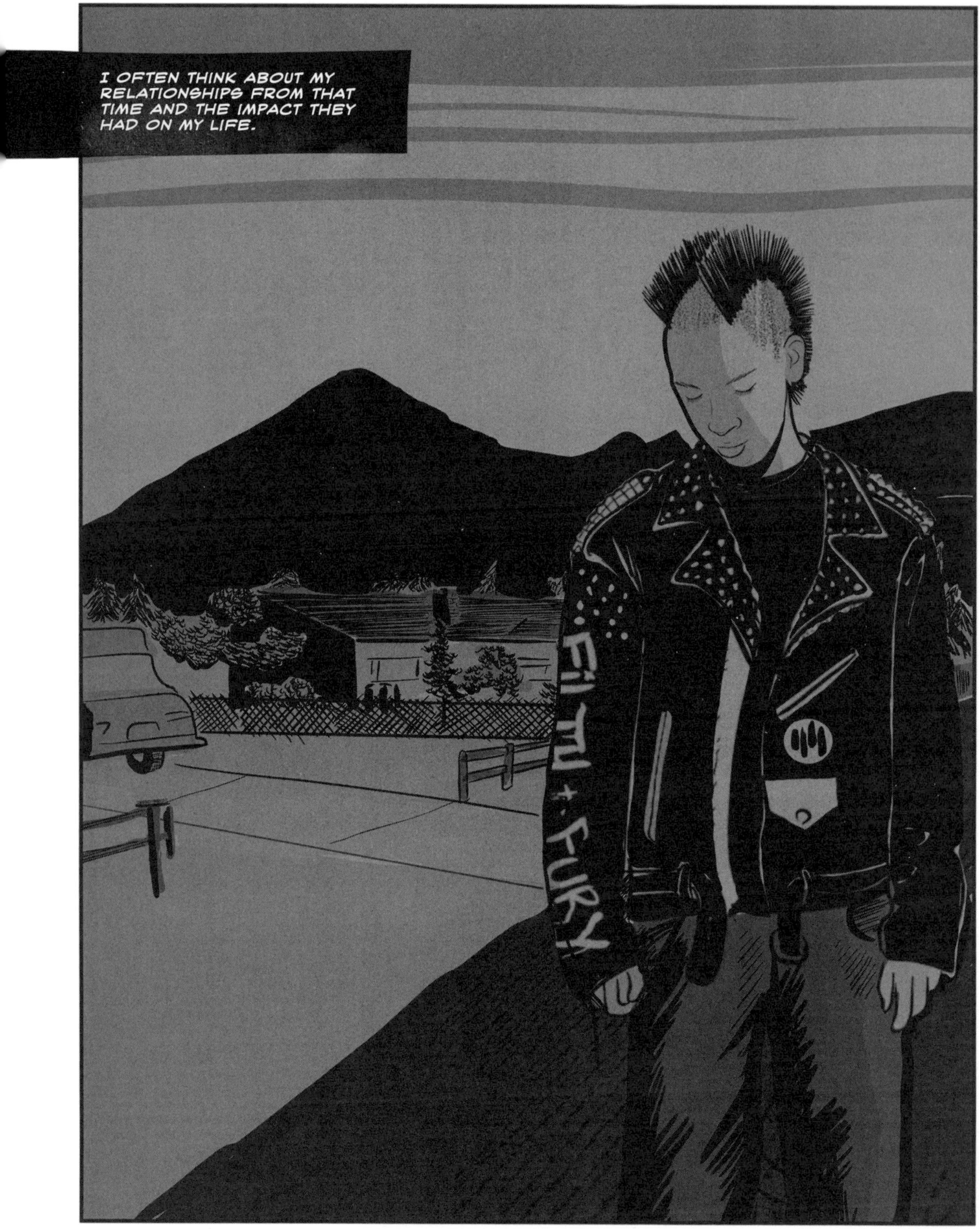
I OFTEN THINK ABOUT MY RELATIONSHIPS FROM THAT TIME AND THE IMPACT THEY HAD ON MY LIFE.
FURY

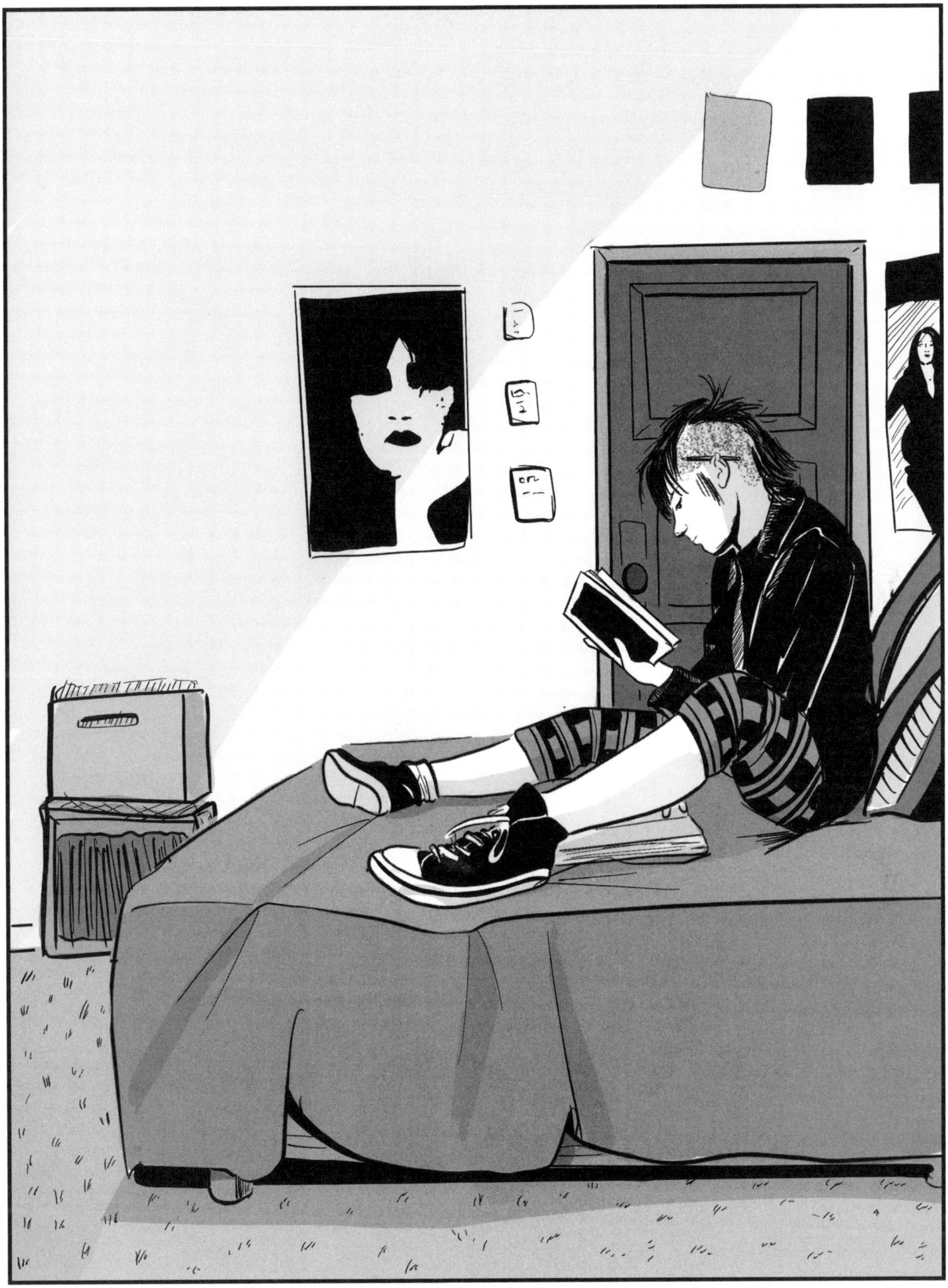

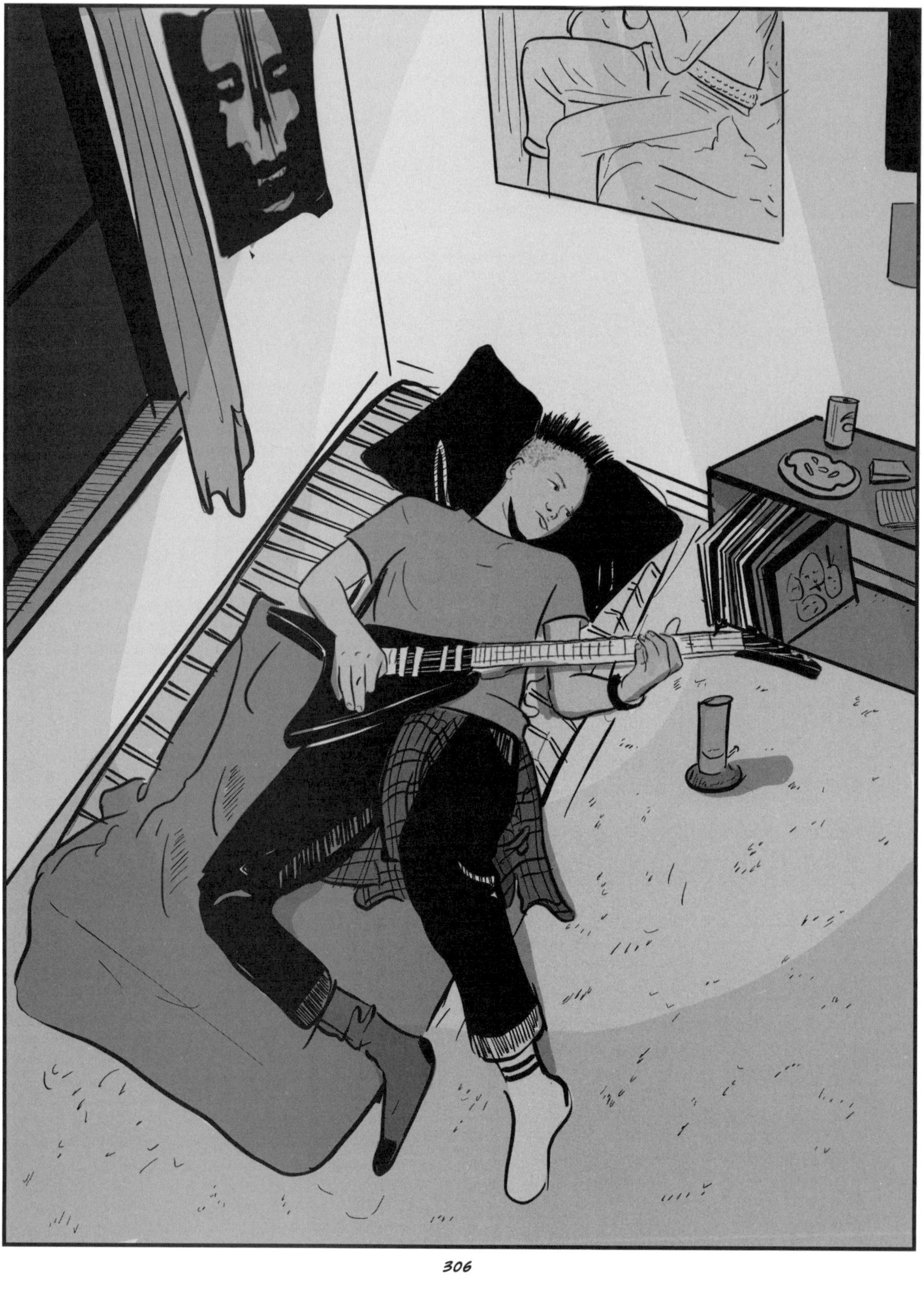

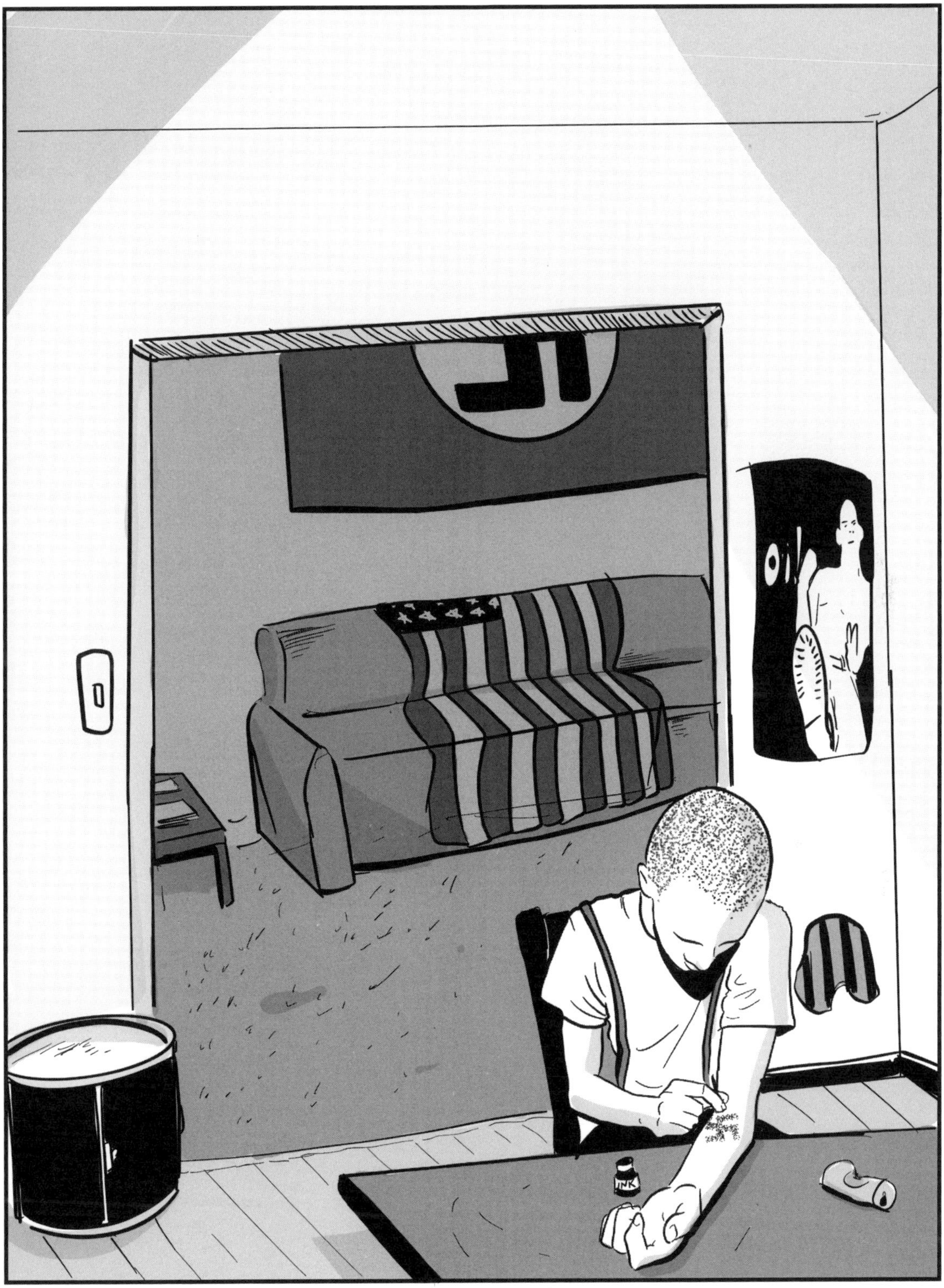
INK

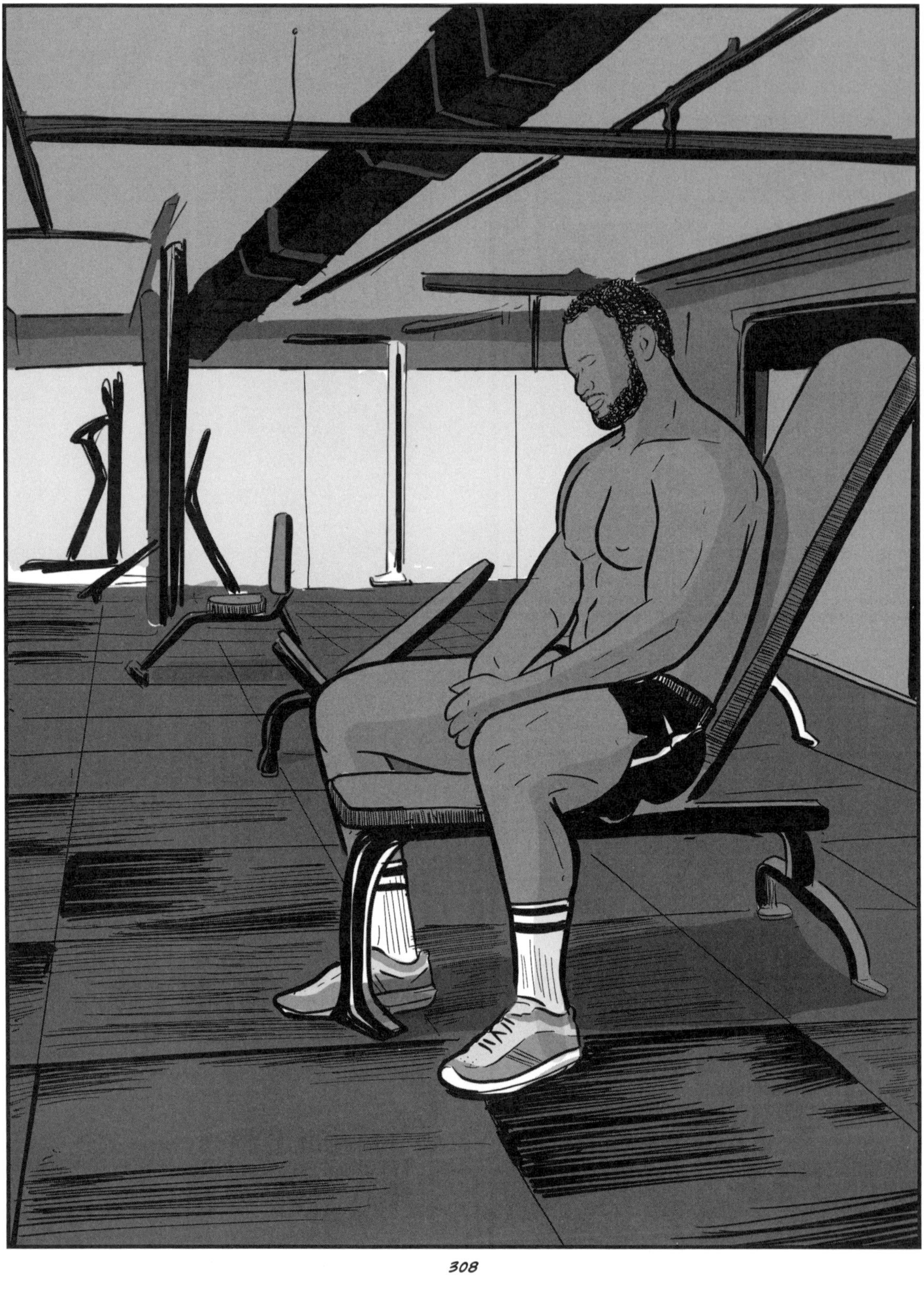

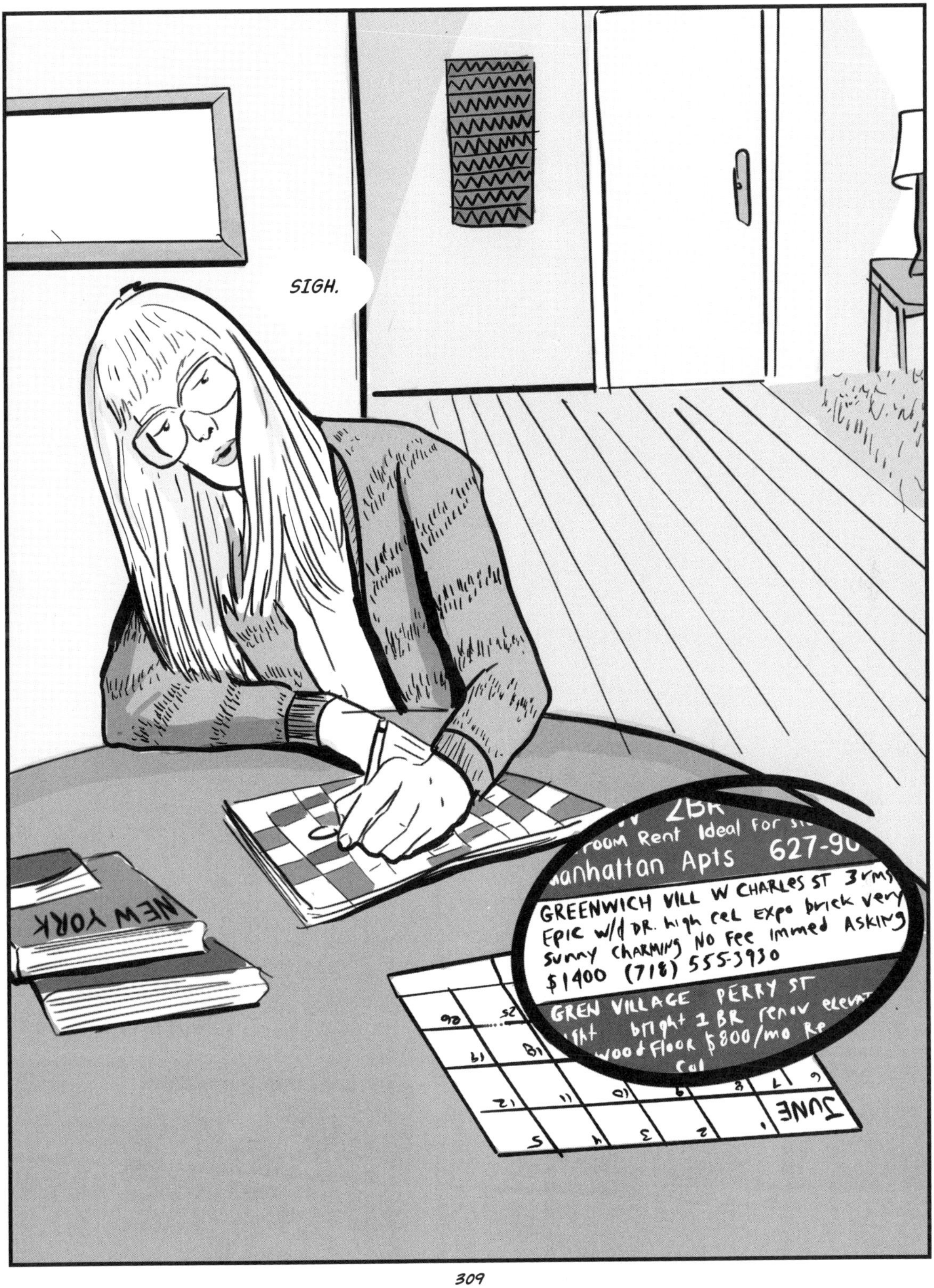
SIGH.
NEW YORK
Rent Ideal For
Apts 627-90
GREENWICH VILL W CHARLES ST
Epic w/d DR. high cel Expo brick very
Sunny Charming No Fee Immed Asking
$1400 (718) 555-3930
GREN VILLAGE PERRY ST
bright 1 BR renov
wood Floor $800/mo
JUNE

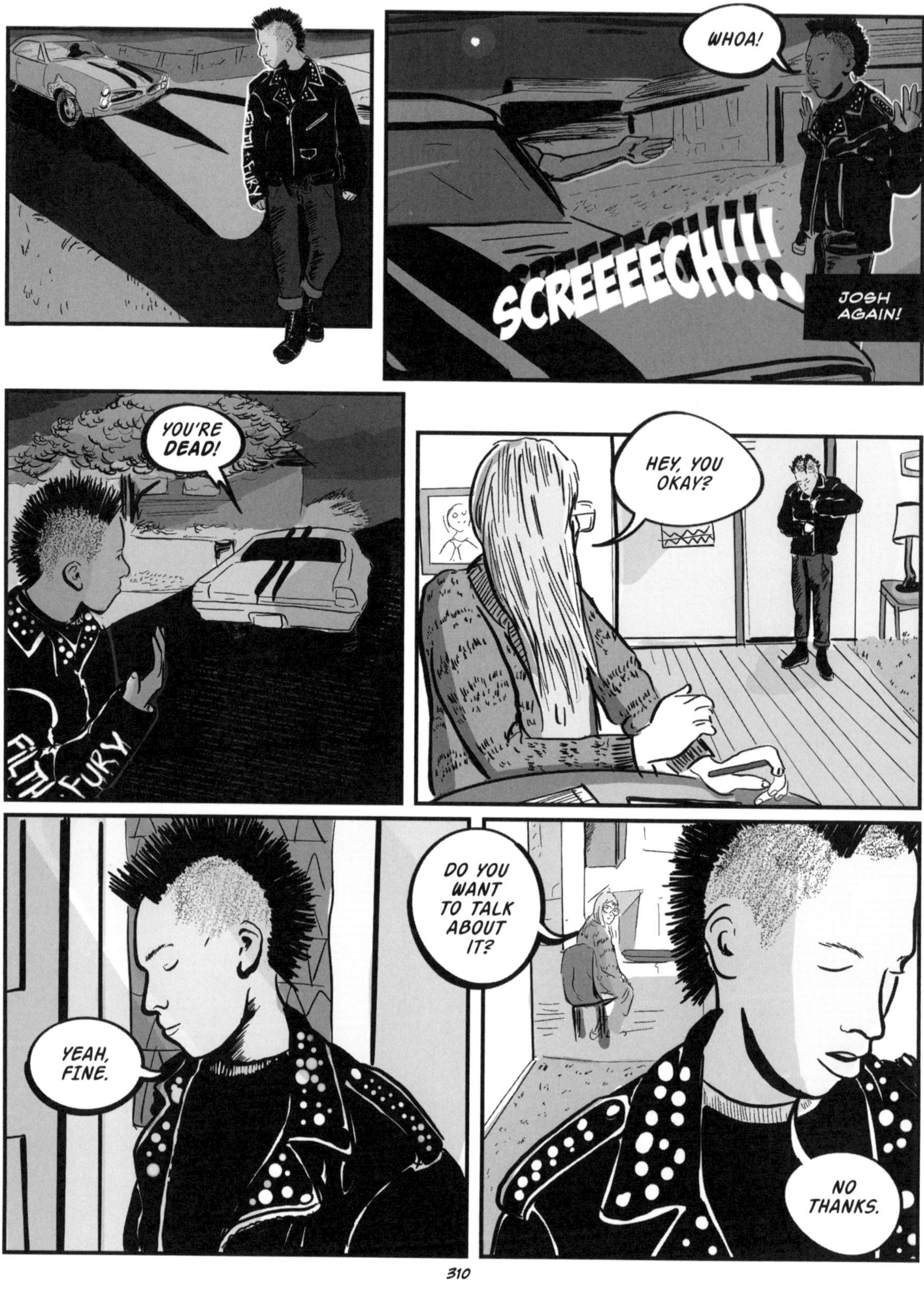
FILTH FURY
WHOA!
SCREEEEECH!!!
JOSH AGAIN!
YOU'RE DEAD!
FILTH FURY
HEY, YOU OKAY?
YEAH, FINE.
DO YOU WANT TO TALK ABOUT IT?
NO THANKS.

CHAPTER 9
WHO'S GOT THE 10½?

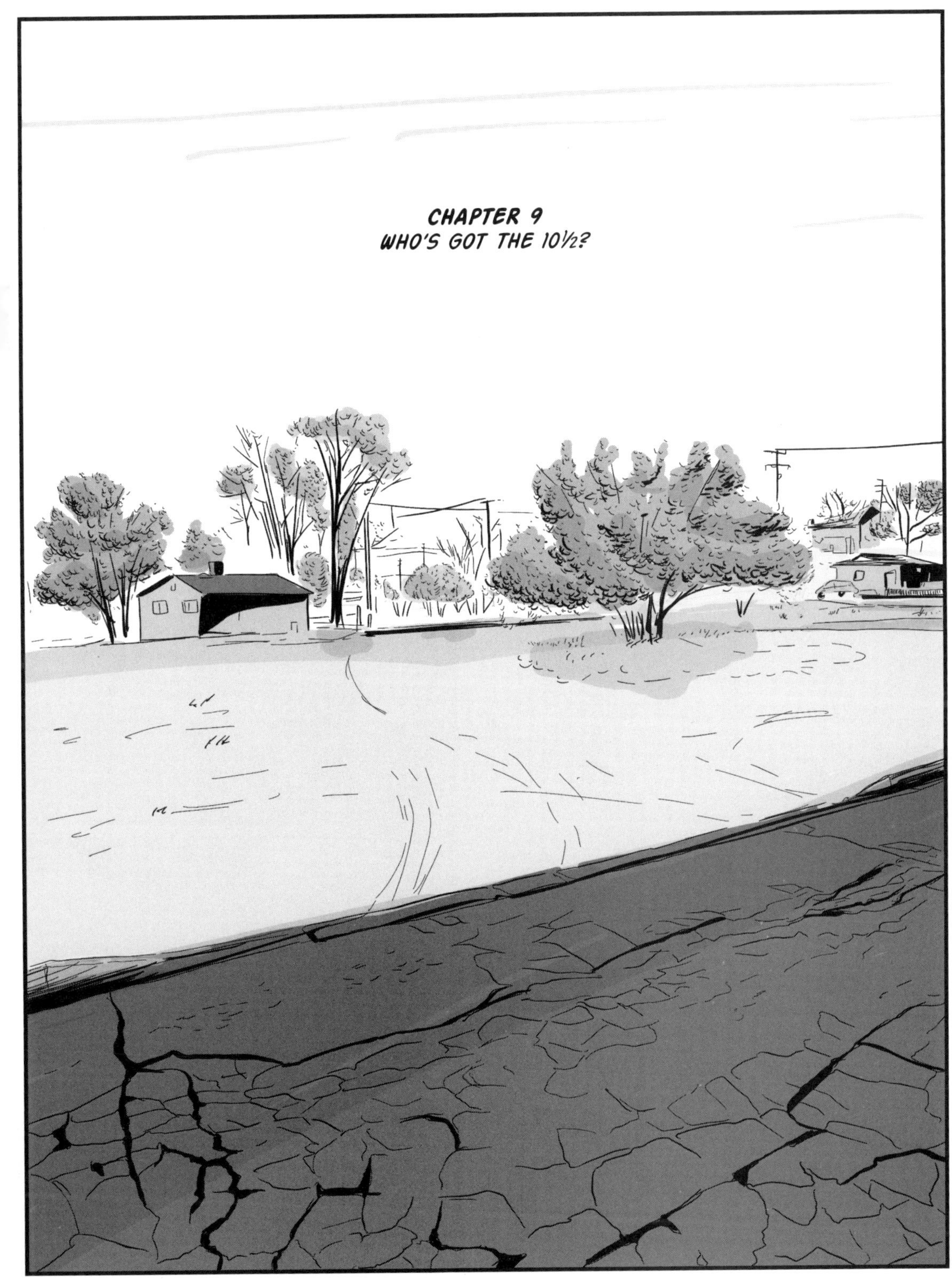

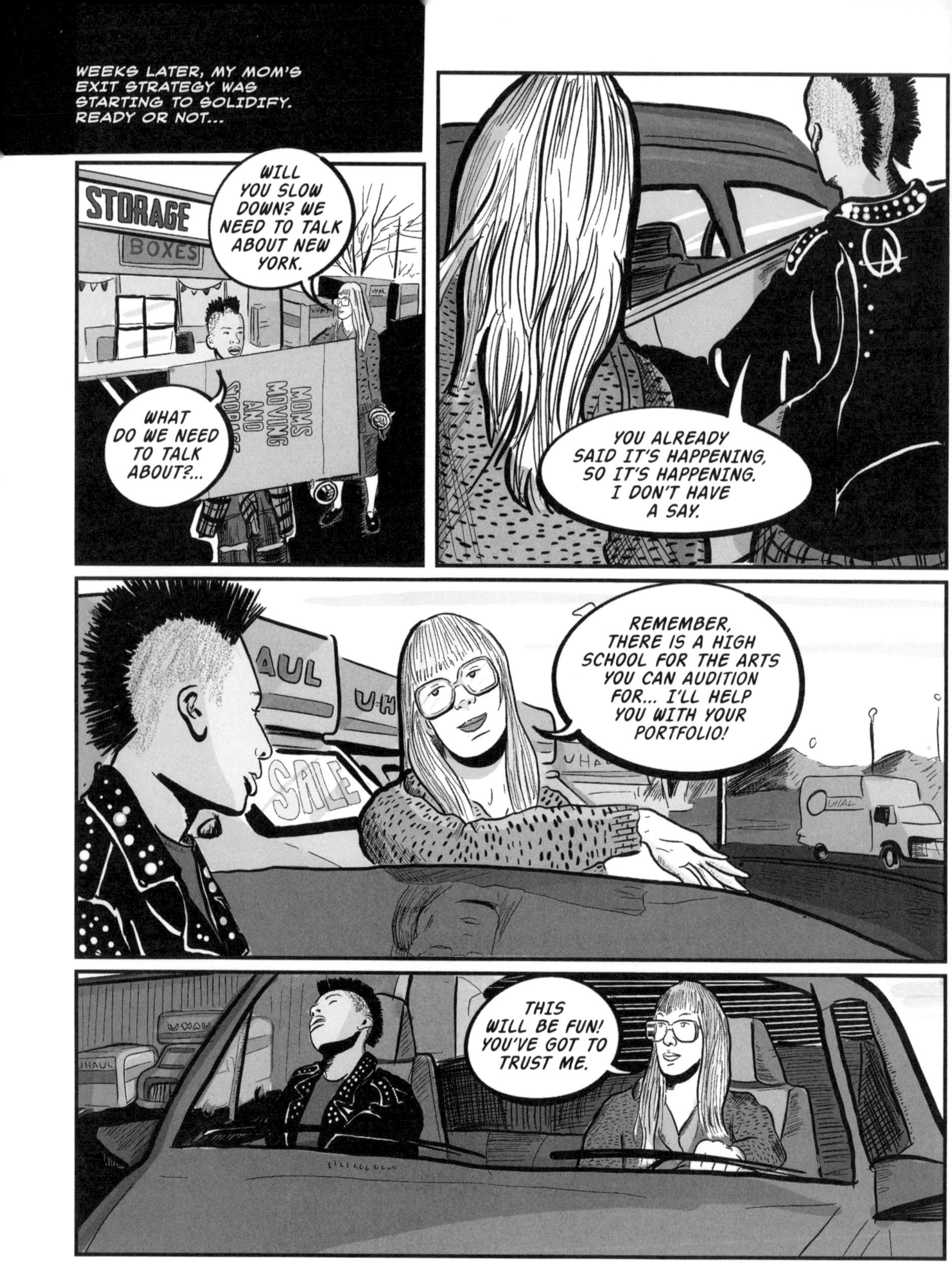
WEEKS LATER, MY MOM'S EXIT STRATEGY WAS STARTING TO SOLIDIFY. READY OR NOT...
STORAGE
BOXES
WILL YOU SLOW DOWN? WE NEED TO TALK ABOUT NEW YORK.
MOMS MOVING AND
WHAT DO WE NEED TO TALK ABOUT?...
YOU ALREADY SAID IT'S HAPPENING, SO IT'S HAPPENING. I DON'T HAVE A SAY.
REMEMBER, THERE IS A HIGH SCHOOL FOR THE ARTS YOU CAN AUDITION FOR... I'LL HELP YOU WITH YOUR PORTFOLIO!
SALE
THIS WILL BE FUN! YOU'VE GOT TO TRUST ME.

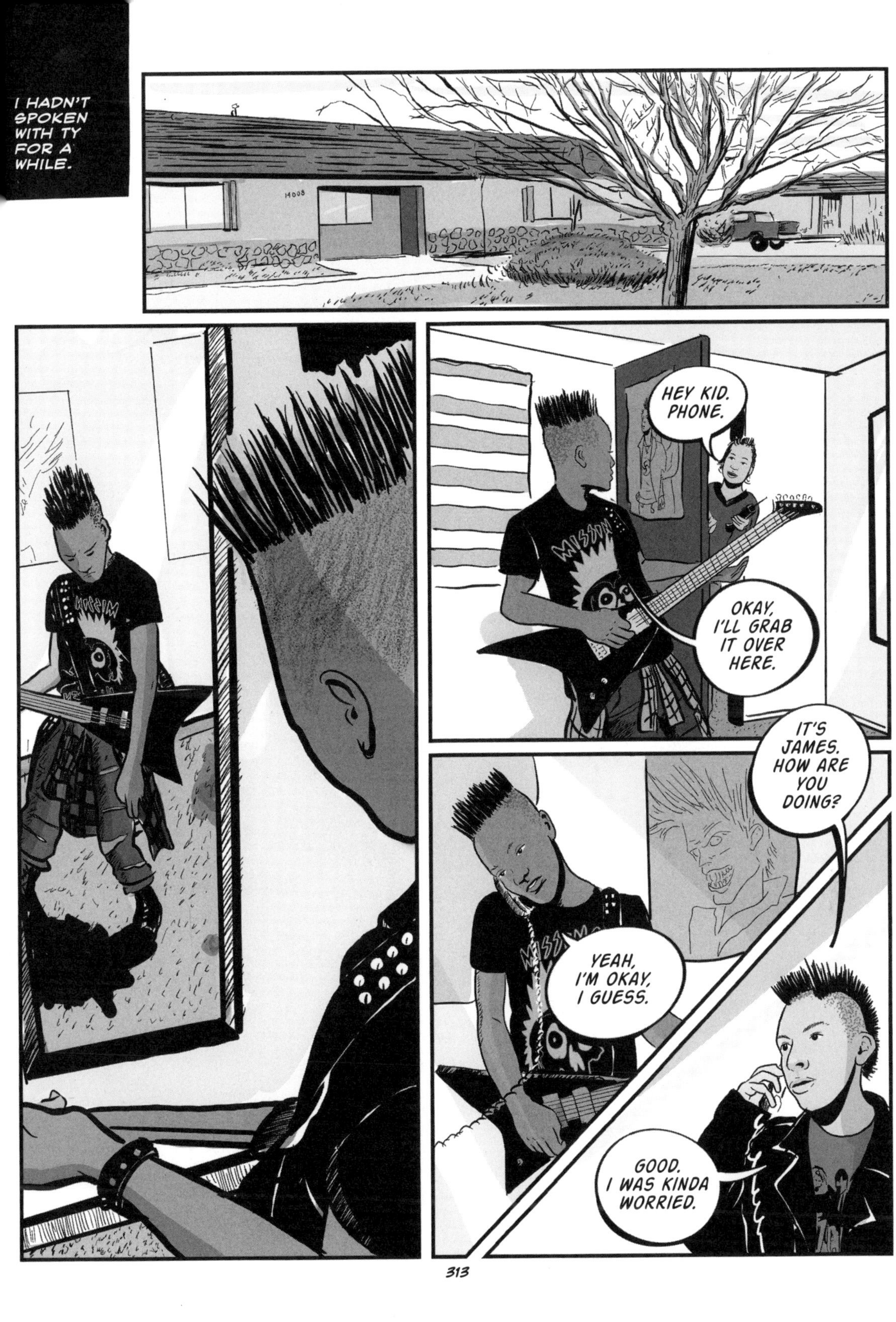
I HADN'T SPOKEN WITH TY FOR A WHILE.
HEY KID. PHONE.
OKAY, I'LL GRAB IT OVER HERE.
IT'S JAMES. HOW ARE YOU DOING?
YEAH, I'M OKAY, I GUESS.
GOOD. I WAS KINDA WORRIED.

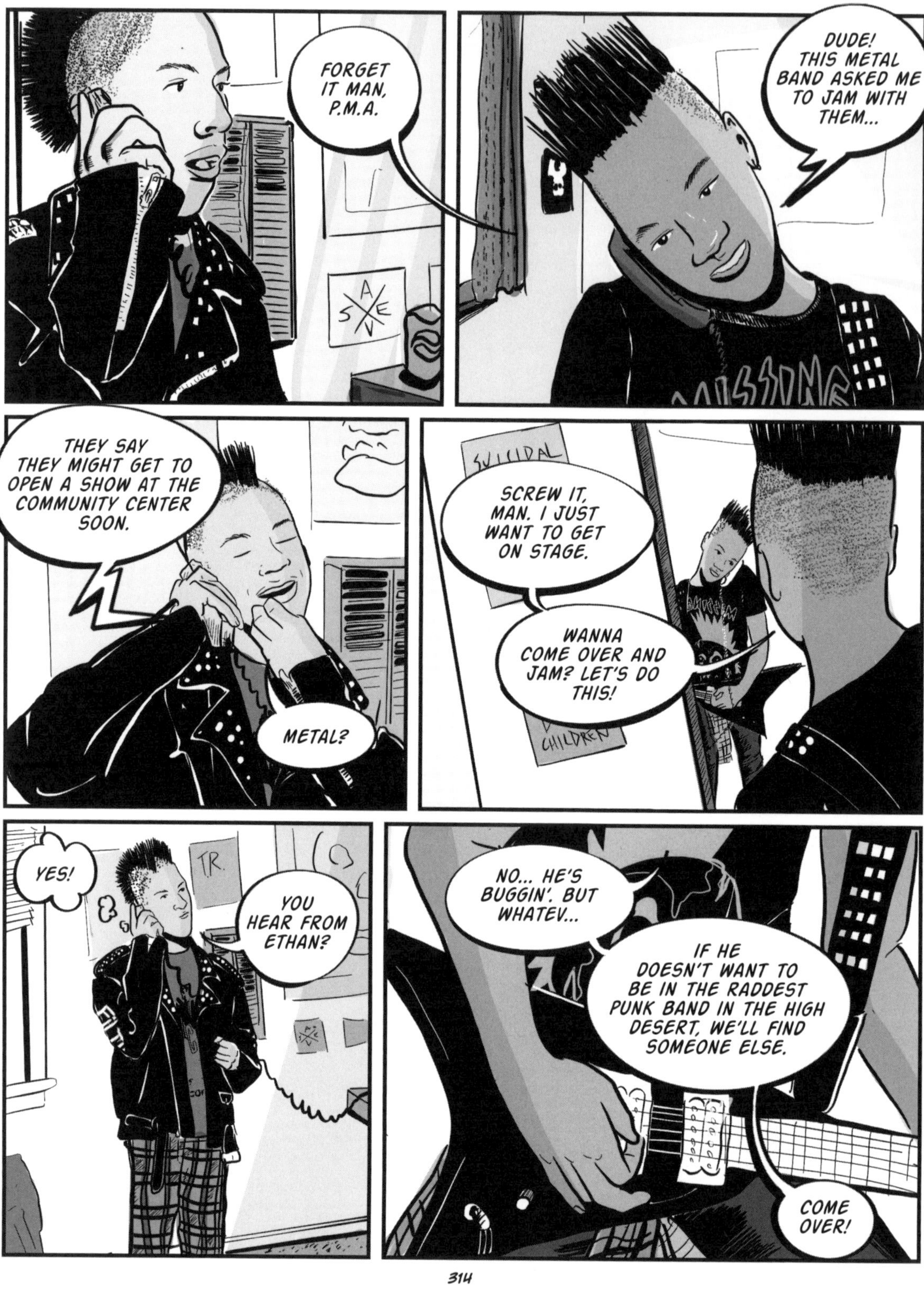
FORGET IT MAN, P.M.A.
DUDE! THIS METAL BAND ASKED ME TO JAM WITH THEM...
THEY SAY THEY MIGHT GET TO OPEN A SHOW AT THE COMMUNITY CENTER SOON.
METAL?
SCREW IT, MAN. I JUST WANT TO GET ON STAGE.
WANNA COME OVER AND JAM? LET'S DO THIS!
YES!
YOU HEAR FROM ETHAN?
NO... HE'S BUGGIN'. BUT WHATEV...
IF HE DOESN'T WANT TO BE IN THE RADDEST PUNK BAND IN THE HIGH DESERT, WE'LL FIND SOMEONE ELSE.
COME OVER!

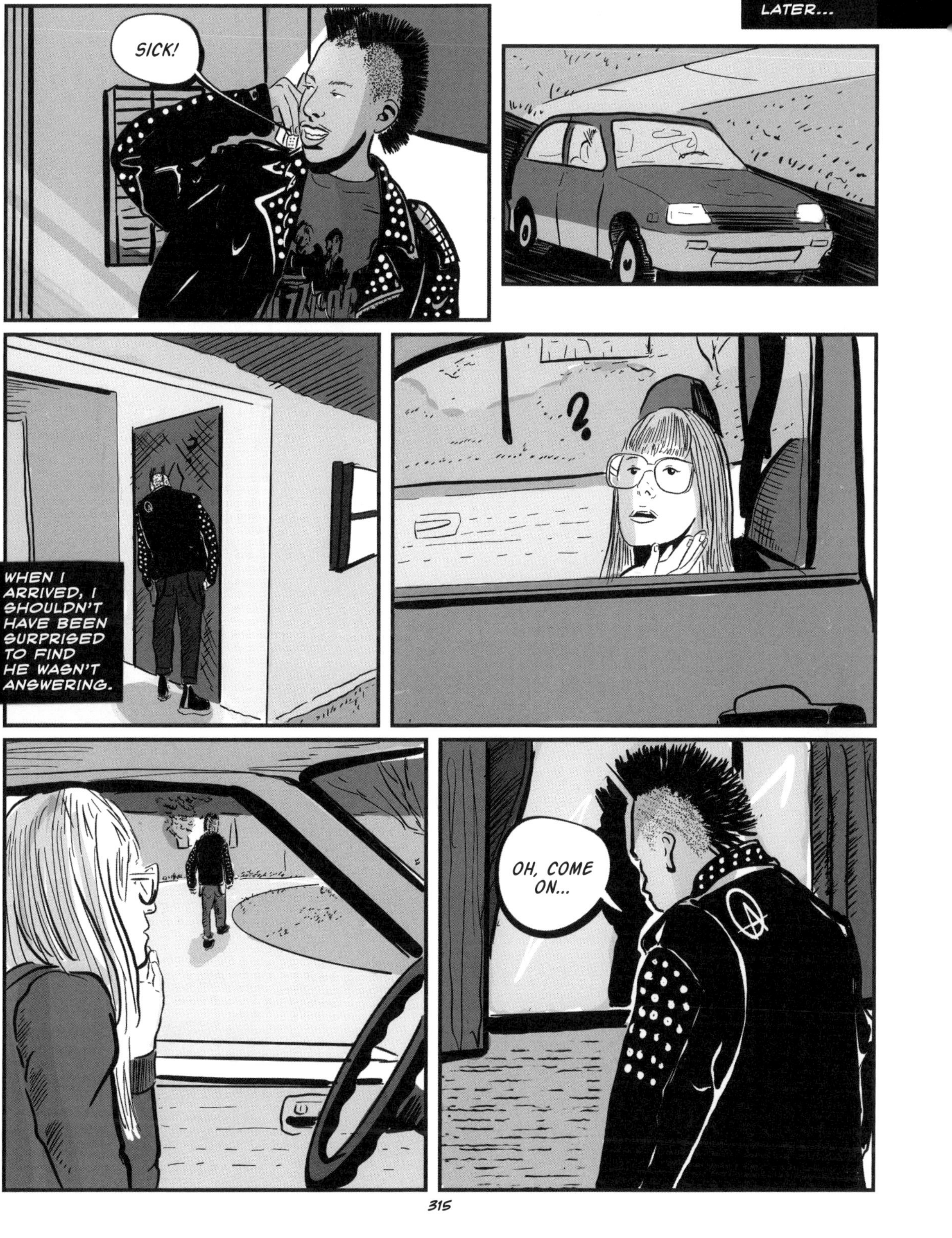
SICK!
LATER...
WHEN I ARRIVED, I SHOULDN'T HAVE BEEN SURPRISED TO FIND HE WASN'T ANSWERING.
?
OH, COME ON...

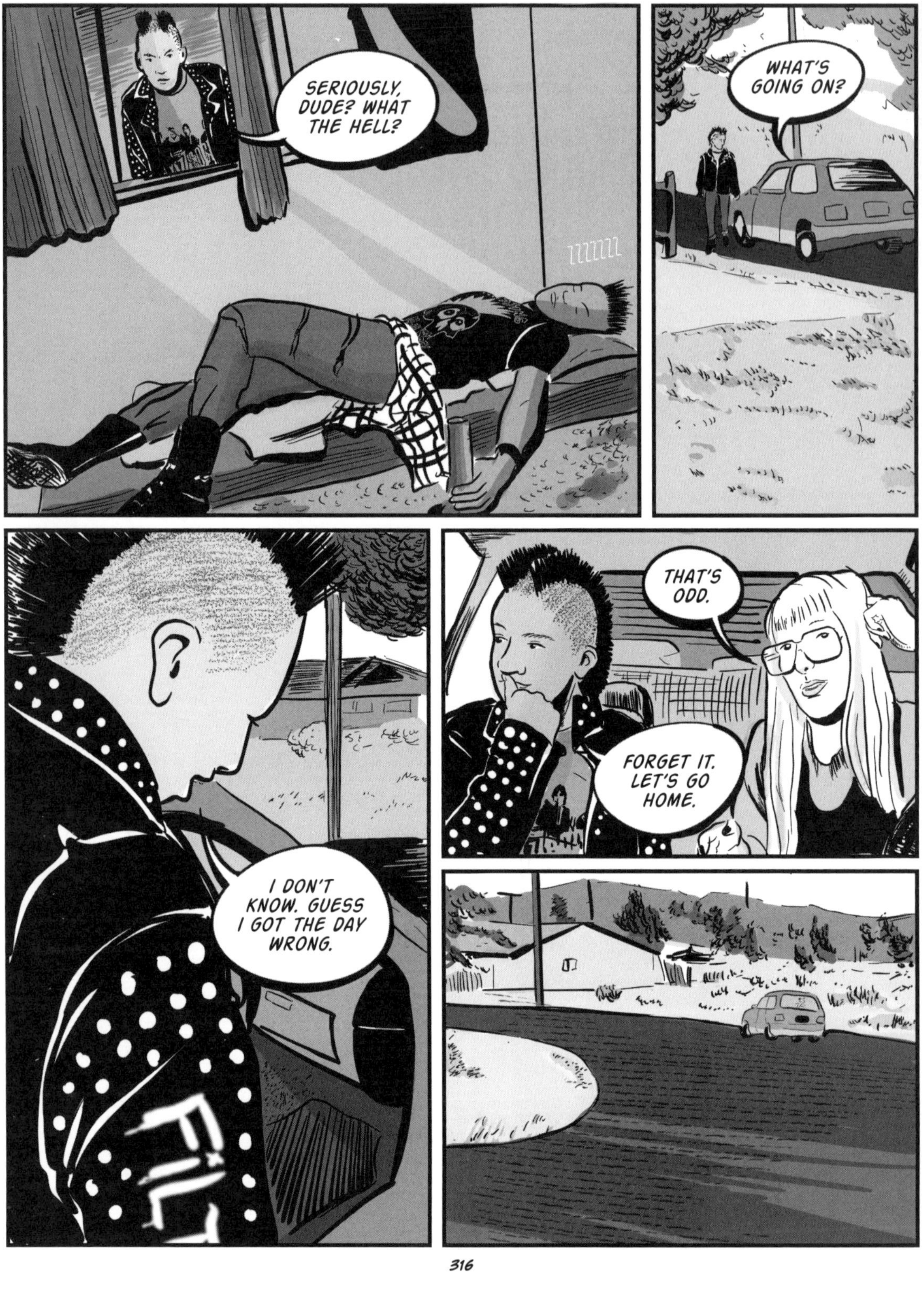
SERIOUSLY, DUDE? WHAT THE HELL?
WHAT'S GOING ON?
I DON'T KNOW. GUESS I GOT THE DAY WRONG.
THAT'S ODD.
FORGET IT. LET'S GO HOME.

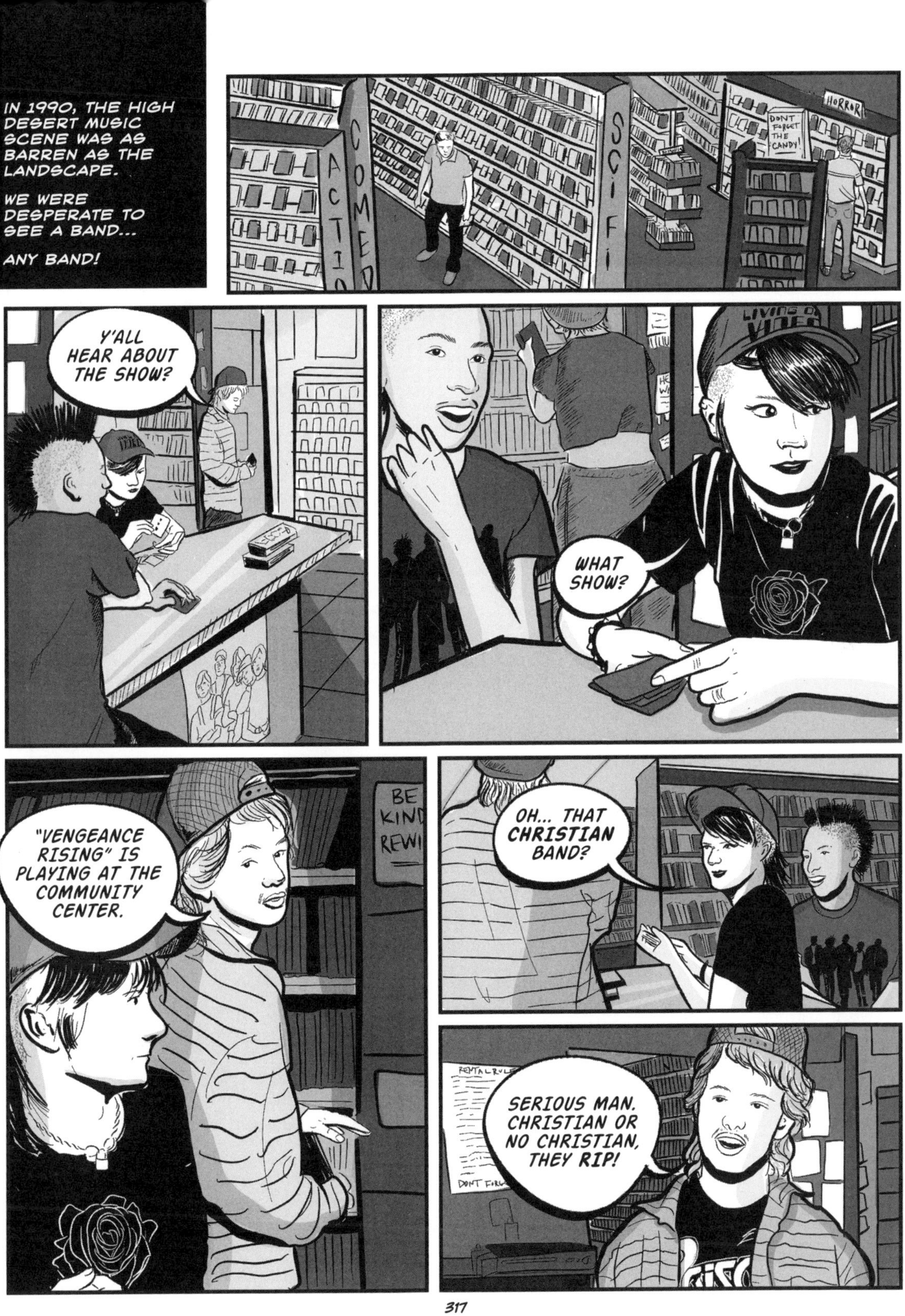
IN 1990, THE HIGH DESERT MUSIC SCENE WAS AS BARREN AS THE LANDSCAPE.
WE WERE DESPERATE TO SEE A BAND...
ANY BAND!
SCI FI
HORROR
DONT FORGET THE CANDY!
Y'ALL HEAR ABOUT THE SHOW?
WHAT SHOW?
"VENGEANCE RISING" IS PLAYING AT THE COMMUNITY CENTER.
OH... THAT CHRISTIAN BAND?
SERIOUS MAN. CHRISTIAN OR NO CHRISTIAN, THEY RIP!

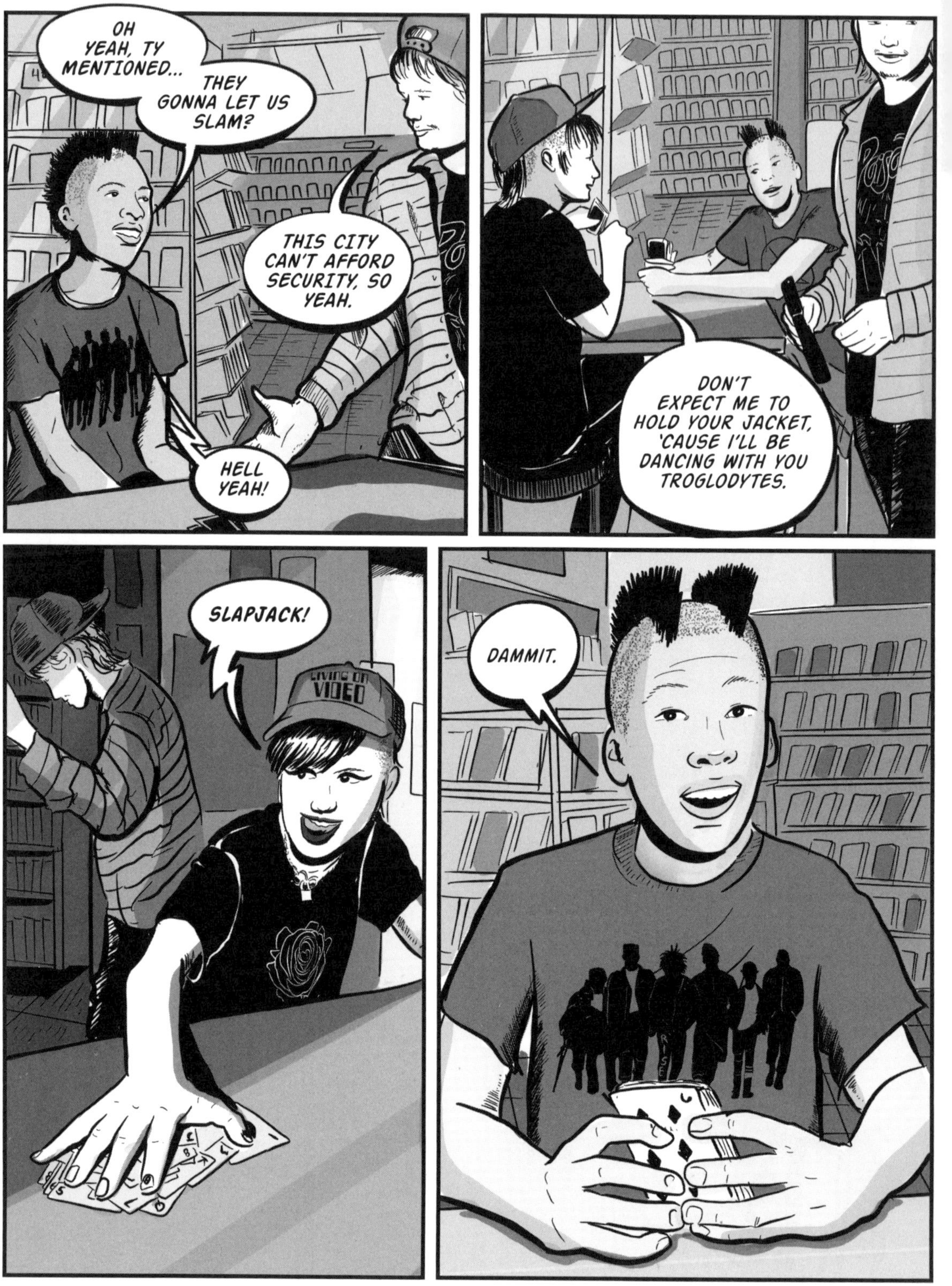

OH YEAH, TY MENTIONED...
THEY GONNA LET US SLAM?
THIS CITY CAN'T AFFORD SECURITY, SO YEAH.
HELL YEAH!
DON'T EXPECT ME TO HOLD YOUR JACKET, 'CAUSE I'LL BE DANCING WITH YOU TROGLODYTES.
SLAPJACK!
LIVING ON VIDEO
DAMMIT.

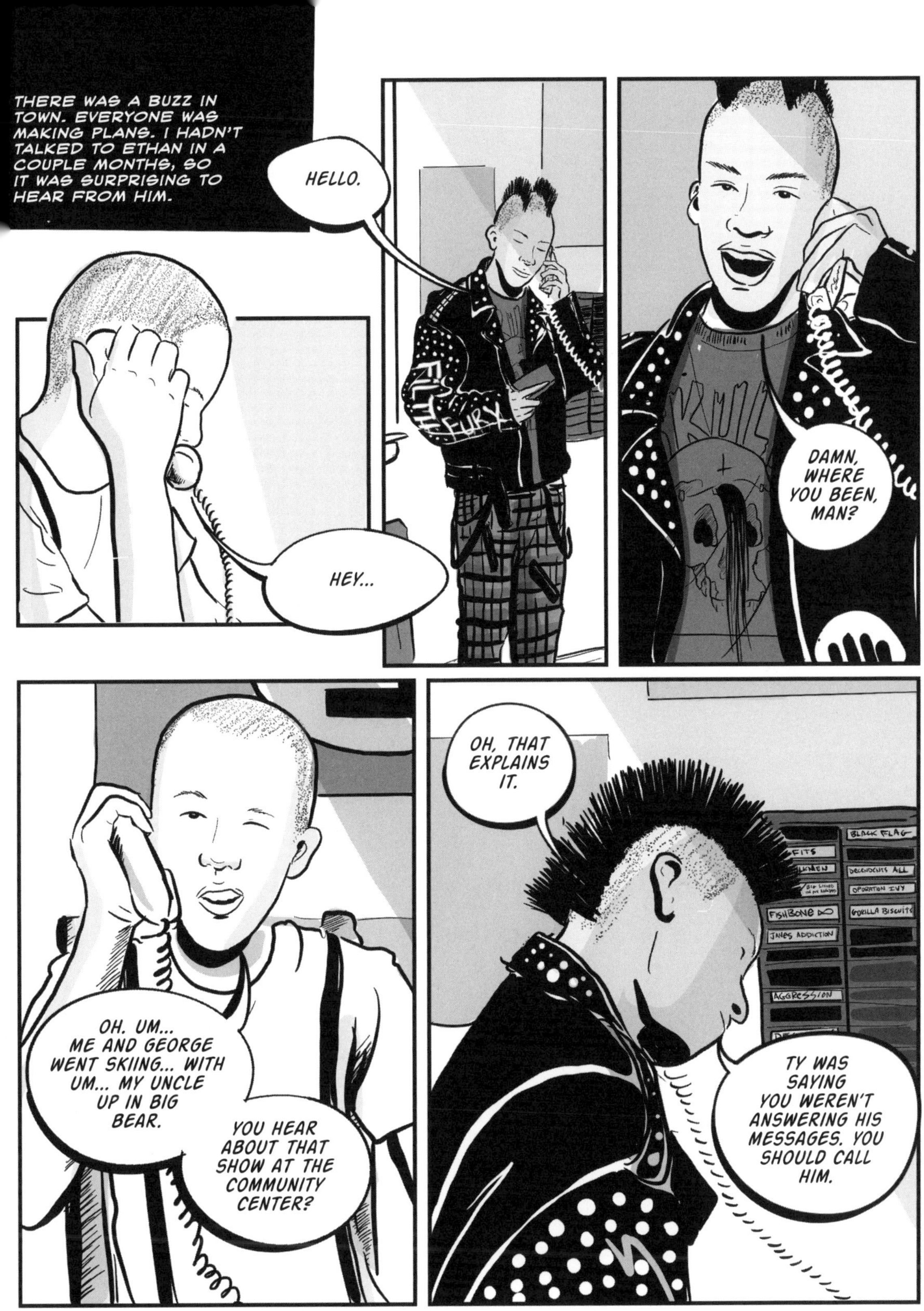
THERE WAS A BUZZ IN TOWN. EVERYONE WAS MAKING PLANS. I HADN'T TALKED TO ETHAN IN A COUPLE MONTHS, SO IT WAS SURPRISING TO HEAR FROM HIM.
HELLO.
HEY...
DAMN, WHERE YOU BEEN, MAN?
OH. UM... ME AND GEORGE WENT SKIING... WITH UM... MY UNCLE UP IN BIG BEAR.
YOU HEAR ABOUT THAT SHOW AT THE COMMUNITY CENTER?
OH, THAT EXPLAINS IT.
TY WAS SAYING YOU WEREN'T ANSWERING HIS MESSAGES. YOU SHOULD CALL HIM.

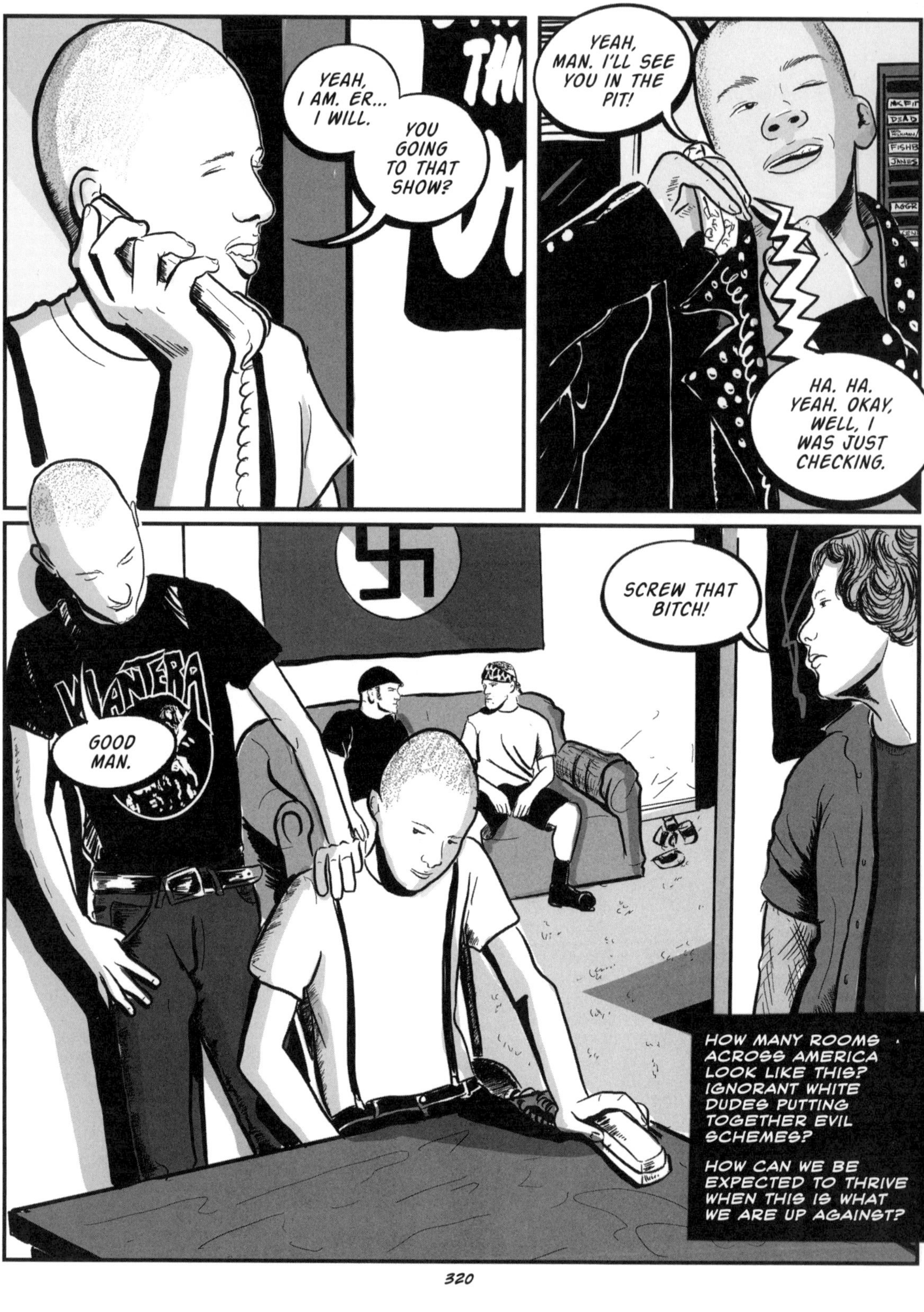

YEAH, I AM. ER... I WILL.
YOU GOING TO THAT SHOW?
YEAH, MAN. I'LL SEE YOU IN THE PIT!
HA. HA. YEAH. OKAY, WELL, I WAS JUST CHECKING.
SCREW THAT BITCH!
GOOD MAN.
HOW MANY ROOMS ACROSS AMERICA LOOK LIKE THIS? IGNORANT WHITE DUDES PUTTING TOGETHER EVIL SCHEMES?
HOW CAN WE BE EXPECTED TO THRIVE WHEN THIS IS WHAT WE ARE UP AGAINST?

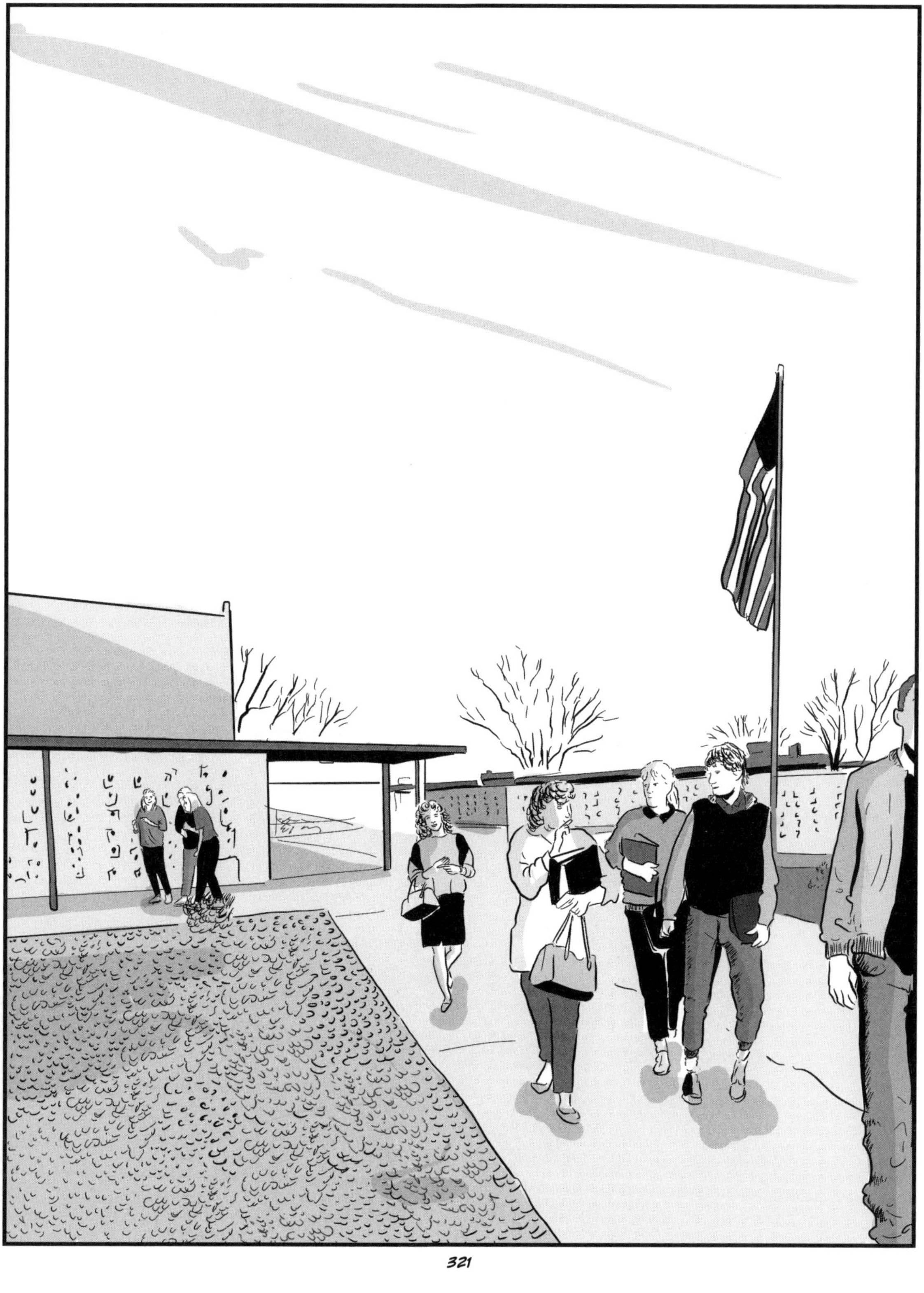

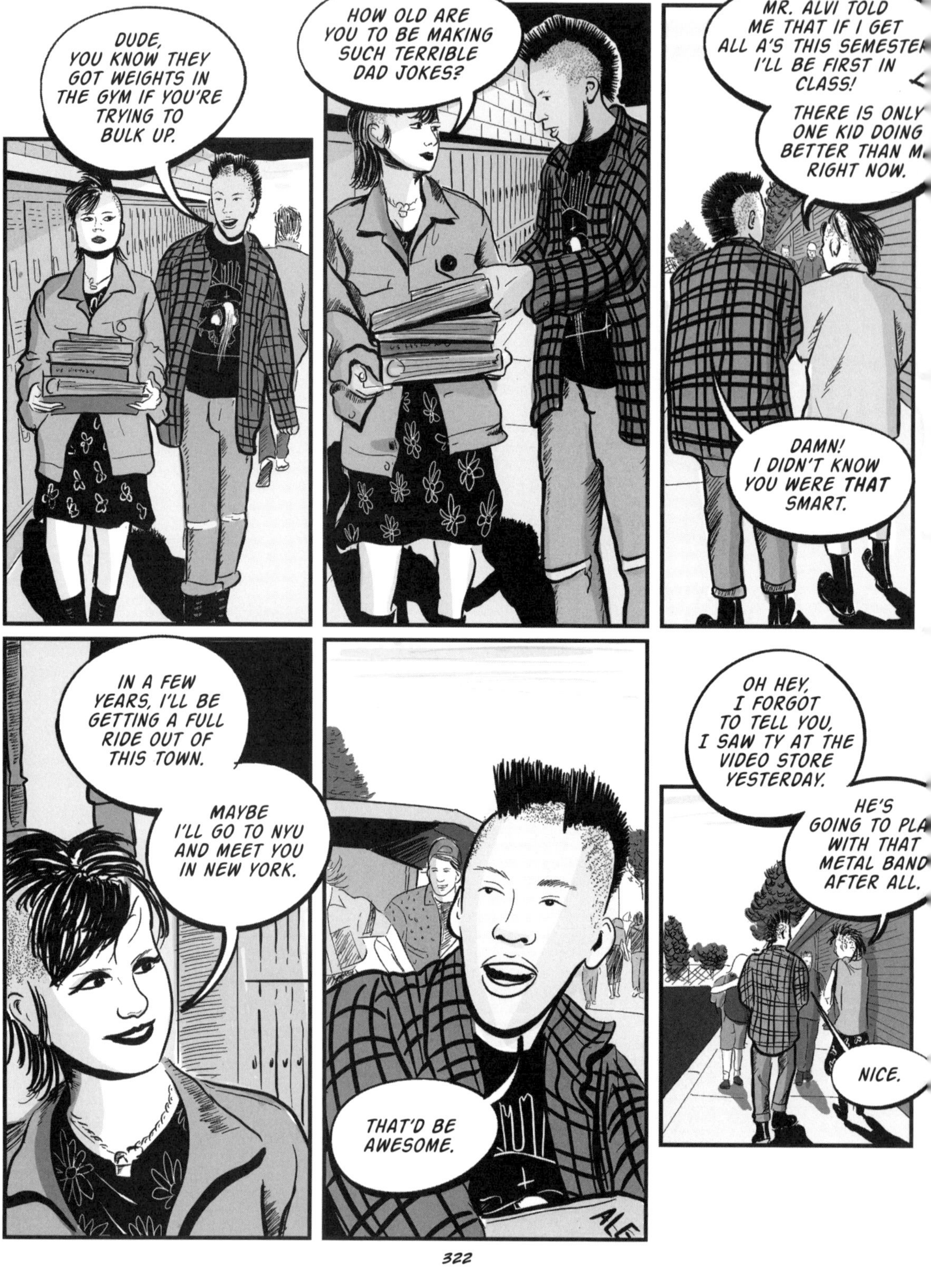
DUDE, YOU KNOW THEY GOT WEIGHTS IN THE GYM IF YOU'RE TRYING TO BULK UP.
HOW OLD ARE YOU TO BE MAKING SUCH TERRIBLE DAD JOKES?
MR. ALVI TOLD ME THAT IF I GET ALL A'S THIS SEMESTE I'LL BE FIRST IN CLASS!
THERE IS ONLY ONE KID DOING BETTER THAN M RIGHT NOW.
DAMN! I DIDN'T KNOW YOU WERE THAT SMART.
IN A FEW YEARS, I'LL BE GETTING A FULL RIDE OUT OF THIS TOWN.
MAYBE I'LL GO TO NYU AND MEET YOU IN NEW YORK.
THAT'D BE AWESOME.
OH HEY, I FORGOT TO TELL YOU, I SAW TY AT THE VIDEO STORE YESTERDAY.
HE'S GOING TO PLA WITH THAT METAL BAND AFTER ALL.
NICE.

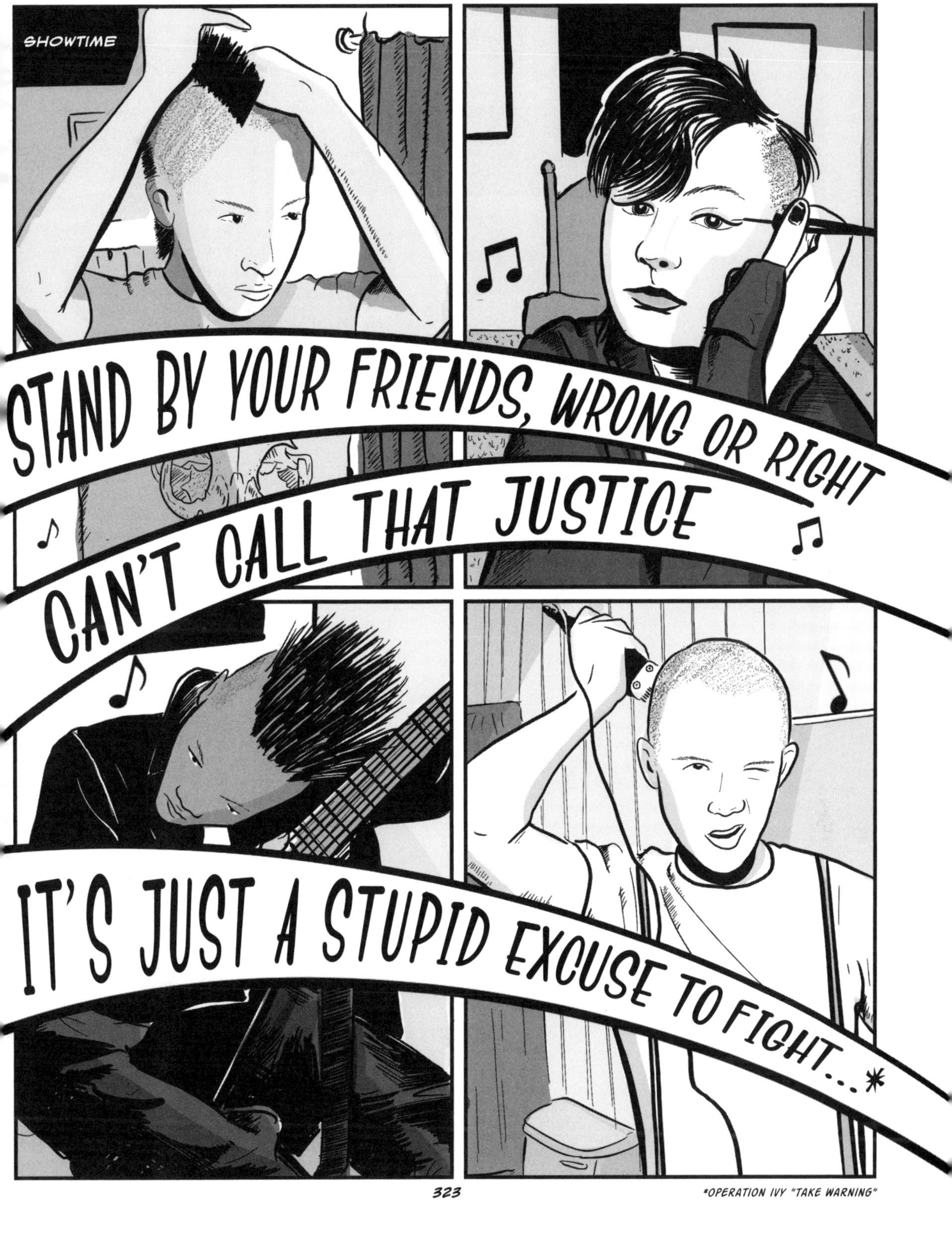
SHOWTIME
STAND BY YOUR FRIENDS, WRONG OR RIGHT
CAN'T CALL THAT JUSTICE
IT'S JUST A STUPID EXCUSE TO FIGHT...*

*OPERATION IVY "TAKE WARNING"

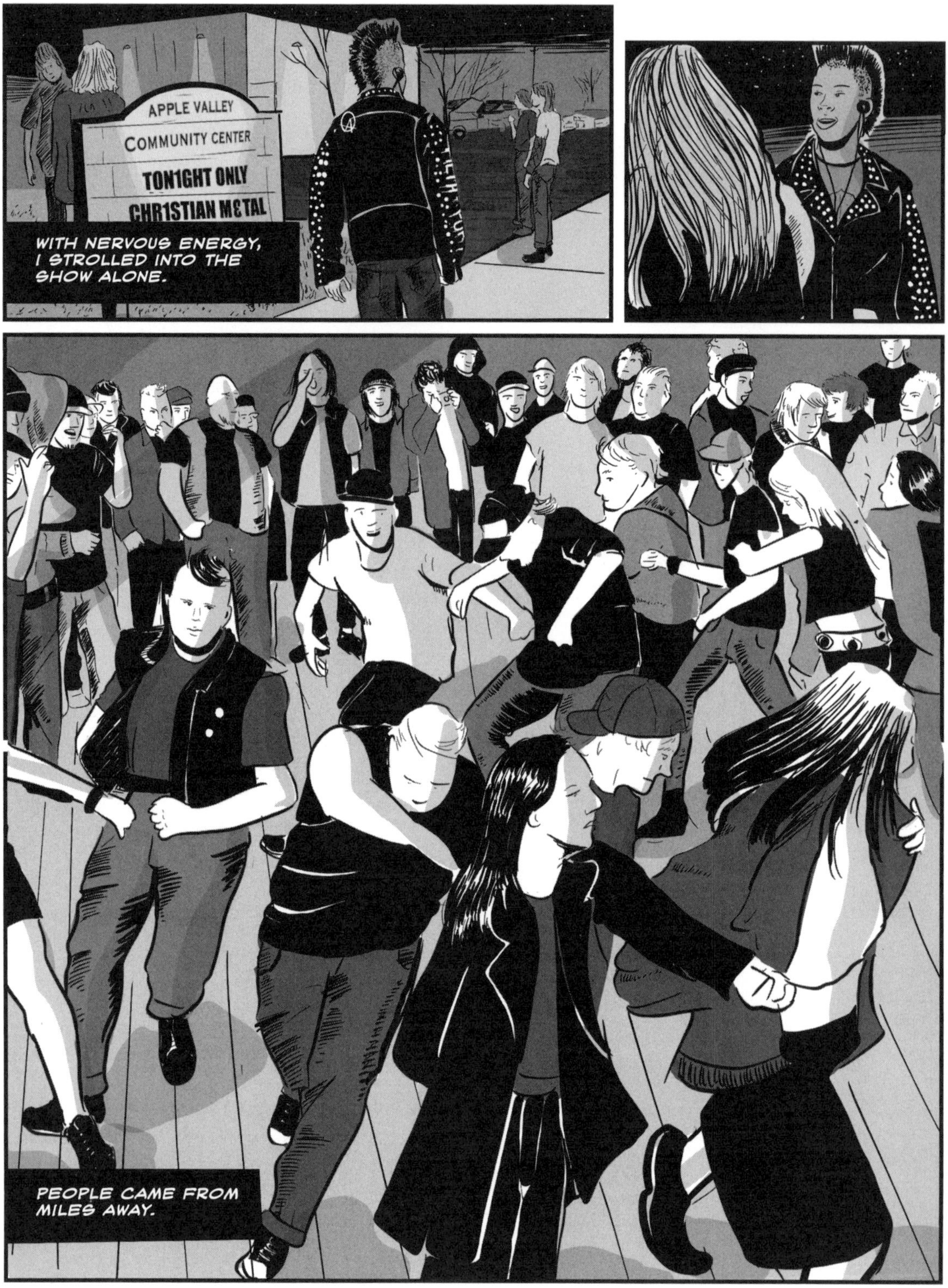
APPLE VALLEY
COMMUNITY CENTER
TON1GHT ONLY
CHR1STIAN M€TAL
WITH NERVOUS ENERGY, I STROLLED INTO THE SHOW ALONE.
PEOPLE CAME FROM MILES AWAY.

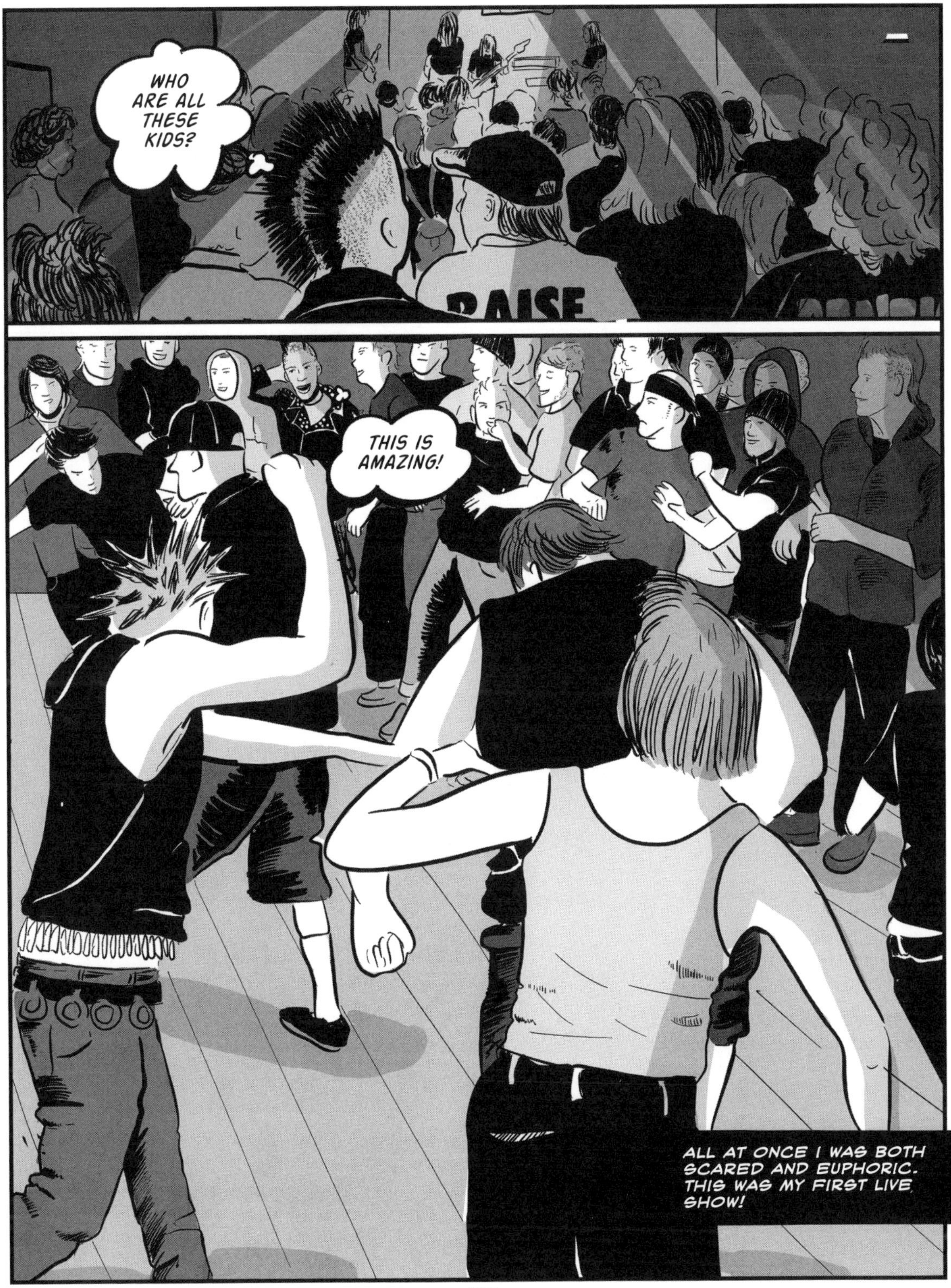
WHO ARE ALL THESE KIDS?
RAISE
THIS IS AMAZING!
ALL AT ONCE I WAS BOTH SCARED AND EUPHORIC. THIS WAS MY FIRST LIVE SHOW!

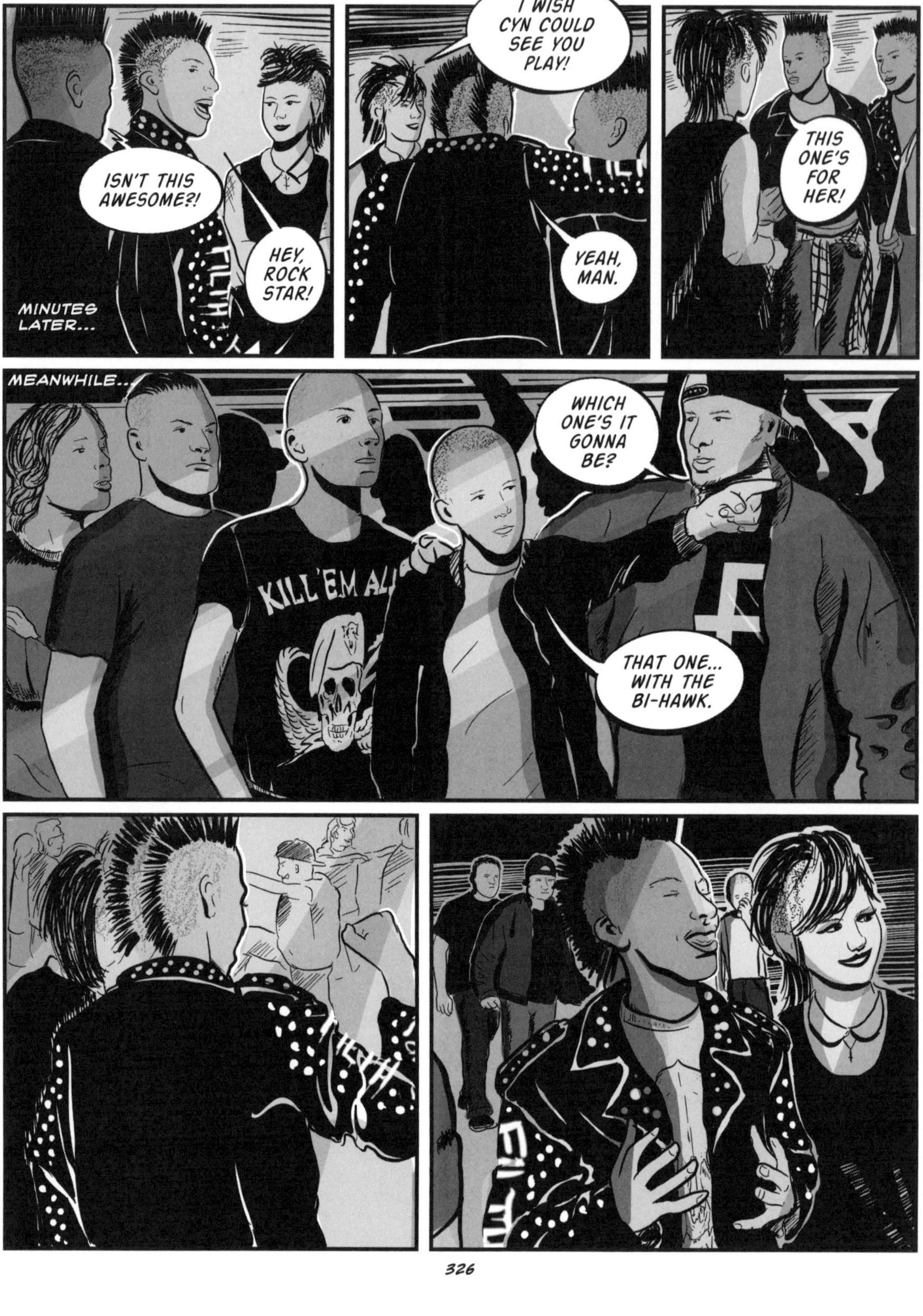
MINUTES LATER...
ISN'T THIS AWESOME?!
HEY, ROCK STAR!
I WISH CYN COULD SEE YOU PLAY!
YEAH, MAN.
THIS ONE'S FOR HER!
MEANWHILE...
KILL 'EM ALL
WHICH ONE'S IT GONNA BE?
THAT ONE... WITH THE BI-HAWK.

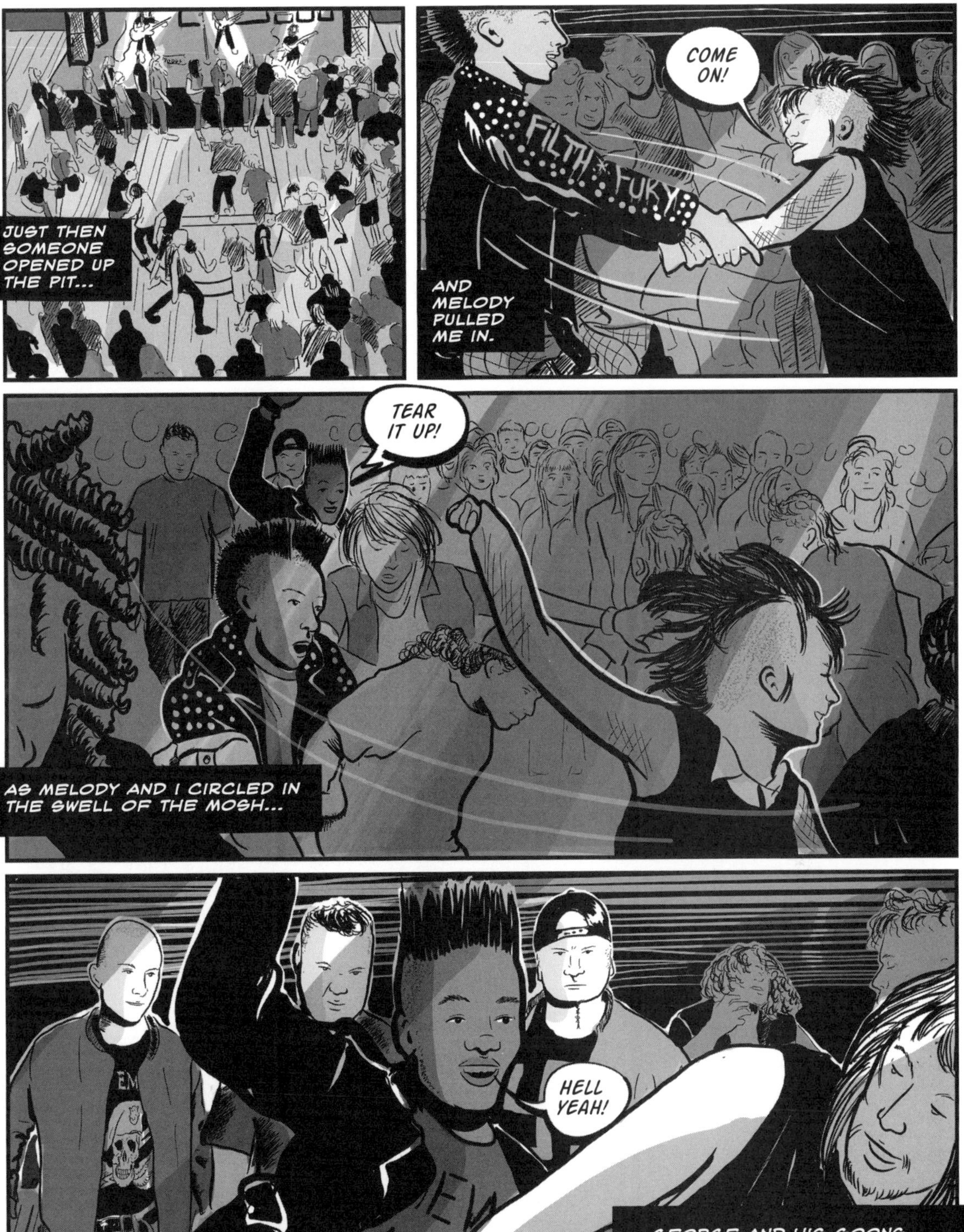
JUST THEN SOMEONE OPENED UP THE PIT...
COME ON!
AND MELODY PULLED ME IN.
FILTH * FURY
TEAR IT UP!
AS MELODY AND I CIRCLED IN THE SWELL OF THE MOSH...
HELL YEAH!
...GEORGE AND HIS GOONS BEGAN CIRCLING THE ONLY OTHER BLACK DOT IN THE ROOM.

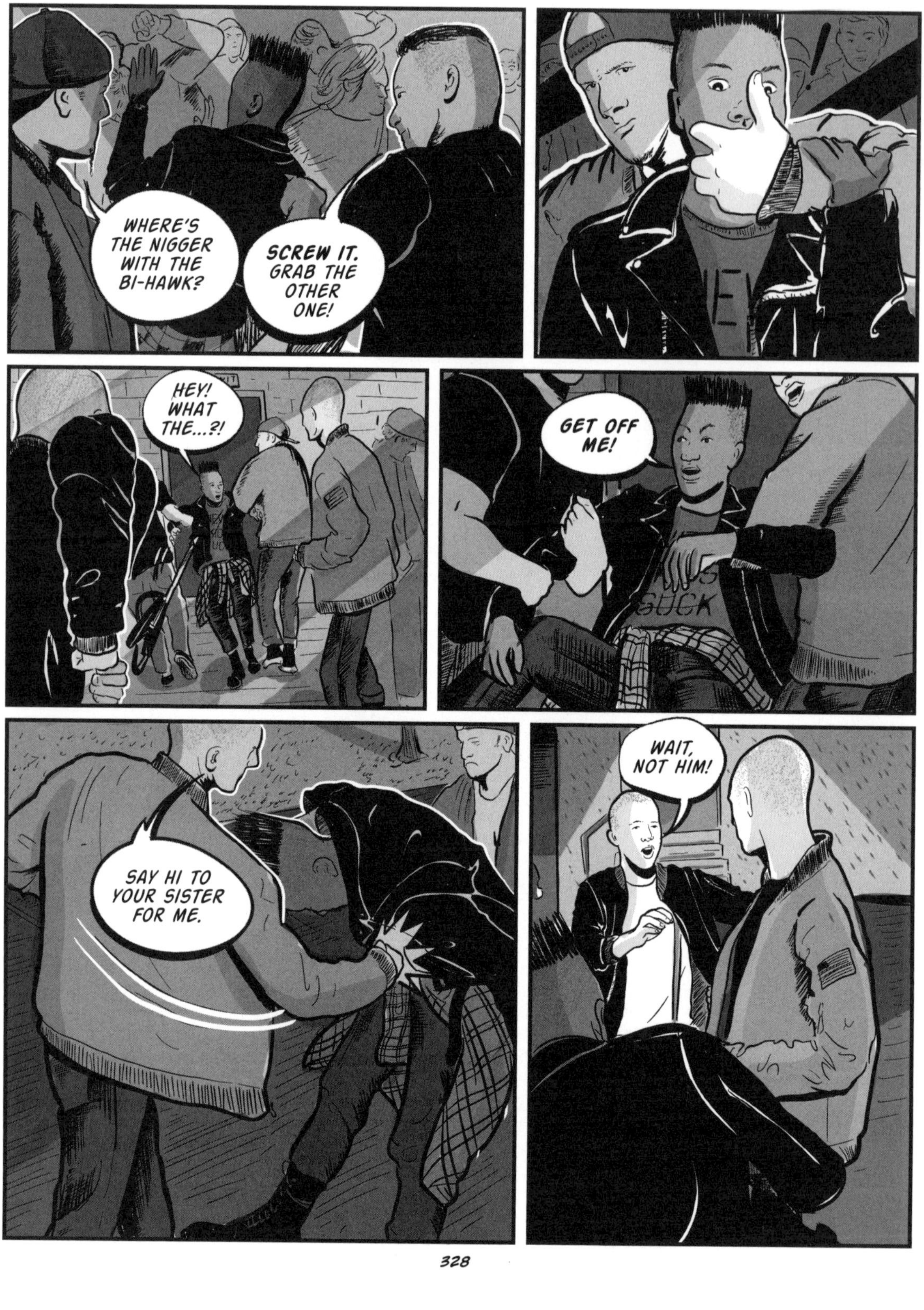
WHERE'S THE NIGGER WITH THE BI-HAWK?
SCREW IT. GRAB THE OTHER ONE!
HEY! WHAT THE...?!
GET OFF ME!
SAY HI TO YOUR SISTER FOR ME.
WAIT, NOT HIM!

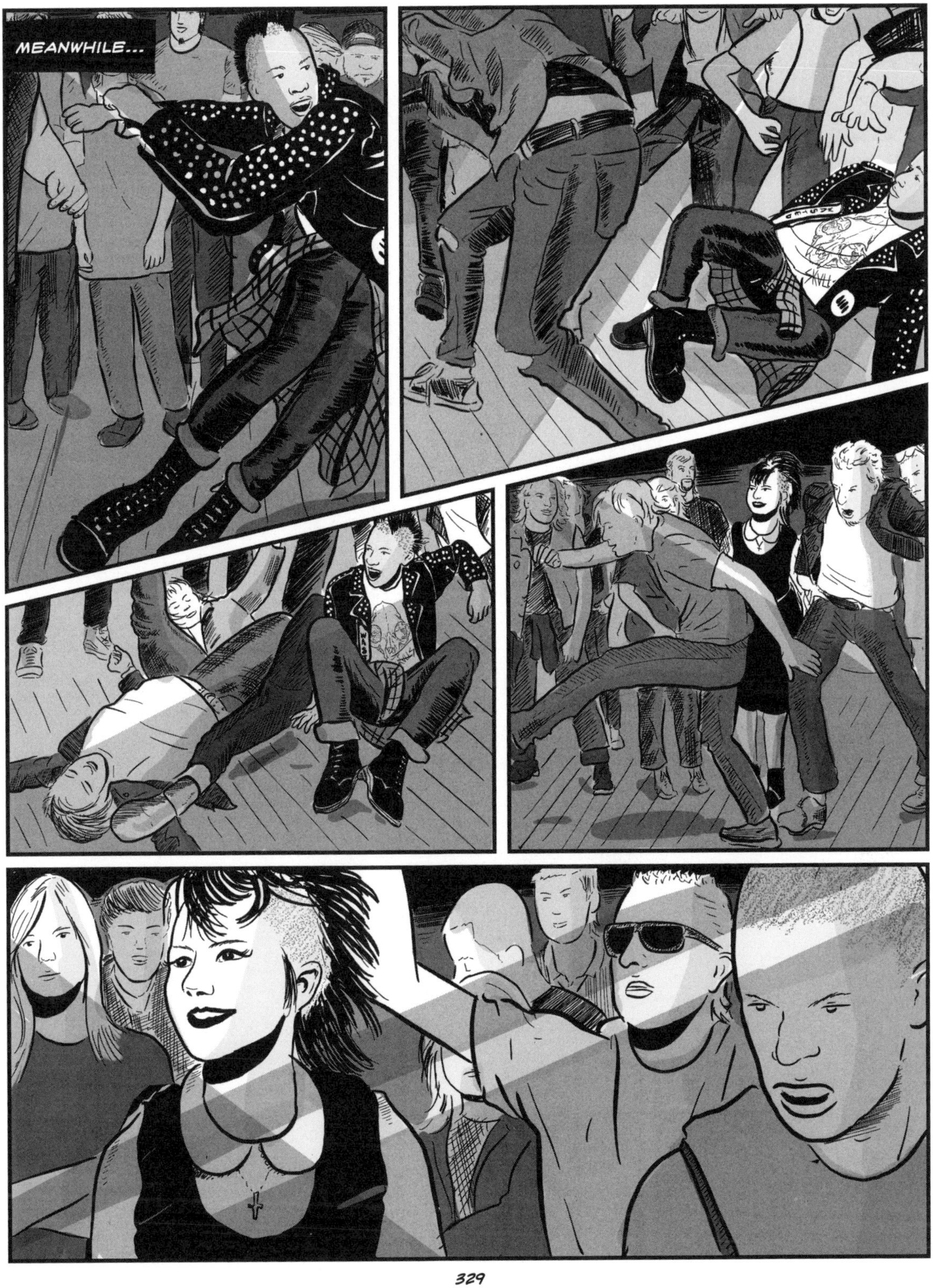
MEANWHILE...

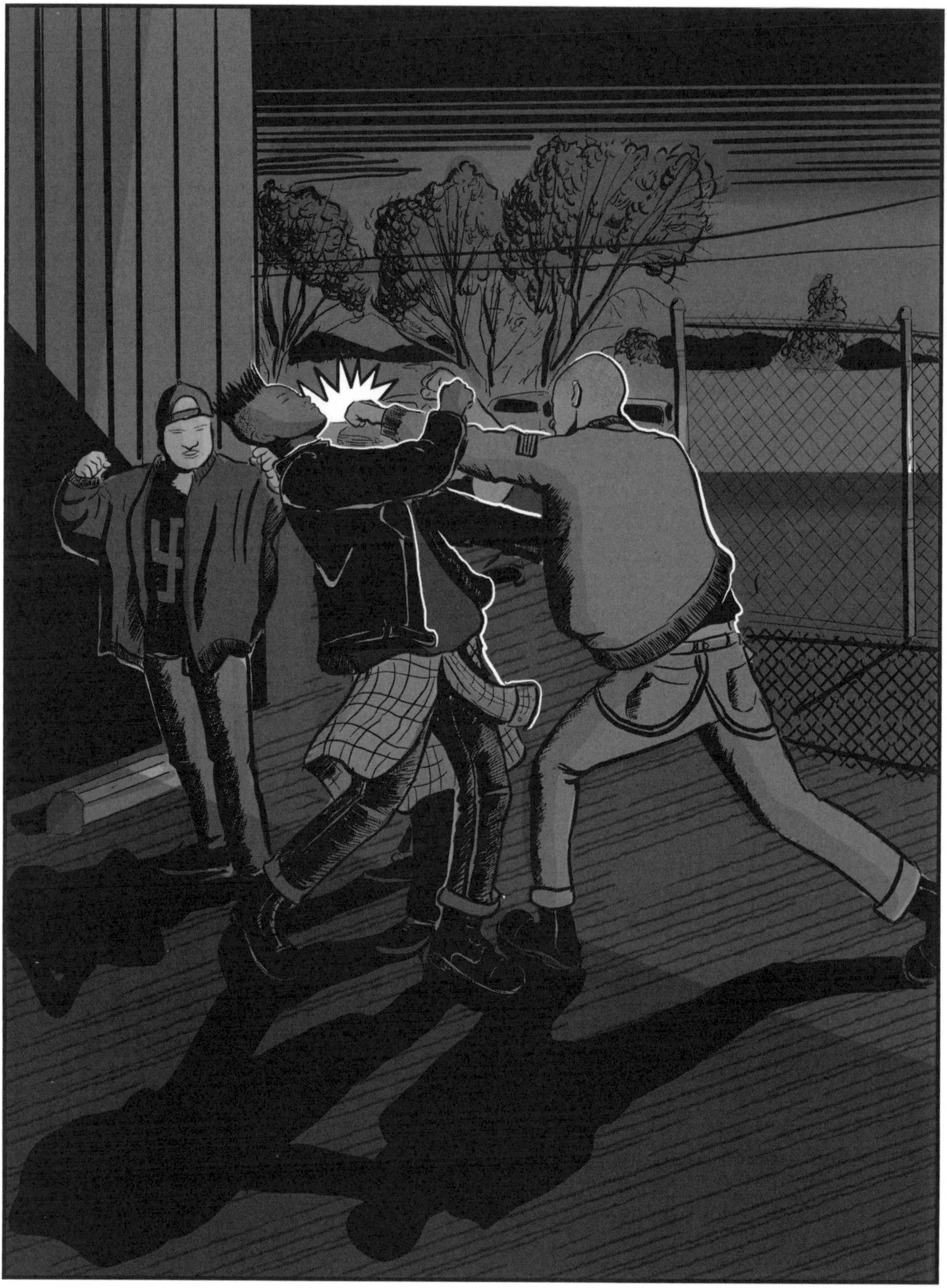

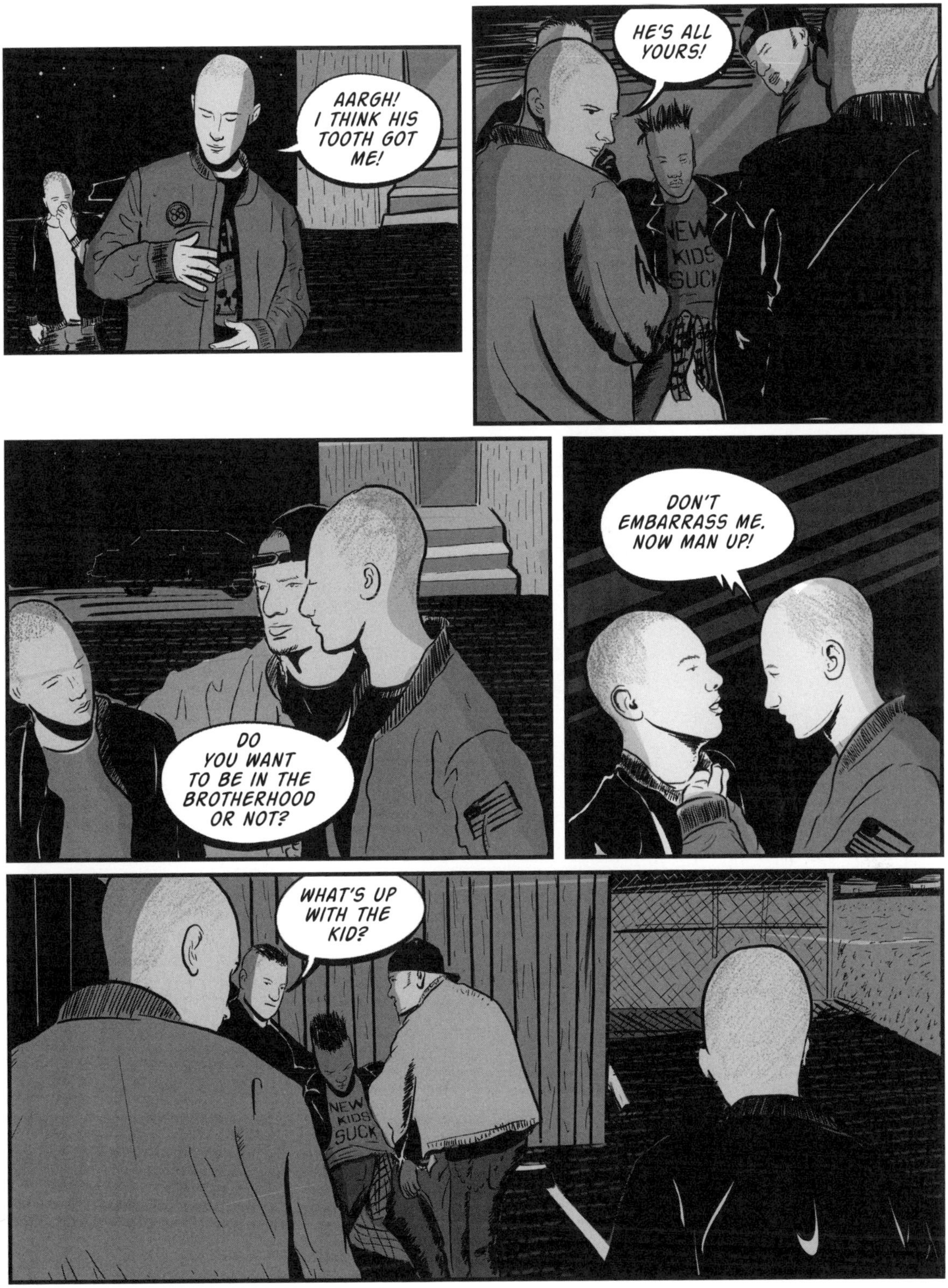
AARGH! I THINK HIS TOOTH GOT ME!
HE'S ALL YOURS!
NEW KIDS SUCK
DO YOU WANT TO BE IN THE BROTHERHOOD OR NOT?
DON'T EMBARRASS ME. NOW MAN UP!
WHAT'S UP WITH THE KID?
NEW KIDS SUCK

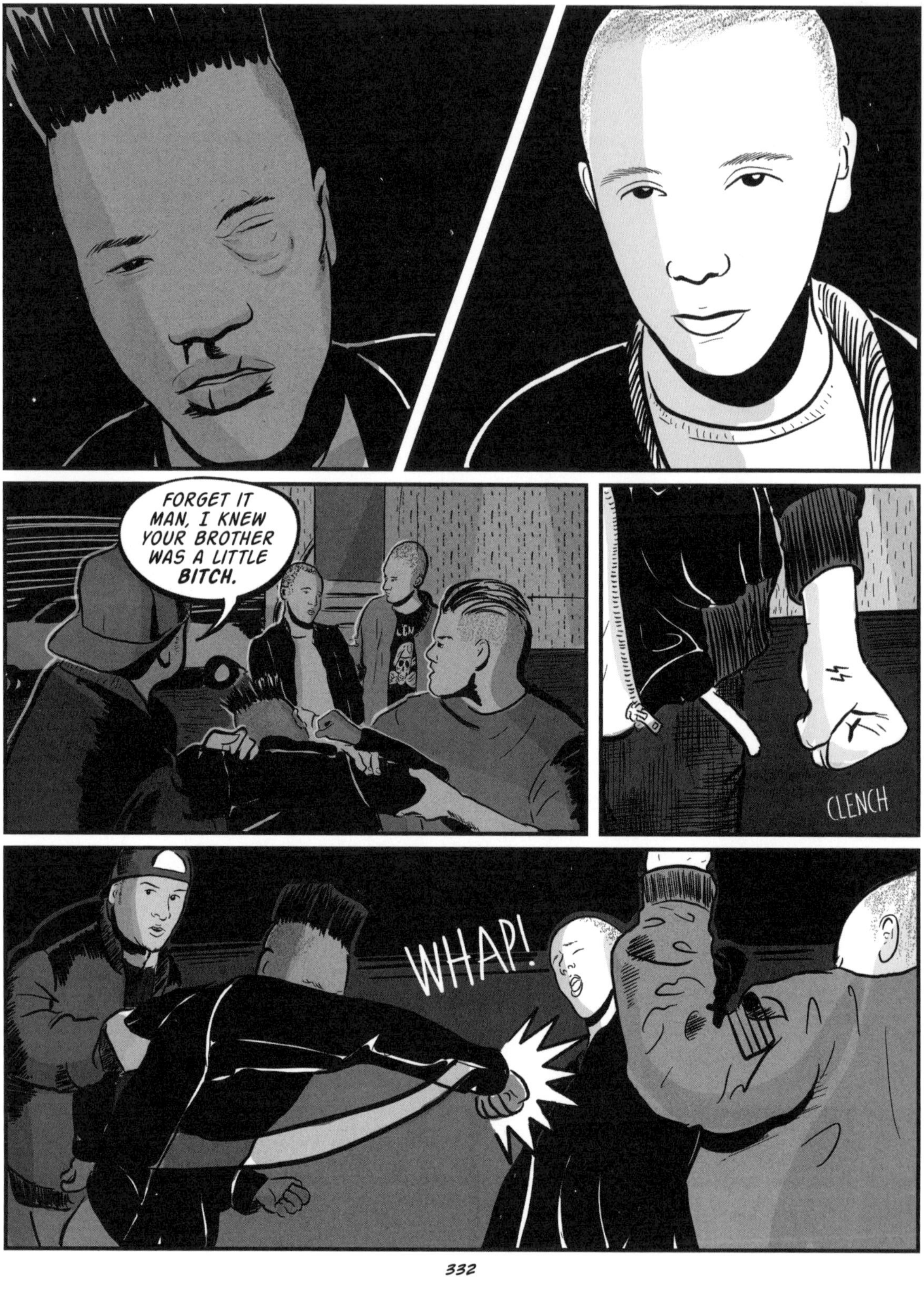
FORGET IT MAN, I KNEW YOUR BROTHER WAS A LITTLE BITCH.
CLENCH
WHAP!

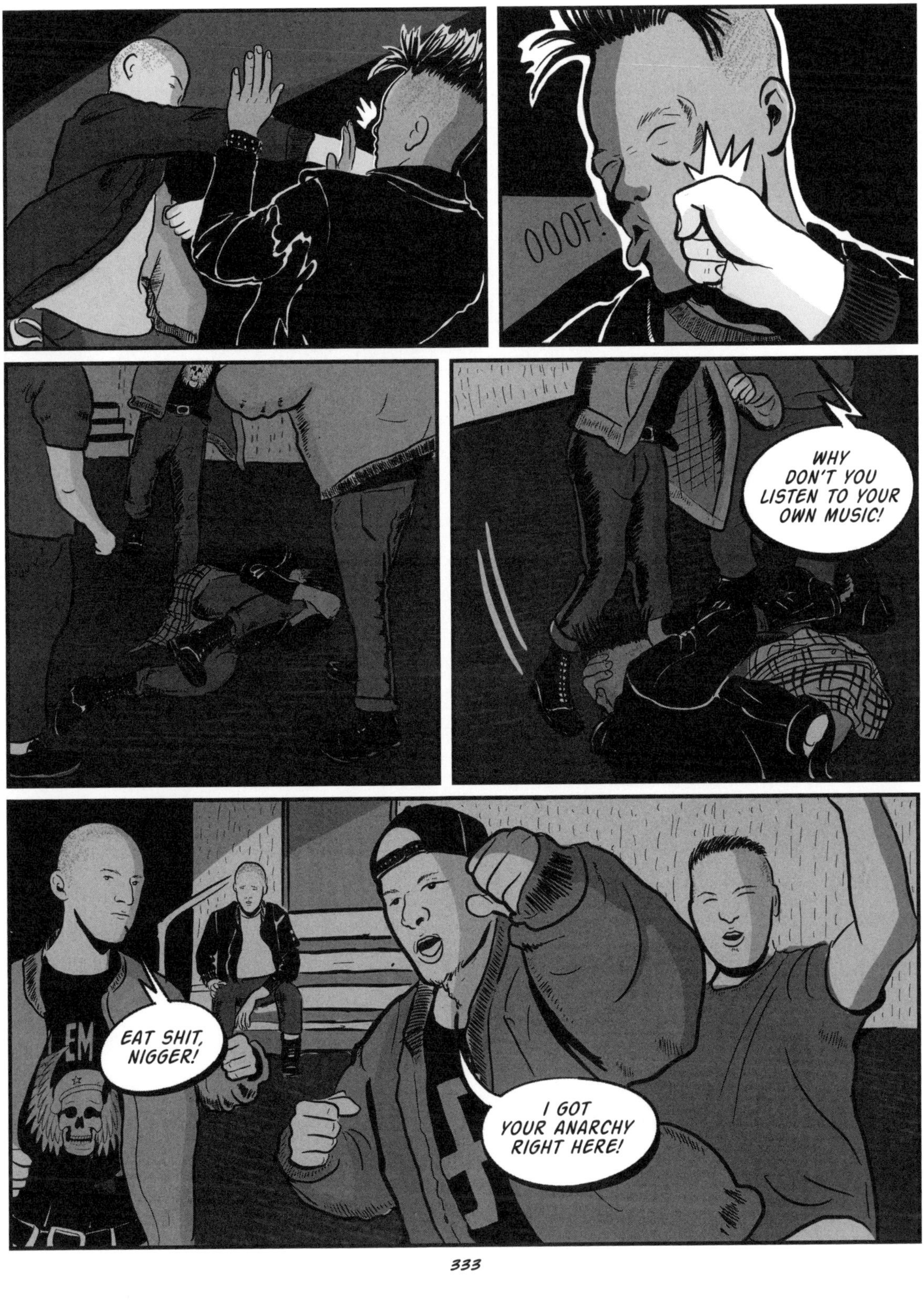
OOOF!
WHY DON'T YOU LISTEN TO YOUR OWN MUSIC!
EAT SHIT, NIGGER!
I GOT YOUR ANARCHY RIGHT HERE!

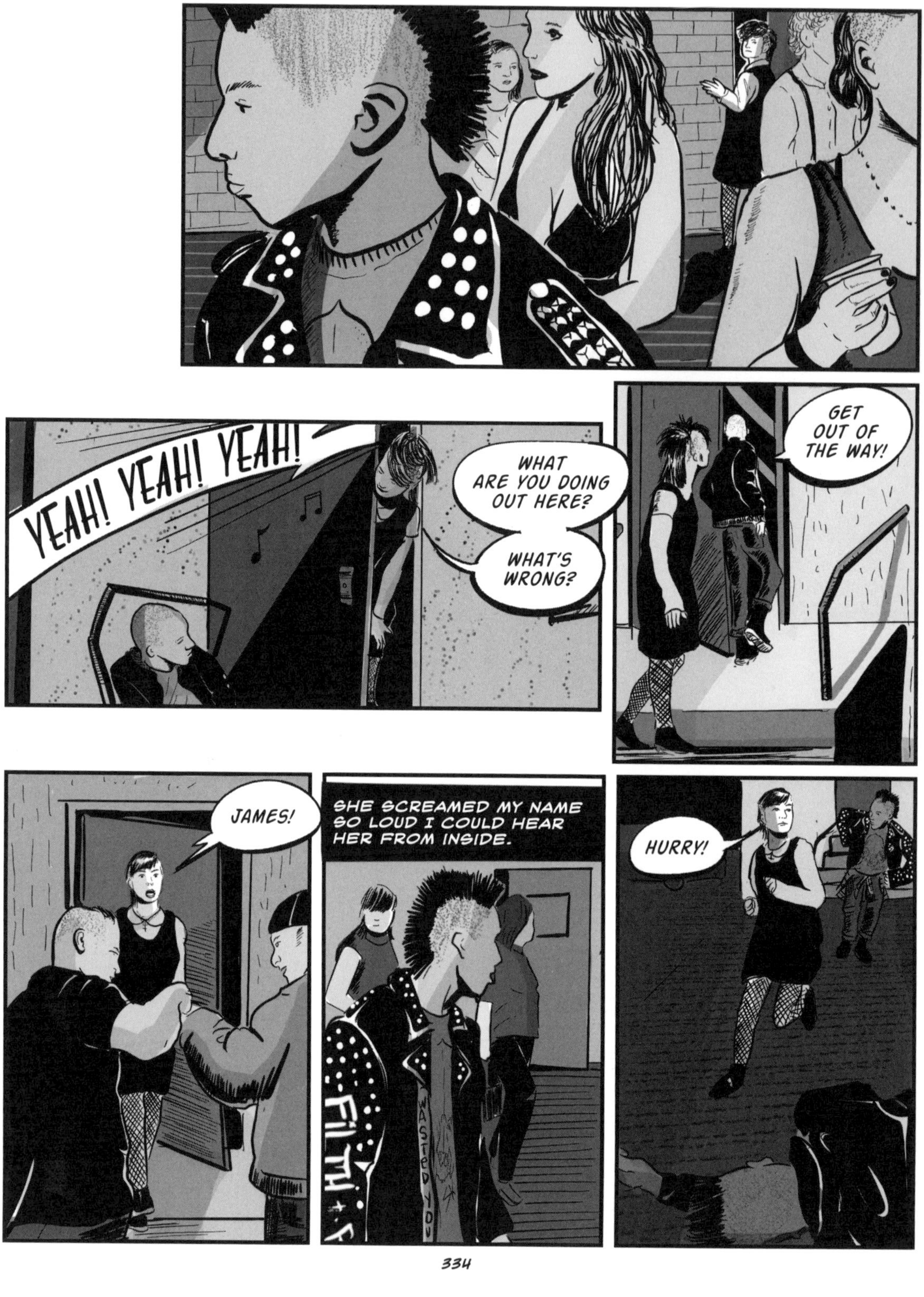
YEAH! YEAH! YEAH!
WHAT ARE YOU DOING OUT HERE?
WHAT'S WRONG?
GET OUT OF THE WAY!
JAMES!
SHE SCREAMED MY NAME SO LOUD I COULD HEAR HER FROM INSIDE.
HURRY!

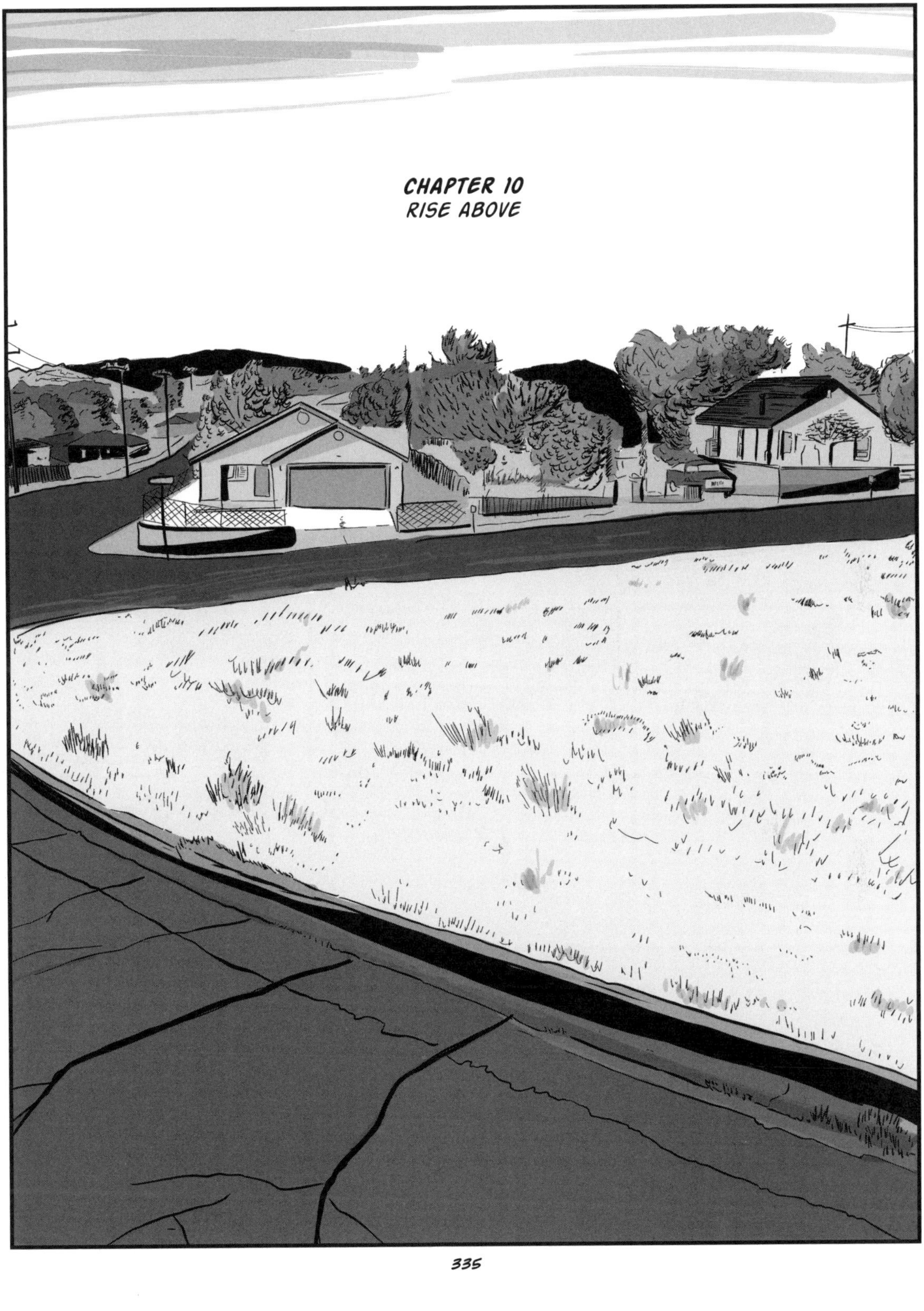
CHAPTER 10
RISE ABOVE

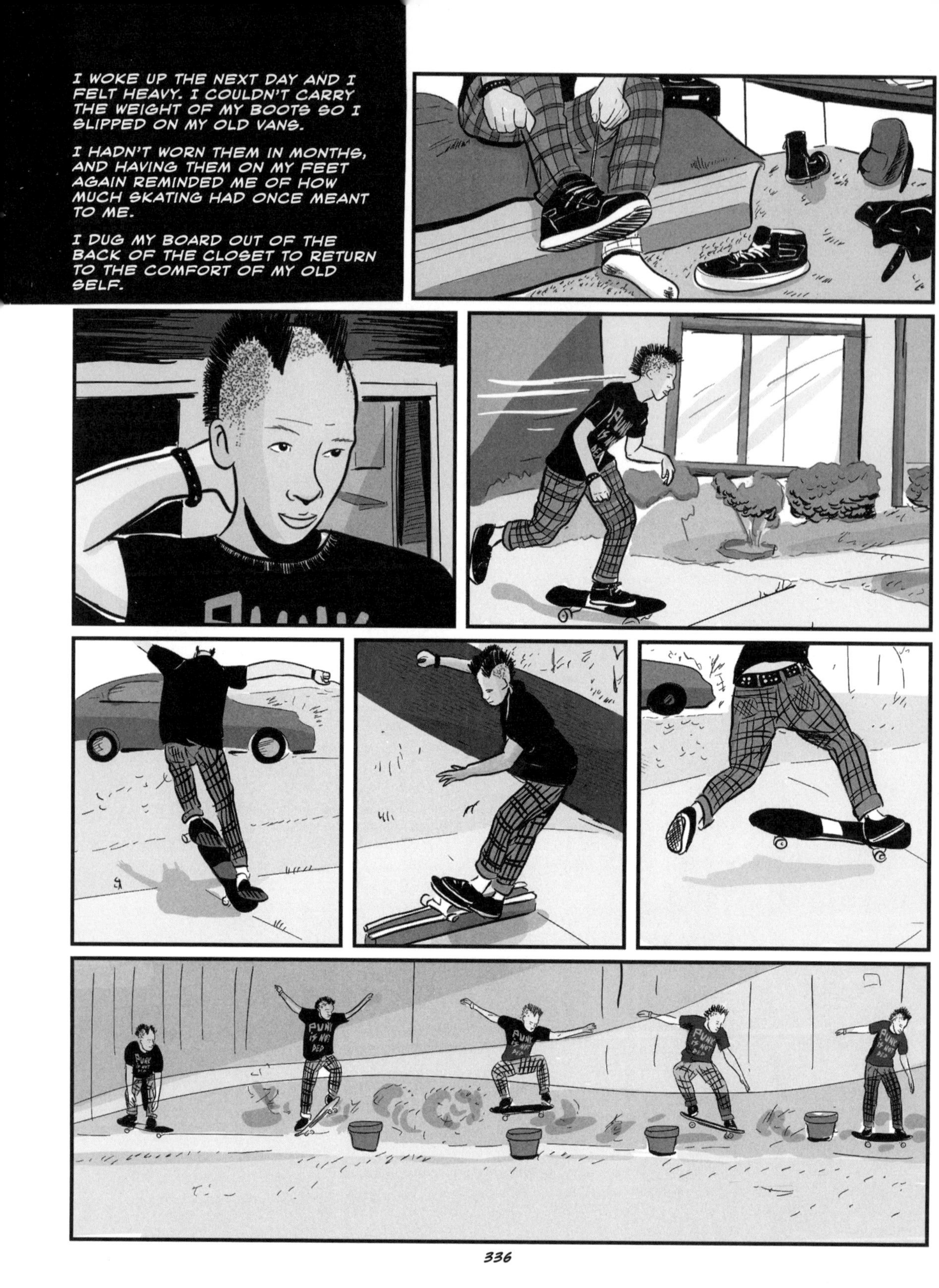
I WOKE UP THE NEXT DAY AND I FELT HEAVY. I COULDN'T CARRY THE WEIGHT OF MY BOOTS SO I SLIPPED ON MY OLD VANS.
I HADN'T WORN THEM IN MONTHS, AND HAVING THEM ON MY FEET AGAIN REMINDED ME OF HOW MUCH SKATING HAD ONCE MEANT TO ME.
I DUG MY BOARD OUT OF THE BACK OF THE CLOSET TO RETURN TO THE COMFORT OF MY OLD SELF.

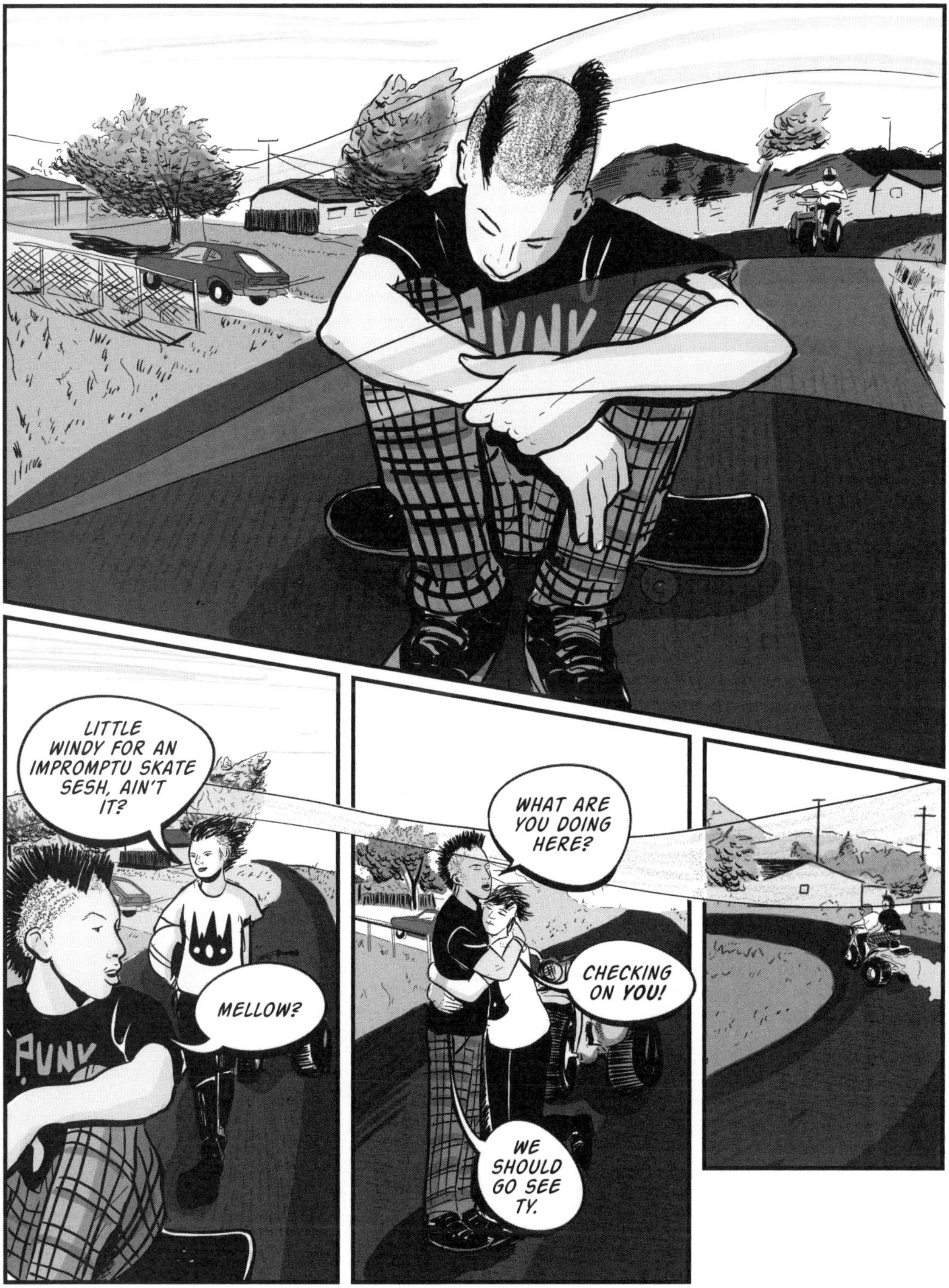
PUNK
LITTLE WINDY FOR AN IMPROMPTU SKATE SESH, AIN'T IT?
MELLOW?
PUNK
WHAT ARE YOU DOING HERE?
CHECKING ON YOU!
WE SHOULD GO SEE TY.

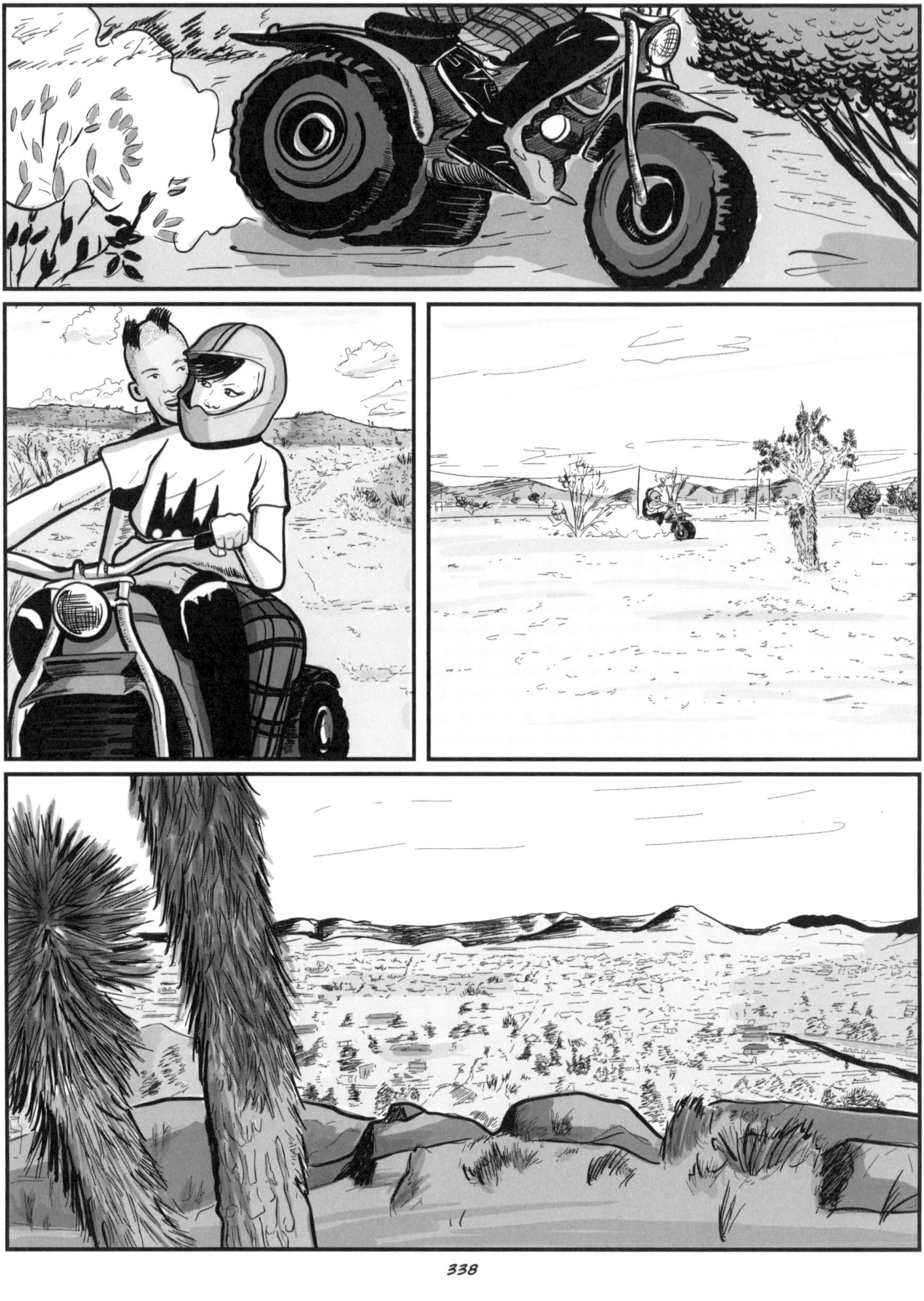

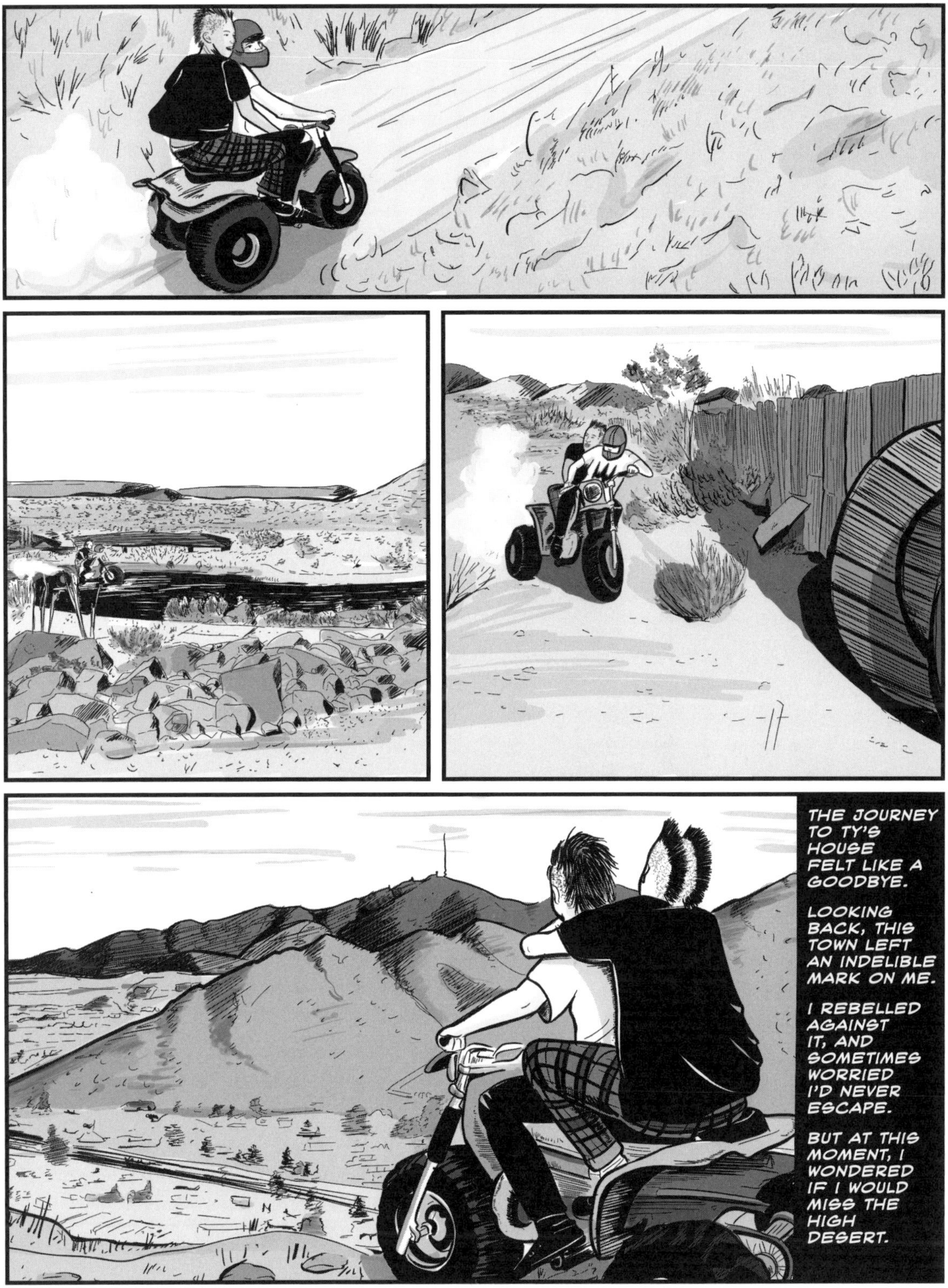
THE JOURNEY TO TY'S HOUSE FELT LIKE A GOODBYE.
LOOKING BACK, THIS TOWN LEFT AN INDELIBLE MARK ON ME.
I REBELLED AGAINST IT, AND SOMETIMES WORRIED I'D NEVER ESCAPE.
BUT AT THIS MOMENT, I WONDERED IF I WOULD MISS THE HIGH DESERT.

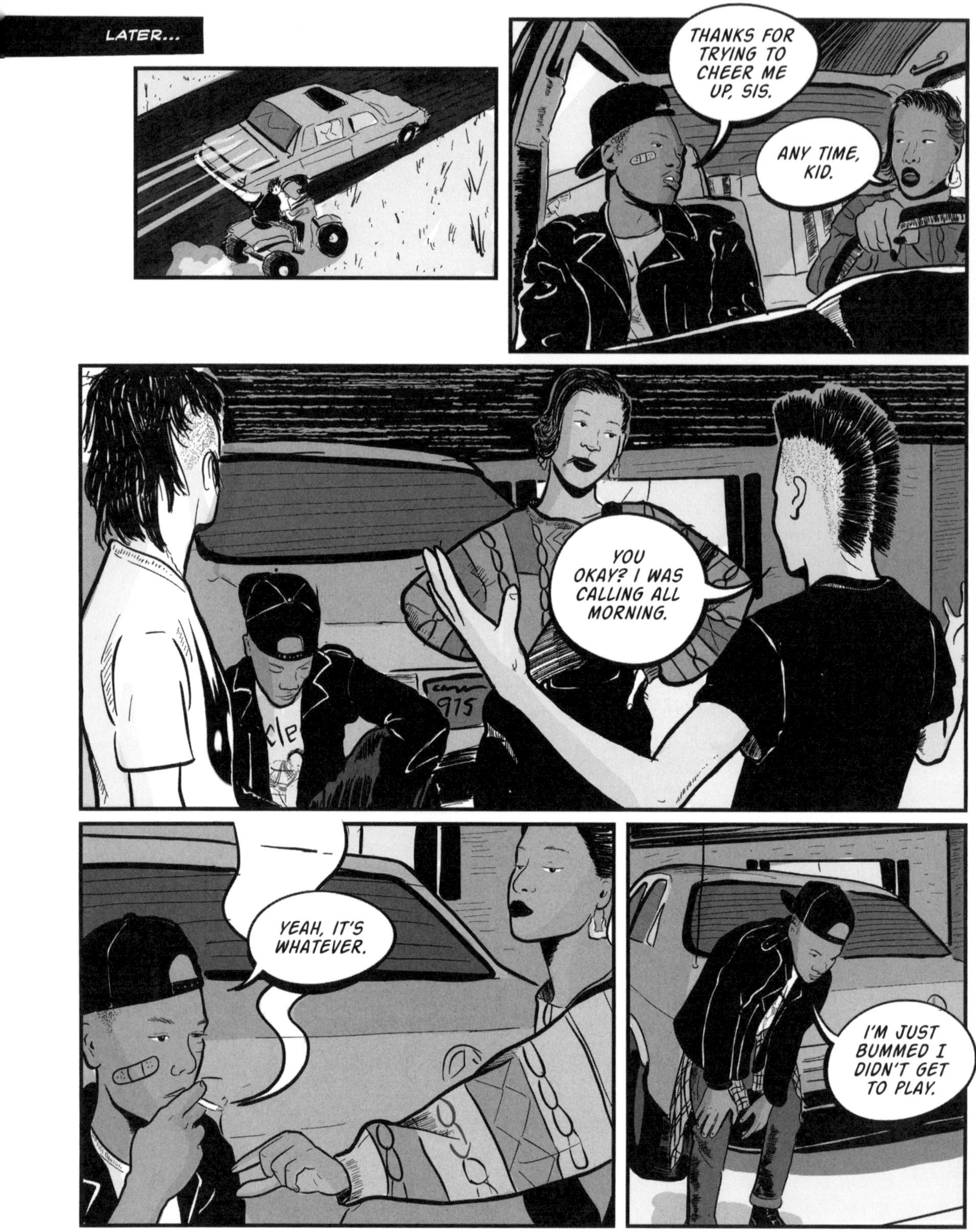
LATER...
THANKS FOR TRYING TO CHEER ME UP, SIS.
ANY TIME, KID.
YOU OKAY? I WAS CALLING ALL MORNING.
YEAH, IT'S WHATEVER.
I'M JUST BUMMED I DIDN'T GET TO PLAY.

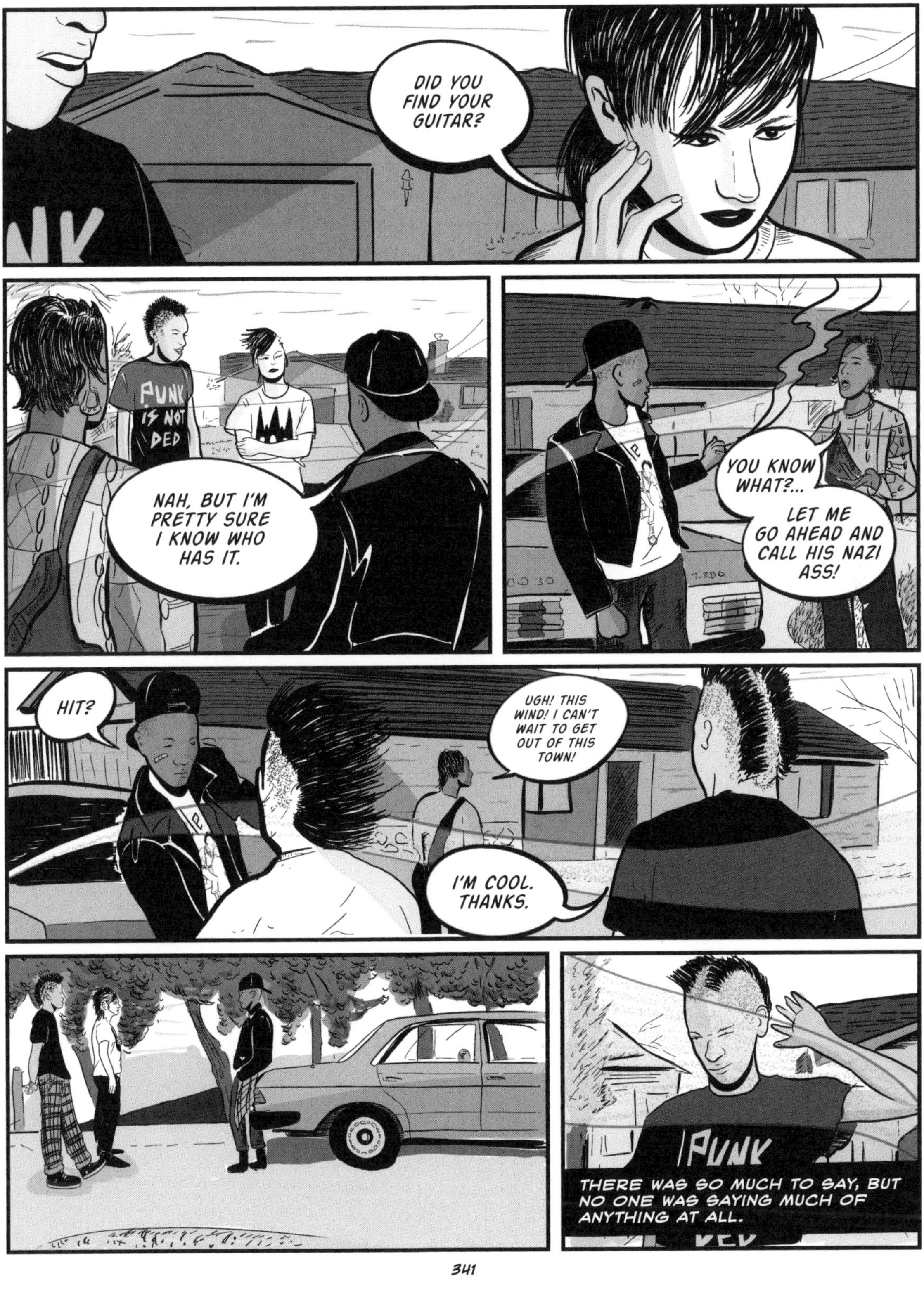
DID YOU FIND YOUR GUITAR?
PUNK IS NOT DED
NAH, BUT I'M PRETTY SURE I KNOW WHO HAS IT.
YOU KNOW WHAT?...
LET ME GO AHEAD AND CALL HIS NAZI ASS!
HIT?
UGH! THIS WIND! I CAN'T WAIT TO GET OUT OF THIS TOWN!
I'M COOL. THANKS.
THERE WAS SO MUCH TO SAY, BUT NO ONE WAS SAYING MUCH OF ANYTHING AT ALL.

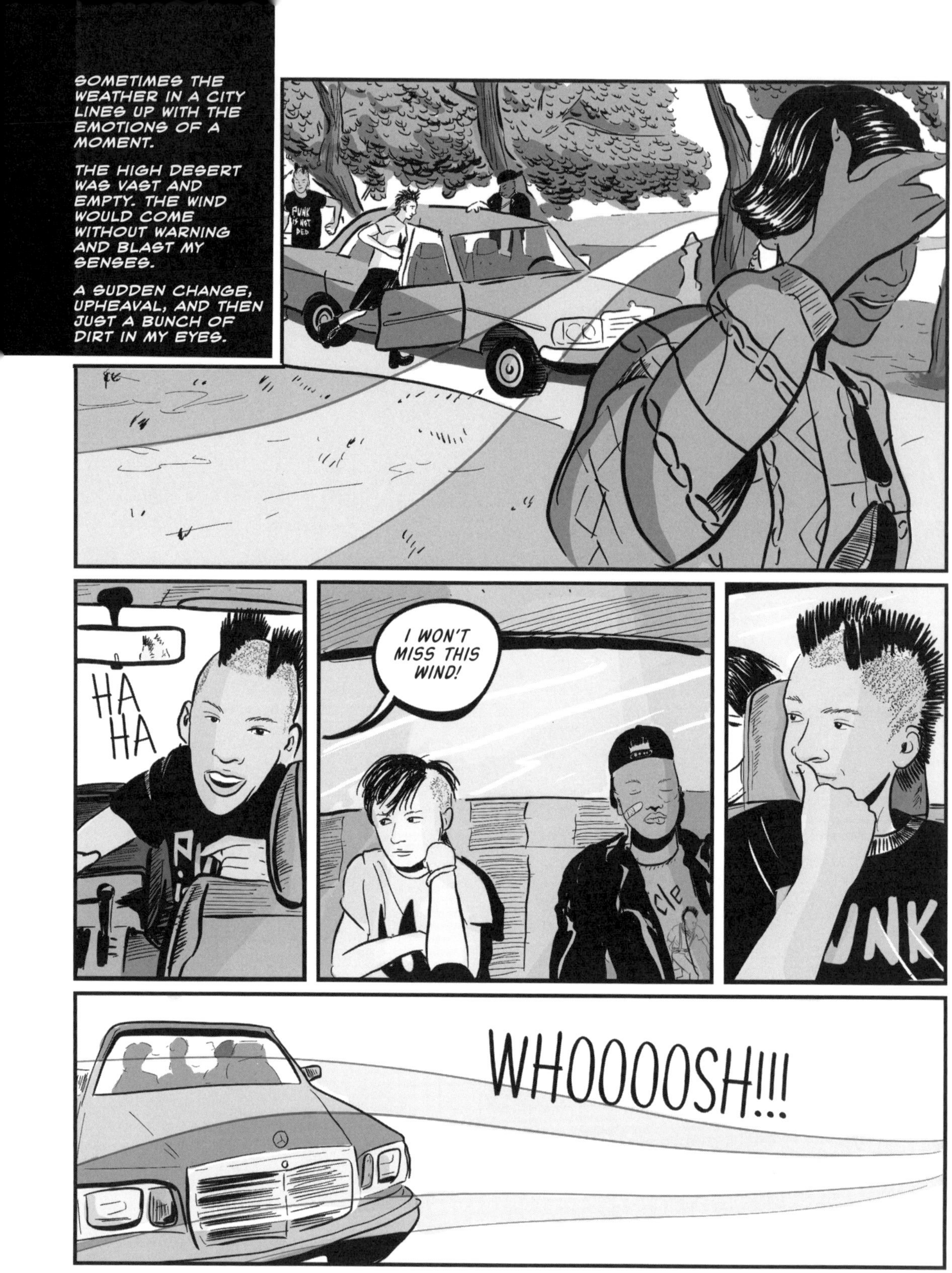
SOMETIMES THE WEATHER IN A CITY LINES UP WITH THE EMOTIONS OF A MOMENT.
THE HIGH DESERT WAS VAST AND EMPTY. THE WIND WOULD COME WITHOUT WARNING AND BLAST MY SENSES.
A SUDDEN CHANGE, UPHEAVAL, AND THEN JUST A BUNCH OF DIRT IN MY EYES.
HA HA
I WON'T MISS THIS WIND!
WHOOOOSH!!!...

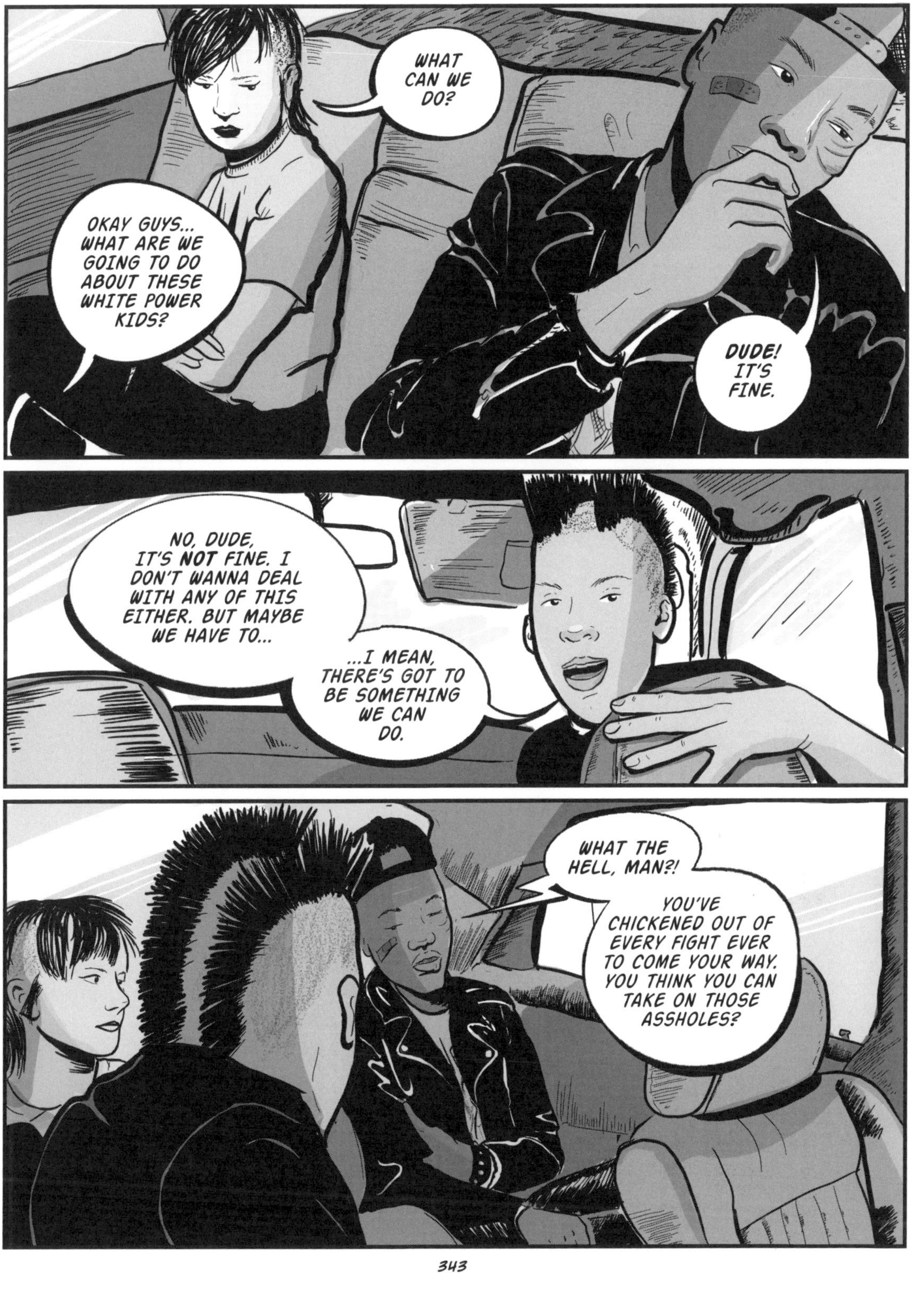
WHAT CAN WE DO?
OKAY GUYS... WHAT ARE WE GOING TO DO ABOUT THESE WHITE POWER KIDS?
DUDE! IT'S FINE.
NO, DUDE, IT'S **NOT** FINE. I DON'T WANNA DEAL WITH ANY OF THIS EITHER. BUT MAYBE WE HAVE TO...
...I MEAN, THERE'S GOT TO BE SOMETHING WE CAN DO.
WHAT THE HELL, MAN?!
YOU'VE CHICKENED OUT OF EVERY FIGHT EVER TO COME YOUR WAY. YOU THINK YOU CAN TAKE ON THOSE ASSHOLES?

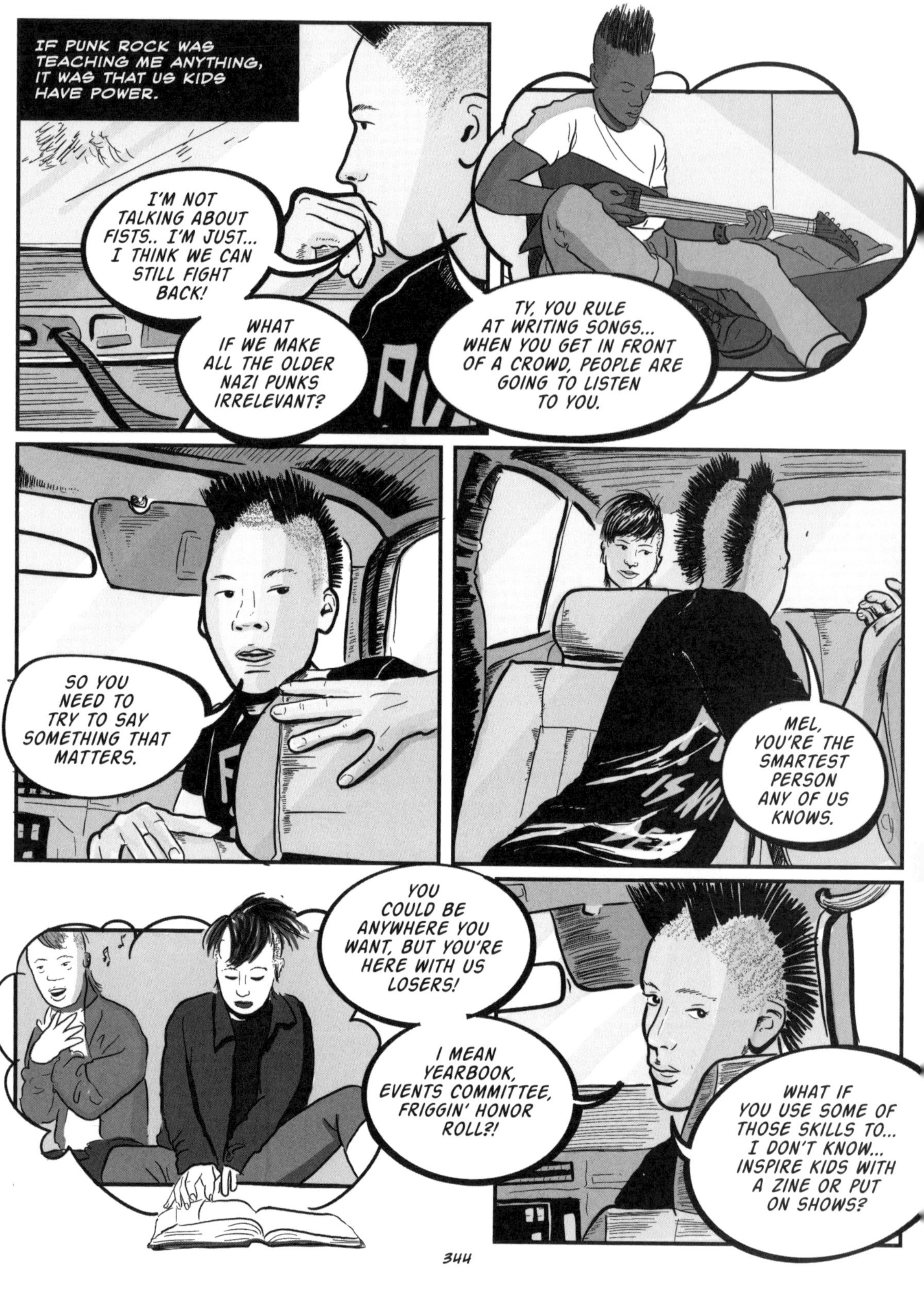
IF PUNK ROCK WAS TEACHING ME ANYTHING, IT WAS THAT US KIDS HAVE POWER.
I'M NOT TALKING ABOUT FISTS.. I'M JUST... I THINK WE CAN STILL FIGHT BACK!
WHAT IF WE MAKE ALL THE OLDER NAZI PUNKS IRRELEVANT?
TY, YOU RULE AT WRITING SONGS... WHEN YOU GET IN FRONT OF A CROWD, PEOPLE ARE GOING TO LISTEN TO YOU.
SO YOU NEED TO TRY TO SAY SOMETHING THAT MATTERS.
MEL, YOU'RE THE SMARTEST PERSON ANY OF US KNOWS.
YOU COULD BE ANYWHERE YOU WANT, BUT YOU'RE HERE WITH US LOSERS!
I MEAN YEARBOOK, EVENTS COMMITTEE, FRIGGIN' HONOR ROLL?!
WHAT IF YOU USE SOME OF THOSE SKILLS TO... I DON'T KNOW... INSPIRE KIDS WITH A ZINE OR PUT ON SHOWS?

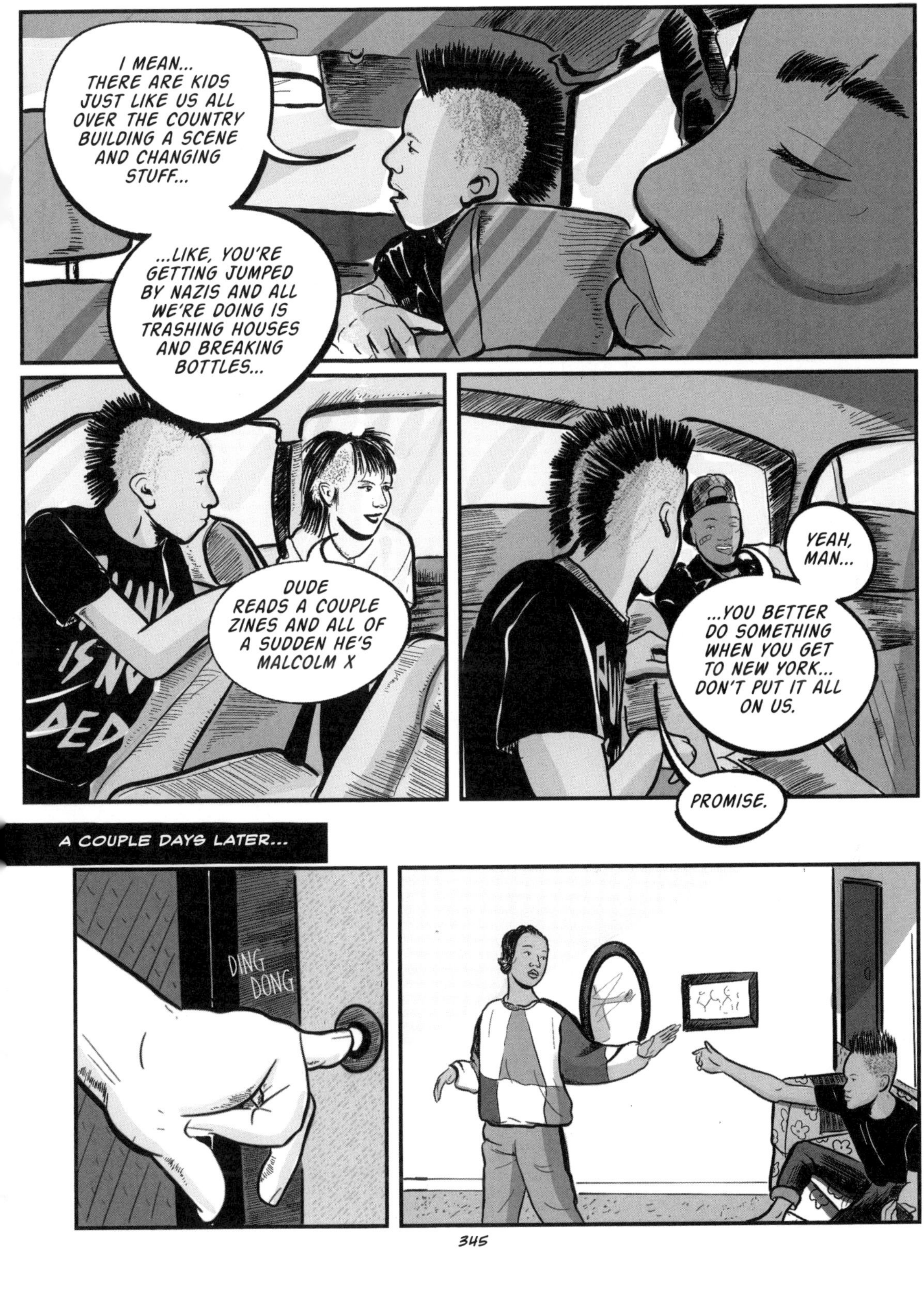
I MEAN... THERE ARE KIDS JUST LIKE US ALL OVER THE COUNTRY BUILDING A SCENE AND CHANGING STUFF...
...LIKE, YOU'RE GETTING JUMPED BY NAZIS AND ALL WE'RE DOING IS TRASHING HOUSES AND BREAKING BOTTLES...
DUDE READS A COUPLE ZINES AND ALL OF A SUDDEN HE'S MALCOLM X
YEAH, MAN...
...YOU BETTER DO SOMETHING WHEN YOU GET TO NEW YORK... DON'T PUT IT ALL ON US.
PROMISE.
A COUPLE DAYS LATER...
DING DONG

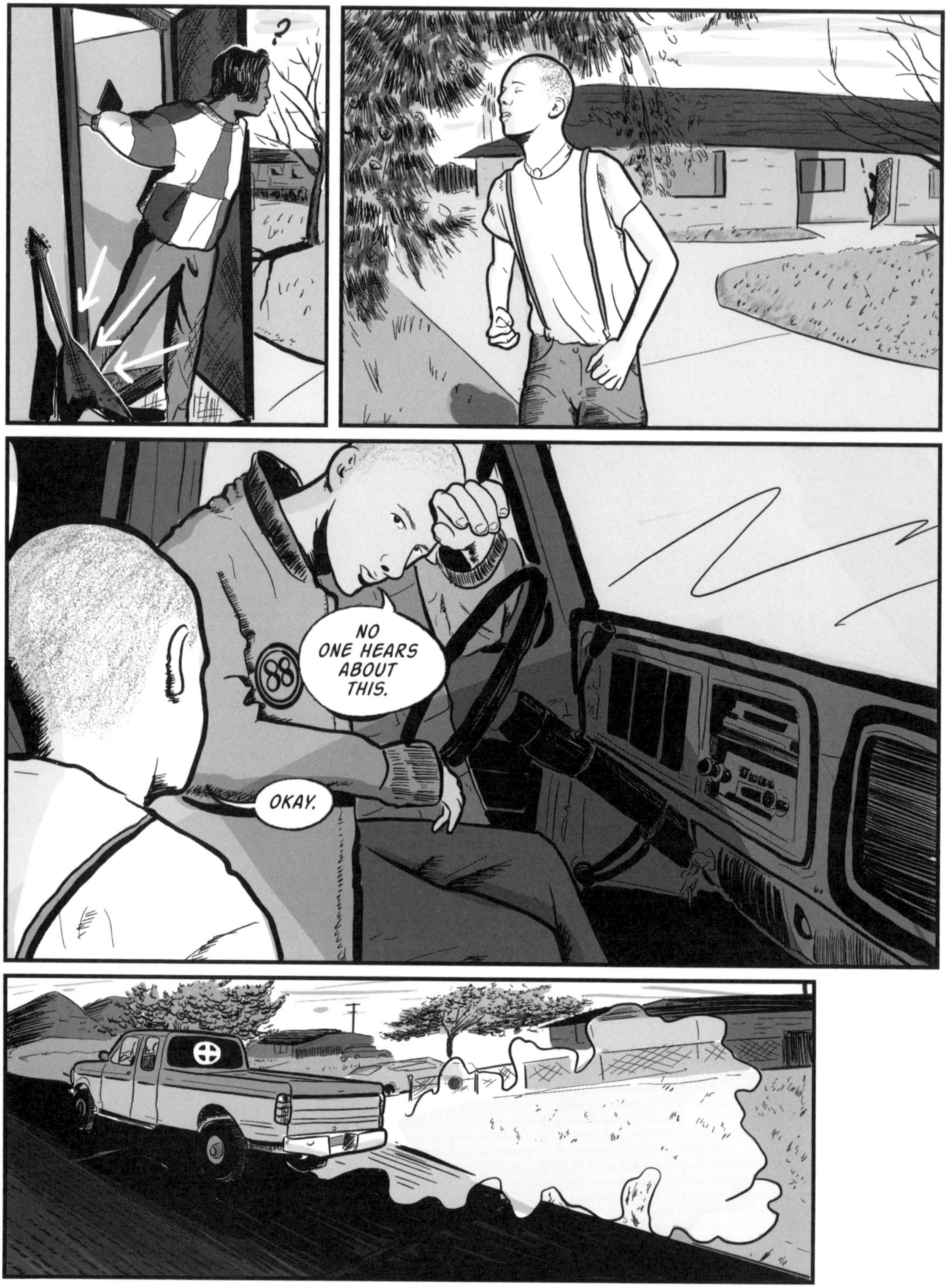
?
NO ONE HEARS ABOUT THIS.
OKAY.
88

CHAPTER 11
GIMMIE GIMMIE GIMMIE

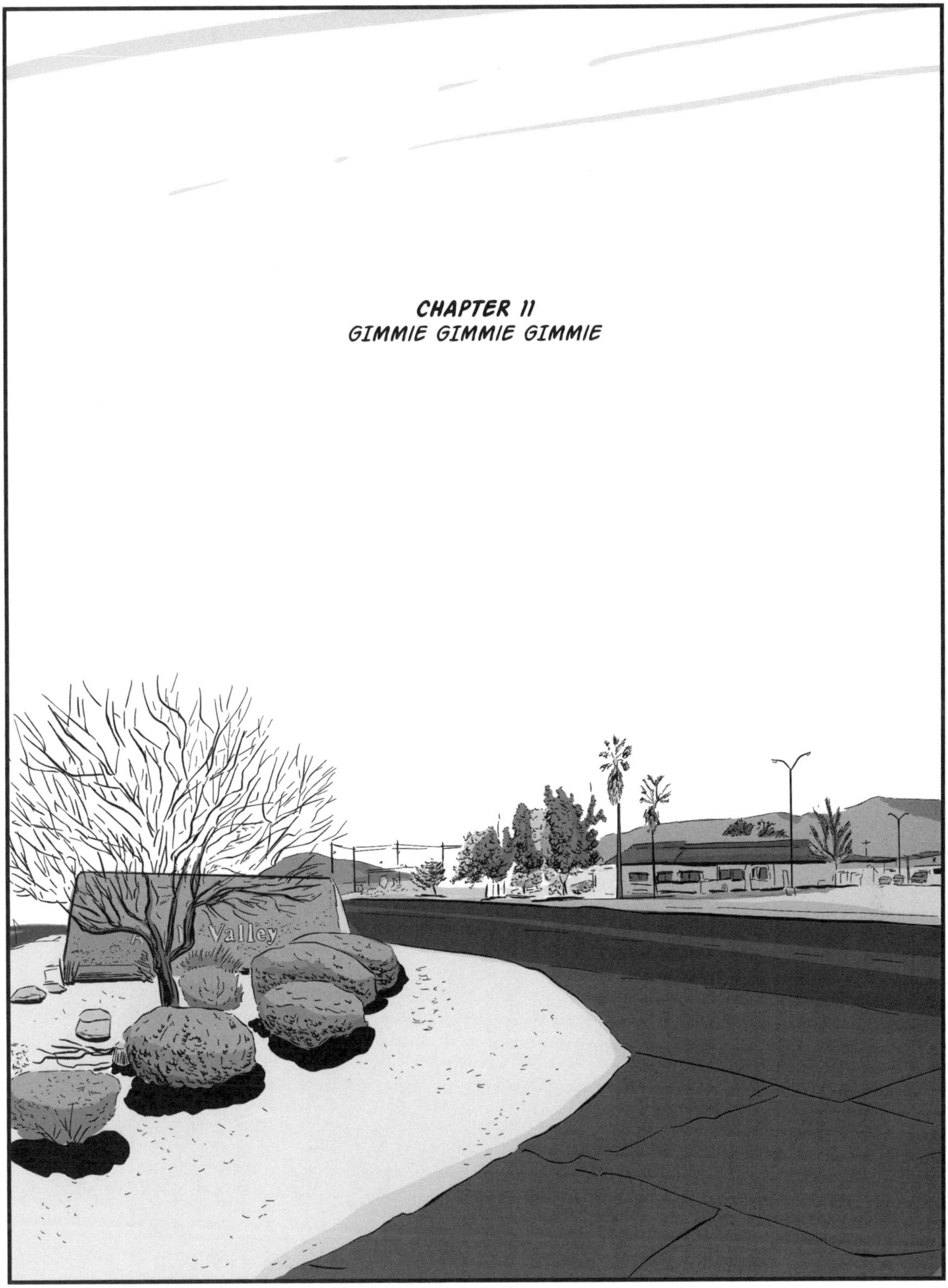
Valley

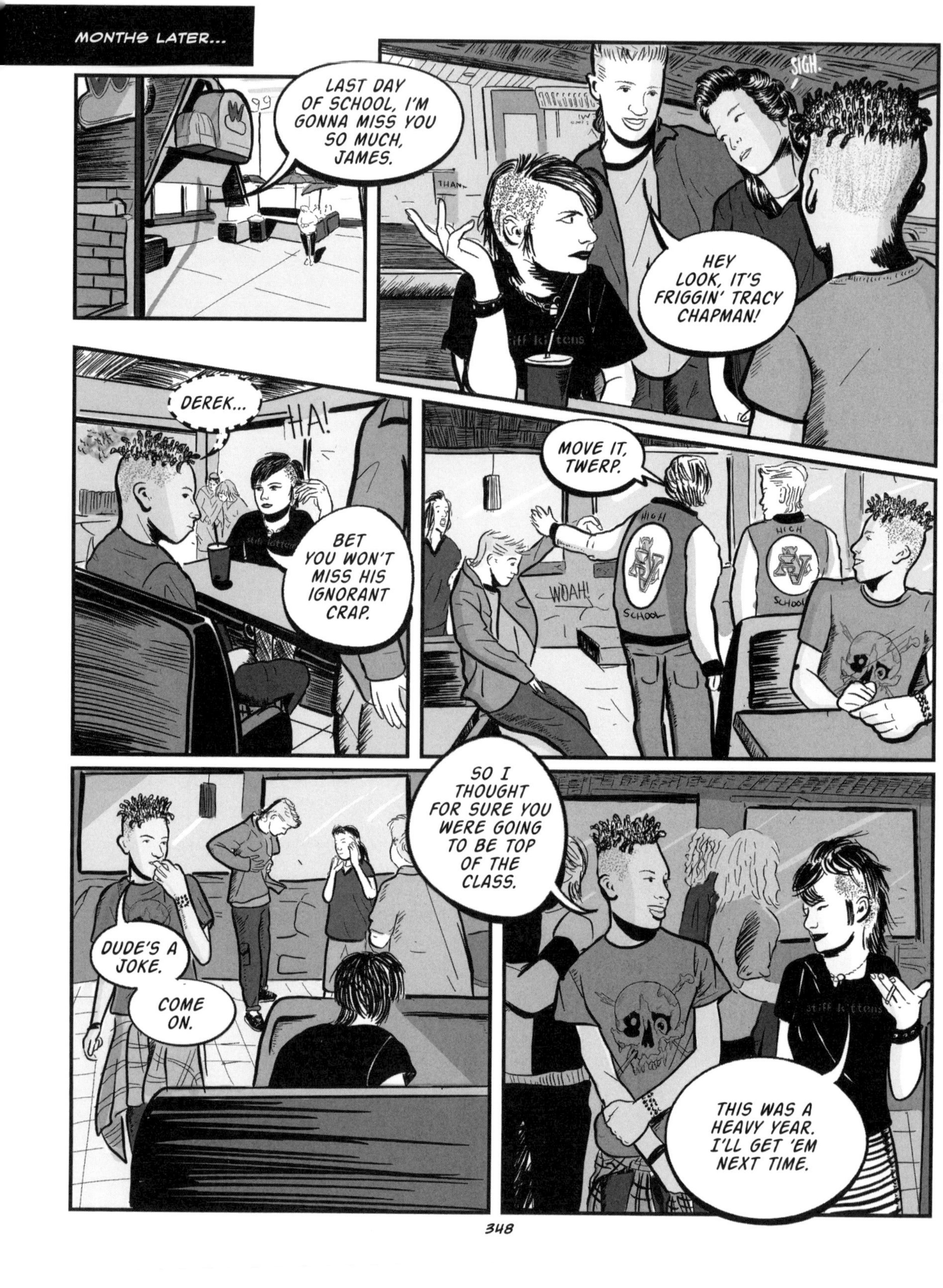
MONTHS LATER...
LAST DAY OF SCHOOL, I'M GONNA MISS YOU SO MUCH, JAMES.
SIGH.
HEY LOOK, IT'S FRIGGIN' TRACY CHAPMAN!
DEREK...
HA!
BET YOU WON'T MISS HIS IGNORANT CRAP.
MOVE IT, TWERP.
HIGH SCHOOL
WOAH!
HIGH SCHOOL
SO I THOUGHT FOR SURE YOU WERE GOING TO BE TOP OF THE CLASS.
DUDE'S A JOKE.
COME ON.
THIS WAS A HEAVY YEAR. I'LL GET 'EM NEXT TIME.

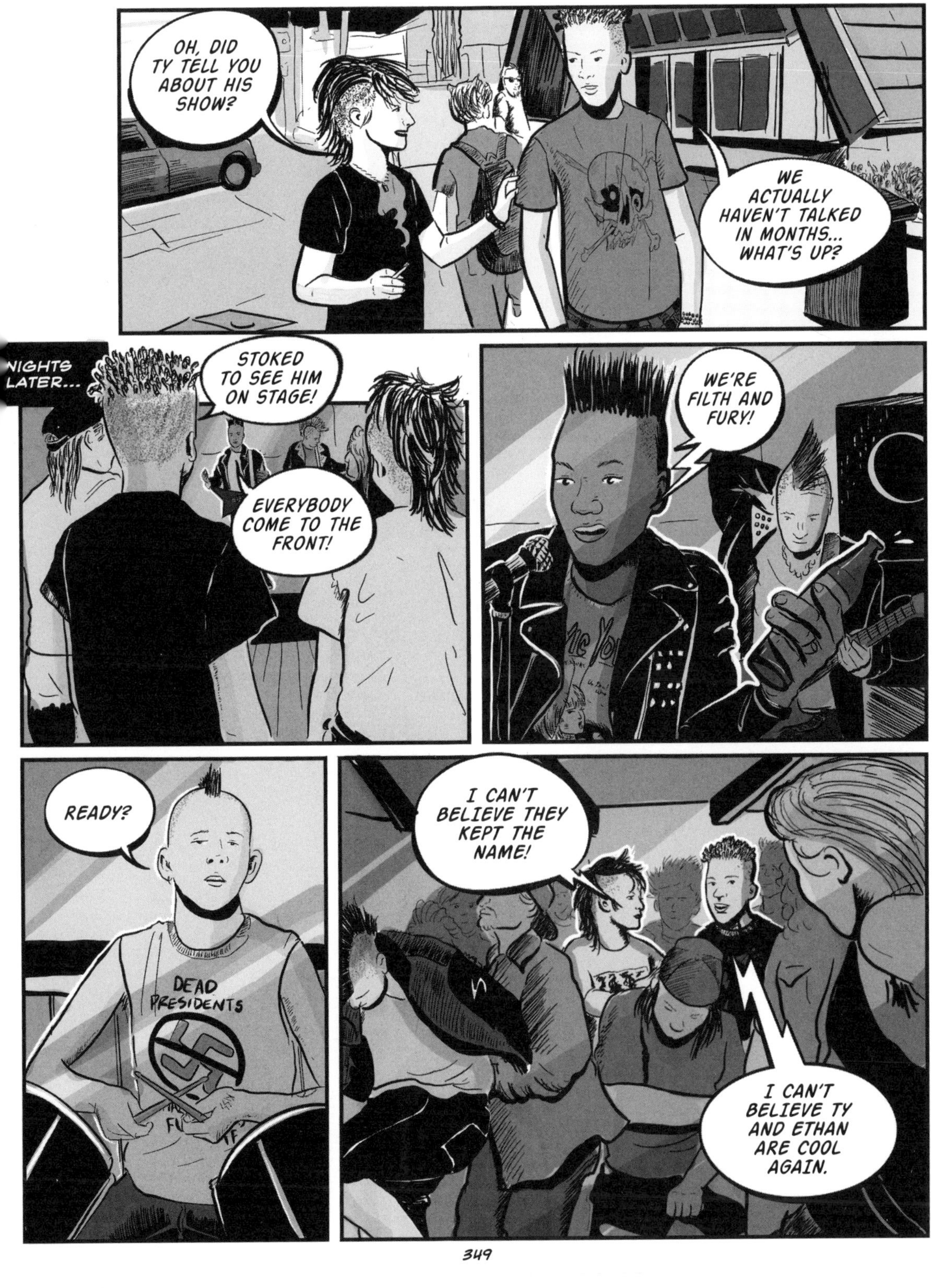
OH, DID TY TELL YOU ABOUT HIS SHOW?
WE ACTUALLY HAVEN'T TALKED IN MONTHS... WHAT'S UP?
NIGHTS LATER...
STOKED TO SEE HIM ON STAGE!
EVERYBODY COME TO THE FRONT!
WE'RE FILTH AND FURY!
READY?
DEAD PRESIDENTS
I CAN'T BELIEVE THEY KEPT THE NAME!
I CAN'T BELIEVE TY AND ETHAN ARE COOL AGAIN.

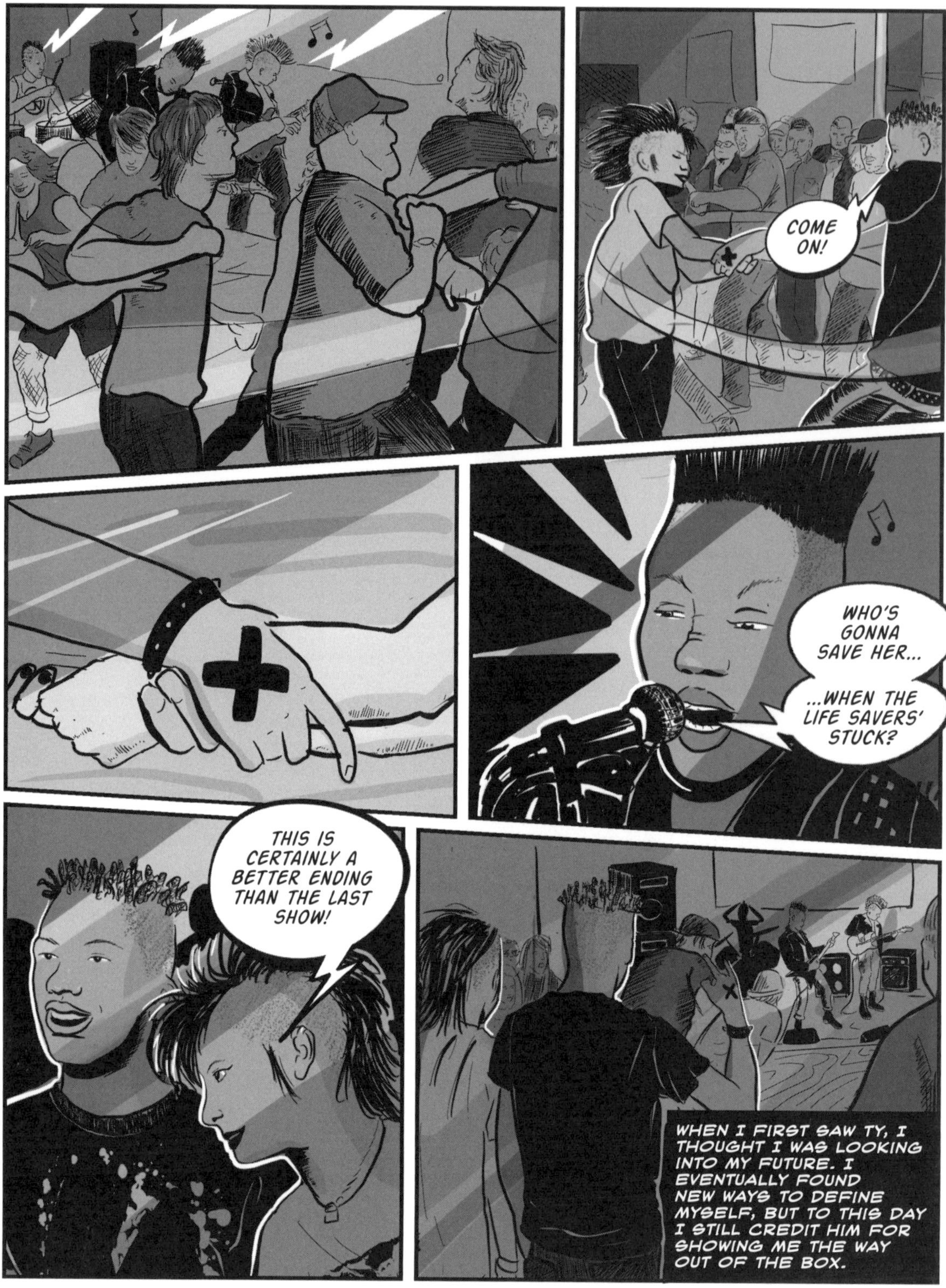
COME ON!
WHO'S GONNA SAVE HER...
...WHEN THE LIFE SAVERS' STUCK?
THIS IS CERTAINLY A BETTER ENDING THAN THE LAST SHOW!
WHEN I FIRST SAW TY, I THOUGHT I WAS LOOKING INTO MY FUTURE. I EVENTUALLY FOUND NEW WAYS TO DEFINE MYSELF, BUT TO THIS DAY I STILL CREDIT HIM FOR SHOWING ME THE WAY OUT OF THE BOX.

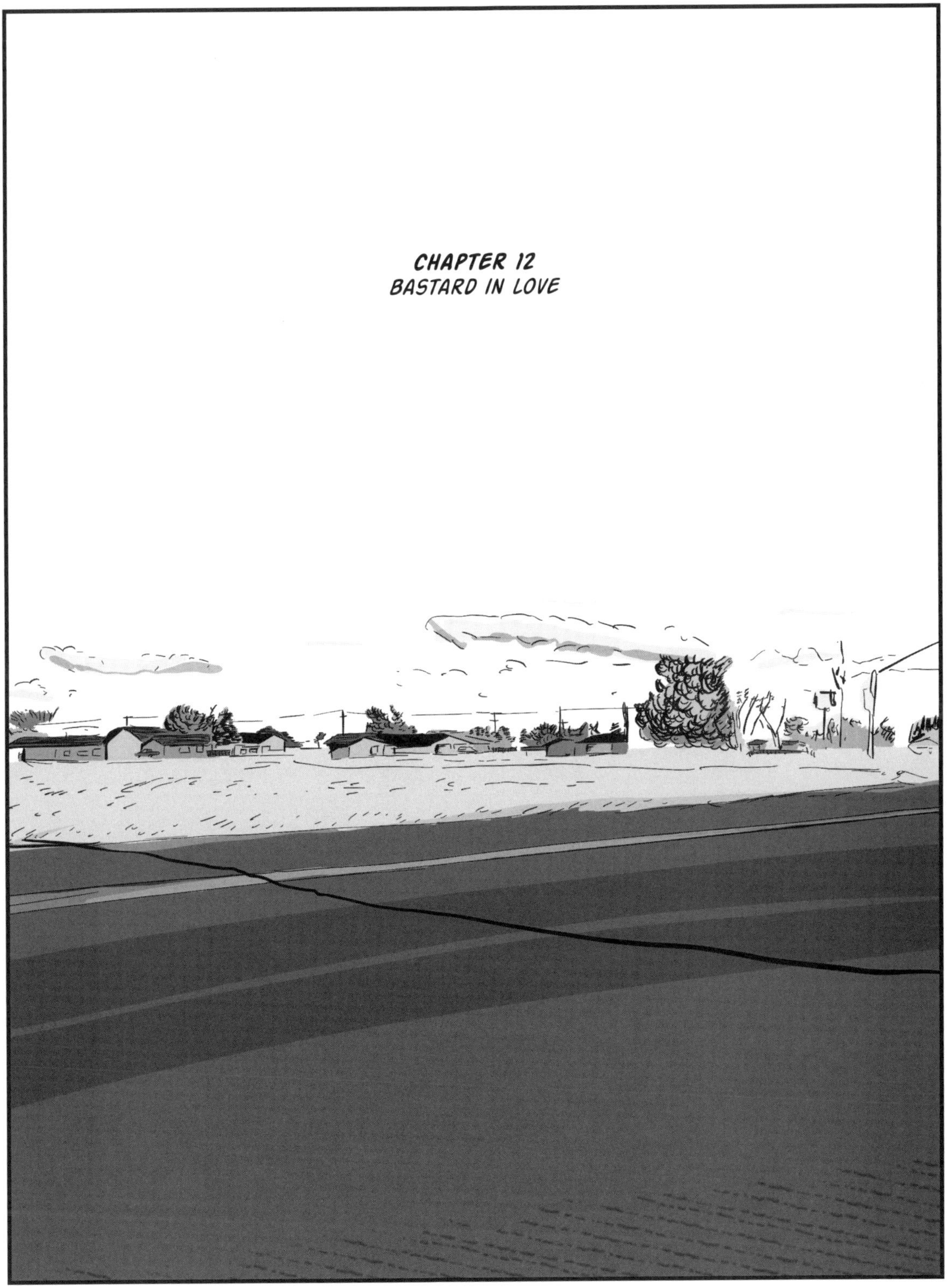
CHAPTER 12
BASTARD IN LOVE

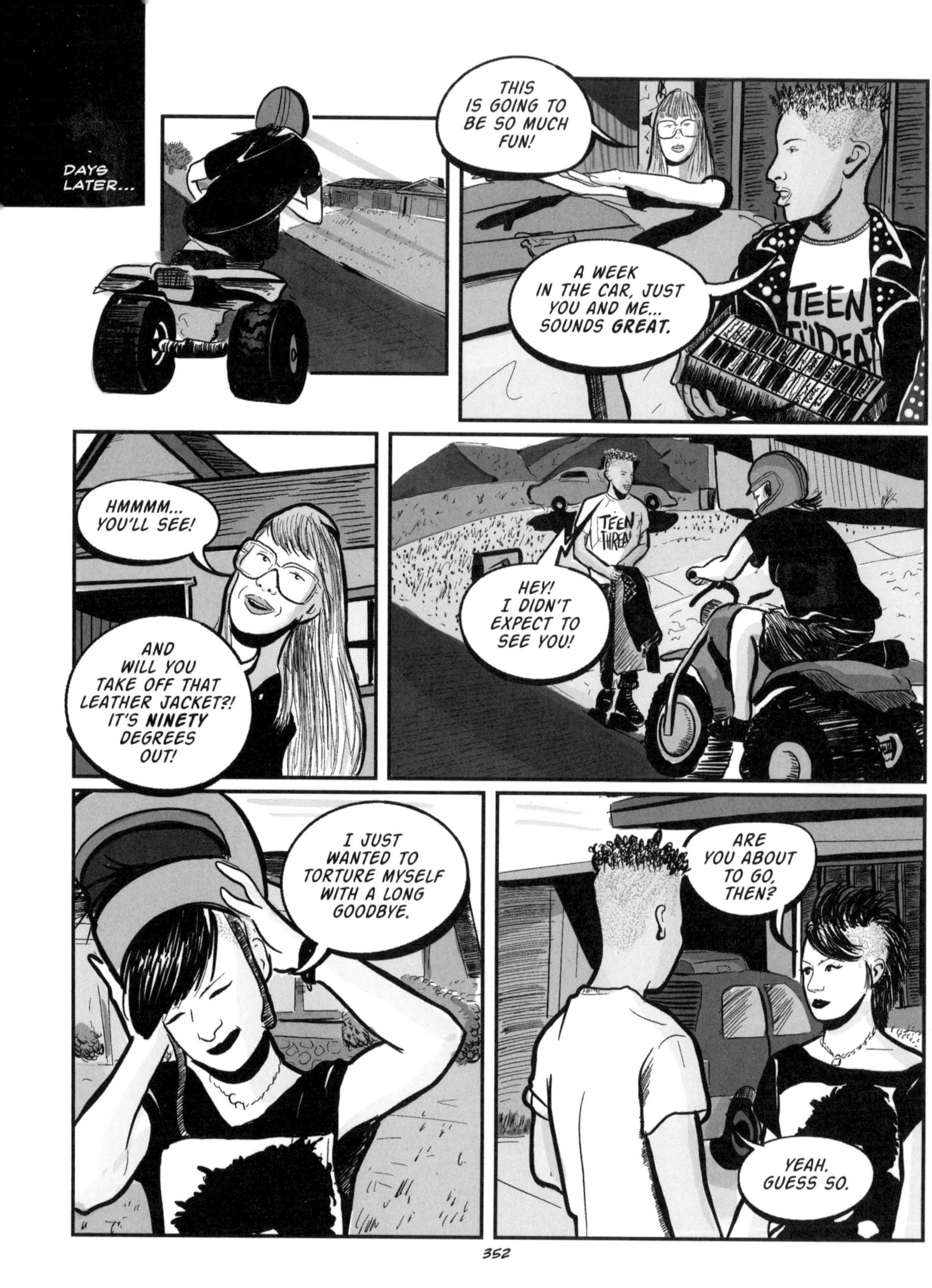
DAYS LATER...
THIS IS GOING TO BE SO MUCH FUN!
A WEEK IN THE CAR, JUST YOU AND ME... SOUNDS GREAT.
TEEN THREAT
HMMMM... YOU'LL SEE!
AND WILL YOU TAKE OFF THAT LEATHER JACKET?! IT'S NINETY DEGREES OUT!
TEEN THREAT
HEY! I DIDN'T EXPECT TO SEE YOU!
I JUST WANTED TO TORTURE MYSELF WITH A LONG GOODBYE.
ARE YOU ABOUT TO GO, THEN?
YEAH. GUESS SO.

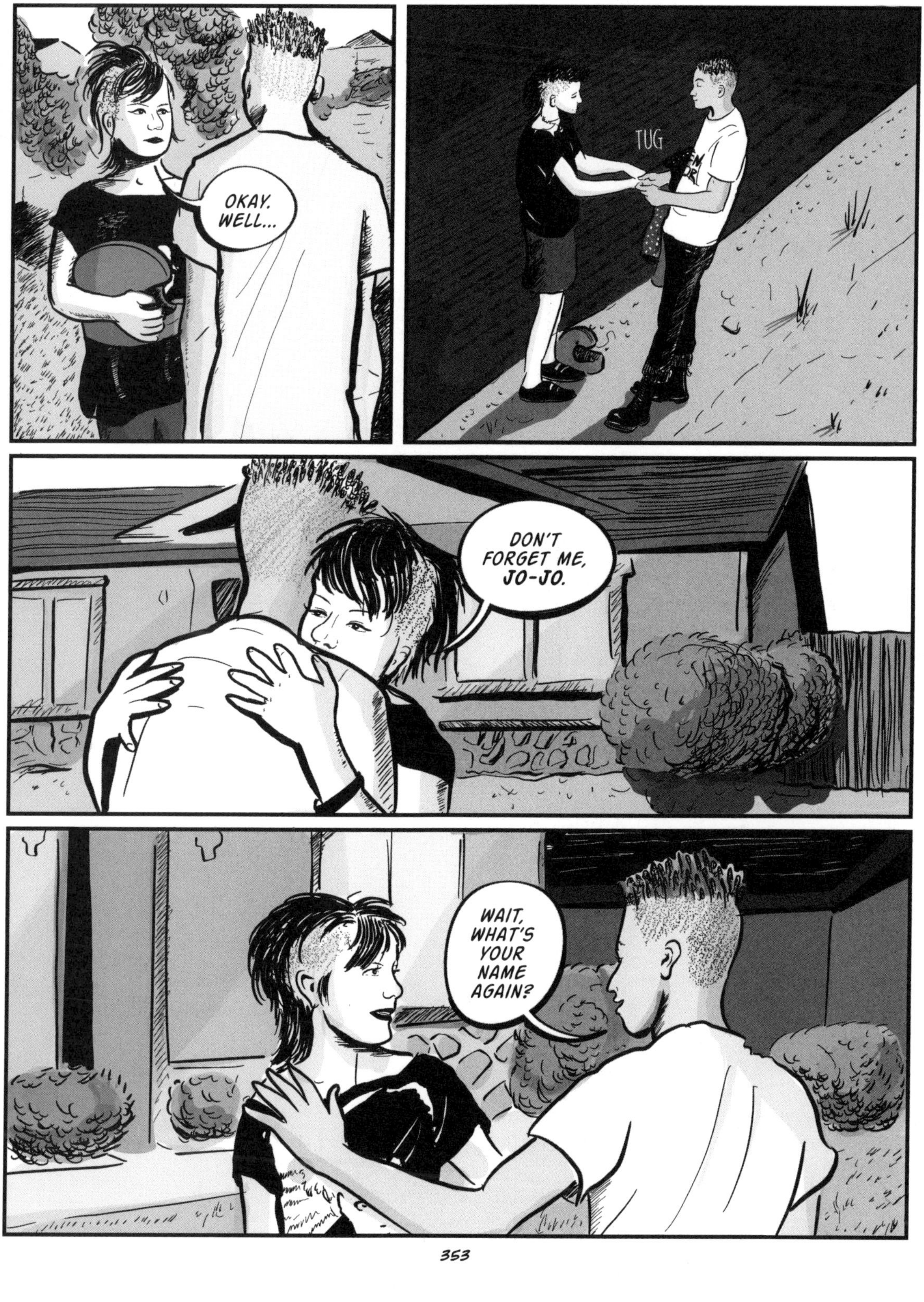
OKAY. WELL...
TUG
DON'T FORGET ME, JO-JO.
WAIT, WHAT'S YOUR NAME AGAIN?

I MADE YOU SOMETHING.
TEEN THREAT
REALLY?
YOU MADE THIS?
JUST A BUNCH OF DEPRESSING SONGS I THOUGHT YOU MIGHT LIKE.
TuRN your GAZE InWARd
DAMN... UM... THANKS.
THAT'S THE LAST OF IT. SAY GOODBYE TO YOUR LITTLE FRIEND.

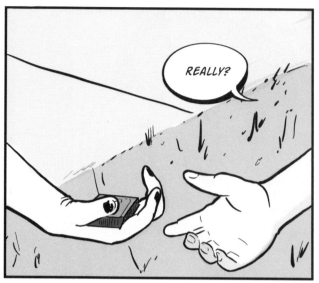

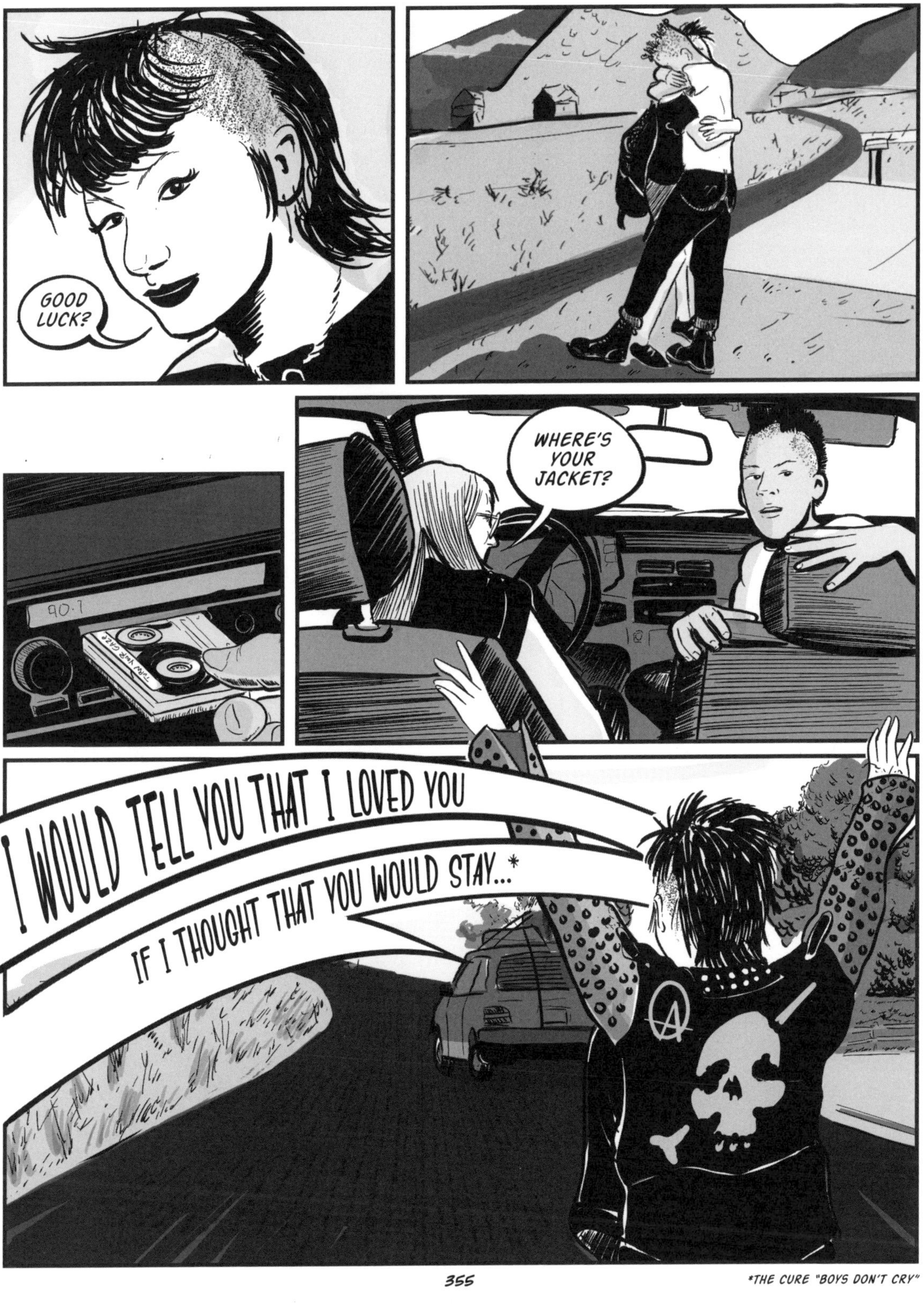
GOOD LUCK?
WHERE'S YOUR JACKET?
90.7
I WOULD TELL YOU THAT I LOVED YOU
IF I THOUGHT THAT YOU WOULD STAY...*

*THE CURE "BOYS DON'T CRY"

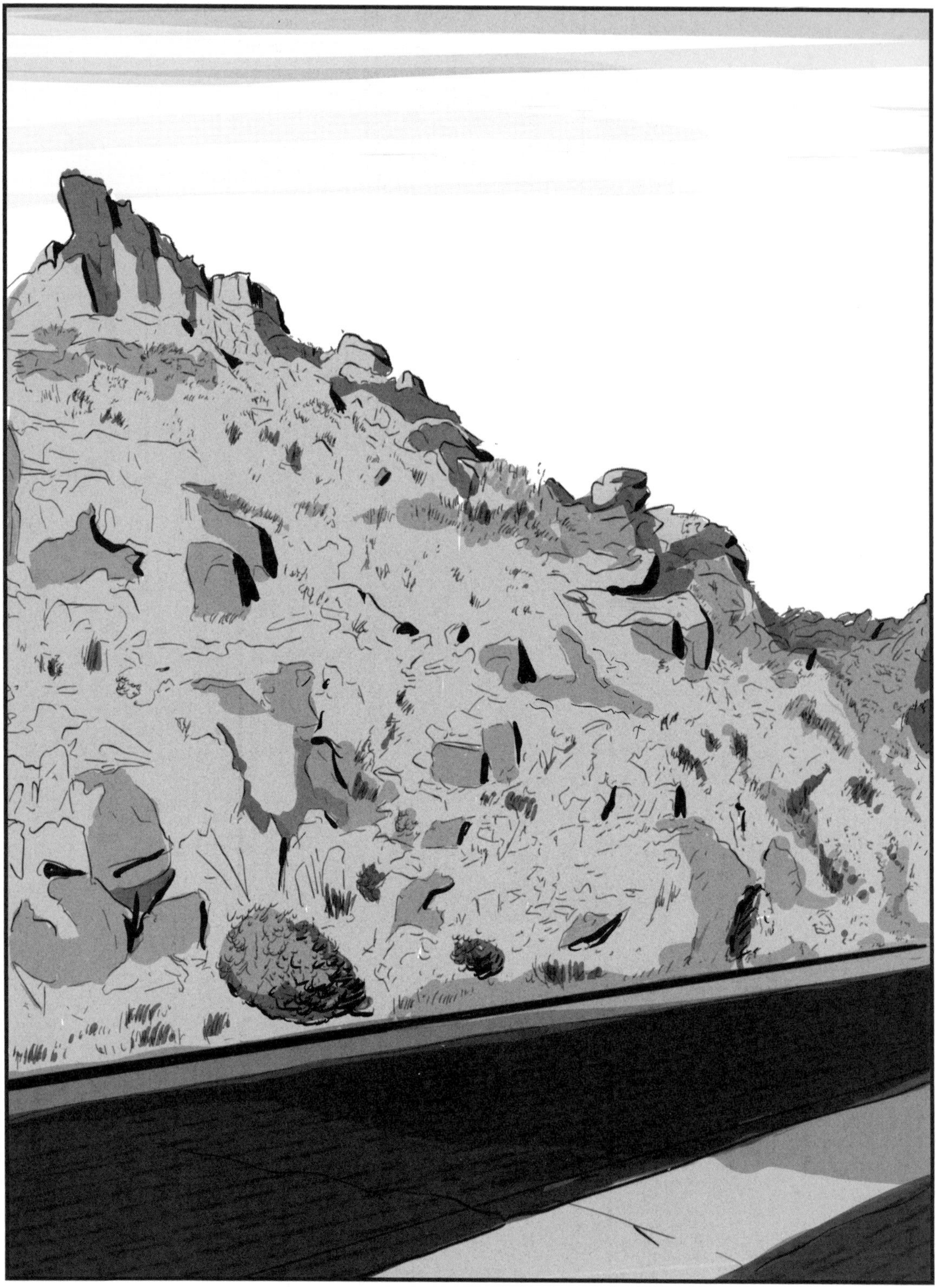

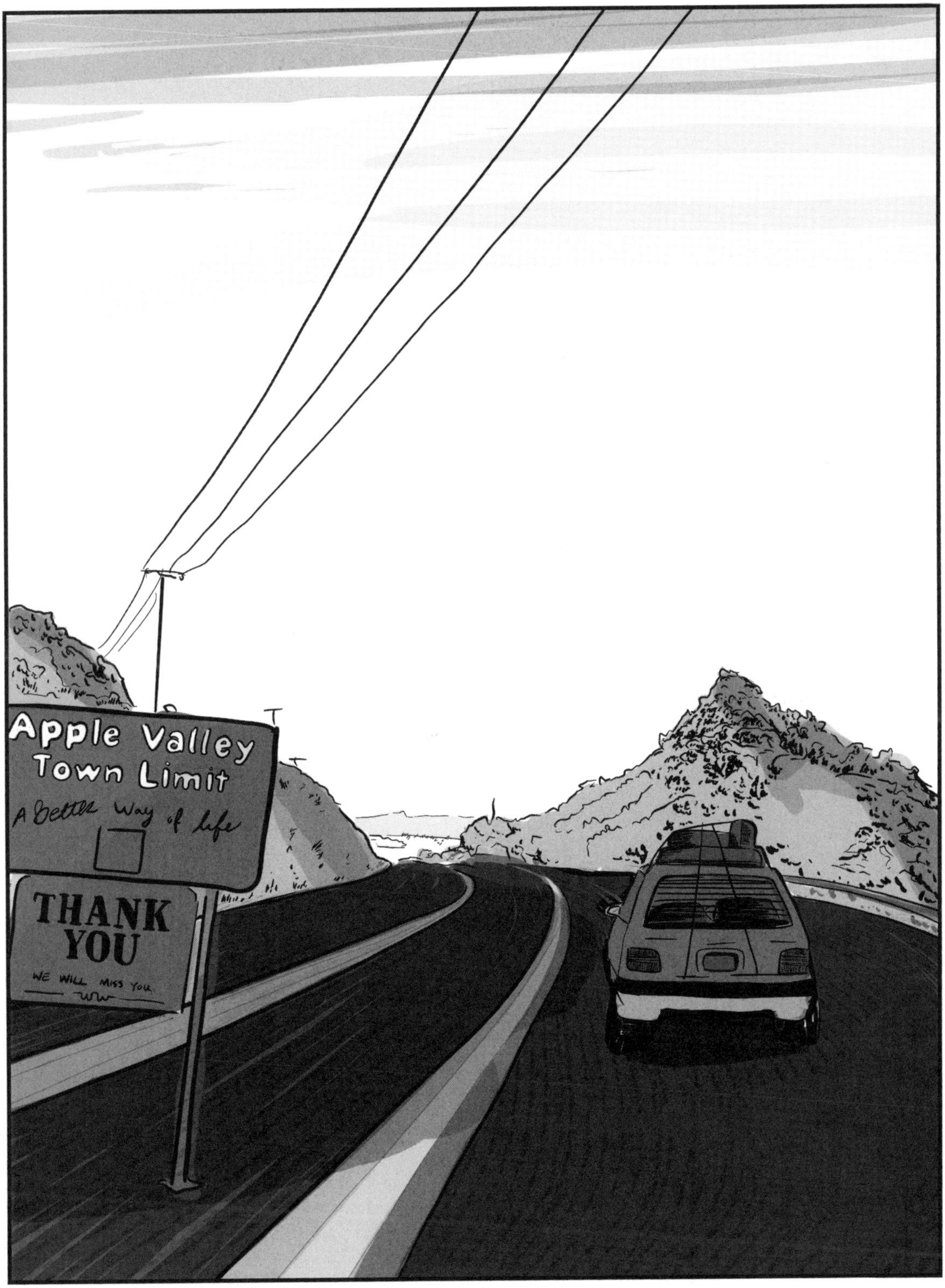
Apple Valley
Town Limit
A Better Way of life
THANK YOU
WE WILL MISS YOU

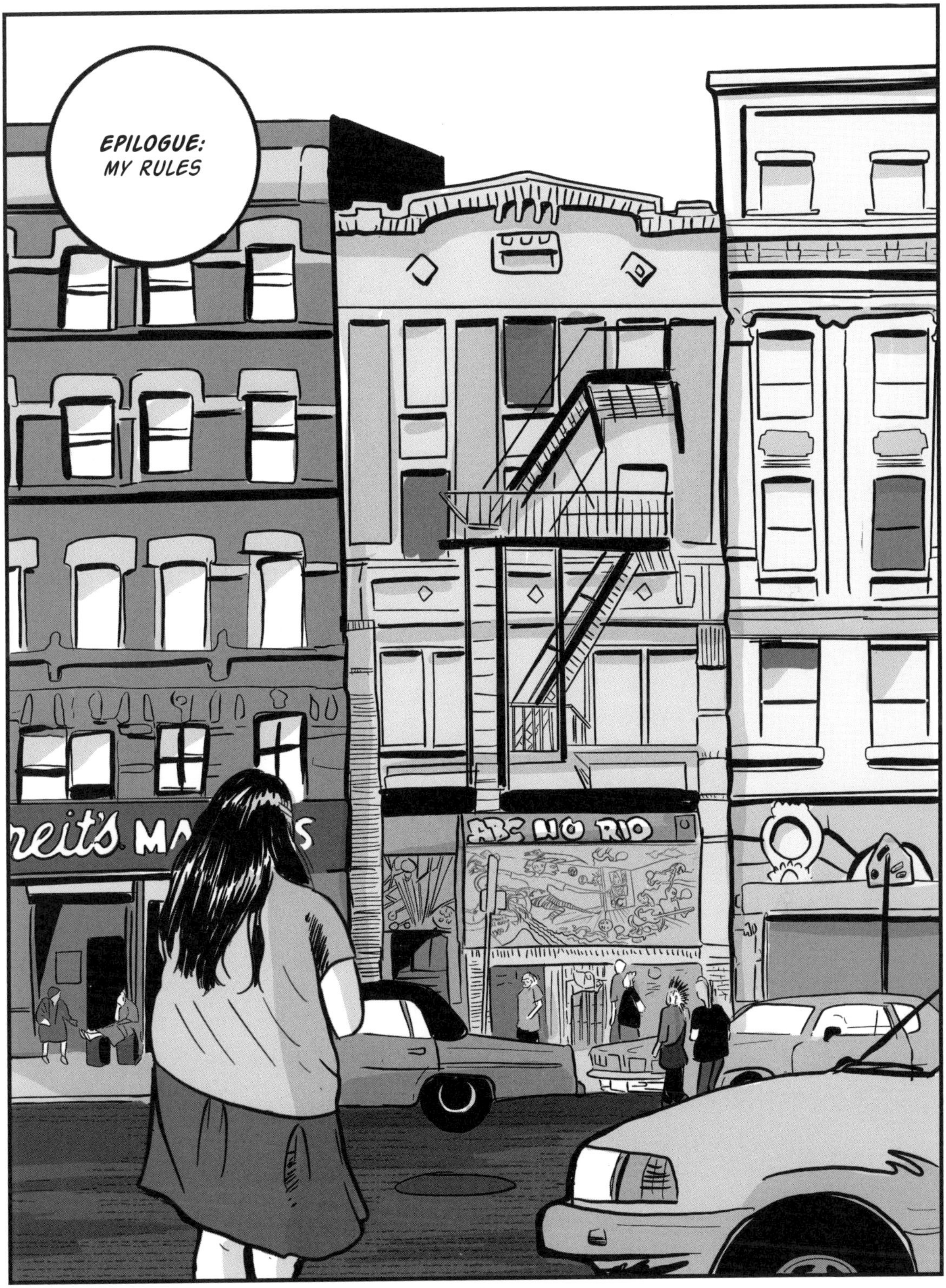
EPILOGUE:
MY RULES
ABC NO RIO

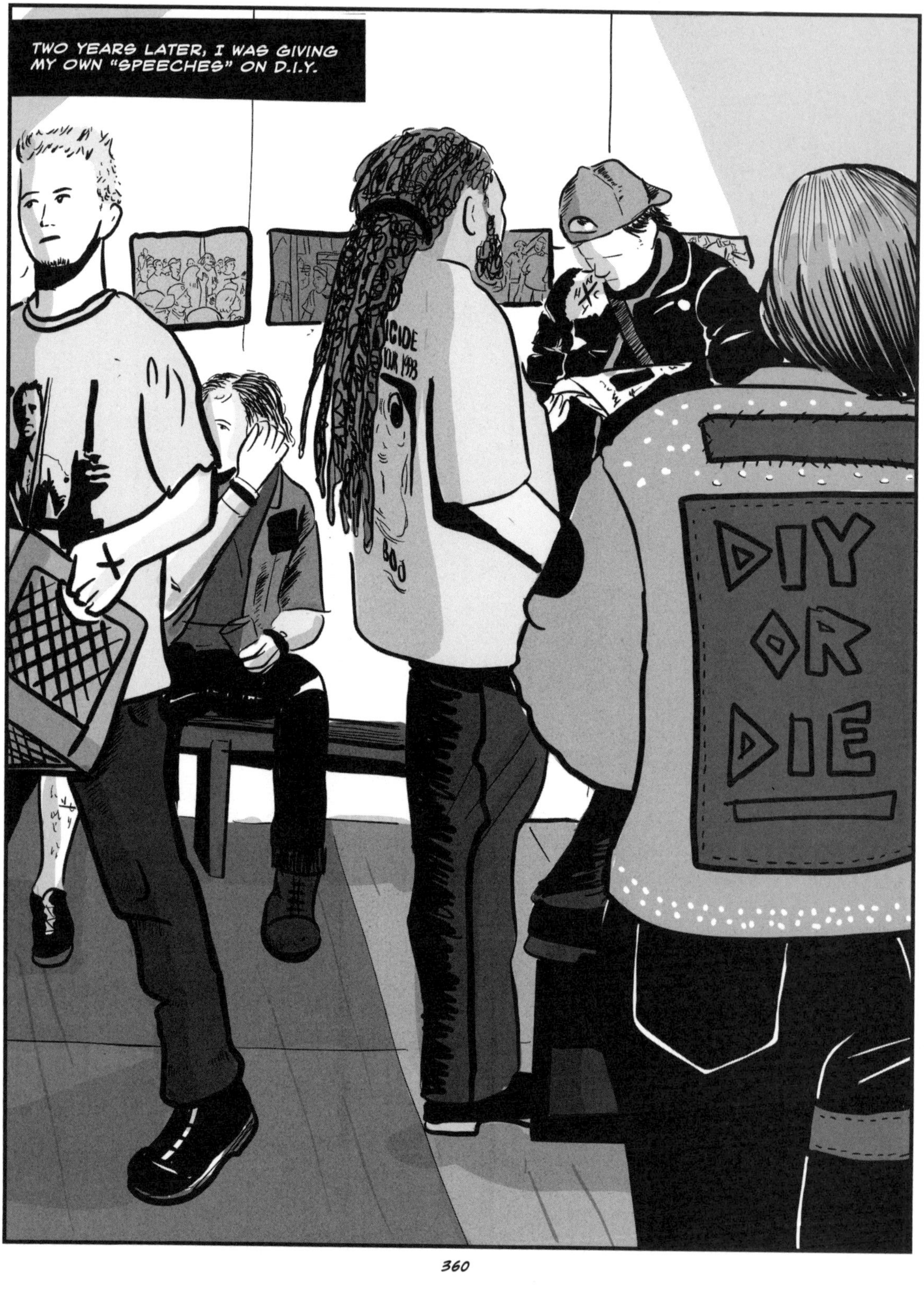
TWO YEARS LATER, I WAS GIVING MY OWN "SPEECHES" ON D.I.Y.
DIY OR DIE

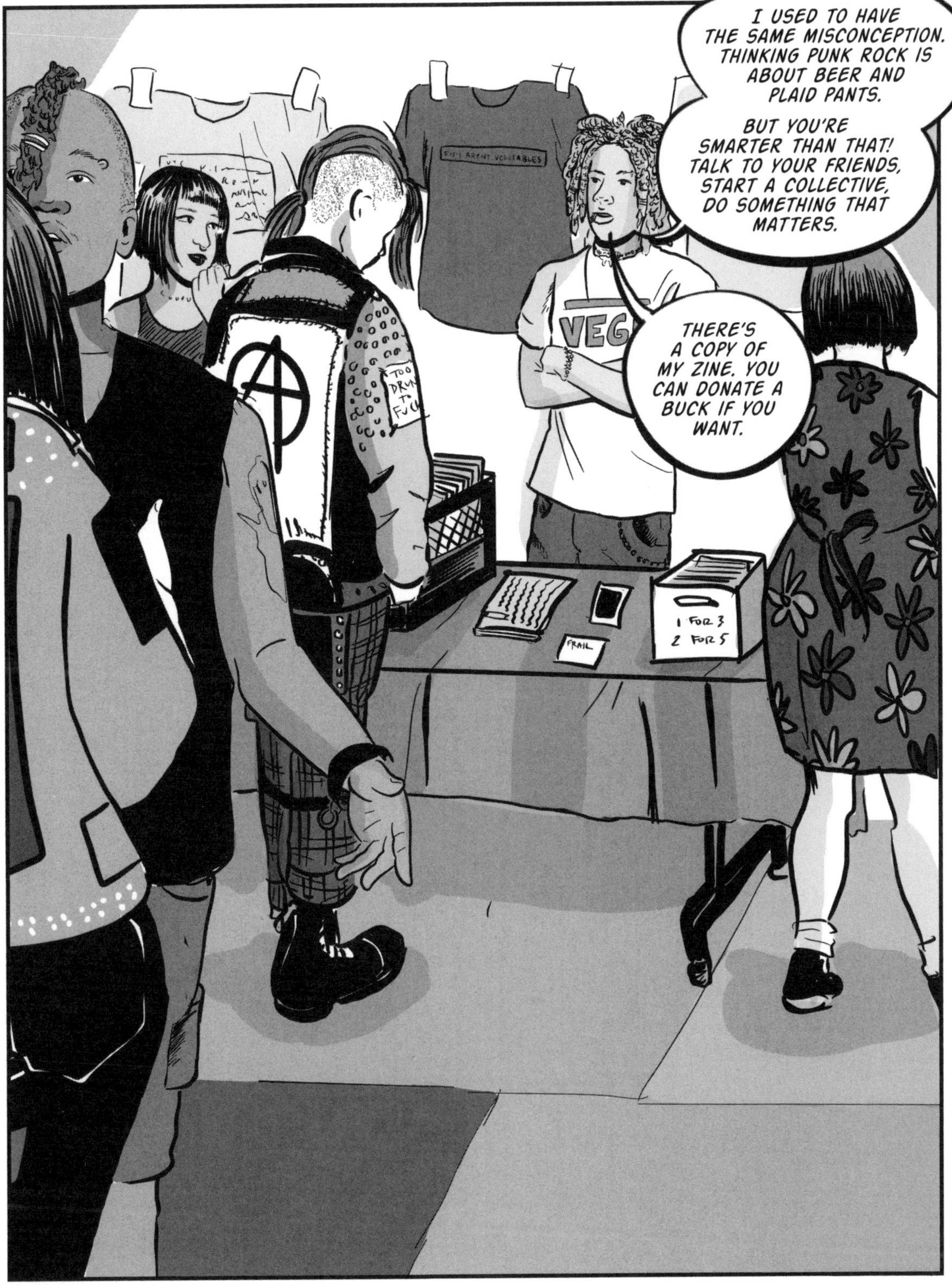
I USED TO HAVE THE SAME MISCONCEPTION. THINKING PUNK ROCK IS ABOUT BEER AND PLAID PANTS.
BUT YOU'RE SMARTER THAN THAT! TALK TO YOUR FRIENDS, START A COLLECTIVE, DO SOMETHING THAT MATTERS.
THERE'S A COPY OF MY ZINE. YOU CAN DONATE A BUCK IF YOU WANT.
VEG
FRAIL
1 FOR 3
2 FOR 5

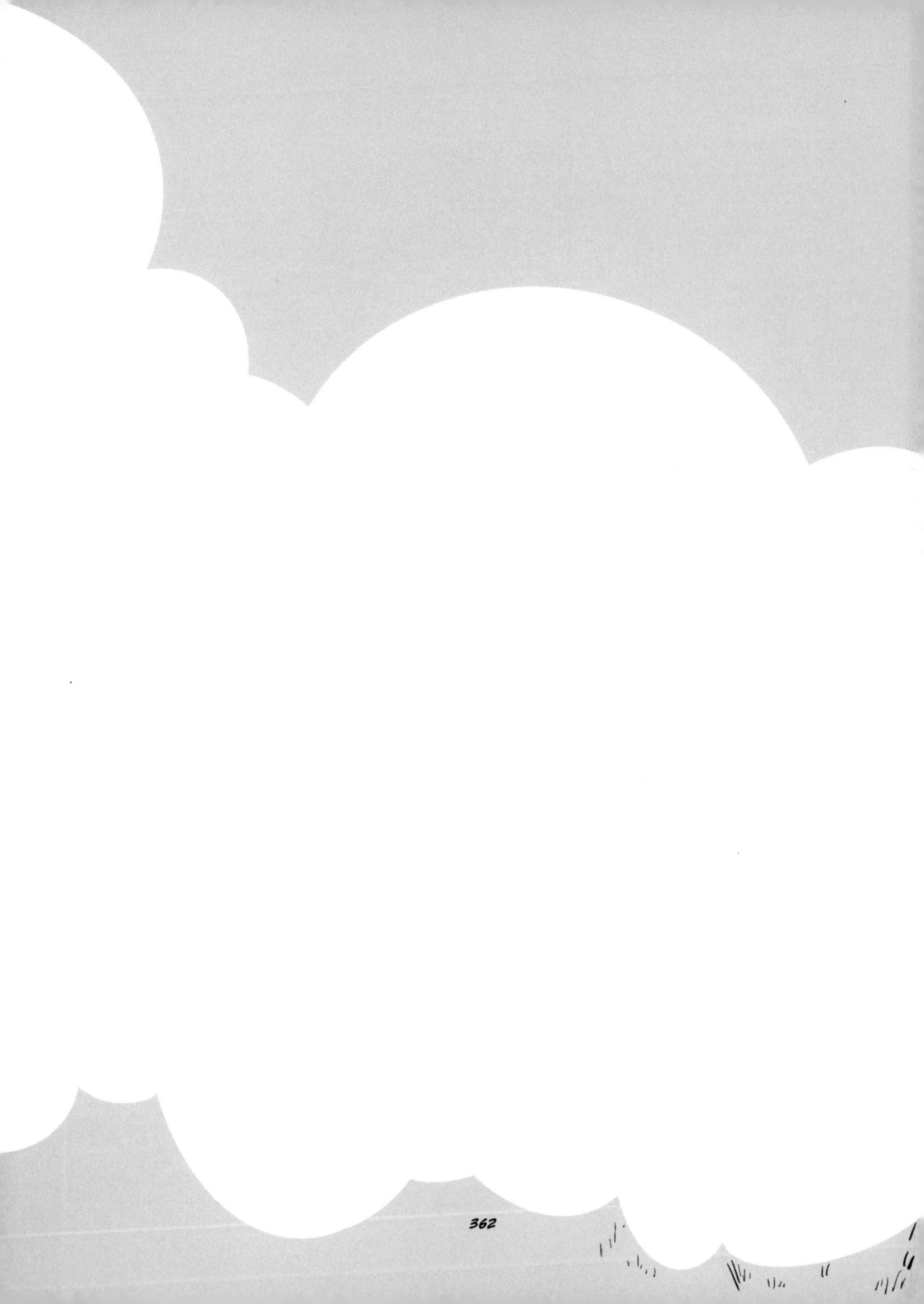

I DISCOVERED PUNK ROCK AT AGE THIRTEEN. IN MANY WAYS, PUNK RAISED ME.

AFTER MOVING TO NEW YORK, I FOUND A TRUE D.I.Y. PUNK AND HARDCORE SCENE. I QUICKLY SUBMERGED MYSELF INTO THE UNDERGROUND. I GOT MY POLITICS ON POINT, BECAME A VEGAN, AN ACTIVIST, AND VOLUNTEERED AND SQUATTED AT ABC NO RIO. I HELPED REKINDLE FOOD NOT BOMBS, MADE SEVERAL ZINES, AND STARTED A RECORD LABEL. THIS IS WHAT PUNK INSPIRED.

I ALSO MADE LIFELONG FRIENDS AND FOUND A COMMUNITY.

COURTESY OF THE AUTHOR

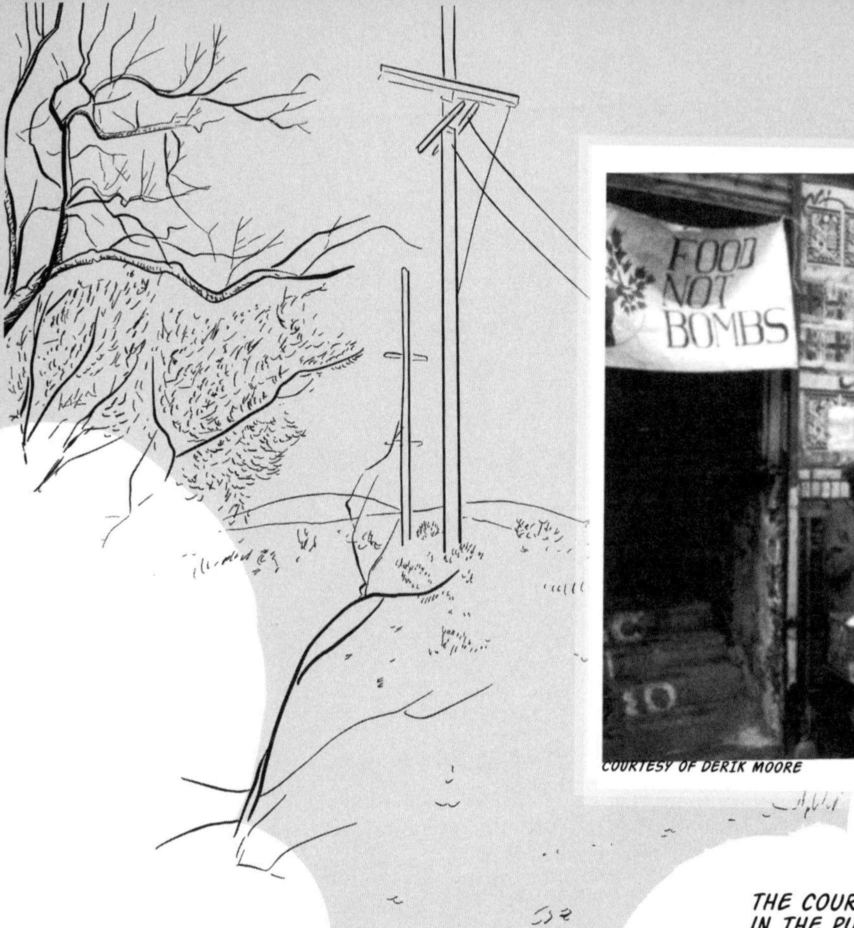

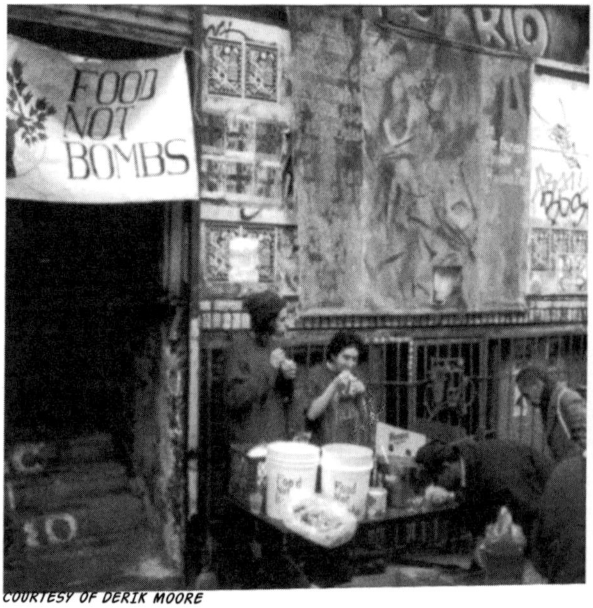
FOOD
NOT
BOMBS

COURTESY OF DERIK MOORE

THE COURAGE AND AUDACITY I GAINED IN THE PUNK SCENE FUELED MY LATER ARTISTIC ENDEAVOR: THE DOCUMENTARY "AFRO-PUNK" (2003). THE FILM, IN TURN, HELPED FOSTER A BLACK PUNK/ INDIE SCENE IN NEW YORK CITY, CREATING THE ALL-BLACK MOSH PIT I ONCE DREAMED OF.

BLACK AND POC PUNK KIDS AROUND THE WORLD CREDIT THE DOCUMENTARY AND THE EARLY AFRO-PUNK EVENTS AS INSPIRATION FOR THEIR OWN COLLECTIVES AND FESTIVALS.

PUNK ASKS ITS LISTENERS TO QUESTION BOTH OURSELVES AND SOCIETY. WE'VE CHANGED THE WORLD IN WAYS MANY NEVER REALIZE, ALWAYS PUSHING UP AGAINST THE MAINSTREAM, BUT NEVER LEAVING THE UNDERGROUND.

THIS BOOK IS MY LOVE LETTER TO THE SCENE, THE BANDS, AND MOST OF ALL, THE KIDS.

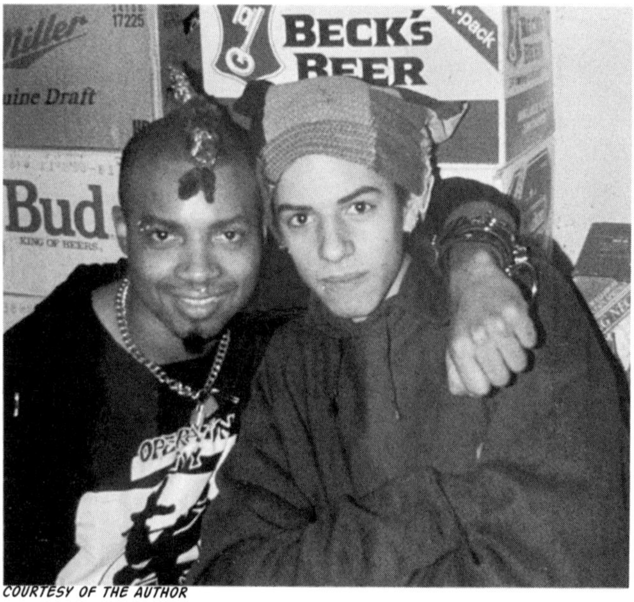
Miller
BECK'S
BEER
Bud
KING OF BEERS

COURTESY OF THE AUTHOR

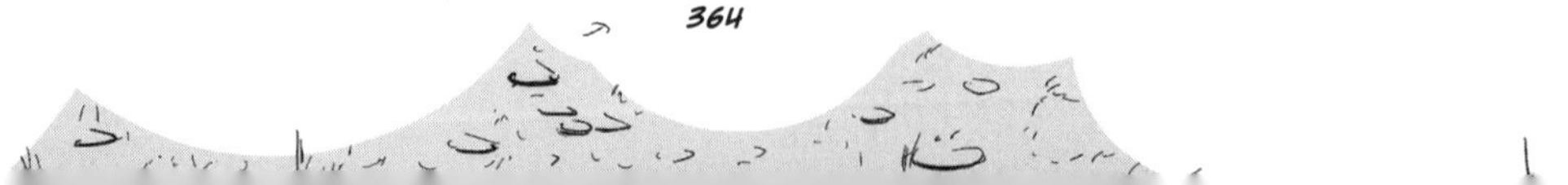

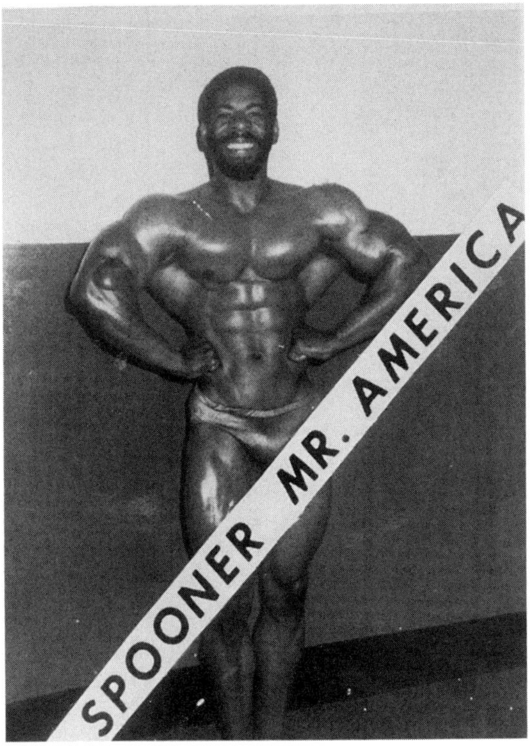
SPOONER MR. AMERICA
COURTESY OF THE AUTHOR

THANKS TO:

BAD BRAINS, BLACK FLAG, BUSHMON, LOS CRUDOS, DESCENDENTS, DOWNCAST, FILTH AND FURY, FRAIL, GORILLA BISCUITS, MINOR THREAT, MOHINDER, MOSS ICON, STRUGGLE, TEAM DRESCH, 13 STITCHES (NY), AND ALL THE BANDS THAT INFLUENCED WHO I AM TODAY.

ALL THE VOLUNTEERS AT ABC NO RIO, RECONSTRUCTION RECORDS, GILMAN ST., EPICENTER, THE NEIL HOUSE, THE PRINCETON GIRLS, EARTH-WELL KIDS, APPLE VALLEY PUNKS. MAXIMUM ROCKNROLL, HEARTATTACK, AND RAZORCAKE. '90S EMO, RIOT GRRRL, CRUST PUNKS AND STRAIGHT EDGE KIDS WHO SHOWED ME PUNK IS INHERENTLY POLITICAL.

ALL THE FOLKS WHO POSED FOR THE BOOK'S ILLUSTRATIONS. MUCH APPRECIATION TO THE KIDS: KT SHELTON, HAYDEN WHYTE, JACK ARREOLA, GRACE DOWELL, AND MOST ESPECIALLY LOUIS "POPS" NAJERA.

PJ MARK, MY PUNK ROCK LITERARY AGENT, AND JENNY XU, MY EDITOR AT HARPERCOLLINS, FOR BELIEVING IN THIS BOOK. DEREK WHIPPLE FOR YOUR SHARP EYE.

TIEASE LEE FOR BEING A GREAT CO-PARENT.

MY MOM, WHO HELPED ME MOVE BEYOND THE DESERT, AND GAVE ME HER BLESSING TO TELL THE STORY.

AND, MOST OF ALL, TO MY PARTNER LISA NOLA, WHO EDITED THIS BOOK TIRELESSLY AND PUTS UP WITH THE 14-YEAR-OLD PUNK INSIDE OF ME DAILY. YOU HELPED ME TURN MY GAZE INWARD. I LOVE YOU.

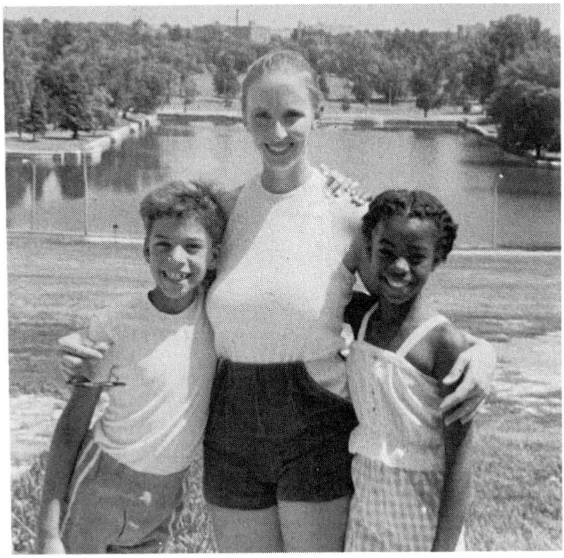
COURTESY OF JANET ASHBAUGH

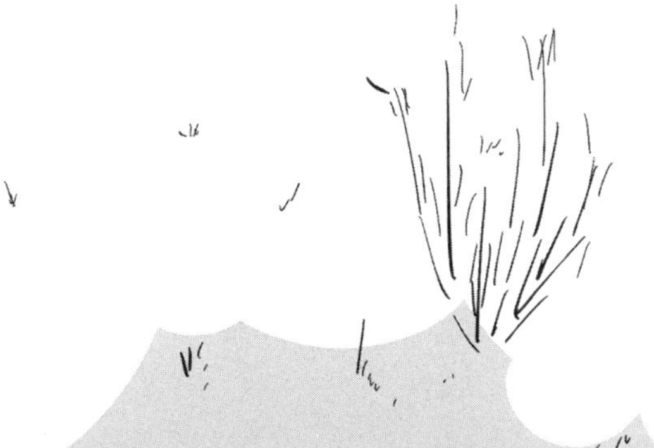

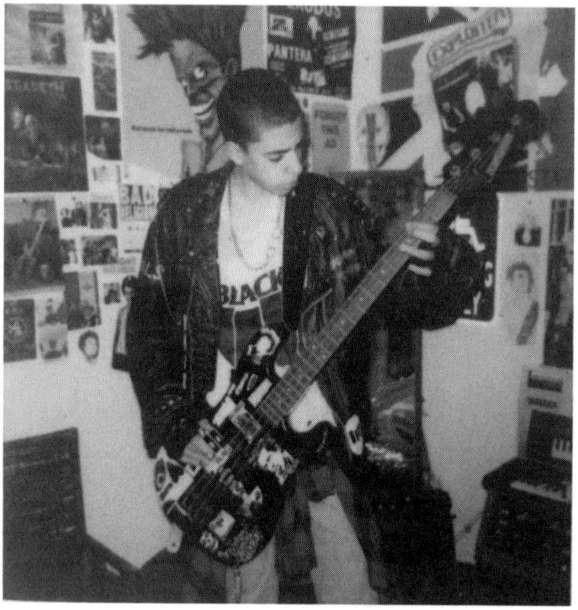
PANTERA

COURTESY OF THE AUTHOR

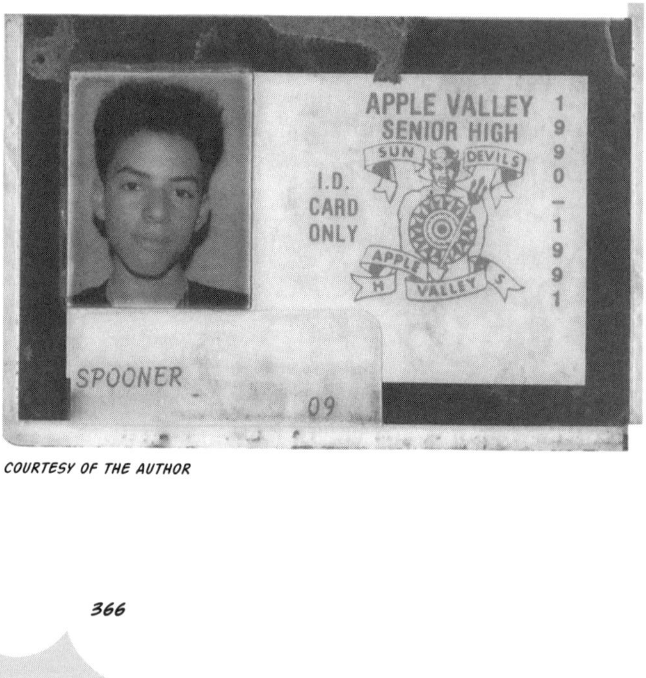
APPLE VALLEY
SENIOR HIGH
SUN DEVILS
I.D.
CARD
ONLY
1990–1991
APPLE VALLEY
SPOONER
09

COURTESY OF THE AUTHOR

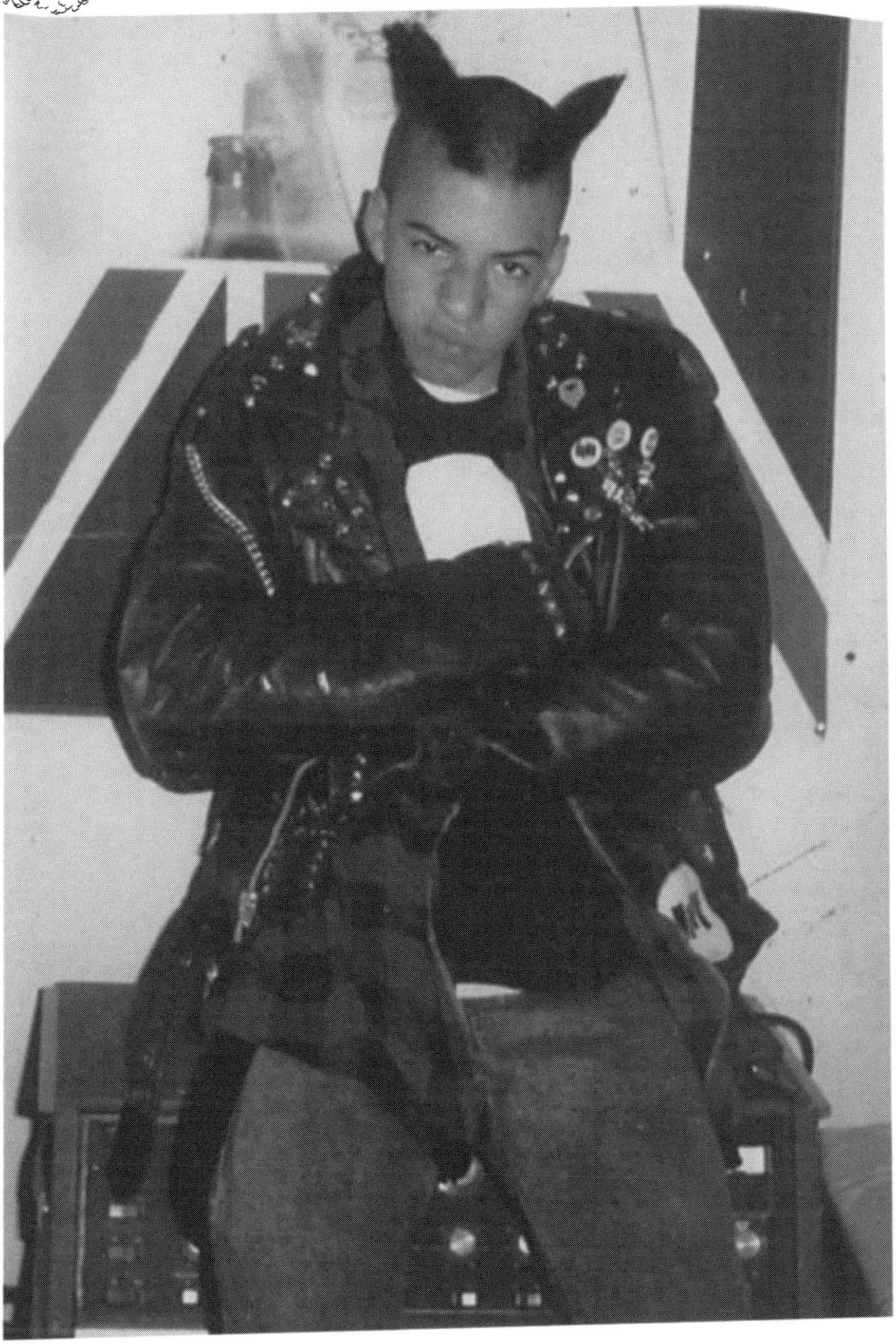

COURTESY OF JANET ASHBAUGH

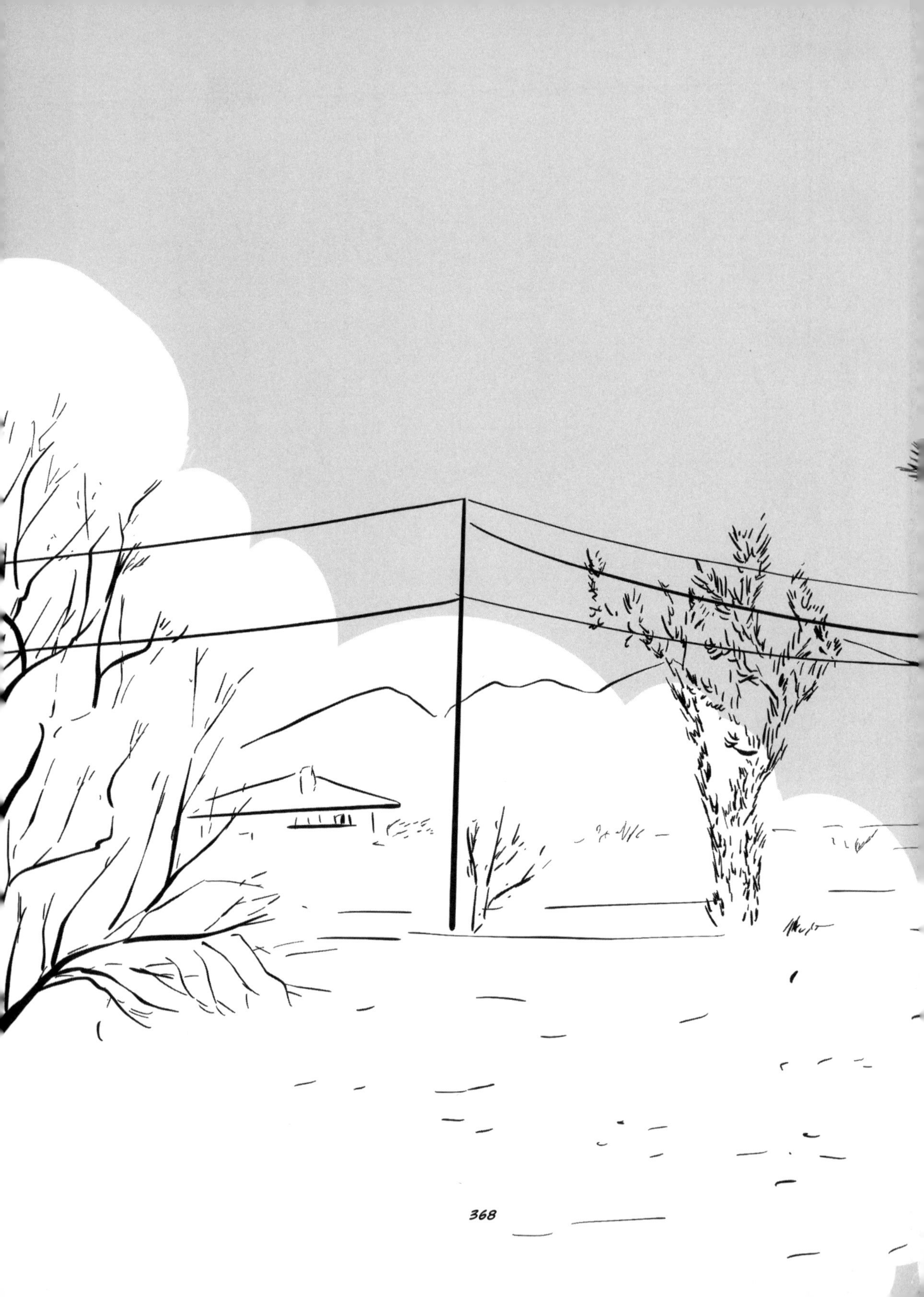

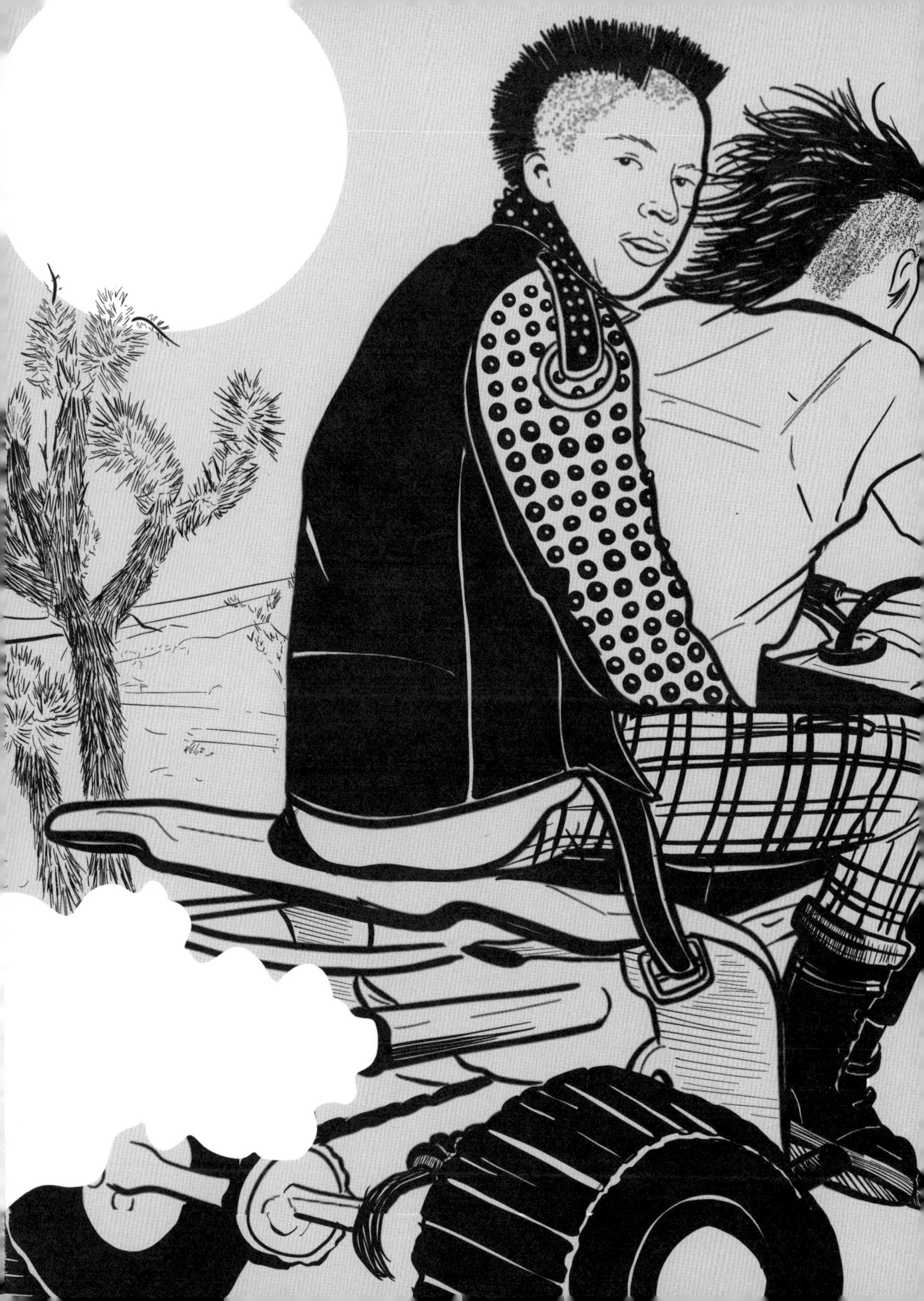

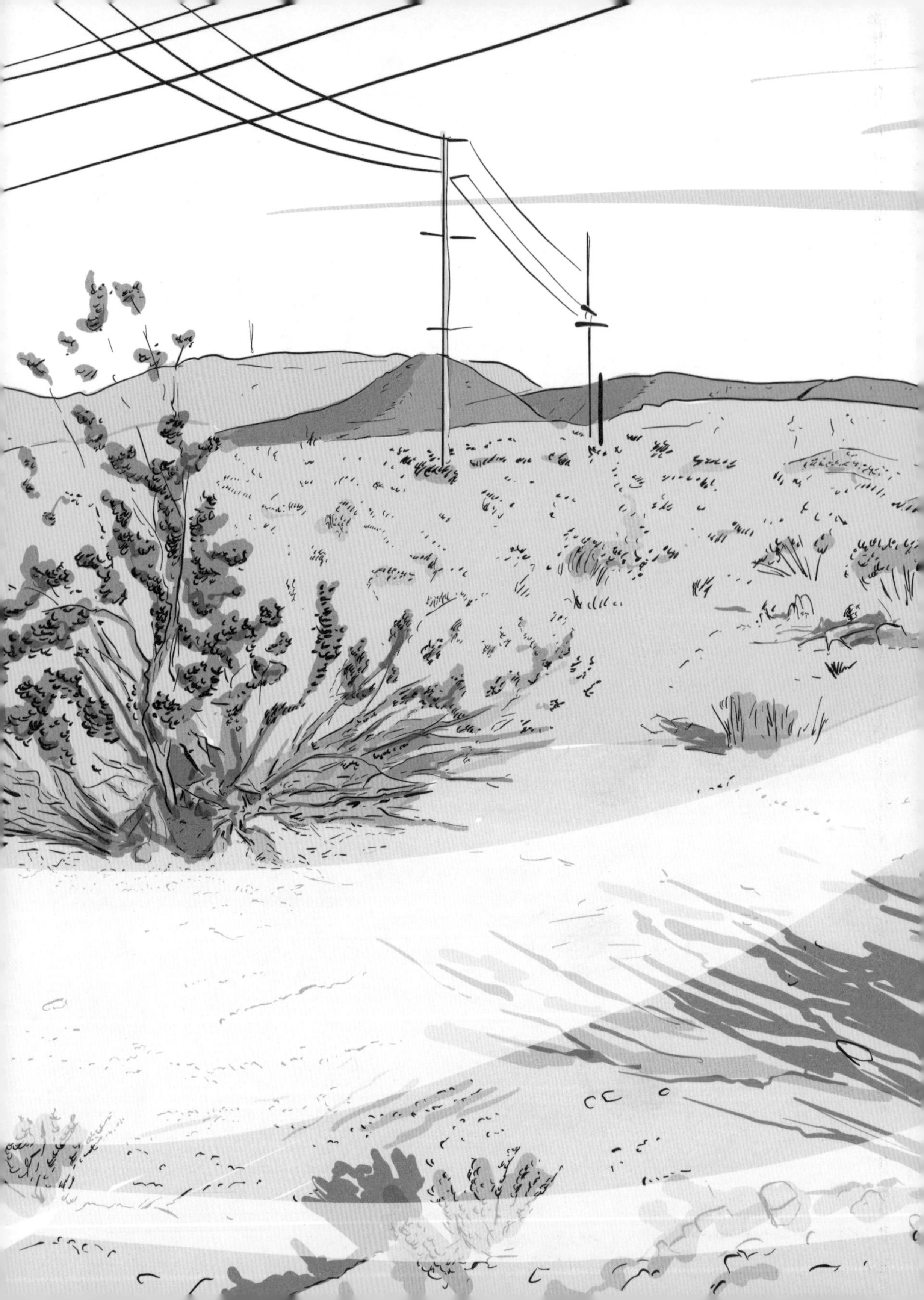